Cognitive Development

Cognitive Development

The Learning Brain

Usha Goswami

University of Cambridge

Psychology Press
Taylor & Francis Group

HOVE AND NEW YORK

Published in 2008
by Psychology Press
27 Church Road, Hove, East Sussex, BN3 2FA

Simultaneously published in the USA and Canada
by Psychology Press
270 Madison Ave, New York, NY 10016

www.psypress.com

Psychology Press is an imprint of the Taylor & Francis Group, an informa business

Reprinted 2009
© 2008 Psychology Press

British Library Cataloguing in Publication Data
A catalogue record for this book is available from the British Library

Library of Congress Cataloging-in-Publication Data
Goswami, Usha.
    Cognitive development : the learning brain / Usha Goswami.
        p. cm.
    Includes bibliographical references and index.
    ISBN 978–1–84169–530–3 (HB)—ISBN 978–1–84169–531–0 (pbk.)
    1. Cognition in children. I. Title.

    BF723.C5G68 2008
    155.4 '13—dc22   2007027300

ISBN: 978–1–84169–530–3 (hbk)
ISBN: 978–1–84169–531–0 (pbk)

Typeset by Newgen Imaging Systems (P) Ltd, Chennai, India
Printed and bound in Great Britain by
Ashford Colour Press Ltd, Gosport, Hampshire, UK

For Roshan Lal Goswami

Contents

Acknowledgments

I have greatly enjoyed re-writing *Cognition in Children* into the current book. The text was largely written in my office at St John's College, Cambridge, which provided a haven from the constant interruptions that I experience when in my Faculty office. I would like to thank both St John's College and the Faculty of Education for providing me with the intellectually stimulating environments that have informed the book. I would also like to thank Victoria Cheah and my secretary Nichola Daily for their willingness to chase down references and their work on the bibliography. Finally, I would like to thank all the lively students and contract researchers at the Centre for Neuroscience in Education for contributing to a really enjoyable working environment, and in particular my colleague and Lecturer in Neuroscience in Education, Denes Szücs.

Usha Goswami
Cambridge, May 2007

Foreword

When does cognitive development begin? Traditionally, it has been assumed that cognitive development—the development of attention, learning, memory, reasoning, language and concepts—can only commence once the baby leaves the womb. Yet more recent studies show that the fetus exhibits learning, memory and volitional motor behaviour. In fact, fetuses have surprisingly active lives. Ultrasonic scanning studies reveal that, by the fifteenth gestational week, the fetus has at least 15 distinctly different movement patterns at its command, including a yawn-and-stretch pattern and a "stepping" movement that enables it to change its position in the womb (via rotation) within 2 seconds (de Vries, Visser, & Prechtl, 1984). Fetuses suck their thumbs by the fifteenth gestational week. This prenatal thumb-sucking predicts later handedness; babies who suck their right thumbs at 15 weeks become right-handed and most babies who suck their left thumbs at 15 weeks become left-handed (Hepper, Wells, & Lynch, 2004). Studies also show that fetuses have some form of cognitive life. Research has shown that memory for the mother's voice is developed while the baby is in the womb (see Chapter 3), and there is also evidence for fetal learning of particular pieces of music (such as the theme tune of the soap opera *Neighbours*; Hepper, 1988). These responses seem to be mediated by the brainstem (Joseph, 2000). However, there is also cortical activity within the womb, for example there are functional hemispheric asymmetries in auditory evoked activity in the fetal cortex (Schluessner et al., 2004). The fetus also shows deceleration of heart rate to certain sounds while in the womb (thought to index attention) and habituation of heart rate to vibro-acoustic stimuli (thought to show rudimentary learning; see Hepper, 1992; Kisilevsky & Low, 1998).

COGNITIVE NEUROSCIENCE: A NEW ERA

The recent advances in cognitive neuroscience mean that a new era is dawning in terms of understanding cognition in children. Cognitive psychology explains cognition via concepts and ideas held in the mind: cognitive representations. These are assumed to be discrete and symbolic ("amodal"). Cognitive neuroscience enables the study of the groups or networks of neurons that are active in the *brain* when cognitive representations are active in the *mind*. In cognitive neuroscience, mental representation is studied directly, in terms of brain structure and function. Neural mental representations are distributed, because many neurons are active at once when a mental representation is activated, and these neurons may be in different parts of the brain. It is likely that a better neural understanding of mental representation will have consequences for our understanding of what cognitive representations are, and of how they develop.

Technical advances in brain scanning now enable us to create images of the active areas of the living brain at any point in time. This enables us to watch the brain at work as it solves a problem or as it makes a causal inference. At the time of writing, three neural imaging techniques are suitable for studying children. One is electroencephalography (EEG), which involves placing sensitive electrodes on the child's scalp to record brain electrical activation. The electrodes measure the low-voltage changes caused by cells firing action potentials during cognitive activity. EEG is very time sensitive and can record changes in brain activity at the millisecond level. However, a drawback of the technique is that the signals it records are difficult to localize.

A second suitable measure is functional magnetic resonance imaging (fMRI), which measures changes in blood flow in the brain. An increase in blood flow to particular brain areas causes the distribution of water in the brain tissue to change. fMRI works by measuring the magnetic resonance signal generated by the protons of water molecules in neural cells, generating a BOLD (blood oxygenation level dependent) response. The BOLD response peaks over time, hence fMRI lacks the millisecond resolution of EEG. Images are typically acquired over 0.5 to several seconds. However, fMRI offers very good spatial resolution in terms of where in the brain neural activity is taking place.

Finally, a new technique that also enables the measurement of changes in blood flow is functional near-infrared spectroscopy (fNIRS). Changes in oxygen availability (blood oxygenation level) are also shown by changes in the quantity of haemoglobin in brain tissue. Near-infrared light is absorbed differentially by brain tissue depending on the concentration of haemoglobin. Hence if optodes emitting near-infrared light are placed at the electrode positions used in EEG, changes in blood volumes can be measured. fNIRS enables the collection of data with better spatial quality than EEG and better temporal quality than fMRI, without a child needing to lie inside a large and noisy cylindrical magnet (as in fMRI). However, fNIRS does not, at present, offer temporal accuracy comparable to EEG, nor spatial accuracy comparable to fMRI.

Currently, most neuroimaging studies are of adults, so we know most about how the *developed* system works during linguistic, perceptual or reasoning tasks. However, studies with children are increasing. We already know that most of the brain cells (neurons) that a child has form before birth, by the seventh month of gestation (see Johnson, 1997; Joseph, 2000; for overviews). Accordingly, the environment within the womb can affect later cognition. For example, certain poisons (e.g. excessive alcohol) have irreversible effects on brain development, which affect later mathematical cognition (see Kopera-Frye, Dehaene, & Streissguth, 1996). Knowledge about brain development also constrains certain kinds of theorizing in developmental psychology. An example is the notion of "critical periods" for cognitive development (which are a "neuromyth"; see Goswami, 2004, 2006). Although there are sensitive periods for developing certain types of mental representation (e.g. the representations for speech sounds; see Chapter 5), the brain retains plasticity throughout the lifespan. Knowledge about when and how different neural regions develop may also offer new insights into long-standing and intriguing developmental problems (such as why infants make the "A-not-B" search error; see Chapter 2).

After birth, brain development consists mainly of the growth of connections between neurons: *synaptogenesis*. This leads the infant brain to double in size during the first year of life. Brain cells pass information to each other via low-voltage electrical signals, which travel from neuron to neuron via special junctions called synapses. As soon as the child is born, the brain is busy sculpting connections between neurons, proliferating some connections and pruning others. The main determinant of this sculpting is the environment experienced by the child. Environmental sculpting establishes specific neural pathways and networks, which will be the basis of perception, attention, learning, and memory. In general, primary sensory systems are established first (e.g. the visual and auditory systems, the motor system); higher-order association areas mature later (Casey, Galvan, & Hare, 2005). The prefrontal cortex is one of the last brain regions to mature. However, the environment does not have to be especially rich to promote optimal development. Rather, the brain is set to respond to normative visual and auditory experience. When many neurons in a network are "firing" together, the patterns of neural activity are thought to correspond to particular mental states or mental "representations". Although few studies currently use neural imaging to understand how a cognitive representation for a concept such as "animate" or "inanimate" develops in a young child, in time this will become possible. Meanwhile, I will mention relevant cognitive neuroscience studies wherever possible when discussing cognition in children in this book.

Two core developmental questions

The study of cognition in children has traditionally focused around two major questions. The first is the apparently simple question of *what develops*. This question can be investigated by observing changes in children's cognitive abilities over time. For example, we can define certain principles of logical thought (such as the Piagetian principles of conservation and transitivity; see Chapter 11) and then track the development of these principles over time with experimental tests. At a very simple level, we can investigate "what develops" by using cognitive neuroscience techniques. We know, for example, that the sensory-motor cortex (vision, audition, action) matures earlier than the language and spatial areas (temporal and parietal cortices), with the prefrontal cortex (reasoning, problem-solving, monitoring one's cognitive behaviour) maturing last of all, during adolescence and early adulthood. Such observations suggest that visual and auditory behaviour will approximate adult levels earlier than reasoning behaviour or self-monitoring behaviour. Remarkably, Piaget's theory of cognitive development began with a sensory-motor phase and ended with higher-order reasoning (see Chapter 11). In this sense, Piaget's theoretical framework parallels the course of brain development.

Information about *what develops* provides data for the second major question in cognitive developmental psychology, the less simple question of *why* development pursues its observed course. This question requires us to develop causal explanations for observed cognitive changes. Traditionally, we try to understand why development pursues the course that it does via experiments. Most of this book will be concerned with such experiments. In the future, it may also be possible to develop causal explanations from neuroscience studies. For example, certain brain structures or certain chemical messengers (neurotransmitters, which pass information across the synapse) may turn out to be important in explaining certain cognitive disorders. An example is schizophrenia, which may be caused in part by abnormal dopamine activity. According to one current theory, neonatal perturbation of the hippocampus disrupts the normal development of prefrontal cortex and its regulation by the neurotransmitter dopamine (see Lipska & Weinberger, 2002). The cognitive effects include heightened reactivity to stress and poor executive control. However, the environment exerts a strong effect on who will become schizophrenic as an adult. For example, Afro-Caribbean adults in the United Kingdom are between 2 and 18 times more likely to develop schizophrenia than genetically matched adults who still live in the Caribbean (Fearon & Morgan, 2006). Hence neurocognitive risk does not necessitate cognitive disorder. This illustrates the complexity of the interactions between brain, environment and cognition (see Munakata, Casey, & Diamond, 2004; Gottleib, 2007; for useful reviews). Neuroscience also offers the potential for new therapeutic interventions. For example, abnormalities in dopamine regulation might be improved by antipsychotic drugs that target dopamine metabolism. Although such drugs indeed improve schizophrenic symptoms, the causal mechanisms by which they exert their therapeutic actions are still very poorly understood (Winterer & Weinberger, 2004).

Two core explanatory systems

Traditionally, two alternative (although not mutually exclusive) explanatory systems have been developed to account for changes in children's cognition. The first type of theoretical account is based on the idea that core modes of learning or reasoning are applied across all cognitive domains. This is a "domain-general" explanation of cognitive development. Whether a child is attempting to understand why another child is upset (the "domain" of psychological causation), why animals usually have babies that look like them (the "domain" of biology), or why objects fall when they are insufficiently supported (the "domain" of physical reasoning), domain-general accounts postulate that certain types of learning, such as causal learning, or certain types of reasoning, such as the ability to make deductive inferences, are applied to the acquisition of all of these understandings.

The second type of theoretical account postulates that the development of cognition is piecemeal, occurring at different time points in different domains. According to this view, cognitive development is "domain specific". For example, deductive inferences may appear in the domain of physical causality long before they appear in the domain of psychological causality. The reason may be that a rich and principled understanding of the physical world is acquired before a rich and principled understanding of the psychological world (a "theory of mind"). Domain-specific accounts of cognitive development acknowledge the importance of the *knowledge base* in children's cognition.

The knowledge that we have affects our cognition when we are adults as well as when we are children. While the ability to (for example) make deductive inferences *per se* might be a domain-general development, the use of deductive inferences may be domain specific. Children may need sufficient *knowledge* to use their deductive abilities in different domains, just as adults do (most of us could not make valid deductions in unfamiliar domains such as nuclear physics). This example illustrates why the two explanatory systems developed to account for changes in children's cognition are not mutually exclusive. In this book, I will argue that certain types of learning, such as statistical learning, learning by imitation, learning by analogy and causal learning, are domain general. However, their use in different domains depends partly on knowledge. Other factors may also affect the observed pattern of cognitive development. These include the richness of the child's environment, the maturation of certain cognitive structures such as the frontal cortex, and the quality of the support and teaching that a child receives at home and in school.

This book focuses on the question of "what develops" rather than on the question of "why". The findings from a given experimental study ("what develops") are generally fixed but the interpretation of what particular findings mean ("why") is fluid. This is one of the most exciting aspects of research. Some of the experiments that will be discussed have alternative interpretations, and every student interested in children''s cognition is invited to develop his or her own ideas about what the different studies mean (preferably along with some ideas about how to find out whether the studies are right or not!). My aim is to provide a selective, but hopefully representative, review of some of the most interesting historic and current work in cognitive development. By considering research on perception and attention, learning, language, conceptual development, memory development and the development of logical, psychological and causal reasoning, we will study the different kinds of knowledge that children acquire, and how they acquire them. At the end of the book, we will assess the impact of recent findings in developmental psychology on the most famous theories of cognitive development, the theories of Jean Piaget and Lev Vygotsky.

Learning and constraints on learning

A central theme, which will become apparent in our discussion of "what develops", will provide a partial answer to the question of "why". As we will see, the human infant is born with certain kinds of learning mechanisms at its disposal. The infant brain can learn statistical patterns in the environment, enabling the extraction of an enormous amount of information. Infants are skilled at associative learning, for example, they readily learn that certain events co-occur. They are also skilled at learning conditional probabilities—that a certain event will reliably occur given that a specific prior event has occurred. The infant brain can also learn by imitation. Perception yields many examples of agents (e.g. parents, sisters and brothers) acting on the world, and infants can imitate what agents do, which appears to help them to represent and understand human action and its causes (social cognition). Infants can also learn by analogy. Imitation may involve an early form of analogy, as infants can recognize others as being "like me" (see Chapter 3). Finally, infants have an impressive ability to learn about causal relations and to acquire causal explanations ("explanation-based learning"; see Chapter 2). This "causal bias" may begin from infants' interest in agents, and bestows a tremendous amount of information upon the infant and the young child. Language acquisition facilitates this further. Anyone with a child of their own, or with a young sibling, is familiar with the constant tendency of young children to ask for causal information ("Why is the sky blue?" "How does the telephone call know which house to go to?" "How come the moon is big and orange now but other times it's little and white?"; see, for example, Hood & Bloom, 1979; Callanan & Oakes, 1992). This relentless questioning is not just a device that children employ to keep a conversation going. Instead, causal questions such as these have an important developmental function.

Children's focus on causal information gives them the ability to explain, predict and eventually even to control events within their everyday worlds. As we will see during this book, this "causal bias" acts to organize early memory, it underlies conceptual development, it helps the child to understand the physical world, it helps to organize the social world of agents and their actions, and it acts as a pacesetter for logical thought. The kinds of objects and events that infants are prepared to link in a causal fashion appear to be constrained in certain ways. For example, some kinds of movement appear more likely to be assigned a biological cause than others (e.g., erratic, unpredictable motion to biological causes, predictable motion to man-made artifacts). Some of these constraints on causal learning are discussed in Chapter 6.

Deduction and induction

Furthermore, children's causal questions demonstrate that abilities such as deductive reasoning are present from an early age. Here is an example of everyday deductive reasoning by a 4-year-old, taken from an interchange that took place at the child's bedtime (from Callanan & Oakes, 1992, p. 221–222):

> *Child (age 4) to her mother: "Why does Daddy, James [older brother] and me have blue eyes, and you have green eyes?"*
>
> *The mother tells the child she got her eyes from Daddy. Then says goodnight and leaves the room.*
>
> *Child (calls her mother back 5 minutes later): "I like Pee Wee Herman [a comedian] and I have blue eyes. Daddy likes Pee Wee Herman and he has blue eyes. James likes Pee Wee Herman and he has blue eyes. If you liked Pee Wee Herman you could get blue eyes too".*
>
> *Mother tells the child that God gave her this colour and they couldn't be changed.*
>
> *Child: "Could you try to like Pee Wee Herman so we could see if your eyes turn blue?"*

The logical deductions here are impressive. The little girl reasons that X (liking Pee Wee Herman) implies Y (having blue eyes) in three cases out of three, and that X' (not liking Pee Wee Herman) implies Y' (not having blue eyes) in one case out of one. This covariation information appears persuasive and so she forms a causal hypothesis (liking Pee Wee Herman determines eye colour). She then thinks of a way to test her hypothesis via an intervention (change X' into X, and see if Y' changes to Y). This exchange incorporates the knowledge that causes and their effects should systematically covary, and illustrates that young children are capable of deductive logic and hypothesis testing—even at the tender age of 4!

Inductive reasoning can be shown to be present at even younger ages. When we make inferences that are not necessarily deductively valid (when we "go beyond the information given"), we are reasoning inductively. For example, we might make a generalization on the basis of a known example, or use an analogy. Conceptual development and categorization depend on inductive reasoning and analogy. For example, when children learn about the category "birds", they may learn about one or two exemplars (e.g. the robins and sparrows in their back garden). However, they are happy to generalize properties like "lives in a nest" to other birds, such as magpies, that they may not have seen before. These generalizations are made on the basis of inductive reasoning. When new exemplars (like magpies) appear typical of a category (like birds), then it seems natural to make generalizations about properties of a typical category member to other category members. Very young children do this all the time as they learn about the world around them, as we will see in Chapter 4.

Making a causal deduction is an example of a mechanism that seems to be *both* domain general and domain specific. Children make causal inferences in different domains at different points in development, for example using causal inferences to learn about the physical world before they use causal inferences in the biological domain. However, physical knowledge develops earlier than biological knowledge partly because the world of objects and events becomes familiar to the young infant before the world of plants and animals. The ability to make causal inferences thus appears to be domain general, emerging at different times in different domains according to the growth of domain-specific knowledge.

Innate vs. acquired accounts of cognition in children

A related theoretical issue to that of domain-specific versus domain-general explanations of cognitive development is that of nature versus nurture. Should the underlying causes of development be explained in terms of a rich genetic endowment of complex behavioural abilities, or in terms of rich experience of the environment? The metaphor of the mind of the infant as a blank slate has long been discredited, and so the "nature versus nurture" debate may appear no longer relevant to developmental psychology. However, recent research demonstrating the relative sophistication of infant cognition has led to a renaissance of quasi-nativist views. Yet genes cannot determine cognitive structures. Aspects of physiological structure that are thought to be totally under genetic control, such as tooth decay, can be dramatically altered by the environment. We can virtually eliminate tooth decay by looking after our teeth properly; we use environmental interventions, like brushing and flossing our teeth. The same principles will apply to psychological development, where organism–environment interrelationships are ubiquitous. Gene expression is controlled by the environment, including the environments within cells and brain tissue (epigenesis). Although genes contribute to neural structures, these structures become active before they are fully mature and this activity itself shapes development ("probabilistic epigenesis"; see Gottlieb, 2007). Knowing whether a particular ability is present at or near birth does not help us to understand its developmental origin. Instead, it is a starting point for the investigation of causes and consequences. The real question for cognitive developmental psychology is how neural and genetic activity *interact* with the environment and with behaviour to produce development. We need to ask questions about how the characteristics and limitations of infant motor, sensory, perceptual, and cognitive functioning produce modes of responding to the environment that help to shape the development of mature cognitive functions.

One famous acquired account of children's cognition was offered by Jean Piaget, who developed a constructivist account of cognitive development. For a long time, Piaget's theoretical framework dominated the field of cognitive–developmental psychology. Piaget is usually characterized as describing cognitive development as a *qualitative* process, because his was a stage theory, involving the emergence of new modes of thinking as revolutions occurred in the structure of thought. Piaget argued for three major modes of thinking, the *sensory-motor* stage, during which cognition was based on action; the stage of *concrete operations*, during which cognition was based on the symbolic understanding of concrete objects and the relations between them; and the stage of *formal operations*, during which cognition was fully detached from the concrete world and was characterized by hypothesis testing and scientific thought. The stage of concrete operations was preceded by a "pre-operational" stage, making four stages in all. Although Piaget's theory no longer dominates cognitive developmental psychology, some of his ideas are once more highly topical. Recent work in cognitive neuroscience highlights the core role of action in mental representations ("embodied cognition"), making Piaget's emphasis on sensory-motor cognition in infancy prescient in terms of explaining early cognitive development. Similarly, symbolic development (whereby cognition becomes detached from the external world) turns out to be quite protracted, and very important in representational terms (e.g. see Chapters 3, 5 and 7). Experiments showing the context-bound nature of human reasoning suggest that we never attain the ability to think purely in terms of formal operations (see Chapter 9). Another famous account of cognitive development was offered by Vygotsky, who focused more on the influences of culture and language. Both Vygotsky's and Piaget's theories are considered in detail in Chapter 11.

The field of cognitive developmental psychology is at a crossroads in terms of theoretical explanations and, at the time of writing, a deeper understanding of brain development looks certain to set the pace for new theoretical perspectives such as neuroconstructivism (see Chapter 11). My focus in this book will thus be on documenting what experiments in psychology tell us about children's cognition, bringing in cognitive neuroscience studies of mental representations where possible. The early chapters in this book focus on cognitive development in the "foundational" domains of human thought: the domains of physics, psychology and biology. We will then consider language acquisition, causal reasoning, memory and logical development. Once a clearer understanding is gained of what the brain learns during childhood cognition, a clearer understanding of the appropriate explanatory frameworks for the "why" of cognitive development should become possible. I will thus end the book by considering how the traditional explanatory frameworks offered by Piaget and Vygotsky can be integrated with the new biologically driven frameworks offered by cognitive neuroscience and connectionism.

CHAPTER 1

CONTENTS

Infancy: The physical world 1

1

What kinds of knowledge are central to human cognitive development? One proposal is that knowledge about the physical world of objects and events; knowledge about social cognition, self, and agency; and knowledge about the kinds of things in the world, or conceptual knowledge, are the "foundational" domains for cognitive development (Wellman & Gelman, 1998). These domains could be described as **naïve physics**, naïve psychology, and naïve biology. Infants need to understand objects and the physical laws governing their interactions; they need to understand social cognition (to interpret and predict people's behavior on the basis of psychological causation) and they need to understand about the kinds of "stuff" in the world (such as animate versus inanimate entities). Clearly, cognitive development in these foundational domains is also dependent on the development of perception, memory, attention, learning, and reasoning. Most areas of cognition involve all of these skills at once.

It was once thought that young infants, who are immobile and whose perceptual abilities are still developing, had very limited cognition. For example, about 50 years ago it was thought that infants did not develop a **full object concept** until around 18 months of age (Piaget, 1954; a full object concept was thought to require an understanding that objects are enduring entities that continue to exist when out of view). This assumption seems to be quite wrong. Recent work in perception demonstrates that a remarkable amount of information about the nature of objects is given simply by watching things happen in the world. This passively acquired perceptual information is probably the source of early cognitive development concerning objects and their interactions. It is rapidly supplemented by information gained through direct action. Much richer information becomes available when the infant becomes able to reach, grasp, sit, and move. Similarly, perceptual information is replete with cues that can facilitate the development of social cognition, and in cues that inform an understanding of the animate–inanimate distinction. The development of knowledge in each foundational domain will be considered in the following chapters. It is important to keep in mind, however, that these types of knowledge are not developing separately in the infant.

At least three types of learning also appear to be functioning from very early in development. One is **associative learning**. Babies appear to be able to make connections between events that are reliably associated, even while in the womb. Once outside the womb, they appear able to track statistical dependencies in the world, such as conditional probabilities between visual events or between sounds. This turns out to be a very powerful learning mechanism. The second type of learning that appears to be available early is learning by imitation. This may be particularly important for the development of social cognition. Learning by imitation is considered further in later chapters. Finally, infants appear able to connect causes and effects by using "explanation based" learning. This "causal bias" was discussed in the Foreword. The causal inferences made by infants provide an extremely

Once an infant is able to reach out and grasp objects, much richer information becomes available to him or her.

powerful mechanism for learning about the world. Infants are not simply detecting causal regularities but appear to be constructing causal explanations for new phenomena on the basis of their prior knowledge. One mechanism that they use is learning by analogy. This fourth type of learning is considered further in later chapters.

MEMORY

Memory is a good place to begin to study infant perception and cognition. After all, without some form of memory infants would live in a constant world of the "here and now". To remember, babies must learn what is familiar.

Memory for objects

Infant memory was originally investigated using rather mundane objects and events. For example, Bushnell, McCutcheon, Sinclair, and Tweedie (1984) studied infants' memory for pictures of simple shapes such as red triangles and blue crosses, which were mounted on wooden paddles. The infants were aged 3 and 7 weeks. Memory for a simple stimulus such as a yellow circle was first developed by asking the infants' mothers to present the stimulus daily for a 2-week period. The mothers were encouraged to show their babies the stimulus "actively" for two 15-minute sessions per day. The babies were then visited at home by an experimenter, who showed them the habituating stimulus and also a random selection of the other stimuli, varying color, shape, or color *and* shape. The aim was to test the infants' memories for these different aspects of the stimuli. For example, to test color memory, the baby might be shown a red circle rather than a yellow circle. To test memory for shape, the baby might be shown a yellow square instead of a yellow circle, and so on. Bushnell et al. found that the infants retained information about every aspect of the stimuli that they had been shown—shape, color, and size.

Cornell (1979) used pictures of groups of such stimuli to study recognition memory in infants aged from 5 to 6 months. In addition to pictures of patterns of geometric forms (Figure 1.1), he also used photographs of human faces. The babies were first shown two identical pictures from Set 1 side-by-side, followed by two identical pictures from Set 2, followed by two identical pictures from Set 3 (the photographs of human faces), and were allowed to study each set for a period of up to 20 seconds. Two days later they were shown the pictures again, first in a brief "reminder" phase in which each previously studied picture was presented on its own, and then for a recognition phase in which the familiar picture from each set was paired with an unfamiliar picture from the same set. Recognition memory was assumed if the infants devoted more looking time to the novel picture in each pair.

Cornell found a novelty preference across all the sets of stimuli that he used. Even though 2 days had passed since the infants saw the pictures, they remembered those that were familiar and preferred to look at the novel pictures in the recognition phase of the experiment. Their recognition memory was not due to the brief reminder

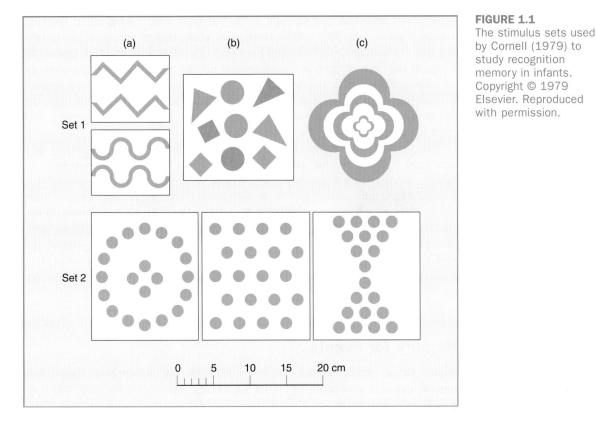

FIGURE 1.1
The stimulus sets used by Cornell (1979) to study recognition memory in infants. Copyright © 1979 Elsevier. Reproduced with permission.

cue, as a control group who received the "reminder" phase of the experiment without the initial study phase did not show a novelty response during the recognition test. Given that the stimuli were fairly abstract (except for the faces) and were presented for a relatively short period of time in the initial study phase, their retention over a 2-day period is good evidence for well-developed recognition memory in young infants.

Working memory in infancy

The capacity to retain information over short periods of time is often called "short-term memory" or "**working memory**". An influential model of memory in adult cognition is Baddeley and Hitch's (1974) model, which distinguishes a short-term from a long-term system. The short-term system, called working memory, is thought to enable the temporary maintenance of information while it is processed for further use (e.g. in reasoning or in learning). Working memory is thought to have both visuospatial and sound-based (phonological) subsystems, which maintain visual versus auditory information respectively.

Working memory abilities in babies have been studied by Rose and colleagues (Rose, Feldman, & Jankowski, 2001). Rose et al. measured how many items could be held in mind by infants as they developed, testing the same babies when they were aged 5, 7, and 12 months. The infants were shown colorful toy-like stimuli, in sets of one, two, three, or four items. Once a particular set had been presented, recognition

KEY TERM

Working memory
The memory system that temporarily keeps in memory information just received that may be processed for further use.

memory was tested by pairing each individual item with a novel item. Working memory capacity was measured by seeing how many objects the babies recognized as novel. For example, if a baby had been shown a set of four items but seemed to recognize only two of them in the subsequent novelty preference pairings, memory span was assumed to be two items. *Primacy* and *recency* effects were also studied: In adult working memory experiments, participants find it easier to remember the first item of a set (primacy) and also the last item (recency). The question was whether babies would show the same effects.

Rose et al. (2001) reported that memory span increased with age. When they were aged 5 and 7 months, rather few babies could hold three or four items in working memory simultaneously (only around 25% of the sample achieved this span). By 12 months, almost half of the babies had a working memory span of three or four items. Recency effects were found at all ages tested—the babies showed better recall for the final item in the set. Primacy effects were not reported but have been reported in 7-month-old infants by Cornell and Bergstrom (1983). Hence the working memory system of young infants appears to operate in a similar way to that of adults. Primacy and recency effects in adults are explained in terms of the extra cues to recall provided by being the first or the last item in the list.

Memory for events

Some striking studies carried out by Clifton and colleagues have shown that 6-month-olds can also retain memories for events, and do so over very long time periods. For example, in one of Clifton's studies, 6½-month-olds were able to retain a memory of a single event that had occurred once until they were 2½ years of age (Perris, Myers, & Clifton, 1990).

Perris et al. (1990) demonstrated this by bringing some infants who had taken part in an experiment in their laboratory as 6-month-olds back to the laboratory at 2½ and retesting them. During the infancy experiment, the babies had been required to reach both in the dark and in the light for a Big Bird finger puppet that made a rattle noise (the experiment was about the localization of sounds). The reaching session had taken about 20 minutes. Two years later, the children were brought back to the same laboratory room and met the same female experimenter, who said that they would play some games. She showed them five plastic toys, including the Big Bird puppet, and asked which toy they thought would be part of the game. She then told them that Big Bird made a sound in the game, and asked them to guess which one it was out of a rattle noise, a bell, and a clicker. Finally, the children played a game in the dark, which was to reach accurately to one of five possible locations for the sounding puppet. After five uninstructed dark trials, during which no instructions about what to do were given, the children were given five more trials in which they were told to "catch the noisy Big Bird in the dark". A group of control children who had not experienced the procedure as infants was also tested.

Perris et al. found that the experimental group showed little *explicit* recall of their experiences as infants. They were no more likely than the control group to select Big Bird as the toy who would be part of the game, or to choose the rattle noise over the bell and the clicker. However, they showed a clear degree of **implicit recall**, as measured by their behavior during the game in the dark. They were more likely to reach out towards the sound than the children in the control group in the first five trials, and they also reached more accurately. If they were given a reminder of their early experience, by hearing the sound of the rattle for 3 seconds half an hour before the test in the dark, then they were especially likely to show the reaching behavior. Again, this was not true of the control group. Finally, the children who had experienced the auditory localization task as infants were much less likely to become distressed by the darkness during the testing than the children who had not experienced the auditory localization task as infants. Nine of the latter children (out of 16) asked to leave before completing the uninstructed trials, compared to only two children in the experimental group. Children who had experienced reaching in the dark as infants thus showed evidence of remembering that event two years later in a number of different ways. Similar results were reported in a study by Myers, Clifton, and Clarkson (1987), who showed that children who were almost 3 years old also retained memories of the laboratory and the auditory localization testing procedures that they had encountered as infants. These children had had 15–19 exposures to the experimental procedures as infants, however, and so their memory is in some sense less surprising than that demonstrated in the experiment by Perris et al. (1990).

Memory for causal events

Event memory can also be studied by teaching infants a causal *contingency* between a response and a reward. This technique of using learned causal relationships between the production of a response and the delivery of a reward was exploited by Rovee-Collier and colleagues in some pioneering studies (e.g. Rovee-Collier, Sullivan, Enright, Lucas, & Fagen, 1980). In these studies, the conditioned response was kicking and the reward was the activation of an attractive mobile hanging over the infant's crib. The contingency was that kicking activated the mobile. Activation of the mobile occurred via a ribbon that was tied to the infant's ankle. As kicking comes naturally to young infants, the kicking response is present whether the mobile is there or not. The important point about Rovee-Collier's paradigm is that the infant must *learn* that kicking makes the mobile start to work. Memory for this cause–effect relation was then measured by returning the infants to the same crib after some time had passed and seeing how much they kicked in the presence of the mobile.

In a typical experiment, the infant is visited at home (see Rovee-Collier & Hayne, 1987, for a review). An attractive mobile is erected on the side of the crib and a second empty mobile stand is also erected (Figure 1.2). The ribbon is first tied to this empty stand, to measure the baseline kick rate in the absence of reinforcement with the mobile. After approximately 3 minutes, the ribbon is attached to the correct mobile stand, and the infant is allowed to kick for about 9 minutes for the reward of activating the mobile. The ribbon is then moved back to the empty stand for a final 3-minute period. The difference in kick rate between this second 3-minute period and the initial baseline period provides a measure of the infant's short-term retention of the contingency. The infant is then visited a second time some days after the original learning phase and the ribbon is again tied to the empty stand. Long-term retention of the cause–effect relation is measured by comparing kicking in the absence of reinforcement during this second visit with the original baseline kick rate.

Rovee-Collier and colleagues have found that 3-month-old infants show little forgetting of the mobile contingency over periods ranging from 2 to 8 days. By 14 days, however, forgetting of the contingency appears to be complete. Furthermore, as the time between the learning and test periods increases, the infants forget

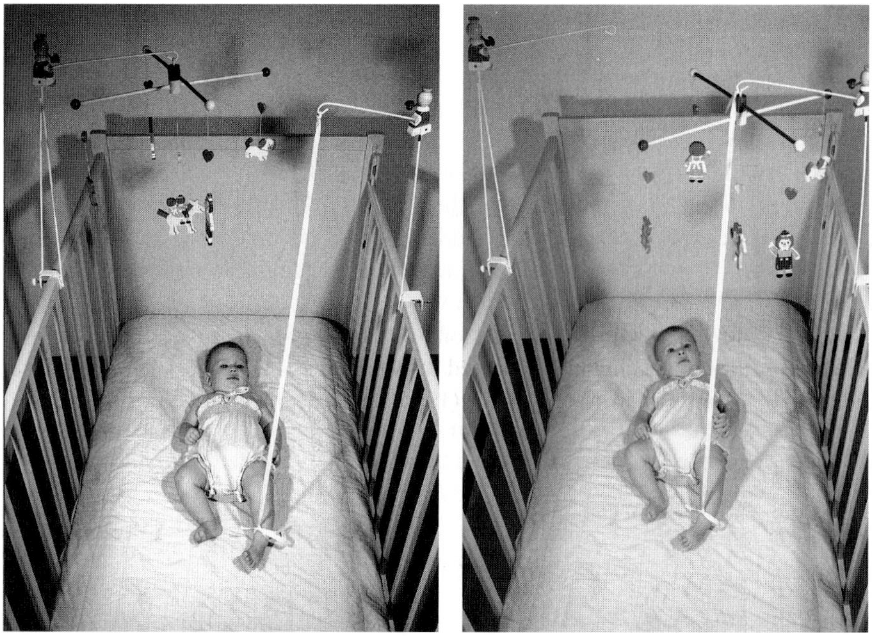

FIGURE 1.2
An infant in Rovee-Collier's causal contingency paradigm (left) during baseline, when kicking cannot activate the mobile and (right) during acquisition, when the ankle ribbon is attached to the mobile. From Rovee-Collier, Sullivan, Enright, Lucas, and Fagen (1980). Copyright © 1980 AAAS. Reprinted with permission.

the specific details of the training mobile (its colors and shapes), and respond as strongly to a novel mobile as to the original. Twenty-four hours after learning, the infants remember the objects on the mobile and will not respond to mobiles containing more than one novel object. By 4 days, however, they will respond to a novel five-object mobile. This suggests that infants, like older children and adults, gradually forget the physical characteristics or attributes of what they have learned, retaining only the gist or the associations between specific attributes and the context of learning.

Interestingly, at the same time as memory for the mobile itself declines, memory for the surrounding context (e.g. the pattern on the crib bumper) becomes more important in reactivating the infant's memory of the contingency. Infants show perfect retention of the contingency at 24 hours, whatever the pattern on the crib bumper. By 7 days, infants who have been trained with a distinctive crib bumper show apparently complete forgetting if they receive a different crib bumper at test, whereas infants who receive the distinctive crib bumper at test remember the contingency. The different cues on the crib bumper, such as its colors and the particular shapes in its pattern, appear to be forgotten at different rates (Rovee-Collier, Schechter, Shyi, & Shields, 1992). It is difficult to escape the conclusion that details of the learning context, such as details of the pattern on a distinctive crib bumper, are acting to cue recall.

KEY TERM

Reactivation paradigm
A procedure in which the participant, usually an infant, is given a reminder of an earlier learned, but apparently forgotten, memory that enables this memory to become accessible again.

If the crib bumper indeed provides an appropriate "reminder" cue for recall, then we can examine whether "forgotten" memories become accessible again when appropriate retrieval cues are provided. Rovee-Collier and colleagues have developed a **reactivation paradigm** to study this question. The retrieval cue that they have studied most intensively is a *reminder* of the mobile contingency, namely showing the infants the moving mobile for 3 minutes prior to measuring kick rate. During the reminder phase, the mobile is activated by a hidden experimenter pulling on the ribbon, and the infants are prevented from kicking by a special seat that also precludes "on-the-spot" learning. The infants are then retested in the crib procedure 24 hours after the reminding event. With a reminder, 3-month-old infants demonstrate completely intact memories for the mobile contingency 14 and 28 days after the training event. Two-month-old infants show excellent memories after a 14-day delay, but only a third of this age group show intact memory after 28 days. By 6 months of age, the retention period is at least 3 weeks (Rovee-Collier, 1993). Thus very young infants can develop long-term memories for causal events, and memory retrieval appears to be governed by the same cues that determine retrieval in adults.

Another way of examining infants' long-term memory for causal events is to use **delayed imitation**, a technique pioneered by Meltzoff in his studies of learning (see Chapter 2). Mandler and McDonough (1995) used delayed imitation to examine 11-month-old infants' retention of causal events over a 3-month period. The events were two-step action sequences, namely "make a rattle" (by pushing a button into a box with a slot), and "make a rocking horse" (by attaching a horse with magnetic feet to a magnetized rocker). Imitation of the events was measured on the following day (24-hour retention period), and three months later. On each occasion the infants were simply presented with the materials (the horse, the rocker) and were then observed. To check that the older infants were not simply more likely to discover the sequences without having seen them being modeled, a control group of 14-month-old infants was also given the materials at the 3-month follow-up.

Mandler and McDonough found that recall was good at both the 24-hour and the 3-month retention intervals, and that there was little forgetting over the 3-month period. By contrast, retention of noncausal events (e.g. "put a hat on the bunny and feed him a carrot") was poorer than that of causal events at 24 hours, and nonexistent after the 3-month interval. Mandler argues that retaining causal relations provides one of the major ways of organizing material that is to be remembered in a coherent and meaningful fashion. The importance of causal relations for memory development is covered more fully in Chapter 8.

Procedural vs. declarative memories?

It is notable that all of the studies discussed above have measured infant event memory in terms of the infants' *behavior*. Rovee-Collier measured the amount of kicking that was produced to the mobile, Mandler the number of action sequences that were reproduced with the props, and Clifton children's reaching behavior in the auditory localization paradigm. This raises the question of whether these memories are somehow different in *kind* to the type of memory in which we bring some aspect of the past to conscious awareness (e.g. Mandler, 1990). Is infant memory an active remembrance of things past, or is it more akin to a conditioned response of the type studied in animals?

In fact, it is widely accepted in cognitive psychology that there are *two* types of memory system in humans. One is automatic in operation, and is not accessible to verbal report. This kind of memory is usually called **implicit or procedural memory**. The second involves bringing the past to mind, and thinking about it. This kind of memory is usually called **explicit or declarative memory**. Only the latter involves information that has been encoded in such a way as to be accessible to consciousness. Infants are generally assumed not to encode explicit or declarative memories until they become verbally competent, a phenomenon that has been called "infantile amnesia". This assumption is probably incorrect, and is discussed more fully in Chapter 8. The development of implicit and explicit memories is also discussed more fully in that chapter.

PERCEPTION AND ATTENTION

Learning and memory in infants and neonates would be impossible if infants lacked adequate perceptual skills and adequate attentional mechanisms. Although there are some important immaturities in the visual system at birth (see Atkinson & Braddick, 1989), recent research has shown that the perceptual abilities of babies are much more sophisticated than was once supposed. We have already seen that visual recognition memory emerges early, as defined by responsiveness to novelty. Attention is clearly a prerequisite if visual recognition memory is to function effectively.

Adequate attentional mechanisms appear to be available shortly after birth. However, it is not clear whether these mechanisms are under the infant's volitional control. It can be very difficult to attract an infant's attention, particularly to a stationary visual stimulus, as many infant experimenters will tell you! At one point it was believed that infants were passive in their selection of visual stimuli. The idea was that attention to certain stimuli was obligatory, and that visual "capture" by these stimuli controlled infant attention (e.g. Stechler & Latz, 1966). This view is no longer widely held. The visual world of the baby is an active one, characterized by a dynamic flow of perceptual events over which the babies themselves have no control. To deal with this dynamic flow of events, infants need to develop expectations of predictable visual events, around which they can then organize their behavior (Haith, Hazan & Goodman, 1988). Thus, one way to study when attentional mechanisms in infants come under volitional control is to study their *expectations* of visual events. The development of visual expectancies requires the volitional control of visual attention.

Attention in infancy

To find out whether babies as young as 3½ months of age can develop visual expectations, Haith and colleagues devised a paradigm that involved showing babies a series of stimuli to the left and to the right of their center of gaze. In Haith et al. (1988), the stimuli used included pictures of checkerboards and bull's eyes, and schematic faces in different colors (the kind of stimuli used by Fantz, 1961, to examine visual perception in babies, see below). Sixty stimuli were used in all. Thirty of these were presented in a left–right alternating sequence, which was thus predictable, and the remaining 30 were presented in a random left–right order. The movements of the babies' eyes were observed during both the predictable and the random presentation sequences. Haith et al. argued that, if the infants could detect the alternation rule governing the appearance of the predictable stimuli, then they should develop expectations of the left–right alternation and should make anticipatory eye movements to the location of the next slide; such eye movements should be less common during the random presentation sequences. This was exactly what happened. The infants showed more anticipatory fixations to the predictable (alternating) sequence than to the unpredictable (random) sequence of pictures, and also showed enhanced reaction times, meaning that they were developing expectations for the visual events quite rapidly. This shows that, at least by the age of 3½ months, babies can control their own perceptual (attentional) activity.

Using a somewhat different task, Gilmore and Johnson (1995) have shown that, by the age of 6 months, infants can also control their visual attention over delays of at least 3–5 seconds. Gilmore and Johnson's paradigm involved showing the infants an attractive geometric display presented center-screen, in order to encourage fixation at the center (Figure 1.3). Once the infants were reliably looking at the central fixation point, a blue triangle (the "cue stimulus") was flashed briefly either to the left or to the right of the center. The screen then stayed dark for a set time period until two rotating, multicolored cogwheel shapes (which were highly attractive to the infant) appeared: one to the left and one to the right of center. The experimenters then scored whether the infants showed a preference for looking at the cued location during the delay period, prior to the onset of the cogwheel targets.

Gilmore and Johnson found strong preferences for the cued location at each of the three different time intervals that they studied, which were 0.6 seconds, 3 seconds, and 5 seconds. They argued that this showed that the infants were maintaining a representation of the spatial location of the cue, and were using it to plan their eye movements several seconds later. In a follow-up study, Gilmore and Johnson cued the eventual left or right location of the target stimulus by presenting different geometric displays at the central fixation point, and omitting the blue triangle. For example, if the center-screen stimulus was a pattern made up of four shifting light- and dark-blue circles, then the target would appear on the right 3 or 5 seconds later, whereas if the

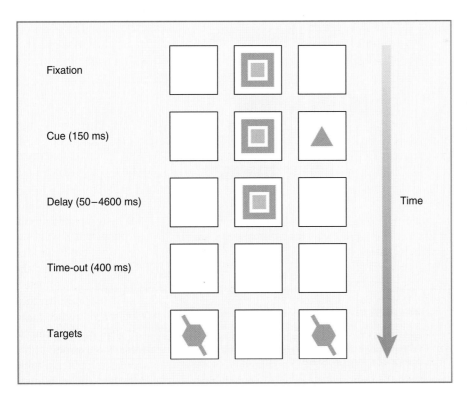

FIGURE 1.3
Example of one of the stimulus presentation sequences used by Gilmore and Johnson to study infant control of visual attention. Each box represents one of the three computer screens. From Gilmore and Johnson (1995). Copyright © 1995 Elsevier. Reprinted with permission.

center-screen stimulus was a pattern made up of small red and yellow squares spiraling around each other, then the target would appear on the left 3 or 5 seconds later. The infants quickly learned this contingency and again showed strong preferences to look to the cued location. Gilmore and Johnson argue that their expectation paradigm also shows the early operation of "working memory" in the infant.

Visual preference and habituation

The existence of visual preferences in infancy provides a useful index of infants' perceptual abilities as well as of their attentional skills. Suppose that we want to discover whether an infant can make a simple visual discrimination between a cross and a circle. One way to find out is to show the infant a picture of a cross and a picture of a circle and to see which shape the infant prefers to look at. The existence of a preference would imply that the infant can *distinguish* between the different forms. The "**visual preference technique**" was first used by Fantz (1961, 1966), who found that 7-month-old infants showed *no* preference between a cross and a circle; instead, they looked at both shapes for an equal amount of time (Figure 1.4).

A "no preference" result in the visual preference paradigm is difficult to interpret. It could mean that the infants were unable to distinguish between the two shapes being tested. Alternatively, it could mean that they found both shapes equally interesting (or equally dull!) to look at. One way to find out whether

FIGURE 1.4
Examples of the visual preference stimuli adapted from Fantz (1961) to study infant form perception, showing the average looking time for each stimulus.

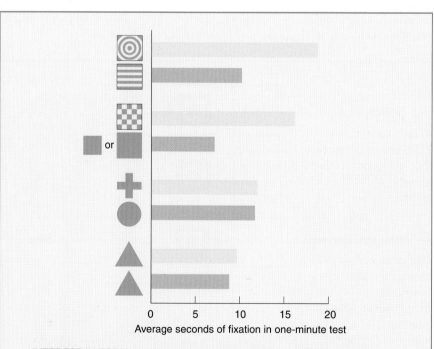

Average seconds of fixation in one-minute test

INTEREST IN FORM was proved by infants' reactions to various pairs of patterns *(left)* presented together. (The small and large plain squares were used alternately.) The more complex pairs received the most attention, and within each of these pairs differential interest was based on pattern differences. These results are for 22 infants in 10 weekly tests.

infants can in fact distinguish two equally preferred visual stimuli is to use the **habituation paradigm**. This has now become one of the most widely used techniques in cognitive research with infants. Habituation is assumed to give the experimenter a way into the infants' conceptual (cognitive) representations.

In simple habituation studies, the infant is shown one stimulus, such as a circle, on repeated occasions. Typically, the infant's interest is at first caught by the novel stimulus and a lot of time is spent in looking at it. Following repeated exposures of the same stimulus, the infant's looking time decreases. This is quite understandable—seeing the same old circle again and again is not that exciting. Once looking time to the stimulus has fallen to half of the initial level, the old stimulus is removed and a new stimulus—such as a cross—is introduced. This is a novel stimulus, so if infants can distinguish between the cross and the circle, renewed looking at the cross should be observed. Renewed looking to a novel stimulus is called "dishabituation". When dishabituation occurs, we know that the cross is perceived as a novel stimulus, and this tells us that infants can distinguish between a cross and a circle.

Research with neonates by Slater and colleagues has shown that infants can indeed discriminate a cross from a circle (Slater, Morison, & Rose, 1983). In Slater et al.'s experiment, the cross and the circle were *both* presented during the dishabituation phase, thereby combining the habituation method with the preference technique. Slater et al. showed that when the cross and the circle were presented after habituation to the circle, then the cross was preferred. When the cross and the circle were presented after habituation to the cross, then the circle was preferred. As neonates in a habituation paradigm can distinguish a cross from a circle, we can conclude that the absence of a preference in 7-month-old infants in Fantz's experiments did not arise out of an inability to distinguish between crosses and circles.

KEY TERM

Habituation paradigm
Infants are presented a stimulus, usually visual or auditory, until it no longer attracts attention: recovery of attention to a new stimulus (dishabituation) indicates discrimination between familiar and new.

Cross-modal perception

The ability to match perceptual information across modalities (cross-modal perception) also appears to be present from early in life. Infants seem to be able to connect visual information with tactile information, and auditory information with visual information, from soon after birth.

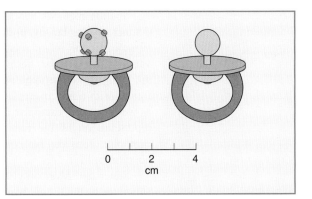

Linking vision and touch

One of the most striking demonstrations of infants' ability to make cross-modal connections between vision and touch comes from an experiment by Meltzoff and Borton (1979), who gave 1-month-old infants one of two dummies, which had different textures, to suck. The surface of one of the dummies was smooth, whereas the other had a nubbled surface (Figure 1.5). The infants were prevented from seeing the dummy when it was placed into their mouths, and so in the first phase of the experiment their experience of the dummy was purely *tactile*. In the second phase of the experiment, the infants were shown enlarged pictures of both dummies, and the experimenters measured which visual stimulus the infants preferred to look at. They found that the majority of the babies preferred to look at

FIGURE 1.5
The two dummies used to study intermodal connections between vision and touch by Meltzoff and Borton (1979). Copyright © 1979 Macmillan Publishers Limited. Reprinted with permission.

the dummy that they had just been sucking: The babies who had sucked on the nubbled dummy looked most at this picture and the babies who had sucked on the smooth dummy looked most at this picture. This suggests an early understanding of cross-modal equivalence.

Linking vision and audition

Infants also appear to be able to make links between the auditory and visual modalities soon after birth. For example, Spelke (1976) showed 4-month-old infants simultaneous films of two rhythmic events: a woman playing "peek-a-boo" and a baton hitting a wooden block. At the same time, the soundtrack appropriate to one of the events was played from a loudspeaker located between the two screens. Spelke found that the infants preferred to look at the visual event that matched the auditory soundtrack. Again, this preference for *congruence* across modalities suggests an understanding of cross-modal equivalence. Dodd (1979) has found similar results in experiments that required infants to match voices to films of faces reading nursery rhymes. When the soundtrack was played "out of synch" with the mouth movements of the reader, the infants got fussy. They preferred to look at faces whose mouths were moving in time with the words in the story. Adults also get fussy when they experience this phenomenon—think of being in the cinema when the soundtrack is out of time with the film. Clearly, we have a strong perceptual preference for congruence across different perceptual modalities, and this preference is present from early in life.

Organizing perceptual information into categories

Habituation methods can also be used to study when babies realize that visually distinct objects belong in the same conceptual category. This paradigm varies the stimuli that the infant sees during the *habituation phase* of the experiment. This variation of exemplars during habituation requires the infants to *categorize* what they are being shown in some way in order to remember it. At test, we can present the infants with a new exemplar of the familiar category that they haven't seen before, as well as a new exemplar from a contrasting category. If the infants have formed a representation of the familiar category then they should prefer to look at the exemplar from the new category, even though both items presented at test are novel stimuli.

Slater and Morison (1987; described in Slater, 1989) used this categorization technique with 3- and 5-month-old babies. During the habituation phase of their study, they showed the babies a variety of types of circle (or of squares, triangles or crosses; Figure 1.6). At test, they showed the "circle" babies a new exemplar of a circle, and an exemplar of another shape, such as a cross. The infants preferred to look at the novel shape (the cross). This suggests that the babies had formed a "prototype", or generalized cognitive representation, of the familiar shape, to which they appeared to be comparing all subsequently presented stimuli.

The ability to categorize exemplars as similar is an important *cognitive* process. The categorization of exemplars as similar suggests that a generalized representation or *prototype* has been formed, to which subsequently presented stimuli can be compared. One idea prevalent in adult cognition is that the use of prototypes enables

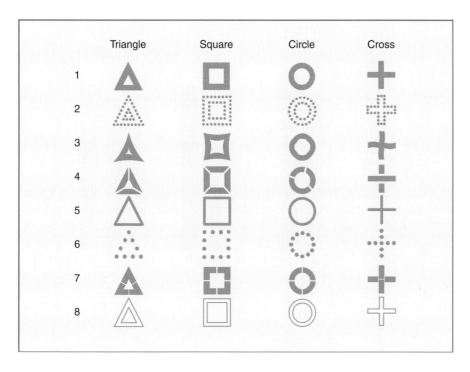

FIGURE 1.6
The different exemplars of triangles, squares, circles, and crosses used during habituation by Slater and Morison. From Slater (1989). Copyright © 1989 Psychology Press.

an organism to store maximal information about the world with the minimum cognitive effort (Rosch, 1978; see Chapter 4). If we were unable to impose categories on the perceptual world then every percept, object or event that occurred would be processed as if it were unique. This would produce an overwhelming amount of information. The ability to organize incoming information into categories is thus essential for cognitive activity. Habituation studies have used a variety of stimuli to discover whether babies can form prototypes of objects.

For example, suppose that you showed a baby a number of pictures of different stuffed animals. You might show a picture of a stuffed frog, a picture of a stuffed donkey, a picture of a stuffed alligator, a picture of a stuffed bear and so on. Although these exemplars would differ in numerous features, the infants might be able to abstract a category like "stuffed animals" from seeing these different instances, in which case they should eventually habituate to these changing exemplars. By the time they saw their fifteenth stuffed animal, even if it was a novel stuffed octopus, they might find the "stuffed animals" category rather *too* familiar and show habituation of looking.

Cohen and Caputo (1978) carried out a habituation experiment that was very similar to the one just described with three different groups of babies, all aged 7 months. The first group saw the same stuffed animal on each trial of the habituation phase of the experiment, the second group saw a different stuffed animal on each trial and the third group saw a set of totally unrelated objects (e.g. a toy car, a ball, a stuffed animal, a telephone). At test, the infants were shown a novel stuffed animal and a rattle. The first group showed dishabituation to both the novel stuffed animal and the rattle. The second group showed dishabituation to the rattle only and the third group (which in any case had shown little habituation) showed no dishabituation. This pattern of results is shown in Figure 1.7. Cohen and Caputo argued that the second group had abstracted a category of "stuffed animals".

FIGURE 1.7
Looking time on the last habituation trial (H) and the first dishabituation trials with the novel stuffed animal (S$_A$) and the rattle (R) in Cohen and Caputo's (1978) experiment with three groups of babies: those shown the same stuffed animal (Same), those shown different stuffed animals (Changing), and those shown totally unrelated objects (Objects). Figure from Younger and Cohen (1985). Copyright © 1985 Academic Press. Reproduced with permission.

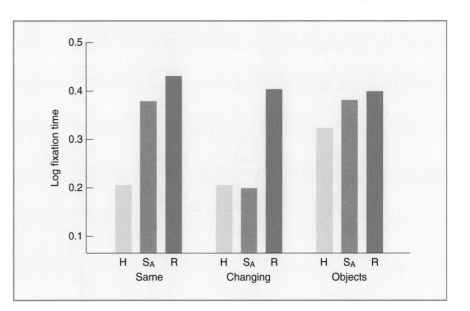

Processing interrelations between features: the differentiation of prototypes

To argue that the infants were abstracting a prototypical "stuffed animal" from all of these instances, we would need evidence that they were attending to the *interrelations* between the different features of each stuffed animal, rather than habituating to a single recurring feature, such as the eyes. If infants can code the perceptual structure of objects in terms of the correlational structure between different features, then this would be good evidence for conceptual representation on the basis of perceptual prototypes. In fact, Rosch (1978) has argued that humans divide the world into objects and categories on just such a correlational basis. Certain features in the world tend to co-occur, and this co-occurrence specifies natural categories such as trees, birds, flowers, and dogs (see also Chapter 4). For example, birds are distinguished from dogs partly because feathers and wings occur together, whereas fur and wings do not. According to Rosch, this process of noticing co-occurrences between sets of features results in a generalized representation of a prototypical bird, a prototypical dog, and so on, and it has been argued that these perceptual prototypes provide the basis for *conceptual* representation.

Younger and Cohen (1983) examined whether infants were able to attend to the interrelations between features as required by prototype theory. They designed a habituation study based on "cartoon animals" to study this question (Figure 1.8). The cartoon animals could vary in five attributes: shape of body, shape of tail, shape of feet, shape of ears, and shape of legs. There were three different forms of each attribute (e.g. the feet could be webbed feet, paws or hooves). During the habituation phase of the experiment, the babies were shown animals in which three critical features varied; two of them varied together, and the third did not. For example, long legs might always occur with short necks, but tails could be any shape. Following habituation, the babies were shown three different cartoon animals. One was an animal whose critical features maintained the correlation; the second was an animal whose critical features violated

FIGURE 1.8
Examples of the cartoon animals used by Younger and Cohen (1983). Reproduced with permission from Blackwell Publishing.

the correlation, and the third was an animal with completely different features. Younger and Cohen found that 10-month-old babies showed dishabituation to the second and third animals, but not to the first. This result suggested that the babies were sensitive to the relationship between the different critical features. They had formed a prototype of an animal with a short neck and long legs.

One way to test whether the infants really were coding the correlational structure between the different features is to show different infants different sets of correlations between features, and then see whether they form different prototypes. Younger (1985) devised an ingenious method to enable such a test. She reasoned that if babies were shown cartoon animals in which all possible lengths of necks and legs could co-occur, then they should form a prototype of the *average* animal. As the different features would be uncorrelated with each other, the infants should abstract a prototypical animal with an average-length neck and average-length legs. However, if they were shown animals in which neck and leg length covaried in two clusters, for example long legs and short necks and vice versa, then they should form two different prototypes. One would be of animals with long legs and short necks, and one of animals with short legs and long necks.

To test her hypothesis, Younger used cartoon animals whose leg and neck lengths could have one of five values (e.g. 1 = short and 5 = long). Infants in a *broad* condition saw animals in which all possible lengths co-occurred except for length 3 (the average value), and infants in a *narrow* condition saw animals in which short legs went with long necks (1,5), and vice versa. At test, Younger found that the infants in the broad group preferred to look at cartoon animals with either very short

FIGURE 1.9
Some of the cartoon animals used by Younger (1985). Reproduced with permission from Blackwell Publishing.

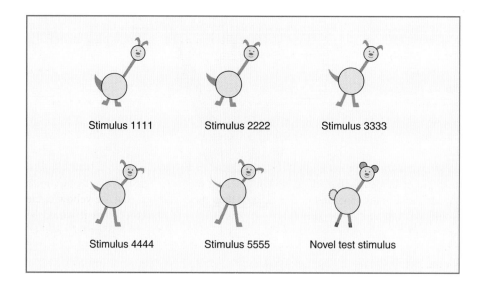

Stimulus 1111   Stimulus 2222   Stimulus 3333

Stimulus 4444   Stimulus 5555   Novel test stimulus

legs and very long necks, or very long legs and very short necks (Figure 1.9). By contrast, the infants in the narrow group preferred to look at cartoon animals whose legs and necks were of average length (3,3). This suggests that the infants in the broad group found the average familiar, even though they had never seen those particular attributes before. They had abstracted a prototypical animal with an average-length neck and average-length legs. The infants in the narrow group had formed *two* prototypes, and thus found the average animal novel. Younger (1990) went on to demonstrate that babies were also sensitive to correlational structure when stimuli were based on features taken from real animals ("natural kinds").

The use of more natural categories and real features to study **prototype formation** is important, as the correlational structure of objects in the real world is quite complex. Recently, developmental psychologists have begun to study whether infants can form prototypes of natural kinds, such as cats, horses, zebras, and giraffes. This work is relevant to infant understanding of the core domain of biology, and is considered in Chapter 4.

Prototypes and statistical learning in infancy

Younger's cartoon-animal experiments demonstrated that infants could code the correlational structure between the different features being manipulated by the experimenters. This suggests a form of **statistical learning**. In effect, the infants were learning about statistical patterns; they were learning which features co-occurred together. Recently, there has been an explosion of interest in infants' ability to track statistical patterns, particularly in the auditory domain (this work is discussed in detail in Chapter 5). However, the same questions can be asked in the visual domain. If the ordering of certain objects in the visual world follows a pattern, will infants track this pattern and show dishabituation when it is violated? This question was studied by Johnson and colleagues, testing infants as young as 2 months of age.

Kirkham, Slemmer, and Johnson (2002) created a visual habituation task based on simple colored geometric shapes. These were presented as a continuous stream by a computer monitor, for example, the participating infants (who were aged 2, 5, and

8 months of age) might see a blue cross for 1 second, followed by a yellow circle for 1 second, followed by a green triangle for 1 second, and so on. Visual attention to the stream of objects was maintained by having the objects "loom" at the infants (essentially this means that the objects increased in size from 4 to 24 cm in height during presentation). The order in which the shapes were seen by a particular infant was varied, so that certain pairs of objects always followed each other. For example, a blue cross might always be followed by a yellow circle. Hence the transitional probability that when a blue cross was on screen the next shape would be a yellow circle was 1.0. Each infant saw a stream of six shapes, with three pairings. This meant that the transitional probability of the next shape after the yellow circle was 0.33. For example, if this particular infant was also seeing the pairs "green triangle, turquoise square", and "pink diamond, red octagon", then the likelihood that the yellow circle would be followed by a green triangle was 0.33, the likelihood that it would be followed by a pink diamond was 0.33, and the likelihood that it would be followed by a blue cross was 0.33. The stream of shapes continued for up to 90 seconds per trial for the 2-month-olds, and for up to 60 seconds per trial for the older infants.

Following habituation to the stream of shapes, the infants saw six test displays. Half of these comprised the familiar sequence and half were a novel sequence of new orderings produced randomly by the computer. The only difference between the familiar and novel sequences lay in the transitional probabilities between the shapes. This ensured that any looking time differences at test would depend on the statistical structure governing the sequence.

Kirkham et al. (2002) found that all groups looked significantly longer at the novel sequence. The 2-month-olds were as good at detecting novelty as the older infants. As there was no a priori relationship between the geometric shapes to provide information for co-occurrence, Kirkham et al. argued that they had demonstrated a true sensitivity to transitional probabilities in very young infants. Again, we see that infants have an impressive ability to keep track of the statistical structure in the input (see also Fiser & Aslin, 2002). The visual input structure in this experiment is quite arbitrary. It is not supported by rudimentary conceptual relations such as "instance of a cartoon animal". This experiment with geometric shapes suggests that infants are able to learn about environmental structure at a fairly abstract level. This facility for statistical learning is also found in other domains, such as the auditory domain (see Chapter 5). The ability to track conditional probabilities provides a very powerful domain-general learning mechanism for extracting structure from the physical world of objects. We can now ask: What about *events* in the physical world? Events can also have predictable structure. Is the visual world of the infant organized into both objects and events?

THE PERCEPTUAL STRUCTURE OF THE VISUAL WORLD

The evidence for prototype formation shows that infants can code the perceptual structure of objects in terms of the relationships (covariations) between different features of these objects. Further, we have seen that they can track conditional probabilities between objects that follow each other in particular sequences. However, if this ability to detect statistical structure was restricted to the static features of natural kinds and artifacts, then even though it would be very useful, its cognitive value would be relatively limited. The ability to detect regularities between perceptual events would markedly increase the cognitive value of this mechanism. Events in the visual world are usually described by *relations* between objects (such as football *collides with* goalpost, child *pushes* truck). The ability to detect structural regularities in these relations would confer great cognitive power, as events in the visual world are frequently *causal* in nature.

The detection of regularities in causal relations like *collide*, *push*, and *supports* between different objects may be an important mechanism in knowledge representation and thus in cognitive development. These regularities can also be described in terms of classes of event, such as "occlusion", "containment", and "support" (see Mandler, 1992; Baillargeon, 2001, 2002). Similarly, other types of relations, such as spatial relations (*above* and *below*) and quantitative relations (*more than* and *less than*), may also be detected. One way of measuring infants' ability to process and represent spatial, numerical, and causal relations is to introduce *violations* of typical regularities in the relations between objects, which then result in physically "impossible" events. This is known as the "**violation of expectation paradigm**", and has been widely used to study infant cognition. For example, an object with no visible means of support can remain stationary in mid-air instead of falling to the ground. The experimental investigation of infants' ability to detect such violations provides an important way of measuring their ability to process relations between events and to represent the causal structure of these relations.

Representing spatial relations

One way to test whether infants are sensitive to spatial relations is to use habituation. For example, if an infant is shown a variety of stimuli that are all exemplars of the same spatial relation, and if the infant shows habituation to these stimuli, then the infant must be sensitive to relational information. If the infant is then shown an example of a *new* spatial relation, dishabituation should occur. This method was used in an experiment by Quinn (1994), who familiarized 3-month-old infants to the spatial relations *above* and *below*. This was achieved by showing half of the infants repeated presentations of a black horizontal bar with a dot above it in four different positions, and half of the infants a black horizontal bar with a dot below it in four different positions. These patterns provided exemplars of the spatial relation *above* and the spatial relation *below*, respectively. At test, the infants were shown a novel exemplar of the familiar relation (a dot in a new position above or below the bar, depending on the habituation condition), and an exemplar of the *unfamiliar* relation (a dot on the other side of the bar). Both groups showed a visual preference for the unfamiliar relation. This finding suggests that infants can categorize perceptual structure on the basis of spatial relations.

Experiments based on the spatial relations between dots and lines might appear to provide rather impoverished tests of relational processing and representation. In fact, monkeys can categorize such relations too (e.g. Spinozzi, Lubrano, & Truppa, 2004). However, there is evidence that infants show the same abilities with far more complex stimuli. For example, Baillargeon and colleagues investigated whether infants of 5½ months realized that a tall rabbit should be partially visible when it passed behind a short wall. During the habituation phase of the experiment, the infants saw a display of a tall painted "wall" (Baillargeon & Graber, 1987). A rabbit appeared at one end of the wall, passed along behind it, and reappeared at the other end. This "habituating" rabbit could either be tall or short, but as both the tall and the

KEY TERM

Violation of expectation paradigm
Infants are shown a physical event and then on test trials shown events that are either incompatible (thus, violating expectation) or compatible with the event. Longer looking at the impossible event indicates that the infants understand the physical principle involved.

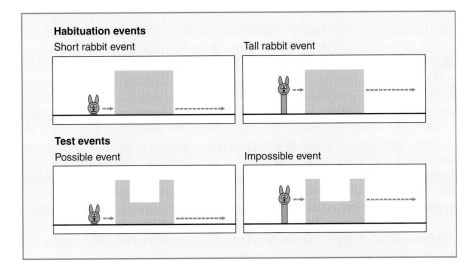

Habituation events

Short rabbit event

Tall rabbit event

Test events

Possible event

Impossible event

FIGURE 1.10
The habituation and test displays in the tall and short rabbit experiment devised by Baillargeon and Graber (1987). Copyright © 1987 Elsevier. Reprinted with permission.

short rabbit were too small to be visible when they were behind the wall, the infants watched the rabbits disappear and reappear as they moved from left to right. At test, the mid-section of the wall was lowered. The wall now had two tall ends and a short middle (Figure 1.10). The short rabbit could still pass behind the entire length of the wall without being visible but the tall rabbit could not. The tall rabbit's head would appear as it passed behind the middle section of the wall.

Both groups of infants then again watched the habituating rabbit (tall or short) passing behind the wall. In fact, they saw the *same* event to which they had been habituated. For the "small rabbit" group, the failure of the rabbit to appear in the mid-section of the apparatus was perfectly acceptable in terms of the spatial relations involved, and accordingly there was no dishabituation. For the "tall rabbit" group, the test event was not acceptable in terms of the spatial relations involved—in fact, it was physically impossible. The tall rabbit's head should have appeared behind the mid-section of the wall, but it did not—just as in the habituating event. Baillargeon and Graber found that the babies in the "tall rabbit" group spent much longer staring at the experimental apparatus than the babies in the "short rabbit" group. The infants' increased looking time at the nonappearance of the tall rabbit suggests that they had represented the spatial relations between the wall and the rabbit. Later work (Baillargeon & DeVos, 1991) has shown that 3½-month-old infants behave in the same way (this was demonstrated in a modified version of the experiment, which used a tall and a short carrot). Thus very young babies appear to be able to represent spatial relations such as relative height, at least in an occlusion paradigm.

Baillargeon and colleagues have also used habituation to measure infants' memory for spatial locations. This is a strong test of representation, as the infants must retain the spatial relations defining location *over time*. In one experiment, Baillargeon and Graber (1988) showed infants a display that had two possible locations in which a toy could be placed, A and B. The two locations were marked by identical mats. As the infants watched the display, an attractive object was placed at location A (in fact, the object used was a plastic styrofoam cup with matches stuck into its sides, an object that the infants found far more visually interesting than the toys that were used when the experimenters tried to pilot the experiment!). Two screens were then slid in front of the two locations, hiding the mats. As the infants continued to watch the display, a hand wearing a silver glove and a bracelet of bells appeared and the fingers danced around—this was also visually interesting, and was designed to keep the infants attending to the display. The hand then reached behind the screen at location B, and retrieved the styrofoam cup.

Of course, this retrieval was an "impossible" event. Location B had been visibly empty when the screens slid in front of the mats, and the styrofoam cup should only have been retrievable at location A. Baillargeon and Graber argued that if the babies could remember the location of the object during the delay, then they would be perturbed at this event, and should show increased looking at the display. This was exactly what they found. The babies stared at the impossible retrieval and looked at the display for a long time. Increased looking time did not occur in a control event, which was a "possible" event. In this event, the hand retrieved the cup from behind the correct screen, and the infants were not particularly interested. The fact that their attention was caught only when the cup was retrieved from the wrong spatial location suggests that they were able to represent the location of the cup even when it was out of view. Baillargeon, DeVos, and Graber (1989) went on to demonstrate that 8-month-old infants could retain these spatial memories for up to 70 seconds: So "out of sight" is not necessarily "out of mind" for infants.

A different test of spatial learning and memory was devised by McKenzie, Day, and Ihsen (1984). They seated 6- to 8-month-old babies behind a kind of semi-circular "news desk" (Figure 1.11). The babies sat on their mothers' laps in a central position (like a "newsreader"), enabling them to scan the entire desk. The shape of the desk meant that there were a number of different locations at which events could occur, both to the left and to the right of the babies. The location at which an event was about to occur was always marked by a white ball. The events were visually exciting to the babies—an adult appeared from behind the desk and began playing "peek-a-boo".

McKenzie et al. found that the babies quickly learned to anticipate an event at the spatial location marked by the white ball. As the white ball could appear either

FIGURE 1.11
The experimental set-up used in the "newsreader" experiment to study spatial learning and memory by McKenzie et al. (1984). Copyright © The British Psychological Society. Reproduced with permission.

to the right or to the left of the midline, the babies could not have learned a specific motor response, such as turning their heads to the right. Instead, they were learning to *predict* the spatial location of the visual events by using the white ball. McKenzie et al. argued that this showed that babies did not always **code spatial position** in memory *egocentrically*, with respect to a motor response based on their own position in space. When given the appropriate opportunity, they could also code spatial location in memory *allocentrically*, with respect to a salient landmark such as the white ball. The representation of spatial relations in 8-month-olds thus involves landmark cues, just as it does in adults.

KEY TERM

Coding of spatial position
Can occur either in relation to one's own position in space (egocentric) or to external landmarks (allocentric).

Representing occlusion relations

So far, we have considered evidence that babies can use the perceptual structure of events in the visual world as a basis for representing relational knowledge about space. However, perceptual events can also provide conceptual knowledge about the continued existence of objects when they are out of view. When an object is occluded by a second object, we as adults believe that it still exists. Even when one object totally occludes another, we assume that the hidden object continues to exist and to occupy the same location in space behind the occluder.

Babies seem to make similar assumptions about the existence of occluded objects. One of the most ingenious demonstrations of their belief in "object permanence" comes from an experiment by Baillargeon, Spelke, and Wasserman (1985). Baillargeon et al. habituated 5-month-old babies to a display in which a screen continually rotated through 180° towards and away from the baby, like a drawbridge (Figure 1.12). Following habituation, a box was placed in the path of the

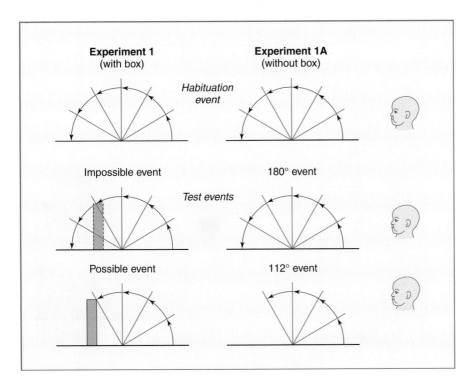

FIGURE 1.12
Diagram of the habituation and test events in the rotating screen paradigm. From Baillargeon et al. (1985). Copyright © 1985 Elsevier. Reprinted with permission.

screen at the far end of the apparatus. As the screen began its 180° rotation it gradually occluded the box. When it reached 90° the entire box was hidden from view. For babies who were shown a "possible event", the screen continued to rotate until it had passed through 120°, at which point it came to rest, apparently having made contact with the box. For babies who were shown an "impossible event", the screen continued to rotate until it had passed through the full 180° rotation. In the physically "impossible" condition, the box had apparently caused no obstruction to the path of the screen's movement. Although the 180° rotation was the familiar (habituating) event, the babies in the impossible condition spent much longer staring at the experimental display than the babies in the possible condition (who were seeing a novel event). This finding suggests that the babies had represented the box as continuing to exist, even when it was occluded by the screen. They looked longer at the display when the screen passed through an apparently solid object.

In later work, Baillargeon has shown that babies as young as 3½ months of age look reliably longer when the screen passes through the box, particularly if they are "fast habituators" (Baillargeon, 1987a). She has also shown that infants can represent some of the physical and spatial properties of the occluded objects, such as whether an object is compressible or not (e.g. a sponge vs. a wooden block; Figure 1.13), and whether it is taller or shorter than the height of the screen (e.g. a wooden box measuring 20 × 15 × 4 cm standing upright vs. lying flat; Baillargeon, 1987b).

FIGURE 1.13
Diagram of the habituation and test events in the rotating screen paradigm with soft vs. hard objects. From Baillargeon (1987b). Copyright © 1987 Elsevier. Reprinted with permission.

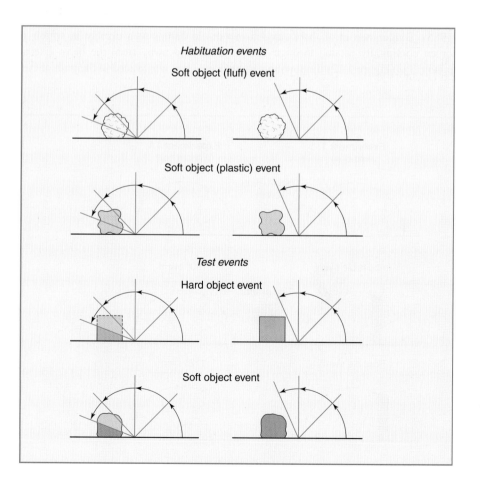

These experiments suggest that not only can young infants represent the existence of hidden objects, they can also represent some of the specific properties of the objects that are hidden. They can then use these physical and spatial characteristics to make predictions about how the drawbridge should behave as it begins to rotate.

Despite the many variations of the "drawbridge" paradigm that Baillargeon has devised, her use of a rotating screen to demonstrate infants' belief in object permanence has proved to be a controversial one. For example, it has been argued that the perceptual structure of events in the "drawbridge" paradigm leads the infants to form a strong expectation that the drawbridge should stop, an expectation that does not necessitate a representation of the occluded object. This criticism is weakened by the demonstration that infants' expectations about the behavior of the drawbridge differ depending on the nature of the object that is hidden (e.g. Baillargeon, 1987b). Furthermore, the series of drawbridge studies that Baillargeon and colleagues have conducted is only one piece of evidence that babies represent hidden objects as continuing to exist. A different paradigm, also devised by Baillargeon (1986), tests the same understanding and does not seem vulnerable to an "expectation" criticism at all.

This paradigm was based on a toy car and a ramp. During the initial phase of the experiment, 6½-month-old infants were shown a display in which a toy car was poised at the top of a ramp. A track for the car ran down the ramp and along the base of the apparatus. When the infants were attending to the apparatus, the middle section of the track was hidden by lowering a screen, and the habituation phase of the experiment began. The car ran down the ramp, passed behind the screen and reappeared at the end of the apparatus. Following habituation to repeated presentations of this event, the screen was raised and a box was placed either on the car's track, or behind it. The screen was then lowered again, hiding the box, and the car began its journey. The apparatus used is shown in Figure 1.14.

All the babies then saw exactly the same set of events as during the habituation phase of the experiment. For babies in the "possible" condition, the box was behind the track and out of the car's path, and so the reappearance of the car was not

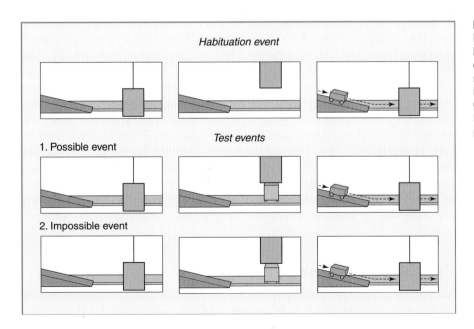

1. Possible event

Test events

2. Impossible event

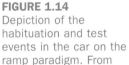

FIGURE 1.14
Depiction of the habituation and test events in the car on the ramp paradigm. From Baillargeon (1986). Copyright © 1986 Elsevier. Reprinted with permission.

surprising. For babies in the "impossible" condition, however, the box was *on* the track, directly in the path of the car—and yet the car *still* reappeared in the familiar way! The babies in the impossible condition spent much longer staring at the apparatus than the babies in the possible condition. The only explanation was that they had represented the box as continuing to exist and as therefore blocking the car's path, and so they were intrigued by the reappearance of the car. Baillargeon and DeVos (1991) later demonstrated that babies as young as 3½ months looked for a reliably longer time when the car reappeared despite the fact that a hidden object (a Mickey Mouse doll) was blocking its path.

This paradigm was subsequently used by Kotovsky and Baillargeon (1998) to investigate babies' understanding of collision events more directly. They explored infants' expectations in situations where a stationary object was hit by a moving object. The moving object was a cylinder that varied in size, and the stationary object was a bug on wheels. When the cylinder collided with the bug, it set the bug in motion. As adults, we would expect the distance traveled by the bug following this collision to depend on the size of the cylinder. Kotovsky and Baillargeon explored whether babies aged from 5½ months also expected there to be a proportional relation between the size of the cylinder and the distance traveled by the wheeled bug. During habituation trials, the infants were shown the ramp, and a stationary wheeled bug sitting at the bottom of the ramp on the track. No occluders were used. As the infants watched, a medium-sized cylinder ran down the ramp, collided with the bug and set it in motion. The bug ran half way along the track and then stopped. In the novel event, either a larger or a smaller cylinder was used. Both cylinders propelled the bug to the *end* of the track. While this was a possible event for the larger cylinder, it should have been impossible for the smaller cylinder. The size of the cylinder should have affected the bug's trajectory. Kotovsky and Baillargeon (1998) found that 6½-month-old babies and 5½-month-old female babies looked reliably longer at the small cylinder event than at the large cylinder event. They argued that the babies were engaging in calibration-based reasoning about the size/distance relations in the perceptual display.

Another type of occlusion event has also been the focus of investigations by Baillargeon's group. Hespos and Baillargeon (2001a, b) studied the looking behavior of babies when potential containers were used as occluders. For example, either a tall or a short container made of PVC piping was used to occlude a brightly colored cylindrical object with a knob on the top. The tall container completely concealed the object, with just the knob on the top remaining visible. However, the short container was only about half as high as the object. Hence the top half of the object should have remained visible behind this short occluder. In fact, via the surreptitious use of two objects, the visual events seen by the babies were the same. When the object was lowered behind the short occluder it also became completely hidden, apart from the knob on the top. Of course, this violated the expectation that the object could not become fully hidden by the short occluder. Hespos and Baillargeon (2001a, b) reported that babies as young as 4½ months looked reliably longer at the impossible event. They apparently realized that the height of an object relative to the height of an occluder will determine whether the object will be fully or only partly hidden behind the occluder.

Representing support relations

Another set of perceptual relations that are commonly encountered in the physical world are the relations involved in support. Adults are well aware that if they put a

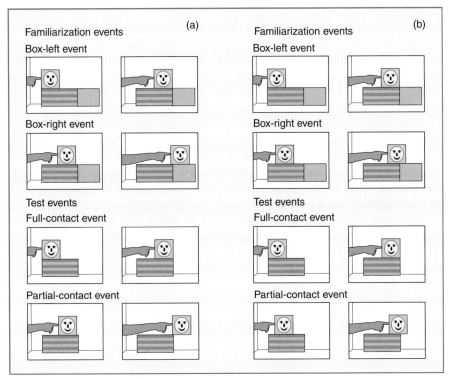

FIGURE 1.15
Depiction of the familiarization and test events in the "box on a platform" paradigm devised by Baillargeon et al. (1992). Panel (a) depicts the 85% protrusion event, and panel (b) the 30% protrusion event. From Baillargeon et al. (1992). Copyright © John Wiley & Sons, Ltd. Reproduced with permission.

mug of tea down on a table and the mug protrudes too far over the edge, then the mug will fall onto the floor. However, if only a small portion of the bottom surface of the mug is protruding over the edge of the table, then the mug will have adequate support and the tea can be drunk at leisure. Baillargeon, Needham, and DeVos (1992) investigated similar intuitions about support in young infants. They studied 6½-month-old infants' expectations about when a box would fall off a platform.

In Baillargeon et al.'s experiment the infants were shown a box sitting at the left-hand end of a long platform, and then watched as the finger of a gloved hand pushed the box along the platform until part of it was suspended over the right-hand edge (Figure 1.15). For some infants, the pushing continued until 85% of the bottom surface of the box protruded over the platform, and for others the pushing stopped when 30% of the bottom surface of the box protruded over the platform. In a control condition, the same infants watched the box being pushed to the right-hand end of the platform, but the bottom surface of the box remained in full contact with the platform. The infants spent reliably longer looking at the apparatus in the 85% protrusion event than in the full-contact control event. This suggests that they expected the box to fall off the platform (the box was able to remain magically suspended in mid-air via a hidden hand). The infants in the 30% protrusion event looked equally during the protrusion event and the control event. Baillargeon et al. argued that the infants were able to judge how much contact was required between the box and the platform in order for the box to be stable.

Interestingly, younger infants (5½- to 6-month-olds) appeared unable to make such fine judgments about support. They looked equally at the 85% and 30% protrusion events compared to the full-contact control event. Baillargeon et al.'s interpretation of this finding was that younger infants perceive *any* amount of contact between objects to be sufficient to ensure stability. They operate with a simpler causal rule that *no contact = object falls*, and *partial contact = object is supported*, even when the partial contact is very partial indeed. In fact, Baillargeon argues that much physical causal reasoning develops according to this all-or-none pattern (see Baillargeon, 2001, 2002). Infants begin with representations that capture the essence of physical events (e.g. contact vs. no contact) and then gradually develop more elaborate representations that identify variables that are relevant to the events' outcomes (such as degree of support). Experience of the physical world has an important role to play in this developmental sequence. For example, at around 6 months of age most babies become "self-sitters". They are able to sit up, with support, and for the first time they can be seated in high-chairs, etc. in front of tables, and can deposit objects on surfaces and watch them fall off. Baillargeon has suggested that these experiences help infants to refine their understanding of the cause–effect relations underlying support. The idea that specific *action experiences* of this kind help in the development of specific aspects of physical reasoning is discussed further in Chapter 2.

Representing containment relations

Another way of investigating what Spelke (1994) has termed the "**continuity principle**"—that objects exist continuously in time and space—is to explore infants' understanding of containment events. When an object is placed inside a container, it leaves the field of view. However, as adults, we know that the object continues to exist inside the container. Do babies share this understanding? In a series of experiments, Baillargeon, Luo, Wang, Paterson, and Hespos studied infants' understanding of containment events (e.g. Hespos & Baillargeon, 2001a, b, 2006; Luo & Baillargeon, 2005; Wang, Baillargeon, & Paterson, 2005). For example, Hespos and Baillargeon (2001a) designed a containment study that was analogous to the occlusion study with the cylindrical object discussed earlier. The container was a piece of PVC tubing identical in perceptual appearance to the PVC tubing occluder. During the containment events, the infants watched as the cylindrical object was lowered inside the container (rather than behind the occluder). This comparison is shown in Figure 1.16. The tall container was large enough to contain the entire object, leaving just the knob on the top visible to the infants; however, the short container was not. In this condition, the top half of the object should have remained visible when it was lowered into the container. Instead, the object disappeared until only the knob was visible, violating expectations based on object continuity. Both the tall and the short container appeared able to contain the entire cylindrical object.

Intriguingly, Hespos and Baillargeon (2001a) reported that infants did not show increased looking times for the short container event until around 7½ months of age. They did not appear to realize that the height of the container relative to the height of the object determined whether the object would be fully or only partially hidden by the container. This was surprising, as infants aged 4½ months were able to use the relative heights of the object versus the container as a cue in the highly similar occlusion condition. In the containment condition, infants of 4½ months, 5½ months, and 6½ months of age did not appear aware of the importance of the height of the container. They did not look reliably longer at the short container event. Baillargeon

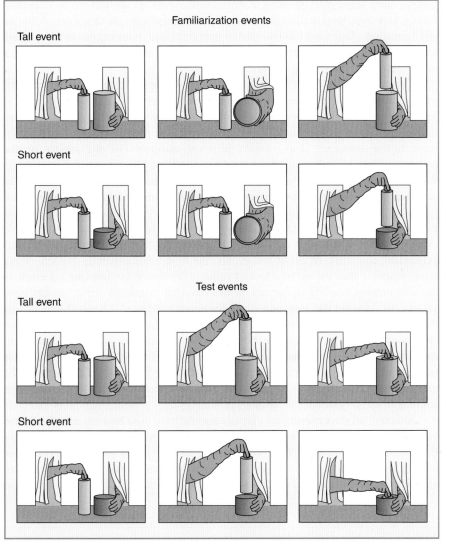

FIGURE 1.16
Familiarization and test events in the container condition of Hespos and Baillargeons's (2001b) study. Reproduced with permission from Blackwell Publishing.

and Wang (2002) suggested that infants treated containment events as distinct from occlusion events. They did not generalize their knowledge of a variable like height from one type of event to the other.

In a separate series of studies, Luo and Baillargeon (2005) studied infants' understanding of transparent containers. The infants were shown a plexiglass box, which was then occluded by a screen. An attractive object was then lowered into the box, although its entry into the box occurred out of view of the infant. When the screen was lowered, the infants either saw the object inside the box (possible event), or the empty transparent container (impossible event). Infants did not look for reliably longer at the empty container until 10 months of age. However, if the plexiglass was used as an occluder, rather than as a container (via a plexiglass screen), then infants from 7½ months of age looked longer at the physical violation. Again, this difference in looking behavior was interpreted in terms of *event categories*.

Infants were apparently treating containment events as distinct from occlusion events, and were working out the perceptual variables relevant to a more elaborate representation of occlusion events earlier than they were working out the perceptual variables relevant to a more elaborate representation of containment events—even when these were the same perceptual variables.

Apparent support for this interpretation based on event categories came from a separate series of studies comparing containment with covering. When a cover is lowered over an object, the same principle of continuity applies as when an object is lowered inside a container. The object continues to exist beneath the cover or beneath the container, and various physical attributes of the object or the cover/container will determine whether any parts of the object remain visible. Wang, Baillargeon, and Paterson (2005) used identical tubes as covers or as containers. For example, in one experiment 9-month-old infants watched as a tall tube was used to cover a tall object (Figure 1.17), or as a tall object was lowered into a tall cylindrical container. These were possible events. In the impossible events, the tall object was covered by a short tube or was lowered into a short cylindrical container. In all of the events, the object became fully hidden. Wang et al. reported that the infants looked reliably longer at the unexpected event in the containment condition, but not in the covering condition. Only infants aged 12 months detected the violation in the covering condition; 11-month-old infants did not. Again, these discrepancies in behavior were explained in terms of event categories. Covering seemed to be treated by infants as an event distinct to containment. Therefore, identical variables (such as tube height) were treated as relevant to one event category before they were treated as relevant to another. The explanation was that infants were sorting physical events into categories, and were learning separately how each category operated.

Although all the experiments discussed so far have used looking behavior in the violation of expectation paradigm as the outcome measure, more recently Baillargeon and colleagues have been testing this model of physical reasoning in infancy by using action-based tasks. For example, Hespos and Baillargeon (2006) exploited search behavior to compare infant actions in containment versus occlusion

FIGURE 1.17
Possible and impossible events used in Wang, Baillargeon, and Paterson's (2005) study. Top: a tall tube was used to cover a tall object (possible); bottom: a tall object was covered by a short tube (impossible). From Wang, Baillargeon, and Paterson (2005). Copyright © 2005 Elsevier. Reprinted with permission.

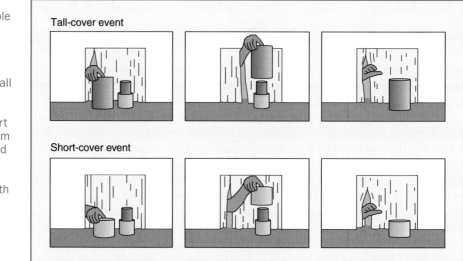

Tall-cover event

Short-cover event

events. They studied the ages at which infants would search consistently for a toy that was either hidden behind an occluder or that was hidden inside a container. The occluders and containers were the same PVC tubes used in previous experiments. This time, infants were given an engaging tall frog toy to play with. The frog was then removed. The infants were shown a screen and, when the screen was lowered, two containers or occluders were revealed—one tall and one short. Frog legs were sticking out of the bottom of each, and the infants were encouraged to find the frog; 6-month-olds and 7½-month-olds were tested.

Based on their findings in the violation of expectation paradigm, Hespos and Baillargeon reasoned that infants identify the variable height as relevant at about 4½ months in occlusion paradigms and at about 7½ months in containment paradigms. They therefore argued that the younger infants should search for the frog behind the tall occluder in the occlusion paradigm, but should not preferentially search inside the tall container in the containment paradigm. The older infants were expected to search for the frog successfully in both paradigms. This was exactly what they found. In the occlusion condition, 12/16 7½-month-olds and 14/18 6-month-olds reached for the tall occluder on three or four of the four search trials. In the containment condition, only the older infants were successful, with 12/16 reliably picking the tall container compared to only 2/18 of the younger infants. Different control conditions were used to rule out alternative explanations. Hespos and Baillargeon (2006) concluded that evidence from action tasks was consistent with evidence from the violation of expectation paradigm concerning physical reasoning in infants. Physical reasoning by infants depends on the formation of distinct event categories (occlusion, containment, support), and infants learn about each category separately. Perceptual variables that are identified in one category may not be generalized to another category, even when they are equally relevant. Hespos and Baillargeon suggested that infants' physical reasoning systems are designed to acquire event-specific expectations rather than event-general principles. This suggestion is consistent with what we know about the neural mechanisms of conceptual learning, as is discussed in Chapter 4.

What is measured in the violation of expectation paradigm?

Recently, a number of criticisms have appeared of studies that use habituation, visual preference, and violation-of-expectation techniques to study cognitive processes in infancy. Some of these critics are highly resistant to the notion that young infants engage in physical reasoning at all (e.g. Haith, 1998). Critics such as Haith point out—correctly—that looking paradigms were developed to study sensory and perceptual questions, not cognitive questions. We saw some examples of these perceptual questions at the beginning of this chapter. An important part of these critiques is the observation that it is simply not possible to generate perceptually identical but conceptually distinct stimuli for habituation paradigms (see Sirois & Mareschal, 2002, although note that this does not mean that looking time as a measure must be abandoned; see Aslin, 2007). Critics such as Haith argue that scientists like Baillargeon must be able to discount every possible *perceptual* interpretation of differences in looking time before proposing cognitive interpretations of infant looking behavior. In a similar vein, Bogartz, Shinskey, and Speaker (1997) argued that simple perceptual mechanisms such as novelty, scanning, and tracking may explain longer looking times by infants in some perceptual conditions versus others. These points are important: It is not clear that behavioral experiments will ever be able to devise conditions that unambiguously demonstrate **cognitive representations** in infants.

In fact, a theoretical point frequently made by such critics regards what it means to attribute cognitive representations to infants at all. For example, Haith (1998) suggests that infants may have lingering sensory information about objects that have been (for example) occluded, and that it is this lingering sensory information, rather than a conceptual representation of the object, that yields the changes in looking behavior. Perceptual mechanisms such as familiarity, novelty, and discrepancy, which operate when objects are visible, may also be operating to create longer looking times to "impossible" events simply because infants are still operating on actual sensory information, albeit degraded information. Haith points out that degraded sensory information is not a cognitive representation in the sense of a recomputation and transformation of sensory information into an (amodal) cognitive entity. He refers to neuroscience work in monkeys that enables the recording of brain activity from single cells, which shows that some of the same neurons that are active when an object is present are also active when it is absent. In other words, there is reduced sensory activity in the same perceptual systems that are active when a real object is present, even though the object has gone from the visual field. Haith suggests that this activity could constitute a neural mechanism for degraded sensory representations.

More recently, work in adult visual perception has shown that object representations in adults ("object files", or mid-level visual mechanisms for treating part of the visual field as the *same* object over time) persist over several seconds (e.g. Noles, Scholl, & Mitroff, 2005). Object files in adults are also affected by violations of key principles of infant perception, such as cohesion (that an object must always maintain a single bounded contour; see Mitroff, Scholl, & Wynn, 2004). A more detailed exploration of how the visual system constructs and maintains object files may throw light on some of the curious discrepancies in infants' use of perceptual variables such as height in the experimental paradigms devised by Baillargeon and colleagues.

However, regarding the question of degraded sensory representations versus amodal cognitive entities raised by Haith, more recent neuroscience work in human adults has superseded these arguments. Such work suggests that the distributed nature of mental representations means that there will always be activity by sensory neurons relevant to experiencing a concept when a cognitive representation is active (Barsalou, Simmons, Barbey, & Wilson, 2003). Concepts are represented in part by the reenactment of neuronal activity in primary sensory systems, and not by redescriptions of these states into an amodal representational form. Multiple representations appear to be involved when the human brain represents conceptual knowledge (see discussion in Chapter 4). If the brain is representing the concept of a cup, for example, motor neurons activated when the cup is grasped and visual neurons activated when seeing a real cup will become active, along with neurons in various association areas that might link cups to specific contexts like breakfast or specific emotions like the pleasure one gets from drinking coffee. There is no set of amodal "cup" neurons that is activated by themselves, without sensory activation. In fact, the new experimental techniques offered by cognitive neuroscience provide us with a way forward in tackling the serious questions about the nature of infant representations raised by scientists like Haith.

KEY TERM

Cognitive representations Conceptual information held "in mind".

COGNITIVE NEUROSCIENCE AND OBJECT PROCESSING IN INFANCY

A series of experiments with 6-month-old infants reported by Kaufman, Csibra, and Johnson (2003a) provides a nice example of this potential way forward. Kaufman et al. used electroencephalogram (**EEG**) imaging as a way of examining what infants' "representations" of occluded objects were actually like. As will be recalled, the EEG is a measure of brain electrical activation obtained by attaching sensitive electrodes to the scalp. The electrodes pick up electrical signaling by cell assemblies in the brain, although the exact generators of the signals are difficult to localize. Kaufman et al. recorded the EEG from electrodes placed over the whole scalp when infants were watching different disappearance events, which were either expected or unexpected. The habituation event was a toy train going into a toy tunnel. The train was shown entering the tunnel and then reversing back out again. Following habituation, the infants watched the train enter the tunnel, and then saw one of the following: (1) a hand lifting the tunnel to reveal the train (expected appearance event); (2) a hand lifting the tunnel to reveal no train (unexpected disappearance event); (3) the train leaving the tunnel and the visual field, and a hand subsequently lifting the tunnel to reveal the train (unexpected appearance event); or (4) the train leaving the tunnel and the visual field, and a hand subsequently lifting the tunnel to reveal no train (expected disappearance event). Behaviorally, the infants looked significantly longer at the unexpected disappearance event compared to the expected disappearance event. The two appearance events were not distinguished by looking time.

Kaufman et al. (2003a) then compared the EEG during the lifting of the tunnel in the expected versus unexpected *disappearance* events. Much higher electrical activity at temporal sites on the right side of the brain only was found when the train was occluded. In addition, when the tunnel was lifted to reveal no train (unexpected disappearance), there was sustained EEG activity, which peaked around 500 ms after the lifting of the tunnel. Kaufman et al. argued that this increased activity showed the brain attempting to maintain its representation of the train despite the competing visual evidence that the train was not under the tunnel. This higher activity could also represent the brain's response to an unexpected event. However, Kaufman et al. argued that the fact that higher activity during object occlusion occurred only in right temporal electrodes ruled out a general explanation of brain activity based on degraded sensory input. It is not clear why degraded sensory representations should be maintained on one side of the brain and not on the other, or why they should involve *increased* neuronal activity.

To investigate further whether the sustained EEG activity shown when the tunnel was lifted was related to the representation of nonvisible objects, a second experiment was conducted using only *appearance* events. As will be recalled, behaviorally, the infants did not distinguish between expected and unexpected appearance in terms of increased looking time. As in the first EEG experiment, it was found that occlusion of the train led to increased EEG activity in the right temporal electrodes during the period that the train should have continued to exist beneath the tunnel. However, there was no change in the EEG when the tunnel was lifted. As the train was always revealed in the appearance conditions, Kaufman et al. argued that there was no need to maintain a representation of the object independently of visual input. Further, as the unexpected appearance was unexpected, the higher activity found for unexpected *disappearance* was unlikely to represent the brain's response to an unexpected event.

KEY TERM

EEG (electroenceph-alogram)
The recording from the scalp of brain electrical activity caused by the firing of neural networks.

Research on how the brain processes objects has also shown that visual objects are processed via two neural pathways (Ungerleider & Mishkin, 1982; Milner & Goodale, 1995). One pathway—the *dorsal* route—is used for spatial and temporal information and is thought to be important for processing information that might be needed to guide action; this is called the "where" pathway. The second pathway—the *ventral* route—is used for processing information that is useful for identifying unique objects, such as color information; this is called the "what" pathway. The ventral route is also used for processing information about faces. Both pathways appear to process information about the size and shape of objects. Recently, it has been argued that this partial separation of the neural processing of different visual features of the same objects needs to be taken into account when interpreting looking experiments with infants (e.g. Mareschal, Plunkett, & Harris, 1999; Mareschal & Johnson, 2003).

For example, it seems quite plausible that younger infants may be poor at integrating information that is processed separately in the dorsal and ventral pathways. This idea was tested in an ingenious experiment reported by Mareschal and Johnson (2003). They exploited the preference of the ventral route for faces and color by examining 4-month-old infants' memory for surface features of objects versus the spatial location of objects in an occlusion paradigm. The infants were habituated to five repetitions of two objects appearing sequentially from behind two occluders on a computer display. In each trial, the infants watched as one object moved out from behind the first occluder for 5 seconds, and then moved back behind it, to be followed by the second object moving out from behind the second occluder and returning behind it. In the test trials, the two occluders moved upwards to reveal the objects behind them. In the *feature change* condition, one of the objects (a face or a cartoon asterisk) changed color or identity. In the *location change* condition, the color of the cartoon asterisks or the identity of the faces remained constant but the location of each was switched. In parallel conditions using pictures of familiar graspable toys, either the identity of one of the toys was changed, or the location of the toys was switched. Faces and colored asterisks were selected because they were expected to be processed by the ventral route. In the parallel conditions, graspable toys were selected because they afforded the infant potential actions and hence should be processed by the dorsal route. In a final baseline condition, the occluders lifted to reveal the expected objects.

Mareschal and Johnson (2003) argued as follows: If 4-month-old infants have difficulties integrating object information processed by the ventral and dorsal pathways, then they should show increased looking time in the feature change condition when the objects were asterisks and faces, but they should show increased looking time in the location change condition when the objects were graspable toys. In each of these cases, one visual route can yield sufficient information for dishabituation. When infants had to process changes in the *conjunction* of features and location (e.g. when the object [toy] afforded action but changed in features rather than moving, or when the faces or colored asterisks preserved their features but changed location), looking time should not differ from baseline. Difficulties in integrating information from the two pathways would prevent the infants from keeping track of conjunctions.

This was exactly the pattern of results found. When the objects in the occlusion paradigm were faces or asterisks, the babies looked significantly longer in the feature change condition only. When the objects were graspable toys, however, the infants showed increased looking time in the location change condition only. They did not show dishabituation when the faces or colored asterisks moved location or when the graspable toys changed in appearance. This is a remarkable result, and illustrates the importance of understanding the neural processing that is underpinning infant looking behavior. As argued by Mareschal and Johnson (2003), it also has implications for the design of studies probing infants' knowledge about objects. Depending on the kind of object used, infants may process features of that object differently. In particular, for real objects that can be grasped, location information appears to be retained at the expense of surface features like color. For objects that do not afford action, information about surface features is retained at the expense of information about location. This does not imply that infants cannot process changes in either surface features or location at the same time. Rather, there appears to be a selective loss of information when aspects of the object that are processed by the **ventral stream** must be integrated with aspects processed by the **dorsal stream** while an occlusion occurs.

Kaufman, Mareschal, and Johnson (2003b) have extended this argument to suggest that the potential graspability of the stimuli typically used in infant studies will influence how the infant brain will process these stimuli. They propose that the ventral/dorsal route framework can explain apparently conflicting results in the infant literature on object segregation, on the processing of surface features of moving objects, and on object individuation. Any experiments using small, familiar and moving objects as stimuli are likely to activate the dorsal route. Any experiments using larger, stationary objects are likely to be processed by the ventral route. Further evidence is needed to evaluate these ideas. For example, neuroimaging may be able to reveal a selective reliance on one route or another. At the moment, evidence of an inability to integrate information from both routes depends on a negative result (no difference in looking time compared to baseline). Negative results can have many causes. A direct measure of neural processing would be better evidence for this plausible hypothesis.

LINKS BETWEEN MEASURES OF EARLY LEARNING, MEMORY, PERCEPTION, AND ATTENTION, AND LATER INTELLIGENCE

A great many studies, only some of which have been mentioned here, provide converging evidence that the perceptual world of even the very young infant is organized into objects and their relationships. These relationships are organized in terms of events such as "containment" and "occlusion". Most of our knowledge about infants' cognitive representations of the physical world depends on experiments that exploit visual recognition memory, such as the visual preference technique and the visual habituation paradigm. One interesting question is whether there is continuity between these measures taken in infancy and later individual differences in cognitive development. Both measures reflect the basic information-processing capacity of an individual, involving learning, memory, perception, and attention. If early learning, memory, perception, and attention are related to later cognitive processing, then speed of habituation and visual recognition memory should be predictive of later individual differences in intelligence.

Speed of habituation and individual differences

The notion that there should be a relationship between the *speed of habituation* in infancy and later differences in intelligence has been proposed by a number of authors (e.g. Fagan 1984). Their argument goes something like this: A baby who is relatively quick to habituate to a stimulus might be relatively fast at processing information, and therefore capable of learning that something is familiar in only a few trials; such babies have been termed "short lookers" (see Rose, Feldman, & Jankowski, 2004). Another baby may take three times as long to habituate to the same stimulus, requiring many more trials to accurately and completely encode a stimulus in memory; such a baby would be a "long looker". As a young child, this second baby may still be slower at processing information and will therefore be slower on a variety of cognitive tasks that contribute to standardized measures of intelligence. However, it is important to be clear that being a "fast looker" is *not* the same thing as having a low attention span. Children who are easily distracted and move quickly from one activity to another may have an "attention deficit disorder" (ADD), and ADD children usually under-perform in various intellectual tasks. These children are unlikely to be fast habituaters, although so far no-one has studied the connection between attention deficit disorder and habituation in infancy directly.

To examine whether individual differences in habituation are associated with later individual differences in intelligence, Bornstein and Sigman (1986) conducted a "meta-analysis" of available studies. This meta-analysis included studies that related decrements in attention (habituation or total fixation time) to later intelligence measures, and also studies that related recovery of attention (novelty preference and response to novelty) to later intelligence. They found that attention scores correlated on average 0.44 with follow-up studies of intelligence conducted at 2–3 years, 0.48 with follow-up studies conducted at 4–5 years, and 0.56 with follow-up studies conducted at 6 years or more. This suggests significant continuity between early habituation measures and later IQ.

One of the longest-running longitudinal studies of the relationship between speed of habituation and individual differences is that of Sigman and colleagues, who have been following the same cohort of children since they were born for over 12 years. For example, Sigman, Cohen, Beckwith, and Parmelee (1986) reported data from a group of 91 of the infants who were tested as neonates. These babies were tested again at 4 months, and were then followed up when they were 8 years old. Two-thirds of the group ($N = 60$) had English-speaking backgrounds and the rest came from varied language backgrounds (the study was conducted at a large hospital in California). As neonates, the infants were shown a single 2×2 checkerboard for three 1-minute trials, and at 4 months they were shown pairs of checkerboards of varying complexity (2×2, 6×6, 12×12, 24×24) for eight trials. Two measures of visual attention were taken: (1) a measure of total fixation time; and (2) a habituation measure of the percentage decrement in looking time across trials.

When the children were revisited as 8-year-olds, they were given the revised version of the Wechsler Intelligence Scale for Children (the WISC-R). This test measures IQ by combining performance scores on a number of verbal and nonverbal measures (e.g. verbal fluency, picture completion, block design, memory span). Sigman et al. found that the neonate measure of total fixation time predicted IQ at

8 years for the whole group, whereas the neonate habituation measure predicted IQ at 8 years for the children from varied language backgrounds only. The measures taken at 4 months did not add to the associations between the neonate measures and later IQ. Sigman et al. concluded that infants who spent a long time looking at the stimuli at 0 and 4 months performed less well on the intellectual assessments given in childhood. It seems as though infants who take a long time to process an unchanging stimulus as neonates are less intelligent later in life. Similar relationships were found when a smaller subgroup of the sample (N = 67) was seen again as 12-year-olds (Sigman, Cohen, Beckwith, Asarnow, & Parmelee, 1991). In addition, more efficient processing of stimuli as a neonate (looking for a shorter amount of time) was related to performance on a test of analogical reasoning at age 12 (e.g. *bread* is to *food* as *water* is to *beverage*).

Visual recognition memory and individual differences

Like habituation, visual recognition memory requires the infant to encode a stimulus, to recognize it as familiar, and to recognize an alternative stimulus as novel. These are all basic information-processing requirements that could be related to intelligence. Fagan (1984) used a visual preference paradigm similar to that of Cornell (1979) to test this hypothesis. He measured looking preference for a novel visual stimulus (a face) over an already-experienced visual stimulus (a different face of the same sex) in a group of 7-month-old babies, and then tested the same group when they were 3 and 5 years of age. The median amount of time that each infant spent looking at the novel stimulus rather than the familiar stimulus formed the dependent measure. Fagan found stable correlations of around 0.42 between the novelty preference measures taken at 7 months and performance on the PPVT (Peabody Picture Vocabulary Test, a measure of verbal ability) at 3 and 5 years. He argued that visual novelty preference measures in infancy are picking up something of *general* importance for later cognition, for example encoding abilities, the ability to detect invariant features or categorization abilities. Fagan's idea that early visual recognition memory is a general rather than a specific measure has received support from a study by DiLalla et al. (1990). DiLalla et al. showed that Fagan's novelty preference measure was a significant predictor of IQ at 3 years as measured by the Stanford–Binet intelligence test.

Another long-running longitudinal study of the relationship between visual recognition memory and individual differences in cognitive development also found a general relationship with broader cognitive abilities (see Rose et al., 2004, for a summary). Rose and Feldman (1995) studied the relationship between visual recognition memory in infancy and visual attention and later intelligence as measured by the WISC-R at 11 years of age. They also studied longitudinal relationships with language development, and measured Piagetian variables thought to provide a key index of cognitive development in infancy, for example object permanence. Rose and Feldman reported that the infancy measure that best predicted IQ at age 11 was visual recognition memory, with a correlation of 0.41. Ninety infants took part in the study, 50 of whom were preterm. The preterm infants were included as a group at risk (preterm infants tend to score on average about 10 points lower on later IQ tests than full-term infants). Rose and Feldman found that the predictive strength of the visual recognition memory measure was very similar for both groups. In addition to overall IQ, infant visual recognition memory predicted performance on the Peabody Picture vocabulary measure at age 11, and predicted performance on particular subtests of the IQ tests used after controlling for overall IQ. These subtests were memory (measured via a speeded task) and perceptual speed. As Rose and Feldman point out, the relationship with perceptual speed may mean that *processing speed* is the common thread underlying cognitive continuity from infancy. For at-risk groups in particular, poorer performance can be tied to slower encoding of the target stimuli. Hence processing speed can play a limiting role in infant visual recognition memory. The importance of processing speed for cognitive development in general has also been highlighted by Anderson (1991) and by Kail (1991).

An alternative suggestion is that, rather than providing an index of information processing in terms of encoding, discrimination etc., both visual recognition memory and habituation derive their predictive power from their ability to provide an index of individual differences in the ability to *inhibit* responding to stimuli that have been seen before. Inhibition as an important cognitive process has received relatively little attention in the field of children's cognition (e.g. Dempster, 1991; Houdé, 2000). However, it has been attracting increasing interest lately with the advent of cognitive neuroscience, which has revealed the importance of inhibition mechanisms in explaining cognitive performance, and also in linking biology to temperament and psychopathology (Fox, Henderson, Marshall, Nichols, & Ghera, 2005). Inhibition (and executive processes more generally) is discussed in Chapter 9.

SUMMARY

There is considerable continuity between measures of learning, memory, perception, and attention in infancy, and later individual differences in cognitive development. Babies as young as 3 weeks show learning and memory for simple objects, and 3-month-olds can learn causal contingencies and retrieve them 28 days later with appropriate retrieval cues. Six-month-olds can form event memories that can be retrieved 2 years later in the presence of the right reminders, and 6-month-old babies have working memories. Event memories seem to be procedural rather than declarative in nature, as both learning and memory are demonstrated via infant *behavior*. The relationship between such memories and bringing some aspect of the past to conscious awareness is discussed in Chapter 8.

Perceptual and attentional abilities are also impressive early in life. Neonates can discriminate between simple visual forms such as crosses and circles. Work with older infants suggests that the basis of these discriminations is fairly abstract perceptual information, as habituation also occurs to different exemplars of the same shape, novel exemplars being seen as familiar. Habituation at an abstract level suggests that rudimentary categorization is occurring, with babies forming a generalized conceptual representation or "prototype" of a particular visual form. Work on prototypes and sequential learning has shown an impressive capacity for tracking conditional probabilities. This provides infants with a very powerful domain-general learning mechanism. In terms of learning about the physical world, it enables infants to construct a world of predictable objects that behave in predictable ways. Infants organize the physical world in terms of events like occlusion and containment. Once they become able to sit up and act on the world, they very quickly elaborate these early representations to encompass fine-grained knowledge about causes and their effects. This further development is discussed in Chapter 2.

CHAPTER 2

CONTENTS

Infancy: The physical world 2

Much of the knowledge that we think of as cognitive may develop initially via the operation of our perceptual systems. In adult cognition, the term "perception" usually refers to the hard-wired aspects of the visual system, such as color and depth perception. Cognition is conceptualized as higher-level judgments or deductions based on that perceptual information, for example making a causal inference based on perceived depth. Yet for both adults and infants, the line between perception and cognition is blurred. Perceptual displays can be experienced by adults as causal or animate, even if the displays themselves consist of simple moving geometric shapes (Scholl & Tremoulet, 2000). It seems likely that babies, too, experience such simple visual displays as causal or animate, suggesting that perception and cognition are intimately linked. One very early link between perception and cognition is demonstrated by studies of infant imitation.

PERCEPTUAL STRUCTURE AND CONCEPTUAL ANALYSES

Imitation

Even neonates can imitate the facial and manual gestures of adults. For example, Meltzoff and Moore (1983) have shown that babies aged from 1 hour to 3 days can imitate gestures like tongue protrusion and mouth opening after watching an adult produce the same gestures (Figure 2.1). In Meltzoff and Moore's experiment, the babies were supported in a seat in a darkened room. A light then came on for 20 seconds, illuminating an adult's face. The adult demonstrated a gesture such as tongue protrusion for the entire 20 second period, and the light was then extinguished. The babies were then filmed in the dark for the next 20 seconds. Following this imitation period, another gesture was modeled by the adult, and so on. An experimenter who was "blind" to the experiment later scored the behavior of the baby in each 20-second segment of video. Significantly more tongue protrusion was scored in periods following modeling of tongue protrusion, and significantly more mouth opening was scored in periods following modeling of mouth opening. The conclusion that the babies were imitating the adults seems inescapable, although initially it proved controversial (e.g. Hayes & Watson, 1981; McKenzie & Over, 1983).

A number of other experimenters have confirmed Meltzoff and Moore's findings, using a variety of different gestures and testing babies from a variety of different countries. For example, Vintner (1986) investigated whether newborn Italian babies could imitate tongue protrusion and hand opening–closing. She contrasted imitation in two conditions, an "active" condition in which the gesture was continuously modeled for a 25-second period, and a "static" condition in which a protruding tongue or an open hand was maintained for 25 seconds. Vintner found

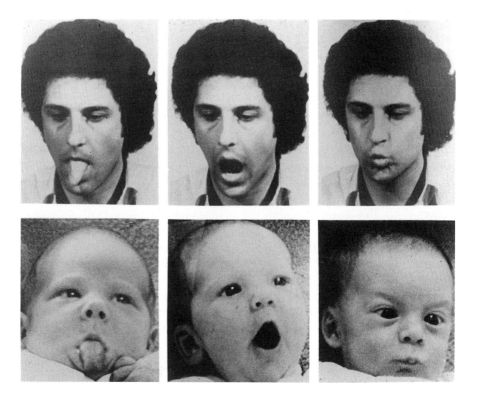

imitation behavior in the "active" group only, even though the babies in the "static" condition spent a lot of time looking at the experimenter. She suggested that movement may be a fundamental property for eliciting imitative responses at birth.

One reason for the controversy generated by the early reports of imitation in babies was that Meltzoff and Moore argued that successful imitation necessitated *representational capacity*. It is simple to demonstrate that a number of cognitive skills are required for successful imitation to take place. At a minimum, the infants need to: (1) represent the action of the adult; (2) retain this representation during the period that the adult is invisible in the dark; and (3) work out how to reproduce the gesture using their own facial musculature. In 1983, the idea that neonates might have a representational system that allowed them to match their own body transformations to those of others was seen as rather incredible. Twenty years later, it seems much more plausible. Although to date no neuroimaging studies have been conducted with infants to explore the nature of these representations, neuroimaging studies with adults suggest that multimodal neurons ("**mirror neurons**") in the ventral premotor and parietal cortex are crucially involved in kinaesthetic-visual matching (Jackson, Meltzoff & Decety, 2006; see Chapter 4). Further discussion of the neural systems involved in recognizing that others are "like me" can also be found in Chapter 7.

The perception of causality

We noted earlier that some perceptual events promote a causal interpretation, in adults as well as in infants. Some of the experiments discussed in Chapter 1 have already provided indirect evidence that infants can represent causal relations. Most of the violation-of-expectation experiments discussed in Chapter 1 involved causal relations as well as the target relations of space, occlusion, containment, etc. This is because, for the physical violations to be unexpected, a representation of the cause–effect relations underpinning the events was necessary. For example, in the study based on the car running down the ramp (Kotovsky & Baillargeon, 1998; see p. 25), it was the expected *collision* between the car and the box that made the reappearance of the car unexpected. In the study with the rotating screen (Baillargeon, et al., 1985), it was the expected *contact* between the screen and the box that made the continued rotation of the screen unexpected. However, all of the causal events in these paradigms occurred *out of view*. This means that we have to infer that, for example, the babies in the car experiment expected the car to collide with the box and thus to stop (they might have looked longer at the display because they expected the car to reappear, shunting the box in front of it!). To assess infants' ability to represent causal events *directly*, we need to study causal events that occur *in full view* of the infant.

Collision events provide a useful set of events for such experiments. For example, when one billiard ball collides with another, the second ball is launched into motion. This is a pure example of a cause–effect relation, and Michotte (1963) showed that adults always have an impression of causality when they view "launching" events, even if they are watching patches of light moving on a wall (see Scholl & Tremoulet, 2000, for more recent examples of adult impressions of causality, using very impoverished displays). This impression of causality even in the absence of a mechanical connection was taken by Michotte to show that adults are subject to a perceptual *illusion* of causality. However, the automatic impression of causality may also mean that the perceptual system *assumes* cause–effect relations in the absence of contradictory evidence. Young infants certainly appear to possess a perceptual mechanism that assumes causality. This mechanism is probably at the root of their causal understanding.

The existence of this mechanism was shown by some experiments devised by Leslie and Keeble (1987), who were interested in 6-month-old infants' understanding of **launching events**. In a typical experiment, infants were shown one of two films. In one film, a red block moved towards a green block and then collided with it, directly setting the green block in motion. In the other film, the red block again moved towards a green block and made contact with it, but the green block only began to move after a delay of 0.5 seconds. Whereas the first launching event gave an impression of causality to watching adults, the second did not. Following habituation to one of the films (either direct launching or delayed launching), the infants were then shown the *same* film in reverse. Although the change in the spatiotemporal relations in the films was the same for both groups, the reversal of the "direct launching" film resulted in a *novel* causal event (green launches red). Leslie and Keeble argued that if the infants in the direct launching condition were perceiving a causal relation (red launches green), then they should show more dishabituation following reversal (green launches red) than the infants in the delayed launching condition.

This was exactly what they found. Leslie (1994) argued that this effect showed that the infants were interested in the *mechanical* structure of launching. In the "direct launching" film, there was a change in the mechanical roles of the two billiard balls; the "pusher" was now the "pushed". In the "delayed launching" film the billiard balls did not have roles and so the roles could not be reversed. Leslie's description of the launching event in terms of mechanics entails a notion of **agency**, an idea that is discussed further below.

KEY TERMS

Launching event
When one object appears to strike another and seems to cause it to move.

Agency
An understanding of instrumentality in events, whether mechanical or human.

The perception of animate relations

The perceptual system also appears to assume animacy in the absence of contradictory evidence. Again, this was first noticed by Michotte (1963), who suggested that simple motion cues provide the foundation for social cognition (this idea is discussed in more detail in Chapter 3). Adults who are shown simple displays of moving geometric shapes will describe the displays as animate ("it's trying to get over there"; see Heider & Simmel, 1944). In an illustrative experiment, Tremoulet and Feldman (2000) created displays in which a dot moved in one direction for 375 ms and then changed direction and speed for another 375 ms. In other displays, a rectangle moved in one direction for 375 ms and then changed orientation when it changed direction and speed (Figure 2.2). In a control condition, a rectangle did not change orientation when it changed direction and speed. Experiments with adults showed that the first two displays were more likely to be perceived as being animate than the control condition. The strongest perceptions of animacy occurred for the rectangle that changed orientation as it changed direction, as in this condition the principal axis of the rectangle was aligned with the direction of motion. Thus, very simple motion cues, such as change in speed or change in direction, can give adults an impression of animacy. The rectangle is seen as an animate agent, "choosing" where to go.

Exactly the same effects are found with infants. Recent data from Gergely and colleagues have shown that the attribution of agency on the basis of perceptual analyses can be quite sophisticated. In an innovative study designed to examine the beginnings of the understanding of agency, Gergely, Nádasdy, Csibra, and Bíró (1995) showed that 12-month-old infants could analyse the spatial behavior of an agent in terms of its actions towards a goal. They argued that the infants applied an **"intentional stance"** to this behavior when it appeared rational. In other words, the infants were attributing a mental cause for the goal-directed behavior. Gergely et al. (1995) also argued that when there is no basis for attributing rationality to goal-directed spatial behavior, then an intentional stance is not adopted.

In their experiment, Gergely et al. took as their starting point the fact that the prediction and explanation of the behavior of agents requires the attribution of intentional states such as beliefs, goals, and desires as the mental causes of actions. This is the adoption of an "intentional stance". The adoption of an "intentional stance" towards agents entails an assumption of rationality—that the agent will adopt

FIGURE 2.2
The shape/alignment conditions used by Tremoulet and Feldman: (a) dot condition (also shown are the motion parameters); (b) aligned condition; (c) misaligned condition. From Tremoulet and Feldman (2000). Copyright © 2000 Pion Ltd, London. Reproduced with permission.

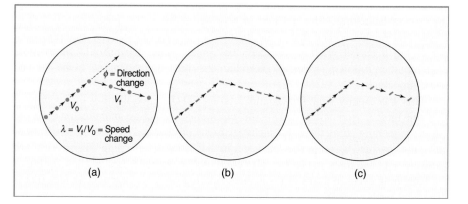

the most rational action in a particular situation to achieve his or her goal. Gergely et al. were interested in whether 12-month-old infants would generate expectations about the particular actions that an assumed agent was likely to perform in a new situation to achieve a desired goal. They designed a visual habituation study to find out, in which a computer display gave an impression of agency to the behavior of circles. The infants saw a display in which two circles, a large circle and a small circle, were separated by a tall rectangle (Figure 2.3). During the habituation event, each circle in turn expanded and then contracted twice. The small circle then began to move towards the large circle. When it reached the rectangular barrier it retreated, only to set out towards the large circle a second time, this time jumping over the rectangle and making contact with the large circle. Both circles then expanded and contracted twice more. Adult observers of this visual event described it as a mother (large circle) calling to her child (small circle) who ran towards her, only to be prevented by the barrier, which she then jumped over. The two then embraced.

Following habituation to this event, the infants saw the same two circles making the same sequence of movements, but this time without a barrier being present. In this "old action" event, there was no rational explanation of the retreat-and-jump action. In a "new action" event, the small circle simply took the shortest straight path to reach the large circle. Gergely et al. predicted that if the infants were making an intentional causal analysis of the initial display, then they should spend more time looking at the old action event than the new action event. This was because even though the former event was familiar, it was no longer rational. This was exactly what they found. A control group who saw the same habituating events without the rectangle acting as a barrier (it was positioned to the side of the screen) showed equal dishabituation to the old and new action events. Gergely et al. argued that the control group had not considered the small circle to be a rational agent, as the behavior of the small circle during the habituation event did not lead the infants to adopt an intentional stance towards it.

This intriguing result shows just how powerful the perceptual relations between objects can be for the young infant. Dynamic interrelations in the everyday world of objects and events appear to give rise to mental representations that supply information about the physical world of inanimate objects and *also* information

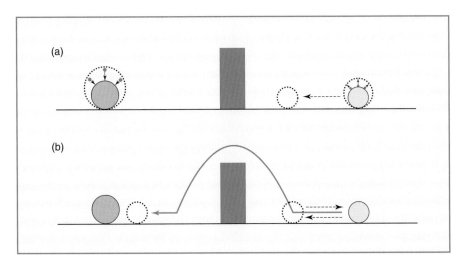

FIGURE 2.3
Schematic depiction of the habituation events shown to the rational approach group by Gergely et al. (1995), with (a) depicting the expansion and contraction events and the first approach, and (b) depicting the retreat, jump, and eventual contact. From Gergely et al. (1995). Copyright © 1995 Elsevier. Reprinted with permission.

about the psychological world of animate agents. These mental representations depend on distributed neural networks. Representations of simple perceptual events seem to lead to the eventual development of two separable causal frameworks, one for explaining the behavior of objects (physical reasoning) and one for explaining the behavior of people (psychological reasoning). Nevertheless, the foundation of both frameworks appears to be the same. The attribution of causal mechanisms such as beliefs and desires seems to develop from the *same* source as the attribution of causal mechanisms such as collision and support—namely from the perceptual (mental) representation of the dynamic spatial and temporal behavior of objects and agents.

In fact, even 3-month-old infants show a preference for "animate" motion. Rochat and colleagues gave infants aged 3–6 months two visual displays involving dots (Rochat, Morgan, & Carpenter, 1997). In one display, one dot appeared to be chasing another around the screen, giving an impression of a social interaction. This dot systematically approached the second dot at a constant velocity, until the latter accelerated away to a comfortable distance. In the other display, the two dots moved randomly and independently on the screen. Except for the relative spatial–temporal dependence of the dots' movements, all dynamic aspects of the two displays were controlled and maintained equal, for example, the average relative distance between the two dots was comparable. Both displays were presented concurrently side-by-side. Rochat et al. found that in general the infants preferred to watch the "chasing" display. They argued that this was evidence that even 3-month-old babies were sensitive to movement information that specified social causality for adult observers.

Cross-modal cues to perceptual structure

In the real world, infants are seldom exposed to events in a single modality at a time. Most perceptual experiences are of unified and unitary objects and events in multiple modalities. We have already seen that infants experience cross-modal equivalence from birth. However, as pointed out by Scheier, Lewkowicz, and Shimojo (2003), modalities like vision and audition can be related in other ways that do not necessarily specify equivalence. For example, hearing something can change the way that we perceive a visual event. Sekuler, Sekuler, and Lau (1997) demonstrated that a sound can cause perceptual reorganization of an ambiguous motion display. Adults who watched a computer display in which two identical disks moved from opposite sides of the screen towards each other, and then past one another, at a constant speed perceived them as streaming through one another. However, if a sound was presented at the moment when the two discs coincided, many adults perceived them as bouncing off one another. This perception occurred even though there was no actual collision. Scheier et al. (2003) asked whether babies, too, would experience this intersensory illusion.

Scheier et al. (2003) tested three groups of infants aged 4, 6, and 8 months. The infants watched as two yellow discs appeared at the edge of the screen, traveled towards one another, coincided without stopping, and continued on until they reached the other's starting point. At the coincidence point, a tone was heard. The tone was expected to cause a percept of bouncing. This event was repeated until the infants habituated to it. At test, the infants saw either another instance of the tone sounding at the coincidence point (no dishabituation expected), or of the tone sounding either 1.3 seconds before or after the coincidence point. Scheier et al. argued that if the infants were perceiving illusory bouncing, then they should dishabituate in the latter two test trials but not in the former. This was exactly what they found, but for the 6- and 8-month-old infants only. In a follow-up experiment, the habituation event was visual streaming (the tone did not sound at the coincidence point, but 1.3 seconds before or after it), and the critical test event was visual bouncing (here the tone sounded at the coincidence point). This time, 6- and 8-month-olds dishabituated to the bounce event only. Scheier et al. argued that sounds can induce the perceptual reorganization of ambiguous visual events from 6 months of age.

This is a very intriguing result. It suggests that the perceptual structure of objects and events in the world is really very rich indeed. Information from all relevant modalities is considered in conjunction by our perceptual systems, at least by 6 months of age. This cross-modal information yields a lot of data about the laws governing physical interactions between objects. Scheier et al. (2003) attribute the apparent failure of the 4-month-olds to perceive the bouncing illusion to immaturities in the attentional systems of young infants. They point out that attentional behaviors become more flexible and voluntary at around 6 months (see Chapter 1). An alternative possibility is that some experience of objects is required in order for infants to associate a complex tone with a collision between two two-dimensional discs on a computer screen. In the real world of objects and events, most collisions will be accompanied by sounds, but the sounds will be meaningful in terms of the objects colliding (e.g. if a child throws a rigid toy at the wall, there will be a thump). For an infant to infer that the complex tone is the sound of two cartoon discs colliding, some experience of such collision events may be required.

Separable causal frameworks for mechanical agency and human agency?

The ability to represent causal relations between objects may appear to be a simple extension of infants' ability to represent relational information in general, but attention to causality is actually a critical cognitive tool. Causal relations are particularly powerful relations for understanding the everyday world of objects and events. For example, in later chapters we will see how a sensitivity to causal relations underlies conceptual development (see Chapter 4), the development of memory (see Chapter 8) and logical development in general (see Chapter 9). A sensitivity to causal relations also appears to underlie the development of a notion of *agency*. Agency may be considered in terms of an understanding of mechanical agency or an understanding of human agency. As we will see in Chapter 6, in mechanical scenarios, young children appear to give priority to establishing the agent of causal events. An analysis of infant development regarding the understanding of mechanical agency has been put forward by Leslie (1994); this is considered here.

Leslie argued that causal analyses of motion in infants serve the important purpose of generating mechanical *descriptions* of the events. Such descriptions are more than a perceptual description of what has occurred, and so the perception of cause and effect cannot be said to be purely visual. Instead, this perception is the basis of a mechanism for understanding the mechanical properties of *agents*. Inanimate objects move in the real world as a result of the redistribution of energy, and these mechanical forces differ in important ways from animate sources of motion. Things that move on their own are agents, and things that move because of other things obey certain cause–effect, or mechanical, laws. Infants' interest in things that move helps them to sort out the source of different cause–effect relations in the physical world.

Evidence that infants make a distinction between mechanical forces and animate sources of motion comes from an experiment reported by Spelke, Phillips, and Woodward (1995). They compared 7-month-old infants' use of the principle of contact as a force that causes motion for inanimate objects versus people. The inanimate objects were meaningless patterned shapes 5–6 feet high, which were moved from behind by hidden people walking at a normal pace. The experiment was based on an occlusion paradigm (Figure 2.4). During habituation, the infants saw either a person or an inanimate object appear to one side of the display and move behind a central screen. A second object or person then

Infants' interest in things that move helps them to distinguish between the sources of different cause–effect relations in the physical world.

appeared from the other side of the screen and exited the display. These events were then repeated in reverse. The timing of the events was identical for objects and people, and for the objects it was consistent with the first object setting the second object in motion via contact behind the screen.

At test, the screen was removed and the infants saw either a contact event or a no-contact event. In the contact event, the two inanimate objects or people followed the same movement paths as in the habituation event, the second object or person moving once the first had made contact with it. In the no-contact event, the two objects or people never made contact, the first stopping a short distance from the

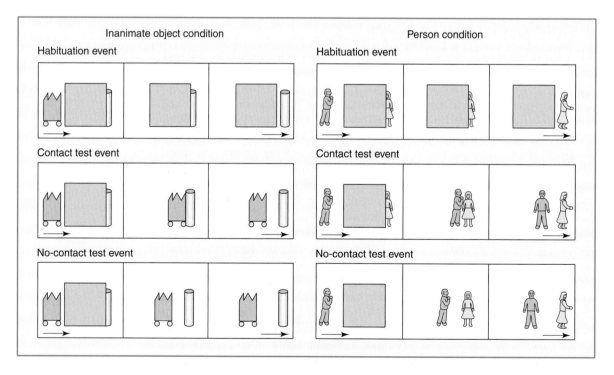

FIGURE 2.4
Schematic depiction of the events used to study infants' understanding of the forceful contact principle. From Spelke, Phillips, and Woodward (1995). Reproduced by permission of Oxford University Press.

second, which began moving after a suitable pause. Both events were then shown in reverse, and were repeated as long as the infants kept looking at them. If the infants were able to distinguish mechanical forces from animate sources of motion, then they should find the no-contact event more visually interesting for the inanimate objects, where the absence of contact should not cause motion. For the people, there should be no difference in the visual interest of the contact and the no-contact events, as people are agents who are capable of self-propelled motion. This was exactly what Spelke et al. found. A control condition established that there was no difference in the intrinsic attractiveness of the contact and no-contact events. Spelke et al. thus concluded that, at least by 7 months of age, infants do not apply the forceful contact principle to people. They reason *differently* about people and objects, appreciating that people are agents who can move on their own.

The development of an understanding of *human* agency has been investigated by Meltzoff (1995a), who showed that older infants can understand the causal *intentions* of others, which is suggestive of an understanding of humans' capacity for agency. In one experiment, Meltzoff (1995a) showed 18-month-old infants an adult who demonstrated an *intention* to act in a certain way. However, the intention was never fulfilled. For example, the adult would try to put a string of beads into a cylindrical container, but the beads would keep falling outside the container rather than inside it. The adult would try to hang a loop of string over a hook, but would continually under- or overshoot the target. A second group of infants saw the adult modeling the same actions but in each case completing the entire action successfully. Both groups of infants then received the beads, string, etc. to manipulate by themselves.

Meltzoff found that production of the target acts (putting the beads inside the container, hanging the loop of string over the hook etc.) was identical in these two groups of infants, even though one group had never actually seen the target acts being performed. A control group of babies given the same objects produced very few of the target acts, suggesting that the target acts were not in themselves a natural way in which to manipulate the objects. Meltzoff concluded that a psychological understanding of the intention of the human actor led the babies in the experimental group to produce the target acts. They were aware of the acts that the adult had intended to produce, even though the acts themselves had failed.

Interestingly, however, the babies did *not* behave in the same way when an inanimate device performed the same movements in space as the human hand. A new group of babies watched a pincer device performing slipping motions matched to those performed by the human hand when failing to complete one of the target acts. The aim was to see whether the babies would respond solely to the physics of the situation, or whether they had been responding previously to the human agent. Meltzoff found that, although the babies' attention was riveted by the mechanical device, they were much less likely to imitate the target acts when the inanimate object failed to demonstrate an intended act than when a human agent failed to demonstrate the same act. In fact, babies who watched the human failing were six times more likely to produce the target act than babies who watched the inanimate device failing.

Meltzoff argued that his results were suggestive of the existence of two *separable* causal frameworks by the age of 18 months: a physical causality for explaining the behavior of things, and a psychological causality for explaining the behavior of people. He suggested that infants represented the behavior of people in a psychological framework that involved goals and purposeful intended acts, and not in terms of purely physical movements and motions (see also Leslie, 1994). Further investigations of the development of the understanding of psychological causality are discussed in Chapter 3. Psychological causation involves the understanding of *unobservable* events such as desires, beliefs, and goals, which are part of the development of a "theory of mind". Data from children with cognitive disorders can be used to support this idea of separable causal frameworks. For example, autistic children understand mechanical cause–effect relations but appear to lack a theory of mind. Developmental disorders such as autism provide evidence consistent with the idea that the development of a theory of mind occurs to some extent independently from the development of an understanding of mechanical agency (see Leslie, 1994, for further discussion).

Perceptual representations of causality or cognitive representations?

Traditionally, the ways in which infants might go beyond perceptual categorization and representation to form concepts and schemas (*meaning-based* knowledge representations) have been hotly debated (e.g. Mandler, 2004a). Meaning-based knowledge representations are usually defined in adult cognition as representations that encode what is significant about an event, omitting the unimportant perceptual details (Anderson, 1990). Concepts and schemas are thought to be sets of ideas in the mind that explain the world, not perceptual copies of how the world is. Cognitive concepts and schemas can be complex units of knowledge that represent what is typically true of a *category*, for example *birds* (has wings, has beak, can fly . . . etc.) or an *event*, such as *going to the doctor* (report to receptionist, wait a long time, enter surgery . . . etc.). Schemas for events are also called **scripts** in cognitive psychology. Previously, it was assumed that infants had categories that were purely sensory or perceptual in nature (Quinn & Eimas, 1986). Clearly, if this were the case, then the problem of conversion to a more cognitive or schematic format that omits perceptual details would be considerable. However, recent cognitive neuroscience studies with adults suggest that the activation of a concept produces neural activity in the sensory modalities associated with those concepts as well as in other networks such as association areas (Barsalou et al. 2003; see Chapter 4). Hence, there might not be a conversion problem to overcome in order to explain the development of cognitive representations from perceptual representations. In terms of brain activation, the key is incremental learning on the basis of exemplars. Perceptual details may never be omitted, although they may be activated less strongly if they are only characteristic of some of the exemplars that are experienced.

Further, we have already seen that infants store a remarkable amount of information that is not purely sensory in nature. For example, infants store information about launching events that goes beyond the perceptual characteristics of the events themselves to a notion of agency based on action (Leslie, 1994). Older infants store information about the movements of simple shapes that assume trajectories based on rational action (the intentional stance). We have also seen (in Chapter 1) that infants can retain two-step causal event sequences like "make a rattle" for long periods of time (3 months), whereas they lose their memories for two-step noncausal or abitrary event sequences like "put a hat on the bunny and feed him a carrot" over the same period. Research such as this suggests that what is being represented and remembered is not simply the perceptual characteristics of the events themselves, but also their causal structure or their meaning. All experienced aspects of an event are stored and together represent its meaning, with aspects that always recur being represented more strongly. This makes it unlikely that infants have to wait until they have acquired language to represent knowledge in a meaning-based fashion, as was once thought. In any case, such a proposal begs an important question, namely what kind of cognitive structures underpin language acquisition.

Infant representations in at least some domains thus incorporate more than the sensory information given. Although early representations of events such as occlusion events or support events may code only some of the important variables (e.g. the presence/absence of support rather than the degree of contact with supporting surface), multiple experience of instances and the capacity for independent action leads infants to augment these variables very rapidly into schemas. Meaning-based knowledge representations are experience dependent. With multiple experiences, what is common across many instances is activated in the brain more strongly than what is not. Hence the "gist", or most significant aspects, of a particular concept or schema is eventually encoded more strongly than the variable perceptual details.

Specialized modules for certain information?

An alternative to this **domain-general** proposal for how perceptual/causal analyses lead to meaning-based knowledge representations is the modular view (Fodor, 2000). For example, Leslie (1994) has argued that specialized information-processing systems in the brain provide the basis for cognitive development. According to Leslie's *domain specificity* view, there are mechanisms in the brain that, by virtue of the position that they occupy in the overall organization, receive inputs from particular classes of objects in the world and end up representing certain kinds of **domain-specific** information. One example given is the mechanism that acquires the syntactic structure of natural language. Other proposed modules include *number* and *music*. In addition, Leslie proposes two core domains that he argues are central to infants' initial capacities for causal conceptual knowledge. These are *object mechanics* and *"theory of mind"*. In these two core domains, the central organizing principle is the notion of cause and effect.

For example, infants' processing of the physical world seems to organize itself fairly rapidly around a core structure representing the arrangement of cohesive, solid, three-dimensional objects that are embedded in a series of mechanical relations such as *pushing*, *blocking*, and *support*. Leslie argues that this organized processing is the result of a specialized learning mechanism adapted by evolution to create conceptual knowledge of the physical world. In Leslie's view, the modular organization of the brain *itself* allows the infant to acquire rapid and uniform knowledge about object mechanics (and also about psychological causality). One way of describing this position is to say that babies have rudimentary "theories", such as a "theory" of mechanics. As we will see in later chapters, the position that babies and young children have emergent theories has also been used to explain cognitive development in areas such as biology. However, the notion of modules is in decline. For example, the notion of a specialized "module" for syntax and grammar, the "language acquisition device", has been challenged on many fronts (see Chapter 5). Cognitive neuroscience has shown that there is no number "module", as important numerical information is stored in the language system (see Chapter 10).

KEY TERMS

Domain general
An ability or skill that applies to several situations or domains.

Domain specific
An ability that applies only to one specific area or domain.

A nonmodular view of development

In this book, therefore, I will follow a nonmodular view of cognitive development (including, perhaps controversially, of language development). The assumption will be one of common learning mechanisms, namely statistical learning, learning by imitation, explanation-based or causal learning, and **learning by analogy**. Using these simple learning mechanisms, the brain appears to build up complex representations about how the world is. Repeated experience of the perceptual/causal structure of objects and events leads to generalization across instances, because the connections between neurons responding to specific aspects of a sensory experience are strengthened less across instances than the connections between neurons responding to more general aspects of experiences that recur frequently. For example, specific perceptual features of two objects in a launching event may vary, but causal structure (the fact that A causes B to move) will not. This representational process allows different types of meaning-based representations to be extracted from sensory input by the same learning mechanisms, in domain-general fashion.

How this might actually work in different domains is considered further in individual chapters. The storage and representation of things that happen in the world—actions and events—is crucial. The way in which an early focus on agency, in particular human agency, contributes to the development of a theory of mind is the subject of the next chapter, Chapter 3. The relationship between spatial/mechanical analyses of the movements of nonhuman objects and agents, and the biological/nonbiological distinction that aids conceptual development, is discussed further in Chapter 4. Communicative acts and language events are very interesting to babies, and the statistical learning of auditory input is discussed further in the chapter on language, Chapter 5. Causal learning is discussed in Chapter 6. Finally, the evidence that even very young children are developing event schemas is discussed in the chapter on memory development, Chapter 8.

REASONING AND PROBLEM SOLVING ABOUT THE PHYSICAL WORLD

In addition to schemas, two other hallmarks of cognitive activity in adults are reasoning and problem solving. Defining reasoning and problem solving is not straightforward. One popular definition of reasoning is that it denotes those processes in information retrieval that depend on the *structure*, as opposed to the *content*, of organized memory (Rumelhart & Abrahamson, 1973). However, this definition leaves us with the problem of deciding which parts of organized memory are structural and which are content. According to Anderson (1990), reasoning and problem solving usually involve three ingredients. First, the reasoner wants to reach a desired end state, which usually involves attaining a specific goal. Second, a sequence of mental processes must be involved in reaching this end state. The involvement of a sequence of mental processes is intended to distinguish reasoning from goal-directed behavior such as opening your mouth when you see a feeding bottle. Third, the mental processes involved should be cognitive rather than automatic. An automatic or routine sequence of behavior, such as playing a "peek-a-boo" game, does not qualify as cognitive. Although we will only discuss a few examples of reasoning and problem solving in infancy here, recent experiments investigating infants' understanding of the physical world have produced many more. Useful reviews include Baillargeon (2002) and Spelke (1991).

Reasoning about objects and events

One ingenious problem-solving experiment concerning the infant's understanding of the physical world asked whether infants understand that, when they have seen a toy bear sitting under an inverted plastic cup, it is impossible to retrieve the *same* bear from a previously empty toy cage. Baillargeon, Graber, DeVos, and Black (1990) examined this question by showing infants a display in which a clear plastic cup and a small cage were sitting side-by-side on a table, with the cage to the right of the inverted cup. A toy bear was visible inside the plastic cup, but the cage was empty (Figure 2.5). A screen was then raised so that the two containers were hidden from the infant's view.

As the infants watched, a hand appeared to the right of the screen, reached behind it, and reappeared holding the cage. The hand then reached behind the screen for a second time and reappeared holding the toy bear. This was an impossible event, and the infants looked significantly longer at this event than at the same event in a control condition in which the bear was first shown to be inside the cage rather than inside the cup. To look longer at the impossible event, the infants had to believe that the bear, cup and cage continued to exist behind the screen and also had to retain a representation of their locations once they were hidden by the screen. On the basis of these premises, they then had to *reason* that it was impossible to retrieve the bear from the empty cage.

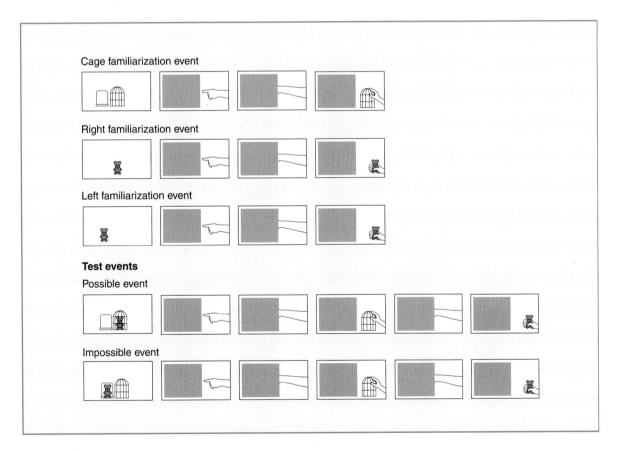

FIGURE 2.5
Depiction of the familiarization and test events in the "bear in the cup" paradigm. From Baillargeon at al. (1990). Copyright © 1990 Elsevier. Reprinted with permission.

Another example of reasoning about physical events in infancy concerns infants' ability to judge the size of a hidden object (Baillargeon & DeVos, 1994). In Baillargeon and DeVos' "hidden object" studies, the infants' task was to work out the size of an object hidden beneath a cloth. In a typical experiment, the infants were first shown a lump covered by a soft, fluid cloth. This array was then occluded by a screen. As the infants watched the display, a hand reached behind the screen and first reappeared holding the cloth cover, then reached again and subsequently reappeared holding a very large toy dog. This toy dog was so big that, to an adult, it was obvious that it could not have been the object causing the original lump beneath the cloth. However, the infants (12½-month-olds) did not look longer at the appearance of this impossibly large "hidden" object.

Subsequent experiments showed that one reason why the infants did not show increased looking was that they found it difficult to retain a memory of the *absolute* size of the lump once it had been occluded by the screen. When Baillargeon and DeVos provided a second, identical protuberance under a cloth as a memory cue which remained visible when the screen concealed the lump, then 12½-month-old infants were able to reason about the plausible size of the hidden object (Figure 2.6). In this study, the infants were able to make a direct comparison between the very large toy dog that emerged from behind the screen and the rather small lump as the hand reached first for the cloth and then for the toy dog. When they could make a relational comparison, the infants looked significantly longer at the emergence of the impossibly large toy dog than at the emergence of a smaller toy dog that was of a suitable size to have caused the lump beneath the cloth. The infants were thus able to use the visible lump to reason about the size of the hidden object.

How can we be certain that infants were indeed *reasoning* about the physical parameters of the situations in the paradigms just discussed? One way is to see whether they would stop being "surprised" at impossible physical events if the mechanism behind the "trick" was revealed. This would be good evidence for problem-solving skills in infancy, as it would involve a sequence of mental processes which were nonautomatic.

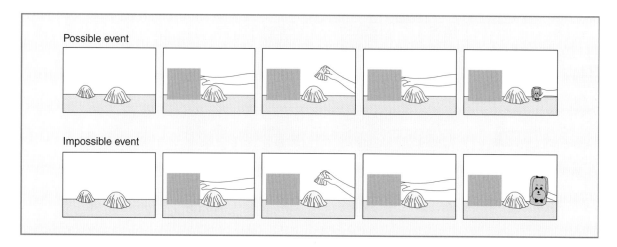

FIGURE 2.6
Depiction of the events used in the "dog beneath the cloth" experiment when a relational comparison was possible. Redrawn from Baillargeon and DeVos (1994). Reproduced with kind permission from the author.

One experiment in which the "trick" behind an impossible physical event was eventually revealed to the infants was the study by Baillargeon and Graber (1987) concerning spatial relations (discussed in Chapter 1). In this study, infants were habituated to either a tall or a short rabbit passing behind a wall. The mid-section of the wall was then lowered, and the impossible physical event was that the tall rabbit passed behind the short mid-section of the wall without the top half of his body becoming visible. This impossible event generated considerable looking among 5½-month-old babies. The impossible event was actually produced by using two rabbits. In a follow-up study, Baillargeon and Graber showed a new group of infants how the "trick" had been produced. These "informed" infants received two pretest trials, during which first two tall rabbits and then two short rabbits were shown standing motionless at each side of the windowless screen. The experiment then proceeded as before. This time, neither group showed extended looking when the rabbit failed to appear behind the short section of the wall, whether they had been habituated with the tall rabbit or the short rabbit. The infants had apparently used the information from the pretest trials to work out that the trick had been produced by using two rabbits.

The disappearance of the dishabituation effect in this experiment is particularly remarkable when it is remembered that the infants did not see the rabbits *in motion* during the pretest trials. They simply saw two short rabbits and two tall rabbits. They apparently then used this information to work out that while one rabbit disappeared behind the fence at the beginning of a habituation trial, a *second* rabbit reappeared at the other end. The infants were apparently using the information about two rabbits to make sense of a surprising phenomenon, and solving the problem of how an impossible event of this nature could have been produced.

Experiments such as these seem to provide convincing evidence of reasoning and problem-solving behavior by young infants. All of the criteria set by Anderson (1990) for defining reasoning and problem-solving behavior appear to be fulfilled. The desired end state is to generate an explanation for an impossible event, which is a specifically cognitive goal. This is achieved by a sequence of mental processes, requiring the combination of a number of premises that are represented in memory. These processes are cognitive rather than automatic as the premises involve information that is not directly observable. It is difficult to disagree with Baillargeon's conclusion that the infants in her experiments are engaging in a knowledge-based, conceptual analysis of the physical world (Baillargeon, 2004).

Responding to numerical relations

The perceptual structure of events in the visual world that involve quantities provides a basis for the representation of numerosity. The understanding of relations such as "greater than" and "less than" is a crucial aspect of the number system. Equally important is the understanding that a quantity remains the same unless something is added to it or taken away from it. Habituation studies have been used to investigate whether babies can represent quantitative relations fairly early in life, and also some numerical relations.

For example, Cooper (1984) devised a habituation paradigm in which infants were habituated to pairs of arrays of colored squares (Table 2.1). These arrays either depicted the relation "greater than" or the relation "less than". For the "greater than" relation the infants might be shown a pair made up of 4 squares in array 1 vs. 2 squares in array 2, then a pair of 4 squares in array 1 vs. 3 squares in array 2, and then 2 vs. 1 square. At test, the infants received either a reversed relation ("less than";

Condition	Numerosity of Array 1	Numerosity of Array 2	Trial type
TABLE 2.1 Examples of numerosity arrays used by Cooper (1984)			
Less than:			
Habituation	3	4	
	2	4	
	1	2	
Test	3	4	Old
	2	3	New
	4	3	Reversed
	2	2	Equal
Greater than:			
Habituation	4	2	
	4	3	
	2	1	
Test	4	3	Old
	3	2	New
	3	4	Reversed
	2	2	Equal
Equal:			
Habituation	4	4	
	2	2	
	1	1	
Test	4	4	Old
	3	3	New
	2	4	Less than
	4	2	Greater than

3 squares in array 1 vs. 4 squares in array 2), an "equal" relation (2 vs. 2), or a novel exemplar of the same relation (3 vs. 2). At 10 months, the infants dishabituated to the "equal" relation only, showing that they could differentiate equality from inequality. By 14 months, the infants dishabituated to the "less than" relation as well, showing an appreciation of relational reversal. Similar paradigms have also been used with younger babies (e.g. Starkey & Cooper, 1980).

There have also been reports of *cross-modal* understanding of number fairly early in life. Starkey, Spelke, and Gelman (1983) used a paradigm similar to that used by Spelke (1976; see Chapter 1) to examine whether infants equated three sounds with three objects, and two sounds with two objects. In their experiment, the infants were given a choice of two visual arrays, one of which contained two objects and the other three objects. The objects in the arrays were changed from trial to trial, but one array always contained *two*, and the other *three*. The infants also heard a soundtrack from a speaker placed in between the two arrays. The soundtrack was either repeated pairs of drumbeats, or repeated triples of drumbeats. Starkey et al. found that the infants preferred to look at arrays of two objects when they were listening to a pair of drumbeats, and at arrays of three objects when they were listening to triples of drumbeats. This preference for cross-modal *congruence* was also found in the cross-modal work discussed in Chapter 1. To recognize cross-modal congruence in Starkey et al.'s paradigm, it was argued that the infants must have been representing the numerosity of the drumbeats. This striking result has proved difficult to replicate, however (Moore, Benenson, Reznick, Peterson, & Kagan, 1987). Further, variables that covary with number (such as the rate of the beats) were not controlled, and even preschoolers find matching abstract events such as handclaps to numbers of dots difficult (Mix, Levine, & Huttenlocher, 1997). Recently, however, Jordan and Brannon (2006) reported a study with 7-month-olds in which the number of voices heard was either congruent or incongruent with the number of "talking heads" on a video. The babies were presented with two videos, one of three unfamiliar women mouthing "look", and one of two unfamiliar women mouthing "look". The babies showed a significant preference for looking at the video that matched the number of voices that were simultaneously saying "look" from a central speaker. The number of voices could be easily distinguished, as they differed in pitch and timbre. Jordan and Brannon argued that this was evidence for the multisensory representation of number in infancy. However, it is unclear whether such skills will generalize beyond faces and voices, which are of crucial social significance for the infant (see Chapter 3).

One of the most famous demonstrations of an apparent understanding of numerosity in infancy is by Wynn (1992), who studied the ability of 5-month-old babies to add and subtract small numbers, using a looking-time procedure. All babies first viewed an empty display area. Once they were attending, a hand appeared in their field of view and placed a Mickey Mouse doll in the display area. Next, a small screen rotated up from the floor of the apparatus, hiding the doll from view. The hand then reappeared and placed a second Mickey Mouse doll behind the screen. When the screen dropped, it either revealed two Mickey Mouse dolls (possible event) or a single Mickey Mouse doll (impossible event). This sequence of events is shown in Figure 2.7.

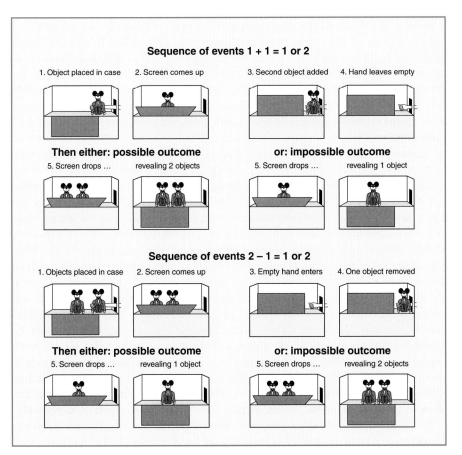

FIGURE 2.7
The addition and subtraction events used by Wynn (1992). Copyright © Macmillan Publishers Limited. Reproduced with permission.

Wynn found that the babies looked significantly longer at the single Mickey Mouse doll, the impossible outcome. A group of babies who initially saw two Mickey Mouse dolls in the display area and then saw one being removed after the screen came up showed the opposite pattern: They looked significantly longer when the screen dropped to reveal two Mickey Mouse dolls (impossible event) than when it dropped to reveal a single Mickey Mouse doll (possible event). Wynn argued that this showed that the infants could compute the numerical results of simple arithmetical operations.

Support for her view comes from a replication of her study by Simon, Hespos, and Rochat (1995). Simon et al. pointed out that Wynn's results could be explained on the basis of violations of infants' knowledge about the physical world, rather than on the basis of an innate possession of arithmetical abilities. In the "impossible addition" condition, objects seen placed behind the screen ceased to exist, and in the "impossible subtraction" condition, objects that did not previously exist magically appeared. Simon et al. noted that this alone could explain increased looking time. However, if Wynn's results depended on the recognition of physically impossible outcomes regardless of arithmetic, then infants should also show increased looking time in "possible arithmetic" conditions in which the identity of Mickey Mouse was changed to someone else. Simon et al. therefore included "impossible identity" and "impossible identity and arithmetic" conditions in their replication of Wynn's study.

Rather than using Mickey Mouse dolls, however, Simon et al.'s "impossible identity" conditions involved a switch between the two Sesame Street characters Ernie and Elmo. This is shown in Figure 2.8. For example (impossible identity), if the infants saw a second Elmo doll being added to a first Elmo doll, which was concealed by the screen, the screen would drop to reveal two dolls, Elmo and Ernie. Similarly, if the infants saw an Elmo doll being removed from behind a screen known to conceal two Elmo dolls, the screen would drop to reveal a single doll, Ernie. Both of these outcomes are arithmetically correct but physically impossible. In the arithmetically impossible conditions ($1 + 1 = 1, 2 - 1 = 2$), the identity of the dolls was also switched (Elmo + Elmo = Ernie, two Elmos − Elmo = Elmo + Ernie). Thus in this condition the outcome was *both* arithmetically incorrect and physically impossible.

Simon et al. found that 5-month-olds in the "impossible identity" condition behaved just like the infants in the "possible arithmetic" condition used by Wynn, whereas the infants in the "impossible identity and arithmetic" condition behaved just like the infants in her "impossible arithmetic" condition. The infants thus looked longer at arithmetically incorrect outcomes, but not at physically incorrect outcomes (a control condition had established that they *could* distinguish between Elmo and Ernie). Simon et al. argued that the spatiotemporal information in Wynn's set-up caused the infants to focus on the *number* of objects behind the screen rather than on their identity.

Other authors have pointed out that in most of these "number" paradigms, the change in number also involves changes in basic perceptual variables. For example, two objects have a larger surface area than one object, and infants could be responding to this feature of the displays rather than to numerosity *per se*. When number versus perceptual variables like total surface area and contour density is varied systematically in *visual* paradigms, then infants do not appear to respond on the basis of number (see Clearfield & Mix, 1999; Feigenson, Carey, & Spelke, 2002). More recently, experiments on number have carefully controlled perceptual variables in the displays and have reported that infants aged 6 months can, for example, discriminate 8 from 16, but not 8 from 12 (see Xu & Spelke, 2000). Similarly, they

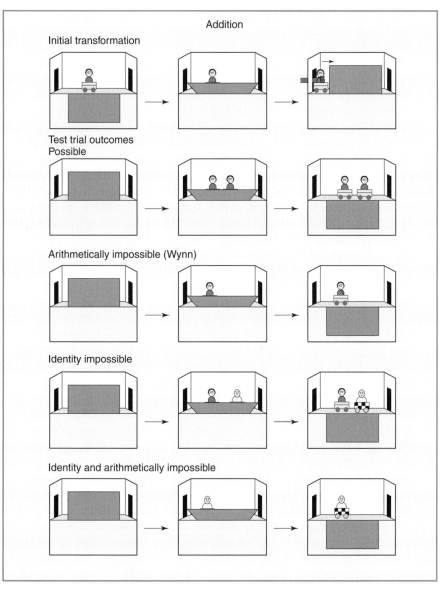

FIGURE 2.8
The addition events used in Simon et al.'s (1995) replication of Wynn (1992). From Wynn (1992). Copyright © Macmillan Publishers Limited. Reproduced with permission.

can discriminate 16 from 32 when perceptual variables are controlled, but not 1 from 2 (Xu, Spelke, & Goddard, 2005).

These surprising findings have led to the proposal that infants deal differently with large versus small numbers. For small numbers, namely 1, 2, and 3, infants are influenced by perceptual variables in the displays. For larger numbers above 3, infants rely on a ratio-sensitive, approximate analogue magnitude representation that is evolutionarily given and that is also found in other species (Dehaene, Dehaene-Lambertz, & Cohen, 1998). This view is discussed further in Chapter 10. For present purposes, it is important to assess these experiments about infant representations of small numbers in the light of the cognitive neuroscience explanation offered by Mareschal and Johnson (2003). This explanation concerned the preference of the dorsal route for information that guides action, and the preference of the ventral route for information that identifies unique objects.

If we apply this knowledge about neural processing to the switch from Elmo to Ernie in the paradigm devised by Simon and colleagues, we can see that in order for the infants to pick up the switch in identity, ventral processing is required. However, if the infants were more interested in the number of graspable objects present in the display, then dorsal processing would be dominant. In this situation, the ventral route may not be engaged, and so information about unique identity would be lost. The spatiotemporal information in Wynn's (1992) paradigm also seems likely to selectively engage the dorsal route. Wynn used small, attractive dolls that could be manipulated by babies, and the dorsal route is interested in information that will guide action. Hence the apparent discrimination of number in these paradigms could reflect the infant's response to the fact that different actions are required when there is one desirable graspable toy present compared to when there are two. If this interpretation is correct, then experiments that do not use attractive graspable toys but rather large nonmanipulable objects to alter the numerosity of visual displays should not yield "numerical" processing.

Another example of the relevance of this neurocognitive analysis concerns a frequently cited experiment about infant numerosity (Xu & Carey 1996). Xu and Carey argued that even though babies as young as 3 months seem to make similar assumptions to adults concerning the continued existence of occluded objects, infants were unable to set up representations of numerically distinct occluded objects until the end of the first year. On the basis of a series of experiments using an occlusion paradigm with two perceptually distinct objects, a toy elephant and a toy truck, Xu and Carey (1996) suggested that infants have a fairly generalized representation of objects until the age of at least 10 months. They argued that infants do not represent the identity of *individual* objects until slightly later in development.

Xu and Carey's basic paradigm contrasted two occlusion conditions, a *property-kind* condition and a *spatiotemporal* condition (Figure 2.9). In the property-kind condition, the infant was shown a single screen. A toy truck was brought out from the right side of the screen and returned behind it. A toy kitten was then brought out from the left side of the screen, and returned behind it. These successive events were repeated three more times. This set of repetitions comprised the habituating event. At test, the screen was removed to reveal either one object or two objects. Xu and Carey reasoned that infants who could set up representations of numerically distinct objects should find the single object outcome surprising, and so look longer at the single object than at two objects. In the spatiotemporal condition, the same sequence of successive emergences of the truck and kitten was preceded by a single trial in which the two toys were brought out *simultaneously* from behind the screen, one to each side. Infants in this condition were again expected to look longer at the single object outcome. Finally, a *baseline condition* assessed infants' intrinsic preference for looking at one object versus two objects in the absence of any occlusion events.

Xu and Carey found that infants looked longer at the two-object outcome in the baseline and property-kind conditions, but looked longer at the single-object outcome in the spatiotemporal condition. This basic finding was then replicated a number of times. Xu and Carey concluded that infants have an intrinsic preference for looking at two objects, and that this preference is overridden in the spatiotemporal condition but not in the property-kind condition. From this, they concluded that 10-month-old infants were unable to use the perceptual differences between the toy kitten and the toy truck to infer that there were two distinct objects behind the screen. An alternative explanation is that both conditions were selectively activating the dorsal visual route, because the stimuli being used were small

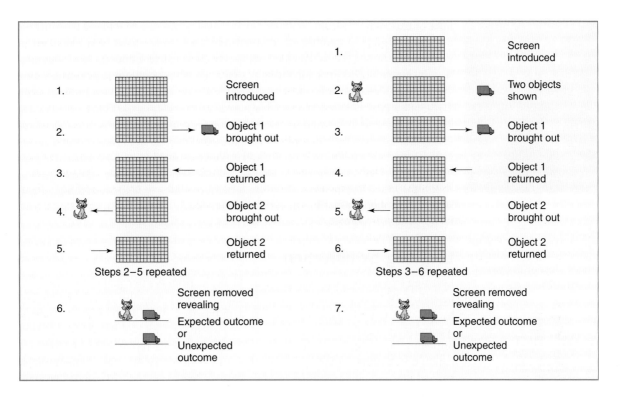

FIGURE 2.9
Schematic representations of the property-kind condition (left) and the spatiotemporal condition (right) used in the experiments by Xu and Carey (1996). Copyright © 1996 Elsevier. Reprinted with permission.

graspable toys (see Kaufman et al. 2003b). The property-kind condition needed to activate the ventral visual route in order to process surface features, but the nature of the toys being used conspired against this. The infants were more interested in what actions they could perform on the toys, and so dorsal processing was prioritized. Kaufman et al. (2003b) argued that objects that are small, within reach, and/or moving are likely to elicit dorsal processing by infants. A consequence of this is that infants will not encode surface features such as color and texture. Only if objects are large and cannot be grasped will ventral stream processing come into play. As we understand more about streams of processing in the brain, it will become possible to test these neurocognitive ideas more precisely.

LEARNING

The dorsal/ventral neural architecture of the human visual system provides a good example of what we can now term "constraints on learning". The advent of cognitive developmental neuroscience allows us to use such terms more precisely. If infants prioritize action, and if it takes time neurodevelopmentally to integrate the information yielded by the dorsal and ventral visual routes, then learning that requires attention to the unique identities of objects will be constrained by the nature of the objects in the visual field. However, there is more than one type of learning. A simple way to define learning is to say that it is the modification of behavior in the

Even very simple organisms, such as *Aplysia*, are able to learn and develop by modifying their behavior in light of experience.

light of experience. Even simple organisms such as *Aplysia* learn according to this definition. In fact, a number of different kinds of learning have been identified in work with animals. These include habituation, associative learning, social learning (e.g. by emulating others), and "insight" learning, when solutions to problems come "in a flash". Habituation and associative learning in infants have already been discussed. In cognitive psychology, learning is usually measured in terms of what has been *remembered* as a result of learning, either via measures of *recognition* or via measures of *recall*. We will examine learning by imitation, learning by analogy, and explanation-based learning here, none of which are found in animals (apart perhaps from exceptional animals such as language-reared chimps). Explanation-based learning is a form of causal learning. Causal learning is extremely important in cognitive development, and is found in animals in some forms, as discussed in greater detail in Chapter 6.

Learning by imitation

Learning by imitation can be defined as "B learns from A some part of the form of a behavior" (Whiten & Ham, 1992). One example is learning the use of a novel tool by imitating the actions of another user with that tool. Most definitions of imitation require that something new is learned, and such learning has proved remarkably difficult to distinguish in animals, even though until quite recently the contrary was believed to be true. In fact, psychologists now believe that learning by imitation is beyond the cognitive abilities of all animals, even animals like monkeys and chimpanzees, who are arguably the most human-like members of the animal kingdom (e.g. Tomasello, 1990; Visalberghi & Fragaszy, 1990). Tomasello has argued that humans differ profoundly from apes in their skills of imitation and imitative learning, because the ability to learn novel behaviors via imitation depends on the ability to understand the *intentions* of others.

Despite its cognitive sophistication, learning by imitation is present by the age of at least 9 months (Meltzoff, 1988a). As we saw earlier, older infants (18 months) can even imitate an adult who demonstrates an *intention* to act in a certain way, although the action is never completed, suggesting that imitation may indeed involve the ability to understand the intentions of others (Meltzoff, 1995a). In fact, most of our knowledge about imitative learning in infants comes from the pioneering work of Meltzoff, who has expanded his early research on the imitation of adult facial gestures in a number of interesting ways. Many of his more recent experiments depend on the use of *deferred imitation* as a test of learning. Meltzoff's test is to see whether infants can reproduce a novel action that they have observed previously even if they were not allowed access to the critical materials at the time of learning. This is a strong test of imitation, as the ability to duplicate actions that have been absent from the perceptual field for some time makes it more likely that the infant is actively reconstructing what he or she has seen and therefore actively imitating. The involvement of "recall" rather than "recognition" memory in deferred imitation also makes it a useful test of memory (see the research by Mandler and colleagues, discussed in Chapter 1).

In one of his first studies of deferred imitation, Meltzoff (1985) devised a paradigm suitable for 14-month-old infants based on the manipulation of a novel toy. The toy, which was specially constructed for the experiment, was a kind of wooden dumbbell made up of two wooden blocks joined by a short length of rigid plastic tubing. The rigid tubing gave it the appearance of a single object. However, the wooden blocks could in fact be pulled apart, but only if sufficient pressure was applied. In the experiment, the experimenter sat across from the baby at a small table, and produced the toy. In the *imitation condition*, he then pulled it apart three times in succession, using very definite movements. In the *control condition*, the experimenter moved the toy in a circle three times, pausing between each rotation. Each action (pulling vs. circling) lasted for the same amount of time. In the *baseline condition*, the experimenter simply gave the infant the toy to manipulate, without any behavioral modeling. In all three conditions, the infants were then sent home.

Twenty-four hours later the infants returned to the laboratory, sat down at the same table and were given the toy to manipulate. The critical question was whether the infants in the imitation condition would be more likely to pull the toy apart than the infants in the baseline and the control conditions. This was exactly what happened. Forty-five per cent of the babies in the imitation condition immediately pulled the toy apart themselves, compared to 7.5% of the control and baseline groups, whose data were added together. The babies in the imitation group were also much faster at producing the pulling-apart behavior than any control babies who managed to do so.

In a later study, Meltzoff (1988b) expanded the novel modeled behaviors to six, and the delay before allowing imitation to one week. In addition to the dumbbell used in the 1985 study (target act = pulling apart), 14-month-old babies were shown a flap with a hinge (target act = hinge folding), a box with a button (button pushing), a plastic egg filled with metal gravel (egg rattling), a bear suspended on a string (bear dancing), and a box with a panel (head touching of the panel, which then lit up). The control group observed six different modeled behaviors with these novel objects, and the baseline group observed no actions. Imitation was again measured in terms of the production of the target acts by each group. Meltzoff found that the infants in the imitation group produced significantly more of the target behaviors than the infants in the control group and the infants in the baseline group, who did not differ from each other. The infants in the imitation group were also significantly faster at producing the target acts. Once again, therefore, Meltzoff found clear evidence for learning by imitation, even after a delay of a week. The fact that six different novel behaviors had to be retained in memory makes this demonstration particularly impressive. In a related paper, Meltzoff (1988a) demonstrated retention of three novel acts by 9-month-olds over a delay of 24 hours, and subsequently he demonstrated deferred imitation in 14-month-olds over delays as long as 2–4 months (Meltzoff, 1995b). Learning by imitation appears to be crucial for infant cognition.

What if infants could learn not only by observing people acting on objects in real life, but by observing people acting on objects in films and videos? Given the ubiquity of the television in the modern home, this would expand infants' potential learning experiences by a huge degree. Meltzoff (1988c) has evidence that infants of 14 months of age can indeed learn novel actions from watching television. In his television study, the target action was again pulling apart (the dumbbell), but this time the infants watched the experimenter model the action on a 22-inch television set and never saw him live. The experimenter was filmed separately for each infant, enabling him to see their reactions on a video monitor so that he could wait until the infant was fixating on the dumbbell before pulling it apart. The experimenter also gained the infant's attention if necessary by calling "Look", or "Can you see me?" to babies who did not immediately begin to watch the television (this was apparently quite rare). Following the demonstration of the pulling-apart action, the infants were sent home. Control and baseline groups were also tested, as in previous studies.

Meltzoff (1988c) found that young infants can reproduce behaviors they witness on TV and proposed that older children would be similarly susceptible to deferred imitation.

When the infants returned to the laboratory the following day, they were given the toy to manipulate. As in real TV viewing, the infants did not see the experimenter "live", but were handed the toy to manipulate by their parents, who followed instructions from the televised experimenter. Meltzoff again found that the imitation group were significantly more likely to produce the target behavior than the control and baseline groups, just as in the "live" version of his study. Forty per cent of the babies in the imitation group immediately pulled the dumbbell apart, compared to 10% of control and baseline subjects. This demonstration of deferred imitation from the TV is a rather sobering one, as Meltzoff himself points out. If such young infants can reproduce behaviors that they see on TV and incorporate them into their own routines, then it is unlikely that TV viewing leaves older children unaffected. However, Meltzoff's demonstration is also an exciting one, as it means that TV can be used in a constructive way to enhance learning in target infant groups. Perhaps we should leave the last word to a toddler quoted by Meltzoff, who, on seeing his father pick up a bottle of beer, pointed to the bottle and exclaimed "Diet Pepsi, one less calorie!"

Learning by analogy

Learning by analogy involves finding certain relational correspondences between two events, situations, or domains of knowledge and then transferring knowledge from one to the other (e.g. Keane, 1988). So far, learning by analogy has only been demonstrated in a few members of the animal kingdom, for example in the highly unusual ape Sarah who had learned a limited language (Gillan, Premack, & Woodruff, 1981). As put memorably by Winston (1980), in learning by analogy "we face a situation, we recall a similar situation, we match them up, we reason, and we learn". We may decide whether a dog has a heart by thinking about whether people have hearts (see Chapter 4), or we may solve a mathematical problem about the interaction of forces by using an analogy to a tug-of-war (see Chapter 6). Reasoning by analogy has usually been measured in children aged 3 years or older (see Goswami, 1992, 2001, for reviews). However, analogies can also be measured in infancy.

One of the earliest demonstrations of analogical mapping by infants comes from an experiment with 3-month-old babies reported by Greco, Hayne, and Rovee-Collier (1990). They used a variant of the reactivation paradigm devised to test babies' memories for causal contingencies in the "kick-to-activate-a-crib-mobile" experiments (discussed in Chapter 1). As will be recalled, the reactivation paradigm involved giving infants a reminder of the mobile contingency 24 hours after learning, namely by showing them the moving mobile for 3 minutes prior to measuring kick rate. During the reminder phase, the mobile was activated by a hidden experimenter pulling on the ribbon. Greco et al. (1990) explored whether the degree of perceptual similarity between the mobile used during learning and the mobile used as a reminder cue affected infant memory. For example, infants who were trained with a mobile made of five hanging cubes were given a mobile shaped like a butterfly perched on a ring as a reminder cue. The butterfly mobile was rated by adults as highly dissimilar physically to the cubes mobile. Nevertheless, the butterfly mobile acted as a perfectly good retrieval cue for the infants. Greco et al. argued that the infants were transferring the learned relational contingency to the dissimilar mobile on the basis of functional relations (they had observed that the mobile could move). The butterfly mobile even acted as a reminder cue for another mobile that was physically dissimilar to the training mobile (this mobile was shaped like a rainbow). Infants shown the butterfly kicked to activate the rainbow 24 hours later. Hence the infants were transferring relational information despite the very different perceptual appearance of the different mobiles. They were making analogies.

Chen and colleagues devised a way of studying learning by analogy in infants of 10 months of age, following a procedure first developed by Brown (1990) for 1½- to 2-year-olds. Brown's procedure depended on seeing whether toddlers could learn how to acquire attractive toys that were out of reach. Different objects (such as a variety of tools, some more effective than others) were provided as a *means* to a particular *end* (bringing the desired toy within grasping distance). The analogy was that the means-to-an-end solution that worked for getting one toy in fact worked for all of the problems given, even though the problems themselves appeared on the surface to be rather different. Brown and colleagues used this paradigm to study analogical reasoning in children aged 17–36 months. Chen, Sanchez, and Campbell (1997) were able to extend it to infants.

In Chen et al.'s procedure, the infants came into the laboratory and were presented with an Ernie doll that was out of their reach. The Ernie doll was also behind a barrier (a box), and had a string attached to him that was lying on a cloth (Figure 2.10). To bring the doll within reach, the infants needed to learn to perform a series of actions. They had to remove the barrier, to pull on the cloth so that the string attached to the toy came within their grasp, and then to pull on the string itself so that they could reach Ernie. Following success on the first trial, two different toy problem scenarios were presented, each using identical tools (cloths, boxes, and strings). However, each problem appeared to be different to the problems that preceded it, as the cloths, boxes, and strings were always dissimilar to those encountered before. In addition, in each problem two strings and two cloths were provided, although only one pair could be used to reach the toy.

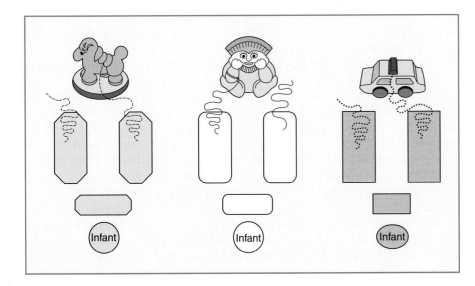

FIGURE 2.10
Depiction of the problem scenarios used to study analogical reasoning in infants by Chen et al. (1997). Copyright © American Psychological Association. Reprinted with permission.

Chen et al. tested infants aged 10 and 13 months in the Ernie paradigm. They found that although some of the older infants worked out the solution for getting Ernie on their own, others needed their parents to model the solution to the first toy acquisition problem for them. Once the solution to the first problem had been modeled, however, the 13-month-olds readily transferred an analogous solution to the second and third problems. The younger infants (10 months) needed more salient perceptual support in order for learning by analogy to occur. They showed spontaneous evidence of using analogies only when the perceptual similarity between the problems was increased (for example, by using the same goal toy, such as the Ernie doll, in all three problems).

Analogical reasoning may be a particularly important form of learning for cognitive development, as it involves reasoning about *relations*. As we will see throughout this book, a focus on relations, particularly *causal relations*, is very important in children's cognition. Analogies, especially analogies involving causal relations, may provide a critical cognitive tool for knowledge acquisition and representation and for conceptual development. More detailed treatment of the view that analogies play a fundamental role in cognitive development can be found in Carey (1985), Goswami (1992), and Halford (1993).

Explanation-based learning

Explanation-based learning in infancy has been explored in detail by Baillargeon and colleagues, who have proposed that explanation-based learning is the core mechanism used by infants to identify new variables as they build their knowledge of the physical world. As we saw in Chapter 1, Baillargeon (2001, 2002) has proposed a detailed model of the development of physical reasoning in infancy (see also Baillargeon, Li, Ng, & Yuan, in press). According to this model, infants identify event categories such as containment and support, and these categories are initially understood in terms of a few fundamental notions deemed to be "**core knowledge**". This core knowledge provides a shallow causal framework for understanding perceptual events, and relies on simple principles such as persistence (that objects exist continuously in time and space). Basic information about physical events such as support is represented, such as *no contact = object falls*, and *partial contact = object is supported*. As infants experience more and more events, more elaborate representations are developed in which variables that are relevant to the events' outcomes are identified and represented, such as *degree of contact* for support events. The process whereby infants identify new variables in event categories is thought to be explanation-based learning.

In the field of machine learning, explanation-based learning depends on constructing causal explanations for phenomena on the basis of specific training examples, using prior domain knowledge (De Jong, 2006). The aim of the mathematicians working on explanation-based learning is to provide machines with ways of applying domain-specific knowledge to formulate valid generalizations from single instances of a phenomenon. The underlying idea is that the ability to generalize from a single example depends on the machine's ability to explain to itself why the training example is an instantiation of a concept that is being learned, guiding itself via its prior domain knowledge. Training examples are explained using prior domain theory, which means that in practice other training examples (which may not be present, but have been previously experienced) are used to evaluate conjectured explanations. De Jong describes this as prior knowledge "magnifying" the information content of the training set. Baillargeon points out that infants are faced with similar problems in learning, and are collecting their own "training sets" of domain-specific knowledge via their prior experiences. Infants might see a variety of instantiations of a particular phenomenon, such as different objects falling from different surfaces. The infants need to extract the generalization that objects fall when they are inadequately supported. To make this generalization, infants need to attend to variables such as the degree of contact between relevant surfaces of the object and the supporting surface, the nature of the object (e.g. is it unevenly weighted?), the nature of the supporting surface (e.g. is it sticky?), and many other variables. Baillargeon has argued that in order to identify these variables, infants engage in three subprocesses that together constitute explanation-based learning. First, infants notice contrastive outcomes (e.g. when an object falls and when it does not). Second, infants search for the conditions that determine the contrastive outcomes (e.g. degree of support). Third, they use core knowledge to supply an explanation for this condition–outcome relationship. Condition–outcome relationships that can be explained via causal explanations are then used to identify new variables relevant to a particular event category.

Baillargeon argues that the experience-dependent nature of explanation-based learning can explain why infants will learn about certain perceptual variables in some event categories before others. For example, we saw in Chapter 1 that infants identified height as a relevant variable for occlusion events at around 4 months, as a relevant variable for containment events at around 7 months, and as a relevant variable for covering events at around 12 months. One reason for this might be that infants have more experiences of the relative heights of occluders and the objects that they occlude than of containers and the objects that they contain. Caretakers are very likely to lower objects directly into containers, whereas many occlusion events may occur when one object (say a cereal packet) is moved in front of another (say a cereal bowl). In the latter event, the infant has the opportunity to observe the relative heights of the object and the occluder.

If infants are really engaged in explanation-based learning, then manipulating the frequency with which they experience key variables in different events should affect the age at which they identify these variables as relevant to the events. Recently, Baillargeon and colleagues have embarked on a series of "teaching" experiments in order to test this possibility. In one such series of experiments, Wang and Baillargeon (in press) explored whether infants aged 9 months could be taught to take account of the variable *height* in covering events. As will be recalled, height is not usually taken into account in covering events until the age of around 12 months. Wang and Baillargeon devised a series of ways of teaching 9-month-old infants to attend to height. For example, in one experiment infants were given three pairs of "teaching trials" regarding the importance of height for covering events. At the beginning of each trial, a cover (tall or short) stood next to a tall object on the apparatus floor. Whichever cover was not going to be used in that pair of trials stood against the back wall of the apparatus. A hand then rotated the cover through 90° to demonstrate that it was hollow, and returned it to the floor. Next it lifted the cover, lowered it over the object, and released it. In the tall cover trial, the cover completely concealed the object. In the short cover trial, a portion of the object remained visible. After a pause, the hand removed the cover and a new event cycle began.

After the infants had seen three pairs of covering trials, they were shown the test event used in the original covering experiments (Wang & Baillargeon, 2005; see Chapter 1). Both a short cover and a tall cover completely hid the tall object once they were lowered over it. The first was an impossible event. The 9-month-old babies who had received the teaching trials looked reliably longer at this "short cover" event. They detected the violation 3 months earlier than babies who had not received any teaching trials. In a second teaching experiment with fewer teaching trials (two pairs of trials only), similar results were achieved. Again, 9-month-old babies looked reliably longer at the "short cover" event. A third teaching experiment then introduced a delay between the teaching trials and the test trials. The infants received the teaching trials on one day, and came back to the laboratory 24 hours later for the test trials. Again, the infants looked reliably longer at the "short cover" event. Wang and Baillargeon argued that exposure to the contrastive outcomes with the tall and short covers during the teaching trials was triggering explanation-based learning. Consequently, infants were identifying relevant variables for covering events on the basis of specific experiences. Further evidence for this account was gained by preventing the infants from experiencing contrastive outcomes. For example, small objects were covered in the training trials, so that the entire object was concealed by both tall and short covers. In these conditions, the infants did not learn about the importance of height in covering events.

These demonstrations of explanation-based learning in infants are extremely important. Explanation-based learning is essentially causal learning. If infants were merely learning condition–outcome relations, as in associative learning, then they would be unable to make predictions about novel events. However, infants who understand *why* (for example) short covers cannot conceal tall objects should be able to reason about height information in any covering event, even if this event is very remote in perceptual terms from the learning events. The infants, like the machines, would be able to formulate valid generalizations from single instances. The need to construct a causal explanation for these instances would rule out spurious generalizations based on condition–outcome regularities (in fact, machine learning algorithms called causal Bayes nets can explain how spurious generalizations are ruled out on the basis of covariation information; see Chapter 6). Even 9-month-olds appear to make causal interpretations of condition–outcome regularities: they appear to engage in causal learning.

To check that the infants were engaging in causal learning, Wang and Baillargeon conducted a final experiment. In this experiment, they created a situation that was perceptually very similar to the teaching events, but for which no causal explanation could be provided. This was done by putting false tops into the tall and short covers, so that both were only 2.5 cm deep. When the covers were rotated at the beginning of the teaching trials, the infants could hence see that they were extremely shallow. It thus made no sense in causal terms when the short cover only concealed a portion of the object, while the tall cover concealed the entire object. There was no plausible causal explanation for the contrastive outcomes. In this final experiment, the 9-month-old infants did not appear to learn about the height variable, as they did not look reliably longer at the "short cover" event. This negative result is consistent with Wang and Baillargeon's claim that explanation-based learning is distinct from associative or statistical learning in infants.

WHAT BABIES CAN'T DO: COGNITIVE NEUROSCIENCE AND APPARENT GAPS IN PHYSICAL KNOWLEDGE

So far, the case for claiming continuity between infant and adult cognition appears to be a fairly strong one. However, some surprising gaps have been documented in infants' cognitive abilities, gaps that have frequently been explained in terms of cognitive immaturities. More recent research in cognitive neuroscience has suggested that these gaps may arise for noncognitive reasons. Rather than reflecting cognitive confusions, they appear to reflect neural constraints such as poor inhibitory processes arising from the immaturity of the **frontal cortex**. The frontal cortex is important for the planning and monitoring of cognitive activity, and the inhibition of action.

One definition of cognitive activity was considered earlier in this chapter, taken from Anderson's (1990) discussion of reasoning and problem solving. Anderson noted that the characteristics of reasoning and problem-solving situations are that the reasoner wants to reach a desired end state, that a sequence of mental processes are involved in reaching this end state, and that the mental processes are cognitive rather than automatic. He pointed out that routine sequences of behavior did not qualify as cognitive. When we examine the documented gaps in infants' cognitive abilities in some detail, most of them turn out to involve repetitive, or perseverative, behavioral routines.

Search errors in reaching

The best known of these apparent gaps in cognitive ability is a search error that emerges at around 9 months of age, which was first documented by Piaget (1954). This search error occurs in simple hiding-and-finding tasks that involve more than one location. Imagine that an object is hidden at one location, location A, for a number of trials. The infants retrieve the object without difficulty. The hiding location is then moved to another location, location B. Although this switch in hiding location occurs in full view of the infants, the infants persist in searching at location A. This is the "A-not-B" error, and is shown in Figure 2.11. The **A-not-B error** was originally thought to stem from a cognitive confusion. Piaget (1954) argued that infants might initially believe that the location of objects was dependent upon their own actions. He proposed that infants might initially rely on egocentric spatial codes, and might therefore link the location of objects to places associated with previously successful actions. In order to find objects, therefore, they would search perseveratively at

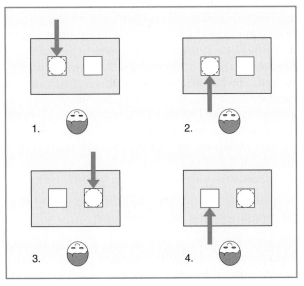

FIGURE 2.11
The sequence of events in the A-not-B error. The experimenter hides an object at location A (1), and the infant reaches successfully (2). The object is then hidden at location B (3), whereupon the infant again searches at A (4). From Bremner (1988). Reproduced with permission from Blackwell Publishing.

locations that had provided them with previous successes. A growing number of studies suggest that the A-not-B error may have a more prosaic explanation. The A-not-B error, and other surprising gaps in infant performance that depend on **perseverative behaviors**, may be due to immaturities in prefrontal cortex.

The frontal cortex of the brain has a number of cognitive functions. Its central role is thought to be the planning and monitoring of action and cognitive activity. The frontal lobe is said to be the site of higher thought processes, abstract reasoning, and motor processing and contains the primary motor cortex, which is involved in the planning and control of movements. Adult patients with lesions to frontal cortex exhibit a tendency to persist in certain motor actions. For example, if a frontal patient is asked to discover the rule (color, shape, or number) for sorting a pack of cards (with feedback), the patient will do so very successfully. If the rule is then switched, however, for example from color to shape, the patient is unable to sort the cards according to the new rule. Instead, the patient continues sorting the cards according to the rule that was previously correct (e.g. Milner, 1963). The patient is aware that the rule has changed, but is unable to use this knowledge to guide action.

Monkeys with frontal cortex lesions demonstrate similar perseverative behaviors. The classic test for prefrontal cortex function in nonhuman primates is "delayed reaching". In delayed reaching tasks, monkeys retrieve a desired object from one of two identical hiding wells after a short delay. The hiding location is varied randomly over trials. Monkeys with lesions to frontal cortex fail the delayed reaching task following delays as brief as 1–2 seconds, although they succeed if there is no delay (Diamond, 1988). Similarly, 9-month-old infants show perseverative searching in the A-not-B task following a delay of 1–2 seconds, but succeed if there is no delay. Older infants *also* show A-not-B errors if they are subjected to *longer* delays. In fact, the delay needed to produce the A-not-B error increases at an average rate of 2 seconds per month (Diamond, 1985). Eight- to 12-month-old infants also fail the delayed reaching task following short delays (Diamond, 1990).

Diamond (and others) has suggested that babies who make "perseverative" errors such as continuing to search in location A when the object has been hidden in location B are doing so because of immaturities in frontal cortex. Her argument is that perseveration is a symptom and not an explanation of the problem faced by these infants when they are searching for desired objects. Their underlying problem is an inability to *inhibit* a predominant action tendency. The predominant action tendency in the A-not-B task is to search at A. When the hiding location is moved to B, infants find it difficult to inhibit their tendency to search at location A, and thus show perseverative errors. Cognitively, they know that the location of the object has changed, but they are unable to use this cognitive knowledge to guide action. The fact that they show these errors even when the object is *in full view* at B supports this explanation (Butterworth, 1977). In the same way, frontal patients who are unable to sort a pack of cards according to a new rule are finding it difficult to inhibit their prepotent tendency to sort by the old rule. They may actually tell you this themselves. Some patients say, as they are sorting the cards by the old rule, "This is wrong, and this is wrong . . ." (see Diamond, 1988).

Search errors in crawling

We will return to the role of inhibition in cognitive development later in this book (see Chapter 9). For the time being, it is worth noting that infants show difficulties in inhibiting prepotent action tendencies in crawling as well as in reaching.

Perseverative crawling has been observed both in studies using random switching of the location-to-be-crawled-to (analogous to the random switches in delayed reaching) and in studies requiring infants to crawl to a consistent location which is then switched following a series of successful trials (analogous to the A-not-B paradigm).

For example, Rieser, Doxey, McCarrell, and Brooks (1982) examined whether mobile 9-month-olds could crawl around a barrier to reach their mothers (Figure 2.12). The barrier went across the center of the experimental room and was too high for the infants to see over it. However, they could hear their mothers calling to them from the far side. Before being allowed to crawl to their mothers, the infants were carried around the apparatus, and were shown that the barrier was open at one end. On the first trial, 85% of the infants crawled successfully to their mothers. However, on subsequent trials 75% of the infants crawled to the *same* side as before, even though the "open" side of the barrier was then varied randomly. In fact, these infants crawled perseveratively to the same side on *every* trial, whether this led to success or failure, despite being shown the open end of the barrier on *each* trial. The infants seemed incapable of inhibiting the previously executed motor pattern. In a second study of infants aged from 9 to 25 months, Rieser et al. showed that the perseverative crawling response dropped out slowly with increasing age. Perseverative crawling was shown by 80% of the 9- and 13-month-olds, 44% of the 17- and 21-month-olds, but only 6% of the 25-month-olds.

McKenzie and Bigelow (1986) carried out a similar "detour crawling" task with 10-, 12-, and 14-month-olds. However, instead of varying the open end of the barrier at random, they kept the open end of the barrier consistent across a series of trials and then changed it. The open path lay either to the right or to the left side of the barrier for four trials at a time. The crucial measure was the direction of crawl on the fifth trial (which is similar to the first B trial in an A-not-B search task). McKenzie and Bigelow found that 75–80% of the younger babies showed perseveration of the now inappropriate motor response on the fifth trial, crawling to the same side as before. In contrast, only 25% of the 14-month-olds made a perseverative response. As the second block of four trials progressed, however, the younger babies, too, were able to learn to crawl to the correct side of the barrier. This suggests that the babies could learn to correct their perseverative errors. It would be interesting to measure the effect of imposing increased delays on infants of different ages in detour crawling tasks. With longer delays, perseverative crawling may be observed in later trials as well.

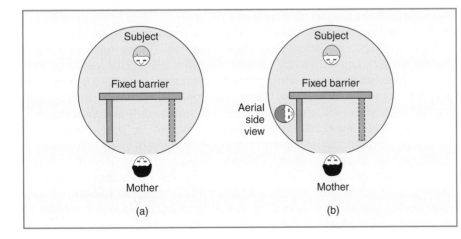

FIGURE 2.12
The experimental set-up used by Rieser et al. to study perseverative crawling, seen (a) from the viewpoint of the infant, and (b) depicting the aerial view shown to the infant. From Bremner (1988). Reproduced with permission from Blackwell Publishing.

The observation that infants have difficulties in inhibiting prepotent motor tendencies in crawling as well as in reaching supports the view that the A-not-B search error does not arise from shortcomings in basic cognitive abilities. Instead of reflecting a difficulty in cognition, it seems to reflect difficulties in gaining control of one's behavior so that one's behavior can *reflect* what one is thinking (Diamond, 1988). The conclusion that knowledge representation, reasoning, problem solving, and learning are progressing well in infancy is therefore not undermined by errors such as the A-not-B error. Instead, it seems that we are justified in concluding that basic cognitive abilities are well-established during the first year of life.

SUMMARY

This chapter examined the development of cognitive knowledge about the physical world in infancy. We found that knowledge representation is rooted in attention to the *perceptual* structure of objects and events, and that aspects of this knowledge are simultaneously *conceptual*, because of the perceptual/causal structure of experienced events. Experienced events are dynamic: objects may be moved or may become occluded. Schemas develop that encode what is consistent about the causal structure of such events as well as encoding the perceptual and sensory details pertaining to each individual event. On the basis of repeated experience, therefore, what is common across many perceptual instances of a dynamic event is activated more strongly than what is not. This simple fact of neural learning means that the "gist" or even the "essence" of a particular concept or schema is eventually encoded more strongly than the (variable) perceptual details.

Perceptual experiences yield conceptual representations via a number of possible mechanisms. For example, Baillargeon suggested that initial perceptually based descriptions of concepts such as support, and core descriptions like "has contact", are gradually refined in the light of active experience of the physical world into more elaborate representations that identify variables that are highly relevant to outcome, such as "degree of contact with supporting surface". Leslie's idea was that, at least for causal analyses of motion, infants generate mechanical descriptions of events that go beyond a perceptual description of what has occurred, enabling them to understand the mechanical properties of agents. On the basis of more recent experiments involving simple dynamic perceptual displays, it was suggested here that the mental (neural) representation of causal events might simultaneously yield conceptual information simply by virtue of the way in which the brain processes different perceptual aspects of an event, such as types of motion (a "constraint" on learning), and the statistical learning algorithms used. Certain motions, for example, suggest agency. Gergely et al.'s (1995) demonstration that passive perception of the spatial behavior of objects can lead infants to adopt an intentional stance to physical events is a particularly intriguing example of this kind of conceptual information.

More sophisticated forms of statistical learning, such as those captured by causal Bayes nets and explanation-based learning, appear to play an important role in the extraction and representation of causal structure. For example, the algorithms underpinning causal Bayes nets rule out spurious associations (those unrelated to underlying causal structure) on the basis of covariation information, and are discussed more fully in Chapter 6. All of these mechanisms probably play a role in the development of cognitive representations from perceptual information. Further, perceptual information is apparently never discarded. Mental (neural) representations are highly distributed, and accordingly cognitive representations (the information held "in mind") will reflect properties of these distributed representations.

Reasoning and problem solving in infancy were also considered. We saw that reasoning and problem solving can be defined as requiring at least three ingredients. The first is a desired end state or specific goal, the second is that a sequence of mental processes is involved in reaching the goal, and the third is that these mental processes are cognitive and not automatic. A series of experiments by Baillargeon and others based on impossible physical events showed that young infants do indeed seem capable of reasoning and problem-solving behavior. Baillargeon described the young subjects in her experiments as engaging in a knowledge-based, conceptual analysis of the physical world, and her experiments in which the "tricks" behind impossible physical events were subsequently revealed supported this contention. The infants' ability to work out how the impossible events were produced suggests that "higher" forms of cognition are also present as young as 5 months of age. Infants' capacities for learning by imitation and learning by analogy, cognitive skills almost universally absent in other species, also support the view that infant cognition is highly sophisticated. The ability to imitate an action seen only on a video is a particularly remarkable demonstration of this sophistication.

Finally, we considered what infants can't do. The conclusion reached was that tasks that depend on aspects of frontal function such as inhibition may suggest very immature cognition in infancy, as the frontal system undergoes protracted development. Frontal cortex is still developing in late adolescence and the early twenties. Unsurprisingly, therefore, like frontal patients, infants find it difficult to inhibit predominant action tendencies. Infants are poor at monitoring their cognitive activities, especially when these activities involve perseverative behavioral routines. They find it difficult to stop themselves searching at a previously successful location or crawling along a previously traveled route. These "cognitive failures" demonstrate the intimate connection between cognitive activity and the underlying neural substrate. Our understanding of this intimate connection is still very preliminary, but in the next decades it is set to increase considerably. Developmental cognitive neuroscience is a particularly promising area for future work in infant cognition (Johnson, 2005; Mareschal, Johnson, Sirois, Spratling, Thomas, & Westermann, 2007).

CONTENTS

Infancy: The psychological world

3

The means by which we come to know others as persons like ourselves has long fascinated philosophers. To explain how we become able to understand that others have unobservable internal entities called minds is quite difficult. Somehow, we come to understand that the actions of other agents will depend on the knowledge and beliefs held in their minds, and that this knowledge and these beliefs may differ from the knowledge and beliefs that we hold in our own minds. This is a sophisticated cognitive feat. We have already seen that one possible mechanism for naïve psychology is the infant's capacity for imitation. Infants appear to be born with a propensity to attend to and interact with other people, finding people intrinsically more interesting than other kinds of entities. Meltzoff has argued that the first common code between self and other is the ability to map the actions of other people onto the actions of our own bodies. As we saw in Chapters 1 and 2, he suggests that this imitative ability is innate, and he argues that basic aspects of the representation of action must therefore also be innate. We have considered evidence that imitation is not simply an immediate mimicry of another's actions, without any representation of those actions. We know that imitation is not due to arousal, and that it cannot be dismissed as a biologically based response that is released in the presence of certain "releasing" stimuli. Rather, infant imitation appears to be creative and open to modulation, and can occur hours or even days after the modeled event.

We also saw that infants prefer to imitate people, not machines. In the last chapter, we saw that Meltzoff originally proposed that this might be evidence for two separable causal frameworks by the age of 18 months. Infants appear to use physical causality for explaining the behavior of things, and may be able to use psychological causality for explaining the behavior of people. In fact, it has been proposed that a "revolution" in social understanding in infancy occurs at around 9 months of age (Tomasello, 1995). At 9 months, babies begin to engage in measurable joint attention activities. They begin to make communicative gestures, and they show social referencing, using the behavior of others as a guide to how to respond to novel objects or events in the world. There is also evidence for a growing understanding of intentionality, which is the rudimentary beginning of developing a "theory of mind". Reading the intentions of others is critical for predicting their unobservable mental states. Further, infants appear to begin developing an understanding of the self as a causal agent. The traditional notion (stemming from Freud) that young infants are initially unable to distinguish themselves from their environments appears to be quite wrong. As we will see, very simple cognitive skills such as the ability to detect causal contingencies between events may underlie the development of an understanding of self and agency in infancy. However, it seems unlikely that there is a sudden revolution in development at 9 months of age. One possibility is that prior developments, such as joint action on objects with caretakers, are preparing the

Infants appear to be born with a natural propensity to finding interaction with other people more interesting than with other entities. © Royalty Free/Corbis.

infant developmentally for joint attention and social referencing (Rodríguez, 2007). According to this view, the "triad" of infant, caretaker, and object is central in very early social development, with shared action on objects acting as a crucial cultural tool.

The propensity for social interaction

Many theorists have commented that infants enter the world predisposed for social interaction. For example, Bowlby (1971) pointed out that newborn babies seem to come equipped with behavioral mechanisms for ensuring proximity to the mother or primary caretaker. Innate actions such as rooting, grasping, crying, and smiling effectively play a role in social interaction; it is very difficult to ignore the cries of a baby! Acoustic evidence suggests that this is no evolutionary accident: These cries are at a particular pitch and amplitude that is highly stressful for the caretaker, prompting immediate attention (e.g. Zeskind, Sale, Maio, Huntington, & Weiseman, 1985). Infants also show strong preferences for the caretaker, preferring the mother's smell and the mother's voice (e.g. Cernock & Porter, 1985). Some of these preferences may be established while in the womb. This was demonstrated in an ingenious study by DeCasper and Fifer (1980), who tested babies' memory for their mother's voice approximately 12 hours after they had been born.

DeCasper and Fifer's (1980) experiment was based on the finding that infants can hear noises while they are inside the womb from at least the third trimester (6–9 months). One sound that they hear a lot is their mother's voice. She may be talking to other people during her daily routines, talking on the telephone or even talking to the infant in her womb. If infants can recognize and remember the sound of their mother's voice then they should be able to distinguish her voice from the voice of a female stranger. To see whether infants were able to do this, DeCasper and Fifer first measured how strongly the infants sucked on a dummy in the absence of any auditory stimulus. They then introduced two tape recordings, one of the infant's mother reading a story and one of a strange woman reading the same story. For some infants, every time their suck rate increased compared to baseline, they were rewarded with the tape of their mother's voice. Every time their suck rate fell below the baseline measure, they heard the tape of the voice of the stranger. For other infants, the contingencies were reversed. A low suck rate relative to baseline was rewarded with their mother's voice and a high suck rate relative to baseline was rewarded with the voice of the stranger.

Both groups of infants rapidly learned to suck at the appropriate rate to hear their mother's voice. This shows that they remembered the sound of their own mother's voice, and that it was a familiar and comforting stimulus. Even more impressive, they could remember the contingency in a second test session given on the following day. Babies who had learned to suck strongly to hear their mother began by sucking strongly on the dummy, and those who had learned to suck slowly began by sucking slowly. The experimenters, however, had reversed the contingencies. Babies who had learned to suck strongly for their mother's voice were now meant to suck slowly, and babies who had learned to suck slowly were now meant to suck strongly.

Around 80% of the babies learned to reverse their suck rate. As well as demonstrating the strength of infants' preference for their mother's voice, this is good evidence for learning and memory in these extremely young babies. In fact, the ability to reverse a learned contingency is considered to be a strong test of cognition in animals. The rapid **reversal learning** demonstrated by these day-old babies shows that they are already cognitively sophisticated as compared with other species.

To provide a strong test of the idea that memory for the mother's voice does indeed occur via learning in utero, rather than from very rapid learning during the first few hours after birth, DeCasper and Spence (1986) conducted a further study in which participating mothers read three stories onto a tape. The mothers then selected one of the three stories and read it every day during the last 6 weeks of their pregnancies. Following birth, the infants' baseline suck rates were established, and the infants were then rewarded for sucking either above or below baseline by their mother's voice reading the familiar story. If sucking fell to baseline, the infants heard their mother's voice reading an unfamiliar story. DeCasper and Spence found that the infants consistently sucked at the rate that was appropriate to produce the familiar story. Interestingly, a second group of infants showed the same pattern of preferences when tested with another mother's voice reading the stories. DeCasper and Spence argued that the target stories were preferred because the infants had heard them before birth. The babies had apparently learned something about the acoustic cues specifying a particular target passage as fetuses, and could recognize these cues even when a strange female voice was reading the story. As we will see in Chapter 5, auditory learning mechanisms in babies are extremely powerful, and provide them with a lot of information about environmental structure.

Infant preferences for the mother's face, voice, and smell are part of the constellation of attachment behaviors that serve to foster and strengthen the relationship with the primary caregiver. This relationship is very important for the healthy psychological development of the infant. However, a discussion of the attachment literature is beyond the scope of this book (see Cassidy & Shaver, 2002, for a comprehensive review). We will focus instead on the more cognitive aspects of understanding the self and the minds of others. We begin by considering the ability to learn contingencies, as demonstrated by the sucking behavior of neonates. **Contingency learning** appears to be a crucial aspect of the development of social cognition.

The role of detecting contingency in awareness of self and other

The early ability to detect and learn contingencies between one's own actions (e.g. sucking) and the auditory environment (e.g. the mother's voice) can also be found in the visual environment. As we saw in Chapter 1, 3-month-old babies can learn a causal contingency involving a relationship between their own actions and visually rewarding objects such as mobiles. Rovee-Collier et al. (1980) showed that babies will learn to kick to activate an attractive mobile at 3 months of age. In these experiments, the mobile's movement was dependent on a ribbon tied to the baby's ankle. The babies learned the contingency between their action and the rewarding event. Following suggestions by Watson (1994), Gergely (2001) has argued that this ability to detect the contingencies of their own motor actions is the mechanism whereby babies first develop a primary representation of the bodily self. He argues that babies can identify the consequences of the motor actions of their own bodies by 2–3 months of age, and that they do this most easily when there is a perfect contingency between their actions and certain consequences.

An interesting study of young babies' ability to notice contingencies based on their own bodily actions was carried out by Bahrick and Watson (1985). They videoed babies aged 3 and 5 months of age as they sat in a seat kicking their legs. The infants could see two video monitors as they kicked. In one monitor, they saw their legs moving in real time. The display showed the current live image, and so there was a perfect contingency between the legs on the screen and the babies' own movements (as they were watching their own legs). The second monitor showed earlier footage of the babies' legs. They were still seeing their own legs, but now there was no contingency between the movements they were in the act of performing and the movements of the legs on the screen. The older babies looked much longer at the noncontingent image, as did half of the younger babies. The other half of the 3-month-olds reliably preferred to watch the contingent image. All infants had a reliable preference, indicating awareness of the contingencies.

Mirror self-recognition

If babies can recognize the contingency between their own actions and the actions of a live video-recording of themselves by 3 months, it seems likely that they would also be able to recognize themselves in a mirror. However, the literature on mirror self-recognition has assumed that this ability emerges rather later, on average at around 2 years. The critical test of mirror self-recognition is the "**mark test**". A noticeable mark is made on the baby in a location that cannot be viewed naturally, such as the face. For example, a spot of rouge is placed on the child's nose. The test of mirror self-recognition is whether the child, while looking in the mirror, notices and touches the spot on their nose. The "mark test" is intended to provide an objective test of mirror self-recognition.

Amsterdam (1972) used the "mark test" as an objective means to establish the age at which a child demonstrates true mirror self-recognition.

Amsterdam (1972) used the mark test with babies aged from 3 to 24 months. The babies were given a mirror in their playpens, large enough to view their entire bodies. Their mothers drew their attention to the mirror, pointing at the babies' faces and saying "See! See! See! Who's that?". The babies were then left to explore the mirror. Amsterdam reported that over half of the babies tested out the mirror, even in the youngest age group (3–5 months), for example by observing their image as they moved different body parts. Some also looked behind the mirror or tried to reach into it. However, only the older babies showed mirror self-recognition in terms of touching the dot of rouge or saying their own name in response to the image (42% of 18- to 20-month-olds, and 63% of 21- to 24-month-olds). Amsterdam concluded that objective evidence for mirror self-recognition was only present from 18 months, although she noted that there were data indicative of emergent awareness (e.g. testing out the mirror) much earlier than this.

More recently, it has been shown that animals like elephants, apes, and dolphins also show mirror self-recognition. For example, Plotnik, de Waal, and Reiss (2006) demonstrated mirror self-recognition in an Asian elephant in New York Zoo.

The researchers mounted an enormous mirror in the enclosure occupied by three elephants, Patty, Happy, and Maxine. They then examined whether the four stages of mirror self-recognition found to be typical in other species would be displayed. These are: (1) social reponses to the mirror; (2) physical mirror inspection, such as looking behind the mirror; (3) repetitive mirror-testing behavior; and (4) self-directed mirror behavior (passing the "mark test"). All of the elephants displayed stage 2 and 3 behaviors during the first 4 days of having the mirror. They touched and sniffed the mirror, checked behind it with their trunks and tried to climb over the wall on which the mirror was mounted. They also tested the mirror repetitively by making nonspecies-typical trunk and body movements. However, when a large white mark was placed on the face on day 5, only Happy passed the mark test. She checked the mark 47 times. Although Patty and Maxine appeared to ignore their marks, they continued to show self-directed behavior at the mirror. Plotnik et al. argued that awareness of the self–other distinction is present in a number of species who show complex sociality and co-operation. This is probably true of human babies, too, even by around 3 months of age.

Adult contingent behaviors

Another reason why infants may develop psychological understanding relatively early in life is that their caretakers treat them as social partners. When caring for infants, adults usually make their behavior contingent upon, rather than ignoring of, infant attempts to communicate. In fact, caretakers may treat their infants as acting communicatively even before infants are intentionally acting in this way (Meins, Fernyhough, Wainwright, Das Gupta, Fradley, & Tuckey, 2002). Striano, Henning, and Stahl (2005) explored infants' sensitivity to social contingencies by studying babies aged 1 and 3 months during face-to-face interactions with their mothers (Figure 3.1).

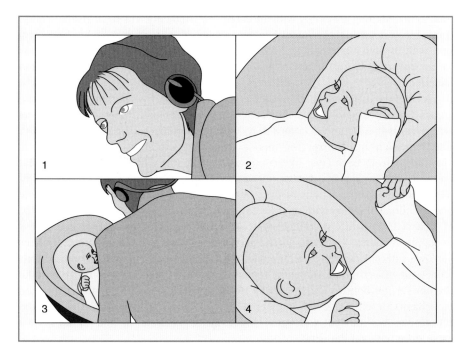

FIGURE 3.1
Set-up for studies 1 and 2.

In Striano et al.'s study, maternal contingencies were manipulated by the experimenters. All mothers were first instructed to interact with their infants "as they normally did". The infants and mothers faced each other with eyes 50 cm apart, and 3 minutes of normal interaction were recorded. Mothers and babies then went home. A week later, they came back to the laboratory and three different contingencies were experienced. The 1-month-olds experienced these different contingencies for 1 minute each, and the 3-month-olds for 3 minutes each. *Normal* interaction was as on the previous visit. In a second condition, *noncontingent* interaction, the mothers wore headsets that played them 1 minute of their interaction from the prior week. They were required to reproduce this interaction as they heard it. The third— *imitation*—interaction required the mother to mirror their infants' facial expressions, arm/hand gestures and vocalizations. The experimenters recorded the gazing and smiling shown by the infant during each of the contingencies. Striano and colleagues found that the 1-month-olds did not distinguish between the different contingencies in terms of their gazing and smiling behavior. By 3 months of age, however, the infants were behaving differently in response to the different contingencies. They showed more gazing in the Imitation condition, and more smiling in the Normal interaction condition. Striano et al. argued that infants were sensitive to social contingencies by 3 months of age.

This sensitivity to contingency and awareness of the bodily self may play an important role in the development of social cognition. Reactive social partners tend to provide high but not perfect contingencies (for example, parents usually "talk back" to a cooing baby, but not always). Gergely (2001) argues that by 3 months of age babies have adapted to this aspect of the social environment, and now prefer imperfect contingencies. They gradually realize via contingency detection that their own states and behaviors exert control over the caretaker's behaviors, and thus pay more attention to these states and behaviors, thereby beginning to develop emotional self-awareness and control. According to Gergely, the very young infant engages in social interactions because these actions have important evolutionary advantages, such as maintaining proximity with the caregiver. Gradually, via mechanisms such as contingency detection, the infant becomes aware of the self as a separate (bodily) self, with its own intentional and affective states. This helps to lay the foundations for an understanding of others as having their own (subjective) mental states and intentions.

A slightly different position to Gergely's is taken by Meltzoff (2002), who argues that the crucial thing about early interactions with other agents such as caregivers is that the infant comes to recognize the other person as "just like me". The important mechanism for this is imitation, which, as we have seen, is operational from birth (just like contingency detection). Meltzoff points out that imitation shows that, at some primitive level, infants are mapping the actions of other people onto the actions of their own bodies. They are connecting the visible bodily actions of others with their own internal states. This cross-modal knowledge of what it feels like to do the act that was seen then provides a privileged access to people as special kinds of entities. Meltzoff suggests that the infant experiences her own internal desires (e.g. she wants her bottle) and experiences the actions (concomitant bodily movements) required to fulfil these desires or goals (she reaches for her bottle). This helps the infant to make sense of the object-directed movements of others. When another person is seen reaching for an object, the action can be imbued with goal-directedness, because of the infant's own experience with similar acts.

THE CENTRAL ROLE OF THE ACTIONS OF OTHER AGENTS

Viewing the actions of others as goal directed

When we as adults observe the actions of others, we assume that they have a purpose. We assume that the actor has certain goals, and that he or she is acting to achieve those goals. Meltzoff's suggestion is that infants' ability to map from self to other (as documented by imitation studies) serves as a catalyst for understanding their own behavior and the behavior of others in terms of goals. For example, infants imitate successful yet arbitrary acts performed by the experimenter, such as turning on a light panel by bending forward and pressing it with the forehead (see Chapter 2). They also imitate unsuccessful acts that they infer that the experimenter had intended to perform successfully, such as putting a string of beads into a cylindrical container (see Meltzoff, 1988b, 1995a). These imitations suggest that certain goals are imputed to the actor. In the first example, infants appear to believe that there must be a reason for the actor using their head rather than their hand to activate the light, and accordingly they follow suit. In the second example, the infants infer the intended goal of the actor and execute this goal, rather than imitating the unsuccessful act. However, neither experiment provides *direct* evidence for these inferences. More recently, a study by Gergely, Bekkering, and Király (2002) demonstrated very nicely that infants who imitate are indeed imputing goals to the actors that they are copying.

For their demonstration, Gergely et al. (2002) extended the light panel procedure invented by Meltzoff (1988b; Figure 3.2). In this procedure, the infant watches as an experimenter switches on a light panel with her head. The panel is set into the top of a box, which sits on a table in front of the experimenter. The experimenter illuminates the light by bending forwards and touching the panel with her forehead. This is a rather odd act, but the infants in Meltzoff (1988b) still imitated it. In Gergely et al.'s (2002) experiment, a rationale was provided for this odd behavior. The experimenter complained of feeling cold, and wrapped herself in a blanket.

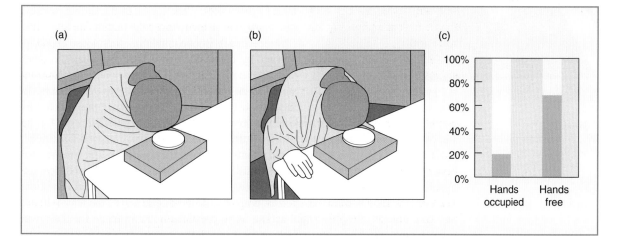

FIGURE 3.2
The light panel procedure showing (a) the "hands occupied" condition, and (b) the "hands free" condition. (c) shows the methods used by infants to switch on the light box after watching the demonstrator under these two conditions. (Blue: head was used, yellow: hands were used.) From Gergely et al. (2000).

Her hands were thus occupied with the blanket, and were not free to press the light panel on the box. Consequently, she used her head to press the panel. The 14-month-old infants who observed this did not use their own heads to illuminate the light panel. When given the box to operate, 79% of them chose to use their hands to illuminate the light, and only 21% used their foreheads. However, in a second condition, other 14-month-old infants saw the same event when the blanket was just draped around the shoulders of the experimenter, whose hands were thus free. In this "hands free" condition, 69% of the infants pressed the light panel with their foreheads, thereby replicating Meltzoff's original findings (Meltzoff, 1988).

This experiment shows neatly that understanding the goals of another transforms the bodily motions of another into purposive behavior. Although the action in Gergely et al.'s (2002) experiment was identical in each scenario, the goals of the agent were assumed to differ. When the experimenter was not clasping the blanket and had her hands free, her use of her forehead was assumed to be intentional and therefore important *vis à vis* the activation of the light panel. This is a robust experimental method. The actions are identical but different intentions are suggested by simple changes in context. Differential imitation of the same action because of changes in context is strong evidence for attributing an understanding of goal-directed action to infants.

Carpenter, Call, and Tomasello (2005) devised a different paradigm based on simple contextual changes to explore how early young infants use context to determine goals. They demonstrated hopping and sliding actions made by an actor with a toy mouse to infants aged 12 and 18 months in two different contexts. In each context, the infants watched an experimenter make a toy mouse take a distinctive hopping or sliding journey across a mat. In the hopping journey, the experimenter made the mouse cross the mat in a series of eight jumping actions, accompanied by suitable hop noises ("bee" "bee" "bee" . . .). In the sliding journey, the mouse was made to cross the mat in one long slide ("beeeeeeeee"). In one condition, the mouse ended its journey by being put into a little house on the other side of the mat (Figure 3.3). The journey followed a straight line into one of two possible goal houses. In the second condition, no houses were present. In this condition, the experimenter appeared to be making the mouse hop or jump just for the fun of the action. The question was what the infants would imitate in each condition.

FIGURE 3.3
Top: the mouse at the start location in the House condition of Carpenter et al.'s (2005) study; bottom: the mouse at the end location in the No House condition. From Carpenter, Call, and Tomasello (2005). Reproduced with permission from Blackwell Publishing.

Carpenter et al. predicted that the infants would put the mouse straight into the goal house in the first condition, where the little houses were present. In this condition, the apparent goal of the adult was to get the mouse into its house. In the second condition, however, the infants were expected to jump or slide the mouse across the mat. Without any goal houses, the differential actions were presumably being made for their own sake. In the test trials, the infants were handed the mouse and told "Now you". Carpenter et al. (2005) found that the infants in the House condition were significantly less likely to imitate the action style of the adult, at both ages, than the infants in the No House condition. In the House condition, most of the infants simply put the mouse into the correct house. In the No House condition, by contrast, the majority of the older infants made the mouse hop or slide across the mat. Carpenter et al. argued that the infants were analyzing the ends and means of the adult's actions, and were thus choosing to imitate either "putting the mouse in the house" or "making the mouse hop up and down". The infants were interpreting the actions of the adult in terms of her assumed goals. They were also making causal analyses of her actions based on context.

In related work, Carpenter, Akhtar, and Tomasello (1998a) have shown that infants aged 14 to 18 months will also imitate the acts of others differentially, depending on whether they perceive these acts to be intentional or accidental. Studying infants' responses to accidental acts is another way of investigating their understanding of the goals of the actor. When something is done accidentally, it was not the goal of the actor to carry out that act. The actor's goal was to carry out a different act. This provides an interesting contrast to Meltzoff's (1995a) paradigm involving unsuccessful acts that *were* intended (such as trying but failing to place a string of beads into a container). In Meltzoff's work, the infants imitated the acts that the actor had intended, but had not actually modeled. In Carpenter et al.'s study, the question was whether they would imitate modeled acts that the actor had *not* intended.

Carpenter et al. (1998a) designed six different objects that afforded two distinct actions by an actor (Figure 3.4). Each object had two parts that could be moved, and an "end result". For example, one object was a bird feeder, which had a top that could be moved up and down and a string attached to its middle with a ring on it. Both pulling the ring or moving the top resulted in a "party favor" being activated—the type of favor that you blow into to make a long paper tongue shoot forwards. The party favor was not activated by the moving parts on the bird feeder but by a hidden experimenter with a small pump. This enabled the experimenters to correlate the end result with certain actions on the object and not with other actions. The experimenter serving as the actor always carried out *both* possible actions on the object. The experimenter said "Watch! I'm going to show you how this works!". She then modeled two actions. For example, for the bird feeder she always both pulled the ring and moved the top. However, one action was done intentionally and the other accidentally. The intentional action was accompanied by the experimenter saying "There" in a satisfied voice, and the accidental action by the experimenter saying "Whoops!". The order of these actions was counterbalanced across infants. Infants were then allowed to interact with the objects themselves, the experimenter asking "Can you make it work?".

Carpenter et al. (1998a) found that the infants were much more likely to imitate the intentional acts. Intentional acts (as marked by "There") were imitated on 78% of occasions, and accidental acts (as marked by "Whoops") on 43% of occasions. The acts themselves, of course, were identical whether they were intentional for some infants or accidental for others. Carpenter et al. argued that the infants were interpreting the adult's overall behavior in terms of the goal of producing the "end state". They were interpreting the adult's behavior as intentional, screening out the accidental and unintended actions. As Carpenter et al. point out, the ability to recognize intentional actions provides a powerful boost to the infant's capacity for imitative learning. An infant who selectively imitates only the intentional acts of others will thereby acquire many significant cultural skills.

Distinguishing different types of intentional action

The actions of others can also stem from very different intentions. The same gesture (e.g. not giving an infant a desirable toy) could occur because the adult does not wish

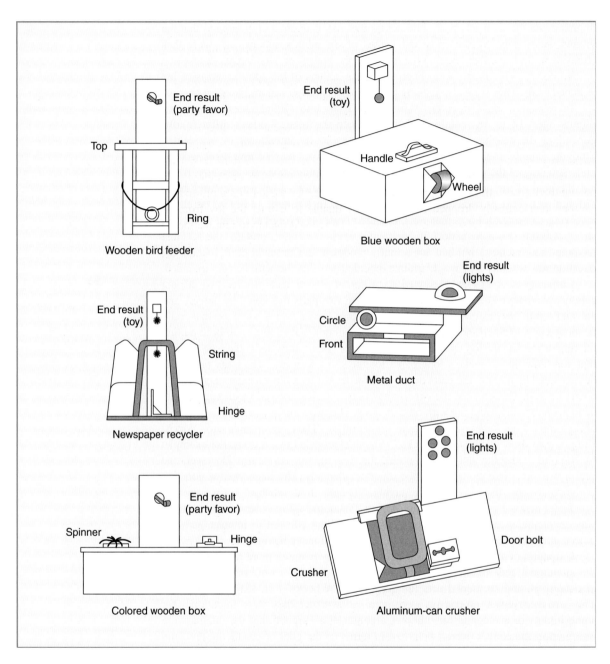

FIGURE 3.4
The test objects used by Carpenter et al. (1998). From Carpenter, Akhtar, and Tomasello (1998). Copyright © 1998 Elsevier. Reprinted with permission.

the infant to have the toy or because the adult is unable at the time to secure the toy. Carpenter and her colleagues have also investigated whether infants can distinguish between different *kinds* of intentional act. They have focused on the distinction between an actor who is *unwilling* to hand the infant a desirable toy and an actor who is *unable* to hand the infant the same toy. In both cases, the infant does not receive the desired toy. However, in the first case this was the intention of the actor, and in the second case it was not. In a third condition, the infant does not receive the toy because the experimenter was distracted from the game. The research question is whether the frustrated infants will behave differently in these three conditions.

To create a context for these different intentional acts, the study was based on a game of handing each other toys (Behne, Carpenter, Call, & Tomasello, 2005a). Each time the experimenter was about to pass a new toy to the infant, she said "Oh, look!". Then she handed over the toy. In some trials, however, the infant did not receive the toy. In the "Unwilling" condition, the experimenter held out the toy and then withheld it in a teasing fashion. In other "Unwilling" trials, she refused to hand it over, leaving the toy sitting in front of her in full view of the infant or continuing to handle the toy herself. In the "Unable" condition, the experimenter either offered the toy but then clumsily dropped it, or appeared unable to extract the toy from its transparent container. In some "Unable" trials, she seemed unable to remove the lid from a different transparent container holding the toy. In the third "Distracted" condition, the experimenter was either about to hand over the toy when the telephone rang, or she got distracted by talking to her assistant, or she appeared to forget to hand the toy over while she searched in a bucket for the next toy. The question in each case was how the infant would react to the withholding of the toy. Groups of 12- and 18-month-old infants were tested.

The results showed that the infants behaved very differently in the Unwilling, Unable, and Distracted conditions. They reached more for the toy in the Unwilling condition and also tended to look away from the experimenter for longer in this condition. When the experimenter was trying to give them the toy but was unable to, they reached less for the toy and looked away from the experimenter less as well. They reacted in a similar way in the Distracted condition, reaching less for the toy than when the experimenter was unwilling to hand it over. They appeared to be adapting their behavior appropriately given the social situation. Behne et al. argued that the infants were basically impatient when the adult refused to give them the toy but patient when the adult was unable to give them the toy. They knew that the goals of the actor in each case were different and responded accordingly.

Younger infants, aged 9 months, showed a similar pattern of performance. They reached more for the toy and banged the table in frustration more in the Unwilling condition than in the Unable condition. Six-month-old infants, however, showed no differential behaviors. Behne et al. thus argued that their results supported the idea that a "revolution" in infant social cognition begins at around 9 months of age. At this age, the first clear evidence for the understanding of the psychological states of others is emerging. However, the negative result in this experiment for the 6-month-olds cannot be taken as evidence that younger babies lack any understanding of differential intentions. As usual in developmental psychology, a negative result simply means that we cannot draw any strong conclusions.

Younger infants also perceive human actions as goal directed

Younger infants certainly seem able to perceive the actions of others in terms of goals. An important paradigm was developed by Woodward (1998), who compared the looking times of babies aged 9 months in a paradigm contrasting a human agent with a nonhuman agent. The infants watched as either a human actor grasped a toy, or a poster tube topped with a sponge made contact with the toy by following the same reach

FIGURE 3.5
The events in the
mechanical condition of
Woodward's (1998)
study. From Woodward
(1998). Copyright ©
1998 Elsevier.
Reprinted with
permission.

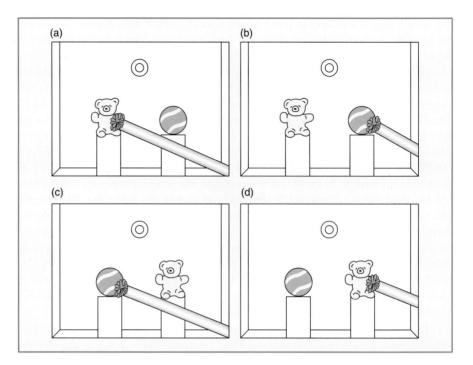

trajectory as the hand (Figure 3.5). The babies watched these events on a small stage. The stage contained two toys: a teddy and a ball. For the human actor condition, the habituation trials comprised an arm appearing at the side of the stage, approaching one of the toys, and grasping it. The actor then remained still. For the mechanical condition, the poster tube (which was similar in size to the actor's arm, and was the same color as the actor's T-shirt) approached the toy, taking the same path as the actor's arm. When the sponge made contact with the toy, it rested there, just as the hand rested in the grasp condition. Babies were either habituated to the mechanical event or to the human actor event. At test, the position of the toys was reversed and two events were shown. In the "new path" event, either the actor or the poster tube approached the same toy as before, thereby following a new trajectory. In the "new goal" event, the actor or the poster tube made the same action as previously, which led to the novel toy being "grasped".

Woodward (1998) found that the babies were most interested when the human actor had a new goal. The babies who were habituated to the human actor looked significantly longer at the "new goal" (same path) event than at the "new path" (same goal) event. The babies who were habituated to the poster tube showed no preference. However, the poster tube babies did show dishabituation to both events, indicating that they were aware that they were seeing something novel. In a follow-up experiment with 6-month-old babies, Woodward showed that even younger infants were also interested in the goals of human actors. The younger babies were shown the hand/grasp event on the toys, contrasted with a mechanical pincer performing the same actions. The babies who watched the human hand grasp one of the toys during habituation were only interested in the "new goal" event at test (same path, new goal), whereas the infants habituated to the mechanical pincer were not, showing reliable dishabituation only when the pincer followed a new path but grasped the same toy. Woodward concluded that her 6- and 9-month-old participants were selectively encoding the aspects of actions that were relevant to the goals of the human agent, thereby construing human actions as goal-directed.

More recently, Sommerville, Woodward, and Needham (2005) have extended this demonstration to 3-month-olds using a similar habituation task. Infants again sat in front of a stage containing two toys: a ball and a teddy bear, which were shown side-by-side. As the infants watched, an actor reached for and grasped one of the toys, but did not move it. This event was repeated until the infants habituated to it. At test, the infants either saw a "new goal" event, in which the actor reached for the other toy, or a "new path" event, in which the location of the toys was swapped and the actor again reached for the familiar toy. They dishabituated to both novel events, but looked equally in the "new goal" and "new path" conditions. This behavior was in marked contrast to a second group of 3-month-olds, who were allowed to manipulate the toys before the habituation and test events. Infants in this group of babies, the "action" group, were allowed to play with the toys for 3 minutes, and were then given a further 3 minutes wearing Velcro® mittens, which caused the toys to adhere to their hands. This gave them experience of different actions on the same toys (in fact, there was significantly more handling of the toys when wearing the Velcro® mittens). When this "action" group watched the two test events, they showed significantly longer looking for the "new goal" event than for the "new path" event. They also showed significantly greater looking on the first habituation trial than the group who had experienced passive watching first (this latter group was also allowed to manipulate the toys before the test trials, but only after watching the agent grasping the toys in the habituation trials). Sommerville et al. (2005) argued that receiving the action experiences first caused the infants to be more attentive to reaching events that they saw performed by another agent. Their ability to detect the goal structure of actions was improved by their initial experience of object-directed behavior, which led them to interpret the habituation trials in terms of the agent's goals. Even 3-month-old babies thus appear to be aware of goal-directed actions, at least when they have had the opportunity to perform these actions themselves.

GOAL-DIRECTED ACTION AND THE ATTRIBUTION OF MENTAL STATES

Teleological vs. psychological analyses of actions

The assumption that the ability to detect the goal structure of the actions of other agents involves an ability to *understand* their goals is controversial. This "rich" interpretation of infant competence credits a baby who can detect such goal structures with the beginnings of an understanding of psychological causality. According to a rich interpretation, the infants are able to understand the goals of other agents because they understand that others have mental states that cause them to act to achieve certain goals. This assumption that very young infants have an emergent understanding of mental states certainly contradicts the idea of a social revolution at the age of around 9 months. It may not be necessary, however. In fact, a strong alternative position has been put forward by Gergely and colleagues. In a refinement of the "intentional stance" (see Chapter 2), they argued that the ability to draw inferences on the basis of goal-directed actions was *not* the same thing as attributing mental states to others. Rather, Gergely and Csibra (2003) proposed that around the age of 12 months, infants adopted a "**teleological stance**" to the

KEY TERM

Teleological stance
The view that it is possible to understand goal-directed actions without the need to evoke mental states to agents.

representation of action. In a teleological stance, goal-directed actions are represented in terms of: (1) the goal state; (2) the action as a means to the goal state; and (3) the relevant aspects of reality as constraints on possible actions. The mental states of the agent are not considered.

One line of evidence supporting the idea that infants do not evoke mental states to understand goal-directed actions comes from demonstrations that infants also attribute goals to nonhuman agents. Relevant experiments have been carried out by Johnson and colleagues (Figure 3.6). For example, Shimizu and Johnson (2004) adapted Woodward's (1998) looking-time paradigm to incorporate nonhuman objects that behaved as though they were agents. In the critical experimental condition, a novel faceless green oval object behaved in self-propelled ways that appeared intentional. For example, it acted as though it could interact with its social environment, beeping contingently in response to small talk from the experimenter. It also acted as though it could choose between the relative merits of two toys, deliberately turning away from one and approaching the other. Infants aged 12 months participated in one of three conditions. In one condition, a human hand performed grasping actions on one of two toys. In the second, the Agent-Object beeped to the infant, and then repeatedly approached one of the toys. In the third condition, the same green object was first shown behaving in a random and nonintentional way, and then repeatedly approached one of the toys exactly as in the Agent-Object condition.

Following habituation, the human hand or the green object either performed the same action as before, but to a new toy (as the location of the two toys had been switched), or performed a novel action by reaching to the old toy in the new location. Woodward (1998) had reported increased looking by infants when the human hand performed a familiar action with a novel goal, but not when a cardboard tube did the same thing. Shimizu and Johnson replicated this effect for the human hand, but found the same effect for the Agent-Object. When the green oval object had been introduced as though it was capable of intentional behavior, infants watched longer when it performed a familiar action with a novel goal than when it performed a novel action with a familiar goal. Infants who saw the same green oval object in the nonagent condition did not differentiate between the two events. Shimizu and Johnson argued that infants do attribute goals to nonhuman agents, thereby supporting a lean rather than a rich interpretation of infant sensitivity to goal-directed action.

The theoretical position put forward by Gergely and Csibra (2003) also follows directly from the computer animation experiments with the rectangle and the large and small circles by Gergely et al. (1995) discussed in Chapter 2. As shown in Chapter 2, the results of these experiments were interpreted in terms of an "intentional stance". Adoption of an "intentional stance" towards agents entails an assumption of rationality—that the agent will adopt the most rational action in a particular situation to achieve his or her goal. This rationality assumption was also

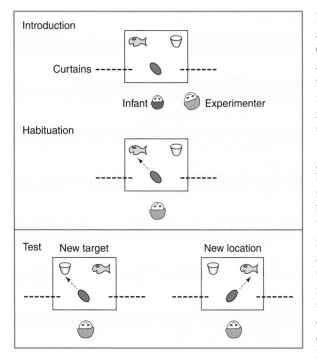

FIGURE 3.6
Top view of the stage for the Agent and Non-agent conditions, showing the introduction, habituation, and test phases of Shimizu and Johnson's (2004) experiment. From Shimizu and Johnson (2004). Reproduced with permission from Blackwell Publishing.

demonstrated in the current chapter, by the imitation experiment concerning the activation of a light panel with the forehead (Gergely et al., 2002).

Teleological explanations depend on the relevant aspects of the actual situation rather than on causal explanatory analyses of the mental states of agents. For example, in the perceptual display of Gergely et al. (1995) discussed in Chapter 2, it was mentioned that adult observers of the movements of the shapes described the event as a mother (large circle) calling to her child (small circle) who ran towards her, only to be prevented by the barrier (rectangle), which she then jumped over. This is a causal explanatory analysis of the perceptual display, which is mentalistic in nature. In contrast, according to a teleological explanation of the same event, the interpreter would be "**mind blind**". He or she would still attribute rationality to the actors, and therefore would expect the novel "straight line" pathway shown in the dishabituating event, whereby the large ball took the most direct path to the small ball. This would be expected because it was the rational way to reach the small ball. However, when the large ball took the familiar "jumping" path, which now appeared to be an inefficient means to the goal of reaching the small ball, the teleological interpreter should be surprised. Nevertheless, this surprise would be based on the perception of the situational constraints concerning direct and indirect paths, rather than on a mentalistic interpretation concerning what the large ball "wanted".

To distinguish between these "rich" and "lean" interpretations of infant behavior, we need empirical tests. The critical empirical test requires a situation in which the infant must attribute rational actions to the agent on the basis of **false beliefs** rather than true beliefs. If the 12-month-old infant is "mind blind", then the assumption of rational action must always be based on visible context, not on hidden context (such as a belief). As long as goal-directed actions are occurring in contexts in which all the variables are visible or known (e.g. visible barriers or hidden barriers whose existence is known to the infant; see Csibra, Bíró, Koós, & Gergely, 2003), then— according to Gergely and Csibra—infants should be able to interpret actions as a means to goals. In such circumstances they should be able to evaluate the relative efficiency of different available means (via the principle of rational action) and generate the relevant inferences (e.g. that it is no longer rational to take a "jumping" pathway). However, if the actor's action is driven by a false belief, infants should not be able to generate the relevant inference. This should be impossible on the basis of teleological reasoning. If infants turn out to be able to evaluate actions based on false beliefs, then the mental states of the actor would have to be represented in order to interpret the actions as rational. At present, most researchers assume that the interpretation of goal-directed action is a foundational mechanism for understanding psychological causation, showing the origins of a "theory of mind". Gergely and Csibra's (2003) teleological analysis points out that this need not be the case.

Although the critical experiments with 12-month-olds have yet to be done, an interesting series of studies reported by Kuhlmeier, Wynn, and Bloom (2003) provide some basis for preferring the mentalistic interpretation of infants' abilities concerning goal-directed action. Rather than using a violation-of-expectation paradigm with infants, Kuhlmeier et al. (2003) created a situation in which one perceptual animation was preferable to another given a specific mentalistic context. The displays were based on squares, triangles, and circles animated on a computer screen that depicted a pair of "hills" to be climbed (Figure 3.7). The infants (12-month-olds) watched as a small red ball set out to "climb" the first, small, hill. Once at the top, it expanded and contracted, and then began to climb the second, larger, hill. When it reached the half-way point, it slid back to the base of this second hill.

KEY TERMS

Mind blindness
A failure to attribute mental states to others.

False belief
An understanding that others may have beliefs that do not reflect current reality.

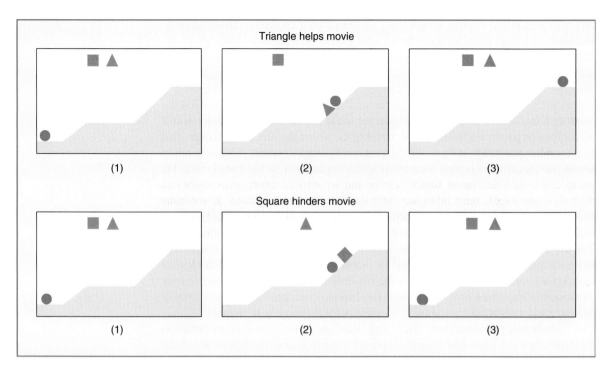

FIGURE 3.7
The habituation movies used by Kuhlmeier et al. (2003). From Kuhlmeier et al. (2003). Reproduced with permission from Blackwell Publishing.

The ball then began a second climbing attempt. In one movie, a green triangle moved down behind the ball and pushed it to the top of the hill. The ball then expanded and contracted once more. This first movie was the "Help" movie, in which the triangle "helped" the ball. In a second movie, a yellow square moved down in front of the ball, and pushed it downwards, so that it "fell" all the way back to its original starting position. This second movie was the "Hinder" movie, as the square "hindered" the ball. Infants saw both movies until they had habituated to them (for half of the infants, it was the triangle who "hindered" the ball and the square who "helped" the ball).

The infants were then shown a second animation. The same three objects were present, with the triangle and square at opposite sides at the top of the display, and the ball in the center at the bottom. There was no "hill". The ball rose to the middle of the screen, paused, wiggled from side to side (as though deciding which direction to move in), and then either moved to rest next to the triangle (its helpmate) or next to the square (its hindrance). Prior piloting with adults had shown that the animation in which the ball "chose" its helpmate was seen as a more coherent continuation of the previous movies. Kuhlmeier et al. (2003) found that the infants shared this view. They looked significantly longer at the movie in which the red ball approached its helper. This result held whether the helper had been the triangle or the square during the habituation trials. This was seen as being consistent with an interpretation of the animations based on mental states. The red ball was seen as "preferring" or "liking" its helper more than its hinderer, and so the movie in which the ball "wanted to be with" its helpmate attracted the infants' attention more. Differential attention was not shown when the square and triangle approached the red ball rather than the other way around. As further experiments using a variety of paradigms are conducted with younger infants, it will become possible to decide between the teleological and mentalistic interpretations of the looking behavior of infants.

Gaze following and gaze monitoring

Another foundational mechanism for understanding psychological causation that is based in action may be infant **gaze-monitoring** behavior. The information from another person's eyes is very important for social cognition. For most of us, it is second nature to monitor another person's gaze. We follow gaze to work out what is capturing the attention of another agent, and we look into their eyes to try and infer their emotions, their intentions and their likely future actions. If someone deliberately avoids or prevents eye contact, it makes us feel uncomfortable. Babies, too, feel uncomfortable when another person stolidly refuses to meet their gaze. This is known as the "**still face paradigm**", in which mothers adopt a "still face" during a playful face-to-face interaction, suspending interpersonal contingency (see, for example, Toda & Fogel, 1993). Babies react to a still face by avoiding gaze and getting upset. During the "still face" periods, they tend to show a decline in visual attention to the mother, and show negative affect. Gaze following and gaze monitoring behavior has been studied in order to find out how early in development babies begin to use the gaze of another as a clue to internal mental states.

One of the first experimental investigations of infants' ability to follow changes in adult gaze direction was carried out by Scaife and Bruner (1975). They were interested in the capacity for joint visual attention in the infant. When the visual attention of the mother–infant pair is directed jointly to objects and events, this facilitates learning. In fact, joint attention episodes have been described as "hot spots" for learning (Tomasello, 1988). For infants to engage in joint attention behaviors, they must be able to follow their mother's gaze. Scaife and Bruner investigated gaze following by infants aged from 2 to 14 months. The infants were tested in a plain room and were supported in an infant seat. After the mother had settled them in, an unfamiliar adult experimenter played with them for a while, and if they appeared content, the mother left the room. The experimenter then established eye contact with the infant, and then looked away, silently turning her head through 90° and gazing at a point on the wall for 7 seconds. The experimenter then turned back to interact with the infant, before repeating the head turn, but this time looking to the other direction.

Gaze following was attributed to the infant if they: (1) looked in the same direction as the experimenter; (2) did not look elsewhere first; (3) looked within 7 seconds; and (4) appeared to be looking for or at something. Using these criteria, the percentage of infants showing gaze following was found to increase steadily with age. Around 30% of the youngest infants followed the experimenter's gaze, compared to around 65% of those aged 8–10 months and 100% of those aged above 11 months. Scaife and Bruner noted that the older infants also showed **social referencing**, looking back to the experimenter and then again at the wall, as though looking for something to look at. In other nonexperimental trials using the mother, this referencing behavior was even more marked, and more infants showed gaze following when alerted by language ("Oh look!").

Gaze following appears to become robust between 6 and 18 months of age. However, not everyone agrees that robust gaze following is evidence that infants are representing the other person as volitionally choosing to "look at" an object in the environment. It has been argued that acts like gaze following could be the result of conditioned learning. For example, infants could learn that when an adult turns their head, something interesting is likely to be occurring at the location that they are now gazing at (see Moore & Corkum, 1994, for this type of analysis). However, if gaze following is a kind of conditioned learning based on adult head turning, then infants should still follow the gaze of an adult who turns their head when their eyes are closed. Brooks and Meltzoff (2002) investigated whether infants aged 12, 14, and 18 months would follow gaze in these circumstances.

In their experiment, Brooks and Meltzoff (2002) contrasted infant looking in two conditions: *open eyes* and *closed eyes*. In each condition, an experimenter first made eye contact with the infant, who was sitting opposite on their mother's lap. She then silently turned her head towards a target, and gazed at it for 6.5 seconds. After this time, she returned her head to mid-line, made eye contact with the infant, and resumed play. In the closed-eyes condition, she first closed her eyes before performing this movement. Four trials were given with 2-minute intervals. Looking by the infant was credited if the infant's head and eyes were aligned with the target for at least 0.33 seconds. Brooks and Meltzoff found that the looking scores were significantly higher in the open-eyes condition than in the closed-eyes condition. Infants also looked significantly longer at the target in this condition (by almost 2 seconds), pointed at it more frequently, and vocalized more. Exactly the same results were found for the older infants when the adult either wore a headband as a blindfold (hence could not see the target) or had the headband around her head (hence could see the target). Brooks and Meltzoff pointed out that not only did these results rule out a conditioned learning explanation of gaze following, but that infant pointing and vocalizing in addition to head turning was also suggestive of the importance of gaze following for joint attention. Infants were interpreting the adult's look as an object-directed act.

More recently, Brooks and Meltzoff (2005) replicated the open-eyes/closed-eyes conditions with younger babies aged 9, 10, and 11 months. They found that the 10- and 11-month-old infants almost only looked at the target when the experimenter's eyes were open. They were also more "talkative" in this condition, producing many spontaneous vocalizations. The 9-month-olds did not distinguish between the two conditions. Furthermore, correct interpretation of gaze + vocalization at 10–11 months predicted language comprehension at 14 and 18 months. Brooks and Meltzoff suggested that infants who were advanced in recognizing the connection between looker and object might have an advantage in using gaze to disambiguate the referent of linguistic utterances. Understanding the line of regard of another person should facilitate language acquisition, as prototypically verbal labels refer to objects that are being looked at. The act of looking thus has referential meaning for both language and behavior (following gaze can disambiguate both another person's emotional behavior and their linguistic behavior).

Brooks and Meltzoff (2005) suggested that infants who were advanced in recognizing the connection between looker and object would in turn benefit from facilitated language acquisition.

Seeing as an intentional act

If infants follow the gaze of another because they want to see what she is seeing, then infants must interpret adult gaze as volitional and intentional. They must understand the looking behavior of adults as a mental act of seeing some *particular* thing. In order to see whether younger infants aged from 7–12 months would interpret adult gaze as intentional, signifying a relationship between actor and object, Woodward (2003) devised an experiment using the visual habituation paradigm. Her method involved an extension of the "teddy and ball" paradigm that she has also used to investigate infants' understanding of goal-directed action (Woodward, 1998).

In Woodward's gaze experiments, the infants were shown a stage containing two objects: a teddy bear and a ball. The two objects were sitting on pedestals a short distance apart. An actor was sitting at the back of the stage, with her upper body and head visible. At the beginning of a habituation trial, she made eye contact with the baby, saying "Hi". When she had the baby's attention, she then said "Look", and turned her head to gaze at one of the objects. She then kept looking at this toy for the duration of the trial. Following habituation, the position of the toys was reversed, and two types of test trial were given. In the "novel trajectory" test, the actor turned her head to gaze in the opposite direction, thereby looking again at the same toy (as the toy locations had been reversed). In the "novel object" test, the actor gazed in the same direction as before, thereby looking at the other toy. The results showed that both the 7-month-old and the 9-month-old infants tested followed the actor's gaze. Thirteen out of 16 7-month-olds and 18 out of 19 9-month-olds looked at the same toy as the actor, irrespective of whether this toy was novel or not. Infants aged 12 months tested in the same paradigm also showed overwhelming gaze-following behavior, but additionally registered the distinction between the old toy and the new toy. They spent longer overall looking at the object holding the actor's gaze when the test trials involved a new toy. Woodward argued that gaze was a powerful attentional signal for young infants. However, she suggested that between 9 and 12 months infants became able to represent gaze primarily in terms of the *relation* between the person and the object of her gaze. This is an important precursor of developments in the second year of life, when infants begin trying to manipulate the gaze-following behavior of others.

If infants follow an adult's gaze because they want to see what she is seeing, then they should also move their location if this is necessary to obtain a good viewing angle. Moll and Tomasello (2004) investigated whether 12- and 18-month-old infants would move their viewing position if an adult was gazing at something behind a barrier. The barrier blocked the child's own line of sight. In their experiment, four different situations were studied. In one, the barrier was a dividing wall, made of wood and cardboard. In the second, the barrier was a cardboard box lying on its side. The third barrier comprised a movable wooden panel. The fourth barrier was the bottom drawer of a filing cabinet which was open, thereby blocking the child's line of sight. All of the barriers had fixed positions in the testing room.

In the experimental trials, an attractive toy was hidden behind one of the barriers. The experimenter looked behind the barrier, and said "Oh!" in an excited fashion. She gazed behind the barrier for about 3 seconds. She then looked back at the child. In the control trials, the experimenter gazed at a toy that was in full view of the child on a wall, in the opposite direction to the barrier. She again said "Oh" in an excited fashion. The dependent measure was whether the child moved to look behind the barrier.

Moll and Tomasello found that all the babies were significantly more likely to crawl around to look behind the barrier in the experimental trials than in the control trials. The 18-month-olds did this in more trials overall than the 12-month-olds. Both age groups also followed the experimenter's gaze in the control trials, looking at the toy on the wall. For the control condition, in which the object of the experimenter's gaze was clearly visible, the 12-month-olds followed the experimenter's gaze almost as frequently as the 18-month-olds. Gaze-following to a visible target appeared to be developmentally easier for infants. In a second study, Moll and Tomasello checked that infants in the experimental condition were not simply having their attention drawn to the barrier by the adult's gaze, and then deciding to crawl around it by themselves. This time, the adult gazed at the barrier in both the experimental and control conditions. In the control condition, the experimenter gazed at a sticker on the side of the barrier. The infants could see this sticker without moving their position. Again, babies were found to be more likely to crawl around the barrier in the experimental condition, at both ages. Although the objects that the adult was gazing at were initially out of the infants' view, even the 12-month-olds wanted to see what the adults were seeing. Moll and Tomasello concluded that 12-month-olds understood that others were intentional agents, just like themselves.

Can we say that the infant understands the adult's communicative intent in gaze-following situations? An adult would gaze with communicative intent if she intended to deliberately direct the infant's attention to something in the visual scene. In the experiments discussed so far, the context of gazing did not necessarily imply communicative intent. Adult gaze was simply used to generate gaze following by the infant. However, in some experimental paradigms, for example those used by Brooks and Meltzoff, the infants did not just follow the adult's gaze, they pointed and vocalized about the object being gazed at as well. This makes it likely that infants who follow gaze systematically can also understand that in some cases the adult is gazing with communicative intent. Gazing at something is not only a mental act for the adult gazer, in some circumstances—particularly during verbal labeling—it is a communicative act as well.

Infant understanding of the *communicative intent* of adult gestures was addressed experimentally in a study by Behne et al. (2005b), who investigated whether infants could use communicative gestural cues, namely gazing and pointing, as clues to the location of hidden objects. The infants were aged 14, 18, and 24 months, and the experiment was introduced as a hiding game. In the hiding game, an attractive toy was hidden in one of two identical opaque boxes placed on a table between the experimenter and the infant. The experimenter then indicated the baited box either by gazing or by pointing. In the gazing condition, she repeatedly alternated her gaze from the baited box to the child and back again. She also raised her eyebrows and used other facial gestures to express communicative intent. In the pointing condition, she did these same things while also pointing at the baited box. Behne et al. (2005b) found that the infants could find the toys by using the gestural cues in both conditions at all ages. There were no differences in finding for the 14- and 24-month-olds whether the hiding place was indicated by gazing or by pointing. The 18-month-olds found significantly more toys from the pointing gesture. Behne et al. concluded that even infants of 14 months of age understand gazing as an expression of communicative intent in certain contexts.

Social referencing

Another way of using gaze to understand the internal mental states of others occurs during social referencing. Social referencing means appraising a current situation on the basis of the emotional expressions and behaviors of others and then regulating your own behavior to it accordingly. The infant modulates his or her reaction to an object or event *by reference to* information gained from the actions of another. An interesting question is why infants regulate their own behaviors in social referencing situations. One possibility is that they modulate their behavior because of a mentalistic interpretation of the reaction of another. For example, they may have an interpretation like "she is reacting like that because she is scared, this is a potentially dangerous toy". A second possibility is that they modulate their behavior simply because the emotional display acts as a signal, telling them what to do (for example, "that expression means that I should stop"). Clearly, only the former possibility implies understanding of the internal mental states of another agent.

The classic study on social referencing used an apparatus called the **visual cliff**. A visual cliff is created by building an apparatus that has a solid transparent surface which allows infants to crawl freely. Beneath the transparent surface, different cues to depth can be manipulated, so that one area of the apparatus appears to fall away like a cliff. This is usually done with geometric shapes, such as black and white squares, which generate powerful depth cues. The visual cliff was originally used to study depth perception in infants. It was found that babies of crawling age (around 9 months) would not crawl over the edge of the "cliff", even though the solid transparent surface enabled them to do so (Gibson & Walk, 1960). This was interpreted as showing that infant depth perception was well developed, enabling them to avoid crawling over dangerous drops. Sorce, Emde, Campos, and Klinnert (1985) demonstrated that crawling behavior on the visual cliff could be modulated by the emotional expression of the mother. They put 1-year-old infants on a visual cliff apparatus with an apparent drop of 12 inches. The infants typically crawled to the edge of the "cliff" and then looked at their mothers. When the mother made a fearful face, 17 out of 17 infants did not cross the cliff. When the mother made a happy face, 14 out of 19 infants crossed the drop.

More recently, social referencing experiments have used procedures based on novel toys. Typically, the toy is faintly alarming, being mechanical and noisy, and possibly able to move. The question is whether the infant will approach and play with the novel toy. In studies in which the social referencing provided by the mother or by another female adult is successful in modulating infant behavior, both facial and vocal signals tend to be given. For example, Hornik, Risenhoover, and Gunnar (1987) showed infants aged 12 months three novel toys, one intended to be pleasant (a musical Ferris wheel), one aversive (a mechanical monkey that clapped cymbals together incessantly), and one ambiguous (a stationary toy robot that recited facts about outer space in a mechanical voice). The infants' mothers were trained to show either positive, negative, or neutral affect when the toys were presented. As the mothers found difficulty in expressing fear in a convincing manner to the toys, disgust was used as the negative emotion. Both facial expression of the emotions and vocalizations were used (e.g. the toys were described as either yucky or fun). Hornik et al. reported that the mothers vocalized almost all the time in the positive and negative affect conditions. The results showed an effect of negative affect only. Infants whose mothers expressed disgust played less with the target toy and also stayed further away from it compared to the neutral condition, irrespective of which toy it was. In contrast, positive affect did not seem to influence the infants' behavior with the toys in any systematic way.

Mumme, Fernald, and Herrera (1996) set out to investigate whether both facial and vocal signals were required for social referencing to be successful, or whether

KEY TERM

Visual cliff
Apparatus that has a solid glass-topped surface but which appears to have a drop (the "cliff" side) on one half. Originally designed to study depth perception in infants.

information from the face alone could be sufficient. If infants can read the emotional expressions of another person in the absence of any vocal cues, then this would suggest that they are interpreting the emotional expressions as reflecting internal mental states with predictable antecedents and consequences. This would be consistent with the idea that social referencing is another building block in acquiring a theory of mind. Vocal emotional signals can also reflect internal states, but with vocal signals intrinsic acoustic properties of the signals may induce emotions directly. For example, properties like loudness and pitch may induce fear (see Fernald, 1993).

Ninety 12-month-old infants were tested in Mumme et al.'s (1996) experiment, using novel mechanical toys that made noises and moved (like Magic Mike, the golden mechanical robot). The infant, mother, and toy were placed so that they formed a triangle. For some infants ("Face-only condition"), the mother's face was fully visible, whereas for others ("Voice-only condition") she was facing away with her back to the infant. In the key experimental trial, the novel toy appeared and the mother either showed fear, happiness, or modeled a neutral reaction. For the Face-only condition, mothers were trained to show the target emotion using facial cues only, producing a "fear" face or a "happy" face. For the Voice-only condition, mothers were trained to show the target emotion using only their voice, saying either "Oh, how frightful!", or "Oh, how delightful", using the appropriate intonation. The phrase "Oh, how insightful" was spoken in a monotone for the neutral condition. The phrases were deliberately chosen to be meaningless to the infants, so that intonation would be the main acoustic cue. The mothers' efforts were later rated, and only successful emotional productions (face or voice) were used to calculate any experimental effects.

Infants were scored for how often they looked to their mother, how close they got to the toy or to their mother, and for their own affect (positive or negative). The results showed that when social referencing depended on facial information alone, there were no systematic effects. The only effect found was for girl infants, who looked at their mothers more when she was making a fearful face compared to a neutral face, and actually also approached the toy more. For the vocal cues, however, infants of both sexes looked longer at their mothers when she was vocalizing fearfully, and also approached the novel toy less compared to the neutral condition. They also expressed more negative affect themselves. The happy vocalizations had no systematic effects on infant behavior. The data suggest that 12-month-old infants may not have a fully referential understanding of facial emotional expression, even though in the visual cliff apparatus infants were able to modulate their behavior by reference to the mother's face. Mumme et al. (1996) suggest that facial expression is a more powerful cue in the visual cliff apparatus, where clear danger is apparent. With the novel toy setting used in their own experiment, there was no particular danger, and this could explain the difference in results.

Recently, an experiment by Vaish and Striano (2004) suggested that Mumme et al. (1996) were correct in emphasizing the potential importance of the context in which social referencing takes place. They compared the contribution of facial versus vocal cues in social referencing on the visual cliff. In their study, 12-month-old infants were placed on a visual cliff with a 28-cm "drop" (Figure 3.8). All infants tested looked up to their mother after looking down at the drop, and the mother was then instructed to act according to one of three possible conditions. In the Face + Voice condition, the mother faced the infant across the cliff, smiled, and vocalized to the infant to encourage him or her to cross the drop. In the Face-only condition, the

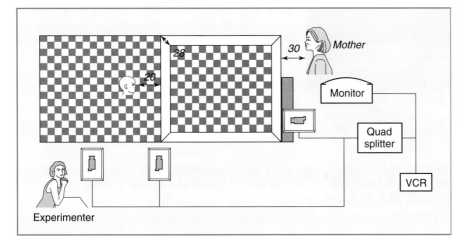

FIGURE 3.8
The visual cliff
experimental set-up used
by Vaish and Striano
(2004). From Vaish and
Striano (2004).
Reproduced with
permission from
Blackwell Publishing.

mother faced the cliff and smiled and nodded to her infant. In the Voice-only condition, the mother had her back to the cliff but vocalized to encourage the infant to cross the drop. Vaish and Striano measured the time it took the infant to cross the visual cliff. They found that infants in the Face + Voice condition crossed fastest, taking around a minute. Infants in the Voice-only condition crossed next fastest, taking just under 2 minutes. Crossing time in these two conditions did not differ significantly. As we will see later (in Chapter 5), language has an important role to play in the development of social cognition. In terms of social referencing, vocal cues can be experienced even when the mother's face cannot be seen (e.g. if she is carrying you on her back). Vaish and Striano pointed out that infant sensitivity to vocal cues deserved greater attention in studies of the ontogeny of human social cognition. Obviously, from the point of view of the mother, vocal interaction is often the most direct way of guiding the responses of her infant.

Infants in the Face-only condition were slowest to cross, taking almost 4 minutes. This was significantly slower than the other two conditions. However, all infants did cross the cliff in the Face-only condition, suggesting that the face is an important social referencing cue in a potentially dangerous situation. It seems that further experiments using more ecologically valid paradigms are needed. This would enable emotional reactions to be natural rather than feigned, and would enable genuine ambiguity about whether the infant should approach or avoid. Such experiments would give us better insights into whether infants can use the emotional facial expressions of others as a basis for developing an understanding of psychological causation.

ACTIONS BY INFANTS

Protodeclarative versus protoimperative pointing

As well as considering infant reactions to the actions of other agents as a source of information about psychological development, it is important to consider what we can learn from the infant's own actions. Pointing is an infant behavior that has interested researchers for decades. A distinction has been made between two kinds of pointing: "protodeclarative" pointing and "protoimperative" pointing. When a

Protodeclarative pointing is used to initiate joint attention, and suggests that the infant is aware that the other person could be thinking about something else.

point has a protoimperative function, it is used to obtain an object. The infant points to communicate "I want that" or "Get me that" (see Baron-Cohen, 1989a). This type of pointing has traditionally been conceived of as an instrumental behavior. Protoimperative pointing does not necessitate an understanding of the mental states of others. The infant could simply be pointing because the usual outcome is getting the desired object (this would be stimulus–response or instrumental learning). When a point has a protodeclarative function, the point is used to "remark on" the world to another person. This is thought to involve a higher, more mentalistic level of communication: The infant appears to want to influence the mental state of another person. The infant is communicating something along the lines of "Look over there!". In **protodeclarative pointing**, the infant's goal is to make the other person attend to or recognize something of interest to the infant. The goal is joint attention.

Protodeclarative pointing is thought to be a precursor for, or early indication of, a "theory of mind" (Baron-Cohen, 1989a). The use of protodeclarative pointing suggests that the infant knows about "thinking", and is aware that another person may be thinking about something else. Pointing is used to initiate joint attention, which is necessary for the turn-taking behaviors that are the foundation of social interaction. The average age at which protodeclarative pointing emerges is around 12 months.

This was shown in a longitudinal study of 24 mother–infant dyads by Carpenter, Nagel, and Tomasello (1998b). They found that, for some babies, protodeclarative pointing emerged as early as 10 months. Butterworth (1998) cites data for protodeclarative pointing in 33% of 8-month-old babies, with an advantage for girls.

To elicit protodeclarative pointing in the laboratory, Carpenter et al. devised a situation in which it was thought likely that the infants would want to engage the attention of an adult. For example, the infant was given a relatively uninteresting toy to play with, and then a much more interesting toy was produced by an experimenter. This was done behind the back of a second experimenter. Carpenter et al. measured when the infant gestured to the second experimenter about the more interesting toy. These "distal" protodeclarative gestures had a mean age of emergence of 12.6 months. The mean age of **protoimperative pointing** was slightly later, at 14 months. There appeared to be a significant developmental change in the likelihood of producing a protodeclarative point between 11 and 12 months, and in producing a protoimperative point between 12 and 13 months.

Joint attention

Both protodeclarative and protoimperative pointing are object directed, in that the goal of pointing is to engage joint attention and focus it on an environmental object. The intended objects of shared attention are in the physical and social environment, they are not unobservable entities in someone's head. The ability to follow the point gesture of someone else emerges slightly earlier. In the study by Carpenter et al. (1998), the average age of the emergence of point-following was 11.7 months. To follow someone's point, infants must understand that pointing is intended to highlight or signal the presence of an object or event worthy of remark. They must understand that the actor is attending to the object that they are pointing to, and that the actor's intention is to bring another person (the infant) into shared attention on the object. Woodward and Guajardo (2002) set out to investigate infants' understanding of the relation between the object being pointed to and the person who points, using a habituation procedure. They argued that understanding the "object directedness" of pointing would be important for a general understanding of pointing as an intentional act.

Woodward and Guajardo (2002) studied babies aged 9 and 12 months of age, in order to capture the period during which it is generally believed that a change in infants' understanding of pointing occurs. They used a variant of the stage apparatus used by Woodward (1998), in which a teddy bear and a ball were displayed each sitting on a pedestal 14 cm apart. During habituation, the infants watched as an actor pointed at one of the two toys, touching it with her finger (Figure 3.9). Only the actor's hand was visible, and the hand either pointed to the object nearest to the right side of the stage, or passed in front of the first pedestal to point to the further object. For some infants, the actor's upper body was visible during habituation as well. For these infants, the actor pointed from above and said "Look" at the same time as she pointed. After the infants had habituated to the actor pointing at the chosen toy, the position of the toys was switched and two types of test trial were given. In the "new object" trials, the actor pointed to the same side as before, which meant that she pointed to a novel object. In the "new side" trials, the actor pointed to the opposite side to before, which meant that she pointed to the familiar object. The 12-month-olds looked significantly longer at the "new object" event. The 9-month-olds did not.

Woodward and Guajardo argued that the 12-month-olds were responding selectively to the change in relation between actor and object. The actor was now pointing at a novel object. This selective response was found whether the infants saw only a hand pointing during habituation, or saw both the hand and the upper body of the actor. During the habituation trials, the 9-month-olds habituated to the pointing events in the same manner as the 12-month-olds. Woodward and Guajardo hence argued that the younger babies were able to attend to the events of interest. In fact, further analyses showed that the point gesture acted as an effective "spotlight" for attention for the younger babies as well as for the older babies. Thirty-seven of the 39 younger babies tested looked longer at the toy being pointed at during the test trials. However, these younger babies did not react selectively according to whether this toy was a novel object of attention for the actor. It was concluded that only the 12-month-olds understood pointing in terms of the relation between the person who points and the object being pointed at. In a second study, Woodward and Guajardo (2002) found some evidence that babies who themselves pointed at objects were more likely to encode the habituation events as object directed. This appears to indicate that the production and comprehension of object-directed points are developmentally linked.

By around 12 months of age, therefore, infants appear to understand pointing as an intentional act. These studies are consistent with the studies on gaze following and pointing discussed earlier (e.g. Behne et al., 2005b). These data support the assumption that protodeclarative pointing is an early indication of a nascent "theory of mind", indicating an effort by the infant to establish joint attention (Baron-Cohen, 1989a). Bates, Camaioni, and Volterra (1975) have also suggested that protodeclarative points are intentionally communicative acts, noting that the pointing infant usually also alternates her gaze between the adult's face and the object being pointed at. Bates et al. argued that this gaze alternation indicates a desire to affect the

FIGURE 3.9
Woodward and Guajardo's (2002) habituation and test events for (a) the hand-only condition, and (b) the face-and-hand condition. From Woodward and Guajardo (2002). Copyright © 2002 Elsevier. Reprinted with permission.

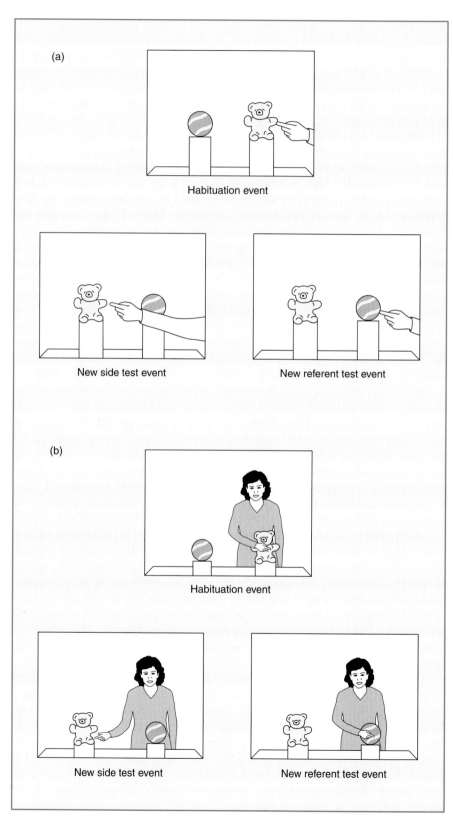

adult's behavior. In the studies discussed above by Brooks and Meltzoff (2002, 2005), the authors reported that their infants pointed at the target object much more frequently when the adult had his or her eyes open. This also suggests an intention to communicate with the adult by pointing—pointing is only useful if the other person is able to move their gaze to the referent.

The possibility that infants who display protodeclarative pointing intend to establish joint attention was examined empirically by Liszkowski, Carpenter, Henning, Striano, and Tomasello (2004). They compared what happened when adults either rewarded infants' protodeclarative pointing with shared attention and interest, or did not. In their study, 75 12-month-old babies interacted with an adult experimenter in one of four conditions. In all the conditions, the experimenter first established herself as a social partner for the infant, who was seated next to her. The infant was facing some curtains, and the experimenter was at 90° to the curtains but could easily see them by turning her head. The experimenter chatted to the infant, made eye contact, and engaged in joint play with a bead toy. Once the infant was relaxed, the experimenter gradually withdrew from the interaction. She then signaled to a second experimenter to produce an interesting event from behind the curtains. For example, a hand puppet might appear from the curtains and dance about (Figure 3.10).

Typically, the infant pointed to this exciting event, and the experimenter then responded in one of four ways. In the Joint Attention condition, she showed shared attention and interest, looking backwards and forwards from the event to the infant's face, talking excitedly about the puppet, and commenting that they were seeing it together. In the Face condition, she continually gazed at the infant's face, talking excitedly but not about the puppet ("Oh! I see you are in a good mood! Did you sleep well?"). In the Event condition, she looked at the puppet, but did not look at the infant and did not vocalize. In the Ignore condition, she took no notice of the infant's protodeclarative pointing, simply gazing at her hands and picking at her nails.

Liszkowski et al. measured how often and how long the infants pointed during a given trial, and how many times they looked at the first experimenter. They expected more pointing and looking when the experimenter was refusing to share her attention with the infant, and this was essentially what they found. Infants were significantly less likely to point frequently in the Joint Attention condition, pointing more within a given trial when the experimenter was not engaging in joint attention behaviors. Their enjoyment of sharing the novel event with a responsive adult in the Joint Attention condition was shown by the fact that their points were of significantly longer duration when shared attention was being engaged. The infants also looked at the experimenter significantly more frequently in the Event condition, when the adult appeared interested in the event but was not sharing her interest with the infant. This condition produced the most gaze alternation between the infants, the adult, and the puppet. Liszkowski et al. argued that protodeclarative pointing indeed had a social motive. The social context within which the pointing took place, in terms of the partner's reaction, had a significant effect on the infants' behavior. Infants point protodeclaratively to share attention and interest with other people. Their pointing behavior has communicative intent.

FIGURE 3.10
Staged photograph of the testing situation in Liszkowski et al.'s (2004) study showing the puppet appearing from behind the curtain. From Liszkowski et al. (2004). Reproduced with permission from Blackwell Publishing.

THE UNDERSTANDING OF FALSE BELIEF

Many of the mechanisms underpinning social cognition are clearly developing rapidly during the first year of life. From birth, infants can detect contingencies between their own behavior and events in the world. During the first year, they come to view the actions of others as goal directed, they follow gaze, they engage in joint attention, and they understand communicative intent. However, in the studies discussed so far, the emergent understanding of the mental states of others has always been correlated with reality. The actual state of affairs in the real world is represented both by the other agent and by the infant. Even in the experiments where the adult used gestures to communicate the location of a hidden toy to an infant who did not know where it was hidden, both agents shared a belief about the location of the toy. The adult had a true belief that she knew where the toy was, and the infant had a true belief that the adult knew where the toy was. There was no contradiction in mental states from the perspective of veridical reality in the world.

Some aspects of mental state understanding must be purely representational, however, and not correlated with reality. An example is understanding *false belief*. In fact, the philosopher Dennett has argued that successful reasoning about false beliefs is the *only* convincing evidence for the **attribution of mental states** to others (Dennett, 1978; see Chapter 7). This is because a person who acts on the basis of a false belief acts in a way that would not be predicted by the real situation in the world. Until a few years ago, it was thought that a fundamental change in children's ability to understand the minds of others occurred at around 4 years of age. This was thought to be the median age at which children became able to respond successfully in false belief tasks (see Chapter 7). This achievement was taken to demonstrate the acquisition of a *representational* "theory of mind". It was thought that the child had come to understand that the minds of others held beliefs that were not necessarily direct reflections of reality. Another person might believe something to be true that you yourself knew to be false.

One of the most frequently used methods to probe children's understanding of false belief involves hiding an object at a location. Then, while the protagonist is absent, the hiding place is changed. Consequently, when the protagonist returns and seeks the object, the rational act is to look in the location at which the protagonist believes the object to be hidden. But this belief of the protagonist is now false—the object is now in a new location. Hence, to find the object, the protagonist must discover this new location. The point at which children understand that the protagonist will *first* seek the object at the wrong location was originally thought to index children's ability to understand false beliefs. This paradigm is now called the "false location" false belief task (see Chapter 7).

Can a similar false location paradigm be devised for infants? We already know that infants can keep track of an object's location across changes in spatial position, even when the object is hidden (e.g. Baillargeon & Graber, 1988). We also know that infants view the actions of others as goal directed, and attribute intentionality to the behaviors of others. Can infants therefore recognize when an actor will be misled by a false belief about the hidden location of an object? Onishi and Baillargeon (2005) set out to find out.

They devised an experiment with 15-month-old infants, using the violation-of-expectation paradigm. The basis of the paradigm was a search task. During the familiarization trials, infants watched as a protagonist hid a toy in one of two possible locations (a yellow box or a green box; Figure 3.11). The openings of the boxes were at 90° to the infants, so that the infants could not see into the boxes, and were concealed by fringing. In the first familiarization trial, the actor put the toy into the green box. In the next two familiarization trials, she put her hand into the green box as though to grasp the toy, and rested her hand there. The infants then saw a belief induction trial. In the false belief condition, they watched as the toy moved location into the yellow box. The actor did not see this event, and the infants observed that she could not see it. In the true belief condition, the actor and infant both watched as the toy moved location into the yellow box. A test trial was then given, during which the actor simply placed her hand into one of the boxes. In the false belief condition, infants were expected to look longer when this was the yellow box, as the actor believed that the toy was in the green box. In the true belief condition, infants were expected to look longer when this was the green box, as the actor believed that the toy was in the yellow box. Further conditions checked the analogous predictions when the first hiding place was the yellow box.

Onishi and Baillargeon found that the infants looked significantly longer when the box that the actor chose to search was inconsistent with her belief about the toy's location. This was also the case when her belief was false. The actor had a false belief that she knew where the toy was, and the infants had a true belief about where the toy actually was. The infants appeared to expect the actor to reach to where she believed the toy to be. Onishi and Baillargeon argued that this was evidence for a rudimentary representational theory of mind in infants. Infants not only attribute mental states such as goals and intentions to other agents, they also attribute beliefs. These beliefs may be true or false, and are used to make sense of others' actions. Again, we see psychological causation being used to explain the behavior of other people. However, in this case the rational interpretation of the agent's action is based on knowledge of the agent's false belief. It is not based on observable aspects of the relevant aspects of reality as constraints on the possible actions of the agent. Hence these experimental results cannot be explained teleologically. Surian, Caldi, and Sperber (2007) have reported experiments with 13-month-old infants that also suggest knowledge of others' beliefs, using a paradigm that involves a caterpillar

(a) Familiarization trial 1

(b) Familiarization trials 2 and 3

FIGURE 3.11
The events shown during (a) the first familiarization and (b) the second and third familiarization trials of Onishi and Baillargeon's (2005) study. From Onishi and Baillargeon (2005). Copyright © 2005 AAAS. Reproduced with permission.

looking for an apple. False belief experiments in even younger infants seem likely to emerge in the near future. A teleological interpretation of goal-directed action may thus describe only very early representations of **goal-directed behavior**, much as infants' reasoning about physical events begins from core principles like "support/no support". These core principles are then refined in the light of experience. In psychological reasoning, early "mind blind" teleological representations based on actual situations may be rapidly supplemented by causal explanations incorporating mental states.

INSIGHTS FROM SOCIAL COGNITIVE NEUROSCIENCE

The importance of information from the face and eyes in the development of psychological understanding has already attracted the attention of cognitive neuroscientists. In neuroimaging studies of adults, it has been found using **fMRI** that a specialized area of the fusiform gyrus (the "**fusiform face area**") responds selectively to faces, whereas EEG studies show that faces elicit a distinctive brain electrical potential, the N170 (a negative potential occurring most prominently over occipital-to-temporal scalp regions). These adult studies provide two neural markers that can be applied to studying the neurocognitive development of face processing in infants. At the time of writing, however, although neuroimaging studies in adults have examined neural processing in the false belief task, no such studies have been carried out with infants.

We know from behavioral work that very young babies prefer to look at face-like stimuli (Fantz, 1961). We also know that they will imitate facial expressions from soon after birth (Meltzoff & Moore, 1977; see Chapter 1). Tzourio-Mazoyer, de Schonen, Crivello, Reutter, Aujard, and Mazoyer (2002) studied whether 2-month-old infants would show activation in the fusiform face area identified by adult studies when viewing unfamiliar female faces. The infants were shown colored slides of women's faces, with a headscarf covering the hair so that only facial information was visible. The women were instructed to show gentle neutral expressions. The faces were interspersed with geometric patterns of circles matched with the faces for luminance. Tzourio-Mazoyer et al. reported that when viewing the female faces, the infants activated a network of brain areas belonging to the core system for the fusiform face area in adults. Even though this neural region is still immature in 2-month-infants, it appears to carry out a relatively specialized activity, namely human face processing.

Converging evidence that face processing is specialized from early in development comes from an EEG study by Farroni, Csibra, Simion, and Johnson (2002). They studied whether 4-month-old infants would display an N170 when processing human faces, and compared faces with direct eye gaze to faces where eye gaze was averted. Clearly, for psychological understanding, eye contact (mutual gaze) is essential for establishing a communicative context. Farroni et al. (2002) predicted that an early preference for eye contact would facilitate the neural processing of faces with direct gaze. Again, female faces without a hair contour and wearing a neutral expression served as stimuli. The females were either directing their gaze straight-on to the viewers, or were looking to one side. Faces with direct or averted gaze were presented in random order and remained on display for as long as the babies were willing to look at them. Analysis of the EEG recordings showed that the "infant N170" (which actually occurred later than in adults, at around 240 ms) showed a significantly greater amplitude (i.e. more negativity) to the faces with direct gaze than to the faces with averted gaze. Farroni et al. concluded that the presence of direct gaze facilitated the neural processes associated with face encoding. They noted that this early facilitation could be important for the interpretation of eye gaze signals as referential communicative acts.

As discussed earlier, one way in which eye gaze signals are important for referential communication is via the establishment of joint attention. Mundy, Card, and Fox (2000) used EEG to measure the neural activation that was predictive of joint attention behaviors at 18 months. As there was little adult work on the neural systems underpinning joint attention at the time of their study, Mundy et al. (2000) measured the baseline EEG from eight sites (left and right frontal, central, parietal and occipital) when infants were sitting quietly at 14 months. Power in the 4- to 6-Hz and 6- to 9-Hz frequency bands was computed. These measures were then correlated with joint attention behaviors at 14 and at 18 months. Using an instrument called the Early Social Communication Scales (Mundy, Hogan, & Doehring, 1996), measures of individual differences in initiating joint attention, responding to joint attention, using behavior to request objects, and responding to behavioral requests for objects were gathered. For example, initiating joint attention might include pointing to an interesting event, while initiating a behavioral request might include pointing to a desired object. Mundy et al. then explored whether baseline EEG activity at 14 months would be associated with the four different measures of early social communication.

They found that the baseline EEG, particularly at left frontal and some central sites, was related to the tendency to initiate joint attention at both 14 and 18 months. By contrast, baseline EEG from parietal sites was related to the tendency to respond to bids for joint attention. The authors speculated that the frontal components associated with initiating joint attention might reflect the need to inhibit visual behaviors to objects in order to focus on sharing attention, whereas the parietal components associated with responding to joint attention might reflect spatial requirements associated with shifting one's own attention in response to the head and gaze shift of a social partner.

These speculations received some support from an electrophysiological study of protodeclarative pointing carried out with 14-month-old infants by Henderson, Yoder, Yale, and McDuffie (2002). They measured EEG power in the 4–6 Hz and 6–9 Hz ranges at 40 sites when the infants were 14 months of age, and correlated their measures with protodeclarative versus protoimperative pointing at 18 months. As discussed earlier in this chapter, only protodeclarative pointing is thought to indicate the desire to influence the mental states of others (i.e. by sharing experiences), and only this kind of pointing is predictive of later language development. Henderson et al. pointed out that contrasting the neural activity related to two acts of pointing enabled them to control for the influence of active motor movements on the brain, so that the neural activity associated with the pragmatic function of the points could be isolated. Once motor responding was equated, they found that EEG power in frontal regions at 14 months was correlated with protodeclarative, but not protoimperative, pointing at 18 months, essentially replicating Mundy et al. (2000). This is a strong result, as brain activity in frontal regions at 14 months predicts pointing 4 months later only when pointing is used to initiate shared attention and not when pointing is used to regulate behavior. Rather than explaining this association via behavioral inhibition, Henderson et al. suggested that baseline frontal activity might reflect the extent to which children find social interactions rewarding. Such an explanation links with imaging studies of older children and adults, which show that ventral medial prefrontal cortex plays a role in representing social stimuli as rewarding or relevant. This evidence is discussed in Chapter 7.

SUMMARY

The development of psychological understanding in the infant, including knowledge of self and agency and the development of social cognition, seems to begin with simple mechanisms for ensuring proximity to the caretaker and facilitating attention to human faces, voices, and odors. Human infants are born with a propensity for social interaction and they notice social contingencies as well as contingencies between their own actions and the environment from the first weeks of life. Contingency detection plays a role in developing a primary representation of the bodily self, and also in fostering social interactions. Infants reward their caregivers with the most smiles when the behavior of their caregivers is contingent on their own responses. These early interactions also enable infants to recognize that other agents are "just like me". In particular, via imitation, infants come to understand that the visible bodily actions of others can provide clues to their internal mental states. This is hypothesized to be worked out by analogy to the self. The infants' own acts are related to their internal desires, and by analogy the object-directed movements of others are related to their internal desires. The ability to interpret actions as goal directed is present by at least 3 months of age.

Goal-directed action has a special role to play in the development of psychological understanding. The interpretation of the goals of other agents is thought to require some insight into intentionality. Although it is possible to interpret goal-directed behavior teleologically, by reference to the relevant aspects of reality as constraints on possible actions, infants go beyond teleological analyses. Infants are more likely to imitate the intentional acts of other agents than their accidental acts, for example, even if the acts are identical. They can also distinguish between actors who are unwilling versus unable to act in certain ways. Depending on the context in which modeled acts are performed, infants will infer the intended goal of the actor. They will then use the most efficient actions themselves to achieve that goal, rather than simply imitating the action sequences modeled for them.

Gaze following and gaze monitoring are also relatively simple mechanisms that can confer psychological understanding of others. The information from the eyes is very important for social cognition, and we look into people's eyes to try to infer their intentions and emotions. Typically developing infants are attracted to direct gaze from early in life, and follow changes in the direction of gaze because they interpret seeing as a mental act. They do not follow changes in gaze if another agent is blindfolded or has their eyes shut. They will also use the facial expressions of others as clues to how to behave themselves, for example inhibiting crawling in potentially dangerous situations if the mother's emotional expressions suggest fear. In social referencing, information from the voice is as important, if not more important, as information from the face.

Joint attention and pointing also play a special role in the development of social cognition. When an infant points to "remark on the world" to another person, pointing has communicative intent. Such protodeclarative pointing emerges as early as 8 months in some infants, with an advantage for girls. Pointing to establish joint attention has been seen as an important indicator of the development of the understanding that others have unobservable mental states. Protodeclarative pointing is usually accompanied by gaze alternation between the face of the social partner and the object being pointed at, and also by increased vocalization. This constellation of behaviors suggests that babies point protodeclaratively with the intention of affecting the mental states of their social partners. Indeed, babies who are skilled at recognizing the connection between looker and object at 10 months have better language development at 14 and 18 months. As discussed, the act of looking has referential meaning for both language and mental states.

Finally, the possibility that babies are able to represent false beliefs was discussed. Successful reasoning about false beliefs has been argued to be the only type of evidence that shows convincingly that humans attribute mental states to others. This is because someone who holds a false belief will act in ways that would not be predicted by the actual state of affairs in the world. The ability to predict these actions demonstrates that the infant or child understands that the contents of the mind of another are not necessarily a direct reflection of reality. Using a false location paradigm, it was demonstrated that babies of 15 months expected the protagonist to seek the object in the location in which the protagonist *believed* the object to be. As this belief was false, this experiment provides intriguing evidence that the development of psychological understanding is proceeding well in the first years of life, before the acquisition of language gives it a major boost. The intimate relationship between language development and the development of social cognition will be discussed in Chapters 5 and 7.

CHAPTER 4

CONTENTS

Conceptual development and the biological world

4

Knowledge about the kinds of things in the world, or conceptual knowledge, is the third of the "foundational" domains in cognitive development. Although originally conceptualized as "naïve biology", I will expand the term here to cover the development of conceptual knowledge about the world in general. Conceptual knowledge covers not simply the objects in the environment (e.g. the distinction between animate and inanimate entities, the development of knowledge about natural kinds such as animals versus plants, the understanding of the properties of the different classes of inanimate objects such as vehicles versus furniture), but also knowledge about other aspects of experience such as actions, events, and mental states. From very early on, infants are using their abilities to detect associations between features, to extract regularities from the environment, to learn conditional probabilities, to connect causes and effects and to perceive relational similarities and make analogies to develop their understanding of the conceptual world around them.

Conceptual development has traditionally been treated in terms of inductive learning and categorization. Generalizing on the basis of a known example is one of the most common forms of inductive reasoning, and is the basis of categorization. Because generalizing on the basis of an object is easiest to study empirically, the majority of studies of conceptual development concern children's knowledge about objects in the world. For example, a child may never have seen a robin before, but may have seen many sparrows. The likely behavior and properties of robins can be inferred from the usual behavior and properties of sparrows. In their everyday worlds, children and adults are frequently required to "go beyond the information given" in this way, and to make inductive inferences. When there are gaps in our knowledge, we have to reason by induction. The ability to reason by induction is widely accepted to be present very early in development. Because inductive reasoning is assumed, the focus of research has been on the extent and organization of the knowledge that determines the ability to categorize entities as instances of the same concept. These core principles that determine induction have been referred to as innate "constraints on learning" (R. Gelman, 1990). An example of such a core principle, which will be discussed in detail later, is the animate–inanimate distinction.

SUPERORDINATE, "BASIC-LEVEL", AND SUBORDINATE CATEGORIES

Categorization is thought of as a cognitive activity because inductive inferences depend on more than purely perceptual similarity. Historically, concepts have been thought to be internalized representations that are relatively abstract. For example, concepts are described as mental structures that are more than the sensory perceptual representation (Quinn, 2002). Robins will be categorized as similar to sparrows because they share many perceptual features such as beaks and wings. However, if the child has seen only muddy sparrows, the feature "being muddy" will not be automatically projected to robins. The child knows that "being muddy" is not an enduring property of a sparrow in the way that "having wings" is, and so irrelevant aspects of the sensory perceptual representation are not generalized (S. Gelman, 1988). Neisser (1987, p. 1) defines categorization as the ability "to treat a set of things as somehow equivalent, to put them in the same pile, or call them by the same name, or respond to them in the same way". For example, a person may indicate the category "bird" by naming a robin, an eagle, a chicken, and an ostrich "bird", or may indicate the category "things that can be sat on" by sitting on a chair, a couch, a stool, and a tree stump (Mervis & Pani, 1980). Categorization is an essential cognitive activity because the world consists of an infinite number of discriminably different stimuli and each object or event cannot be treated as unique. Recognizing novel objects or events as familiar because they belong to a known category enables us to know more about those objects or events than is possible just from looking.

Categorizing is thus more than another form of perceiving, even though perceptual and conceptual processes are intertwined. They are intertwined both because of the intimate connections between perceptual information and cognition (for example, between modes of movement and inferences about animacy), and because categories involve *beliefs* about the world. These beliefs are discussed later in this chapter. Nevertheless, the perceptual structure of the world must be an important source of information for the development of these beliefs. Perception of the attribute structure of the world provides a reasonable basis for the assignment of objects to particular categories. This point was made by Rosch (1978), who argued that the world comes naturally bundled into sets of attributes, and that this attribute structure is most accessible at the so-called "basic level". The "basic level" involves both seeing directly what things are, and having a theory that tells us how they should be classified. This theory is prototype theory.

"Basic-level" categories and prototypes

As we saw in Chapter 1 when considering perceptual development, the categorization of exemplars as similar suggests that a generalized representation or *prototype* of a category has been formed. Subsequently presented stimuli are then compared to this prototype. The experiments discussed in Chapter 1 showed the key role of statistical learning in prototype formation, for example that infants can code the correlational structure between different features of cartoon animals (e.g. Younger, 1985). The infants in these experiments were learning which features co-occurred together: they were tracking conditional probabilities and constructing prototypes. Rosch pointed out that many naturally occurring categories in the world can be distinguished by perceptual similarity. Rosch (Rosch & Mervis, 1975; Rosch, Mervis, Gray, Johnson, & Boyes-Braem, 1976) argued that at the so-called "basic level" of category abstraction, concepts such as "cat", "bird", "cow", "tree", and "car" were perceptually "given" by covariations in the constituent features of category members.

According to this account, the world contains intrinsically separable things because features co-occur in regular ways. For example, feathers reliably co-occur

Basic-level category exemplars contain the greatest number of features in common with one another, and the fewest with members of contrasting classes. The robin and the sparrow have more features in common with each other (as birds) than, for example, with dogs.

with wings, with flight, and with light body weight, and this co-occurrence helps the child to distinguish the category "bird". Basic-level category exemplars are thought to have the greatest number of features in common with one another, and the fewest number of features in common with members of contrasting classes. For example, birds share more features in common with each other than they share with dogs. Rosch further proposed that the basic level was the level of categorization that offered the greatest *psychological utility*. She argued that at this level, an organism could obtain the most information about a category with the least cognitive effort. Her views have also been widely interpreted to imply that the most efficient means of storing conceptual information will be in terms of *prototypes*, or highly typical basic-level objects (Rosch herself argued that "Prototypes do not constitute a theory of representation for categories"; Rosch, 1978). In terms of *conceptual development*, it has been assumed that if children indeed categorize the world around them at the basic level, distinguishing between objects such as cats, birds, cows, trees, and cars, then this will result in the development of a conceptual system that codes categories by prototypes.

As we have seen, the perceptual abilities of infants are certainly sophisticated enough to respond to the featural co-occurrences that distinguish a prototypical category member (e.g. Younger & Cohen, 1983). Although the experiments discussed in Chapter 1 involved man-made categories such as stuffed animals and cartoon animals, similar experiments have been done with pictures of real animals. For example, Eimas and Quinn (1994) studied whether infants can form prototypes of natural kinds such as cats, horses, zebras, and giraffes. They habituated 3- and 4-month-old infants to colored photographs of horses, using 12 different photographs. Following habituation, the infants were given three different kinds of test trial in a looking preference paradigm: a novel horse paired with a cat, a novel horse paired with a zebra, and a novel horse paired with a giraffe. The infants reliably preferred to look at the photograph of the new animal on each type of test trial, showing that they could distinguish between horses, zebras, giraffes, and cats. Research such as this shows that the information-processing systems of young infants can cope with the natural featural variation found among exemplars of real species, and can form categorical representations of these species which are perceptually based. In the world of real objects as opposed to photographs, other perceptual features such as relative size, characteristic sounds, and movement patterns would also help to differentiate between these natural kinds.

In fact, babies aged 3 months can categorize objects as effectively on the basis of motion cues as on the basis of rich visual perceptual features. Arterberry and Bornstein (2001) showed infants photographs of real vehicles and real animals on natural backgrounds, or showed them "point light" displays of vehicles and animals in motion (Figure 4.1). Point light displays remove all attributes except motion. These displays are usually created by putting points of light on key joints (animals) or intersections (vehicles) of objects and filming them as they move. When the points of light are then viewed against a plain background, a strong impression of an animal moving or a vehicle moving is experienced by the perceiver. The stimuli created by Arterberry and Bornstein (2001) were computer generated but were judged by adults with 100% accuracy as either animals or vehicles.

The infants then viewed either the static pictures of animals and vehicles or the point light displays. Half of the infants in each condition were habituated to animals and the other half to vehicles. At test, they were shown either new novel exemplars from the familiar category, or an exemplar from the contrasting category. For example, infants habituated to point light displays of different animals either saw a point light display of a new animal, or of a vehicle. Arterberry and Bornstein reported that all infants distinguished the novel category from the familiar category, irrespective of whether they had seen static pictures or point light displays. All infants also failed to dishabituate to the novel exemplar from the familiar category. Categorization of animals versus vehicles was equivalent whether perceptual cues were provided, or only information about motion. This suggests that if both kinds of cue were provided together, infant categorization of basic-level categories would be very sophisticated.

However, the prototype effects demonstrated by experiments have been argued to provide evidence for *perceptual* rather than *conceptual* categories (Mandler, 2004a).

FIGURE 4.1
(a) Examples of the type of photos used as color static images of exemplars in the animal and vehicle categories used by Arterberry and Bornstein (2001). (b) Single frames from the dynamic point light displays of the dog and the sports car. Adapted from Arterberry and Bornstein (2001).

To provide evidence for basic-level conceptual categories, developmental psychologists need to demonstrate that these perceptual differences have *conceptual significance* for children. One way of investigating this has been to study sorting behavior in preverbal children. If children reliably group objects by their basic-level category, for example by putting toy dogs with other toy dogs and toy cars with other toy cars, then this might imply conceptual significance.

Sequential touching as a measure of basic-level categorization

One way to examine sorting behavior is to measure touching. Infants and children like to handle objects that interest them, but spontaneous grouping of objects is rarely seen before 18 months of age. However, **sequential touching** is often observed: Children tend to touch objects from the same category in sequence more often than would be expected by chance, and this systematic touching behavior gradually develops into systematic sorting. Children's tactile behavior was used to measure emergent categorization in a set of studies designed by Mandler and Bauer (1988). They used sequential touching to see whether there was any evidence that children would sort toys into basic-level categories.

The toys used in Mandler and Bauer's studies were: (1) dogs vs. cars (a basic-level contrast); and (2) vehicles vs. animals (a superordinate-level contrast). In the basic-level task, the children were given a toy poodle, collie, bloodhound, and bulldog and a toy sports car, sedan, station wagon, and Volkswagen beetle. Sequential touching of the cars or the dogs was taken as evidence for differentiation of these basic-level categories. In the superordinate-level task, the children were given a toy horse, spider, chicken, and fish, and a toy airplane, motorcycle, truck, and train engine. A set of kitchen things vs. bathroom things was also used (mug, spoon, plate, pan vs. soap, toothbrush, toothpaste, comb), to explore "contextual categories". These were defined as categories of objects that are associated because they are found in the same place or are used in the same activities. The sequential touching behavior of infants aged 12, 15, and 20 months who were faced with these pairs of categories was then measured, and any spontaneous grouping of the objects was also noted.

Spontaneous grouping of objects is indicative of conceptual organization, but is rarely witnessed in children prior to 18 months of age.

Mandler and Bauer found that the touching behavior of the 12- and 15-month-old infants as a group indicated categorization at the basic level only, as their touching was nonrandomly sequential only for the dogs vs. cars. Sequential touching within the contextual and superordinate categories was reliably nonrandom only at 20 months. However, there were large individual differences within this overall pattern. For example, 25% of the 12-month-olds were responsive to the superordinate categories.

In a second experiment, Mandler and Bauer compared sorting behavior with basic-level categories when the objects either came from the *same* superordinate class or *different* superordinate classes. Objects from the same superordinate classes (animals) shared a high degree of within-category similarity while *minimizing* between-category differences (e.g. dogs vs. horses), whereas objects from different

KEY TERM

Sequential touching
Children from around 18 months of age tend to touch objects from the same category in sequence more than one would expect by chance, and this is thus a measure of categorization.

superordinate classes (animals vs. vehicles) shared a high degree of within-category similarity while *maximizing* between-category differences (e.g. dogs vs. cars). Only older children were tested (16- and 20-month-olds). The results showed that basic-level categories were clearly distinguished when animals were compared with vehicles, but not when animals were compared with animals. Mandler and Bauer argued that the role of superordinate classes in the development of categorization may be greater than was previously supposed. In their studies, what had been scored as "basic level" sorting apparently occurred only when the basic level coincided with *different* superordinate categories.

Another way of describing these results, however, is to argue that the children's sorting behavior reflected the differing amounts of *perceptual similarity* evident in the stimuli. The contrast between basic-level objects from the same or different superordinate categories does not hold perceptual similarity constant. For example, the distinction between dogs and cars is an easy one to make in terms of perceptual similarity, because dogs are more similar to each other than they are to cars (all dogs have heads, tails, four legs etc., whereas all cars have wheels, no legs, seats, and so on). The distinction between dogs and horses is less easy to make in terms of perceptual similarity, as both dogs and horses have heads, tails, four legs, and so on, and so it is more difficult to differentiate between them (at least, when one is looking at toy dogs and horses!). Mandler and Bauer's negative result does not necessarily imply an inability to differentiate at the basic level within the same superordinate category.

Furthermore, features that suggest membership at the basic level also suggest membership at the superordinate level. For example, feathers suggest "animal" as well as "bird", "fur" suggests "animal" as well as "cat" (see Murphy, 1982). This is recognized in Rosch's theory, as she argues that perceptual similiarity *correlates with* structural similarity. The perceptual similarity between dogs and horses reflects a deeper underlying structural similarity, namely that both dogs and horses are natural kinds. Similarly, cars have wheels and no legs because they are artifacts, and are thus more perceptually similar to airplanes and trains, with whom they share a deeper underlying structural similarity. Of course, in the real world, dogs and horses are easily distinguished at the basic level by a striking difference in size, texture of coat, barking versus neighing, smell, and so on, distinctions that are not a feature of plastic toy animals. In this sense, both basic-level and superordinate concepts originate from perceptual knowledge. The differing degrees of perceptual similarity between horses, dogs, and cars are an intrinsic part of Rosch's hypothesis.

However, Pauen (2002) has produced evidence that infant behavior can also be based on pre-existing conceptual insights. She used an object examination paradigm to show that infant generalizations were not based simply on the variability in the perceptual characteristics of the particular set of objects being used in a particular experiment. In the object examination task, infants are given a series of objects from one category to examine manually, one at a time, until they are familiar. For example, they may be given a series of animals. Following familiarization, they are given a novel exemplar from the familiar category (a new toy animal) and a novel exemplar from a new category (a toy chest of drawers) to manipulate in turn. If they spend longer manipulating the chest of drawers, this is evidence for categorical discrimination. To explore the question of whether infants form on-line perceptually based representations in categorization tasks, Pauen systematically varied the degree of perceptual similarity between objects from different superordinate categories. Her categories were animals and furniture.

Pauen's manipulation was to create toy furniture that was matched with toy animals for overall perceptual similarity. The animals were made of wood but did not appear naturalistic. The furniture was also made of wood, and each piece had black-and-white dots that could be interpreted as eyes, had the same global shape as one of the animals, had the same colors as another animal, and had the same surface pattern as a third animal. For these artificial stimuli, adult raters judged that there was more perceptual similarity *between* the animals and furniture than within each category. Hence, perceptually, the individual animals were more different from each other than they were from the individual pieces of furniture. Different, more naturalistic toy animals and toy furniture were also used. These toys differed markedly in perceptual similarity. Examples of Pauen's stimuli are shown in Figure 4.2.

Pauen was interested in whether categorization would be better with the realistic toy replicas of animals and furniture than with the artificial replicas. If infant categorization in the object manipulation task depends on the similarity of the perceptual attributes of particular objects, then categorization should be very difficult with the artificial replicas. This is because the artificial toy animals and furniture were more similar to each other than the animals were to other animals and the furniture was to other pieces of furniture. However, if infants use pre-existing knowledge to group objects in this task, then there should be no difference in responding across the artificial and naturalistic conditions. Pauen found the latter result. Infants spent much more time examining an object when it was from a new category than when it was from a familiar category, irrespective of perceptual similarity. Pauen therefore argued that infant behavior in the object manipulation task was knowledge based.

FIGURE 4.2
The stimuli used by Pauen (2002). Top: natural-looking models of toy animals and furniture with low between-category similarity. Bottom: artificial-looking toy models of the same animals and furniture items with increased between-category similarity. Adapted from Pauen (2002) with permission from Blackwell Publishing.

The matching-to-sample task

Another way to look at category knowledge is to use a **matching-to-sample task**. In matching-to-sample tasks, children are given a sample or target object, and are asked to select the correct match for the target from a pair of alternatives (this task is often used with monkeys!). Bauer and Mandler (1989b) used a matching-to-sample task to contrast superordinate and basic-level matches in children aged 19, 25, and 31 months. The distinction between superordinate matches and basic-level matches was created by varying the objects in the choice pair. For example, triads like *bird*, bird, nest or *toothbrush*, toothbrush, toothpaste enabled basic-level matches. Triads like *chair*, table, person or *monkey*, bear, banana enabled superordinate matches (Table 4.1). The children were told that they were going to play a "finding" game. The experimenter would indicate the target object (e.g. the toothbrush or the monkey), and then say "See this one? Can you find me another one just like this one? Can you show me the other one like this?".

KEY TERM

Matching-to-sample task
In which children are given a sample or target object and asked to select the correct match for the target from a pair of alternatives.

TABLE 4.1 Examples of triads of stimuli from Mandler and Bauer (1988)

Column 1	Column 2	Column 3
Bird	Nest	Bird
Toothbrush	Toothpaste	Toothbrush
Mug	Juice can	Glass
Brush	Mirror	Comb
Pear	Knife	Apple
Chair	Person	Table
Baby	Bottle	Adult
Flower	Vase	Plant
Bed	Pillow	Crib
Spoon	Plate	Measuring scoop
Coat	Umbrellla	Sweatshirt
Pot	Spatula	Skillet
Hammer	Nail	Pliers
Wagon	Child	Trike
Monkey	Banana	Bear
Pail	Shovel	Flowerpot
Lion	Cage	Elephant
Shirt	Hanger	Pants
Sink	Soap	Bathtub

Basic-level triads comprised two nonidentical objects from Column 1 and one object from Column 2. Superordinate-level triads comprised one object each from Columns 1, 2, and 3. The first three rows of stimuli formed the example triads.

Bauer and Mandler found that, although basic-level sorts were slightly easier overall, the children were highly successful at categorical sorting in both tasks at all ages. For the basic-level sorts, correct responses by age were 85% for the 19-month-olds, 94% for the 25-month-olds, and 97% for the 31-month-olds. For the superordinate-level sorts, the figures were 91% correct for the 19-month-olds, 81% for the 25-month-olds, and 93% for the 31-month-olds. We can conclude that a sensitivity to *both* basic-level and superordinate-level categories exists by at least 19 months.

The core developmental role of the superordinate level

Rosch's assumption that the basic level of categorization would have developmental primacy has been challenged by more recent research. Mandler and colleagues have proposed that sensitivity to superordinate-level categories may *precede* sensitivity to basic-level categories, reversing the sequence of development proposed by Rosch (Mandler, 2004b). Quinn and colleagues have proposed that the development of categorization proceeds from more general to more specific representations (Quinn, 2002). Both proposals assume that more global category representations are differentiated with development into narrower ones (such as basic-level ones). However, whereas Mandler makes a distinction between perceptual (infant basic level) categorization and conceptual (older infant object examination) categorization, Quinn assumes that perceptual learning processes are sufficient to account for the "global to basic" sequence.

Mandler's position is based on a series of studies contrasting basic-level objects within the *same* superordinate categories, such as horses and dogs (both animals, e.g. Mandler, Bauer, & McDonough, 1991; Mandler & McDonough, 1993). For example, Mandler et al. (1991) used the sequential touching technique to investigate basic-level distinctions between toy dogs and toy horses (which have a low degree of perceptual contrast), toy dogs and toy rabbits (which have a medium degree of perceptual contrast), and toy dogs and toy fish (which have a high degree of perceptual contrast) in 19-, 24-, and 31-month-olds. They found that only the 31-month-olds could differentiate the dogs from the horses with any degree of reliability ($P < .08$). For the medium degree of perceptual contrast (dogs vs. rabbits), both the 24- and 31-month-olds could reliably differentiate the animals, and for the high degree of perceptual contrast (dogs vs. fish), all groups could differentiate the animals reliably. All groups could also differentiate animals from vehicles (a superordinate-level contrast with high perceptual dissimilarity). From these data, Mandler et al. argued that categorization proceeds from the differentiation of a global domain (such as animals) through successively finer distinctions until the basic level of abstraction is approximated. Alternatively, it can be argued that toddler sorting behavior is correlated with perceptual similarity. The failure to distinguish toy dogs from toy horses in this task need not imply the *absence* of the conceptual distinctions (a negative result cannot be used to argue for the lack of knowledge because it might reflect other aspects of the experimental task).

Further negative evidence against Rosch's view that categorization begins at the basic level and then differentiates upwards to the superordinate level and downwards to the subordinate level has been reported by Mandler and McDonough (1993), working with 7-, 9-, and 11-month-old infants. They again compared the basic-level contrasts of toy dogs vs. toy fish, and toy dogs vs. toy rabbits, but this time they used an object examination task rather than the object manipulation task that they used in their studies with older children; an object examination task was also used by Pauen. To use the object examination task to explore basic-level distinctions, infants are first presented with a series of exemplars at the basic level. For example, they may be given a series of toy fish. Following familiarization, they are given a novel exemplar from the familiar category (a new toy fish) and a novel exemplar from a new category within the same superordinate (a toy dog) to manipulate in turn. If the infants show increased examination time for the object from the new basic-level category (dog) compared to the novel object from the familiar basic-level category (fish), then they are assumed to differentiate the two categories. Using this technique, Mandler and McDonough found no evidence that dogs were discriminated from fish, or that dogs were discriminated from rabbits. However, animals were discriminated from vehicles (a superordinate-level contrast). On the basis of these data, Mandler and McDonough argued that infants have a fairly undifferentiated concept of animals that does not include basic-level information. Again, however, a weakness is that the study depended on toy animals, not on real animals. Toys only preserve some of the features of the objects that they represent (such as overall appearance, number of legs, and number of eyes), and omit many others (such as relative size, smell, sound, and texture of skin). These other features may make a key contribution to basic-level distinctions between, for example, dogs, horses, fish, and rabbits (real fish and real dogs look, feel, and smell very different!). Again, the failure to distinguish toy dogs from toy fish in this task need not imply the *absence* of the relevant conceptual distinctions

Quinn's view of a perceptually based **global to basic sequence** of category development derives from **connectionist modeling**. Quinn and Johnson (1997, 2000; see Quinn, 2002, for a summary) essentially gave a computer model information about different environmental features of mammals and furniture. For example, the model was given information about the different leg lengths associated with tables, chairs, dogs, and cats. This information was given to input nodes in the model and had to be mapped to output nodes via a layer of hidden units. The hidden units had the job of forming representations (i.e. connection strengths) from the featural information given to the input nodes that would yield the relevant concepts at the output nodes. Such computational models learn via progressive extraction of statistical regularities in the input, just like babies. A variety of different simulations converged on the same result: global categories emerged prior to basic-level categories.

Quinn's argument (see Quinn, 2002) is that connectionist modeling has the advantage of showing what kinds of representation are, in principle, possible given perceptual features as input. The connectionist networks tended to devote large numbers of hidden units initially to coding the global level. Large differences in a small number of attributes were focused on (e.g. faces and tails being present in mammals and absent in furniture). Subsequently, more and more hidden nodes were allocated to coding more subtle distinctions in attributes that were relevant to the basic level (e.g. leg length of different types of furniture). As learning progressed, the models overall were dedicating more nodes to basic-level distinctions, and fewer to global level distinctions. Hence as more and more exemplars were encountered, coding favored the basic level. As we will see later in this chapter, connectionist accounts are more consistent with results emerging from cognitive neuroscience. It seems that the earliest concepts are at a global level but that, quite quickly, representations come to favor the basic level of categorization proposed by Rosch. Highly typical basic-level objects are called *prototypes*, yet so far the role of typicality in conceptual development is relatively underresearched. Presumably, by varying the typicality of the objects that the model learns about, the degree to which the hidden units focus first on global-level attributes could be varied as well.

Typicality effects in sequential touching tasks

A prototype is an exemplar of a category that is considered highly representative of that category. Prototypes are either conceived of as the category member with *average* values on the features or attributes associated with the category (Rosch & Mervis, 1975), or as an individual exemplar that is judged as highly typical in terms of the number of other exemplars of the category that it resembles (Medin & Schaffer, 1978). In practice, the two measures usually generate the same prototype: the category member with average values is often the exemplar that is most typical.

Bauer and her colleagues have tackled the question of whether prototypicality facilitates category formation by using the sequential touching measure. Bauer, Dow, and Hertsgaard (1995) tested 13-, 16-, and 20-month-old infants' categorization of sets of objects that either consisted entirely of prototypical exemplars, or of nonprototypical exemplars. The categories that they used were *animals* and *vehicles*, at either the superordinate or the basic level. For example, a set of prototypical animals at the superordinate level might include a cow, a dog, a pig, and a cat. A set of prototypical vehicles at the superordinate level might include a bus, a motorcycle, a truck, and a car. A set of nonprototypical animals at the superordinate level might include a snail, a rhinoceros, an alligator, and an ostrich, and a set of nonprototypical vehicles at the superordinate level might include a canoe, a tank, a space shuttle, and a battleship. The basic-level sets contrasted prototypical and nonprototypical fish, dogs, cars, and airplanes (e.g. trout, salmon, bass, pike; or sunfish, eel, fancy goldfish, nurse shark; Table 4.2). If prototypicality is important in category formation, then prototypicality should affect sequential touching at *both* the superordinate and basic levels. For example, children should sequentially touch the cow, pig, dog, and cat as frequently as they sequentially touch the trout, salmon, bass, and pike.

Bauer et al. found that the categorization of the prototypical object sets was indeed superior to that of the nonprototypical object sets. However, for the 13-month-olds, categorization of the prototypical object sets occurred at the basic level only, whereas for the 16- and 20-month-olds, categorization of the prototypical objects sets occurred at both the basic and the superordinate levels. Categorization of the nonprototypical object sets was more variable. For the 16-month-olds, categorization of nonprototypical objects (e.g. sunfish, eel, fancy goldfish, nurse shark) was found only at the basic level. Sequential touching of all the other

TABLE 4.2   Examples of the stimuli used by Bauer et al. (1995)

Stimulus type/ Category	Global level	Basic level	
	Animal vs. vehicle	Dogs vs. fish	Cars vs. aeroplanes
Prototypical			
Category 1	pig	German shepherd	Mercedes-Benz
	house cat	collie	Mustang convertible
	dog	Labrador-retriever	Renault sedan
	cow	brown mongrel	Thunderbird
Category 2	school bus	bass	KLM airliner
	motorcycle	trout	Pan Am airliner
	pick-up truck	walleyed pike	Comanche prop
	4-door sedan	salmon	airforce jet
Nonprototypical			
Category 1	alligator	bulldog	Indy racer
	snail	Chihuahua	drag racer
	rhinoceros	spitz	Lotus
	ostrich	terrier	3-wheeled roadster
Category 2	wooden canoe	sunfish	glider
	armoured tank	eel	stealth bomber
	battleship	fancy goldfish	WWI bomber
	space shuttle	nurse shark	X-wing fighter

nonprototypical object sets did not differ from chance. Again, it is difficult to draw strong conclusions from this negative result. For the 24-month-olds, categorization of the nonprototypical object sets was only found at the superordinate level, whereas for the 28-month-olds categorization of the nonprototypical object sets was found at both levels (basic and superordinate). Finally, prototypicality accounted for more variance than either age or categorical level (basic vs. superordinate). This finding demonstrates the importance of prototypicality in categorization. More studies exploring the links between prototypes and different levels of categorization are obviously important, particularly as in adults inductive inferences are partly governed by typicality. Typicality also seems likely to be important given recent findings in cognitive neuroscience, which are beginning to address the question of how concepts are represented by the brain.

Child-basic categories and cognitive neuroscience

As cognitive developmental neuroscience provides more data on brain development, a deeper understanding of how concepts are represented by infants and young children should emerge. Some of the behavioral data discussed so far has been quite contradictory, for example regarding the primacy of basic level versus global level concepts. However, it may turn out that the infant brain is attending to aspects of the stimuli that have not been considered by the experimenters (and accordingly, have not been built into a connectionist simulation). The aspects of a stimulus that a child or an infant considers to be important and therefore assigns the greatest weight in computing similarity and making inductive inferences may differ from those aspects used by an adult. For example, in Chapter 1 we saw that Mareschal and Johnson (2003) were able to demonstrate that 4-month-old infants treated "being graspable" as an important feature of toys. "Being graspable" was an important aspect of the stimuli to be categorized for the infants, because it meant that these toys afforded the infant the same potential actions. Using data from cognitive neuroscience, Mareschal and Johnson's idea was that any studies using small, familiar, and moving objects as stimuli were likely to activate the dorsal route of visual processing, while any studies using larger, stationary objects were likely to be processed by the ventral route. Other studies in developmental cognitive neuroscience may show that other features or factors are also important. Features that afford actions, either actions by the perceiver or by the entity itself, seem likely to be particularly important.

We already know from adult studies that actions on objects are coded by a special neural system, the mirror neuron system. Mirror neurons fire both when one makes an action oneself, such as picking up a cup, and also when one is sitting passively watching someone else pick up a cup (Rizzolatti, Fogassi, & Gallese, 2001). Mirror neurons are found in frontal, parietal, and premotor cortex, and are also active when one imagines making a movement. When reading *words* for action concepts such as "kick", "pick", and "lick", the motor areas in the brain that are used when moving the feet, fingers, and tongue become activated respectively (Hauk, Johnsrude, & Pulvermuller, 2004). When imagining the colors of objects, the color area of the brain is activated (Barsalou et al., 2003). Cognitive neuroscience studies with adults thus essentially show that the activation of particular concepts produces neural activation in the sensory modalities associated with experienced instances of those concepts.

Experiments such as these suggest that the brain codes objects, actions, events, and other concepts in terms of the sensory modalities that are active when the concepts are being directly experienced. Following repeated experiences of objects, events or actions, what is common across instances will be activated more strongly than what is not. Hence for events and actions, causal structure will be strongly represented. The brain also keeps track of which areas associate together. Object categories have very distributed representations, and any category is represented by activation in multiple modalities at the same time. When a child activates the concept "robin", knowledge about how robins look, sound, move, and what they feel like to touch, as well as the emotions associated with seeing robins, are simultaneously active and together constitute the child's conceptual knowledge. Neurally, therefore, there is no amodal or abstract "concept" for "robin" that is held in a separate conceptual system (semantic memory; see Chapter 8). Rather, people's knowledge of the world may be held in lots of different parts of the brain, comprising the sensory systems first used to experience the different concepts, and associated neural areas that represent the conjunctions of particular sets of sensory information (Barsalou et al., 2003).

Note that such a modality-specific system would lend itself naturally to development. As infants and children gain more conceptual knowledge about the world, modality-specific knowledge would change, and this would in turn change the conjunctions in association areas (analogous to the connection strengths for the hidden units in a connectionist model; see Chapter 11). In fact, children's concepts could naturally differ from those of adults, depending on the sensory and emotional information being attended to. Similarly, knowledge about subordinate, basic-level, and superordinate categories could depend on the overlap between the particular patterns of activation associated with exemplars of those categories. Because two superordinate categories like vehicles and animals, or two basic-level concepts like car and dog, are likely to activate different networks of sensory neurons and different conjunctions in association areas, these distributed representations also lend themselves naturally to the simultaneous development of categorical representations at more than one level. We already know from magnetoencephalogram (MEG) studies that if adults are asked to make simple decisions ("man-made or natural?") about different superordinate categories such as animals, flowers, clothes, and furniture, spatially distinct neural networks are activated by basic-level exemplars of these categories, even though the basic-level exemplars are different. For example, seeing pictures of a bear, wolf, deer, and fox all activate a particular neural network distributed widely across the scalp, and this network of neurons is geometrically partially distinct from the network activated by seeing pictures of a rose, sunflower, orchid, and tulip (Low et al. 2003). Depending on the particular exemplars that have been experienced, these networks may differ at different ages. Clearly, the field of conceptual development is ripe for exploration using cognitive neuroscience methods.

The idea that what is core conceptual knowledge for a child may differ from what is core conceptual knowledge for an adult has been proposed before. This idea was proposed in terms of "**child-basic categories**", which were thought to be distinguished from "adult-basic" categories, and was originally proposed by Mervis and colleagues (e.g. Mervis, 1987). Mervis pointed out that children might notice or emphasize different attributes of the same object than adults do, for example because of their different experiences and their different knowledge of the culturally appropriate functions of objects. They may thus form slightly different basic-level categories from adults. Children's categories may thus be broader than, narrower than, or overlap with the corresponding adult categories.

KEY TERM

Child-basic categories
Categories that can differ from "adult-basic" categories because children might notice or emphasize different attributes of objects than adults.

FIGURE 4.3
Examples of the objects included in and excluded from Ari's initial duck category. Top: objects included immediately (plush mallard, carved grebe, porcelain snow goose, wind-up chicken). Second row: objects that were included as soon as they were available for testing (plush Canadian goose, swan, great blue heron, ostrich). Bottom: objects initially excluded (plastic duck rattle, Donald Duck head, porcelain song bird, plush owl). From Mervis (1987). Copyright © Cambridge University Press. Reproduced with permission.

To illustrate her theory about "child-basic" categories, Mervis kept a detailed record of the development of her son Ari's first category, which was duck. The objects that he was first prepared to countenance as members of this category are shown in Figure 4.3, which also shows the objects that he excluded. Ari's category boundaries were tested by giving him sets of four objects, and asking "Can Ari get the duckie?". Over time, Ari's duck category evolved to include first pictures of ducks, then the plastic duck rattle shown in Figure 4.3, and finally the plush duck head rattle and the Donald Duck head. At this point, he began to spot instances of ducks that his mother failed to notice, such as a picture of a duck inner-tube in a magazine that she was reading and a swan soap dish in a shop. The fact that Ari initially considered some toys to be ducks and not others is obviously important for the design of future studies of basic-level distinctions that rely on toys.

Beyond the role of perceptual similarity in categorization

In the studies of categorization at the basic, superordinate, and subordinate levels discussed above, a recurring factor in children's categorization behavior has been the degree of perceptual similarity between different category exemplars. As noted above, one reason for this is that perceptual similarity is correlated with structural similarity. Perceptual similarity can act as a guide to structural similarity, providing an indication that objects share deeper characteristics (such as the nonobservable features shared by biological kinds: has a heart, has blood inside, and so on). However, we can also study how children behave when perceptual similarity and conceptual similarity are not correlated. When perceptual similarity is pitted against category membership, children prove surprisingly adept at categorizing on the basis of deeper structural characteristics. However, younger children perform better when language helps their intuitions about category membership (2-year-olds), whereas slightly older children do not (3-year-olds). This has been demonstrated in a series of experiments by S. Gelman and her colleagues, who devised a picture-based technique that allowed category membership and category appearance to be independently manipulated (e.g. Gelman & Markman, 1986, 1987; Gelman & Coley, 1990).

For example, Gelman and Coley (1990) asked 2-year-old children questions about the properties of typical and atypical members of familiar categories like birds and dinosaurs. The children were shown pictures of birds and dinosaurs, and were asked questions such as "This is a bird. Does it live in a nest?", and "This is a dinosaur. Does it have big teeth?". Each category comparison was introduced by showing the children a target picture of a typical category member, such as a typical bird. The children were then asked one question about the target picture ("Does it live in a nest?"), and this picture remained in view during the presentation of the test pictures. Pictures of other category members and of the members of a contrasting category were then shown to the child one by one. The same question ("Does it live in a nest?") was asked for each picture in turn.

The key manipulation was that one of the members of the contrasting category looked highly similar to the target picture, and one of the members of the same category looked highly dissimilar to it (Figure 4.4). For example, for the bird category just mentioned, the highly dissimilar test picture was a *dodo* (atypical category member) and the highly similar test picture was a *bluebird* (typical category member). In the contrasting category of dinosaurs, the highly dissimilar test picture was a *stegosaurus* (typical category member) and the highly similar test picture was a *pterodactyl* (atypical category member). If the children answered the questions on the basis of overall appearance, then they should have judged that the bluebird and

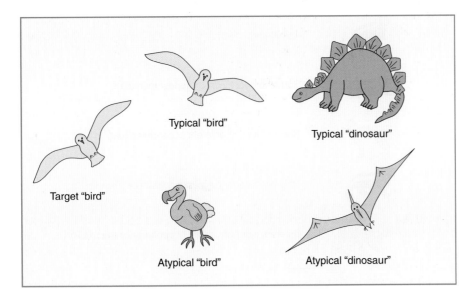

Typical "bird"

Typical "dinosaur"

Target "bird"

Atypical "bird"

Atypical "dinosaur"

FIGURE 4.4
Examples of the stimuli used to test the "bird" category by Gelman and Coley (1990). Copyright © American Psychological Association. Reprinted with permission.

the pterodactyl both live in a nest, whereas the stegosaurus and the dodo do not. However, if they were sensitive to the deeper structural properties that specify category membership, then they should have judged that the bluebird and the dodo both live in a nest, whereas the stegosaurus and the pterodactyl do not.

Gelman and Coley found that the 2-year-olds correctly ascribed the different properties to the atypical category members only 42% of the time (dodo), compared with 76% for the typical category members (bluebird). The 42% level of responding was significantly *below* chance, suggesting that appearance does seem to control judgments about category membership in the absence of linguistic support in this age group. However, if category membership labels were provided during questioning, for example by saying "This is a bird/dinosaur. Does this bird/dinosaur say 'tweet tweet'?", then the 2-year-olds correctly ascribed the different properties to the atypical category members 69% of the time, and to the typical category members 74% of the time. Adults given the same task succeeded even without labels. Of course, this is unsurprising as all the atypical members were unfamiliar to the children, but not to the adults. Nevertheless, Gelman and Coley's experiment demonstrates clearly that, when children are provided with category labels, category membership rather than perceptual appearance guides inferences about the extension of category properties.

In related work, Gelman and Markman (1986, 1987) demonstrated that 3- and 4-year-olds succeed in a similar categorization task, even without labels. For example, in their work with 3-year-olds the children were shown a picture of a target object, such as a cat, and were told a new fact about it, such as that it "can see in the dark". They were then shown pictures of four more animals (Figure 4.5), one that looked like the target picture and was of the same category (another cat), one that looked like the target picture but was of a different category (a skunk), one that did not look like the target picture but was of the same category (a cat with different coloring), and one that did not look like the target picture and was of a different category (a dinosaur). The children were asked in each case whether the animal shared the

FIGURE 4.5
Examples of the stimuli used to test the "cat" category. From Gelman and Markman (1987). Reproduced with permission from Blackwell Publishing.

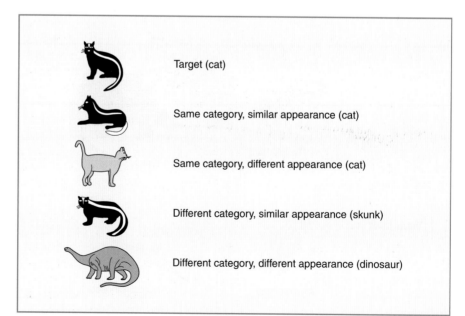

Target (cat)

Same category, similar appearance (cat)

Same category, different appearance (cat)

Different category, similar appearance (skunk)

Different category, different appearance (dinosaur)

property ascribed to the target picture ("can see in the dark"). Gelman and Markman found that the children consistently assigned properties on the basis of category membership rather than perceptual appearance. This finding suggests that 3- to 4-year-old children can use category information *alone* as a basis for drawing inductive inferences about biological kinds.

However, these findings should not be interpreted as evidence that category membership is *more important* than perceptual similarity in guiding inferences about the extension of category properties by the age of 3–4 years. This is because the perceptual stimuli in these experiments were line drawings, and so were fairly impoverished in perceptual terms. Jones and Smith (1993) have argued that perceptual and nonperceptual knowledge do not play distinct roles in our concepts, and the experimental work discussed so far appears to support this view. Instead, it seems that "Surface appearances, just like nonperceptual properties, support theoretical relations within and among different bits of knowledge" (Jones & Smith, 1993, p. 126).

THE ROLE OF LANGUAGE IN CONCEPTUAL DEVELOPMENT

The potentially critical role of language in conceptual development is clearly illustrated by the finding of S. Gelman and colleagues that category membership labels promote accurate conceptual distinctions in 2-year-olds. In fact, there is a lot of experimental work on the relation between language and conceptual development (a detailed discussion of the relation between language and thought is beyond the scope of this book, although some examples are discussed in Chapter 5). Here, I give a brief flavor of the kind of research that has been carried out into the role of language in conceptual development. A key finding in such work is that children seem to have *linguistic biases* that guide their conceptual organization at the different hierarchical levels identified by Rosch.

Learning new words apparently teaches children about conceptual relations between objects and classes of objects. For example, names in natural language designate relations between basic-level objects and superordinate and subordinate relations. The provision of a common label like "animal" for multiple referents like dogs, horses, and fish *acts in itself* to classify these referents as members of the same superordinate class. In particular, work in language acquisition has shown that children interpret the introduction of *novel nouns* as highlighting superordinate categories, but the introduction of *novel adjectives* as highlighting subordinate categories.

One researcher whose studies have led to this conclusion is Waxman, whose experimental technique involves teaching children novel labels (Japanese words) for objects from familiar categories which have been sampled at different hierarchical levels. For example, Waxman (1990) taught 3-year-olds novel labels for superordinate categories like *animal*. Here, the basic-level objects were photographs of dogs, cats, and horses, and the subordinate-level objects were photographs of collie dogs, Irish setters, and terriers. The children were shown some Japanese dolls, who were introduced as being unable to speak English and also as being "very picky" (choosy). Each doll only liked a certain kind of thing, and three examples of the thing that the doll liked were given by the experimenter. If the doll liked *animals*, the experimenter placed photographs of a dog, bird, and fish by the doll (superordinate level), and if the doll liked *dogs* then the experimenter placed photographs of a setter, a bulldog, and a poodle by the doll. The children were then given a variety of other photographs to assign to the dolls (e.g. *superordinate sort*: horse, elephant, duck, pig, mixed in with photographs of clothing and food; *basic-level sort*: photographs of four other varieties of dog mixed in with photographs of varieties of cats and horses).

Some of the children were given the sorting task in the context of novel nouns and others were given the sorting task in the context of novel adjectives. For example, in the novel noun condition the experimenter would say "This doll likes only *suikahs*, and these are the *suikahs*". In the novel adjective condition, the experimenter would say "This doll only wants *sukish* ones, and these are the ones that are *sukish*". Waxman found a striking cross-over effect in sorting behavior, with the 3-year-olds in the novel noun condition classifying more pictures correctly at the superordinate than at the subordinate level (e.g. doing better with animals than with dogs), and the 3-year-olds in the novel adjective condition classifying more pictures correctly at the subordinate than at the superordinate level (e.g. doing better with dogs than with animals). This indicates that nouns are interpreted as indicating superordinate categories, and adjectives are interpreted as indicating subordinate categories. Note also that the perceptual cues were equivalent in both conditions, as the children were sorting the same sets of photographs.

Furthermore, classification at the basic level was close to ceiling in both conditions, with linguistic cues neither facilitating nor inhibiting performance. Waxman argued that, at nonbasic levels, children used syntactic cues to aid the establishment of taxonomic classes. She also argued that children have a linguistic bias to behave like this, because they are sensitive to the powerful links between conceptual hierarchies and the language that we use to describe them. Novel labels can thus promote classification at precisely those levels which are most subject to cultural influence and variation—the nonbasic levels.

THE BIOLOGICAL/NONBIOLOGICAL DISTINCTION

As noted earlier, however, categories also involve *beliefs* about the world. At the same time as they are developing conceptual hierarchies *within categories* like animal and vehicle, children are also developing knowledge about some fundamental conceptual distinctions. One of the first and most important of these conceptual distinctions is that between biological and nonbiological entities. Biological entities engage in certain distinctive processes. They can move on their own, they can grow taller, fatter or (in some cases) change their color or form, and they can inherit the characteristics of their forebears. They also share certain core properties, such as blood, bones, or cellulose. Nonbiological entities do not engage in self-generated movement, and do not exhibit growth, metamorphosis, or inheritance, although they can also share certain core properties (e.g. they may be made of plastic). Infants and young children are aware of some of these differences between animates and inanimates at a surprisingly early age. This basic understanding of the biological/nonbiological distinction is then enriched by the child's growing experience of the world.

Evidence from studies of biological movement

One way to examine whether infants and young children are sensitive to the animate–inanimate distinction is to see when they distinguish biological from nonbiological movement. Bertenthal, Proffitt, Spetner, and Thomas (1985) used "**point-light walker displays**" to find out. These displays were first created by Johansson (1973), who placed small lights on the major joints and head of a person, dressed him in black, and then filmed him walking in the dark. Johansson found that adults easily recognized these 10–12 points of moving light as a person walking. Adults could also recognize people doing push-ups, people dancing, and people riding a bicycle. Later work showed that the gender of the person could also be determined just from seeing the moving points of light (Cutting, Proffitt, & Kozlowski, 1978). As discussed earlier in this chapter, Arterberry and Bornstein (2001) found that 3-month-olds could distinguish between animals and vehicles on the basis of point-light displays only.

One of the key cues in recognizing the points of light as a human form turns out to be the patterns of occlusion created by the act of walking. Imagine a person walking past you. Each time the lights on the limbs on the far side of his or her body (e.g. wrist, knee, elbow, ankle) pass behind the near-side limbs or torso, they will be briefly occluded. Bertenthal et al. used this occlusion cue as a test of 9-month-old infants' recognition of the point-light displays as human walkers. They created computer displays of points of light, allowing occlusion to be manipulated experimentally, and then showed the babies point-light displays with and without occlusion. Babies were either habituated to an occluded display and then shown the nonoccluded version, or vice versa. Additional control groups of babies saw scrambled point-light displays with and without occlusion, which tested their detection of occlusions that did not specify biological motion.

Bertenthal et al. found that the babies dishabituated to the point-light displays that specified biological motion ("canonical" displays) but not to the scrambled displays. This suggested that they were indeed preferentially sensitive to the occlusion information characteristic of biological motion. In a later experiment, Bertenthal et al. demonstrated that the babies' sensitivity was due to their implicit detection of the body of the point-light walker. The babies discriminated the canonical walker from a random occlusion display, but did not show the same discrimination when the walker was presented up-side down.

Basic movement cues other than occlusion also seem to be used to distinguish biological from nonbiological motion. Lamsfuss (1995) suggested that the predictability and regularity of motion was another useful cue to the biological/ nonbiological distinction, as whereas we can usually make fairly accurate predictions about the movement patterns of nonbiological kinds such as cars and other machines, we cannot make accurate predictions about the movements of biological kinds such as house flies. To test her idea, Lamsfuss showed 4- and 5-year-old children different pairs of "tracks" that had purportedly been left by either an animal or a machine. The tracks were simple dot patterns (Figure 4.6), one of which was always more regular than the other. Dot patterns were used so that no additional perceptual information about the object that produced the motion would be provided by the displays. Lamsfuss found that, when asked which of the two tracks looked more like it could have been left by a machine, the children chose the regular track significantly more often than when asked the same question about animals. She argued that this

KEY TERM

Point-light walker displays
Displays resulting from the movements of small lights that are placed on the major joints and head of a person in dark-colored clothes who is filmed walking in the dark.

FIGURE 4.6
Some of the simple dot
patterns used to test
children's intuitions
about biological and non-
biological movement by
Lamsfuss (1995).

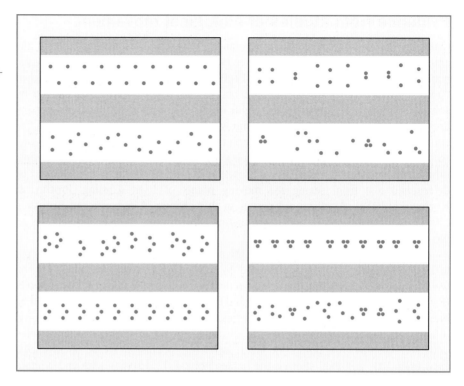

FIGURE 4.6
Some of the simple dot patterns used to test children's intuitions about biological and non-biological movement by Lamsfuss (1995).

indicated that children expect animals to move in unpredictable ways, regular as well as irregular, whereas they expect machines to produce highly predictable, regular movements. Adults and biology experts who took part in the study showed the same response pattern as the young children. Thus movement cues seem to be an important source of information about the biological/nonbiological distinction.

Evidence from knowledge of movements

Another way to assess young children's ability to make a conceptual distinction between biological and nonbiological entities is to see whether young children recognize that biological entities can move on their own. Massey and R. Gelman (1988) investigated 3- and 4-year-olds' understanding of self-initiated movements by showing them photographs of unfamiliar objects and asking them whether the objects could move up and down a hill on their own. The photographs depicted unfamiliar exemplars of two animate categories, mammals (e.g. tarsier, marmoset) and nonmammals (e.g. tarantula, lizard), and exemplars of three inanimate categories, statues of animals, wheeled objects (e.g. golf caddy, bicycle), and complex rigid objects (e.g. camera, exercise machine). Notice that the golf caddy and the bicycle can move down a hill on their own. This choice of categories was intended to pre-empt responding on the basis of shared perceptual features, such as linear vs. nonlinear edges. Only the animate objects could move *uphill* on their own.

Massey and Gelman introduced the children to the task by showing them a picture of a hill, and asking them whether photographs of some practice items (a man, a little girl, a fork, and a chair) could go up and down the hill "all by itself". The target pictures were then shown in a randomized order, and the child was asked to decide whether these objects, too, could go up and down the hill by themselves. Overall, the 3-year-olds made correct decisions about 78% of the photos, and the 4-year-olds made correct decisions about 90% of the photos. Even though the animals were not depicted as moving, and feet were seldom evident, the children's comments often focused on the feet and legs. For example (about an echidna) "It can move very slowly . . . it has these little legs. Where's the legs? Underneath?" and "It has feet and no shoes". [*Experimenter*: "Can you point to the feet?"] "I can't see them". In contrast, when feet were depicted for inanimate objects (e.g. the statues), the children denied that they were feet because they were not movement enabling. Most of the errors made by the 3-year-olds concerned the unfamiliar animate nonmammals, such as the tarantulas and lizards. The younger children who made errors with these pictures nonetheless appeared to be basing their decisions on the animate/inanimate distinction. For example, they would say that "bugs" (the spider) could not go up the hill by themselves because they were too little to go up such a big hill.

Similar results concerning young children's assumptions about self-generated movement have been reported by S. Gelman and Gottfried (1993; discussed in S. Gelman, Coley, & Gottfried, 1994). They showed 4-year-old children videotapes of animals, wind-up toys, and household objects moving across a surface. The animals and toys were deliberately chosen from unfamiliar categories, for example a chinchilla and a wind-up toy sushi (a kind of food). The household objects (e.g. a pepper mill) were all transparent, in order to see whether this would make it more difficult for the children to assume an internal cause for movement. In a control condition, all of the animals, toys, and objects were moved manually, and the hand doing the moving was clearly visible on the video.

The children were asked three critical questions about each animal and object. These were: Did a person make this move? Did something inside this make it move? Did this move by itself? Gelman and Gottfried found a clear distinction between the animals and the toys and objects in the children's responses to these questions. In the manual carrying condition, the children said that the animals moved on their own, whereas the toys and the objects were moved by a person. In the self-generated movement condition, the children attributed movement to internal mechanisms, even for the transparent objects. However, they were unable to explain how this movement occurred. Many children suggested the involvement of a supernatural agent, hidden persons, or invisible natural causes such as electricity. So even children as young as 4 are quite clear that animals are different; animals can move on their own, whereas toys and objects can only move with the help of an external agent. Finally, the concept of goal-directed movement is receiving increasing attention. Goal-directed movement is particularly informative about animacy, as we saw in the experiments with infants discussed in Chapters 2 and 3. Young children, too, treat goal-directed movement as a core property of living things. In an experiment by Opfer (see Gelman & Opfer, 2002), children aged 4, 5, 7, and 10 years observed blob-like shapes in motion. In one condition, the blobs were apparently pursuing a goal, whereas in another condition the same blobs made the same motions without a goal being present. From age 5, the children decided that the blobs in the goal-directed movement condition were living things. They attributed life, biological properties, and psychological properties to these blobs, describing them as jellyfish or bugs. In the control condition, where no goal was present, the blobs were not attributed any biological or psychological properties, and were described as clouds or meteors.

Evidence from the assumption of shared core properties

A third way of probing children's understanding of the biological/nonbiological distinction is to ask children to make judgments about similarities and differences in the "insides" and "outsides" of objects. "Insides" are more important than "outsides" for understanding the true nature of an object. For example, biological kinds share key internal properties (dogs and birds both have blood and bones), and these differ from the key internal properties of nonbiological kinds (chairs and doors may be wood or metal). To examine young children's understanding of the "inside–outside" distinction, S. Gelman and Wellman (1991) asked 3- and 4-year-old children to make a series of judgments about which pictured objects shared insides or outsides.

In their study, the children were asked "Which has the *same kinds of insides as x?*" (insides), or "Which looks *most like x*" (outsides). The pictures were always presented in threes, two of which were similar in their insides, and two in their outsides. For example, in the triad *orange, lemon, orange balloon*, the orange and the lemon had the same insides, whereas the orange and the balloon had the same outsides (appearance). In the triad *pig, piggy bank, cow*, the pig and the cow had the same insides, and the pig and the piggy bank had the same outsides. Gelman and Wellman found that both the 3-year-olds and the 4-year-olds performed at levels above chance, although the 4-year-olds were correct on more trials than the 3-year-olds (73% correct and 58% correct, respectively). Additional analyses showed that errors were not due to a reliance on similarity of appearance (a perceptual error, such as saying that the pig and the piggy bank had the same insides). Although such errors occurred, an equal number of errors were made on the basis of using insides to assess appearances (saying cows and pigs looked similar). Gelman and Wellman argued that what developed with age was the ability to deal with conflicts between insides and outer appearances (as in the piggy bank), rather than the ability to distinguish insides from outsides.

This conclusion is supported by the results of a study by R. Gelman and Meck (cited in R. Gelman, 1990). Gelman and Meck asked 3-, 4-, and 5-year-old children about the insides and outsides of animate and inanimate objects. The animates were person, elephant, cat, bird, and mouse; the inanimates were rock, ball, doll, and puppet. The children's answers showed a clear distinction between the animates and the inanimates. The animates were said to have blood, bones, and hearts inside, whereas the inanimates had hard stuff (rock, ball) or material and cotton inside (dolls and puppets). All the inanimates were said by some children to have "nothing" inside, whereas none of the animates were ever thought to contain "nothing". The children also tended to say that the animates would have different insides from outsides (the outsides included skin, hair, and eyes), whereas the inanimates were judged to have the same outsides as insides ("hard stuff", "material").

Concrete or abstract knowledge?

Although these responses appear to indicate that young children have fairly concrete ideas about the insides and outsides of animates and inanimates, Simons and Keil (1995) have argued that the basis of young children's judgments about insides and outsides are *abstract expectations* about the sorts of things that should differentiate the two. Rather than having concrete knowledge about which insides are appropriate for biological vs. nonbiological kinds, Simons and Keil argue that children have an abstract framework of *causal expectations* about natural kinds and artifacts that guides their search for concrete differences. To test their idea that younger children lack concrete knowledge about these differences, Simons and Keil conducted a series of experiments designed to examine the kinds of things that 3-, 4-, and 5-year-old children expected to be inside biological and nonbiological kinds. They argued that their hypothesis was consistent with the findings discussed above, as the tasks used by Wellman and S. Gelman and by R. Gelman and Meck actually required abstract knowledge about category membership.

In their experiments, Simons and Keil introduced children to a toy alligator, Freddy, who had the ability to "see right through the outsides of things into the inside". The children were told that Freddy had never been to Earth before, so he sometimes got confused about what was inside different sorts of things. The children were asked to help Freddy to decide which of a pair of things had the real insides. For example, in one study the children were shown two pictures of either a natural kind (such as a sheep, a frog, or an elephant) or an artifact (such as a clock, a telephone, or a bus). Each picture had a computer-generated inside depicted in its middle (Figure 4.7). One inside was always animal-like and the other was machine-like. For example, one of the two pictures of a sheep had cogs and gears inside it, and the other had some internal organs. The children were asked to show Freddy which picture showed "a sheep with real sheep insides". In another study, the children were just shown a single picture of a sheep without any depicted insides, and had to choose the appropriate insides from a set of three glass jars. One jar contained gears, dials, and wire (machine insides), a second contained the preserved abdominal organs of two cats (biological insides), and the third contained some small white rocks suspended in gelatin (representing a mixture of biological and nonbiological insides, or "aggregate insides"). The children were asked to point to the sort of insides that Freddy would see if he looked right through the outside of each animal or machine.

The findings across these different studies were quite consistent. The younger children had more difficulty in selecting the correct insides than the older children, but they did not err randomly. Instead, they showed a clear distinction between the natural kinds and the artifacts. Even the youngest children were highly accurate at selecting the correct insides for the machines, but for the natural kinds they tended to choose the aggregate insides as frequently as the biological insides. Simons and Keil argued that the younger children did not know what insides are like, but that they did know that some things were more likely to be inside animals than inside machines, and vice versa. These general ideas about what insides should look like were taken to indicate that even the youngest children had *abstract expectations*

FIGURE 4.7
The sheep with animal vs. machine insides. Adapted from Simons and Keil (1995). Copyright © 1995 Elsevier. Reprinted with permission.

about the sorts of things that can be inside animals and machines. However, they lacked experience with *concrete examples* of insides.

Another way of examining children's knowledge about **shared core properties** is to ask them to make *verbal* judgments about the internal properties of biological and nonbiological kinds. Without the aid of pictures, children are forced to reason about categories as abstract wholes. Gelman and O'Reilly (1988) asked 5- and 8-year-old children whether different biological and nonbiological kinds, such as dogs, horses, snakes, and tractors, had "the same kinds of stuff inside". These comparisons were made sequentially. The children were asked, in a random order: (1) whether all dogs had the same kinds of stuff inside; (2) whether dogs and horses had the same kinds of stuff inside; (3) whether dogs and snakes had the same kinds of stuff inside; and (4) whether dogs and tractors had the same kinds of stuff inside. Gelman and O'Reilly found that the children knew that animals had the same kinds of internal parts, and differentiated the animals from the artifacts such as the tractor. For example, they told the experimenters "Every dog has the same stuff unless they're missing a tail or something", and "All chairs aren't the same. Some of 'em have metal, some of 'em have wood. Some of 'em have iron".

Structure vs. function in categorizing natural kinds and artifacts

The research on children's intuitions about "insides" and "outsides" rests on the assumption that the shared core properties that are important for categorization are similar for biological and nonbiological kinds. However, Keil (1994) has pointed out that, while children may judge *shared structure* (insides and outsides) as important for categorizing living kinds, they may judge *shared function* as more important for categorizing artifacts. While shared function in artifacts does not necessitate similarity of appearance, shared structural similarity in animals frequently does. For example, the handles of bags can look quite different. They may be rigid or flexible, thick or thin, and long or short. Nevertheless, we do not categorize bags according to the appearance of their handles as long as these differences have no *functional* implications. Different varieties of rodent, however, may have tails that vary in appearance as much as the handles of bags (thick or thin, bushy or hairless, long or short), and yet these variations in appearance may be very important for classification purposes. Such differences do not necessarily affect the function of tails, but they may indicate important differences between species (e.g. squirrels vs. rats). In the case of animals, differences in the appearance of parts thus often imply other underlying differences, such as differences in specific genetic structure.

To test the idea that children judge *shared function* as important for categorizing artifacts and *shared structure* (insides and outsides) as important for categorizing living kinds, Pauen (1996a) created pictures of pairs of artifacts and pairs of biological kinds which shared a key part. Her idea was that the perceptual similarity of this key part could be manipulated across the pairs. The function of the key part was the same within each biological or nonbiological pair, but its appearance differed. For example, a pair of mice had either a wide tail or a narrow tail, and a pair of tape recorders had the same perceptual feature forming either a wide handle or a narrow handle (the two mice or tape recorders were otherwise identical in appearance; Figure 4.8).

Children aged 4–5 years old were shown the different matched quadruples of pictures, and were told a cover story about needing to tidy a room. Tidying required putting the pictures together "that were the same kind of thing", and the experimenter began this by separating the artifacts from the living kinds. An "expert" then appeared, and told the children that this was not the proper way to organize things, as some of the pairs of pictures that had been put together were "not really the same kind of thing". It was necessary to separate one of the two pairs (either the artifacts or the living kinds). The children were then asked which of the experimenter's pairs could be separated. Pauen found that the majority of the children said that the biological kinds could be separated rather than the artifacts. This supports the idea that perceptual dissimilarities are taken to specify different subcategories within biological kinds. The same does not appear to apply to artifacts, at least as long as the function of the dissimilar feature remains the same.

Evidence from studies of growth

A fourth way of examining children's understanding of the difference between biological and nonbiological kinds is to study their understanding of growth. As time goes by, biological kinds change in their appearance. They may grow bigger (a tree), they may change color (a tomato), and they may even change their appearance (a caterpillar changing into a butterfly). Artifacts do not alter as time goes by. They may become scuffed or worn, but they cannot grow, change their shape, or change their color.

In a series of studies examining young children's understanding of growth, Rosengren and colleagues have shown that children as young as 3 are aware of these distinctions. For example, Rosengren, Gelman, Kalish, and McCormick (1991) showed 3- and 5-year-old children pictures of baby animals and brand-new artifacts, and then asked them to choose which of two other pictures showed the animal or the artifact after it had been around for a very long time (Figure 4.9). In some example pairs the children had to make a choice between a picture showing the target the same size and a picture showing the target as larger (*same-size–bigger* condition), and in others they were given a choice between a picture showing the target the same size and a picture showing the target as smaller (*same-size–smaller* condition). In the case of the artifacts, the same-size pictures were drawn to show the passing of time, with cracks and scuff marks. The animals depicted included alligators, bears, and squirrels, and the artifacts included mugs, light bulbs, and televisions. If children understand that animals grow but that artifacts do not, then they should consistently select the picture of the artifact that is the same size in each type of pair, and they should never select the picture of the animal that is smaller.

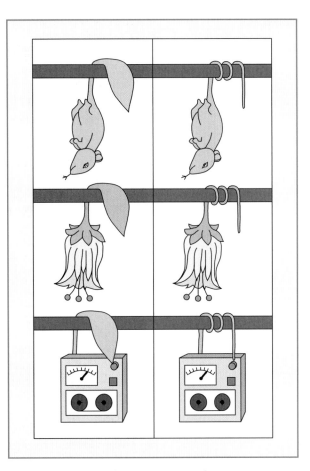

FIGURE 4.8
The same perceptual feature functioning as a mouse's tail, a plant stem, or a tape recorder's handle. From Pauen (1996a).

FIGURE 4.9
Examples of the artifact (top row) and natural kind (bottom row) stimuli used to study children's understanding of growth, From Rosengren et al. (1991). Reproduced with permission from Blackwell Publishing.

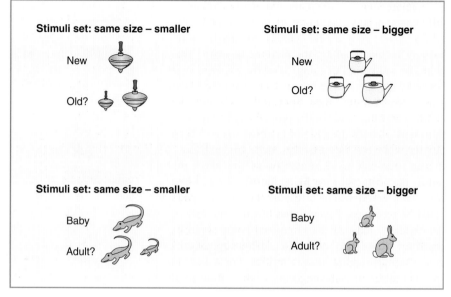

Rosengren et al. found that the 5-year-olds' performance on the task was at ceiling level for the animals, being 100% correct for the same-size–smaller comparison, and 97% correct for the same-size–bigger comparison. The 3-year-olds also performed at high levels in the animal task, at 78% correct for the same-size–smaller comparison, and 89% correct for the same-size–bigger comparison. Performance with the artifacts was also at ceiling for the older children. By contrast, the 3-year-olds performed at 78% correct for the artifacts in the same-size–smaller comparison, and were at chance in the same-size–bigger comparison. Both age groups thus expected animals to change in size over time, and knew that they got larger and not smaller. However, the 3-year-olds seemed uncertain as to whether artifacts grew over time, occasionally selecting the larger artifact rather than the aged and scuffed one in the same-size–bigger condition.

Rosengren's work suggests that the **principle of growth** is understood first in the biological domain. Even young children expect animals to undergo changes over time that do not affect their identity, understanding that biological kinds only grow bigger and not smaller over time. Artifacts are less well understood. Although an emerging understanding of the fact that artifacts do not grow with the passing of time was clear in these studies, the younger children did not seem to have fully grasped the kind of changes that artifacts actually undergo. Nevertheless, by the age of 5 the children were drawing a principled distinction between animate and inanimate patterns of transformations.

Analogy as a mechanism for understanding biological principles

Convergent evidence for the idea that 5- to 6-year-old children have grasped that the principle of growth applies only to biological kinds comes from a study by Inagaki and Hatano (1987). They were interested in how often children base their predictions about biological phenomena on analogies to people. As human beings are the

KEY TERM

Principle of growth
Understanding that animals undergo changes over time that do not affect their identity and that they only grow bigger and not smaller over time.

biological kinds best known to young children, and as we already know that analogical mappings can be made quite early in development (see Chapter 2), it seems plausible that children may use their biological knowledge about people to understand biological phenomena in other natural kinds. To study this question, Inagaki and Hatano asked 5- to 6-year-olds to make biological predictions about a person, a rabbit, a tulip, and a stone. The growth question was "Suppose someone is given a baby X and wants to keep it forever the same size because it's so small and cute. Can he or she do that?". Inagaki and Hatano found that 89% of the children said that he or she couldn't do that for the person, 90% said that he or she couldn't do that for the rabbit and 81% said that he or she couldn't do that for the tulip. Eighty per cent of the children also said that he or she could keep the stone the same size. The understanding that growth is inevitable for biological kinds thus appears to be present in this age group. Inagaki and Hatano also found that the children had some idea about the biological mechanism underlying inevitable growth. They tended to make statements like "No, we cannot keep the baby the same size forever, because he takes food. If he eats, he will become bigger and bigger and be an adult".

In fact, analogies to people appear to provide an important source of preschoolers' understanding of a variety of biological phenomena. Inagaki and Sugiyama (1988) asked 4-, 5-, 8-, and 10-year-olds a range of questions about various properties of eight target objects, including "Does x breathe?", "Does x have a heart?", "Does x feel pain if we prick it with a needle?" and "Can x think?". The target objects were people, rabbits, pigeons, fish, grasshoppers, trees, tulips, and stones. Prior similarity judgments had established that the target objects differed in their similarity to people in this order, with rabbits being rated as most similar and stones being rated as least similar. The children all showed a decreasing tendency to attribute the physiological properties ("Does x breathe") to the target objects as the perceived similarity to a person decreased. Apart from the 4-year-olds, very few children attributed physiological attributes to stones, tulips, and trees, and even 4-year-olds only attributed physiological properties to stones 15% of the time. A similar pattern was found for the mental properties ("Can x think?"). This study supports the idea that preschoolers' understanding of biological phenomena arises from analogies based on their understanding of people.

Evidence from studies of inheritance

Another biological principle is that living things transmit some of their properties to their offspring. Baby kangaroos have the properties of adult kangaroos, and baby goats have the properties of adult goats. Artifacts are different. They do not reproduce, and so they cannot transmit their properties. A coffee-pot cannot transmit its shape or color to a smaller coffee-pot, as coffee-pots are created by man. Young children appear to know certain facts about biological inheritance from quite an early age.

One important fact about inheritance is that "genes will out". If you are a baby kangaroo, you will grow up to be an adult kangaroo, even if you live with goats. S. Gelman and Wellman (1991) investigated young children's understanding of this essential fact by telling 4-year-olds about baby animals that were raised among members of a different species. For example, the children were shown a picture of a baby kangaroo, which looked like a shapeless blob, and were told that it was taken to a goat farm as a baby and raised with goats. A picture of the goat farm was then shown to the children, and they were asked how the baby kangaroo behaved when she grew up. For example, was she good at hopping or good at climbing? Did she

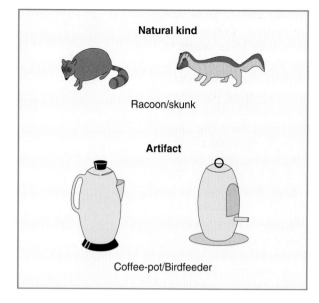

Natural kind

Racoon/skunk

Artifact

Coffee-pot/Birdfeeder

FIGURE 4.10

A racoon transformed to resemble a skunk, and a coffee-pot transformed into the birdfeeder. Two of the examples used by Keil (1989). © Massachusetts Institute of Technology, by permission of the MIT Press.

have a pouch? The children were almost all sure that the grown-up kangaroo was good at hopping, and had a pouch.

Another important fact about inheritance is that identity is maintained over transformations in appearance. For example, if a doctor bleaches the hair of a tiger and sews a mane onto its neck, it looks like a lion, but it is still really a tiger. If the same doctor paints the skin of a zebra to conceal its stripes, it is still a zebra. However, if a doctor saws off the handle and the spout of a coffee-pot, seals the top, and then attaches a bird's perch, a little window at the side and some birdseed, it not only looks like a birdfeeder, it can function as a birdfeeder (Figure 4.10). Keil (1989) has shown that younger children behave as though such transformations in appearance change identity for both the natural kinds (e.g. tiger–lion) and the artifacts (coffee-pot –birdfeeder), whereas older children (7- and 9-year-olds) accept identity changes only for the artifacts. Keil's explanation is that the older children are operating on the basis of a biological *theory*, in which natural kinds are identified by underlying essences and deep causal relations. In contrast, artifacts are identified by virtue of the functions that they serve by children of all ages.

For example, when the younger children were asked "After the operation, was the animal a tiger or a lion?" for the bleached tiger with a mane, they would say things like:

> *Child:* "*I think he changed it into a real lion.*"
> *Exp.:* "*OK. Even though it started out as a tiger, you think now it's a lion?*"
> *Child:* "*Um hmm.*"
> *Exp.:* "*Why do you say that?*"
> *Child:* "*Because a tiger doesn't have long hair on his neck.*"

Ina similar paradigm, older children would say things like:

> *Child:* "*It looks like a lion, but it's a tiger.*"
> *Exp.:* "*Why do you think it's a tiger and not a lion?*"
> *Child:* "*Because it was made out of a tiger.*"

By contrast, a typical response to the coffee-pot–birdfeeder example at all ages was:

> *Child:* "*I think they made it into a birdfeeder because it doesn't have a spout, and coffee-pots need spouts, and it doesn't have a handle . . . and how are you supposed to hold onto it if it doesn't have a handle?*"
> *Exp.:* "*Can it be a birdfeeder even though it came from a coffee-pot?*"
> *Child:* "*Yes*".

However, even the youngest children seemed to realize that transformations that appeared to change an object from a natural kind into an artifact or vice versa were impossible (e.g. porcupine to cactus). This fits with Keil's notion that biological knowledge is theory driven, with natural kinds being identified on the basis of deeper structural characteristics like being alive and having offspring. For example, the same young child who had argued that a tiger could be changed into a lion denied that a porcupine could be changed into a cactus:

> *Child:*   *"I think he's still really a porcupine."*
> *Exp.:*   *"And why do you say that?"*
> *Child:*   *"Because he started out like a porcupine."*
> *Exp.:*   *"Oh, OK. And even though he looks like a cactus plant, you think*
>   *he's really a porcupine?"*
> *Child:*   *"Um hmm."*
> *Exp.:*   *"OK. Can you think of any other reasons why he's still a*
>   *porcupine? Something you know about him?"*
> *Child:*   *[Shakes head]*

Finally, whereas some bodily characteristics such as eye color and gender are inherited and so cannot be changed or modified, others such as running speed and body weight can be modified by training or diet. Inagaki and Hatano (1993) investigated whether Japanese children aged 4 and 5 years were aware of such distinctions. For example, the children were told "A boy, Taro, has black eyes. He wants to make his eyes blue like a foreigner's (Caucasian). Can he do that?", and "Taro is a slow runner. He wants to be a fast runner. Can he do that?".

Inagaki and Hatano found that the children were very good at distinguishing between whether Taro could change his eye color if he wanted to (no), and whether Taro could become a faster runner if he wanted to (yes). For the modifiable characteristics, they gave explanations like "He can run fast if he practices more". Inagaki and Hatano concluded that even rather young children understand biological phenomena like inheritance. Perhaps the younger children studied by Keil demonstrated a poorer understanding of inheritance because Keil's modifications were based on non-natural transformations like surgery, which may not have been well-understood.

Evidence from studies of natural cause

Finally, we can examine children's understanding of natural cause, which is not quite the same as inheritance but taps the same underlying conception that features can be inborn. For example, a rabbit may not hop at birth, but the ability to hop is inborn. In contrast, the behavior of artifacts is not a result of natural cause. A ball can bounce, but this is because someone made it that way—the cause is man-made.

S. Gelman and Kremer (1991) asked 4- and 7-year-old children about the behaviors of a variety of natural kinds and artifacts (e.g. rabbits hopping, birds flying, leaves changing color, salt melting in water, balloons going up into the sky, cars going up hills, telephones ringing, guitars playing music, crayons drawing). For example, the children might be shown a picture of a rabbit, and told "See this? It's a rabbit. It hops". They were then asked "Why does it hop?". This open-ended question was followed by two direct questions, such as "Did a person make it hop?" and "Is there anything inside it that made it hop?". For the balloon, the equivalent questions would be "Did a person make it go up into the sky?" and "Is there anything inside it that made it go up into the sky?".

Gelman and Kremer found that the children tended to overgeneralize the involvement of man-made causes to the less familiar natural kinds. For example, human influence was attributed to the dissolution of salt in water (42%) but not to the color change of leaves (0%). However, the children were extremely accurate at identifying man-made causes in the case of the artifacts, knowing for example that guitars couldn't play music on their own. Although natural causes were ascribed to artifacts in some cases, the ascription of internal cause depended on the artifact. Internal causes were largely attributed to *self-sustained properties* of artifacts, such as a telephone ringing, a balloon going up into the sky, or a car going up a hill. Internal causes were seldom attributed to properties that were not self-sustained, such as guitars playing music or crayons drawing.

Gelman and Kremer concluded that children as young as four realized that natural causes existed independently of human influences. The children applied *different causal mechanisms* to natural kinds and to artifacts, and realized the importance of internal causes, which were applied to all of the natural kinds: "The leaf just makes itself change colors", "Rabbits are made to hop", "Flowers open up theirselves", "It grew that way". Gelman and Kremer argued that children can develop a core understanding of natural cause for objects, their properties, and their behaviors before knowing the precise origins of such natural causes. Also, children appreciate that causal mechanisms can be inferred rather than directly observed. As we will see, the idea that young children can go beyond information that can be directly observed and can grasp the significance of nonobvious properties for surface appearances is becoming increasingly important in explaining conceptual development. Conceptual development seems governed by children's beliefs about the world, beliefs which (as we have seen) are based on their direct experience of things moving, growing, dying, and having shared core properties.

THE REPRESENTATION OF CATEGORICAL KNOWLEDGE: A HISTORICAL PERSPECTIVE

Before we discuss relevant theories of conceptual development, however, we need to address the question of how conceptual knowledge is represented in memory. Despite the recent work in cognitive neuroscience discussed earlier, suggesting that conceptual knowledge is held multiply in modality-specific neural systems, the dominant view of conceptual representation is still that of amodal concepts, with adults organizing their semantic memories on the basis of *categorical knowledge*. At one time, it was thought that young children did not share this categorical bias. Instead, it was thought that young children organized conceptual knowledge in terms of **thematic relations**.

The role of thematic relations in organizing conceptual knowledge

The belief that young children organize semantic memory according to thematic associations arose from some experiments that suggested that younger children were more inclined to learn about thematic relationships than about categorical relationships. A thematic relationship is an associative one: dogs go with bones, and bees go with honey. As the young child tends to experience instances of different categories along with associated instances of other categories, the notion that categories are first represented in terms of thematic relations seemed quite plausible.

For example, a picture-sorting study carried out by Smiley and Brown (1979) found a preference for thematic over categorical relations in 4- and 6-year-old children. Only 10-year-olds appeared to prefer categorical relations. In Smiley and Brown's study, children were given a matching-to-sample task using triads of pictures. The triads used included *bee*, honey, butterfly; *dog*, bone, cat; and *bird*, nest, robin (Table 4.3). The children were asked "Which one goes best with the [bee], the [honey] or the [butterfly]?". Children who chose *honey* were scored as preferring a thematic match, and children who chose *bee* were scored as preferring a category match. Smiley and Brown found that the conceptual preferences of the younger children were consistently for the thematic match.

However, the instructions used in this task were very open-ended. More recent work has shown that even 1-year-olds are able to sort objects by category relations rather than by thematic relations when they are given more direct sorting instructions. For example, Bauer and Mandler (1989b) used the matching-to-sample task with 16- and 20-month-olds in a paradigm similar to that used by Smiley and Brown, except that triples of real objects were presented rather than triples of pictures. For example, the toddlers were shown a toothbrush, and were asked to select the correct match from another toothbrush (category relation) and some toothpaste (thematic relation). Alternatively, they might be shown a hammer and asked to make a choice from some pliers (category relation) and a nail (thematic relation). Bauer and Mandler changed the verbal instructions given to the children to "find the other one just like this one". They also checked that the thematic relations were familiar to their young subjects.

Under these circumstances, a preference for thematic selections was shown on only 26% of trials by the 16-month-olds, and 15% of trials by the 20-month-olds. Although it could be argued that the children were matching on the basis of object identity, a follow-up study using slightly older children found similar results, even though this time the triads were at the superordinate level (*monkey*, banana, bear; *hammer*, nail, pliers; *bed*, pillow, cot; this study was discussed earlier). Bauer and Mandler's work suggests that children organize semantic knowledge in the same way as adults do, in other words, on the basis of categorical relations. They only show a preference for thematic relations under the influence of certain task instructions.

However, the demonstration that very young children can organize conceptual knowledge according to *either* thematic *or* categorical relations again suggests that cognitive neuroscience studies will transform our understanding of conceptual development. If conceptual knowledge is represented in *both* the sensory systems first used to experience the concept and associated neural areas that represent the conjunctions of particular sets of sensory information, then knowledge about both categorical and thematic relations between concepts would be developing at the same time.

Children, like adults, can organize conceptual knowledge according to categorical knowledge when required. The next question is how this categorical knowledge is represented. Work on adult concepts

TABLE 4.3	Examples of the stimulus sets used by Smiley and Brown (1979)	
Standard	**Thematic**	**Taxonomic**
Bee	Honey	Butterfly
Cow	Milk	Pig
Crown	King	Hat
Spider	Web	Grasshopper
Dog	Bone	Cat

has suggested that at least two sets of features could be used to store conceptual information in semantic memory. Concepts could be coded on the basis of their *defining features* or on the basis of their *characteristic features*.

Representing categories in terms of characteristic vs. defining features

A characteristic feature is a feature that is typically associated with a concept. For example, a characteristic feature of grandmothers is that they are old. A defining feature is a feature that applies to 100% of all the instances of a concept. A defining feature of a grandmother is that she is the mother of your parent. One possibility that has interested developmental psychologists is that children initially represent concepts in terms of *characteristic features*, which tend to be perceptually salient. As they learn more about the world, children pass through a period of conceptual reorganization, developing conceptual representations that take account of *defining features*. According to this hypothesis, the basis of categorization changes developmentally from being based on well-known characteristic features to being based on more sophisticated defining ones. This hypothesized reorganization was called the "**characteristic-to-defining shift**" (Keil, 1991). Earlier investigators have talked in similar general terms of a "concrete to abstract" shift in conceptual development, a "perceptual to conceptual" shift, and a "holistic to analytic" shift (see Keil, 1987).

One way to examine the possibility that children's conceptual representations pass through a "characteristic-to-defining" shift is to pit characteristic features against defining ones, and then to examine whether younger children prefer characteristic features and older children prefer defining ones. Keil and Batterman (1984) used this technique with 5-, 7-, and 9-year-old children. They told the children pairs of stories about familiar concepts like *uncle*, *robber*, and *island*. The first of the stories in each pair had no information about the characteristic features of being an uncle, a robber, or an island, but did include a defining feature. The second story in each pair had no information about the defining features of being an uncle, a robber, or an island, but included a number of characteristic features. The children were then asked "Could [x] be an uncle/robber/island?".

Examples of the "defining feature" stories include:

Suppose your mommy has all sorts of brothers, some very old and some very, very young. One of your mommy's brothers is so young that he's only 2 years old. Could that be an uncle?

This very friendly and cheerful woman came up to you and gave you a hug, but then she disconnected your toilet bowl and took it away without permission and never returned it. Could she be a robber?

Examples of the "characteristic feature" stories include:

This man your daddy's age loves you and your parents and loves to visit and bring presents, but he's not related to your parents at all. He's not your mommy or daddy's brother or sister or anything like that. Could that be an uncle?

This smelly, mean old man with a gun in his pocket came to your house one day and took your colored television set because your parents didn't want it anymore and told him he could have it. Could that be a robber?

Keil and Batterman reported that the 5-year-olds relied on characteristic features in making their judgments, whereas the 9-year-olds relied on defining features. Although the children did not shift at the same time for all concepts, the younger children usually said that the "characteristic feature" stories were instances of the concept, while the older children chose the "defining feature" stories. Keil and Batterman concluded that the children seemed to represent the concepts in different ways at different ages. Of course, this could reflect increasing knowledge. As children learn more about defining features, these could replace characteristic features as the basis for representation.

However, cognitive neuroscience offers a different interpretation. The evidence for **distributed mental representations** means that concepts and categories are represented in the brain in terms of multiple sensory modalities, with additional activation in neural association areas recording the conjunction of those particular modalities at each point in time that instances were previously experienced. These distributed representations would mean that aspects of experimental situations would be crucial for guiding which particular conjunctions were deemed relevant. As real-world experience increases, children's "robber" concept might still incorporate aspects like "looking mean" and "having a gun", but the fact that a parent had told this person that they could take the television would activate conjunctions associated with charity and giving away old things. The evidence for multimodal representational systems is growing, and is a developmentally appealing one, as discussed earlier. Lakoff (1986) argued that the properties that are relevant for the characterization of human categories do not exist objectively in any case. Instead, what we *understand* as properties depends on our interactive functioning with our environment. Thus our theories about the world are important for our decisions about what is categorically similar. This notion has recently been incorporated into developmental psychology by reference to the importance of "essences" for conceptual understanding.

CATEGORIES AND BELIEFS ABOUT THE WORLD: "ESSENCES" AND NAÏVE THEORIES

Some researchers in adult cognitive psychology have argued that category membership is defined not only in terms of characteristic and defining features, similarity to prototypes etc., but in terms of "essences". One of the major proponents of this view is Medin (1989), whose view can be summarized by the following: "People act as if things (e.g. objects) have essences or underlying natures that make them the thing that they are" (p. 1476). In other words, people have implicit assumptions about the structure of the world, and about the underlying nature of categories, and these beliefs are represented in the categories that they develop. This view is sometimes called "psychological **essentialism**". According to this view, categories are not discovered via the passive observation of correlations between features. Rather, they are created by "carving nature up at its joints".

KEY TERMS

Distributed mental representations
Concepts and categories are represented in the brain in terms of multiple sensory modalities and therefore highly distributed networks of neurons.

Essentialism
Implicit assumptions or beliefs that may be innately determined about the structure of the world that guide cognitive development and categorization by setting important limits or constraints on the information that can and cannot be learned.

We can illustrate how category membership can go beyond clusters of characteristic features by returning to our example of birds. It is true that feathers reliably co-occur with wings, with flight, and with light body weight, and that these co-occurrences help to distinguish the category "bird". But adults also have a "theory" about why these features go together. This theory involves the causal relations necessary to enable flight. Adults believe that low body weight, feathers, and wings facilitate flight, thereby imposing a degree of *causal necessity* on the covariation of these features in birds. This tendency to create causal explanatory constructs may not be limited to adults. Children, too, may create intuitive theories to understand conceptual structure. These "theories" would correspond to core sets of interconnected beliefs about category membership.

The essentialist bias

Such sets of causal beliefs about the co-occurrence of core properties apply to a great many concepts (although not all). They apply particularly to categories of natural kinds, such as animals, birds, and plants. A number of developmental psychologists have suggested that children's growing understanding of the category of natural kinds is partly governed by their implicit appreciation of the causal/explanatory relations that explain featural clusterings within this category (e.g. Carey & Spelke, 1994; S. Gelman et al., 1994; Keil, 1994). For example, S. Gelman et al. suggested that young children have an essentialist "bias", and that this "bias" constrains the ways in which they reason about natural kinds. Their early understanding of living things is theory-like, leading them to search for invisible causal mechanisms to explain object actions (Gelman, 2004).

Gelman (2004) argues that psychological essentialism may be an early cognitive "bias". She suggests that young children have an early tendency to search for hidden, nonobvious features that make category members similar. Some of the evidence reviewed in this chapter is consistent with Gelman's idea that even young children go beyond observable features when developing biological concepts. For example, young children appear to assume that living things maintain their identity over superficial transformations and transmit some of their properties to their offspring. Evidence discussed in previous chapters also supports her idea, as we have seen that children have an inherent tendency to search for causal explanations of phenomena in their everyday worlds, and that they show an early ability to go beyond surface features to focus on structural characteristics (e.g. when reasoning by analogy; see Chapter 2). Children also prioritize causality in deciding which properties members of a category should share. One appealing aspect of essentialism is that it does not propose dichotomous development, for example from perceptual to conceptual categories, or from concrete to abstract categories. Rather it assumes that categories have two distinct, interrelated levels: the level of observable reality and the level of explanation and cause. The level of explanation and cause is essentially a placeholder for as-yet unknown properties of concepts.

However, a strong version of the "psychological essentialism" theory argues that the theories and core principles that guide essentialism are *innate*. This innate knowledge is thought to guide cognitive development by setting important limits (or "constraints") on the information that can and cannot be learned (e.g. Carey & R. Gelman, 1991). The origins of this innate knowledge are not well-specified. Another intriguing proposal is that in addition to conceiving of causality as either mechanistic or intentional, young children conceive of it as "vitalistic" (Inagaki & Hatano, 2004).

Children assume a "vitalistic causality", namely a vital life force taken from food and water which makes humans and other animals active. This vital power explains target biological phenomena such as growth and health. As we understand more about the ways in which perceptual structure in itself gives rise to conceptual assumptions (for example, our tendency to experience moving geometric shapes as being animate or goal-directed depending on aspects of the perceptual display; see Chapter 2), it may turn out that the learning mechanisms used by our perceptual systems are themselves the source of these core principles and causalities. Using statistical learning algorithms, which may be very complex (e.g. explanation-based learning and causal Bayes nets), learning about the perceptual structure of the world may *in itself* yield the levels of explanation and cause. Hence the basic learning mechanisms used by the brain may support the patterns of early conceptual development that have been documented in this chapter, giving rise to the patterns of inductive inference currently described by "cognitive biases" such as essentialism, vitalism, and constraints on learning. Once language is acquired, then children can use language to help to organize concepts and categories, and to reflect on hidden features that may make category members similar. The role of explanation in concepts and intuitive theories is discussed at length by Keil (2006), who also foregrounds the importance of causal explanations in cognitive development (see Chapter 6).

CONCEPTUAL CHANGE IN CHILDHOOD?

Although we have reviewed a large amount of evidence indicating that young children have rich conceptual structures that they have abstracted from their everyday experience of the world, this does not mean that they never experience conceptual change. The level of knowledge that can be abstracted from perceptual causal information about different entities has in many cases been transcended by modern physics and biology. By and large, such information must be taught. It seems likely that conceptual change in such instances (for example, from medieval theories of motion to Newtonian theories; see Kaiser, Proffitt, & McCloskey, 1985; Chapter 6) depends on tuition.

However, it is unclear whether taught knowledge really causes *conceptual change* (see also Chapter 6). Some developmental psychologists have argued that children do experience spontaneous conceptual change, without direct tuition. When such conceptual change occurs, then new principles are said to emerge that "carve the world at different joints" (see Carey & Spelke, 1994, for a fuller discussion). However, such apparent change may result from incremental knowledge acquisition. This could change the relative activation strength of various core features of particular concepts, suggesting to the external observer that new principles have emerged. For example, at some point children may need to distinguish plants as biological entities that are essentially similar to animals, even though plants differ markedly from animals in terms of their capacity for self-generated movement. It seems likely that incremental real-world experience is sufficient for this kind of distinction.

Carey has argued that conceptual change in childhood (and in science) depends on children and scientists making *mappings* between different domains. Such mappings entail relating objects in one system (e.g. people) to objects in another (e.g. plants). If such a mapping is created, then the principles that govern children's understanding of people can be applied to their understanding of plants. We have already seen that children use analogical mappings from people to decide whether animals and plants can be kept small and cute forever or whether they would feel pain if pricked by a needle (see the work of Inagaki and her colleagues discussed earlier in this chapter). Furthermore, there is a growing body of work which demonstrates that analogical mappings are used by children as young as 3 in other areas of cognition such as causal reasoning (Goswami & Brown, 1989), physical reasoning (Pauen & Wilkening, 1997), and reasoning about natural kinds and artifacts (Goswami & Pauen, 2006). The availability of the mapping mechanism proposed by Carey is thus well-documented.

Carey (1985) has also argued the case for the importance of analogical mappings to conceptual change, using the domain of biology as an example (although see Kuhn, 1989). Carey has argued that preschool children's understanding of biological phenomena differs radically from that of older children. Her data suggest that younger children base their understanding of animals on their understanding of people, projecting behavioral and psychological properties onto other animals according to how similar these animals are to human beings. For example, the attribution of the property "breathes" was made to humans by 100% of the 4-year-olds studied by Carey, to aardvarks by 78% of the children, to dodos by 67%, and to stinkbugs by 33%. The property "breathes" was never attributed to plants. Only older children showed a coalescence of the concepts *animal* and *plant* into the new concept, *living thing*. Carey thus argued that children's understanding of biology emerged *out of* their understanding of people. It is unclear whether this coalescence should be termed conceptual change. The tendency to attribute physiological and mental properties to other objects on the basis of their similarity to people has also been termed a "personification analogy" (Inagaki & Hatano, 1987; Inagaki & Sugiyama, 1988).

Not everyone agrees with Carey's views on biological development (e.g. Atran, 1994; Keil, 1989; Kuhn, 1989; and see Wellman & S. Gelman, 1992, for a useful review). A different way of conceiving of conceptual development can be derived from the notion of foundational domains, summarized by Wellman and Gelman (1998), and adopted in this book. Wellman and Gelman pointed out that young children are probably developing several alternative conceptual frameworks *at the same time*. Rather than developing a monolithic understanding of the world, infants and young children are probably developing distinct yet interlinked conceptual frameworks to describe the "foundational domains" of biology, psychology, and physics. In fact, this would be a natural consequence of representing knowledge via distributed representations. Many concepts will of course be represented in *more than one* of these foundational frameworks. For example, persons are psychological entities, biological entities, *and* physical entities. These foundational domains will then engender, shape, and constrain other conceptual understandings. At the same time, children will use at least two levels of analysis within any framework, one that captures surface phenomena (mappings based on attributes) and another that penetrates to deeper levels (mappings based on relations). The need to compare, share, merge, and create new conceptions is likely to be encouraged by the assumptions of surrounding children and adults, by the technology of the culture, and by systematic teaching received in school. It is not clear that these mechanisms of sharing and merging conceptual understandings across foundational domains are the same as the kind of conceptual change envisaged by Carey and Spelke (1994) however. Although new conceptions and understandings will be created, these may not "carve the world at different joints". These are empirical questions, and can be investigated by cognitive neuroscience studies. The issue of whether development is ever characterized by conceptual change is discussed further in Chapters 9 and 10, for example in relation to conceptual change in understanding number.

SUMMARY

Data from cognitive neuroscience seem particularly likely to impact the field of conceptual development. Many of the historically important debates about conceptual development, such as the potential developmental primacy of the basic level of categorization, the distinction between perceptual versus conceptual categories, and the role of "constraints" on learning (the core principles that govern induction), may turn out to be natural products of the way that our neural architecture activates, represents, and stores knowledge about the world of natural kinds and artifacts. Connectionist modelers have already demonstrated that concepts have distributed representations (e.g. Quinn, 2002). However, connectionist models can only work with features that are thought to be used by the infant brain when attending to aspects of the stimulus. A deeper understanding of how the brain processes perceptual information may show that primary features additional to those built into existing connectionist simulations are important for induction. These additional features would thereby also be important for early representations of conceptual structure, and as domain knowledge increased and other features became salient, incremental learning could be responsible for apparent conceptual change.

The sheer variety of studies discussed here on different aspects of conceptual development demonstrate the complexity of the knowledge that is built up by the infant and by the young child. Three- and 4-year-olds already make assumptions about shared core properties such as "insides" and "outsides", as well as about other unobservable features of entities such as natural kinds. Again, this may originate in perceptual knowledge. Even relatively simple perceptual mechanisms, such as whether a movement originates from a biological or a nonbiological entity, yield rich information about animacy and agency (see also Chapter 3). The study discussed by Arterberry and Bornstein (2001) showed that babies of 3 months can make distinctions between the motion of vehicles versus the motion of animals on the basis of very impoverished cues. As we will see in Chapter 7, cognitive neuroscience studies with adults show that mirror neurons are tuned to respond only to biological motion (Tai, Scherfler, Brooks, Sawamoto, & Castiello, 2004). As more discoveries of this nature are reported, the many important observations about conceptual development yielded by behavioral work may fit into a clearer "bigger picture" about how young children develop conceptual knowledge about different aspects of their experience (natural kinds, artifacts, actions, events), and about why experimenters observe behavioral effects such as the apparent shift in categorization from characteristic to defining features.

CHAPTER 5

CONTENTS

Language acquisition

So far in this book, we have considered cognitive development largely independently of language. This is not accidental. Language acquisition has traditionally been studied separately from cognition, and as we saw in Chapter 4, there is strong commitment to the idea that basic concepts are preverbal. Another reason for the traditional distinction between language and thought was that language acquisition seemed such a remarkable feat for the infant brain that it was assumed that special capacities must be at work. These capacities were thought to be distinct from the capacities underpinning broader cognitive development. For example, it was suggested that infants were born equipped with a "**language acquisition device**" or **LAD**, which had the special job of acquiring the spoken language of whichever culture the infant entered. Chomsky, the original proponent of the LAD, argued (and still argues) that infants are born with innate knowledge of the general rules that all languages obey, along with innate knowledge of permitted variations (e.g. Chomsky, 1957). Hence an infant can as readily acquire a language that makes heavy use of the passive tense (The boy was bitten by the dog), like Sesotho, as a language that does not, like English (The dog bit the boy; see Bates, Devescovi, & Wulfeck, 2001).

More recently, it has become clear that language acquisition depends on the same kinds of learning mechanisms that underpin broader cognition. We have already seen in Chapters 1 to 4 that infants acquire a remarkable amount of information simply by perceiving things in the world. In the case of the physical, conceptual, and psychological worlds, the primary sense that has been studied is vision. In the case of language, infants acquire a remarkable amount of information simply by listening to what the people around them say. Infants use the same abilities to acquire language that they use to acquire knowledge about the physical and psychological worlds, namely associative learning, learning by imitation, tracking statistical dependencies, tracking conditional probabilities, and making analogies. Auditory perceptual information is replete with statistical cues to the **phonotactic patterns of language** (the sounds that make up the language, and the orders in which they can be combined), cues to word boundaries (e.g. speech rhythm), and cues to the emotional content of speech (e.g. stress, volume). As in the visual world of objects and events, information gained passively is rapidly supplemented by information gained through direct action by the infant, for example by imitation. In the case of language, infants act by babbling and trying out sound combinations for themselves, and by attempting to initiate verbal interactions—in other words, by attempting to communicate. Children also use analogies to create novel utterances, and to extract grammatical structures.

Social interaction is fundamental to natural language learning, and plays as important a role as the statistical patterning described above (Kuhl, 2007). The importance of making shared meaning probably explains why no-one has yet managed to build a computational system that can learn language (Kuhl, 2004). When learning a natural language, auditory statistical information is augmented by other kinds of perceptual information that convey meaning and reference. Parents usually

KEY TERMS

Language acquisition device (LAD)
An innate device, first suggested by Chomsky, with the special job of acquiring the language the infant encounters.

Phonotactic patterns of language
Speech sounds and relationships among speech sounds used to make lawful words that make up spoken language.

"Motherese" or infant-directed speech (IDS) is an exaggerated prosodic register that emphasizes word and phrase boundaries, often with target words receiving primary stress at the end of the utterance. "What a pretty DAISY!".

talk to babies about things that are happening right now, in the direct visual field, and the situational context often makes the meaning of their vocalizations highly predictable. The facial expressions of interlocuters, their gestures and touch, the things that they are attending to as they speak, as well as the current situation that everyone is in (e.g. a meal time) all convey cues concerning what is being spoken about. The learning task for the baby is further facilitated by two things. One is the use by caretakers of a special register to speak to babies, called "**motherese**" or **infant-directed speech (IDS)**. IDS is an exaggerated prosodic register that emphasizes word and phrase boundaries, and appears to make the segmentation of the speech stream easier for the infant. The second is the apparently inborn propensity for attachment, social interaction, and communication described in Chapter 3. Infants learn language because of social interactions with partners, and not simply because of exposure to sequences of sounds. The same factors that underpin the emergence of psychological understanding, for example the capacity for joint visual attention, the appreciation of communicative intent, and the desire to imitate, also underpin the acquisition of human language.

PHONOLOGICAL DEVELOPMENT

Although you may be a fluent speaker of English, and may be able to get by in a couple of other languages, you are unlikely to speak all of the 6000 plus languages of the world with fluency. In fact, if someone speaks to you in Chinese, the context might give you a general idea of what they are talking about but you would probably have no way of understanding the sounds that they are making as individual words. For example, if a Chinese person holding a map, carrying a camera, and close to the Tower of London stops you with a questioning air, they are probably asking you directions. You can infer this from the situational context and perhaps from global cues such as whether their utterances end by rising in a questioning fashion. However, you probably have no idea of the individual words in the utterance, because you have no idea of the patterns of sound combinations that constitute words in Chinese. This type of learning is phonological learning. It has two aspects. One is to learn the sounds and combinations of sounds that are permissible in a particular language, so that the brain can develop phonological representations of the sound structure of individual words. The second is to learn to produce these words yourself. Both types of learning undergo protracted development. Although children are usually fluent comprehenders and producers of spoken language by the age of 5 years, new challenges (such as learning to read) require further development of phonological representations (see Chapter 10).

Categorical perception

Early experimental research on phonological development focused on when infants learn the **phonemes** that make up their particular language. "Phoneme" is the short-hand term used for the individual elements that make up words in languages. For example, words like *bat* and *bit* differ by one phoneme, the middle phoneme. *Bat* and *pat* differ by one phoneme, the initial phoneme, and *bat* and *back* differ by one phoneme, the final phoneme. The notion of a phoneme is an abstraction from the physical stimulus, which is why it is a short-hand term (e.g. the "a" phoneme in *bat* and *back* is not exactly the same sound), but it is a useful term for explanatory purposes. Languages are based on two types of phoneme: consonant phonemes and vowel phonemes. These are selected from a repertoire of around 600 consonants and 200 vowels that are distinctive to the human brain. In practice, most languages use a very small set of all the possible phonemes, for example English uses about 40. An important job for the infant learner, therefore, is to learn the phonemes or speech sounds of their native language. This has been a fertile area of research. It is now apparent that infants come to learn the phonemes of their native language very quickly indeed, within the first year of development. At the same time, they lose their ability to distinguish the phonemes of other languages.

Phoneme perception is categorical in adults. In terms of the actual physical sound, there are many similar but nonidentical sounds that we would recognize as the phoneme /b/, and many other similar but nonidentical sounds that we would recognize as the phoneme /p/. However, there is a measurable point at which sounds that are highly similar physically stop being perceived as /b/ and begin being perceived as /p/. This is called categorical perception. For /b/ versus /p/, the brain is exposed to a physical continuum of sound, the vocal cords are vibrating to produce the sound, and the airflow of the sound is obstructed at the lips to produce a "plosive" (for plosives like /b/ and /p/, this obstruction is complete). However, the brain imposes a category of /b/ sounds, and a category of /p/ sounds. At some degree of voicing (i.e. degree of vibration of the vocal cords, which will vary in physical terms with the age, gender, and communicative intent of the speaker), the adult brain decides that it is no longer hearing "bat", but is hearing "pat". How quickly does the infant brain reach a similar conclusion?

In a classic study, Eimas and colleagues investigated the categorical perception of phonemes in infants aged 1 and 4 months (Eimas, Siqueland, Jusczyk, & Vigorito, 1971). The infants began the experiment by sucking a dummy to a background sound, for example the syllable "ba" being repeated over and over again. The rate of sucking gradually declined. The experimental question was whether the rate of sucking would increase to a new syllable "pa". Six stimuli were used over the experiment, each varying in voice onset time by 20 ms. The voice onset time values were −20, 0, 20, 40, 60, and 80 ms. For an adult, the +20 ms stimulus was heard as "ba", and the +40 ms stimulus as /pa/. Hence for an adult, the change in voice onset time (VOT) of 20 ms from +20 ms to +40 ms signaled a novel perceptual event: the category boundary between /b/ and /p/ had been crossed. Eimas et al. (1971) reported that both groups of infants showed significant dishabituation in suck rate to the change from the +20 ms stimulus to the +40 ms stimulus. In contrast, changes of the same absolute magnitude (−20 ms to 0 ms VOT, and 60 ms to 80 ms VOT) did not lead to dishabituation in suck rate for either age group. Clearly, the month-old infants had already developed categorical perception for these sounds.

In another classic study, Werker and Tees (1984) showed that young infants had categorical perception for phonemes in other languages as well. Two contrasts were compared, the English contrast /ba/–/da/, and the native-American contrast /ki/–/qi/. Infants were rewarded for turning their heads when the sound changed from /ba/ to /da/, or from /ki/ to /qi/. Adult English listeners had to press a button when they heard the sound change. Werker and Tees found that English babies aged 6–8 months and native-American adults could perceive both contrasts. However, most English adults tested could not perceive the distinction between /ki/ and /qi/. Older English babies were then tested, aged 8–10 months and 10–12 months. At 8–10 months, 57% of the infants could discriminate the non-native /ki/–/qi/ contrast (8 infants out of 14). By 10–12 months, only 1 baby out of 10 showed categorical perception of this contrast. Comparable patterns were found for Hindi contrasts (Figure 5.1). Werker and Tees (1984) were also able to test a couple of native-American infants aged 10–12 months, who had no difficulty in distinguishing the /ki/–/qi/ contrast. A longitudinal study following the same babies from 6 to 12 months of age confirmed these cross-sectional patterns. Werker and Tees concluded that the ability to discriminate non-native phonetic contrasts declines during the first year of life.

Further work has established that the physical changes where languages place phonetic boundaries are not random (Kuhl, 1986). General auditory perceptual abilities seem to influence where these "basic cuts" are made, and in fact other mammals such as chinchillas seem to partition sounds in the same ways. This probably explains why infants are sensitive to the acoustic boundaries that separate phonetic categories in all human languages from birth. The choice of sounds that comprise the phonetic repertoire of the languages of the world capitalize on natural auditory discontinuities (Kuhl, 2004). The important point is that these basic cuts are rather rough, so further learning is required. During development, infants need to learn the locations of the phonetic boundaries that are important for their language.

FIGURE 5.1
Proportion of infant subjects from three ages and various backgrounds reaching criterion on Hindi and Salish contrasts. From Werker and Tees (1984). Copyright © 1984 Elsevier. Reprinted with permission.

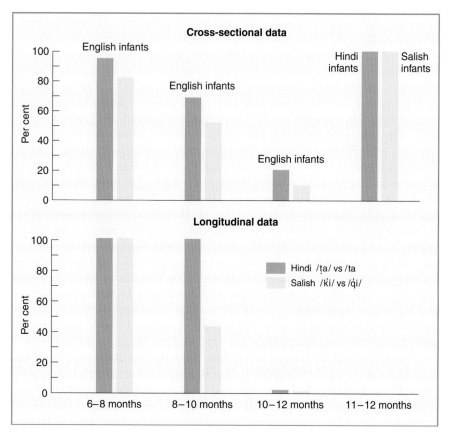

As they continually hear the sounds of, say, English rather than Hindi, or English rather than Chinese, their brains specialize in the sounds of English. Language-specific patterns of listening develop, so that infants become highly adept at discriminating phonemes in their native language, and lose the ability to discriminate phonemes in other languages. They develop "prototypes" of the phoneme categories special to their language (Kuhl, 1991). This specialization is well under way by 1 year of age, leading to the idea that there is a sensitive period for language acquisition.

Just as in other areas of development, the formation of prototypes depends on statistical learning. Prototypes are generalized representations of a category, to which subsequently encountered stimuli can be compared. For language, we can think of a prototypical /p/, or a prototypical /b/. Other sounds that we would categorize as /p/ or /b/, even if they are relatively distant from the prototype, are called allophones. In the visual world, infants track conditional probabilities to create prototypes. They learn which visual features in a given stimulus typically occur together, and they use perceptual information about correlational structure to construct the prototype. Exactly the same mechanisms appear to govern phonological learning. The infants track the distributional properties of the sounds in the language that they hear, and register the acoustic features that regularly co-occur. These relative distributional frequencies then yield phonetic categories.

Once a prototype is formed, we know that nonprototypical members of a category are perceived as more similar to the category prototype than they are to each other. This occurs even though the actual physical distance between the stimuli may be equal. This effect is called the "**magnet effect**". If magnet effects reflect experience with specific languages, then babies should only show the magnet effect for prototypes from their native language. This possibility was tested by Kuhl and colleagues (Kuhl, Williams, Lacerda, Stevens, & Lindblom, 1992). They played 6-month-old English-learning versus Swedish-learning babies vowel sounds from both languages. The babies heard prototype vowels from either English (/i/) or Swedish (/y/) as a background stimulus. They were then trained to turn their heads when the prototype changed into a variant, that is, when the prototype changed into an acoustically similar but not identical sound that would still be classified as /i/ or /y/ by an adult. Kuhl and colleagues found that the English and Swedish babies behaved differently. The English babies perceived the English vowel variants as different from the prototype on 33% of trials, whereas the Swedish babies perceived the Swedish vowel variants as different from the prototype on 34% of trials. For the non-native prototype, performance was 49% and 44%, respectively. Hence the English babies grouped together the English vowel variants and the Swedish babies grouped together the Swedish vowel variants. Vowel variants from the non-native language were not grouped perceptually in the same way. The prototypical sounds in each language were functioning as a kind of "magnet" for perceptually similar sounds. However, what was experienced as perceptually similar depended on the input. The distributional properties of the sounds comprising English versus Swedish respectively determined which sounds were perceptually assimilated to the prototype. Kuhl et al. (1992) had demonstrated that linguistic experience alters phonetic perception by the age of 6 months.

Finally, social interaction plays a critical role in perceptual learning. As noted earlier, infants learn language because they are motivated to interact with partners and to communicate. They do not learn language simply because they are passively exposed to sequences of sounds. The core role of social interaction in language learning was demonstrated in an ingenious study by Kuhl and colleagues

KEY TERM

Perceptual magnet effect
Prototypical sounds in a language that act as a "magnet" for perceptually similar sounds so as to perceive such sounds as belonging in the same category.

(Kuhl, Tsao, & Liu, 2003). This study exploited the decline in sensitivity to the phonetic units of non-native languages that occurs between 6 and 12 months of age. Kuhl et al. (2003) exposed 9-month-old American infants to native Mandarin Chinese speakers, and then tested their speech perception for Mandarin contrasts. The infants experienced around 5 hours of spoken Mandarin during play sessions with an adult Mandarin speaker, who entertained them with toys and books. A control group of 9-month-olds experienced identical play sessions, but the language used was English. The adult entertainers spoke in motherese, made frequent eye contact with the infants, and used their names during the sessions, which on average exposed the infants to 33,000 Mandarin syllables. At test, the infants were given a Mandarin Chinese phonetic contrast that does not occur in English. The group exposed to Mandarin Chinese was significantly more sensitive to the critical contrast, performing as well as infants tested in Taiwan who had heard Mandarin for their entire lives.

Kuhl et al. (2003) then replicated the study using videotapes of the Mandarin Chinese adults. A new group of 9-month-olds got the same amount and quality of Mandarin Chinese input from a film. The toys and books were visible on screen and the adults appeared to be looking directly at the infants, as the films were taken from the infants' perspective. Analysis of the language used showed that on average 50,000 Mandarin Chinese syllables were heard over the course of the videos. The infants were very interested in the videos, touching the screen and attending avidly to the entertaining adults. However, when their sensitivity to the critical Mandarin Chinese contrast was tested at the end of the experiment, they were indistinguishable from the control infants tested in the first experiment (Figure 5.2). Watching and

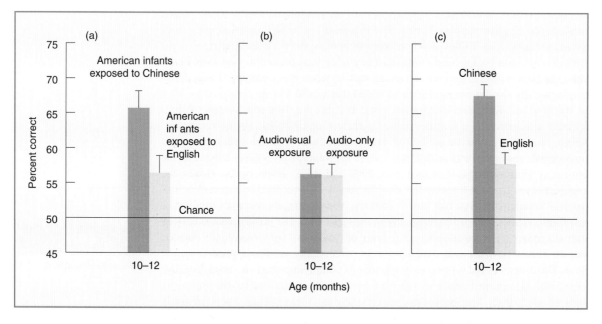

FIGURE 5.2
The results of Kuhl et al.'s (2003) study. (a) Effects of live foreign-language intervention in infancy.
(b) Mandarin Chinese foreign-language exposure in the absence of a live person (audio-visual or audio only) shows no learning. (c) The same Mandarin speech discrimination tests on monolingual Mandarin-learning and English-learning infants. From Kuhl, Tsao, and Liu (2003). Copyright © 2003 by the National Academy of Sciences. Reproduced with permission.

listening to films of foreign-language material did not result in any measurable perceptual learning. Kuhl and colleagues argued that the live speakers provided many subtle social cues that facilitated language acquisition. For example, the speaker's gaze tended to focus on the toys or pictures that they were talking about, and the infants' gaze followed. This conveyed referential information, while the live presence of the adult also provided interpersonal cues that attracted attention and possibly motivated learning. The infants were learning language for a purpose, namely communication. Simply being exposed to the raw auditory sensory information is apparently insufficient to trigger perceptual learning of phonology.

Phonotactic learning

So far we have seen that infants rapidly learn to discriminate between individual phonemes, but words are composed of sequences of phonemes. The infant needs to group together the phonemes that comprise individual words, and learn which phonemes belong to one word and which phonemes belong to the next word. Some sequences of phonemes are more frequent than others, and some cannot occur at all. The rules that govern the sequences of phonemes used to make words in a particular language are called phonotactics. Information about phonotactic probabilities helps us to determine where one word ends and another word begins. In English, for example, syllables can end in "ant", but cannot end in "atn". If a sequence like "atn" is heard, it probably crosses a word boundary (as in "at night").

Infants become able to extract words from continuous speech by about 7 months of age (Jusczyk & Aslin, 1995). They seem to do so on the basis of various cues, one of which is phonotactic probability. Phonotactic probability is a good cue, because the sequencing of sounds within particular words is usually heavily constrained. Usually, the transitional probability between two sounds is greatest when the two sounds are within the same word. The probability of sounds following each other tends to dip at word boundaries (as in "atn"). Hence the ability to track these statistical probabilities is a powerful cue both to the sequences of sounds that make words, and to word boundaries.

An elegant demonstration of the fact that infants use transitional probabilities to segment speech comes from Saffran and colleagues (Saffran, Aslin, & Newport, 1996). They gave 8-month-old infants novel "words" to learn on the basis of transitional probabilities. The "words" were novel three-syllable units like "bidaku" and "padoti". These "words" were repeated in random order in a monotonous stream (no stress cues or pauses) by a computer speech synthesizer that sounded like a female voice, for 2 minutes ("bidakupadotigolabubidaku . . ."). The transitional probabilities were 1.0 for syllable pairs within words (like bi–da), and 0.33 for syllable pairs that crossed word boundaries (like ku–pa; as will be recalled, the same transitional probabilities were used in the visual sequencing experiment by Kirkham et al., 2002, discussed in Chapter 2). These transitional probabilities told infants where the word boundaries were (i.e. bidaku padoti golabu bidaku . . .). After this 2-minute learning trial, a series of 12 test trials was given, half comprising "words" familiar from the learning phase (like "bidaku") and half comprising new sequences (like "dapiku"). Although the elements of the new "words" had been experienced during learning, their transitional probabilities had been 0 (i.e. the probability of "da" being followed by "pi" had not been experienced, as "da" was always followed by "ku" during learning). Saffran et al. (1996) reported that the 8-month-olds dishabituated to the novel "words" like "dapiku", showing that they were computing the necessary sequential statistics.

In a second experiment, Saffran et al. (1996) studied whether 8-month-old babies could also keep track of sequential statistics when the transitional probabilities were relative rather than absolute. For example, learning from the string "bidakupadotigolabubidaku . . ." was tested with novel items like "kupado". For novel items like these, the serial order of the syllables (ku pa do) has been experienced previously. However, the transitional probability between the first two syllables (ku pa) was 0.33 (as this sequence spanned the boundary between "bidaku" and "padoti"), and the transitional probability between the second two syllables (pa do) was 1.0 (as this sequence was in "padoti"). These "part words" provided a strong test of statistical learning, as in order to distinguish the "words" the infants had to pay attention to statistical patterns over the whole learning corpus. Again, the 8-month-old babies showed dishabituation when the novel "part words" were presented, showing longer listening time to these test stimuli. They were picking out the three-syllable strings with the highest transitional probabilities. In other words, they were learning the structural properties of the input.

Infant-directed speech, rhythm, and prosody

As noted earlier, everyone talks to babies in a special way, originally called motherese. When making eye contact with a baby, it is very difficult to stop oneself from speaking in a sing-song intonation that is higher than usual, and that exaggerates certain words by using increased duration and stress. The universal tendency of adults (and children) to talk to babies using infant-directed speech (IDS) suggests that this special prosodic patterning has a developmental purpose. The characteristically higher pitch and exaggerated intonation of IDS may help the infant to pick words out of the speech stream. Although we do not yet know exactly how IDS helps infants to do this, we have extensive evidence that babies prefer to listen to motherese, and that cues such as duration and stress help them to identify words.

Evidence that motherese plays a role in word identification has been gathered by Fernald and colleagues. Fernald and Mazzie (1991) argued that if the function of IDS was simply to gain the infant's attention and encourage social interaction, then there should be no relationship between prosodic structure and linguistic structure. Similarly, if **prosody** is simply used to mark new information in all speech, then mothers should use pitch to mark particular words just as frequently when speaking to adults as when speaking to infants. To control experimentally which new information was to be marked in natural speech, Fernald and Mazzie designed a picture book called "Kelly's New Clothes". The book depicted a child getting dressed, with a new item of clothing introduced on each page. Each item was shown as brightly colored when first introduced, and then appeared in grey on the following page. Mothers of 14-month-old babies were then asked to "tell the story" to either their infant or to an adult listener on separate occasions. Acoustic measures of prosodic emphasis were made of the target words (the new items of clothing, for example shoes, hat, shirt etc.).

Fernald and Mazzie found that the target words were those receiving primary stress on 76% of occasions when the mothers told the stories to their infants, compared with 42% of occasions when the mothers told the stories to another adult. When the new information was mentioned a second time, it was again highly stressed on 70% of occasions to the infants, compared to just over 20% of occasions to the adults. Furthermore, the mothers tended to place the target words at the end of their sentences, increasing their salience further (e.g. "Then he put on his yellow SOCKS").

For the infants, 75% of new words were in utterance-final position, compared to 53% for speech directed to another adult. Hence the mothers were using distinctive prosodic patterns to speak to their infants about new information. Target words were most likely to occur on an exaggerated pitch peak at the end of the utterance. Fernald and Mazzie (1991) argued that pitch is widely used to highlight new words in speech to infants, even in languages that do not typically use stress for emphasis, suggesting that mothers across cultures converge on this strategy because of its perceptual effectiveness.

Prosodic cues, that is, changes in duration and stress, also carry important information about how sounds are ordered into words when the words are multisyllabic. For example, 90% of English bisyllabic content words follow a strong–weak syllable pattern, with the stress on the first syllable (e.g. monkey, bottle, doctor, sister). Jusczyk and colleagues explored whether infants could use prosodic strategies to segment words from continuous speech. For example, if infants can learn that word onsets are aligned with strong (stressed) syllables, then this would be a useful strategy for picking out words in speech (Cutler & Norris, 1988). Jusczyk, Houston, and Newsome (1999) carried out a series of experiments to see whether infants were successful in segmenting words following the typical strong–weak pattern from fluent speech, and whether they tended to mis-segment words (such as guitar and surprise) that followed an atypical weak–strong pattern. In general, strong syllables are louder and longer than weak syllables, and have a higher pitch (frequency). Using a habituation paradigm, Jusczyk et al. found that infants aged 7½ months could segment words with strong–weak patterns from fluent speech, and treated the words as bisyllables (i.e. they were responding to the total word "doctor" and not just to the strong syllable "doc"). At this age, infants appeared to mis-segment words following a weak–strong pattern, like "guitar". For example, if they heard a sentence like "her guitar is too fancy", they segmented "taris" as a plausible word (treating "taris" rather than "guitar" as familiar during the dishabituation test). By 10½ months of age, infants did not make these mistakes with words comprised of weak–strong syllables. Sensitivity to the predominant stress patterns of English words is clearly important for segmentation.

More recently, Curtin, Mintz, and Christiansen (2005) have shown that stress combines with transitional probabilities in an additive way. They analyzed a corpus of phonologically transcribed speech directed to British infants aged between 6 and 16 weeks, to see whether a connectionist model would be able to learn word representations better when stress provided an additional cue. The addition of stress to the syllable representations led to better segmentation performance by the model. This result suggests that lexical stress makes it easier to distinguish transitional probabilities in the speech stream. Hence it is possible that infants code lexical stress as part of their initial phonological representations. This possibility was tested experimentally. Using an adaptation of the paradigm designed by Saffran et al. (1996), Curtin et al. (2005) familiarized 7-month-old infants with novel words presented in real English sentences. The novel words either had the lexical stress typical of English (DObita), or atypical stress (doBIta). The question was whether the two types of word, which contained the same phonemes and transitional probabilities, would be represented as distinct by the infants on the basis of whether they contained initial or medial stress. The results showed that the infants preferred the sentences with the words with initial stress. Curtin et al. concluded that lexical stress is retained in the proto-lexical representation. Early phonological representations of potential word forms encode lexical stress as well as segmental information. Therefore, word forms with identical phonemes but differential stress patterns are treated as different words (and in natural language may indeed have different meanings, as in CONtent and conTENT).

There is also some evidence that when word forms differ by one phoneme but have identical stress, infants do not distinguish between them. Swingley (2005) explored whether the phonological representations of 11-month-old infants showed high specificity for familiar words. For example, would the infants differentiate between *dog* and *bog*, or between *dirty* and *nirty*? Swingley used an infant-controlled **head turn preference procedure**, in which infants are played speech stimuli for as long as they continue to fixate a flashing light. In these paradigms, infants usually spend longer looking at the light when stimuli are familiar. Swingley compared looking time for familiar words like *dog* and nonwords that either varied in the onset consonant, like *bog*, or in the final consonant, like *daub* (in British English, this would be *dob*). His data showed that American infants were able to spot the mispronunciations based on onset consonants (as in *dog/bog*), but not in offset consonants (as in *dog/daub*), for stressed syllables. Swingley therefore argued that the 11-month-olds were already building a lexical phonological system that enabled the distinction of minimal pairs (real words differing by a single phoneme). Using a similar paradigm, Vihman, Nakai, DePaolis, and Halle (2004) showed that infants' recognition of mispronounced words depended on the stress system of a language. As we have seen, in English stress is usually placed on the first syllable of a bisyllabic word. Hence English infants could recognize *nirty* as a mispronunciation of *dirty*, but did not recognize *dirny* as a mispronunciation of *dirty*.

In fact, infants are sensitive to general prosodic and rhythmic patterning in language from very early indeed. Mehler and colleagues have shown that infants as young as 4 days use information about rhythm and stress (accentuation) to distinguish their native language from other languages (Mehler, Lambertz, Jusczyk, & Amiel-Tyson, 1987). Mehler et al. tested 4-day-old babies who had been born in France, and who had thus been exposed to the rhythms and intonations of French while in the womb. For the experiment, recordings were made of a bilingual speaker of French and Russian telling the same story in French and in Russian. Fifteen-second segments of these stories were then played to the babies. The babies showed a clear preference for listening to the native language, in this case, French. The researchers then played the tapes backwards. This meant that whereas the absolute parameters of the signal such as voice pitch were preserved, the relative cues such as intonation and melody were modified. With the reversed speech, the babies could no longer tell the difference between French and Russian. Mehler and colleagues argued that the infants were relying on rhythmic and prosodic cues to distinguish the two languages. In a control experiment in which the speech was filtered so that only the rhythmic cues were preserved (filtered speech sounds a bit like someone speaking under water), the 4-day old infants could again distinguish between Russian and French. Monkeys and rats can also discriminate languages from different rhythm classes (e.g. rats can distinguish Dutch from Japanese; see Toro, Trobalon, & Sebastien-Galles, 2003). This is suggestive of the involvement of general perceptual abilities. Related work by Mehler and colleagues suggests that the same rhythm-based cues could be important for learning grammar for humans (Bonatti, Peña, Nespor, & Mehler, 2005). Vowels in syllables are the main carriers of prosody, and in many languages vowels provide cues to **syntax**, e.g. via prominence and lengthening, or via vowel harmony. A relatively high percentage of vowels compared to consonants is found in languages using agglutinative **morphology**. This means that the duration, intensity, and pitch of vowels, which comprise the prosodic information, can also carry information about the syntactic structure of a language.

Early phonological production

Infants begin vocalizing from very early on. Infants first signal to their caretakers by crying, and also make other early nonvocal sounds such as grunting, sneezing, and coughing. However, some vocalizations are speech-like, and it is thought that speech-like vocal development goes through a number of stages. During the first stage, from 0 to 2 months, infants produce "comfort sounds" that have normal speech-like phonation. These comfort sounds most typically sound like vowel phonemes. By 2–3 months of age, infants enter the so-called "gooing" stage (Oller, 1980), producing phonetic sequences that are precursors to consonant phonemes. This is followed by an expansion stage, typically from 4 to 6 months, during which infants produce a variety of new sound types, including trills, squeals, growls, whispers, and protosyllables, which are termed "marginal babbling" (Oller & Eilers, 1988). Mature syllables appear in the canonical stage, which is when "**canonical babbling**" begins, at around 7–10 months. Now infants produce the reduplicated sequences of consonant–vowel (CV) syllables that we typically consider babbling, saying /mamamamama/ or /dadadadada/. The onset of the canonical stage is considered critical, as it represents the point in development at which infants produce mature syllables that can function as the building blocks of words.

Cross-language work has shown that infants across cultures typically babble the same kinds of sounds in the same order. For example, stops like /b/ and /p/ and nasals like /m/ are easier to produce than fricatives like /f/ and liquids like /l/. The most frequent sounds to be babbled early are /d/, /b/, /m/, /n/, /g/, and /t/. Hence babbling /dadada/ and /mamama/ emerges early in all cultures. However, the relative frequency of easily produced sounds in children's babbling is very similar to the frequency of those sounds in the ambient language. For example, French uses the sounds /p/, /b/, /m/, /f/, and /v/ more frequently than English. Accordingly, French babies babble those sounds more frequently than English babies. Babbling also reflects the rhythmic properties of the adult language. de Boysson-Bardies, Sagart, and Durand (1984) took samples of babbling from 6-month-old babies who were learning one of French, Cantonese, or Arabic. They then played them to French-speaking adults. The adults were asked to pick out the babbling of the French babies. They managed to do this very accurately, apparently by relying on the intonational prosodic patterning of the babble.

It is often reported anecdotally that deaf babies produce the same kinds of babbling sounds as hearing infants. This belief has been very important theoretically. If deaf babies babble in the same way and at the same age as hearing infants, it would suggest that babbling is biologically predetermined, and can unfold without auditory experience. The first systematic study of babbling in deaf infants was carried out by Oller and Eilers (1988). They were able to collect vocalizations from nine deaf infants aged from 1 month. This was a significant achievement, as hearing impairment is not often diagnosed early, and is often accompanied by other learning difficulties. These nine babies were compared to 21 hearing infants, and all infants were followed longitudinally. Oller and Eilers found that all the hearing infants started canonical babbling between 6 and 10 months of age. For the deaf infants, the earliest age for canonical babbling was 11 months, and the latest age was 25 months. Further, the nature of their babbling was quite different. They produced far fewer

KEY TERM

Canonical babbling
Babbling that begins around 7–10 months in which infants produce reduplicated sequences of consonant–vowel (CV) syllables that sound mature in that they can function as the building blocks of words.

vocalizations, and the quality of what they produced was restricted. Oller and Eilers concluded that the idea that audition played no role in normal babbling was a myth.

One interesting question is whether there is any link between rhythmic babbling and other forms of rhythmic patterning. For example, babies shake rattles and make rhythmic hand movements. Babbling, however, follows the rhythmic timing and stress patterns of natural language prosody, suggesting that it is not simply another motoric rhythmic behavior; rather, it is specifically linguistic. The linguistic hypothesis of babbling assumes that the production of the structured rhythmic and temporal patterns of the ambient language is a crucial part of language acquisition. An alternative, motor hypothesis of babbling attributes the rhythms of babble to the physiological properties of the jaw. Petitto, Holowka, Sergio, Levy, and Ostry (2004) contrasted the motoric and linguistic accounts of infant babble by studying the rhythmic hand movements of two groups of babies. One was a group of hearing babies born to hearing parents, and the second was a group of hearing babies born to deaf parents. The latter were learning sign language rather than spoken language, even though they could hear.

Petitto et al. reasoned as follows. Babies exposed to sign rather than to spoken language might go through a developmental stage of "babbling" on their hands. In an earlier study of deaf babies, Petitto and Marentette (1991) had indeed found a unique set of hand movements in deaf babies that appeared to contain a reduced subset of the sign units of natural sign language. This "hand babble" was produced repetitively in accord with the general prosodic contours of natural sign languages, duplicating the rhythmic timing and stress of hand shapes in natural signs. However, if hearing babies who are not exposed to sign language also produce **manual babbling**, then this would not be specifically linguistic in the sense of indexing production of a reduced form of the ambient language. Rather, it would be suggestive of a universal rhythmic motor activity, but produced with the hands rather than with the mouth. The hearing babies studied by Petitto et al. all produced vocalizations, but the key question was whether they would also produce the same kind of manual hand movements as each other.

KEY TERM

Manual babbling
Hand movements of deaf babies who are signed to that approximate the auditory babbling of hearing infants.

To get very detailed information about hand movements, Petitto et al. attached infrared emitting diodes onto the babies' hands. Sensitive sensors then tracked the trajectory and location of the babies' hands while the babies played with a parent. During the videotaped play period, the parent offered toys like rattles and soft toys, played peek-a-boo, or talked and signed to the baby. The trajectory and hand locations emitted by the diodes were then calculated independently of the video and blind of whether the babies were being exposed to speech or sign. The resulting movement segments were then matched to the videos. Petitto et al. found that only the hearing babies who were being exposed to sign language produced a low-frequency hand activity that was rhythmic at around 1 Hz (i.e. one hand movement cycle per second). Both groups of hearing babies produced high-frequency hand activity at around 2.5–3 Hz (three cycles per second), which was designated as nonlinguistic excitatory activity. The low-frequency activity was designated as manual babbling. Video matching showed that around 80% of this manual babbling was produced within

If infants are exposed to spoken language, they will babble sounds. If they are exposed to sign language, they will babble signs. © Louis Quail/Corbis.

"signing space"—the restricted spatial area around the face and chin used for linguistic signs. By contrast, only around 20% of high-frequency hand movements were restricted to the signing space. These data suggest that babbling is not simply another motoric rhythmic behavior, but is rather specifically linguistic. If infants are exposed to spoken language, they will babble sounds. If they are exposed to sign language, they will babble signs. In each case, the babies are discovering and producing the most rudimentary structures of the natural language to which they are exposed. These rudimentary structures are rhythmic ones.

Cognitive neuroimaging of phonological development

Our understanding of speech perception in adults has been transformed by neuroimaging. Old controversies, such as whether the brain has a specialized system for language processing in addition to a general system for the processing of nonlinguistic sounds, have been reinvigorated. Studies using fMRI with adults have shown that, as in the visual system, there are two pathways for processing incoming signals in the auditory system. An anterior pathway, analogous to the "what" pathway for vision, is interested in information about vocalizations and acoustic-phonetic cues ("what are they"). The second posterior pathway, analogous to the "where" pathway for vision, is more interested in information about sound localization and how sounds are made, hence articulatory information (Scott & Johnsrude, 2003). Speech perception appears to depend on multiple representations of the input, such as acoustic-phonetic representations and motor/articulatory representations. Speech is processed both as a sound and as an action. These multiple and complementary representations appear to help to explain why speech perception is robust across different speakers, noise contexts, and variability in accent.

The EEG methodology, which measures the time course of neural processing with great specificity (to millisecond accuracy), turned out to be perfect for studying phonemic processing in adults. The best-established response in this EEG literature is the **mismatch negativity**, or **MMN**. When a stimulus such as /p/ is repeated many times, there is decreased activity in the network of neurons that respond to auditory /p/ signals (i.e. there is habituation). However, if the stimulus is changed to /b/, there is renewed activity. The brain was expecting to hear another /p/, and so the mismatch /b/ triggers an increased response. This is marked as an increased negative potential at around 270 ms following stimulus onset, and has been labeled the mismatch negativity (Naatanen & Picton, 1987).

Studies using fMRI and EEG in infants and young children are only just beginning to be reported in the literature. However, neuroimaging could transform the study of language acquisition in young children, because meaningful responses can be measured without attention. In fact, sleeping babies can show robust MMN responses, because the auditory system does not "switch off" during sleep. Dehaene-Lambertz and Gliga (2004) have summarized neuroimaging studies carried out with infants. They showed that EEG responses in phonetic perception tasks with infants were remarkably similar to the EEG responses found with adults. They argued that this implied a common neural basis for phonetic perception in the posterior temporal lobe. When syllables varying along a place of articulation are used as stimuli (e.g. /ba/ to /da/), infants show a large MMN for a change that crosses the phonemic boundary. A change of similar amplitude within the phonemic category yields a significantly smaller mismatch response. Cheour et al. (1998) used MMN to measure the neural response to native versus non-native phonemes in infants aged 6 months and 1 year. They recruited Finnish and Estonian infants to their study, and used: (1) vowel phonemes present in both languages; and (2) a vowel phoneme that was present in Estonian but not in Finnish. Finnish infants aged 6 months showed very similar MMNs to this vowel phoneme and to the Finnish vowel phonemes, suggesting that all three vowels were distinguished, probably on the basis of acoustic cues. By the time the Finnish infants were aged 12 months, differential responding was found. The MMN shown by the Finnish infants was significantly smaller to the absent vowel phoneme compared to the vowel phonemes that were part of the Finnish language. The MMN shown by the Estonian infants was similar for all vowel phonemes, as all were phonemes in the Estonian language. Hence neural responding mirrors the behavioral effects documented earlier by researchers such as Werker and Tees (1984).

The MMN has also been used to study infant processing of the stress patterns of natural language. These studies suggest that different stress patterns are distinguished early, and that the stress patterns characteristic of the ambient language rapidly attain a special status in long-term memory. For example, Weber, Hahne, Friedrich, and Friederici (2004) studied German infants' sensitivity to stress patterns using the MMN. Ninety per cent of bisyllabic German nouns are stressed on the first syllable (the trochaic pattern) rather than on the second syllable (the iambic pattern). Weber et al. investigated infant sensitivity to changes in trochaic and iambic patterns. They reported that infants aged 4 months did not distinguish between two-syllable items stressed on the first versus second syllable. By 5 months of age, however, infants clearly separated the iambic and trochaic patterns, showing a strong MMN for the trochaic items. These neural findings complement the behavioral demonstration by Curtin et al. (2005) that infants of 7 months of age are coding lexical stress as part of their initial phonological representations. Adults investigated in the Weber et al. (2004) study showed clear MMNs to both syllabic stress patterns. This pattern of EEG findings suggests that language experience helps the infants to focus on the stress patterns characteristic of their spoken language, a template for which is then stored in the phonological lexicon. This phonological representation of the typical rhythm and stress patterns enables the distinction of atypical patterns. As rhythm and stress are exaggerated in motherese and are critical to word identification, EEG offers the potential for distinguishing early "markers" of possible language impairment, long before the production of spoken language has commenced.

Dehaene-Lambertz and colleagues have been able to use fMRI with very young infants to study the functional organization of speech processing in the infant brain. For example, Dehaene-Lambertz, Dehaene, and Hertz-Pannier (2002) played awake and sleeping infants aged 3 months a recording of a female voice reading a story in a vivid theatrical manner. The infants heard 20-second excerpts of the story, played either forwards or backwards, and images of the brain were acquired. Dehaene-Lambertz and colleagues found that both forward and backward speech led to specific activation in the left temporal lobe, particularly in Heschl's gyrus, a region that is particularly important in speech processing in adults (although it is not speech specific). There was also significantly greater activation to the forward speech in some left temporal sites, in particular the angular gyrus and the precuneus. Dehaene-Lambertz and colleagues argued that the infant cortex is already structured into several regions of functional importance for speech processing by the age of 3 months.

In a subsequent study, Dehaene-Lambertz et al. (2006) played 3-month-old infants sentences from these stories which were repeated, and studied the time course of the hemodynamic response. Fast responses to the sentences were observed in Heschl's gyrus, with slower responses in left anterior temporal and inferior frontal regions. In adults, left inferior frontal gyrus (**Broca's area**) is related to the overt production of speech, silent rehearsal, and short-term memory. In infants, this was the only brain area sensitive to sentence repetition, producing a stronger response when a sentence was heard for a second time. Dehaene-Lambertz and colleagues argued that a memory system for speech (and possibly other auditory) stimuli was already active in 3-month-old infants, based on Broca's area.

Mills and colleagues extended the use of EEG to word learning (Mills, Prat, Zangl, Stager, Neville, & Werker, 2004). Event-related potentials (ERPs) to familiar and novel words were studied in 14-month-olds and in 20-month-olds. Three categories of word were compared. The first category comprised words already known to the infants, such as "bear", "cup", and "milk". The second category comprised nonwords generated by changing the initial phoneme, as in "gare", "tup", and "nilk". These nonwords shared high phonemic similarity with the familiar words. A third category of nonwords was selected to be phonetically dissimilar to the familiar words, for example "kobe", "mon", and "keed". Each item was presented six times randomly interspersed with other items from the same category, and ERPs were recorded for the different categories. Mills et al. (2004) found age differences in the brain responses shown by the 14-month-olds versus the 20-month-olds. The younger infants showed similar brain responses to the familiar words ("bear") and the phonetically similar nonwords ("gare"). These items were distinguished from the phonetically dissimilar nonwords ("kobe") but were not distinguished from each other. The 20-month-olds showed differential brain responses to all three categories. The amplitude of the brain responses around 200–400 ms after onset (N200–N400) was significantly larger for the familiar words; the two types of nonword ("gare" and "kobe") did not differ from each other. Mills et al. argued that, at 14 months, the neural responses indicated mistaken recognition of items like "gare" as the real word targets (although note that Swingley, 2005, found behavioral differentiation of "dog" and "bog" at 11 months). By 20 months, the children were showing neural responses only to known words that were phonologically correct in all details. This "word recognition" ERP was said to indicate that the development of phonological representations for familiar words is well specified by 20 months. Further studies are clearly required using different age groups, and studying ERPs in different language contexts (like sentences), using real objects. Nevertheless, phonological development is clearly a rapid process and the brain is particularly sensitive to phonological information in the first years of life.

LEXICAL DEVELOPMENT

Although phonological development is central to language acquisition, the primary function of language is communication. Infants need to learn what words mean. To learn word meanings, infants must map acoustic patterns to specific concepts. **Lexical development** (building a vocabulary) is hence intimately tied to conceptual development. Words often name things that are in the world. As we saw in earlier chapters, infants understand a lot about the kinds of things that are in the world. They also understand the kinds of events and actions named by language long before

Carers will typically name the objects that are the focus of the child's interest long before the child is talking, employing highly frequent constructions.

they are fluent speakers of language themselves. Nevertheless, words are part of meaning-making experiences from very early in development. Carers will typically name the objects that are the focus of the child's interest long before the child is talking, and will comment on joint activities or on the child's behavior or apparent feelings. The situational context in which words are used is an important cue to what they might mean.

A study of mothers' utterances to their toddlers showed that children heard an estimated 5000–7000 utterances a day (Cameron-Faulkner, Lieven, & Tomasello, 2003). Around a third of these utterances were questions. In Cameron-Faulkner et al.'s study, more than half of maternal utterances began with one of 52 highly frequent constructions, such as "Look at . . .", "Are you . . .", "Let's . . .", and "Here's . . .". The utterances that children heard were thus quite repetitive and frequent, with some constructions experienced literally hundreds of times per day. Similar estimates have been made by other researchers. Hart and Risley (1995) estimated that children from families of high socioeconomic status (SES) heard around 487 utterances per hour; children from families on welfare heard around 178 utterances per hour. By the time they were aged 4 years, it was estimated that high SES children had been exposed to around 44 million utterances, compared to 12 million utterances for the lower SES children. These differences are remarkable. The brain has received far more language input as a basis for learning in the higher SES children.

Word learning usually takes off some time after the end of the first year. The earliest age for producing your first word is around 9 months. By 16 months of age, median spoken vocabulary size is 55 words (Fenson, Dale, Reznick, Bates, Thal, & Pethick, 1994). By 23 months, it is 225 words. By 30 months, median vocabulary size is 573 words, reflecting a tenfold increase in 14 months. By age 6, the average child has a spoken vocabulary of around 6000 words and a comprehension vocabulary of around 14,000 words (Dollaghan, 1994). Clearly, some powerful learning mechanisms are at work.

What are children's first words like? Most children produce words that are highly relevant to their daily lives, such as words for salient individual objects (Mummy, teddy), words for salient categories of objects (cookie, cup), words for actions (up, gone), words for recurrence (more, again) and words for social routines (bye-bye, night-night). Word learning is particularly interesting because it is symbolic. Words are linguistic symbols, they *refer* to an object or to an event, but they are not the object or the event itself. This use of linguistic symbols in systematic patterns that in themselves convey meaning (i.e. grammatical patterns, see below) is uniquely human (Tomasello, 2006). Linguistic constructions have meaning independent of the meaning of the individual words making up the utterances. Following the one-word stage at about 16 months, and the two-word stage at 20–24 months, children from around 30 months rapidly acquire and produce many different kinds of linguistic constructions.

Early in language acquisition, the comprehension of words outstrips the production of words—**comprehension precedes production**. Benedict (1979) studied eight infants from when they were 9 months of age until they were 1 year 8 months old. She visited the infants at home twice weekly to observe and record their vocabulary, and in between her visits the mothers kept a diary of their children's new words. Benedict reported that the rate of word acquisition for comprehension was twice that of production. On average, she found that the children understood 50 words before they were able to produce 10 words. When 10 words could be produced, the number of words comprehended ranged from 30 to 182. There was a gap of approximately 5 months between attaining the 50-word level in comprehension and attaining the 50-word level in production. Thus comprehension developed earlier than production, and it developed much more rapidly. For the first 10 words comprehended, over 50% were action words (give, kiss). Most of the early words produced were words that referred to things.

Much of our knowledge concerning early lexical development has relied on parental report. For example, Fenson, Bates, and colleagues (1994) developed the Child Language Checklist to give to parents. This comprised the first few hundred words and phrases typically acquired by American English children. Fenson et al. (1994) asked parents to mark how many of the words they thought their children knew at different ages. This checklist has now been translated into at least 12 languages, enabling cross-language comparisons of lexical development. Three key findings are: (1) that word comprehension appears to onset between 8 and 10 months across the world's languages; (2) that word production onsets between 11 and 13 months across languages; and (3) that there is huge variation in the lexical growth shown by individual children. For example, at 2 years, the range in word production is from 0 words to more than 500 words. In terms of what the words are, cross-language checklists suggest that all children produce similar first words, words that are salient to the concerns of their everyday lives. However, there are some interesting culturally related differences. For example, the child's word for "grandmother" is on average the fifth social word produced by an Italian toddler, but the thirtieth social word produced by an American toddler. This difference probably reflects the fact that Italian children tend to live in closer proximity to the extended family (Bates et al., 2001).

The checklist studies also revealed that a sudden acceleration or "burst" in vocabulary acquisition did not describe the language development of most children. Rather, vocabulary acquisition was incremental, and was best fit by a smoothly accelerating exponential function (Fenson et al., 1994). This was surprising, as the **"vocabulary spurt"** observed in longitudinal studies of individual children was widely held to be a central aspect of early language acquisition. These individual studies had documented a sudden surge in the number of new words acquired just prior to the achievement of a 50-word lexicon, at around 17–19 months of age (Bloom, 1973; Benedict, 1979). Theoretically, this sudden "spurt" had been interpreted to show that children had achieved a new level of referential understanding—they had achieved the "insight" that words can name. It was thought that the vocabulary burst marked an important change in the symbolic status of words. However, other authors had pointed out that this "naming explosion" may only characterize young children who were focused on learning names for things. In a longitudinal study reported by Goldfield and Reznick (1990), 30% of the children studied never showed a dramatic acceleration in word learning. These children maintained a steady balance of nouns and other kinds of words throughout early lexical development. More recent experimental work (discussed below) shows that the "insight" that words can name probably develops much earlier than 17–19 months of age, some time during the first year of life.

Another aspect of development revealed by the checklist studies was the important mediating role of gesture. The first communicative skill to emerge was word comprehension. The second was communication gestures and routines. These gestures were usually elicited in response to verbal input, for example waving "bye-bye". Gestures recognizing the function of common objects appeared shortly afterwards, such as holding a telephone receiver to the ear. Verbal naming then began.

Gesture is a form of production rather than comprehension, and it has communicative intent—children are gesturing to convey information. Young children are using action to express or lexicalize meanings that could have been put into words (Volterra & Erting, 1990). Gesture thus provides a kind of cognitive bridge between comprehension and production.

The use of gestures to communicate between the ages of 10 and 21 months was studied by Zinober and Martlew (1985). They studied four types of gesture: instrumental gestures (e.g. gestures intended to control the caretaker's behavior, such as pointing to a desired toy); expressive gestures (e.g. gestures conveying emotions); enactive gestures (e.g. imitating the turning of a door handle to convey opening the door); and deictic gestures (for focusing joint attention). These intentional signals by the infant were co-ordinated with emergent vocalizations including babbling, protowords, and single words, in two contexts, free play with the mother and a shared picture-book session. The use of gesture was found to increase between 10 and 18 months, and then to decline. Vocalization showed a steady increase, and by 21 months was the dominant form of communication. Usually, even at 10 months, gestures and protowords were used together to convey the same message. For example, one child always accompanied his gesture for opening and shutting with the protoword "shuh". In general at this period, the gestures were easier to understand than the vocalizations. Later in development, from around 18 months, vocalizations and gestures were used together to convey more complex meanings than either could convey alone. For example, William conveyed the message "You choose the book, Mummy" by responding to his mother's invitation "Billy choose one" with the word "No" (shaking his head), and then "Book", at the same time placing his mother's hand firmly on the pile of books. Gesture thus plays a key role in enhancing the effectiveness of communication in early language development.

Word learning by infants

What learning mechanisms do children use to acquire all these words? Clearly, the perceptual mechanisms reviewed above play an important role in stabilizing the acoustic patterns that constitute words, but these patterns must be linked to concepts for a lexicon to develop. In preceding chapters, we have seen that infants are developing a number of physical concepts (such as containment) during the first year of life, and are making distinctions between animates and inanimates as well. These pre-existing conceptual categories can then be linked to words. However, language is primarily part of the social world. Infants first make sounds to communicate. Furthermore, the social world provides some of the most salient and important early concepts for the infant—the infant's mother, and the infant's self. In fact, word learning seems to begin with learning one's own name.

Infants as young as 4½ months of age can reliably recognize their own names and appear to have a relatively detailed phonological representation of this salient word. This was demonstrated in a habituation study by Mandel, Jusczyk, and Pisoni (1995). Each infant listened to repetitions of four different names, their own name and three foils. One foil matched the stress pattern of the infant's name. For example, an infant called Joshua might be tested with the foil Agatha, whereas an infant called Becca might be tested with the foil Aaron. Two foils had a different stress pattern. Here Joshua might be tested with Maria and Eliza, while Becca might be tested with Rumiz and Michelle. A different set of foils was used for each infant, in case some names were inherently more appealing than others. The names were recorded by a female speaker using a lively intonation pattern, as though she were calling to the infant.

During the experiment, the infant sat on their caretaker's lap and watched a centrally placed flashing green light. Once the infant was fixating at center, a red light on one side (either left or right) came on, and when the infant turned his or her head towards this red light, a name was played. The name continued until the infant stopped looking at the red light. Mandel et al. reported that the infants looked significantly longer when rewarded with their own name. They could distinguish their name both from the foil with the same stress pattern, and from the other foils. There was no difference in looking time to the different kinds of foils. Clearly, one's own name is one sound pattern that has been learned by 4 months of age.

The salient cue of your own name or of your word for "Mummy" can help in learning adjacent words as well. Bortfeld, Morgan, Golinkoff, and Rathbun (2005) played 6-month-old infants passages containing novel words, in which the novel word either followed their own names or an unfamiliar name. For example, an infant named Maggie might hear "The girl rode Maggie's bike" if participating in the "familiar name" condition, and "The boy played with Hannah's bike" if participating in the "unfamiliar name" condition. There were six such sentences in each passage. Learning of the novel words (bike, cup, feet, dog) was then tested via a head-turn procedure. When the infant turned her head to look at a blinking light, the same (female) voice that had read the passages would begin speaking a particular word. At test, the infant either heard words that had been paired with their own name spoken repeatedly (words like "bike" in the example above), or heard words that had been paired with unfamiliar names (e.g. "cup"). The infants chose to listen significantly longer to the words that had been paired with their own (familiar) name.

In a second experiment, the same effect was found using the name most often used for the infant's mother (e.g. Mama, Mommy). Infants listened significantly longer to words like "dog" after hearing sentences like "Mommy's dog barked only at squirrels" than after hearing sentences like "Lola's dog barked only at squirrels". Bortfeld et al. (2005) argued that the infants were using their own name or their word for mummy as an "anchor point" in the speech stream, enabling top-down processing that also identified novel words. Such top-down processing would be a potent language-learning device. In such cases infants, like adults, would be using stored lexical knowledge to segment other likely words from speech. The infants must have been matching a stored representation of a phonological form (like Mommy) against the input, and hence segmenting out adjacent words as well.

So far in this chapter, we have considered the "bottom-up" perceptual and statistical mechanisms available to infants. These learning mechanisms are based solely on the perceptual characteristics of the input. By the age of 6 months, babies can also use top-down learning mechanisms as a basis for word acquisition. This top-down processing begins with their own names.

Cognitive expectations about language and labels

What about nonsocial words? Waxman (e.g. Waxman & Lidz, 2006) argues that to acquire specific meanings, which she calls "word-to-world" links, infants must expect that words highlight commonalities among named entities. The early lexicon has more nouns (words for objects) than verbs (words for actions). Waxman argues that the consistent pairings of certain nouns with certain objects will lead the infant to understand a particular noun as the label for that category of objects. As early words also tend to refer to basic level categories (dog, cup), these objects will be salient in the environment, facilitating learning of this referential relationship. Once infants understand referential function with respect to nouns and objects, they will begin to evolve more specific expectations about referential function, linking particular types of words (nouns, verbs, adjectives like "pretty") to particular types of relations among objects (object categories, actions, object properties). Interestingly, content words like nouns, verbs, and adjectives also tend to be perceptually salient (they tend to receive greater stress and have more interesting melodic contours). Hence perceptual saliency supports infants in this important task of mapping words to objects and events in the world.

In a classic study, Baldwin and Markman (1989) explored the first steps in acquiring word–object relations. They argued that children were unlikely to pay much attention to correlations between labels and objects unless they had a general expectation that the sound patterns uttered by adults were connected to things in the external environment. They proposed that a way to test for the presence of this expectation was to investigate whether infants would pay greater attention to objects that were labeled. They showed infants aged 10–14 months completely novel objects, like snorkels, padlocks, and flippers. Some of the novel objects were labeled by adults ("See the snorkel? That's a snorkel"), and others were presented in silence. The question was whether the infants would show more attention to the novel objects that were labeled. During the experiment, the toys were placed within reach of the infants for 60-second periods and the infants were allowed to play with them. During the labeling condition, the toy was repeatedly labeled during the 60 seconds (resulting in approximately 10 repetitions of the label). In the control condition, the toy was presented in silence. Looking time at the toy was measured in each case. The results showed that, even by the age of 10 months, the infants showed more looking to the

objects that were named than to the objects that were not named. In a follow-up study, Baldwin and Markman (1989) compared the effects of pointing to the novel toy to increase attention to it with both labeling the toy and pointing to it at the same time. This time, two toys were presented in one trial, and the experimenter picked out one of them by either pointing to it repeatedly, or pointing to it while naming it. The time that the infant spent looking at each toy during a subsequent play period was then measured. The infants spent reliably longer looking at the toys that were both labeled and pointed to. Baldwin and Markman argued that labeling sustained infants' attention to objects, facilitating the establishment of word–object relations.

Waxman and Markov (1995) explored how infants make links between a particular kind of word–object relation, that between nouns and categories. They argued that infants approach the task of lexical acquisition with a bias to interpret words applied to objects as referring both to that object and to other members of its kind. This hypothesis was tested by giving infants aged 12–13 months different sets of objects to manipulate, and measuring how long they attended to each subsequent object. In the Noun condition, the objects were named for the infant. For example, four toy cars might be presented one by one for

30 seconds each, with the experimenter saying "Look, a car" (basic level) for each one, and adding "Do you like the car?" as she removed each toy; in a control condition (No Word condition), the experimenter simply said "Look at this" for each toy. Waxman and Markov argued that, if infants interpret nouns applied to objects as referring both to that object and to other members of its kind, then attention to each subsequent object should decline more rapidly in the Noun condition compared to the No Word condition. Basic-level nouns were also compared to nouns at the superordinate level. Here, the infants might be handed four different toy vehicles, with the experimenter saying "Look, a vehicle" for each toy.

In a subsequent test phase, infants were then given both another novel object from the familiar category (e.g. another car), and an object from a different category, such as a toy airplane (or a toy tool for the superordinate condition). The question was whether they would prefer to manipulate the object from the novel category (here, either the airplane [basic level] or tool [superordinate level]). Waxman and Markov (1995) found different results depending on whether the objects were labeled at the basic level or at the superordinate level. At the superordinate level, both predictions were confirmed. The infants showed significantly less attention to the labeled objects ("Look! A vehicle") than to the objects in the No Word condition; they also showed significantly more attention to the novel object at test (the airplane). At the basic level, performance in the two conditions was comparable. Waxman and Markov argued that nouns at the superordinate level do indeed highlight categories of objects for infants.

More recent work has shown that labeling distinct objects with distinct names appears to highlight their individuality. Recall the experiment by Xu and Carey (1996), analyzed in Chapter 2. In that study, infants aged 10 months appeared to have difficulty distinguishing perceptually distinctive toy objects. The experimental paradigm involved bringing each object out alternately from behind a screen, for example first showing a toy kitten, and then a toy truck, three times each. At test, the infants did not look longer when only a single object was revealed behind the screen. The explanation given in 1996 was that the infants were incapable of object individuation: they had not categorized the toy kitten as distinct from the toy truck. An alternative possibility, discussed in Chapter 2, is that the experimental procedure was selectively activating the dorsal visual route, and hence leading infants to ignore information about the surface features of the toys. A related possibility is that the information-processing demands of the task confused the infants. Xu (2002) therefore explored the effects of labeling the objects for the infants. In an object individuation task of similar complexity, 9-month-old infants heard the appropriate labels for the toys.

Xu (2002) contrasted a toy duck with a toy ball. The objects were again shown emerging from behind the screen one at a time, but each appearance was labeled with a distinctive noun ("Look, a duck", or "Look, a ball"). In a control condition, each appearance was labeled with the phrase "Look, a toy". At test, the infants were shown either one or two objects. The expectation was that the infants would look longer at the single object. In the experimental condition, 10 of the 12 participating infants looked significantly longer at the unexpected, one-object outcome. This did not happen in the control condition, where 10 out of 12 infants spent more time looking at the expected two objects. Labeling clearly plays an important role in establishing objects as distinct. Xu (2002) also argues that language may bring together the representations for objects established by the "what" (ventral) and "where" (dorsal) visual systems. This argument is at present purely speculative.

Perhaps unsurprisingly, consistency of labeling appears to be important for highlighting commonalities among named objects. Waxman and Braun (2005) used the same experimental procedure as Waxman and Markov (1995) to investigate learning new words when a consistent novel noun was introduced to babies compared to a variable novel noun. Small toys were used to make up sets of objects. Infants were then shown a set in one of three different conditions. In the two labeling conditions, the experimenter named each toy with either a consistent novel label ("Look, it's a keeto! . . . yes, it's a keeto" for each toy), or with a variety of labels ("Look, it's a —! Yes, it's a —" [keeto, bookoo, dimbee], respectively). In a control condition, no label was provided, the experimenter simply said "Look! Look here!" for each toy. At test, the infants were shown two objects, a new object from the familiar category, and a new object from a new category (e.g. tools). Exploratory behavior (looking, manipulating) to each object was then recorded. Waxman and Braun found that infants in the consistent noun condition showed a significant preference for the toy from the labeled category. Infants in the variable noun condition did not. Infants in the variable noun condition were in fact indistinguishable from infants in the control condition, suggesting that simply hearing novel labels in the presence of a new set of objects does not lead to the formation of inclusive categories. Applying the *same* name to a set of distinctive objects has the conceptual effect of supporting categorization.

A consequence of Waxman's argument about mapping commonalities is that early word learning has a reciprocal effect on conceptual development. As infants seek the perceptual and conceptual similarities between objects that share a common name, there is a corresponding effect on their understanding of the concept that the name is labeling.

Linguistic influences on early concepts

The influence of language on conceptual understanding is not limited to labels for objects, however. As Clark has pointed out (Clark, 2004), whereas children's earliest conceptual representations of objects, relations, and events underpin early word learning, languages differ subtly in how they encode experience. As children begin to learn particular languages, therefore, it might be expected that linguistic differences will affect which aspects of conceptual categories become most salient. Words will draw attention to some aspects of a category and not to others. A good example is the domain of spatial relations. As we saw in Chapters 1 and 2, infants are aware of spatial relations such as support and containment in the first year of life. Clark notes that different languages partition these spatial concepts differently (Figure 5.3). In English, we use "in" to match containment, and "on" to match support. However, we also use "on" to match attachment to a surface. We say "the cup is on the table" and "the fridge magnet is on the fridge", even though in the first case the cup is on top of the table (support in the horizontal plane), and in the second the magnet is attached to the door of the fridge (support in the vertical plane). By contrast, Dutch has three different words for these three types of spatial relation. In Dutch, being "on" the table is denoted by "op", and being "on" the door is denoted by "aan". In Spanish, the same word "en" is used for all three types of spatial relation. The word "en" is used for "in", "on", and for attachment in the vertical plane. Clark's argument is that these linguistic differences will lead to differences in the conceptual encoding of space. This interesting idea remains to be tested empirically.

A different way in which language might shape concepts is suggested by the phenomenon of **overextension** in children's language production. Overextension is when a child uses a single label to refer to multiple objects. For example, the child might use the label "dog" to name not only dogs, but also lions, cats, and horses

(Fremgen & Fay, 1980). Overextension is generally found before around 2½ years of age. Other examples of overextensions include using the label "ball" for apples, grapes, bell-clappers, and other round objects, or the label "tee" for sticks, a cane, an umbrella, a wooden board, and other stick-like objects (Clark, 2003). One hypothesis is that overextensions reflect the fact that children have less well-differentiated conceptual categories than adults do. For example, objects of similar shape may be grouped into the same category of "long, thin, inanimate things" (see Clark, 1973). According to this hypothesis, as more words are acquired they will cause the child to differentiate objects within these rather general conceptual groupings. The acquisition of more verbal labels will result in meanings no longer being underspecified. Hence language will change conceptual groupings. If overextension really does reflect the child ascribing a more general meaning to a word than adults do, then overextensions should be as frequent in comprehension as in production. This does not seem to be the case.

Fremgen and Fay (1980) provided an empirical test of the frequency of overextensions in comprehension versus production. They studied children aged from 1 year 2 months to 2 years 2 months, visiting them at home. Following a play period with the experimenter, the child was shown a series of black-and-white line drawings of objects or animals for which the child's mother had previously reported overextension. The child was asked to name each picture. For example, if the child used the label "dog" to refer to other animals, the child might be shown pictures of a cow, a cat, a horse, and finally a dog. This formed the production test. In a subsequent comprehension test, the child was shown sets of four pictures. Two of these pictures in a given trial were irrelevant to the label being tested, and one of them had been overextended in production. For example, if the child was being asked to show the experimenter the "dog", the pictures might be of a dog, a cat, a vase, and a car. The results of the experiment were extremely clear. The children in the study never overextended the meanings of words during the comprehension test, even though the test was based on overextensions produced by the same child during the production phase of the experiment. Fremgen and Fay (1980) argued that children's knowledge of the meaning of words was much more precise than was suggested by their utterances. They suggested that overextensions occur because young children are stretching their vocabularies to the limit in their efforts to communicate. When the correct vocabulary item is lacking, the child simply substitutes an item that is present that is similar enough in meaning to what she wants to express. Again, communication is at the heart of linguistic behavior.

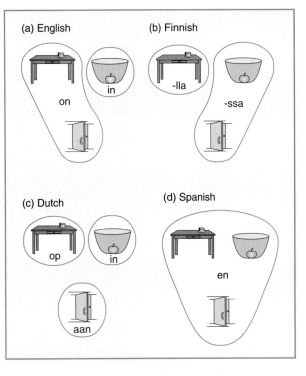

FIGURE 5.3
Linguistic terms for three static spatial relations compared for English, Finnish, Dutch, and Spanish, for talking about the locations of the cup, apple, and handle in the settings picture. From Clark (2004). Copyright © 2004 Elsevier. Reproduced with permission.

Fast mapping

By the age of around 2 years, children are acquiring approximately 10 new words a day. This high rate of learning novel "word-to-world" links suggests that a powerful form of exclusion learning must be at work. Children must be rather good at rapidly narrowing down the potential meanings of a new word. This ability to form quick and rough hypotheses about the meaning of a new word has been termed "**fast mapping**" (Carey, 1978; Heibeck & Markman, 1987). Using the context in which new words are encountered (nonlinguistic information), and their position in a sentence (linguistic information), "fast mapping" enables the learner to eliminate potential candidates for the meaning of a new word rapidly and efficiently. Even 2-year-olds can quickly infer the meaning of new words for color, shape, and texture on this basis (Heibeck & Markman, 1987).

To explore "fast mapping" experimentally, Heibeck and Markman taught children aged 2, 3, and 4 years novel words such as "turquoise", "rectangle", and "fibrous" using a "helping" task. The children were asked to help the experimenter by fetching her certain items from a chair in the corner of the room. For example, in the color condition, the child might be told "Oh, there's something that you could do to help me. Do you see those two books on the chair in the corner? Could you bring me the turquoise one, not the red one, the turquoise one?". The novel color words were presented via books, and were contrasted with familiar color words like "red" and "blue". The novel shape words were presented via different trays, and the novel texture words via different little boxes covered with material. Familiar shape and texture words like "round", "square", "fuzzy", and "smooth" were used to contrast with the unfamiliar shape and texture words in each case.

Heibeck & Markman (1987) reported that the children comprehended the novel words at levels well above chance at all ages. Strongest performance was found for the shape words, followed by the color words and finally by the texture words. This reflected existing vocabulary entries: in a vocabulary assessment, the children knew 80% of the color and shape terms tested, but only 36% of the texture terms. Girls comprehended the novel words better than boys. As a further test of word learning, the children were asked to provide a proper contrast for the new word (e.g. to contrast a new texture word with a known texture word). The experimenter would select a novel item, and say "See this box? It's not fibrous, because it's —?". If the child said a texture word like "soft" or "fuzzy", the child was credited with domain comprehension. If the child said a familiar word from a different domain (e.g. "It's not fibrous because it's blue"), domain comprehension was not credited. Heibeck & Markman (1987) found that older children were better than younger children at this task. Sixty-three per cent of 2-year-olds answered these questions correctly, compared to 90% of 3-year-olds and 96% of 4-year-olds. Shape words were again easier than color words, which were easier than texture words. Finally, the children were asked to produce the novel words that they had learned. Novel word production was much poorer than comprehension, with only 43% of children being able to produce the novel shape words, 4% the novel color words, and 8% the novel texture words. There were no age or gender differences. Clearly, fast mapping is a very efficient comprehension strategy, but more protracted learning may be required for accurate production.

Although first conceptualized as a dedicated language mechanism, "fast mapping" can be found for other types of learning as well. Markson and Bloom (1997) taught 3- and 4-year-old children novel names for objects, and novel facts as well. Retention of the novel names and facts was tested immediately, following a 1-week delay, or following a delay of 1 month. The novel words were taught via a measuring game. Children were given novel objects to measure with the experimenter, such as a plastic tube and a rubber disc. Some familiar objects were also present, such as a pencil and a ruler. During the game, the child was introduced to a novel label such as "koba". The

KEY TERM

Fast mapping
The ability to form quick and rough (but usually accurate) hypotheses about the meaning of new words.

child was told "Let's measure the koba. We can count these to see how long the koba is" or "Let's use the kobas to measure which is longer. Line up the kobas so we can count them". The novel facts were also introduced via the game. For example, in the latter scenario the experimenter said "We can use the things my uncle gave me to measure which is longer. My uncle gave these to me". To test retention, all 10 objects used in the measuring game were presented together. The children were asked to show the experimenter which one was the koba, and which object had been given by the uncle. Children remembered the correct word–object mapping at levels significantly above chance at all retention intervals, and also remembered which novel object had been given to the experimenter by her uncle. Markson and Bloom argued that because novel facts were retained as well as novel labels, fast mapping was not special to word learning. However, a control condition requiring learning of a novel fact presented visually suggested that there did seem to be a connection between fast mapping and information conveyed through language. In this control condition, the children had to remember where to place a sticker on a novel object ("Watch where this goes. This goes here. That's where this goes"). When asked to put the sticker where it should go, they showed significant forgetting, and by 1 month performance was at chance levels. Hence fast mapping does not apply to any arbitrary retention task: it seems most effective for new information delivered linguistically.

Further evidence that fast mapping might be a general cognitive ability of exclusion learning comes from evidence that dogs, too, can learn novel words. As dogs do not develop language, this implicates general auditory learning and memory mechanisms rather than a dedicated language-learning mechanism. The dog "Rico" was a pet border collie whose owners claimed that he knew the words for over 200 items (mainly for children's toys and balls). Rico had been learning label–object pairings since the age of 10 months, and was rewarded with food or play for fetching named items from around the owners' flat. His abilities to fast map were tested experimentally by Kaminski, Call, and Fischer (2004). First, Rico's knowledge of familiar labels was tested by asking him to fetch things ("Fetch the sock"). Rico correctly retrieved 37 out of 40 items. A novel object was then placed in another room along with seven familiar objects. Rico was first requested to bring one of the familiar objects, and was then asked for the novel object. There were ten trials with novel objects overall, and Rico was correct in seven out of ten trials. Retention was tested for these items 1 month later. Each novel object was placed in a room with four other novel objects and four familiar objects. Rico was correct on 50% of trials. Rico is probably an exceptional dog but this study shows that dogs, too, can acquire the expectation that sound patterns uttered by adults are connected to things in the external environment. Furthermore, they can learn specific word–object pairings by fast mapping, and store the novel pairings in memory for at least a month. Perhaps surprisingly, the perceptual and cognitive mechanisms required to compute word-to-world links are not special to humans.

Cognitive neuroimaging of lexical development

It is technically challenging to use neuroimaging to explore how infants build a lexicon, as a measure is needed that tracks the integration of the acoustic patterns representing specific concepts into the meaningful contexts provided by other acoustic patterns representing other concepts. That is, words have to be interpreted within sentence or conversational contexts. This means that a brain response like the MMN, which is very sensitive to acoustic differences (e.g. between phonemes, stress patterns, or words), is not in itself a semantic measure. Further, measures of semantic integration will also inevitably measure conceptual development and the organization of semantic memory (see Chapters 4 and 8), hence such measures will not be language specific.

In adult studies, the most widely used measure of semantic integration in the mental lexicon is an EEG response called the N400. The amplitude of the N400 is thought to reflect the integration of a potentially meaningful stimulus into the current semantic context. For example, adults show an MMN when integrating a word into a sentence, or a picture into a picture story (see Friedrich & Friederici, 2006). The classic technique for eliciting an N400 is to give adults sentences to read. The electrophysiological response to a specific word that is either semantically congruent or semantically incongruent with the rest of the sentence is then measured. For example, the second word in the sentence "the *shirt* has been ironed" makes sense semantically; the second word in the sentence "the *storm* has been ironed" does not. The electrophysiological response to the second word in each sentence can then be compared. Recognition of the semantic incongruency of the second sentence is shown by an increased negativity at around 400 ms when reading this sentence. This increased negativity is the N400.

To date, there have been few studies of N400 responses with infants and children. This is partly because there is debate about how to characterize an N400 in the immature brain. For example, the "word learning" negativity shown by Mills et al. (2004, discussed earlier) occurred at around 200–400 ms, but it was not tied to semantic integration. As Mills et al. (2004) explored the comprehension of individual words (e.g. "bear" vs. "gare"), lexical familiarity rather than semantic processing could explain the increased negativity. In order to measure semantic integration in early language comprehension, Friedrich and Friederici (2004) therefore developed a paradigm linking words to pictures. All words selected for the study were at the basic level (see Chapter 4). During the experiment, the infants, who were aged 19 months, watched a screen which displayed pictures of familiar objects. After each picture appeared, it was named using either the correct or an incorrect label. The same pool of 44 early acquired words was used as labels and each word appeared twice, so that semantic congruency depended on the picture context. An N400-like semantic congruency effect was then sought in a broad temporal range (200–1500 ms). The response to incongruous words was found to be significantly more negative in these 19-month-olds from around 700 ms. Friedrich and Friederici argued that this broadly distributed negativity to the incongruent words was an infant N400. An earlier negativity between 150 and 400 ms (similar to that measured by Mills and colleagues) was also observed, but this negativity was greater to *congruous* words. Friedrich and Friederici argued that this early response reflected a priming effect of the picture (an early "context" effect). The presence of a picture made the infants expect to hear a real word containing certain phonemes.

Friedrich and Friederici (2005) then extended their paradigm to 12-month-olds. For these younger infants, no effect of semantic incongruency was observed in the picture–word paradigm. The 12-month-olds did, however, show the early negativity to congruous words shown by the 19-month-olds, between around 100 and 500 ms. Friedrich and Friederici argued that this early negativity demonstrated that the younger infants did have lexical-semantic knowledge about the words used in the study. Extra experimental conditions including pseudowords and nonwords showed that the 12-month-old infants also had well-developed knowledge of the phonotactics of the language, as they distinguished real words from pseudowords and nonwords. Friedrich and Friederici (2005) argued that mechanisms of semantic integration were not yet mature in 12-month-old infants.

As in behavioral work, of course, the absence of an effect (a negative result) is not strong evidence that a certain capacity is lacking. Current EEG techniques are not specific enough at the individual level to allow us to be confident about the meaning of negative results. Nevertheless, longitudinal investigation (e.g. showing the emergence of an N400 at different ages in different children) could be informative. Friedrich and Friederici (2006) were able to introduce a longitudinal component for the 19-month-olds measured in their 2004 study. When the children in Friedrich and Friederici (2004) reached 30 months of age, they were given a standardized language development test. They were then grouped on the basis of their expressive language abilities. Children with age-adequate skills at 30 months were found to have displayed an N400 at the age of 19 months. For children who had deficits in expressive language skills at 30 months, however, the N400 at 19 months of age was found to be absent. The N400 may hence provide another neural marker of risk for later language impairment. Clearly, more comprehensive longitudinal studies using a variety of EEG markers (MMN, N400) to different aspects of language (phoneme discrimination, word identification, semantic integration) in the same children would be very valuable (Goswami, 2003a).

GRAMMATICAL DEVELOPMENT

Grammatical development encompasses syntactic development (the set of grammatical rules that determine how words can be combined into sentences and phrases) and morphological development (the set of rules governing the internal structure of words: we can say "burglary" but not "stealery"). The basic unit of morphological analysis is the morpheme. A word like "dog" is a single morpheme, but the word "dogs" comprises two morphemes, since the additional phoneme /s/ conveys plurality and hence is also a morpheme. Sometimes morphology is inflectional, as when we add verb endings like —ing and —ed. At other times, morphology is derivational, as when we create new words by adding affixes ("un" + "happy" = "unhappy") or suffixes ("make" + "er" = "maker"). All of these grammatical rules appear to be acquired by young children on an implicit basis, by listening to the adults around them.

When young children first produce combinations of words, at around 20–24 months, their usual aim is to convey additional meaning. The two-word stage marks a turning point in grammatical development, with many core constructions rapidly acquired between the ages of 2 and 3 years. A child who says "No bath" is conveying a different meaning from a child who says "Bath". A child who says "Wet doggie" is conveying a different meaning from a child who says "Doggie". These first word combinations have various semantic functions (in the examples here, these functions are negation and "property of *X*"; see Bates et al., 2001). Cross-language data suggest that young children everywhere are trying to get across the same basic stock of meanings. These are possession, location, volition, disappearance/reappearance, and aspects of transitivity (in, on, etc.). Examples of the basic stock of meanings are shown in Table 5.1.

Originally, children's facility in acquiring grammatical rules was interpreted as meaning that grammar was a language universal. All children were thought to acquire language on the same schedule and in the same way. It was thought that telegraphic combinations of uninflected words in ordered strings appeared first ("more biscuit", "Mary come"), followed by inflections like —ing and —ed ("me ironing

TABLE 5.1 Semantic relations underlying first word combinations in English and Italian (adapted from Braine 1976)		
Semantic functions	**English examples**	**Italian examples**
Attention to X	See doggie!	*Gadda bau*
Property of X	Big doggie	*Gande bau*
Possession	My truck	*Mia brum-brum*
Plurality or iteration	Two shoe	*Due pappe*
Recurrence	Other cookie	*Atto bototto*
Disappearance	Daddy bye bye	*Papà via*
Negation or refusal	No bath	*Bagno no*
Actor-action	Mommy do it	*Fa mamma*
Location	Baby car	*Bimbo casa*
Request	Have dat	*Dà chetto*

that") and then by function words ("Where's the spoon?"). However, cross-language research quickly showed these universals to be nonexistent. For example, English has relatively little inflectional morphology but word order is very important. Hence an English child is just beginning to produce inflected forms like "foots" and "breaked" by around 2½ years of age. By contrast, each inflection in Turkish is a stressed syllable and there are almost no irregular forms (like "break–broke"). This exceptional regularity and phonological salience means that children growing up in Turkey have pretty much mastered inflectional morphology for nouns and verbs before the age of 2.

Spoken language errors like "foots" and "breaked" seem to be quite frequent between the ages of 2 and 5. Originally, this was thought to provide good evidence that young children were figuring out the syntactic rules underlying linguistic utterances. **Over-regularization** of the past tense construction "—ed" in English was particularly intensively studied. Once children had acquired the past-tense morpheme "—ed", it was thought that they overapplied it to all verbs, thereby displaying so-called "U-shaped" developmental growth. Development was "U shaped" because this over-regularization followed a period of correct usage. Prior to the age of around 2½ years, children use the past tense forms that they hear from adults. They say "broke", "came", "went", and so on. However, this correct usage is then followed by a period of over-regularization. The same children start saying "breaked", "comed", and "goed". Finally, children appear to learn that there are exceptions to the rule and begin to display appropriate use of irregular and regular past-tense forms. This U-shaped pattern of over-regularization errors was for a long time taken to support the idea that grammatical development depends on the acquisition of rules.

However, when more systematic studies of over-regularization were conducted, it was found that over-regularizations were actually quite rare. In a study by Marcus, Pinker, Ullman, Hollander, Rosen, and Xu (1992), 11,521 irregular past-tense utterances from the spontaneous speech of 83 children were comprehensively analyzed. It was found that only 2.5% of irregular verbs were over-regularized, suggesting that over-regularization errors are quite rare. Once frequency was taken into account, it became clear that irregular forms that were heard frequently by

KEY TERM

Over-regularization
A tendency to over-regularize irregular forms of words such as past tense and plurals (e.g. "goed" and "mans").

children were rarely over-regularized (e.g. "goed" was rare). In fact, there was a direct connection between how often a parent used an irregular form and how often a child over-regularized it. The more often a parent used a particular irregular form, the less likely the child was to over-regularize it. Over-regularizations were more likely for verbs that were not frequent in spontaneous conversation (e.g. "build"), and many individual verbs were used in both the correct and over-regularized forms for a period of some months or even years. However, all children showed a period of correct usage before the first over-regularizations appeared. Marcus et al. suggested that over-regularizations were a consequence of children beginning to mark tense intentionally. When they first did this, they relied on memory of the relevant irregular forms. When memory failed, they treated irregular forms as though they were regulars, and consequently they made errors.

Children's ability to use rules can also be studied directly. In a seminal study, Berko (1958) tested children's implicit knowledge of grammatical rules by using an analogy task based on nonsense words. The children, who were aged 4–7 years, were told that they were going to look at some pictures. The pictures were of objects, cartoon-like animals, and of men performing various actions. The experimenter would point to a picture, and read some accompanying text (Figure 5.4). The child was required to fill in the missing word. In the example concerning plural endings shown in Figure 5.4, the children were meant to say "Now there are two wugs". Berko also explored the use of appropriate rules for creating the past tense ("This is a man who knows how to spow. He is spowing. He did the same thing yesterday. What did he do yesterday? Yesterday he —?" [spowed]), the rules for generating possessives ("The niz's hat"), and knowledge about the rules for adjectives ("This dog has quirks on him. This dog has more quirks on him. And this dog has even more quirks on him. This dog is quirky. This dog is —? [quirkier]. And this dog is the —?" [quirkiest]).

Berko reported that the children were in general able to handle plural endings, although performance varied with different nonsense words (e.g. 91% of children tested could complete the analogy "wug–wugs", whereas only 36% succeeded with "gutch–gutches"). Similarly, children could handle the past tense, although again there was variation depending on the phonological form of the nonsense word (e.g. 78% could complete "hing–hinged", whereas 33% completed "mot–motted"). For the possessive, 84% were correct for "wug" ("the wug's hat), compared to 49% for "niz" ("the niz's hat"). The adjectival inflections were too difficult for most children, with only one child able to generate "quirkier" and "quirkiest". Berko concluded that young children had a good grasp of English morphological rules. The large variation in performance with the phonological patterning required was explored in terms of the child's possible rules for forming plurals. Alternatively, it could reflect the number of real-world analogies that the child may have learned (e.g. many analogies for the plural "wugs", e.g. bug–bugs, jug–jugs, mug–mugs, plug–plugs, rug–rugs; but only one analogy for the plural "gutches", namely hutch–hutches, as clutch–clutches and touch–touches are not plurals).

The invention of new words by children also reveals their knowledge of word-formation paradigms in the language. Becker (1994) documented new words invented by one boy between the ages of 2 and 5 years. The boy produced many delightful inventions over this period. He produced different types of novel nouns, as in "He's a cock-a-doodle-doo" (a rooster), "You have good earsight, Daddy" (meaning sensitive hearing), "He has real sneak shoes" (to refer to the quiet shoes Father Christmas uses to tiptoe into houses) and "That's a nose beard" (meaning a

This is a wug.

Now there is another one. There are two of them. There are two _____.

FIGURE 5.4
An example of the text used by Berko (1958) to test children's implicit knowledge of grammatical rules.

moustache). He also produced novel verbs, as in "I'm gonna horn you—do you want to be horned?" (= have a horn blown in your face), and "I wanna tennis it" (= hit it with a tennis racket). Verb innovations were rarer than noun innovations.

Becker found that most innovations reflected common word-formation devices, such as compounding or combining single words (e.g. "earsight"). Bowerman (1982) pointed out that children's gradual learning of implicit constraints on word formation can also be revealed by the decline of certain kinds of innovations. For example, the prefix "un" can only be used with verbs of a specific type. These verbs denote enclosure or surface attachment. Between the ages of 4 and 7, Bowerman's daughter Christy produced various innovations involving "un", but these innovations only reflected inappropriate affixing when Christy was 4. At this age, she produced phrases like "I hate you! And I'll never unhate you or nothing!". By age 7, she was producing innovations like "I'm gonna unhang it", innovations that do follow the hidden rule.

How do adults respond to children's innovations or errors? The role of feedback from caretakers in shaping grammatical development has long been debated. The first naturalistic studies suggested that overt correction of grammatical errors was rare. Caretakers did not often use direct correction and, when they did, it was seldom successful, as illustrated in this example (from Braine, 1971):

> Child: "Want other one spoon daddy."
> Father: "You mean, you want the other spoon?"
> Child: "Yes, I want other one spoon please daddy."
> Father: Can you say 'the other spoon'?"
> Child: "Other one spoon."
> Father: Say 'other'."
> Child: "Other."
> Father: "Spoon."
> Child: "Spoon."
> Father: Other spoon."
> Child: "Other—spoon. Now give me other one spoon?"

More recently, it has been demonstrated that adults in fact provide extensive feedback when their children make errors in language production, but that they do this by reformulating the child's utterance rather than by overtly correcting it. This was nicely demonstrated in a study by Chouinard and Clark (2003), who selected all the spontaneous utterances recorded from five children in the child language database **CHILDES** between the ages of 2 and 4 years, and the subsequent utterances made by the parent. They then took random samples of 200 utterances from 6-month slices of the data. They reported that almost 70% of children's erroneous productions at age 2 years were reformulated by their caretakers. All types of erroneous production were likely to be reformulated, whether the errors were grammatical, morphological, phonological or semantic (errors of word choice). There was no prioritizing of grammatical errors. Examples of reformulations include:

> Child: "I want butter mine."
> Father: OK, give it here and I'll put butter on it."
> Child: "I need butter on it."

KEY TERM

CHILDES
Child language data exchange scheme, a database of utterances made by children in the age range 2–4 years and their caregivers.

Similar patterns were found irrespective of language:

Child: *"Une petit de lait."* [= a little of milk]
Mother: *"Une petite boite de lait."* [= a little carton of milk]
Child: *"Petite boite de lait."*

Reformulations also occur via adult use of expansion. Adults often repeat an ungrammatical utterance made by a child by expanding it, at the same time providing the correct grammatical form. Again, this is conversationally more natural than simply correcting the child's production. For example, if the child says "Muffy step on that", the mother might say "Who stepped on that?" and the child might reply "Muffy", and the mother then says "Muffy stepped on it". An experimental study by Cazden (1970, cited in Peccei, 2005) compared the effects of expansion on the utterances of 2- to 3-year-old children at a day-care centre. Three types of feedback were given to the children for 40 minutes a day. One group was given extensive and deliberate expansions of their utterances, a second group spent 40 minutes in which the researcher provided models of adult forms by continuing the conversation (e.g. *Child*: "I got apples". *Experimenter*: "Do you like them?"), and a third group received no special treatment. When language progress was assessed at the end of the study, the children in the expansion group had made no more progress than the children in the control group. It was children in the "conversation" group who had made the most progress.

Syntactic development is also measured in terms of a concept called the "**mean length of utterance**", or **MLU**. This term was coined by Brown and Hanlon (1970), who followed the language development of three children—Adam, Eve, and Sarah—in great detail from the age of around 18 months. Mean length of utterance is measured in morphemes, or units of meaning. "Dog" has one morpheme, "dogs" has two morphemes, "big dogs" has three morphemes and "big dogs ran" has five morphemes (because the use of the past tense of "run" adds two morphemes). These utterances would yield MLUs of 1, 2, 3, and 5, respectively. Eve, Adam, and Sarah showed strikingly different rates of grammatical development using the MLU measure. Whereas Sarah was already producing utterances with an MLU of 4 by age 2 years 2 months, Eve and Adam did not reach an MLU of 4 until they were 3 years and 5 months old.

Bates made the important point that the MLU measure was dominated by the child's ability to use two aspects of grammar, inflectional morphology (—s, —ed) and grammatical function words such as "the" and "he". In the checklist study (Fenson et al., 1994), children first began to use morphemes like —s and —ed at about 16 months. At this age, rather few children used grammatical suffixes. However, by 22 months, the majority of children were using all four of the morphemes studied (—s, —ed, —ing, and possessive "s", as in "Maggie's dolly"). Fenson et al. (1994) argued that sentence complexity might be a better estimate of grammatical development than MLU, particularly after the age of 30 months. They collected data on sentence complexity by giving parents a forced choice task. The parents were asked which kinds of sentence sounded most like "the way your child talks right now". Sentences were paired to reflect increases in complexity, for example "doggie table" versus "doggie on table", or "I want that" versus "I want that one you got". A steady expansion in the complexity of sentences used was documented, with large individual variation. Furthermore, the best predictor of grammatical complexity was vocabulary size.

KEY TERM

Mean length of utterance (MLU)
A measure of language development in terms of the number of morphemes in utterances; shows increases in language development in early childhood.

It thus seems quite possible that children's early utterances do not in fact reflect the range of grammatical constructions imputed to them by adults. Rather, children are acquiring pieces of language. Consequently, grammatical development is intimately related to vocabulary development. This viewpoint has been argued quite compellingly by Tomasello (2000, 2006), who has suggested that children's early linguistic constructions are most likely to reflect the types of utterance that they hear around them. Grammatical development is suggested to centre around the piecemeal acquisition of particular constructions that are good grammatical forms, rather than on the acquisition of general syntactic categories. Children are then thought to build upon these early linguistic constructions by using the same pattern-finding mechanisms that underpin learning in other areas of development (statistical learning, categorization, induction, analogy). In this way, children create the more abstract dimensions that we recognize as grammar. Tomasello's argument is that early linguistic constructions are learned as concrete "pieces" of language. Children are learning "communicatively effective speech act forms", and these may well correspond to whole adult utterances (e.g. "I wanna do it", "Lemme see"). For the child, these utterances represent a single relatively coherent communicative intention.

Tomasello (2006) marshalls a variety of experimental evidence in support of this viewpoint. Tomasello, Akhtar, Dodson, and Rekau (1997) showed that one word or phrase in a multiword utterance often acts as a "pivot" in determining the effective "speech act" (see also Braine, 1963). This pivot utterance can then be paired with a wide variety of words to create novel utterances (e.g. "More juice", "More milk", "More grapes"; "Want cup", "Want cookie", "Want dollie"). Tomasello et al. (1997) showed that 22-month-old children could combine totally novel nouns with their pivot words. When taught the label "wug" ("Look! A wug!") the children could produce phrases like "More wug!" and "Wug gone". In the case of questions, Rowland and Pine (2000) showed that 2- to 4-year-old children either produced certain linguistic constructions 100% correctly ("How did . . . ?", "How do . . . ?", "What do . . . ?") or 100% incorrectly ("Why I can . . . ?", "What she will . . . ?", "What you can . . ."). Again, the children appeared to be acquiring single "pieces" of language that had a certain communicative function, and sticking with them. Only later did children appear to develop a more abstract knowledge of language. Tomasello proposes that the main learning mechanism underpinning this change is reasoning by analogy.

According to Tomasello's account, the acquisition of grammar depends on learning, and development is consequently slow but steady throughout early childhood. Tomasello argues that more studies using nonsense constructions are required in order to get an accurate picture of development, and that these studies must be done across languages. In his own studies with nonsense words, Tomasello consistently finds evidence for slow and steady progress. For example, he finds that children have difficulties in interpreting totally novel verbs. Akhtar and Tomasello (1997) used novel verbs like "dack" with children aged 2 years 9 months and 3 years 8 months. The children were shown a variety of toy scenarios to depict "dacking", and were then asked "Make Cookie Monster dack Big Bird". Only 30% of younger children succeeded at this task, although all children succeeded with familiar verbs. By 3 years 8 months, all children could "dack" without difficulty. Experiments such as these suggest that children learn from the input, using the same general learning mechanisms that they deploy in other cognitive domains. Children learn language by recognizing patterns, and using these patterns to determine the set of rules governing the internal structure of words and the ways in which words can be combined into sentences and phrases.

PRAGMATIC DEVELOPMENT

Language is about communication, and the "**pragmatics**" of language development are about learning how to communicate competently. For example, to have a meaningful conversation with another person, you need to take turns in speaking. You also need to judge your contributions to the conversation, making sure that the other person can understand the information that you are conveying. Anyone who has had a telephone conversation with a young child is aware that it takes time for children to learn these aspects of communication. Young children frequently talk about things that have happened to them, assuming that a listener who was not present at the event will understand them. They seem to assume that adults always know what they are talking about. Young children fail to adopt the perspective of their conversational partner. Young children may also switch conversational topic without warning, breaking the implicit "rules" of discourse. Finally, pragmatics involves being able to use language both socially and appropriately. Young children may be oblivious of the social aspects of dialogue, for example they may be unaware of what is "rude" or "polite" in a given context. They may also be unaware of differences in the social status and familiarity of conversational partners that would lead an adult to modify the language that they use.

One of the first attempts to measure early pragmatic development came from Dale (1980). He argued that early pragmatics had been studied in terms of "speech acts" or "pragmatic functions", which measured children's ability to produce declarative or imperative functions (e.g. "That's mine", "Gimme that"). Further dimensions requiring inclusion were affirmation versus negation, requests for objects versus requests for information, and reference to immediately perceivable objects and events versus reference to absent objects and events. Dale (1980) decided to try and devise a measurement tool for pragmatic functions during the second year of life.

Dale's pragmatic measurement tool was based on two sets of structured tasks. The first set was designed to elicit declaratives from the child, words or phrases commenting on a state of affairs in the world. The idea was to set up a repetitive task, and then introduce a new element, to see whether the child communicated about this new element. The declarative tasks included dropping blocks into a bucket and then offering the child a doll, rolling balls to the child and then rolling a baby bottle, and tapping a xylophone with a stick and then offering the child a hammer. The imperative tasks were designed so that the child would have to request assistance from the experimenter. For example, a dancing tiger toy was wound up by the experimenter and then allowed to run down, or some attractive toys were presented packaged in a clear plastic container that required opening. Children aged 1 year, 1 year 3 months, 1 year 6 months, 1 year 9 months and 2 years were tested. The children were credited for utterances that responded to the newness of the objects introduced in the declarative tasks, and for the way in which they communicated (e.g. pointing versus verbalizing). They were also credited for any imperatives produced, again whether verbal or nonverbal (e.g. removing the experimenters' fingers from a desired toy).

Dale found that the number of pragmatic language categories produced was highly correlated with age. Naming emerged first, followed by greetings and ritualized forms, and then comments about objects and their attributes. Requests concerning the here and now emerged next, followed by affirmation and then denial. Reference to past and future and requests for absent objects emerged last. There was no relationship between pragmatic development and MLU. Dale concluded that the

KEY TERM

Pragmatics
Study of language use in communicating effectively.

range of pragmatic functions developing in the second year of life was measurable, and was tapping information about language development that was separate from syntactic development. However, the imperative tasks were more successful at eliciting communicative behaviors than the declarative tasks. This made it difficult to generate an overall measure of communicative performance for an individual child.

How do children acquire the social roles for language use? It is difficult to see how children could acquire social speech and politeness routines without direct input from adults. As pointed out by Gleason (1980), learning the social roles for language use is part of the development of social cognition. The language used in many social routines has no intrinsic meaning, rather the child is required to recognize a certain kind of social situation and apply the appropriate formula. For example, the child may have to say "thank you" for a present that she does not actually like, or say "God bless you" when someone sneezes. Adults are not concerned with the truth value of the routine involved, but with the performance of the child.

We will consider the development of social cognition in greater depth in Chapter 7. As we will see, language and social cognition are connected in important ways. The development of both language and social cognition depends on communicative intent, as already outlined in Chapter 3. The pragmatics of communication require some insights into the mind of another person. For a conversation to be meaningful, an assessment must be made of how much your conversational partner understands. These aspects of pragmatics are as important as conventions like turn taking, and involve the skills that comprise a "theory of mind". These aspects of pragmatics will be discussed further in Chapter 7.

SUMMARY

Language acquisition is a remarkable feat, yet most children are competent speakers of their language within 3 years of being born. They seem to achieve this via powerful general learning mechanisms coupled with a desire to communicate. Children do not learn language from the television or the radio. They learn language when conversational partners are interacting with them, and they learn the language structures used by those partners. The communicative intentions of their conversational partners play a key role in which words are learned, and so does the context of learning. The context within which new words are heard usually provides rich cues to the meanings of those new words, and mechanisms such as joint attention facilitate the use of the relevant context by infants.

For phonological learning, the input is crucial. Infants rely on auditory statistical learning, attending to the distributional properties of the sounds in the language to extract the crucial phonetic contrasts. Although the brain is particularly sensitive to the prototypical phonetic contrasts that are used by a particular language early in life, continued exposure to more than one language preserves the ability to make phonetic distinctions that are not used by the dominant language. Nevertheless, within the first year of life, monolingual babies focus on the phonetic contrasts that are important for their native language, showing reduced sensitivity to the phonetic contrasts that are important for other languages.

General auditory perceptual abilities seem to influence where the physical boundaries for phonetic contrasts are placed by human languages, and general physiological properties of the mouth and jaw seem to influence which sounds are easiest to make and hence which sounds are frequent across languages. Rhythmic and prosodic patterning are also important. Infants use stress patterns as a way of segmenting words from the speech stream, and prosodic cues also determine how individual sounds are ordered into words. Producing sounds yourself (babbling) appears to be important for perceptual learning, and babbling reflects the frequent sounds and the intonation patterns of the ambient language.

Word learning takes off around the end of the first year. Here the input that requires attention is more complex. Children need to be aware of the context in which new words are being used by their caretakers, and of the communicative intent of the speaker. Adopting a basic premise that the sound patterns uttered by adults must be connected to things in the external environment, infants rapidly make these "word-to-world" links. Most children acquire the meanings of hundreds of words during their second year. In fact, it is estimated that 2-year-olds acquire around 10 new words per day. Children's early words tend to be highly relevant to their daily lives, with a special role for their own name and for extremely salient labels like "Mummy". Production tends to lag behind comprehension, and so gesture is used to increase communication. By combining gestures with words, 2-year-olds can get quite complex messages across. Language also has a reciprocal effect on conceptual organization, for example of spatial relations.

At the same time as busily acquiring words, children are learning how to put words together. They are learning the set of grammatical rules that determine how words can be combined into sentences and phrases, and the set of rules governing the internal structure of words. Again, the learning involved appears to depend on general learning mechanisms. Children initially learn "pieces of language" that can correspond to whole adult utterances. Children want to communicate, and so they use statistical learning, categorization, induction, and analogy to appropriate structures that enable them to fulfill certain communicative intentions. In fact, the best predictor of grammatical complexity at any age is vocabulary size. Children's brains do not have a special learning device for learning grammar. Rather, children learn grammar from the phrases used by those around them and, when they produce ungrammatical utterances, their caretakers reformulate these utterances as a way of extending conversation. Children notice these reformulations, once again learning from the input but in a communicative context. Children do not seem to learn much from direct correction. At the same time, children must learn the pragmatics of effective communication. The "pragmatics" of language development are about learning how to communicate competently, and this depends particularly on social cognitive development. As we saw in Chapter 3, and will see again in Chapter 7, social development and language development are intimately linked.

CHAPTER 6

CONTENTS

The central role of causal reasoning

In the Foreword to this book, I suggested that causal learning was a domain-general skill that played a core role in cognitive development. I also argued that the perceptual system may be set up to assume causal relations in the absence of contradictory evidence. This could yield the apparently innate "bias" to learn about causal relations and to acquire causal explanations. So far, we have seen that perceptual information supports causal learning in the foundational domains of cognitive development. Perceptual information gives the infant and the young child important insights into the nature of objects and their interactions, enabling the emergent understanding of the physical world. Perceptual information yields multiple cues about agency and intentionality, facilitating the development of social cognition. Finally, perceptual information supplies rich information about animates and inanimates, informing conceptual development.

Perception is a rich source of causal information because perception involves more than simply registering the physical structure of the world. The causal structure of physical events is registered as well. For example, in Chapter 2 we saw that simple perceptual events such as launching events yield strong impressions of causality to infants and adults (see Schlottmann, Allen, Linderoth, & Hesketh, 2002, for experiments with young children). We also saw that watching moving objects that change in their speed or direction yield strong impressions of animacy. The evidence considered so far suggests that the causal structure of events plays an important role in representing, interpreting, and remembering events from very early in development. Observing the world yields important clues to causal structure, and causal structure is given to some extent by perception.

We have also seen that infants' abilities to notice associations, to track statistical dependencies (conditional probabilities), and to connect causes and effects enables powerful learning from perceptual information. In Chapter 2, the tendency of the perceptual system to assume cause–effect relations in the absence of contradictory evidence was suggested to lie at the heart of causal understanding. As proposed by Michotte (1963) and by Scholl and Tremoulet (2000), the origins of causal cognition may lie in neurally hard-wired mechanisms that give rise to causal perception. Children's early focus on causal information is clearly an essential building block for cognition (see Goswami, 1998), and causality can be thought of as a "developmental primitive" (Wellman & Gelman, 1998). However, although the spatiotemporal dynamics of visual events in themselves yield rich information about causal relations, infants and young children quickly come to evolve explanatory frameworks for making sense of events in the world around them. They seek hidden features to help them to understand what makes objects and events similar (S. Gelman, 2004; see Chapter 4). These explanatory frameworks depend in part on action: Once the child can actively manipulate different causes and observe the effects, causal learning benefits enormously. Having an explanatory framework enables *predictions* to be made about future states of the world. Explanatory frameworks also enable informed and purposive intervention. Once a child has worked out how an event was caused, the child can control that event, causing it to happen by intervening in the world in a principled way. An intervention involves imposing a change on a variable in a causal system from outside the system (see Lagnado, Waldmann, Hagmayer, & Sloman, 2007). A simple example is a baby crawling to unplug the vacuum cleaner while his or her parent is trying to do the cleaning.

How do children learn about causal structure? Some causal explanatory frameworks can clearly emerge from consideration of the relevant perceptual variables. For example, when examining the development of naïve physics, we saw that perceptual information about object trajectories and relative size and weight leads infants to infer notions like "transfer of force" to explain whether the collision of one object with another can be expected to set the other object in motion (e.g. Kotovsky & Baillargeon, 1998; see Chapter 1). In other foundational domains, for example naïve psychology, we discussed how key variables for the construction of an explanatory framework may be unobservable, requiring infants to infer their existence (e.g. mental states; see Chapter 3). In the case of psychological causality, we may only be able to predict certain actions (such as an adult searching a box that we know to be empty; see Onishi & Baillargeon, 2005) if we can understand that the adult has a *false belief* that the box contains a desired object. The development of the understanding of psychological causality is discussed further in Chapter 7. In the case of physical causality, when key variables are unobservable, we have to infer **causal mechanisms** to predict the effects that one object may have upon another. The kind of causal mechanisms that we infer will also depend on our experience. In most causal learning situations, we have some prior knowledge about basic causal features, and this prior knowledge guides our causal inferences.

I therefore begin this chapter by reviewing studies concerning whether children have the ability to make causal inferences. As argued by Shultz (Shultz & Kestenbaum, 1985), children would only be able to understand causal mechanisms if the underlying processes of causal reasoning were functioning efficiently. Shultz defined these underlying processes by reference to the principles of causal inference defined by the philosopher David Hume (1748). Hume assumed that people are exposed to patterns of data, and infer causality from these patterns. He argued that we infer causality (that event X causes event Y) when X precedes Y in time, when X is contiguous with Y in time and space, and when the contiguity is regular (see Koslowski & Masnick, 2002). These Humean indices can be defined as the principle of causal priority, the principle of temporal contiguity, and the covariation principle.

More recently, it has been argued that causal Bayes nets are a better way of representing the statistical relations present in a body of evidence (see Lagnado et al., 2007, for a discussion of how to go beyond covariation information to extract causal structure). Causal Bayes nets derive from research on machine learning and can represent conditional relations, such as relations of conditional independence. Even though Bayes nets are very sophisticated, statistical data alone are usually insufficient for inferring a unique causal model and so structural constraints are also important. Principles such as temporal order, intervention in situations, and real-world knowledge about likely causes and effects (e.g. that a switch is probably a cause of something) are all important for inferring causal structure (see also Waldmann, Hagmayer, & Blaisdell, 2006). Understanding the importance of interventions (e.g. the effects of pressing the switch yourself: Think of toddlers operating DVD players and televisions) also involves the ability to recognize the relationship between hypotheses and evidence. From this perspective, causal reasoning is also central to the development of scientific reasoning. After all, a major goal of science

KEY TERM

Causal mechanisms
The causal features that determine the effects that one object may have on another.

is to identify and understand the causes of different phenomena. These different aspects of causal reasoning will be discussed in turn.

REASONING ABOUT CAUSES AND EFFECTS

By the age of around 3 years, children have experienced many different physical causes and their effects. For example, they have many experiences of *cutting* (apples, paper, hair), of *melting* (chocolate, snow, butter), of *breaking* (a toy, a cup, a chair), of *wetting* (washing clothes, rain, having a bath), and so on. One way to investigate the development of causal reasoning is thus to ask whether children know that causal agents can produce transformations in objects, changing them from one state to another. For example, if children are shown a picture of a cup and a picture of a shattered cup, do they know that a hammer is a more likely agent of the causal transformation than a knife or scissors?

Reasoning about the causal transformations of familiar objects

R. Gelman, Bullock, and Meck (1980) used three-picture causal sequences based on such transformations to investigate cause–effect reasoning in 3- and 4-year-old children. They first trained children to read the picture sequences from left to right. Following this training, they showed the children picture sequences that either depicted an object being transformed from its *canonical* form (an intact cup) to its *noncanonical* form (a broken cup), or from its noncanonical form (a broken cup) to its canonical form (an intact cup). The middle picture in the sequence always depicted the causal agent (the correct agents in this example were a hammer or some glue). As well as familiar causal transformations like cups breaking, the children were shown unfamiliar causal transformations like a cut banana being restored to its canonical form using a needle and thread.

In the experiment, the children were shown the picture sequences in an incomplete form, with one of the three pictures missing. Their job was to select the correct picture to fill the empty slot from three alternatives. For example, if the picture of the agent was missing, then pictures of three possible agents were provided as alternatives. If the first or the final picture in the sequence was missing, then the children were shown pictures of the correct object with either a correct or an incorrect causal transformation, and a picture of an incorrect object with the correct causal transformation. Examples of each type of trial are depicted in Figure 6.1.

Gelman et al. found that 92% of the 3-year-olds and 100% of the 4-year-olds could select the correct causal agent when the middle picture was missing from the canonical stories (e.g. cup to broken cup), and that 75% of the 3-year-olds and 100% of the 4-year-olds could select the correct causal agent when the middle picture was

Gelman et al. (1980) found that 92% of 3-year-olds and 100% of 4-year-olds could select the correct causal agent of the causal transformations presented in their task. Children of this age are able to infer that the sun is causing their popsicle to melt.

FIGURE 6.1
Examples of the three-picture causal sequences used by Gelman et al. (1980). Story A has the final picture missing, story B the initial picture, and story C the picture of the agent. From Gelman et al. (1980). Reproduced with permission from Blackwell Publishing.

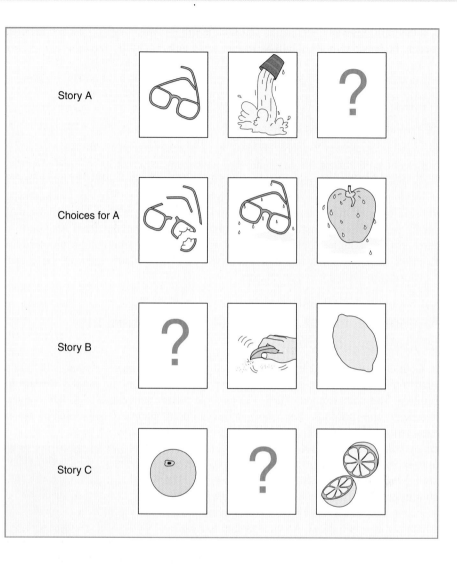

missing from the noncanonical stories (e.g. broken cup to cup). Performance fell slightly for the younger children when the missing picture was the final item (83% and 100%, respectively, for canonical sequences; 58% and 100%, respectively, for noncanonical sequences), and fell more markedly when the missing picture was the first item (66% and 92%, respectively, for canonical sequences; 58% and 100%, respectively, for noncanonical sequences). Nevertheless, performance was significantly above chance in all cases. Gelman et al. concluded that preschool children could predict or infer the states of objects changed by a causal transformation, and could also infer the kind of transformation that related two object states.

Reversible reasoning about causal transformations of familiar objects

In a second study, using the same children, the **reversibility of causal reasoning** was investigated. In this study, the missing picture was always the middle picture,

KEY TERM

Reversibility of causal reasoning
The ability to think about the same objects in different (reversed) causal relationships.

and the children were first asked to select a picture of an agent for a *left-to-right* reading of the causal sequence, and then a picture of an agent for a *right-to-left* reading of the causal sequence. This request required the children to think about the same object pairs (e.g. cup and broken cup) in two different (reversed) ways. The 3-year-olds found this task quite difficult, and were correct on only 49% of trials; the 4-year-olds succeeded on 75% of trials. Gelman et al. argued that the 3-year-olds scored poorly because they tended to impose their *own* causal ordering onto the task. They preferred canonical to noncanonical readings over noncanonical to canonical readings, and so were scored as being wrong on half of the trials. Overall, however, Gelman et al. claimed that the 3-year-olds' representations of the causal transformations were abstract enough to permit reversibility.

Although Gelman et al.'s work suggests an early understanding of many cause–effect relations and of their reversibility, Das Gupta and Bryant (1989) criticized their studies on methodological grounds. Das Gupta and Bryant argued that it was possible to "solve" the reversible causal sequences by associative rather than by causal reasoning. This is an important criticism, as associative reasoning is thought to be a less sophisticated type of reasoning than causal reasoning. Das Gupta and Bryant argued that, rather than considering *both* the initial *and* the final states of the object when choosing the causal instrument, the children could simply have focused on the *more salient* noncanonical state of the object (e.g. the broken cup). They could then have selected the instrument associated with that noncanonical state. Thus the children could have solved the problems without taking the object's initial state into consideration at all.

Das Gupta and Bryant argued that a *genuine* causal inference depended on the children being able to work out the *difference* between the initial and final states in a causal chain. To examine whether 3- and 4-year-olds could do this, Das Gupta and Bryant showed them three-picture causal sequences in which the objects *began* as noncanonical in one way (e.g. a broken cup), and ended up as noncanonical in *two ways* (e.g. a wet, broken cup). Trials were paired, so that later in the experiment the children also saw a picture sequence that began with a wet cup and ended with a wet, broken cup. As in Gelman et al.'s procedure, the children's job was to select the missing middle term in the three-picture sequences, which was the causal agent. However, in Das Gupta and Bryant's task, the selection of the agent *most highly associated* with the noncanonical form of the object (a hammer) would be an *incorrect* response in the picture sequence broken cup to wet, broken cup, but the *correct* response in the picture sequence wet cup to wet, broken cup (Table 6.1). Thus if the same causal agent was chosen on a given pair of trials (e.g. the hammer for broken cup to wet, broken cup *and* for wet cup to wet, broken cup) then a genuine causal inference was unlikely to be made.

Following Gelman et al., the children were again required to choose from three possible causal agents, in this case *hammer*, *water*, and *feather* (an irrelevant agent). Das Gupta and Bryant found that the 3-year-olds chose the same causal agent (e.g. the hammer) in 49% of trials for the pairs of sequences, whereas the 4-year-olds only chose the same causal agent on 21% of trials. The younger children got the correct answer to both sequences in a pair on 39% of occasions, and the 4-year-olds on 78% of occasions. Das Gupta and Bryant concluded that 3-year-olds were often distracted by the salience of particular causal effects (such as breaking), which led them to disregard

TABLE 6.1	One of the pairs of causal sequences used by Das Gupta and Bryant (1989)		
1. Wet cup	[Blank]	Wet *broken cup*
2. Broken cup	[Blank]	Broken *wet cup*

the relation between initial and final states. This made the causal status of their inferences questionable.

The salience of noncanonical states in early causal reasoning

In a second experiment, Das Gupta and Bryant went on to argue that the best test of children's ability to make genuine causal inferences was to use noncanonical (broken cup) to canonical (whole cup) sequences. Such sequences necessitated a causal inference based on the *difference* between the object's initial and final state. In contrast, canonical to noncanonical sequences (cup to broken cup) could be solved on the basis of the departure from canonicality. The salience of the broken cup could lead children to "correctly" select a hammer as an agent in a canonical to noncanonical sequence, but would probably also lead them to choose a hammer in the noncanonical to canonical sequence. In support of their claim, Das Gupta and Bryant showed that 3-year-olds were significantly poorer at reasoning from a noncanonical initial state to a canonical state (broken cup to cup) than from a canonical initial state to a noncanonical one (cup to broken cup), success rates being 47% correct and 88% correct, respectively. Their conclusion was that the ability to make genuine causal inferences developed between 3 and 4 years, rather than being already present at age 3. However, the use of static picture sequences may not be the optimal method for probing the development of causal understanding. Real-world reasoning tasks suggest that children behave as though they are making genuine causal inferences as young as 2 years of age. This evidence is discussed below, when we consider causal Bayes nets. It is also worth noting that studies with adults demonstrate clear effects of reasoning from effect to cause on the speed of causal reasoning. For example, when deciding whether two events can be causally related, adults are significantly faster to say yes for the events "spark, fire" (*predictive condition*) than for the events "fire, spark" (*diagnostic condition*, see Fenker, Waldmann, & Holyoak, 2005). Fenker et al. argued that "causal directedness" is stored as part of the causal understanding of real-world events. It would clearly be interesting to investigate the importance of causal directedness for young children.

KEY TERMS

Causal principles
The principles underlying causal contingencies.

Priority principle
Understanding that an event can be caused by another event occurring prior to it and not by a subsequent event.

Covariation principle
Understanding that the true cause of an effect is likely to be the event that regularly and predictably covaries with the effect.

REASONING ON THE BASIS OF CAUSAL PRINCIPLES

A number of experimenters have explored whether children's causal reasoning follows the **causal principles** identified by Hume (1748). Take the simplest kind of causal contingency, when one event A causes another event B: For A to cause B, a number of causal principles must apply. One is that A must either precede B or occur at the same time as B; it cannot occur after B. This asymmetry of causal relations is called the **priority principle** (that causes precede or co-occur with their effects). Other important principles in assigning causality are the **covariation principle** (that causes and their effects must systematically covary), the **temporal contiguity principle** (that causes and effects must be contiguous in place and time), and the similarity principle (that causes and their effects should have some similarity to each other, for example that a mechanical effect should have a mechanical cause).

The priority principle

The age at which children develop the understanding that causes precede their effects has been measured largely with action-based tasks. For example, imagine that you see a puppet dropping a marble into an apparatus, and that soon afterwards a jack-in-the-box pops out of the middle of the apparatus. You are likely to attribute the appearance of the jack to the action of the marble. It is unlikely that you will attribute causation to a second marble that is dropped into the apparatus by a second puppet *after* the jack has appeared.

Bullock and R. Gelman used this "jack-in-the-box" apparatus to investigate whether 3- to 5-year-old children understand that the jack-in-the-box can only be activated by an event *preceding* the jack's appearance, and not by an event that occurs after his jump. In their task, the children were shown a long black box. This box was divided internally into three sections (Figure 6.2; these divisions were not visible to the children). The two outer thirds of the box each had a tunnel for marbles to roll down, with each tunnel running on a sloping path towards the center of the box. The tunnels were visible through plexiglass windows, so that only their ends (in the middle third of the box) were hidden from view. The central section of the box was opaque, and concealed the ends of the tunnels and the jack-in-the-box. The experimenter could make the jack jump by dropping a marble down either tunnel, although the jack was in fact controlled by a hidden pedal and not by the marbles themselves.

To test the children's understanding of the unidirectional order of causes and effects, the experimenter (via two puppets) dropped a marble down one tunnel before the jack jumped, and another marble down the second tunnel after he had jumped.

KEY TERM

Temporal contiguity principle
Causes and effects must by contiguous in time and place.

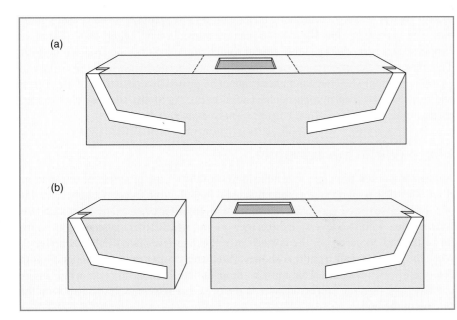

FIGURE 6.2
The apparatus used in Bullock and Gelman's (1979) "jack-in-the-box" study, showing (a) the complete apparatus, and (b) its appearance when the causally appropriate runway was separated from the remaining two-thirds of the box. From Bullock and Gelman (1979). Reproduced with permission from Blackwell Publishing.

The children's task was to infer which puppet's marble had made the jack jump. Bullock and Gelman found that the majority of children at all ages tested could work out that the first marble had made the jack jump. This was the case for 75% of the 3-year-olds, 88% of the 4-year-olds, and 100% of the 5-year-olds. Bullock and Gelman then made the task more difficult by physically separating the causally appropriate runway from the other two-thirds of the box. Following the separation, one tunnel was in apparent contact with the jack, and the other tunnel was not. The experimenter dropped a marble down the detached tunnel before the jack jumped, and a marble down the attached tunnel after he had jumped. Even under these more stringent conditions, causality was attributed to the first marble by 75% of the 3-year-olds, 94% of 4-year-olds, and 100% of 5-year-olds. The children in Bullock and Gelman's study appeared to assume that temporal ordering cues were more critical than spatial proximity in determining causality in the jack-in-the-box apparatus. Nevertheless, they were surprised that action-at-a-distance was possible in the detached tunnel condition, and assumed that it needed some explanation ("It's a trick, right?", "It's magic", "When I wasn't looking, the ball slided over").

However, it is not necessary to assume from these data that the children assigned *more* causal importance to temporal priority than to spatial proximity. The simplest conclusion from Bullock and Gelman's data is that the children were basing their judgments on what was *causally relevant* to the experimental set-up. Consistent with this conclusion, Shultz (1982) has shown that children will favor spatial factors over temporal ones when spatial factors are more causally relevant to a particular outcome than temporal ordering factors. Shultz's demonstration was based on an apparatus in which two electric air blowers were directed at a lit candle. The candle flame could be protected from the jets of air by a three-sided plexiglass shield, which could be rotated to field the air emitted by one of the blowers at a time. Shultz showed 5-year-old children this apparatus, and then switched on one of the blowers when the shield was in a position to protect the candle. Five seconds later the second blower was switched on, and at the same time the shield turned to protect the candle from this second blower. The flame immediately went out. The children correctly attributed the flame's extinction to the action of the first blower, even though the onset of the second blower was the event that was temporally contiguous with the candle going out. The *particular mechanisms* of causal transmission, rather than spatial or temporal parameters *per se*, thus appear to determine children's causal attributions. This illustrates the importance of context and background knowledge in children's causal reasoning. The Humean indices cannot be treated independently of the objects and relations involved in a particular causal event. As Shultz showed, children are aware of the importance of the *causal agent* in a given set-up.

The covariation principle

Another important principle in establishing causality is the principle of covariation. If an effect has a number of potential causes, then the true cause is likely to be the one that regularly and predictably covaries with the effect. For example, if a child is shown a box with two levers, and has to work out which lever causes a light on the lid of the box to come on, the correct answer is the lever that is always activated when the light is on. If a child is shown a box with two holes in the top, and has to determine which hole a marble must be dropped into in order to make a bell inside the box ring, then the correct answer is the hole that is always associated with the ringing of the bell.

Shultz and Mendelson (1975) gave causal problems such as these to 3- to 4-year-old and older children to determine their ability to use the covariation principle. Covariation information was varied by manipulating the number of times that the cause and the effect were associated with each other. For example, if lever 1 caused the light on the lid of the box to come on, then the children might receive the following pairings of the light and the two levers: lever 1, light; lever 2, no light; lever 1, light; levers 1 and 2, light; lever 2, no light; levers 1 and 2, light. Shultz and Mendelson found that even the 3- to 4-year-olds could use this kind of covariation information to determine causality, with the majority of children choosing the correct cause across all the different kinds of apparatus used. Shultz and Mendelson thus concluded that the ability to make causal attributions on the basis of covariation information for simple physical phenomena was present by at least 3 years of age (see also Siegler and Liebert, 1974, for work on covariation with older children).

The temporal contiguity principle

The principle of temporal contiguity, which states that causes and effects must be contiguous in time and place, is intimately related to the covariation principle. In many causal situations, the same cause is implicated by both temporal contiguity and covariation (an example is Bullock and Gelman's jack-in-the-box study, discussed above). Temporal contiguity is also intimately related to the priority principle, which states that causes must temporally precede or co-occur with their effects. However, the temporal contiguity principle refers to the fact that, in addition to covarying systematically, causes and effects must be linked to each other by an intervening chain of contiguous events (Sedlak & Kurtz, 1981). If there is a physical rationale for a temporal delay between cause and effect, then the principle of temporal contiguity may still hold.

For example, imagine that you are shown an apparatus consisting of a box painted half green and half orange which sits on top of a wooden stand. The box is linked by a piece of rubber tubing 34 inches long to another box, which has a bell inside it. The green and orange box has two holes in it, one on the green side and one on the orange side. If a marble is dropped into the hole on the green side, a 5-second delay ensues, and then the bell in the second box rings. If a marble is dropped into the hole on the orange side, then the bell in the second box does not ring. If a marble is dropped into the hole on the green side, and then 5 seconds later another marble is dropped into the hole in the orange side, the bell rings immediately. Which side of the box is responsible for making the bell ring, the orange side or the green side?

On the basis of covariation information, it seems as though the green side is responsible for making the bell ring. However, on the basis of temporal contiguity, the orange side is a more plausible candidate – except that the marble must pass through the rubber tubing before it can reach the second box which contains the bell. Mendelson and Shultz (1975) showed children this apparatus in two conditions. In one condition the rubber tubing was present, and in the second condition the first box sat directly on top of the second. They found that when the tubing was present, most of the children (who were aged 4–7 years) attributed the ringing of the bell to the green side of the box. However, when the tubing was absent, most of the children attributed the ringing of the bell to the orange side of the box, even though they knew that in some cases dropping a marble into the hole in the orange side failed to make the bell ring. Mendelson and Shultz concluded that, in the absence of a physical rationale for a temporal delay, children assigned more causal importance to information about temporal contiguity than to information about covariation. However, when they could see a reason for the temporal delay, then they attributed causality to the consistent covariate (the green side), despite the lack of temporal contiguity. Again, it seems that prior knowledge of potential reasons for delays between causes and effects, coupled with a focus on the identification of potential causal agents, has an influence on assumed causal mechanisms.

The principle of the similarity of causes and effects

So far, we have seen that young children's causal reasoning follows the principles of priority, covariation, and temporal contiguity. When attempting to reason about causality in the absence of any information about temporal contiguity or covariation, however, then the *similarity* of potential causes and effects can be useful. For example, imagine that a box is equipped with a heavy lever and a delicate lever, and can either emit a loud electric bell sound or a very gentle sound. The typical assumption in these circumstances is that the delicate lever is the cause of the gentle sound and the heavy lever is the cause of the loud sound. Similarly, if you are shown two small bottles of clear fluid, one with a pink cap and one with a blue cap, and you are also shown a flask of water that is tinged pink, then the typical assumption is that the pink coloring was caused by fluid from the bottle with the pink cap. Of course, if you are then shown that a drop of fluid from the bottle with the blue cap turns the water pink, and a drop of fluid from the bottle with the pink cap has no effect on the color of the water, then this covariation information is likely to change your causal attribution. Similarly, if you are shown that a drop of fluid from the bottle with the blue cap has no effect on water color, and then 5 seconds later that a drop from the bottle with the pink cap immediately turns the water blue, this temporal contiguity information is likely to change your causal attribution as well.

Shultz and Ravinsky (1977) used a number of physical reasoning problems of this type to see whether, in the absence of information about covariation or temporal contiguity, young children would make causal inferences on the basis of the **similarity of cause and effect**. They were also interested in whether young children would abandon the similarity principle when it conflicted with temporal and covariance information. Shultz and Ravinsky tested children aged 6, 8, 10, and 12 years with a variety of physical problems, presenting a variety of covariation and temporal contiguity information in addition to similarity information. In the *absence* of information about temporal contiguity or covariation, all of the children used similarity information to make their causal attributions. When information about *covariation* conflicted with similarity information, then the older children (10- and 12-year-olds) abandoned the use of similarity information. The younger children appeared confused about which principle to apply, and did not make consistent attributions. A similar pattern was found when information about *temporal contiguity* conflicted with similarity information, although in this case only the 6-year-olds showed the confused pattern of responding. Shultz and Ravinsky concluded that similarity of causes and their effects is a potent principle of causal inference for children at all ages, but that the abandonment of this principle in situations of conflict occurs at an earlier age for conflicting temporal information than for conflicting covariation information.

Does this mean that, developmentally, temporal information is recognized to have causal importance prior to covariation information? As Shultz and Ravinsky point out, this would fit Mendelson and Shultz's (1975) data (described earlier) based on the experiment with a marble and some rubber tubing. Here, too, children preferred to attribute causality to a temporally contiguous but inconsistent event rather than to a temporally noncontiguous but consistent event. Recently, however, it has been argued that information about temporal order provides an important clue to *causal structure*, while information about covariation provides important information about *causal strength* (see Lagnado et al., 2007). Historically, experiments on causal reasoning have been more concerned with causal strength than with causal structure. This is true of most of the experiments carried out by Schulz and colleagues. However, causal structure is prior with respect to human cognition, because the qualitative causal relations that hold between variables are more important than their strength. It is first important to know whether a given causal relation exists at all (does smoking cause lung cancer?), and only then to know about the strength of the relation (is there a dose–response relationship?).

In any event, given the data discussed so far, it seems that children's judgments in any particular causal reasoning paradigm will depend on their background knowledge about what is *causally relevant* to the experimental set-up. Shultz himself argued for a version of this position 20 years ago, pointing out that an effect is most likely to be attributed to a cause that seems capable of directing the appropriate sort of transmission (Shultz, Fisher, Pratt, & Rulf, 1986). In other words, contextual knowledge governs children's interpretation of statistical patterns of covariation. Other researchers stress the key role for children of the identification of the causal agent(s), which may precede the effort to clarify potential causal mechanism(s) (see Koslowski & Masnick, 2002).

CAUSAL BAYES NETS

More recently, interest has grown in whether the development of causal reasoning can be described by **causal Bayes nets** (Gopnik, Glymour, Sobel, Shultz, Kushnir, & Danks, 2004). Causal Bayes nets were originally a mathematical tool for implementing machine-learning algorithms. They arose from algorithms that required different sets of probabilities according to whether a given variable in the algorithm was on or off. Formally, causal Bayes nets enable algorithms for the induction of causal structures from covariation data by representing both straightforward relations (A, B, and C all covary) and conditional relations (A covaries with C only in the presence of B). The requirement for B to be present means that either A causes B, which in turn causes C (A $\rightarrow$ B $\rightarrow$ C); or that B causes both A and C (A $\leftarrow$ B $\rightarrow$ C); or that C causes B, which causes A (A $\leftarrow$ B $\leftarrow$ C; example from Lagnado et al., 2007). Causal Bayes nets can represent all of these possible causal structures on the basis of the statistical input that A, B, and C all covary. Information about temporal order or real-world knowledge could then come into play (for example, if A precedes B in time, then A $\rightarrow$ B $\rightarrow$ C is the only possible causal structure).

In terms of modeling causal inference, it has been shown that causal Bayes nets can represent the formal distinction between seeing and doing (Waldmann & Hagmayer, 2005). This is a very interesting point with respect to cognitive development, as young infants inevitably have to see before they can do, given

KEY TERM

Causal Bayes nets
Machine learning algorithms that can represent the causal structure underlying covariation data.

limited motor capacities in the first months of life. To date, however, the causal distinction between seeing and doing has only been studied in adults and in animals. Seeing versus doing is also relevant to the role of intervention in working out causal structure. The probability of a given event B covarying with an *observed* event A may differ from the probability of event B if event A is caused to happen via an *intervention*. For example, the probability of observing a thunderstorm (event B) following a change on the barometer to "Rain" (event A) is not the same as the probability of observing a thunderstorm if the barometer is set by a human agent to point to "Rain". The difference between seeing and doing as a basis for causal knowledge, or between making causal inferences about covariations between states of events that are observed, and between states of events that are caused by *interventions*, deserves systematic investigation in developmental psychology. Causal Bayes nets can be used to predict the effects of interventions in both simple and complex causal structures.

Recently, Gopnik, and colleagues have conducted some investigations into whether children can use covariation data to induce causal structure in the same ways that machine algorithms like causal Bayes nets can. Gopnik and colleagues focused on whether young children are able to "screen off" spurious associations between variables. For example, the association between the barometer reading and rain is spurious—the association is spurious with respect to causal structure in that the barometer does not *cause* the rain. Gopnik proposed that if young children reason in accordance with the graphs of cause–effect relations generated by causal Bayes nets, they should make only causal inferences about genuine relationships. She suggested that even very young children might be able to draw correct causal inferences from patterns of evidence without necessarily having an explicit understanding of what they were doing.

Gopnik, Sobel, Schulz, and Glymour (2001) examined whether children aged from 2 to 4 years could use *screening off* to work out which objects (called "blickets") had the causal power to make a novel machine called a "blicket detector" work. The children had to work out which objects were blickets by observing what happened when the objects were placed on the machine. The blicket detector was a box that lit up and played music when a blicket was placed on it (Figure 6.3). Gopnik et al. (2001) also investigated whether the children could design appropriate interventions.

During the experiments, the children were told "blickets make the machine go", and were asked to "find out which things were blickets". In fact, the blicket detector was controlled by a hidden experimenter, who activated it according to various sets of covariation relations. These sets of covarying relations were observed by the children. Following training to ensure that the children understood the relationship between an object setting off the machine and being labeled a blicket, children experienced both "one-cause" and "two-cause" tasks. In the *one-cause task*, the children saw two blocks, A and B. Block A activated the machine and block B did not. When both blocks were placed on the machine together, it lit up and played music (the dual block event was shown twice). From observing this set of causal relations, we should infer that A is a blicket but that B is not. In the *two-cause task*, the children again saw two blocks A and B, but this time each block was placed on the machine by itself on three occasions. Block A activated the machine on all three occasions, and block B on two-thirds (two) of occasions. In this case, we should infer that both A and B are blickets. The presence of each block on its own increases the likelihood that the machine will be activated.

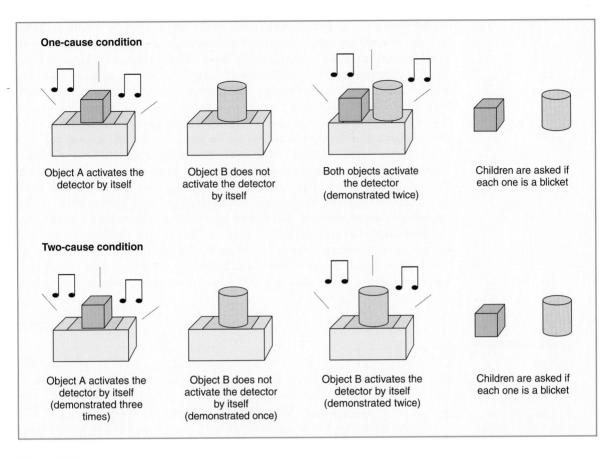

FIGURE 6.3

The procedure used in Gopnik et al. (2001), Experiment 1. From Gopnik, Sobel, Schultz, and Glymour (2001). Copyright © American Psychological Association. Reproduced with permission.

Note also that, in both tasks, the children see the same contingencies. Block A is associated with activation of the machine on three occasions, and block B is associated with activation of the machine on two occasions. However, in the one-cause task, the fact that B is associated with the activation of the blicket detector on two out of three occasions is spurious with respect to causality. The requirement that block A is also present "screens off" the possibility of a causal relation between block B and the activation of the machine. Using this simple paradigm, Gopnik et al. (2001) were able to demonstrate that children as young as 2 years behaved in accordance with screening off. Block A "screened off" block B as a potential cause of the effect in the one-cause condition, even for the 2-year-olds.

Gopnik et al. (2001) then investigated whether the children would intervene appropriately to make the machine stop. They reasoned that if the children really believed that blickets had the causal power to make the machine go, then they should be able to infer that removing the blicket would make the machine stop. This was tested by showing a new group of children the following pattern of dependent probabilities. First, block B was placed on the machine, and nothing happened. After a few seconds, block A was also placed on the machine, and it began to work. After a while, the children were asked "Can you make it stop?". The majority of children removed just block A. In a second scenario, the machine was shown being activated by block B, which was then removed. Next, it was shown being activated by block A when placed alone, and then block B was added next to block A (Figure 6.4). In this scenario, the majority of children removed both blocks in order to make the machine stop. Gopnik and colleagues argued that this showed that the children were using screening off information to make genuinely causal judgments. Schulz and Gopnik (2004) went on to show that young children also used screening off to make causal judgments in the domains of biology (which flowers make Monkey sneeze?) and psychology (which animals make Bunny scared?). They argued that children's causal inferences were consistent with the relationships between causality and probabilistic dependence represented by causal Bayes nets across domains. Even very young children appear to have the implicit ability to draw these powerful causal inferences from patterns of evidence about dependent and independent probabilities.

Intriguingly, however, so do rats. Although Gopnik et al. (2004) suggested that children have specialized cognitive systems that enable them to recover accurate causal maps of the causal relations among events, Blaisdell, Sawa, Leising, & Waldmann (2006) produced data suggesting that rats, too, have such a system.

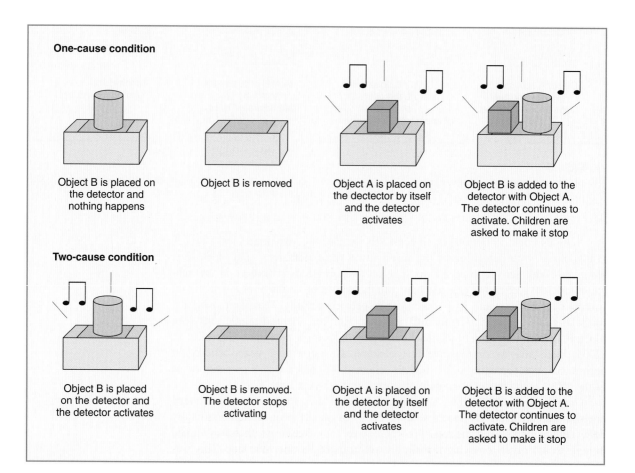

FIGURE 6.4

The procedure used in Gopnik et al. (2001), Experiment 3. From Gopnik, Sobel, Schultz, and Glymour (2001). Copyright © American Psychological Association. Reproduced with permission.

Blaisdell et al. (2006) were interested in whether rats understand the relation between observations and interventions in causal reasoning as predicted by causal Bayes nets. They devised experimental situations analogous to the barometer example described above (if the barometer is set by a human agent to "rain", then a thunderstorm is unlikely to be observed). These situations involved predicting the arrival of food on the basis of cues like tones and lights. For example, if an animal learns from observation that a light coming on causes a tone to sound and that the light also causes the arrival of food, then the animal should expect that the tone alone should also lead to the arrival of food, on the basis of covariation data. However, if the animal also experiences that pressing a lever causes the tone to sound, then there is no reason to expect food, as the light is absent. Blaisdell et al. (2006) trained rats with a variety of such causal relations, including whether they themselves pressed the lever to generate the tone (intervention) or whether they merely observed presentations of the tone without the involvement of the lever. They reported that rats made the correct causal inferences as predicted by causal Bayes nets on the basis of purely observational learning. The rats also correctly differentiated between common-cause models, causal chains, and direct causal links. These data cannot be explained in terms of associative learning. Blaisdell et al. argued that causal learning in rats is consistent with causal Bayes nets.

THE UNDERSTANDING OF CAUSAL CHAINS

Another way of examining whether children can reason from patterns of evidence is to study their understanding of three-term causal chains. The experiments discussed so far have all involved two-term causal chains (A → B). In a three-variable chain (A → B → C), the reasoning task is more complex, as the presence of a *mediate cause* requires a transitive inference as well as an understanding of physical causal contingencies (see Shultz, Pardo, & Altmann, 1982). Understanding the causal structure of a three-term causal chain is crucial for making accurate causal inferences. If an event A causes an event B to occur, which in turn results in an event C, then there is no direct causal link between A and C. For example, a tennis ball (A) can be rolled so that it strikes a golf ball (B), which in turn strikes a light plastic ball (C), dislodging it from its resting position. The golf ball is a mediate cause of the covariation between A and C (and is analogous to the middle term in a transitive inference problem; see Chapter 11). Although event C is caused by event A in this causal chain, does the child understand that this only holds true when B functions as a causal mediator?

The understanding of mediate transmission

Shultz et al. (1982) gave 3- and 5-year-old children simple causal chains of the type described above in two conditions. In one condition, the mediate causal event (B) was effective; in the other it was not. For example, to administer the tennis ball problem, Shultz et al. devised an apparatus in which balls of different sizes could roll along converging lanes (Figure 6.5). The first pair of lanes was wide enough for tennis balls, the second pair for golf balls, and the lanes then converged onto a single lane for a light plastic ball. The light plastic ball was positioned at the

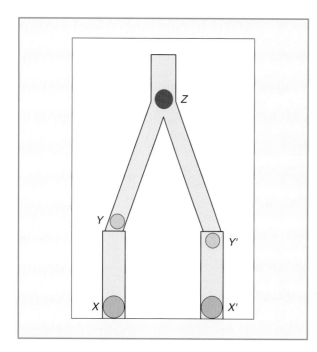

FIGURE 6.5

The runway apparatus used to study children's understanding of mediate causal transmission by Shultz et al. (1982). From Shultz, Pardo, and Altmann (1982). Copyright © The British Psychological Society. Reproduced with permission.

point of convergence, so that following impact from the golf ball, it would roll to the end of the apparatus. On each side of the apparatus an arch was created that separated the tennis ball lane from the golf ball lane. These arches were too narrow for the golf ball to pass through. In order for the golf ball to act as a mediate cause, it therefore had to be on the far side of an arch. In order to create the two conditions, on one side of the apparatus the golf ball was on the near side of the arch (at Y': ineffective mediate cause), and on the other it was on the far side of the arch (at Y: effective mediate cause).

The children's job was to choose which of the lanes to roll the tennis ball along to dislodge the light plastic ball from its position at the point of convergence of the lanes. If the child chose lane Y', then the plastic ball would not be dislodged, whereas if the child chose lane Y then the desired outcome could occur. The sides of the ineffective and effective mediate causes were varied at random over 10 trials. Shultz et al. found that the children were able to select the correct lane for the tennis ball on the majority of trials. The correct lane was chosen on 69% of trials by the 3-year-olds and on 86% of trials by the 5-year-olds. Most of the errors were on the first trial, and also on the third trial for the 3-year-olds. From the fourth trial, children of both ages were consistently correct in choosing the lane with the effective mediate cause.

Children's understanding of three-term causal chains has also been investigated by Baillargeon and R. Gelman (1980, described in Bullock, Gelman, & Baillargeon, 1982). They designed a "Fred-the-Rabbit" apparatus, in which the final step in the causal chain consisted of a rabbit (Fred) falling into his bed (a mat at the end of the apparatus). Fred was first presented to the children standing on a platform above his bed. The mediate cause for getting Fred into his bed was a series of wooden blocks, which were arranged in a row in front of the platform like a series of dominoes (Figure 6.6). Each block in turn could fall onto the block in front (in a "domino effect"), thereby causing the final block to fall onto a lever, which pushed Fred off his platform and into his bed. The initial cause in the chain was a rod positioned in a post, which could be pushed through the post to activate the first block in the series. The children's task was to explain how to get Fred into his bed.

The children were first shown the entire apparatus during pretest demonstration trials. The mid-portion of the apparatus (the blocks) was then covered, leaving only the rod in its post and Fred on his platform visible to the child. The rod and Fred were separated by a distance of around 1 metre. The children (4- and 5-year-olds) correctly predicted that Fred could be got into his bed by pushing the rod through the post. The experimenter then introduced two new rods, a short one that was of insufficient length to reach the first block, and a long one that was of sufficient length. Both rods then failed to get Fred into his bed (the longer rod was prevented from working by a trick). The children were asked to explain why each rod had failed to get Fred into his bed.

Baillargeon and Gelman found that the children were able to offer causally coherent explanations in both cases, distinguishing between relevant (short rod) and irrelevant (long rod) modifications. For the short rod they said that the rod was too short to reach the first block, and for the long rod they said that the experimenter must have done something to disrupt the mediating event, such as taken some of the blocks away. Baillargeon, R. Gelman and Meck (1981, reported in Bullock et al., 1982) then extended the Fred-the-Rabbit task to 3- and 4-year-olds. The children were asked to predict whether Fred would fall into his bed following a variety of modifications to either the initial or the mediate event. Modifications to the initial event included substituting a soft, flexible rod for the wooden rod, and substituting a rod with a stopper on the end that could not pass through the post. Modifications to the mediate event included the experimenter moving Fred's platform away from the final block in the series, and the experimenter moving the platform to one side of the blocks. Children's predictions were highly accurate whether the initial or the mediate event was changed (81% and 78% correct, respectively, for the 3-year-olds; 87% and 85% correct, respectively, for the 4-year-olds).

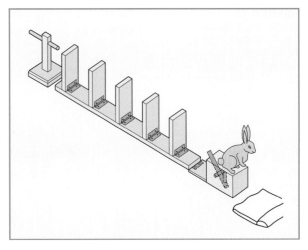

FIGURE 6.6
The "Fred-the-Rabbit" apparatus used by Bullock, Baillargeon, and Gelman (1982). Copyright © 1982 Elsevier. Reproduced with permission.

From the research discussed above, it seems that even very young children can use information about three-term causal chains to reason about event sequences. This holds true whether causal reasoning is measured via a prediction task (Baillargeon et al., 1981; reported in Bullock et al., 1982) or via a problem-solving task (Shultz et al., 1982). As performance in prediction tasks is often inferior to performance in problem-solving tasks (e.g. Goswami & Brown, 1990), Baillargeon et al.'s data provide particularly strong evidence that children understand **mediate transmission** by 3 years of age.

The understanding of logical search

A different way of measuring children's understanding of the causal constraints on event sequences is to use search tasks. For example, imagine that you are on a visit to the zoo and that you want to photograph the chimpanzees, but you find that you have lost your camera. As the chimpanzees are about the eighth group of animals that you have visited, one strategy for finding the camera is to try to remember the last animals that you photographed. If you clearly remember taking a photo of the lions, but you don't recall taking a photo of the elephants, then you probably lost your camera somewhere after the lion enclosure but before you reached the elephants. If young children can use this kind of causal logic when searching for objects, then this must entail some understanding of causal chains and causal necessity.

In a playground version of the **logical search** task described above, Wellman, Somerville, and Haake (1979) took children aged 3, 4, and 5 years around eight different locations in a playground (Figure 6.7). Each location was visited in turn. Upon arrival in each new location, the experimenter and the child played a distinctive game, such as jumping in the sand box or hopping in tyres. At location 3, the experimenter took a photograph of the child doing the long jump as this made a good "action shot". At location 7, the experimenter was about to take another photograph when he discovered that his camera was missing. The children's job was to help him to find it. Wellman et al. were interested in whether the children would limit their

FIGURE 6.7

Schematic depiction of the playground used in the logical search study devised by Wellman et al. (1979), showing the eight locations and their associated games. From Wellman, Somerville, and Haake (1979). Copyright © 1979 American Psychological Association. Reprinted with permission.

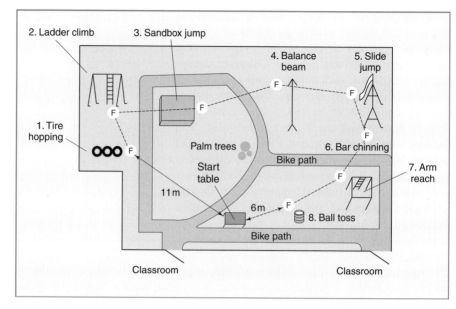

searching behavior to the critical area (between locations 3 and 7), or would search all of the areas that had been visited in turn. In a control condition, the experimenter discovered the loss of a calculator that had been in his bag throughout the experiment. The loss was discovered at location 8, and so in this control condition searching at each location in turn was an appropriate search strategy.

The important measure was the number of searches that were in the critical area (between locations 3 and 7) in both conditions. Wellman et al. found that most of the children concentrated their searches in the critical area in the camera condition, but not in the calculator condition. There were no marked age differences. The 3-year-olds seemed as capable of logical searching behavior as the 5-year-olds. However, closer inspection of the data revealed that half of the searches in the critical target area were actually searches at location 3, the location where the camera had last been seen. Because of this, it is not clear whether the children in Wellman et al.'s study understood that each of the locations between 3 and 7 was *equally likely* to contain the missing camera.

This point was made by Somerville and Capuani-Shumaker (1984), who set out to investigate more directly the question of whether young children understand the causal implications of a sequence of events. Again using a search task as their critical measure, they devised a hiding and finding task in which two locations were at any one time equally likely to contain a hidden toy. This toy was a small Minnie Mouse doll, which could be concealed at one of four possible locations by the experimenter. However, in some of the hiding and finding trials it was more logical to go *forwards* and search in the next two locations from where the Minnie Mouse doll had last been seen, and in others it was more logical to go *backwards* and search in the previous two locations. Somerville and Capuani-Shumaker were interested in whether young children would recognize that some search sequences were more logical than others.

The experimental set-up consisted of a dark tablecloth with the four possible hiding locations marked by smaller stiff white cloths. Each cloth was pulled up into a peak so that it was unclear whether it concealed a Minnie Mouse doll or not. In a given *hiding trial*, the experimenter showed the children the Minnie Mouse doll in her hand, closed her hand, and then moved it beneath the first two cloths, pausing beneath each in turn. She then opened her hand to show the children whether the doll was still present or not, closed her hand again, and moved it beneath the second two cloths. If the Minnie Mouse doll was still *present* after cloth 2, then the children were meant to infer that the hiding location had to be cloth 3 or cloth 4. If the Minnie Mouse doll was *absent* after cloth 2, the children were meant to infer that the hiding location had to be cloth 1 or cloth 2.

The *finding tasks* were the inverse of the hiding tasks (Figure 6.8). This time the children's job was to find Minnie Mouse's *sister*, who always liked to hide together with Minnie under a cloth. In the finding trials, the adult's hand was always empty to begin with, and then after passing beneath cloth 2 was either shown to be still empty or to now contain Minnie Mouse. The question was whether the children could infer that Minnie's sister must be hiding under cloth 3 or cloth 4 when Minnie Mouse was still absent after cloth 2, but must be hiding under cloth 1 or cloth 2 when Minnie Mouse was present after cloth 2. Three- and 4-year-olds were tested.

Somerville and Capuani-Shumaker scored the first location at which the children searched. They found that the children were able to narrow down the potentially correct locations to two out of the possible four, as searching behavior was above chance at both age levels. Interestingly, first searches were also significantly more likely to be correct when the children had to reason from the continued *presence* of Minnie after location 2 in the hiding task, and from the continued *absence* of Minnie after location 2 in the finding task. This suggests that the causal implications of the event sequences were easier to understand when the cause and the effect were temporally more contiguous. This reflects one of the principles of causal reasoning discussed earlier.

However, when the experimenters scored the children's second searches, they found that they were by no means always correct. This was surprising, given that an

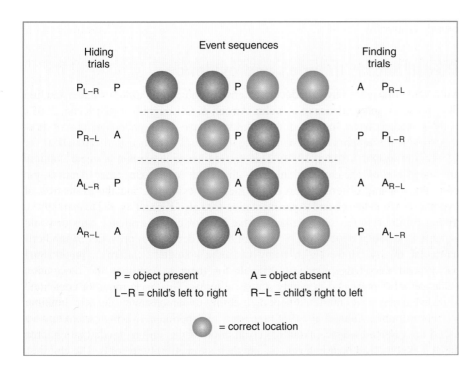

P = object present   A = object absent
L–R = child's left to right   R–L = child's right to left

 = correct location

FIGURE 6.8
Schematic depiction of the sequences of events in the hiding and finding tasks devised by Somerville and Capuani-Shumaker (1984). Copyright © The British Psychological Society. Reproduced with permission.

incorrect first search in the target area left only one plausible alternative hiding or finding location. Subsequent experiments replicating and extending Somerville and Capuani-Shumaker's basic design have shown that, although even 2-year-olds respond logically on their first searches (Haake & Somerville, 1985), children younger than 4 years appear to search by considering only one possibility at a time (Sophian & Somerville, 1988). Having searched in the critical area on their first search, they sometimes search outside the critical area on their second search. It appears that the causal implications of the hiding and finding event sequences studied by Somerville and her colleagues are not fully understood before the age of 4 years. It is not clear, however, whether this reflects a general problem with understanding causal implications or a problem specific to hiding and finding. Research on children's scientific reasoning offers an alternative way of exploring children's understanding of causal necessity.

SCIENTIFIC REASONING

The research discussed so far has shown that young children's causal reasoning is usually in accord with accurate representational models of causal structure. However, even though the different causal principles appear to be available to young children, difficulties appear to arise when they have to *rule out* potential causal variables as the cause of a particular effect. This involves an understanding of the "**scientific method**". When young children are asked to determine the causes of a particular phenomenon, they may fail to test a hypothesis in a systematic way, omitting to control for confounding variables. They may also fail to seek evidence that could disconfirm their hypotheses, and they may accept causes that account for only part of the available data (Sodian, Zaitchek, & Carey, 1991). In short, younger children appear to have little explicit understanding of the components of scientific reasoning. Scientific reasoning is complex, as it usually involves the understanding of multiple causal variables.

Co-ordinating theories and evidence

Kuhn and colleagues have conducted extensive studies of children's understanding of hypotheses and evidence (e.g. Kuhn, Amsel, & O'Loughlin, 1988; Kuhn, 2005). Kuhn's studies have suggested that children have little understanding of how hypotheses are supported or contradicted by causal evidence until around 11 or 12 years of age (e.g. Kuhn, 1989). This has led her to argue that younger children are incapable of "scientific thinking"—the kind of thinking that requires the co-ordination and differentiation of theories and evidence, and the evaluation of hypotheses via evidence and experimentation (see also Klahr, Fay, & Dunbar, 1993). Young children do not seem to know what kind of causal evidence does or could support a particular hypothesis, or what kind of evidence does or would contradict a particular theory. However, in many of Kuhn's studies, children's pre-existing background knowledge made it difficult for them to consider the covariation evidence being presented in purely statistical terms. This background or contextual knowledge may have interfered with their ability to demonstrate scientific thinking.

For example, Kuhn et al. (1988) reported an experiment in which subjects were asked to evaluate evidence about the covariation of the various foods that children ate at a hypothetical boarding school, and their susceptibility to colds. The children, who were aged 11 and 14 years, were given the covariation information about the different foods pictorially (Figure 6.9). For example, in the figure, apples and french fries covary perfectly with colds, and Special K® and Coca-Cola® do not. The children were then asked questions like "Does the kind of drink the children have make any difference in whether they get lots of colds or very few colds?". Only the older children showed an ability to evaluate the covariation evidence effectively, although their performance was far from perfect. The spontaneous evidence-based responses given by the 11-year-olds constituted 30% of responses, and of the 14-year-olds, 50% of responses. Adults performed at the same level as the 14-year-olds.

One reason for these performance patterns could be the background knowledge that participants brought with them to the experiment. We are often told (e.g. by advertisers of orange juice) that what we choose to drink does affect our susceptibility to colds. For example, children may have learned that drinks high in vitamin C, such as orange juice, will actually protect them against getting colds. In studies like Kuhn's, children are only credited with true scientific reasoning if they can override such background information and focus purely on the covariation

FIGURE 6.9
Four examples of the pictorial covariation evidence concerning foods eaten and susceptibility to colds (Kuhn et al., 1988).

information being presented during the experiment. The children did not do this, but real scientists may not do this either. In science, information about mechanism can guide the assessment of covariation, while systematic and unexpected covariations can also guide the discovery of new mechanisms (see Koslowski & Masnick, 2002). For example, car color may be systematically correlated with driving speed, but pre-existing background information about mechanism makes us unlikely to conclude that red paint causes cars to go faster than blue paint. We already know that paint color is not a mechanism for speed. However, if we learn that cautious drivers tend to choose blue cars, then a possible mechanism for the correlation becomes evident. Blue cars may go slower because they are more likely to be driven by cautious drivers.

Kuhn et al. (1988) also reported that children showed a strong tendency to make incorrect inferences about causality based on "inclusion errors". Inclusion errors involve the attribution of causal status to variables that only covary with the outcome on a single occasion. In our example, the children would accept a single instance of a food covarying with colds as evidence that the food was a cause of susceptibility to colds (e.g. Granola in Figure 6.9). Such incorrect single-instance inclusion inferences were made on 47% of occasions by the 11-year-olds and on 65% of occasions by the 14-year-olds. Kuhn points out that this is an error-prone strategy for inferring causal relations, because even though inclusion inferences may on occasion be correct, they may also be false.

Kuhn et al.'s investigations (e.g. Kuhn, Garcia-Mila, Zohar, & Andersen, 1995) have suggested that an important source of the persistence of inclusion errors is the prior theories that children hold about the causal status of the variables being investigated. These prior beliefs influence the selection of instances that are attended to, and which instances are relied upon when justifying conclusions about causality. Work with adults has shown similar effects. Even eminent scientists in their laboratories are more likely to attend to data that is consistent with their prior theories (Fugelsang, Stein, Green, & Dunbar, 2004). Inconsistent data is not treated as "real" until repeated observations of unexpected relationships force theory revision. There is a "confirmation bias" in human reasoning—a tendency to seek out causal evidence that is consistent with one's prior beliefs. This is a major source of inferential error in fields as disparate as science, economics, and the law, and is not restricted to young children. Kuhn et al.'s observations about the influence of prior theories on reasoning also fit with the importance of background knowledge and context in scientific reasoning. Both children and adults may be concerned with arriving at a plausible causal explanation of a given scientific phenomenon, and in certain cases this may justify reliance on a single instance. Koslowski (1996) has argued that the aim of scientific reasoning is to assess plausibility rather than possibility or certainty. Scientific inquiry can seldom conclude that a given explanation is definitely correct, as new evidence may always emerge in the future to show that it is wrong.

Testing hypotheses

Sodian et al. (1991) were interested in how children would perform in reasoning tasks that were not set in contexts (like "catching a cold") that were probably already the subject of strongly held beliefs. To see whether young children have any insights into the relationship between hypotheses and evidence in a novel context, Sodian et al. asked children to choose between a conclusive and an inconclusive test of a hypothesis. They used a simple paradigm in which pre-existing beliefs were unlikely to be evoked, which also involved a single test that was sufficient to draw a causal conclusion. The test concerned how two brothers could decide whether they had a small or a large mouse in their house.

In Sodian et al.'s experiment, 6- and 8-year-old children were told a story about two brothers who knew that they had a mouse in their house, even though they had not actually seen it (because it only came out at night). One brother believed that it was "a big daddy mouse" and the other believed that it was "a little baby mouse". The problem was how they could decide who was right. To test their hypotheses about the size of the mouse, the brothers were planning to put some cheese into a box for the mouse to eat. Two boxes were available, one with a large opening that could take either the large or the small mouse, and the other with a small opening that would only allow the small mouse to enter. The children had to decide which box the brothers should use in order to determine the size of the mouse. The majority of children in both age groups realized that the box with the small opening was required. As one child remarked "They should take the house with the small opening, and if the food is gone, this tells them that it is a small mouse, and if it's still there it is a big mouse" (p. 758). Sodian et al. concluded that even quite young children understand the goal of testing a hypothesis, and can distinguish between conclusive and inconclusive tests of that hypothesis in simplified circumstances.

Ruffman, Perner, Olson, and Doherty (1993) devised a "fake evidence" task to investigate whether even younger children can work out how a pattern of evidence relates to a hypothesis when only a single cause is involved. The children's task was to work out which kind of food was more likely to lead to tooth loss, green food or red food (the "food" consisted of bits of colored paper). Four- and 5-year-olds were shown consecutive pictures of 10 boys in the act of eating food. Five of them were eating green food and had healthy teeth, and five of them were eating red food and had teeth missing. The children were asked "Which type of food makes kids' teeth fall out?". All of them answered that it was red food (showing use of the covariation principle).

The children were then shown a picture of 10 boys' heads, five with missing teeth and five with intact teeth. Directly in front of each boy's mouth was a piece of red or green food, depicting the covariation information. The experimenter then "faked" the evidence, rearranging the food so that the opposite pattern of tooth loss was suggested (that green food caused tooth loss). A doll, Sally, was introduced, who didn't know that the evidence had been faked. The children were asked "When Sally sees things the way they are now, which food will she say makes kids' teeth fall out?". The majority of the 5-year-olds correctly said that Sally would arrive at a mistaken hypothesis. In a second experiment in which the faked covariation evidence was not perfect (so that the pattern was in favor of a particular hypothesis), 5-year-olds were unsuccessful, but 6-year-olds were successful (4-year-olds were not tested). Ruffman et al. concluded that, by the age of around 6 years, children understand how simple covariation information forms the basis for a hypothesis.

In fact, the best conclusion is probably that both children and adults are poor at scientific reasoning if scientific reasoning is defined in terms of giving priority to evidence over background knowledge and context. When children have to make causal inferences in situations involving *many* potential causal variables, they experience difficulty, even though their basic causal intuitions are sound. The same is true of adults, as Kuhn et al. (1995) pointed out. Many adults also perform poorly in fully fledged scientific reasoning tasks, for example, tasks that require them to examine a database and draw conclusions. Conducting scientific investigations into the relations between variables in real-world situations is simply not an easy task when many variables are present, because human beings find it difficult to ignore their pre-existing knowledge and to keep multiple variables in mind at once (see Hagmayer, Sloman, Lagnado, & Waldmann, 2007, for a recent summary of these factors in adults). Although the essential principles for making valid causal inferences are available early in childhood, the ability to draw multivariable causal inferences remains difficult even beyond childhood.

MULTIVARIABLE CAUSAL INFERENCES

Many situations encountered in real life do require some ability to draw multivariable causal inferences. One example is the need to *integrate* information about different causes, which is characteristic of a number of aspects of causal reasoning in everyday life. In fact, we seldom have to reason about causes and their effects in isolation. Instead, we frequently have to reason about more than one cause at a time. Even everyday problems require us to take into account many causal factors and their effects, and some of the causal factors relevant to a particular problem may interact with each other. Causal reasoning is thus *usually* multidimensional.

To take a trivial example, imagine that you are trying to decide whether you have enough time to go to the post office during your lunch hour. You need to consider not only how far the post office is, how long your lunch hour is, and how fast you can walk, but also whether it is raining (this could affect speed and time), whether sufficient cashiers will be available to prevent long queues (this could affect time in the post office itself), and whether there are any potential hold-ups en route. In other words, you will need to consider many causal factors and how they may interact with each other before deciding whether it is actually worth trying to go to the post office.

The integration of knowledge about two dimensions

The question of when young children become able to interrelate information about different causal relations has been investigated using a variety of paradigms. We will begin by considering experiments that investigate children's ability to interrelate information about two causal dimensions, and we will then consider experiments that investigate children's ability to interrelate information about three causal dimensions. One of the best-known paradigms for investigating children's ability to interrelate information about two causal dimensions is the **balance scale task**.

The balance scale task measures children's ability to interrelate information about weight and distance. A typical apparatus consists of two arms of equal length that extend from a central fulcrum, like a see-saw (Figure 6.10). Each arm can have weights attached to it at different distances from the fulcrum. The child's task is to predict which side of the balance scale will go down when different combinations of weights are placed at different distances from the center.

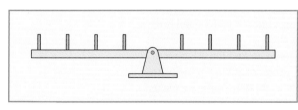

FIGURE 6.10
A balance scale apparatus.

To judge this correctly, children must take into account *both* the relative number of weights and their relative distance from the fulcrum, and then combine these variables multiplicatively. For example, if three weights are placed on one arm of the balance scale 20 cm from the fulcrum, and six weights are placed on the other arm 10 cm from the fulcrum, the scale will balance. However, if both groups of weights are placed 10 cm from the fulcrum, then the side with six weights on it will go down.

Siegler (1978) used a balance scale to assess the different rules that children use to interrelate information about weight and distance during development. His method was to ask children to make judgments about which arm of the balance scale would go down in a choice format that held one variable (weight or distance) constant while varying the other. For example, in *distance problems*, the same number of weights was placed on each arm, but at different distances from the fulcrum. In *weight problems*, different numbers of weights were placed on each arm, but at the same distance from the fulcrum. In *conflict-weight problems*, there were more weights on one arm, but the fewer weights on the other arm were at a greater distance from the fulcrum (e.g. two weights 8 cm from the fulcrum vs. three weights 6 cm from the fulcrum: weight wins), and so on. Girls aged 5, 9, 13, and 17 were tested.

Siegler's results led him to postulate that the development of physical understanding in the balance scale task proceeded through four different rules. Only the final rule involved information integration (Figure 6.11). The first three rules depended on considering the dimensions of weight and distance *separately*, without

Rule 1: is weight the same?	If **YES**, then **balance** If **NO**, then **greater weight down**	
Rule 2: is weight the same?	If **YES**, then check distance Is distance the same? →	If **YES**, then **balance** If **NO**, then **greater distance down**
	If **NO**, then **greater weight down**	
Rule 3: is weight the same?	If **YES**, then check distance Is distance the same? →	If **YES**, then **balance** If **NO**, then **greater distance down**
	If **NO**, then check distance Is distance the same? →	If **YES**, then **greater weight down** If **NO**, then check — if greater weight is same side as greater distance? If **YES**, then **greater weight and distance down** If **NO**, then **muddle through**
Rule 4: is weight the same?	If **YES**, then check distance Is distance the same? →	If **YES**, then **balance** If **NO**, then **greater distance down**
	If **NO**, then check distance Is distance the same? →	If **YES**, then **greater weight down** If **NO**, then check — if greater weight is same side as greater distance? If **YES**, then **greater weight and distance down** If **NO**, then check — are cross products the same? If **YES**, then **balance** If **NO**, then **greater product down**

FIGURE 6.11
The four rules proposed by Siegler (1978) to explain the development of physical understanding in the balance scale task.

trying to integrate them. Children who used rule 1 always said that the arm with the most weights would go down. Children who used rule 2 took into account distance information, but only when the two arms had equal weights. In all other cases, they ignored distance and made judgments on the basis of relative weight. Children who used rule 3 showed a developmental progression to considering distance information as well as weight information, but only when the two variables did not conflict. When one side had a greater weight and the other side had a greater distance, as in the conflict-weight problem given earlier, performance was at chance. Only children who used rule 4 showed an ability to integrate weight and distance information multiplicatively.

However, Wilkening and Anderson (1991) argued that Siegler's task could *underestimate* younger children's ability to apply integration rules because of a problem with "false positive" responses. They pointed out that younger children might be using a simpler integration rule of *adding* weight and distance information rather than a more sophisticated rule of multiplying weight and distance. Such children would be scored by Siegler as following a nonintegration rule (one of rules 1–3, and therefore a "false positive"), whereas in fact they were following a *simpler form* of an integrative rule. To test their idea, Wilkening and Anderson asked children to *adjust* the position of a fixed set of weights on one arm of the balance scale in order to balance a set of varying weights on the other.

The adjustment task required the children to adjust either weight or distance. For example, if the fixed set was three, weights placed 12 cm from the fulcrum and the variable set was one, two, three, or four weights placed at 6, 12, 18, or 24 cm from the fulcrum, then the children had to adjust the distance of the fixed set in order to balance the scale. To balance one weight at 6 cm, the children would have to move their fixed set to 2 cm from the fulcrum, to balance one weight at 12 cm the children would have to move their fixed set to 4 cm from the fulcrum, and so on. This was the *distance adjustment* task. An analogous *weight-adjustment* task was also used, in which a fixed set of two weights at 24 cm had to be adjusted by adding more weights to balance either one, two, three, or four weights placed at 8, 16, 24, or 32 cm from the fulcrum. Using the adjustment methodology, Wilkening and Anderson found that 9-year-olds, 12-year-olds, and adults all used multiplicative integration rules to combine information about relative weight and distance. The youngest children tested (6-year-olds) tended to focus on either weight or distance, without trying to integrate the two. Nevertheless, Wilkening and Anderson argued that their data showed that children's causal understanding in the balance scale task was seriously underestimated by Siegler's methodology. More recently, Amsel, Goodman, Savoie, and Clark (1996) tested children aged from 5 to 12 years in the balance scale task, and reported that children tended to recognize the importance of number of weights at about 5–6 years of age. By 9 years of age, the majority of children tested also identified distance from the fulcrum as an important causal variable.

Integrating information about the causal effects of forces

Another type of physical information that must be integrated in the real world is information about forces. Consider a tug-of-war. This is a simple force problem. Two teams of men are pulling on the ends of a rope. Both teams hope to move the center of the rope beyond a certain pre-agreed point. If one team consists of 20 men and the other of 10 men, then most people would predict that the team of 20 men should win the tug-of-war. The reason is that this team should exert the stronger force. However, if the team of 10 men all weigh 20 stones or more, and the team of 20 men all weigh 8 stones or less, then the prediction might go the other way. Perhaps the combined force of 10 strong men will be greater than the combined force of 20 weak men. Alternatively, if the teams are *equal* in number and in strength, then the center of the rope may not move at all. The forces may cancel each other out.

Pauen (1996b) gave a version of this force problem to young children. As well as the special case of two forces acting at 180° to each other (the tug-of-war), she used problems in which two forces acted at 45°, 75°, and 105° to each other. The forces, which were represented by weights, were in the ratios 1 : 2, 1 : 3, and 1 : 6, respectively. To solve these problems correctly, the children had to combine two force vectors. The problem was presented using a special apparatus called a force table (Figure 6.12).

The force table consisted of an object that was fixed at the center of a round platform. Two forces acted on this object, both represented by plates of weights. The plates of weights hung from cords attached to the central object at 45°, 75°, or 105° to each other. The children's job was to work out the trajectory of the object once it was released from its fixed position. Although the central object was never actually released, the children had to move a barrier surrounding the platform until an opening in the barrier was in exactly the right position to catch the object. Their predictions were measured and scored in terms of whether the opening in the barrier was positioned closer to one or the other plate of weights, or was equidistant from both.

The force table problem was presented to the children in the context of a story about a King (central object) who had got tired of skating on a frozen lake (the platform) and who wanted to be pulled into his royal bed on the shore (a box behind the opening in the barrier). The children were asked to turn the barrier so that the royal bed would be in the right place for the king to slide into it. Different combinations of weights were used, and children aged 6, 7, 8, and 9 years of age

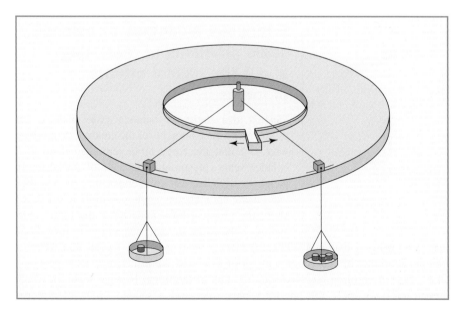

FIGURE 6.12
The force table used by Pauen (1996b).

were tested. Pauen found that most of the younger children (80–85%) predicted that the king would move in the direction of the stronger force only. For example, if there were three weights on one plate and one weight on the other, these children would move the opening in the barrier so that it was directly below the cord holding the plate with three weights (the "one-force-only" rule).

An ability to consider the two forces simultaneously was shown by some of the 9-year-olds (45%). These children realized that the correct location for the opening in the barrier was near the cord holding the heavier weights, but not exactly below it. However, although they showed this insight on some trials, they reverted to the one-force-only rule in other trials. Pauen thus judged them to be in a transitional stage regarding the integration rule. Very few children (5–10% across all groups) showed pure integration rule behavior. Such behavior required placing the opening in the barrier between the bisector of the angle and the stronger force. Such integration rule responses were shown by the majority of the adults tested (63%), however.

In the special cases when the forces were at 180° to each other (analogous to the tug-of-war situation described earlier), the majority of children at all ages tested gave the correct answer to the force problem. Pauen thus decided to change the situational context of the force problem, to see whether it would be easier for children to use the integration rule if the forces were represented by men pulling on ropes rather than by weights sitting on plates. In a second experiment using the force table, she replaced the plates of weights with teams of toy people pulling on ropes (Figure 6.13). The children were told that two groups of cowboys were trying to pull a barrel to the shore in order to take it to their camp.

In this replication, fewer of the younger children used the incorrect one-force-only rule (40–50% instead of 80–85%). However, correct integration solutions did not increase. Furthermore, the solution of the special-case (180°) problems actually *decreased* when Pauen used the cowboys context with the younger children. Pauen speculated that this may have been because the children who received the plates of weights applied a balance scale analogy to the force integration problem. A balance scale analogy gives rise to one-force-only solutions, which are correct in the case of the 180° problems, but not in the cases of the 45°, 75°, or 105° problems.

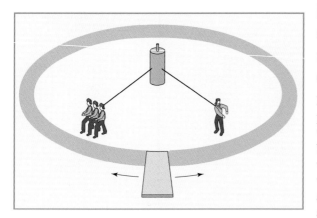

FIGURE 6.13
The force table used in Pauen's (1996b) cowboys paradigm.

Erroneous analogies to balance scale problems in reasoning about the causal effects of forces

Pauen's idea about the balance scale analogy was prompted by the comments of the children themselves, who said that the force table reminded them of a balance scale (presumably because of the plates of weights). This led her to propose that the children were using spontaneous analogies in their reasoning about the physical laws underlying the force table, analogies that were in fact misleading. To investigate this idea further, Pauen and Wilkening (1997) decided to give 9-year-old children a training session with a balance scale prior to giving them the force table problem. One group of children received training with a traditional balance scale, in which they learned to apply the one-force-only rule, and a second group of children received training with a modified balance scale that had its center of gravity below the axis of rotation (a "swing boat" suspension). This modified balance scale provided training in the integration rule, as the swing boat suspension meant that even though the beam rotated towards the stronger force, the degree of deflection depended on the size of *both* forces. These two balance scales are depicted in Figure 6.14. In each case, the children had to predict the location of a pointer attached to the center of the beam for different ratios of weights. When the beam was balanced, the pointer pointed straight up.

Following the balance scale training, the children were given the force table task with the plates of weights. A third group of children received only the force table

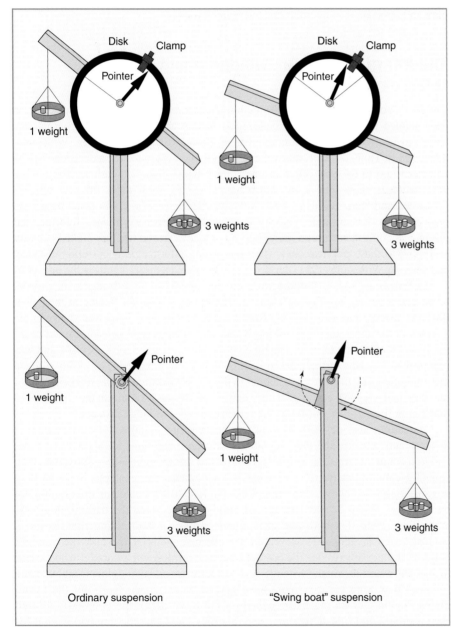

FIGURE 6.14
The balance scale apparatus used to provide training in (a) the "one force only" rule vs. (b) the integration rule. From Pauen and Wilkening (1996). Copyright © 1996 Elsevier. Reproduced with permission.

task, and acted as untrained controls. Pauen and Wilkening argued that an effect of the analogical training would be shown if the children who were trained with the traditional balance scale showed a greater tendency to use the one-force-only rule than the control group children, while the children who were trained with the modified balance scale showed a greater tendency to use the integration rule than the control group children. This was exactly the pattern that they found. The children's responses to the force table problem varied systematically with the solution provided by the analogical model. These results suggest that the children were using spontaneous analogies in their reasoning about physics, just as we have seen them do in their reasoning about biology (children's use of the personification analogy was discussed in Chapter 4) and in language acquisition. Analogies seem to play an important role in children's everyday reasoning.

The integration of knowledge about three dimensions

Children's ability to interrelate information about three different dimensions has also been studied by Wilkening and colleagues. In this work, they examined children's ability to interrelate information about time, distance, and velocity (e.g. Wilkening, 1981, 1982). Time, distance, and velocity information is crucial for a decision such as whether to go to the post office in one's lunch hour (discussed earlier). The critical information is "how long is my lunch hour?" (time), "how far is the post office?" (distance), and "how fast can I go?" (velocity). These variables are related by simple physical laws. For example, velocity is equivalent to distance divided by time, and distance is equivalent to time multiplied by velocity. To see whether children reason according to these physical laws when integrating information about time, distance, and velocity, Wilkening (1981) devised a task involving a turtle, a guinea pig, and a cat.

In Wilkening's task, children were shown a model of a footbridge with a turtle, a cat, and a guinea pig fleeing along it. The animals were all fleeing at their own different speeds, and were running from a fierce barking dog, who was shown at the left side of the apparatus. The children's task was to judge how far each animal could run in a certain period of time. The time period was either 2, 5, or 8 seconds, and was represented in terms of the amount of time that the dog barked. The children made their judgments by moving each animal to the correct location on the footbridge after the dog had stopped barking. This version of the task required the children to integrate information about time and velocity in order to judge distance.

Wilkening also devised versions of the task that required the integration of distance and velocity, and the integration of distance and time. He argued that if the children could integrate these different sources of information successfully, then they should use multiplicative rules to make their judgments. For example, in the barking dog task described above, they should use the rule "distance equals time multiplied by velocity". When 5- and 10-year-old children were given the barking dog task, Wilkening found that both age groups indeed used a multiplying rule, as did a control group of adults. However, in the other versions of the task the younger children did not always use the correct integration rules. For example, when asked to use information about distance and velocity to make judgments about time (judging how long the dog must have barked when shown the point the turtle, the cat, or the guinea pig had reached on the footbridge), the youngest children used a subtraction rule. This suggested that they knew that the dog had barked for different amounts of time for each animal, but that they could not estimate these differences proportionally.

Even the adults used the wrong integration rule in some versions of the task, however. When asked to use information about distance and time to make judgments about velocity (deciding which animal would have been able to reach a certain point on the footbridge in the time that the dog barked), adults used a subtracting rule, just like the younger children in the time judgment task. From Wilkening's perspective, however, the fact that children and adults did not always select the correct rules was not critical. The important finding was that even 5-year-olds attempted to apply algebraic rules when trying to reason about different physical dimensions. This meant that they had some conceptual understanding of the separate variables involved, even though they (and the adults) occasionally selected the wrong algebraic rules to integrate these variables. Although the psychological rules used in information integration did not always mirror the physical rules of mechanics, Wilkening argued that his results implied an implicit understanding of dimensional interrelations—a naive or "intuitive" physics. Children were adopting a practical approach to the psychological integration of separate variables in which the procedures chosen did not *violate* the physical rules, but simplified them.

BIASES AND MISCONCEPTIONS IN CAUSAL REASONING

So far in this book, it has been argued that intuitive physics is rooted in the perception of objects and events (see also Wilkening & Huber, 2002). Children's perception of the world around them has been shown to yield rich information about the structure and action of physical systems, and in general physical structure has proved a reliable guide to the causal structure of physical events. Hence perceptual information provides a reliable basis for causal reasoning. However, this is not always the case. Intuitive or naïve physics can also yield misleading models of the physical causal structure of the world. This was first documented in pioneering work by McCloskey and colleagues (e.g. McCloskey, 1983).

Intuitive physics and misconceptions about projectile motion

Our intuitions about projectile motion provide a good example of how our intuitions about physical causation are not always correct. In fact, when reasoning about projectile motion, most children and adults employ a pre-Newtonian, medieval theory of motion, called the **impetus theory** (e.g. Viennot, 1979). According to this theory, each motion must have a cause. Our everyday experience makes this a very plausible assumption. If an object is inanimate, it cannot be set into motion without a physical cause being involved. If a ball is thrown by a person, it will move in a trajectory determined by the force of the throw, and will fall to earth when this force diminishes. However, if a ball drops from a moving train, no impetus appears to be involved—the ball has fallen passively from the train. In this latter case, according to an impetus theory of motion, the ball will fall downwards in a straight line. If we were standing by a railway and saw a ball fall from a passing train, this would indeed appear to be the case. The train would continue moving forwards, while the ball

KEY TERM

Impetus theory
The theory that every motion must have a cause.

would be perceived as falling straight down (see Wilkening & Huber, 2002, for a fuller analysis).

McCloskey and colleagues showed that, when asked to predict the trajectories of objects, adults as well as children seem to follow a "straight down" rule. They seem to believe that if an object is dropped by a walking person, then it will fall downwards in a straight line. In fact, it will fall forwards in a parabolic arc (e.g. Kaiser et al., 1985). By Newtonian physics, the moving carrier of the object imparts a force, just as if the object was pushed from a table top. With respect to the frame of reference of the ground, the object will fall forwards in both cases. Similarly, when asked to predict the motion of a ball ejected at speed from a curved tube shaped like the letter "C", adults and children judge that the ball will continue to move in a curvilinear arc, whereas in fact it follows a straight line with respect to the horizontal plane (e.g. Kaiser, McCloskey, & Profitt, 1986; Figure 6.15). Medieval physical theories, such as the medieval theory of impetus, depend on perceptual experience, and in the case of impetus theory, children are unlikely to receive many perceptual experiences that contradict the "straight down" rule. Because of this, Newtonian physics can only be understood via direct instruction.

Gravity errors

Other research confirms that intuitive but misleading concepts of mechanics can be very difficult to dislodge. For example, the "straight down" rule noted above is applied not only to projectile motion, but also in tasks that test children's understanding of the effects of gravity. One example is the "tubes task" invented by Hood (1995). In the tubes task, young children (2- to 4-year-olds) are asked to find a ball that is dropped into one of three tubes. The tubes are all opaque and they can be interwoven to form a visuospatial maze. When the tubes are interwoven, a reliance on the "straight down" rule will lead the child to search in the *wrong* location for the ball. The tubes task can be administered at different levels of difficulty by increasing the number of tubes and the complexity of their intertwining (Figure 6.16).

FIGURE 6.15
Schematic depiction of six alternative trajectories for the curved tube problem (Kaiser et al., 1986).

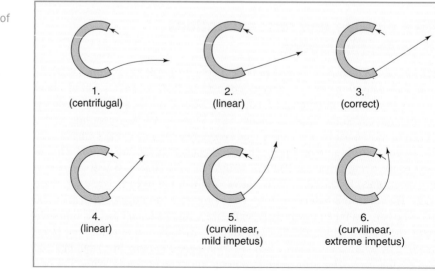

1.
(centrifugal)

2.
(linear)

3.
(correct)

4.
(linear)

5.
(curvilinear, mild impetus)

6.
(curvilinear, extreme impetus)

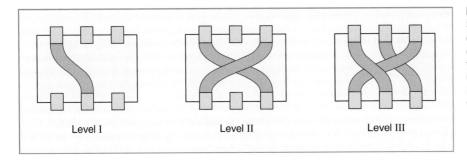

Level I   Level II   Level III

Hood found that children who erred in the tubes task consistently searched in the location directly beneath the point at which the ball was dropped. He termed this a "gravity error". Gravity errors were the most frequent kind of error at every difficulty level tested, although the ability to solve the tubes task at different levels was related to age (older children passed the easier levels) and sex (boys showed superior performance to girls). All erroneous search behavior seemed to be predominantly determined by the straight-down trajectory, irrespective of the trajectory of the tube.

In later experiments using transparent tubes instead of opaque tubes, Hood showed that even the youngest children tested (2-year-olds) were able to search successfully for the ball when they could see its trajectory, and that this success occurred at all difficulty levels. Surprisingly, however, he found no evidence for transfer. Children who searched successfully with the transparent tubes were immediately given problems at the same level of difficulty with the opaque tubes, and promptly failed them. Even extensive training on the tubes task with a single tube failed to dislodge the prepotent gravity error in a group of 2-year-old children. Hood concluded that his task documented a growing understanding of the operation of tubes, and of how they constrain the movements of invisibly falling objects. This explanation suggests that the gravity error is also dependent on intuitive physics. Children appear to believe that all objects fall straight down. Hence the gravity error might well recur in children who have become quite sophisticated in the tubes task if they were presented with a different apparatus or if task demands were varied.

Hood, Wilson, and Dyson (2006) gave children aged 5½ years who had passed the tubes task a modified version of the task involving two balls. Using a three-tube apparatus, in which no (opaque) tube connected to the container directly below it, the experimenter dropped both a red and a green ball simultaneously down two randomly determined tubes, and asked the child to find either the red ball or the green ball (also determined randomly). A successful search required the children to monitor two potential targets: They had to assess the spatial layout of the tubes, work out which container went with which tube, and remember which tube the red versus the green ball was dropped down. Hood et al. reported that success decreased significantly in comparison to the one-ball condition, and that many search errors were gravity errors. They argued that the increased attentional demands of the "two ball" paradigm decreased the children's ability to inhibit the gravity error. Children need to actively suppress their naïve physical theories to respond correctly in the modified tubes task. Again, the role of inhibiting incorrect knowledge for accurate responding by children is highlighted. Even children who demonstrated correct understanding in the easier version of the tubes task became confused in the "two ball" paradigm. The problem developmentally may thus be in resisting interference rather than in grasping underlying causal structure: a problem of executive inhibition (see Chapter 9).

Knowledge versus action

It is notable that most of the multivariable causal reasoning tasks discussed so far have measured knowledge via action. For example, Shultz et al. (1982) asked children to roll tennis balls to measure their understanding of mediate transmission, Wilkening and Anderson (1991) asked children to move weights on a balance beam to measure their understanding of the integration of weight and distance information, and Wilkening (1982) asked children to move toy animals along a bridge to measure their understanding of the integration of three physical variables (time, distance, and velocity). One interesting possibility is that intuitive physical knowledge as measured by action may be *distinct from* intuitive physical knowledge as measured by judgment tasks. Judgment tasks require *reflection* on one's physical knowledge. For example, action-based knowledge about projectile motion may be fairly sophisticated, whereas explicit judgments about the same motions may be naïve. Action-based knowledge and verbalizable knowledge may also follow different developmental paths (see Chapter 8, for a discussion of the different developmental paths followed by implicit/ procedural and explicit/ declarative memory). The possibility that intuitive physics is best measured directly, via action, was investigated by Krist, Fieberg, and Wilkening (1993), in a task using projectile motion.

The task used by Krist et al. was a throwing task. Six-year-olds, 10-year-olds, and adults were asked to throw a tennis ball from different heights so that it would hit a target on the floor. The subjects were asked to use a horizontal motion when throwing the tennis ball, which was somewhat awkward to produce as it involved sliding one's arm along a horizontal "throwing" board before releasing the ball. This meant that the speed with which the ball was released was critical if the ball were to reach its target. In addition, the height of the throwing board was varied during the experiment (a lower board requires a faster throw), and so variable throwing speeds were required. As well as requiring the subjects to throw the ball themselves, Krist et al. asked them to make judgments about how fast the ball should be released in order for it to reach the target when the throwing board was raised or lowered. These judgments were either required prior to, or following, the action phase of the experiment.

Krist et al. found that the functional relation between speed and height was present in the *action data* at all age levels tested, whereas it was only present in the *judgment data* for the adult subjects. Whereas the adults judged that a lower throwing table would require a faster speed of release, the 10-year-olds did not differentiate between the speeds required for the different height levels, and some of the 6-year-olds showed an *inverse pattern*, judging that greater heights would require greater speeds. In contrast, mean speeds of actual throwing represented the physical law very closely, across all age groups. Thus whereas performance in the judgment condition reflected a strong age trend towards integrating height and distance in an appropriate way, performance in the action condition showed an intuitive understanding of this relationship. These data imply that intuitive knowledge develops from the acquisition of perceptual-motor knowledge and skills, which in turn provide a basis for the development of intuitive concepts of mechanics.

Insights from cognitive neuroscience

At the time of writing, there are no cognitive neuroscience studies of causal reasoning in children. However, there are some interesting neuroimaging studies of reasoning in adults, which are suggestive with respect to some of the ideas that we have discussed. For example, very similar neural networks are activated by causal reasoning tasks, analogical reasoning tasks, problem solving, hypothesis testing, and deductive reasoning tasks (Dunbar & Fugelsang, 2005). These different reasoning tasks all activate areas of the brain thought to be important for attention, inhibition, and working memory, such as the dorsolateral, prefrontal, and parietal areas. Imaging work thus suggests that scientific reasoning is not a "special" form of reasoning, but rather draws on core cognitive processes. Furthermore, imaging studies suggest that when we learn particular scientific concepts, such as the Newtonian theory of motion, this does not replace the medieval impetus theory of motion that is given by perceptual information. Instead, rather than undergoing conceptual change, the brain appears to maintain both theories. The adult who has learned a Newtonian theory of motion activates both theories during scientific reasoning, and the incorrect impetus theory is then inhibited so that the correct answer to a problem can be generated (Petitto & Dunbar, in press). This neural imaging work is consistent with some behavioral studies, which use reaction times to argue that generating the correct Newtonian answer to a problem about motion requires active inhibition of the incorrect answer based on impetus principles (Kozhevnikov & Hegarty, 2001). It is also consistent with the explanation given by Hood and colleagues concerning the re-emergence of the gravity error in search tasks based on twisting tubes with young children. The gravity error re-emerged because of inefficient inhibition of the incorrect response based on the "straight down" rule.

Importantly, such data are not consistent with the notion that scientific knowledge undergoes radical restructuring with development, driven by new information that cannot be accommodated within existing conceptual frameworks (Carey, 1985; see Chapter 4). Rather, imaging data suggest that naïve theories are stored alongside more comprehensive theories, with the naïve theories requiring inhibition in order for reasoning to proceed correctly. Given the distributed nature of representations (see Chapter 4), it may be that true conceptual change is not characteristic of the development of human reasoning. What changes developmentally may be the accretion of relevant knowledge and the increasingly efficient inhibition of irrelevant knowledge. This possibility is discussed further in Chapter 9.

Neural imaging has also been used to study the brain-based mechanisms underlying causal reasoning on the basis of covariation information by adults (Fugelsang & Dunbar, 2005). Fugelsang and Dunbar varied the plausibility of potential causal theories for explaining whether certain drugs were likely to relieve symptoms of depression in an experiment with college students. For example, some students were told that research has shown that levels of happiness were directly linked to levels of the neurotransmitter serotonin in the brain, and that a particular pill worked by increasing serotonin levels (plausible causal theory). Other students were told that the same pill affected the number of staphylococci in the body, and that staphylococci had no direct link to how happy people feel. The students were then given covariation information about how often people taking those or other pills felt less depressed. Behaviorally, it was found that both covariation data and information about causal plausibility influenced the students' judgments about the effectiveness of the pills. The effects of covariation were larger when the students were evaluating plausible causal theories.

Brain imaging (fMRI) of neural activity during causal reasoning showed differences depending on whether participants were evaluating a plausible versus an implausible theory. When evaluating a plausible theory, neural regions associated with working memory, executive processing, and primary visual cortex were more active.

When theory and data were inconsistent (e.g. implausible theory but strong covariation data), neural regions associated with error detection and conflict monitoring, such as the anterior cingulate, were more active. Fugelsang and Dunbar (2005) argued that they had demonstrated specific neural response patterns as a function of the relationship between theory and data. Participants appeared to devote more attentional and working memory resources to evaluating *plausible* causal theories. The importance of *plausibility* is also relevant to the centrality of explanation-based causal reasoning for conceptual development, discussed in Chapter 4. As argued by Keil (2006), people do have skeletal explanatory schemes (often implicit) of the causal structure of the world, and they seek additional explanatory knowledge to improve these schemes from a variety of sources. These sources include situational support (e.g. from context), and explanatory knowledge in other minds (e.g. the minds of one's teachers).

SUMMARY

Causal reasoning is fundamental to cognitive development. It is particularly important for learning about the empirical relations in the world, that is, for learning how the world is. Causal reasoning enables children to learn about likely causal agents and causal mechanisms in all of the foundational domains. For example, children need to understand agency in terms of animate agents with intentions, and they also need to understand agency in terms of physical causal agents and mechanisms. Children also need to develop explanations for why an agent has a certain effect. In the psychological domain these explanations comprise a theory of mind, and in the physical domain these explanations concern plausible causal mechanisms. Children develop these understandings and explanations by noticing associations, tracking statistical dependencies (conditional probabilities), making analogies, acting on causal systems, and connecting causes and effects. In the developed world, many physical mechanisms have to be taken on trust. For example, most people do not understand the causal mechanisms behind facilities such as electricity, or how simple devices such as zips function. This does not impair their ability to operate electrical appliances or zips. Background or collateral knowledge enables them to make sensible choices (e.g. they assume that experts have built certain artifacts like irons and vacuum cleaners because electricity works; see Koslowski & Masnick, 2002). Casual reasoning and explanation-based learning continue to be important throughout the lifespan.

One theory discussed in this chapter was that causal reasoning could offer impressive cognitive benefits only if it followed recognized causal principles. A variety of evidence has shown that children do indeed reason in accordance with causal principles such as the principle of causal priority and the principle of covariation. Further, they do so from surprisingly early in development (e.g. Shultz & Kestenbaum, 1985). Similarly, children seem to have some understanding of the relationship between hypotheses and evidence, although this understanding is less robust early in development (Somerville & Capuani-Shumaker, 1984; Sodian et al., 1991). Even teenagers and adults have difficulties in reasoning about multiple causal variables, and in integrating causal information on a variety of dimensions (Wilkening, 1982; Kuhn et al., 1995). Nevertheless, overall the evidence suggests that causal reasoning shows impressive continuities from childhood to adulthood. Causal inferences that come easily to adults also come easily to children, and causal inferences that are difficult for adults are also difficult for children. Both children and adults also hold some *intuitive misconceptions* about physical phenomena, not all of which decline with age (Kaiser et al., 1985). These misconceptions have to be inhibited if correct causal inferences are to be drawn in certain situations. Improvements in metacognition and executive function enable misleading prior knowledge to be actively inhibited as children get older (see Chapter 9). These developments enable taught information, which may more accurately reflect the causal structure of physical systems, to underpin causal reasoning when perceptual information is misleading with regard to causal structure.

CHAPTER 7

CONTENTS

Social cognition, mental representation, and theory of mind

The term "**theory of mind**" was first used by Premack and Woodruff (1978) to refer to the ability of a person to impute mental states to the self and to others. Clearly, having a theory of mind is very important for social cognition. Understanding the mental states of others enables you to predict their behavior on the basis of their beliefs and desires. Essentially, having a theory of mind enables an analysis of psychological causation. However, analyses of psychological causation will only work if we generally attribute to others beliefs that are true and actions that are rational. In this chapter, I review the development of the ability to impute mental states, both to the self and to other agents.

As we saw in Chapter 3, research on the psychological world of infants suggests that many mechanisms that support social cognitive understanding are at work early in life. These mechanisms include gaze following, joint attention, the monitoring of goal-directed actions, and the monitoring of intentions. By at least 12 months, infants also appear to adopt a rational stance in their analyses of action. Infants can also make psychological inferences from social-cognitive information, suggestive of an emergent understanding of the mental states of others. For example, infants of 15 months seem to expect an agent to seek an object on the basis of its last known location by that agent, rather than on the basis of where it is now (Onishi & Baillargeon, 2005). This implies some understanding that beliefs can be false. If infants expect other people to act on the basis of their beliefs, they are developing a theory of mind. Accordingly, by 15 months, some form of **metarepresentational ability** appears to be present. By this age, infants appear to have some ability to represent the knowledge states (mental representations) of others.

This capacity for "metarepresentation" is at the heart of our ability to understand the mental states of others and to use knowledge about their mental states to make predictions about their behavior. These predictions require causal analyses of their likely goals and desires. Metarepresentational abilities seem to develop from at least three sources in addition to the early mechanisms discussed in Chapter 3. These sources are the capacity for imitation, the development of **pretend play**, and language. The importance of metarepresentational abilities for developing a "theory of mind" was first discussed in detail by Leslie (1987).

KEY TERMS

Theory of mind
The ability to impute mental states to the self and to others.

Metarepresentational ability
The ability to represent the knowledge states (mental representations) of the self and others.

Pretend play
To pretend that one object or event is another, often called symbolic play.

Leslie (1987) suggested that pretend play was one of the earliest manifestations of a child's ability to characterize and manipulate both their own and others' cognitive relations to information. ©LWA-Dann Tardif/Corbis.

Pretend play, symbolic development, and metarepresentation

In a seminal paper, Leslie (1987) suggested an important link between the development of a theory of mind and pretend play. His idea was that pretend play was one of the earliest manifestations of a child's ability to characterize and manipulate their own (and others') cognitive relations to information. To pretend that (for example) a banana is a telephone, the child must decouple the *primary* representation of the banana given by the sensory systems (yellow, edible object) from the pretend representation (telephone receiver) that is necessary for playing at answering the telephone. The primary representation is a direct representation of the object—the child is seeing and touching a banana. The pretend representation is part of the game. It is crucial for cognition that our primary representations are veridical. To pretend that the banana is a telephone, therefore, this primary representation must be marked off or "quarantined" from the pretend representation of a telephone receiver. This quarantining suspends the true semantics of being a banana. The pretend representation is not a representation of the objective world. Rather, it is a representation of a representation from that world; it is a *metarepresentation*. Leslie argued that the fact that early pretence is usually shared with others (e.g. a pretend tea party) shows that young children also have some understanding of pretending by others. Hence the act of pretending suggests some understanding that others also have metarepresentations.

According to this analysis, the emergence of pretence marks the beginning of a capacity to understand cognition itself—to understand thoughts as entities. Social partners frequently use language to help young children to understand pretend representations. For example, they may say "Do you want a turn with my telephone?". As we will see later, language plays other roles as well in helping children to understand mental states. For example, a theory of mind emerges earlier in children who live in families who talk explicitly about their emotions and feelings (Dunn, Brown, & Beardsall, 1991a).

An important aspect of Leslie's (1987) analysis of metarepresentation was the explicit connection that he drew with pretend play. Prior to this analysis, pretend play had been analyzed largely in terms of the development of a symbolic capacity. Therefore, pretend play had been considered largely in relation to language development. Both language and pretending were thought to require a general capacity for creating "symbols in thought". In pretend play, objects are used for symbolic purposes irrespective of their appearance. For example, a baby bottle may be used as a comb (Ungerer, Zelazo, Kearsley, & O'Leary, 1981). Similarly, in language, words are used for symbolic purposes. The sound patterns that constitute words have no direct link to the objects or to the events that they refer to. Language and pretend play were hence thought to depend on the same cognitive capacities. It was thought, for example, that the ability to sequence pretend acts (e.g. cook a pretend meal and then feed it to a doll) and the ability to sequence words into sentences depended on the same symbolic mechanism. Certainly, a large number of studies produced evidence consistent with a joint timetable for the development of language and of pretend play.

One example comes from a detailed analysis of the sequence of pretend play behaviors that develops between 8 and 30 months, carried out by McCune-Nicolich (1981). McCune-Nicolich was able to document a number of parallel developments in pretend play and in language. Young children's pretending begins by being closely tied to the veridical actions that people make on objects. For example, below 12 months, pretending might constitute "drinking" from an empty cup while making playful slurping noises. During the second year, pretending gradually becomes more abstract, and divorced from the immediate context. For example, a doll might be made to drink from the empty cup, or the child might play at "cleaning" something that isn't dirty. Initially, pretending seems to depend on the child's knowledge of the structures and functions of real objects. Gradually, action schemes are combined, so that, for example, a doll might be given a drink, do some cleaning, and then be put to bed. Late in the second year, the child becomes able to plan games mentally before embarking on them. At this stage, the child will search for the particular objects that are required for the planned pretend game, or will substitute different objects (e.g. a stick becomes a horse). Planned pretend is clear when the child announces the planned pretend act, or searches deliberately for a required prop. Whereas 2 years is the median age for planned pretend, longitudinal studies reveal its emergence as early as 18 months, or as late as 26 months (Nicolich, 1977).

The shared requirement of pretend play and language for "symbols in thought" was assumed on two grounds. First, both activities involve the communicative function of sharing objects with others. Second, children use both pretend play and language for "trying out" various representational equivalences. Accordingly, McCune-Nicolich (1981) went on to document some structural developments in language that appeared to parallel different levels of pretend play. For example, first words tend to co-occur with first pretend behaviors. McCune-Nicolich suggested that this signaled a separation between the means of signifying a meaning and the meaning itself. A second parallel was that the combination of words tends to co-occur with the sequencing of pretend behaviors. This coupling was suggested to arise from a fundamental cognitive development that allowed the child to construct *relations* between symbols. As a third example, the production of rule-based (syntactically structured) utterances appeared to emerge at the same time as planned pretending. The essential common element for this coupling was thought to be an internal cognitive structure that allowed symbolic elements to be related to one another directly.

The apparent correspondences between pretend play and early language were also appealing because of the view that a general capacity for symbolic representation set human cognition apart from cognition in other animals. The symbolic capacity was thought to account for representation across many domains, for example play, language, drawing, and mental imagery. Leslie's (1987) paper pointed out that the development of "symbols in thought" was better understood as a "meta-representational" capacity. He argued that this "meta-representational" capacity was also at the core of the developing understanding of the internal states of others. One reason that it might be useful to separate pretend play from language was demonstrated in a study by Fenson and Ramsey (1981), who showed that the developmental sequence of pretending could be influenced when adults modeled pretend behaviors for the child to imitate. Fenson and Ramsey demonstrated that pretend play following modeling was more advanced than pretend play in the absence of modeling. Fenton and Ramsey focused on combinatorial pretend acts, which are typically observed being performed spontaneously at around 24 months. An example is pouring imaginary liquid from a tea-pot into a cup and then giving a doll a drink from the cup.

Fenson and Ramsey studied infants aged 12, 15, and 19 months. Examples of the modeled combinatorial behaviors included stirring a spoon in an empty pan and then feeding a doll pretend food, and placing a doll into a bed and tucking her in with a blanket. A substantial number of both the 15-month-olds and the 19-month-olds in the study were found to imitate the combinatorial pretend acts, and a couple of the 12-month-olds did so as well. Two subsequent studies confirmed this developmental pattern. Fenson and Ramsey concluded that the general ability to imitate sequences of pretend acts was present by 19 months of age rather than by 24 months of age. In language development, single words are usually present by about the same age (see Chapter 5). Fenson and Ramsey speculated that in both domains (pretend play and language) the appropriate cognitive components were in place before combinations began to occur. An alternative way of thinking about these results is that imitation is a powerful tool for social cognition. Children will imitate pretend acts modeled by others as a way of sharing communication, and they will imitate pieces of language for the same purpose (see Chapter 5). In neither case is it necessary to propose a particular cognitive development enabling such behaviors. Learning by imitation has been present from birth. The child may be utilizing imitation in the realms of both language and action as a means of gaining a deeper understanding of representational activities. Initially, the imitation may occur for purely social purposes. Eventually, it may give the child fundamental insights into human social cognition.

Converging evidence that imitation enables a deeper understanding of representational activities comes from a study reported by Bigelow, MacLean, and Proctor (2004). They were interested in pretend play during episodes of sustained joint attention, where an adult and an infant share attention to an object. As we saw earlier, joint attention can be considered a "hot spot" for learning. Bigelow and colleagues expected infants to show increases in more advanced play with objects during episodes of joint attention. The infants studied were aged 12 months, the youngest age group studied by Fenson and Ramsey (1981). Twelve months is the age at which infants begin to be intentional in their play with objects: rather than simply sucking or banging objects, infants now begin to attend to the specific functional uses of their toys, and play gradually becomes symbolic. Bigelow et al. provided some enticing objects for the infants to play with, including a tea set, a doll with her bed, and a toy telephone.

Following a period of free play by the infants alone, mothers and infants were encouraged to play as they normally would. Infants' activities with the toys were then scored in both conditions. Bigelow et al. found that the infants had significantly more advanced play within joint attention episodes, and significantly more stereotyped play outside joint attention episodes. Bigelow et al. argued that mature play thus depended on more than simply the presence of the mother. Adult scaffolding of play within joint attention episodes had a particular effect on symbolic development. This supports social learning theories about the potential importance of "collective intentionality" in pretend play and psychological development. The view that psychological development is dependent on cultural imitative learning and "collective intentionality" has been proposed by Rakoczy, Tomasello, and Striano (2005). Rather than conceiving the individual mind as the main driver in the child's attainment of an understanding of mental states, Rakoczy et al. argue that the developmental process is a more social one. Carpendale and Lewis (2004) also offer a social interaction view of the child's developing understanding of mind.

The argument that imitation is crucial for gaining a deeper understanding of mental states and mental representations has been made in a stronger form by Meltzoff and Decety (2003). They pointed out that infants not only imitate the actions of others, but are also aware when others are imitating the actions of the infant. On this basis, Meltzoff and Decety argued that when infants see others acting "like me", they project that others have the same mental experience that is mapped to those behavioral states in the self. The evidence that infants know when they are being copied comes from a series of experiments reported by Meltzoff (1990). In these studies, Meltzoff asked adults to become "social mirrors" for babies aged 14 months. The adults simply had to copy every action that the infant made, behaving like a kind of "shadow". In fact, during the experiments two adults were sitting opposite to the infants. One shadowed the infant's behavior with a novel toy. If the infant banged her toy three times, the shadow banged her toy three times. If the infant mouthed the toy, the shadow mouthed her toy. The other adult served as an active control and imitated the infant's past behavior with the toy, which was shown on a video screen out of the infant's line of view. Meltzoff found that the infants preferred to look at the adult who was imitating them. They smiled more at this adult, and also tested out her reactions, for example suddenly stopping an action to see whether the shadow would follow suit. Meltzoff argued that caretakers who act as social mirrors take infants beyond the initial starting point of behavior. Caretaker reflections of infant behavior capture not only the motor aspects of this behavior, but add in intentions and goals. For example, if an infant waves a toy, the caretaker might interpret this as waving in order to shake and make a sound. Hence intentionality and desire become part of the imitative episode, reflecting psychological attributions back to the infant. In this way, imitation serves to aid the development of both a notion of the self and a notion of other minds.

Bigelow et al. (2004) found that the infants had significantly more advanced play within joint attention episodes, and that adult scaffolding of play (for example by the mother) had a particular effect on symbolic development.

On this view, action and imitation are critical to developing a theory of mind. Meltzoff and Decety (2003) argued that human acts are especially relevant to infants, because other humans look like the infant feels himself or herself to be. The infant recognizes "that seen event is like this felt event". Human acts are also events that the infant can intend. This enables infants to make inferences about the visible behavior of others, and the underlying mental states of others, such as what they intend. Infants thus infer the internal states of others through an analogy to the self. Meltzoff and Decety argued that this analogy is the root of empathic behavior, the uniquely human capacity to identify with others. However, empathy undergoes protracted development. Becoming a sophisticated mentalizer requires experience, and the extended development of metarepresentational capacities.

Early desire-based psychology?

Inferring the internal states of others through an analogy to the self might be easier for some internal states than for others. For example, it has been proposed that the ability to understand the internal state of desire might develop earlier than the ability to understand the internal state of belief. It may be cognitively easier to infer the desires of others from their actions than to infer the beliefs of others from their actions. This view, that early psychological understanding is based on desires, and that later psychological understanding is based on the interaction between beliefs and desires, has been proposed for example by Wellman and colleagues (Wellman, 2002; Wellman & Woolley, 1990).

For example, Wellman and Woolley (1990) argued that young children (2-year-olds) first construe human action in terms of desires. This "**simple desire psychology**" was thought to precede "**belief-desire psychology**" because desires motivate behaviors, and desire–behavior action sequences are relatively easy to map. Beliefs frame behaviors, and are less easy to map. It is easier to predict the actions and reactions of another person that are related to desires, than to predict the actions and reactions of another person that are related to beliefs. Wellman and Woolley hence argued that younger children will be simple "desire psychologists" and older children (from 3 years on) will be "belief-desire psychologists". For example, if you are hungry, that is a physiological state. Hunger is a drive that can be overcome by eating anything that is edible. However, if you want an apple, that is a psychological state. The desire for an apple cannot be overcome by eating a banana. Using examples such as these, Wellman and Woolley showed that desires are intentional constructs, whereas basic physiological drives (hunger, fear, pain) are not. They then argued that whereas beliefs always entail metarepresentations, desires might not. To understand the beliefs of another person, it is necessary to understand thoughts as entities—to understand representations of representations. To understand the desires of another person, it is only necessary to understand objects and events—primary representations.

Wellman and Woolley characterize simple desire psychology as attributing to other agents internal dispositions towards or against certain primary representations (i.e. actions or objects). An actor might not want a drink of milk, or might want a certain toy. These desires then cause the actor to do certain things. Usually, he or she engages in goal-directed actions, e.g. refuses the milk or fetches the toy. These goal-directed actions can be predicted by understanding desires. Simple desire reasoning can proceed without a conception of belief. The child can predict that the other person will go and get the desired toy from wherever the child knows the toy to be. The child can make this prediction without attributing knowledge of where the toy is to the actor (a belief-representational state). Simple desire reasoning does not allow a child to explain why an actor may engage in an action that is contrary to prediction (for example, going to fetch the toy from a wrong location—this might occur because the actor believes that the toy is in that location). However, although simple desire reasoning does not require a conception of belief, it does require a conception of intention or internal disposition.

To test their claim that 2-year-olds engage only in desire-based reasoning about the actions of others, whereas 3-year-olds engage in belief-desire reasoning about the actions of others, Wellman and Woolley devised experiments contrasting desire reasoning with belief-desire reasoning. For example, children were asked to predict the actions of story characters in different situations. The children might be told "Here's Johnny. He wants to find his dog to take it to the park, 'cause that's what he really wants to do. His dog might be in the house, or it might be in the garage. So, he's looking for his dog to take it to the park. Watch, he's looking for his dog in the garage. Look. He doesn't find his dog. What will Johnny do next?". This scenario can be solved by simple desire reasoning. If Johnny doesn't find his dog in the garage, the child can predict that he will next look for his dog in the house. The 2-year-olds were extremely good at making these desire-based predictions.

To contrast predictions based on desire psychology with predictions based on belief-desire psychology, Wellman and Woolley changed their scenarios slightly. In their second experiment, the correct prediction in each case required the child to go against their own desires or beliefs. This was done so that the child could not give the correct prediction on the basis of happening to have that desire or belief him- or herself. For example, the child might be told "At Betsy's school, they can play with puzzles in the classroom or they can play with sand on the playground". The child was then asked which option they would choose. If the child said the sand, the experimenter would say "Betsy wants to play with puzzles today, she doesn't want to play with sand". The child was then asked to predict where Betsy would go. This experimental design enabled a parallel scenario to be constructed requiring belief-desire reasoning. Here the child might be told "Sam wants to find his puppy. His puppy might be in the garage or under the porch. Where do you think Sam's puppy is?". If the child said under the porch, the experimenter would say "Sam thinks his puppy is in the garage, he doesn't think it is under the porch". Again, the child was asked to predict where Sam would go.

Wellman and Woolley predicted that the 2-year-olds in their study would be good at desire reasoning and poor at belief-desire reasoning. In fact, the children taking part in the study were quite good at both. As a group, the 20 children tested were 73% correct on the belief stories, and 93% correct on the desire stories. Both performance levels were significantly above chance. However, when a stricter criterion was adopted requiring correct responding in all three story scenarios based on either belief or desire, then 85% of the 2-year-olds passed the criterion for the desire stories and only 45% passed the criterion for the belief stories. Based on this and further experiments, Wellman and Woolley (1990) concluded that 2-year-olds understand others' mental states in intentional terms, but not in representational terms. Two-year-olds understand that others can want certain objects (have desires), but not that others can believe certain states of affairs (have beliefs). Simple desire psychology grants young children a beginning awareness of how people's internal intentional states can guide their behavior. However, it does not grant young children awareness of other people's cognitive relations to information. Hence by this account, children's first understanding of the mind is nonrepresentational. Very young children's analyses of psychological causation do not depend on an understanding of belief.

Although the view that younger children have only a nonrepresentational understanding of the mind is controversial (e.g. recall Onishi & Baillargeon's [2005] false-belief task with 15-month-olds discussed in Chapter 3, and see Perner & Ruffman, 2005), many studies since Wellman and Woolley (1990) have confirmed an early-developing desire psychology in very young children. For example, Repacholi and Gopnik (1997) devised a paradigm for exploring reasoning about desires in children aged 14 and 18 months. This paradigm entailed a food-request procedure, in which the toddlers were asked to select one of two foods to give to an experimenter. One of the foods had previously been preferred by the same experimenter. For example, in a contrast between crackers and broccoli, the experimenter might have tasted the crackers and pulled a face of disgust saying "Eew! Crackers! I tasted the crackers! Eew". The same experimenter might have tasted the broccoli and shown happiness, saying "Mmm! Broccoli! I tasted the broccoli! Mmm". The experimenter then placed her open hand mid-way between the two foods and said "Can you give me some?". The experimental measure was whether the toddler gave the experimenter the food that was the target of her positive affect (for some toddlers, this was the crackers and not the broccoli). Repacholi and Gopnik found that of the 14-month-olds, only 54% of children offered the preferred food. For the 18-month-olds, 73% offered the preferred food. As almost all the children themselves preferred the crackers to the broccoli, adjustments were necessary depending on whether the child was in the matched condition (both child and experimenter prefer crackers) or in the mismatched condition (child prefers crackers, experimenter prefers broccoli). These analyses indicated that while the 18-month-olds reliably offered the food preferred by the experimenter, the 14-month-olds reliably offered the food preferred by themselves. Repacholi and Gopnik concluded that, by 18 months of age, children have a psychological understanding of desire. They understand that desire is an internal psychological state, and that two people can have different internal dispositions towards the same entity (i.e. the broccoli).

In terms of the development of the understanding of psychological causation, of course, belief and desire are equally important in determining human action (Astington, 2001). Desires might be understood first because they are more closely tied to observable motivational states and to observable emotional expressions. Astington suggests that desires may be easier to observe because of their direct volitional connection to the world, as one can observe goal-directed actions. However, demonstrations of an early-developing desire psychology do not rule out an early-developing belief-desire psychology. Recall that at the group level, even 2-year-olds could solve belief-desire tasks at above-chance levels in Wellman and Woolley's (1990) paradigms. The most likely explanation is that the same developmental mechanisms, for example intention reading, imitation, and interpreting goal-directed actions, underpin the development of the psychological understanding of both desires and beliefs. Nevertheless, it is easier to demonstrate experimentally an understanding of desire than an understanding of belief. However, others argue that the transition from desire psychology to belief-desire psychology represents a theory change. Whereas 2-year-olds can predict and understand the actions and emotions of another as stemming from internal states of desire, a 3-year-old can understand why two actors with the same desire but opposing beliefs can act and react to the same outcome in very different ways (Wellman & Woolley, 1990; Wellman, 2002).

Mental representations, belief, and false belief

Despite ongoing controversies in the field, it is generally agreed that metarepresentation is not present from birth and develops relatively slowly. So far, we have seen that pretend play is an early manifestation of the infant's growing metarepresentational abilities. For example, the substitution of objects in pretend games (as in using a banana as a telephone) requires the ability to conceive *simultaneously* of two contradictory models of reality. Other types of metarepresentational understanding are more complex. A good example is the reasoning required to succeed in the standard false-belief task. The understanding that others can have beliefs that are *false* has occupied a special place in developmental studies of children's understanding of mind. For example, the philosopher Dennett argued that successful reasoning about false beliefs was the *only* convincing evidence for the attribution of mental states to others (Dennett, 1978).

Dennett made this argument because the predictions that we make about the behavior of others based on reasoning about their false beliefs differ from the predictions that we make if we reason on the basis of current reality. For a long time, it was believed that children had no understanding of false belief until the age of 3–4 years (Wimmer & Perner, 1983). Passing the false-belief task was equated with having a theory of mind. Therefore, it was argued that important changes in social cognitive development occurred between the ages of 3 and 4 years. During this period, children were thought to acquire a previously absent representational concept of belief, and they were thought to become able to represent the contents of other people's beliefs. It is still argued by many that children do not begin to use beliefs in order to explain the actions of others until relatively late in development (Saxe, Carey, & Kanwisher, 2004). However, the concept of a fundamental representational change between 3 and 4 years is being increasingly questioned.

The copious developmental literature using false-belief tasks began with a classic paper by Wimmer and Perner (1983). They devised a simple and ingenious paradigm for measuring children's understanding of false belief based on a change of location. A story character Maxi puts chocolate into cupboard X. He then goes out to play. While he is absent, his mother moves the chocolate into cupboard Y. The children are then asked where Maxi will look for his chocolate when he returns. In order to answer correctly, children need to distinguish their own true belief concerning the location of the chocolate (cupboard Y) from Maxi's false belief (cupboard X). Wimmer and Perner argued that children need to have an explicit and definite representation of Maxi's wrong belief in order correctly to select cupboard X. When children aged 4–6 years were tested with toy scenarios, 50% of those aged 4–5 years wrongly chose cupboard Y, whereas 92% of those aged 5–6 years correctly chose cupboard X. This dramatic difference occurred despite evidence that the younger children remembered where Maxi had left his chocolate. This was shown by the inclusion of a memory control question in the experimental paradigm ("Do you remember where Maxi put the chocolate in the beginning?"). This memory question was usually answered correctly. Wimmer and Perner concluded that a novel cognitive skill emerged between the ages of 4 and 6 years. This was the ability to represent wrong beliefs. More generally, Wimmer and Perner suggested that it was only between the ages of 4 and 6 years that children became able to represent the relationship between two people's epistemic states.

In fact, the ability to represent false beliefs in the false-location task appears to emerge between the ages of 4 and 6 years in children in all cultures so far studied when variants of Wimmer and Perner's paradigm are used. For example, Callaghan and colleagues (2005) tested false belief understanding in 267 children aged between 30 and 72 months in five different cultures. The participating countries were Peru, where children from a rural Andean town were tested; Samoa, where children from traditional Polynesian agrarian villages were tested; Canada, where children from a rural town were tested; India, where children from a large city were tested; and Thailand, where disadvantaged children attending a Buddhist temple school in a large city were tested. All children were tested by local female experimenters using a change of location false-belief task. Callaghan et al. (2005) found that in all settings, a majority of 3-year-olds failed the false-belief task, whereas a majority of 5-year-olds passed it. The 4-year-olds were usually evenly split—around half demonstrated understanding of false belief by passing the task, and around half did not. Callaghan et al. concluded that a shift in understanding false belief was a universal milestone of development, and that it occurred between 3 and 5 years of age.

Despite many replications (see Wellman, 2002), Wimmer and Perner's original claim that their change of location task measured children's understanding that beliefs can be false has not gone unchallenged. For example, it was argued that the context within which the children were questioned in the false-belief task could mislead children into thinking that they were being asked where Maxi would *need* to look to find his chocolate. Siegal and Beattie (1991) suggested that a more child-friendly way of asking children about Maxi's false belief would be to change the question that they were asked to "Where will Maxi look *first* for his chocolate?" Siegal and Beattie tested 40 3-year-olds and 40 4-year-olds in a false-belief paradigm involving lost puppies and kittens. For example, the children were told "Sam wants to find his puppy. Sam's puppy is really in the kitchen. Sam thinks his puppy is in the bathroom. Where will Sam look first for his puppy?" Children tested with the "look first" question tended to give the correct answer. For the 3-year-olds, 85% were correct in answering on the basis of a false belief in at least one of the story scenarios used, compared to 40% in the standard paradigm. For the 4-year-olds, the figures were 75% and 50%. Siegal and Beattie argued that it was unlikely that conceptual limitations prior to the age of 4 explained children's performance in Wimmer and Perner's false-belief task. Rather, the successful performance shown by 3-year-olds in the "look first" paradigm indicated that the nature of the conversational environment was critical to explaining children's response patterns.

A different suggestion was that developmental deficits in executive function (see Chapter 9) lay at the root of the wrong answers given by younger children in the false-belief task. It was argued that younger children might fail the false-belief question because they were worse than older children at inhibiting themselves from giving an answer based on their very salient current mental representation of reality. Russell and colleagues developed the "windows task", a measure of young children's capacity for strategic deception, to explore this alternative explanation (Russell, Mauthner, Sharpe, & Tidswell, 1991). In the windows task, children learned to play a competitive game with the experimenter to win chocolate for themselves. The game was based on two little boxes, one of which always contained chocolate. The child's job was to point to one of the two boxes on each trial, to tell the experimenter "where to look" for the chocolate. If the competitor opened the empty box, the child got the chocolate. If the competitor chose the box containing the chocolate, the competitor kept the chocolate. Thus the winning strategy was to point to the empty box.

When the child was learning the game, the boxes were opaque. Once the child had learned how to play (after 15 trials), however, the opaque boxes were replaced with boxes that had windows facing the child (and facing away from the competitor). The child could now see via the windows which of the two boxes on a given trial contained the chocolate. It was explicitly pointed out to the child that it was now easier to make the competitor go to the wrong box. Twenty trials with the windows then commenced, and 3- and 4-year-olds were tested. The results showed that, on the first windows trial, most of the 3-year-olds pointed to the box containing the chocolate, whereas most of the 4-year-olds pointed to the empty box. The 4-year-olds hence won the chocolate for themselves and the 3-year-olds lost the chocolate. Remarkably, 65% of the 3-year-olds continued to point to the baited box for all 20 trials, thereby never winning the chocolate. No 4-year-olds showed this pattern. Russell et al. argued that the younger children's difficulty lay in inhibiting pointing to a salient object (i.e. the chocolate). Their physical knowledge concerning the location of the chocolate was so salient that it controlled their behavior.

Russell et al. went on to argue that younger children faced similar problems in the false-belief task. Here, the younger children's physical knowledge of the new location of Maxi's chocolate controlled their verbal responding. Indeed, Russell et al. (1991) demonstrated that the same children who failed in their windows task were likely to fail a traditional false-belief task. More recently, however, Hughes (1998) has shown that developmental deficits in executive function can account for many instances of younger children failing to inhibit very salient information when initiating action (see Chapter 9). The large variety of situations in which this does and does not occur suggest that executive deficits do not provide a parsimonious explanation of younger children's performance in false-belief tasks. For example, Carlson and Moses (2001) showed that inhibitory control tasks shared substantial common variance with theory of mind tasks, but that the two sets of tasks did not tap entirely coextensive abilities. Performance in both theory of mind and inhibitory control tasks was also related to age, gender, and verbal ability. Inhibitory control is an important component of executive function, and the general relationship between the development of executive functions and metacognitive development is currently a major focus of developmental research. This research is considered further in Chapter 9.

What about Wimmer and Perner's original interpretation, that younger children were poorer at co-ordinating different mental representations? This idea received apparently strong support from a related series of experiments on children's understanding of **the appearance–reality distinction**, conducted by Flavell and colleagues. Flavell, Flavell, and Green (1983) were interested in situations in which appearance and reality differed, for example in children's understanding of a sponge that looked like a lump of rock. They thought that young children might not be able to keep the difference between appearance and reality clear in their minds if appearance and reality differed. Younger children might confuse their representations of appearance and reality. To investigate this question, Flavell et al. gave children aged 3–5 years a series of tasks involving contrasts between appearance and reality. The objects used included the rock/sponge, an imitation pencil made out of rubber, a hand puppet covered with a white handkerchief so that it looked like a ghost, and a piece of white card placed beneath a pink transparency, so that it appeared pink. The children were then asked a series of questions, including "What is this really really? Is it really really (a rock) or really really (a piece of sponge)", and "When you look at this with your eyes right now, does it look like (a rock) or does it look like (a piece of sponge)?". Flavell et al. reported that the 4- and 5-year-olds rarely confused appearance and reality, whereas about half of the 3-year-olds did so. They concluded that the younger children had a general metacognitive difficulty in dealing with mental representations. Although young children have and use mental representations, Flavell et al. suggested that they are less able to "stand back" from their representations and reflect on their veridicality. What develops is thus the ability to reflect on and index one's own representations, tagging their internal source so that both appearance and reality can be kept in mind together. This conclusion implies a role for metacognition, as source monitoring (from where did I gain this knowledge?) is an important aspect of metacognitive behavior. This is considered further in Chapter 9.

Pictorial versus mental representations

A different paradigm for exploring children's ability to hold two competing representations in mind at once was developed by Zaitchik (1990). She decided to develop a task that did not depend on mental representations, but on nonmental representations. Her solution was a "false-photograph" task. In this task, a photograph was taken of an object A at one location, location X. The object was then moved to location Y. The child was then asked "In the picture, where is object A?". The correct answer was, of course, location X. Three-, 4- and 5-year-olds were tested, and all received prior experience with a Polaroid camera. This type of camera takes real pictures and develops them instantaneously. The child took pictures of familiar soft toys (e.g. Ernie from Sesame Street), and watched them develop. During the experimental test, the child watched a little show in which Bert and Ernie

KEY TERM

Appearance–reality distinction
Awareness that appearance and reality may differ, both in terms of physical objects (e.g. a sponge that looks like a rock) and psychological states (e.g. appears interested but is actually bored).

Zaitchik's (1990) "false-photograph" task explored children's ability to hold two competing representations in mind at once, using the familiar figures of Bert and Ernie from Sesame Street. © Kay Nietfeld/dpa/Corbis.

were taking a picture of Rubber Duckie with a Polaroid camera. Bert took a photo of Rubber Duckie on the bed, and developed the picture. Ernie then moved Rubber Duckie to the bathtub, so that he could go to bed. The child was asked "In the picture, where is Rubber Duckie?".

Zaitchik found that both the 3-year-olds and the 4-year-olds were at chance in working out where Rubber Duckie would be in Bert's picture. In fact, they were worse in the false-photograph task than in a standard false-belief task given at the same time. Zaitchik (1990) suggested that mental representations are difficult not because they are mental, but because they are representations. When children must reason about representations that are supposed to describe the real state of affairs in the world, be these photos or beliefs, they run into difficulty when the representations in fact do not describe the veridical state of affairs in the world. Zaitchik suggested that it is misrepresentations rather than mental representations that cause younger children difficulties.

Zaitchik's conclusions have been called into question by more recent studies. For example, Slaughter (1998) gave 3-year-olds five different tasks involving representations, including a false-belief task, a false-photograph task, and a false-drawing task. The false-photograph task involved a Polaroid camera, which was used to take a photo of a toy frog on a chair. The frog was then removed, and a teddy bear was put onto the chair instead. The child was asked "What is on the chair in this picture?". The false-drawing task was similar. A doll was placed on the chair, and the experimenter drew a picture of the doll on the chair. The child checked the picture, which was then turned face down, and a car was put on the chair in place of the doll. The child was asked "What is on the chair in this picture?". Slaughter reported that the false-photograph and false-drawing tasks were significantly easier than the false-belief task for her 3-year-olds. For example, 76% of her participants passed the false-photograph task, compared to 32% passing the false-belief task. Slaughter suggested that children's understanding of pictorial versus mental representations was not developmentally related.

Mental representation in the deaf

This view of the developmental independence of mental versus pictorial representations has been supported by a quite different line of investigation. This innovative research examines deaf children's understanding of mental states. Siegal (e.g. Peterson & Siegal, 1998) pointed out that conversations about mental states were likely to be important in the normative development of an understanding of mind, and that deaf children were unlikely to have such conversations. The reason for this is that most deaf children are born to hearing parents, and so miss out on many rich early communicative experiences. Typically, deafness is not diagnosed early and, once it is diagnosed, both the hearing parents and the deaf child need to learn sign language before adequate communication can take place between them. Suprisingly, most deaf children do not learn sign language prior to schooling, and many hearing parents with deaf children lack fluency in signing. Accordingly, most deaf children experience a relatively isolated early social environment. This is bound to have effects on the development of social cognition and the understanding of mental representation. As we saw when considering pretend play, social partners are very important for the early development of an awareness that others have their own minds and representations. For example, regarding representational understanding, caretakers frequently use language to help young children to understand thoughts as entities.

Peterson and Siegal (1998) studied signing deaf children's performance in two representational tasks, the false-photograph task and the standard false-belief task involving the change of location of a desired object. The deaf children ranged from 5 to 11 years in age, and were compared with typically developing 3- and 4-year-olds. Peterson and Siegal found that the deaf children had no difficulty with the false-photograph task but were at chance in the false-belief task. The deaf children were significantly poorer in the false-belief task than 4-year-old children, being comparable to typically developing 3-year-olds (who also failed the false-belief task while passing the false-photograph task). Peterson and Siegal concluded that deaf children have a special difficulty with the concept of false mental representations. They do not have a difficulty in conceiving of pictorial representations, because the latter are not facilitated by conversations. Peterson and Siegal suggested that the absence of pervasive family talk about abstract mental states lay at the root of deaf children's poor performance in theory-of-mind tasks.

Clearly, family talk about abstract mental states should not be absent in deaf families where the parents are fluent signers. Indeed, it has been shown that native deaf signers (deaf children who learn to sign from birth) acquire a theory of mind at the same developmental rate as other children. Woolfe, Want, and Siegal (2002) recruited two groups of deaf children aged 4 to 8 years to their study, a group of native-signing deaf children being raised by deaf signing parents, and a group of late-signing deaf children being raised by hearing parents. The children were tested by a native deaf signer who tested them in sign language. The tasks used to test the children's understanding of mental representations were false- and true-belief tasks, shown pictorially. For example, in the false-belief task a boy was shown fishing, and then shown looking happy and excited when he felt a weight on his rod. However, the child was shown that he had actually caught a boot. The child was then required to select an item to go into a new picture of the boy showing a "think bubble" above his head (i.e. the child had to choose a picture to represent the boy's belief). The child also had to select the picture of the item that was really at the end of the rod. In order for the child to be credited with having a theory of mind, they were required to pass both the belief and the reality measures successfully.

Woolfe et al. (2002) found that the native deaf signers performed at a similar level to hearing 4-year-olds in the belief tasks, showing an understanding of false belief; the late deaf signers did not. Both native and late deaf signers succeeded on the false-photograph test, which was also administered. This success demonstrated that both groups understood pictorial representations. Woolfe et al. argued that the late deaf signers were likely to be cut off from communication about mental states with their parents and siblings by their lack of a shared language. The native deaf signers were not. The importance of conversations about mental states for a normative development of an understanding of mind was emphasized.

THE ROLE OF LANGUAGE AND DISCOURSE IN METAREPRESENTATIONAL DEVELOPMENT

The idea that conversations and communication about the mind might play a pivotal role in acquiring an understanding of other minds is an idea that has been around for a long time. Bretherton and Beeghly (1981) suggested that the exchange of

Piaget (1962) suggested that pretend play and language development were linked, as both reflected an emerging ability to manipulate symbols. © Bettmann/Corbis.

information via language played a central role in the development of social cognition, an idea expressed more broadly in Vygotsky's theory of cognitive development (Vygotsky, 1978; see Chapter 11). Theorists such as Piaget (1962) also suggested that pretend play and language development were linked, as both reflected an emerging ability to manipulate symbols. In fact, the kind of discourse found during pretend play might have a special role in explaining why conversations help to develop young children's mindreading abilities. There are a number of converging sources of evidence for these links between language as a symbol system, language as a communication system, pretend play, and the development of metarepresentational understanding. Here we consider some of this evidence, focusing on the development of children's spontaneous use of mental state language, the kinds of communicative experiences that seem to matter within families, and the role of siblings and peers in developing social cognition, particularly as focused around pretend play.

The use of internal state terms

Children begin using mental state terms in their everyday conversations some time during the second year. Internal state language, that is, the use of labels for one's own states such as fatigue, disgust, pain, distress, and affection, is found in children aged as young as 20 months. Although some of these internal states are emotions, other internal states such as fatigue are not emotional states. Between 20 and 28 months, there is a large increase in the use of mental state terms in children's discourse. This was demonstrated in a study by Bretherton and Beeghly (1982). They asked mothers of children aged 20 and 28 months to keep a record of their child's internal state language in six different categories. The first category was perception (sight, hearing, touch), for example "Hear wind Daddy? Blowing, blowing" and "I'm going to be a cloud in the sky so that you can't see me". This category also incorporated skin senses (pain, temperature), for example "I'm too hot, I'm sweating!". The second category was physiology (hunger, thirst, states of consciousness), as in "Are you awake?" and "I not hungry now". The third category was positive and negative affect (joy, surprise, love, anger, fear, distress, kindness, disgust), for example "You boo-hoo all better?", "Don't be mad, Mummy!" and "Daddy surprised me!". The fourth category was volition and ability (desire, need, ability to do something difficult), as in "My baby needs me" and "Do you think I can do this?". The fifth was cognition (knowledge, memory, uncertainty, dreaming, reality versus pretending), for example "Jim knows where it is", "Those monsters are just pretend, right?", and "I had a dream about a dog". The final category was moral judgment and obligation (moral transgression, permission, and obligation), as in "Matthew won't let me play!", "Was he naughty?", and "If I'm good, Santa will bring toys".

Bretherton and Beeghly found wide individual differences in the children's utterances. Nevertheless, 90% of the children at 28 months produced labels for pain, fatigue, disgust, love, and moral conformity. Distress was the most commonly labeled emotion, and knowing was the most commonly labeled cognition. The scores for cognition labels (knowing, remembering, thinking, pretending, dreaming) lagged significantly behind the scores for affect and morality labels. As Bretherton and Beeghly pointed out, it is much more difficult to infer processes like thinking than to infer emotions and intentions, as the latter have more explicit behavioral correlates. Unasked, the mothers also collected examples of their children's causal utterances involving mental states. These included utterances like "I scared of the shark. Close my eyes", "I give a hug. Baby be happy", "I'm hurting your feelings, 'cause I was mean to you", and "You sad Mommy. What Daddy do?". Most causal utterances were emotion related, indicating some grasp of the causes and consequences of mental states even at 28 months. Bretherton and Beeghly concluded that linguistic evidence suggested that the ability to analyze the goals and motives of others was already well-developed in the third year. They argued that the exchange of information via language played a central role in the development of social cognition. Theoretically, they predicted that the acquisition of psychological knowledge about the self and about others should be greatly facilitated by intentional communication (see also Chapter 3).

The role of communicative experiences

Subsequent work by Dunn and colleagues suggested that this idea was correct. For example, Dunn, Brown, and Beardsall (1991a) investigated the links between family dialogue about feelings and children's later understanding of the emotions of others. The children were observed at home when aged 36 months in conversation about feeling states with their mothers and older siblings. They were then followed up at 6 years of age using an affective-perspective-taking task. The naturalistic observations revealed that a number of different emotional themes were discussed in family talk, with positive themes (pleasure, affection, sympathy) and negative themes (fear, anger, distress) discussed about equally. No gender differences were found in the frequency of children's references to feeling states, and mothers did not discuss feelings more frequently with girls than with boys. However, discussions about feeling states were most common when the child was engaged in a dispute, either with their mother or with a sibling.

At 6 years, the children's ability to identify the emotions of others was measured using video vignettes of acted emotion scenarios between adults (happiness, anger, anxiety, sadness). In these vignettes, the emotions portrayed changed from the beginning of the scenario to the end. The children were asked to identify how the protagonist was feeling at the beginning of the interactions, and at the end. Dunn et al. found that there were highly significant associations between early differences in family talk about feelings (measured in terms of frequency of discussions, causal feeling-state discussions, diversity of themes, and disputes) and the children's ability to identify emotions in others at age 6. These associations were independent of the verbal ability of the children and the total amount of mother–child talk in different families. Dunn et al. concluded that there was a continuity between early family discourse about feelings and children's understanding of the emotions of others. It seems likely that this continuity reflects the linguistic exchange of information about emotions and their causes, particularly in situations which may be highly emotionally charged for the child, such as a dispute with a sibling.

What about possible links between family dialogue and children's understanding of the *beliefs* of others? Family discourse about the causes of behavior and events might well be linked to individual differences in the later ability to understand the connections between another's beliefs and another's behavior. Dunn, Brown, Slomkowski, Tesla, and Youngblade (1991b) suggested that family conversations about causality offered young children opportunities to enquire, argue, and reflect about why people behave in the ways that they do. Dunn et al. tested their hypothesis in a study using methods analogous to those used by Dunn et al (1991a). Participating children (this time aged 33 months) were observed at home in conversation with their mothers and older siblings during spontaneous interactions. At a later time point (at age 40 months), the children were given both false-belief and affective-perspective-taking tasks. The latter involved emotion-inducing situations enacted by puppets (e.g. having a frightening dream). The false-belief tasks involved puppets believing that a Band-Aid box would contain sticking plasters ("false contents" task), and finding out that it did not. Instead, the sticking plasters were in a plain, unmarked box. The child was then asked to predict where a new puppet (who had a cut) was likely to look for sticking plasters. Dunn et al. found that their different measures of feeling state talk in family conversations when the children were aged 33 months (total amount of talk, mother-to-child talk, causal talk) were related to both the children's emotional understanding and to their understanding of false belief when aged 40 months.

The existence of significant correlations over time between explicit family conversation about mental and feeling states at time 1, and later emotional and false belief understanding at time 2, is strongly suggestive of a causal link. However, a training study is required to demonstrate whether a specific causal relationship in fact exists. Lohmann and Tomasello (2003) provided an example of such a study. Lohmann and Tomasello highlighted the potential role of requests for clarification and discourse concerning misunderstandings as being particularly important for developing an understanding of family members' different perspectives about situations. Two training conditions were devised. These conditions enabled the comparison of the effects of perspective-taking discourse that also involved the frequent use of mental state words, with the effect of perspective-taking discourse alone. The basic training procedure was based on deceptive objects. For example, an object might appear to be a plastic flower, but turn out to be a pen. In the mental state condition, the deceptive nature of the objects was highlighted and discussed using mental state verbs like "think" and "know" ("What do you think this is? . . . You thought it was a flower"). In the contrasting condition, the experimenter only used phrases like "What is this?" and "A flower". The effects of training were assessed using: (1) further deceptive objects; (2) the traditional Wimmer and Perner false-belief task involving change of location; and (3) Flavell's appearance–reality distinction tasks.

Lohmann and Tomasello (2003) reported that the 3-year-olds tested showed significantly more improvement in the metarepresentational post-tests if they experienced training with perspective-taking discourse involving mental state terms. Their conclusion was that mental state language was necessary for young children to make progress in false-belief understanding, with this language used by other persons to structure the children's perspective-taking experiences. Lohmann and Tomasello linked their findings to those of Siegal and colleagues with deaf children, discussed earlier. They argued that it seems to be difficult for children to construct an understanding of the representational nature of mental states from visual scenes alone. Rather, rich linguistic communicative experiences are required for children to develop adequate social understanding.

"Mind-mindedness" talk by mothers, security of attachment, and metarepresentational understanding

Meins (1997; Meins & Fernyhough, 1999) has developed an interesting idea concerning how children internalize representations of the self and others via family discourse about mental states. She has suggested that a crucial factor in explaining individual differences is whether parents and other caregivers treat young children as individuals with minds. She terms this parental stance "**mind-mindedness**", and links mind-mindedness to security of attachment. Although an analysis of the attachment literature is beyond the scope of this book, theories linking aspects of cognitive development with aspects of attachment are very welcome. Originating with Bowlby's (1969, 1973) analysis of security of attachment as a key variable in explaining social and emotional development, the attachment literature offers an alternative way of analyzing how children internalize the notion of self and come to characterize others as distinct mental agents expected to act in certain ways. A core notion in attachment theory is the "internal working model" of the self, which is thought to be developed from parenting experiences. Via experiencing either consistent or inconsistent responding from caretakers, the infant develops a notion of the self as an entity that is more or less deserving of loving attachment from others. The development of the internal working model therefore involves understanding other people and their psychological characteristics, particularly in terms of their likely behavior towards the self (see Symons, 2004, for a useful overview). Children who experience secure attachments develop more positive inner working models.

Meins (1997) pointed out that individual differences in parenting experiences in infancy might have effects on later metarepresentational understanding. The ways in which caregivers initiate, maintain, and control interactions with their infants might be important, in particular how they choose to interpret their infants' acts. The proclivity to treat one's child as an individual with a mind from an early age might well have a positive effect on the child's developing understanding about other minds. This proclivity was "mind-mindedness". Meins and Fernyhough (1999) set out to explore whether maternal mind-mindedness assessed when infants were aged 20 months would be predictive of maternal mind-mindedness at age 3, and also predictive of the children's performance in theory of mind tasks at 5. Maternal mind-mindedness at 20 months was assessed using two measures. The first was whether the mother reported that their infants used nonstandard vocalizations to reliably intend certain meanings, systematically using such vocalizations to replace a given English word. Mothers who interpreted infant vocal behavior as intending meanings were deemed more mind-minded. The second was whether the mother reported that their infants made many vocalizations that they could not understand (such vocalizations were frequently referred to by the mothers as "double Dutch" or "gobbledegook"). Mothers who did not report that their infants used meaningless speech were deemed to be more mind-minded. Continuity in mind-mindedness when the children were 3 years was assessed by asking the mothers to describe their children, and then scoring the use of mental descriptors as a proportion of the total descriptors produced. For example, a mother who described her child in terms of height, weight, hobbies, position in the family, etc. would score low on mind-mindedness ("He's a typical lad"). A mother who described her child in terms of the child's emotions, desires, mental life, and imagination would score high on mind-mindedness ("She knows what she wants").

Meins and Fernyhough (1999) found that mothers of securely attached infants were more likely to be mind-minded. Maternal attribution of meaning to their infant's early vocalizations was significantly related to the likelihood that the mothers would describe their children in terms of mental characteristics 16 months later. All three maternal mind-mindedness measures were significantly related to the children's performance in the false-belief tasks at age 5. Meins and Fernyhough suggested that the proclivity to treat one's child as an individual with a mind was important for the child's own developing understanding of other minds. Relating this to the family discourse work of Dunn and colleagues, they pointed out that mothers in those studies who employed mentalistic strategies to diffuse disputes, explaining why a sibling had behaved in a certain way using mental state terms, were similarly treating their children as mental agents.

Pretend play/mental state discourse between siblings and peers, and metarepresentational understanding

Of course, older siblings are also likely to treat younger children as mental agents, and a child with an older sibling is likely to be involved in many episodes of pretend play. Indeed, there is some evidence that children with siblings acquire a theory of mind somewhat earlier than children without siblings, and that older siblings may cause larger developmental effects (e.g. Perner, Ruffman, & Leekam, 1994). In Perner et al.'s study of 76 children aged between 3 and 4 years, those with two siblings were found to be almost twice as likely to pass false-belief tasks as those who were only children. There was also a trend for older siblings to have a greater effect on false-belief development than younger siblings, although this trend was nonsignificant. However, Perner et al. did not collect information about the children's verbal and cognitive abilities, and so the association between family size and false-belief understanding could be mediated by children from larger families having higher cognitive or verbal abilities. Jenkins and Astington (1996) therefore investigated the potential association between false-belief understanding and family size by systematically measuring these variables as well.

Jenkins and Astington studied a cohort of 68 children, 22 of whom were only children. The others had either one sibling (32 children), two siblings (13 children), or three siblings (one child). All of the children were given four different false-belief tasks, including versions of the standard Wimmer and Perner (1983) task, as well as comprehensive language and memory assessments. Jenkins and Astington reported that general language ability and verbal memory were significantly associated with false-belief understanding after controlling for age. General language ability was also related to family size, with children from larger families generally having more advanced language skills. The central question was whether family size would be related to false-belief understanding once individual differences in language ability were controlled. Jenkins and Astington found that even with age, language ability, and birth order controlled, family size contributed a significant amount of unique variance to individual differences in false-belief understanding. They also found that the effects of having siblings were actually stronger for children with lower language abilities, and that whether the sibling was older or younger than you did not matter. Hence it seems to be having a sibling *per se* that is important. A sibling provides a ready playmate as well as a competitor for parental attention, and the intensity of children's interactions with their siblings seems likely to provide a large number of opportunities for reflecting upon both one's own and another's desires, beliefs, and emotions.

The presence of siblings does more than provide rich linguistic communicative experiences that may contribute to the development of understanding other minds. Siblings also offer different kinds of play experiences to mothers. Regarding pretend play, Youngblade and Dunn (1995) pointed out that pretend play with siblings differs from pretend play with the mother, as siblings are more likely to be actors in the drama themselves. Pretend play with siblings is thus more likely to be social pretence, and may be highly charged emotionally. It may thus have particular effects on the development of metarepresentational understanding. To investigate this hypothesis, Youngblade and Dunn observed naturally occurring pretend play episodes between children aged 33 months and their older siblings. The pretend play episodes were rated for factors such as diversity of themes, role enactment, and role play. The experimenters then measured the same children's performance when aged 40 months on the Band-Aid false-belief and puppet affective-perspective-taking tasks used by Dunn et al. (1991b). The median age gap between the target children studied and their siblings was 3 years.

Youngblade and Dunn (1995) found that pretend play with siblings differs from pretend play with the mother, as siblings are more likely to get involved in the drama themselves.

Youngblade and Dunn (1995) found that the target children spent much more time in pretend play with their siblings than with their mothers. Further, conversations about feelings were much more frequent during pretend play with the sibling than with the mother. To examine predictive relations with understanding of false belief and emotional states, longitudinal correlations were computed for four measures of pretending, namely total amount of pretend play, diversity of themes, role enactment during pretend, and role play during pretend. Of these four measures, only the role enactment measure was found to be significantly related to later performance in the false-belief task. For the affective understanding task, only total amount of pretending showed a significant longitudinal correlation. Youngblade and Dunn concluded that certain aspects of children's interactions with their siblings were particularly closely linked to developments in understanding other minds.

Interactions with siblings are of course only possible if you have siblings, and interactions with friends may also be important in developing an understanding of other minds. There may also be important developmental changes in when and why children talk about mental states. Brown, Donelan-McCall, and Dunn (1996) reported that at 33 months of age, children's talk about mental states was predominantly within their families, whereas by 47 months mental state talk was more frequent with siblings and friends. Many children begin nursery in their fourth year of life, which gives them access to multiple friendships. The role of play with their friends in children's growing understanding of the beliefs, desires, and intentions of others is becoming an increasing focus of developmental studies. Pretend play between friends makes high demands for imaginary and co-operative interaction.

For example, Hughes and Dunn (1998) recruited 25 pairs of friends (mean age 3 years 11 months), who met daily at their nurseries, to study whether dyadic play was characterized by mental state talk. They videorecorded each dyad during 20 minutes of pretend play on three occasions spread over the course of a year. The 25 pairs comprised 10 boy–boy dyads, 10 girl–girl dyads, and 5 boy–girl dyads. Hughes and Dunn also studied the children's understanding of mental states and emotions at the same three time points. To ensure that rich interactions would occur during the sessions being recorded for the study, Hughes and Dunn (1998) supplied novel and exciting dressing-up materials and role-play toys at each recording session. These props included walkie-talkies, police clothes, and handcuffs, and an extensive set of toy cooking equipment including a blender and a cooker. Children's mental state talk during the dyadic play sessions was measured, and related to the different outcome measures of theory of mind and emotion understanding development. These measures included variants of the false-belief and puppet affective-perspective-taking tasks used in prior studies, along with additional measures of false belief including deception.

Hughes and Dunn found that the rate of mental state talk between the dyads and performance on the false-belief and emotion understanding tasks was highly correlated at all three measurement points. Within individual dyads, individual differences in the frequency of mental state talk remained reliable across the year of the study. These individual differences between dyads were significantly associated with theory of mind performance a year later: Higher rates of talk at session 1 led to better theory of mind performance when measured at session 3. Interestingly, mental state talk was both more advanced and more frequent in pairs of girls than in pairs of boys. Hughes and Dunn concluded that children's friendships provided a rich social context for learning about others' minds.

Individual differences in friendships and in topics selected for pretending

Of course, children's friendships can vary markedly in quality. Dunn and Cutting (1999) explored whether the nature of interactions with friends might have differential effects on the development of a theory of mind. For example, while some friendships are characterized by amity, shared amusement, and positive affect, others are characterized by frequent dramatic quarrels, conflicts, and then making up. Dunn and Cutting studied the friendships of 128 4-year-olds from both middle-class and deprived backgrounds. The children's theory of mind development was measured in terms of false-belief and deception understanding. Their understanding of emotions was measured using puppet vignettes and other measures, and assessments were also made of their language development, family background, and temperament. Each friendship pair was videoed for two separate 20-minute periods of playing by themselves, in a separate room supplied with a set of props similar to those used by Hughes and Dunn (1998). Dyadic play was then rated for the frequency of co-operative pretend play, co-ordinated play, conflict, communication, and amity.

Dunn and Cutting reported that the nature of the friendships between children differed dramatically between the dyads. Whereas some children shared an imaginary world together with great skill and enjoyment, others created shared pretence rarely, preferring to engage in boisterous games or even "shared deviance" (e.g. killing flies together). Children with more shared pretend play were those who scored more highly on the theory-of-mind measures. These were also the children who talked more to their friends, showed fewer "failed bids" at communication, and showed less dyadic conflict. When both friends had higher mind-reading scores, there was more pretending within the dyad. Maternal education and family background also made important contributions to better performance on the theory-of-mind measures. The amount of connected conversation between children did not in itself contribute unique variance to the understanding of other minds. In fact, this kind of conversation often focused on competitive discussions (e.g. who had the better toys at home) rather than on sharing thoughts and feelings. Clearly, it is mental state discourse rather than discourse *per se* that is important for the development of mind-reading skills.

There is also evidence that skilled mind-reading does not always go hand-in-hand with amicable play characterized by low conflict. Studies of older children have shown that those who bully others may show advanced performance on theory-of-mind tasks. For example, Sutton, Smith, and Swettenham (1999) studied possible links between social cognition and bullying in a cohort of 193 children aged between 7 and 10 years. They pointed out that whereas the popular stereotype of a bully combines physical power with intellectual backwardness (the "oaf"), bullies can actually be manipulative experts who organize gangs of other children and use subtle and indirect methods for control. This latter kind of bully would require superior mind-reading skills. Sutton et al. characterized the children in their sample into six groups on the basis of peer and self-nomination. These were Bully (13%), Victim (18%), Assistant (helps bully, 6%), Reinforcer (encourages the bully indirectly via watching and laughing, 8%), Defender (sticks up for the victim, 44%), and Outsider (resolutely refuses to become involved, 11%). Theory-of-mind development was measured using a comprehensive assessment of 11 types of social cognition (e.g. understanding deception, "double bluff", and emotion).

Sutton et al. reported that the Bullies scored higher in terms of total social cognition scores than any other group. They scored significantly more highly than victims, followers, and defenders, but not significantly more highly than outsiders. Initiative-taking, ringleader behavior by bullies was the type of bullying most highly correlated with total social cognition score. Sutton et al. argued that possessing theory-of-mind skills that were superior to those of their followers and victims put bullies at an advantage. Bullies appear to perceive and interpret social cues very accurately. However, Sutton et al. also noted that their study was a correlational one. Hence they could not distinguish between the possibility that having advanced theory-of-mind skills enables a child to become a bully and the alternative explanation that the experience of bullying itself aids children's social cognitive development.

For younger children, it appears that pretend play with peers has effects on the development of a theory of mind because it entails frequent discussion of mental states. For older children, other developmental factors may also come into play, such as a propensity to manipulate others. Younger children who engage in antisocial play are not necessarily good mind readers. This was shown in a study of "hard-to-manage" preschoolers reported by Hughes, Dunn, and White (1998). They studied 40 children nominated by their parents as being difficult to manage, and compared their performance on theory of mind and emotion understanding tasks with 40 age- and gender-matched 4-year-olds from the same urban area. Family background, language development, and nonverbal ability were also measured.

Hughes et al. found that the hard-to-manage preschoolers showed delayed understanding of emotion, showing poorer affective perspective-taking skills even when family background, language, and cognitive ability were controlled. These children were basically poorer at understanding how others might feel in particular situations. Once language abilities were controlled, the hard-to-manage preschoolers were equivalent to their controls on most of the theory-of-mind tasks. An exception was the emotion false-belief task, which involved a protagonist experiencing either a nice surprise or a nasty surprise. The hard-to-manage preschoolers found it easier to pass the false-belief task involving a nasty surprise. As Hughes et al. (1998) pointed out,

Hughes et al. (1998) found that the hard-to-manage preschoolers were more likely than controls to snatch toys and to engage in rule-breaking behavior. Moreover, these 4-year-olds went on to display deficient moral understanding as 6-year-olds. © Royalty-Free/Corbis.

rather than showing a bias in understanding nasty intentions before nice intentions, this difference could simply reflect the home lives of the hard-to-manage children, which may have included more hostile interactions. Hughes et al. found that the hard-to-manage preschoolers were more likely than controls to snatch toys, to call their friends names, and to engage in rule-breaking behavior. Hughes et al. speculated that these permissive attitudes towards social transgressions could reflect norms within the families.

In fact, the hard-to-manage preschoolers were also significantly more likely to engage in violent pretend play at the age of 4 years, Violence that involved killing or inflicting pain on another was particularly frequent, and in fact the friends of the hard-to-manage preschoolers often refused to continue with these games (child brandishing sword "Kill! Kill! Kill me!"; friend drops his sword "No"). When the hard-to-manage preschoolers were followed up as 6-year-olds, Hughes and Dunn (2000) found that they showed deficits in moral awareness and in social understanding. Language abilities, theory-of-mind performance, and moral sensitivity were all related in this sample, suggesting developmental continuity in mentalizing and language abilities. However, there was also an independent relationship between the violent pretend play measure and individual differences in later moral understanding (see also Hughes, White, Sharpen, & Dunn, 2000). The children showing more violent pretend play as 4-year-olds had deficient moral understanding as 6-year-olds.

Pretend play, mental state discourse, and metarepresentational understanding: what are the causal connections?

The consistent finding that language development plays an important role in the development of metarepresentational understanding deserves deeper consideration. From the evidence discussed so far, it seems that language development facilitates metarepresentational understanding because play (particularly pretend play and role play) provides a context in which discussions about feelings, thoughts, and desires take place. This discourse about mental states enhances understanding, leading to further development of theory-of-mind skills. In fact, as noted by Lillard (2002), as children get older less time is spent in actual play, whereas more and more time is spent in negotiating the plot in planned pretend play and in negotiating what each other's roles will be. This negotiation requires sophisticated language abilities and seems likely to engender further metarepresentational insights.

More recently, Russell (2005) has suggested a complementary reason for thinking that language should play a central role in the development of representational understanding. He points out that even the most basic aspects of language acquisition entail a conception of beliefs. This is because language acquisition involves becoming a labeler of objects. First, a true labeler of objects seeks the correct word for the object—there is a requirement for veridicality. Second, the true labeler realizes that the source of this veridicality is label use by other language users. It is only correct to label a cat as "cat" if there is a social consensus that "cat" is the correct label for small furry animals. Russell argues that this insight entails a notion of intersubjective truth—and thereby also of intersubjective error. If two people are fixating the same object, but using different labels, one is mislabeling the object.

Koenig and Echols (2003) demonstrated that infants as young as 16 months will correct a human mislabeler and will spend more time looking at a mislabeler than at a human who labels objects correctly. Koenig and Echols pointed out that words carry information both about the world and about the people who use the words. The choice of label made by human speakers who use labels is a reflection of their internal mental life. If someone says assertively "That's a cat", then it is likely that her utterance reflects her belief that the object being viewed is indeed a cat, and that she is informing an audience of that fact about the real world. Koenig and Echols termed this type of assertion a "belief report" and pointed out that even a simple statement such as "That's a cat" is a belief report, because it reflects the speaker's beliefs about the world (as well as the state of affairs in the world itself, i.e. that there is indeed a cat present).

To explore this idea about belief reports experimentally, Koenig and Echols showed 16-month-old infants color slides of five different familiar objects (shoe, ball, duck, cat, chair) while the infants were sitting on their parent's lap. The parents wore eye shields so that they could not influence their infant's looking behavior. As each slide appeared, an adult experimenter who was sitting looking at the slides with the infant provided a label, for example "That's a cat". On half of the trials, the label provided was false. Koenig and Echols reported that the infants looked significantly longer at the pictures when the label was true, but looked significantly longer at the experimenter and at their parent when the label was false. The infants also corrected the false labels, produced other vocalizations or shook their heads to the false labels, and attempted to get support from their parents by trying to remove their eye shields. In fact, 15 of the 16 infants in the study showed corrective labeling behavior, and some infants began crying at the false labeling. Koenig and Echols argued that infants expect truthful labeling from human labelers who have visual access to the objects being named. Infants take labels to reflect the intentional states of human speakers, and expect veridicality in labeling. In an attempt to ensure veridical labeling, some infants became very active, for example pointing at their own shoes when the experimenter was mislabeling a picture of a cat as a "shoe".

Russell argues that this infant behavior shows recognition of a kind of false belief. This is the false belief about social reality that was apparently held by the mislabeling adult (the social reality "what do people call it?"). Russell points out that young children also have difficulty in reporting true beliefs. For example, when the true belief was true in the past but is currently false, 3-year-old children experience difficulties. Russell suggests that this is because they are being asked about nonveridical mental representations. To illustrate his point, Russell gives an example from a study by Riggs and Simpson (2005). Riggs and Simpson gave 3-year-old children story vignettes in which a true belief was manipulated. For example, "Linda left her book on the floor of the living room before going into the kitchen to fetch a glass of milk. In her absence, her sister took the book upstairs to read". Linda then returned to the living room, and the child was asked the following true-belief question "When Linda left the living room, where did she think her book was?".

Riggs and Simpson reported that 3-year-olds were just as likely to say "upstairs" in response to this true-belief question as when asked the more usual false-belief question "Where does Linda think her book is?". However, a memory question established that they had no difficulty in telling the experimenter where the book actually was when Linda left the living room. Russell argues that the key to the children's erroneous responses is that the past true belief under consideration is currently false. The problem is not simply with belief, but with nonveridical mental representations more generally. Russell argues that it is developmentally easier to understand false beliefs about social reality (e.g. what people call things) than to understand false beliefs about objective reality (e.g. where things are). He suggests that language plays a role in the development of both kinds of metarepresentational understanding.

Just as language may facilitate metarepresentation in ways additional to the need to use language to discuss the feelings, thoughts, and desires of others, for example of characters in pretend play, so pretend play is also likely to facilitate metarepresentation in ways additional to this requirement for mental state discourse. Two other ways in which pretending might facilitate metarepresentational development are via the need to interpret the intention of the playmate in pretending, and the need for active quarantining of what is pretend and what is real. Researchers have explored both of these demands of pretence in empirical studies. Tomasello, Striano, and Rochat (1999) investigated whether children aged 18, 26, and 35 months could interpret adult pretend gestures in the context of a game about giving the adult desired objects. For example, the adult would gesture wanting a hammer by making a hammering motion with their fist, or gesture wanting a book by opening their hands in a cupped form like a book. Tomasello et al. reported that children in all three age groups were able to hand the adult the desired object in this game. The pretence was then made more abstract, by involving substituted objects. For example, a cup was substituted for a hat, with the adult demonstrating putting the cup on her head. A ball was substituted for an apple, with the adult demonstrating biting motions on the ball and pretending to chew. The child was then again asked to play the object-giving game. This time, the adult gestured putting a hat on her head when she wanted the cup, and gestured biting into an apple when she wanted the ball. Now only the 26-month-olds and the 35-month-olds were able to interpret the intention of the gestures at above-chance levels. These findings are consistent with the earlier work of McCune-Nicolich (1981). She showed that on average the ability to substitute one object for another during pretend play emerges at around 2 years of age.

Children's capacity for active quarantining during pretend play has been explored by investigating the occasions on which young children do confuse the pretend and the real. An example is scary pretence. Games involving scary monsters can be actively upsetting for children. Harris, Brown, Marriott, Whittall, and Harmer (1991) asked children aged 4 and 6 years to play a pretend game in which they had to imagine a scary creature such as a monster, and then to pretend that it was inside a large black box that was actually present in the room. In fact, two black boxes were present in the room, and the children were asked to pretend that a little puppy was inside the other black box. Each box was about 1 meter square, and had a small hole in the front. The children were asked to imagine that if they put their finger in the hole, the puppy would lick it, whereas the monster would bite it off. The children were then asked to choose which box they would put their finger into, and whether they would prefer to poke a stick through the hole rather than their finger. Harris and colleagues found that the majority of the children chose to put their finger into the box with the imaginary puppy. Situations involving scary pretence hence seem to present children with some difficulties in quarantining the pretend from the real. However, even adults show pretend–real boundary problems for certain pretend entities such as witches and the devil. Lillard (2002) has suggested that in cases where emotions color real-world behavior, there will be failures in quarantining. However, she argues that these failures bear little relation to children's everyday pretending.

Cognitive developmental neuroscience and theory of mind

Is there a special neural substrate for reasoning about beliefs? In Chapter 2, we saw that Leslie (1994) argued that there were specialized information processing systems in the brain that provided the basis for cognitive development. One of these was a "theory of mind" module or specialized neurocognitive mechanism (Leslie, 2005). Although Leslie's proposals about brain mechanisms are theoretical, the idea that there might be a specialized region in the brain for representing beliefs has become very popular. At the time of writing, all relevant studies have been conducted with adults, and there is no particular consensus (see Frith & Frith, 2003, 2006; Gallagher & Frith, 2003, Saxe et al., 2004; for reviews). Imaging studies of adults have identified an extensive network of neural regions that are typically active when adults are engaged in false-belief reasoning, involving the temporal poles, posterior superior temporal sulcus and the temporoparietal junction, and medial prefrontal cortex. Animal studies (Rolls, 1999) suggest that emotional/ social responding begins with visual input from the environment to the amygdala, which evaluates the emotional significance of the stimuli. Input then travels to the ventral medial prefrontal cortex, where the reward value of the stimulus is stored, and then to the anterior cingulate, where rewards are calculated. Duncan and Owen (2000) demonstrated that a wide range of executive function tasks activate the posterior portion of the anterior cingulate, whereas mentalizing tasks appear to activate the rostral portion (Bush, Luu, & Posner, 2000). Nevertheless, it is still unclear which portions of recorded activity in these extensive regions reflect the complex demands made by false-belief tasks on general abilities like memory and language. Interestingly for the executive deficit account of failure in false-belief tasks, however, neuroimaging studies do not find a shared neural substrate for theory of mind and executive tasks.

Research examining how actions are represented in the brain, and how action, imitation, and intention are linked, may be more promising for understanding the neurocognitive development of metarepresentation. Groundbreaking work in this respect has been described by Rizzolatti and colleagues, who have identified the "mirror neuron" system in monkey and man for representing action. As we have seen in earlier chapters, action is fundamental to infant cognitive development (Rizzolatti & Craighero, 2004). To represent human action, the brain must activate certain networks of neurons when the self makes a certain action, and must also activate certain networks of neurons when someone else makes a certain action. As the actions of both self and other usually have intentions, possibly the brain will thereby also represent the likely intention of another person who is performing a certain action. Rizzolatti and colleagues have argued that a special neuronal system, the mirror neuron system, is active in all three of these cases. The mirror neuron system may thus be the neural substrate for imitating the actions of others, and possibly also for understanding their intentions.

Mirror neurons were first discovered in primate premotor cortex. It was found that mirror neurons fired when the monkey performed object-directed actions such as tearing, grasping, holding, and manipulating (single-cell recording is possible in the monkey). Furthermore, the same neurons also fired when the animal observed someone else performing the same class of actions, and were even activated by the sound of an action, such as paper ripping or a stick being dropped (Rizzolatti & Craighero, 2004). The researchers pointed out that action recognition has a special status, as action implies a goal and an agent. Hence action recognition may involve an understanding of the agent's intentions. To find out whether the mirror neuron system had a role in coding intentions, Iacoboni, Molnar-Szakacs, Gallese, Buccino, Mazziotta, and Rizzolatti (2005) devised a paradigm in which the context for performing an identical action varied. Adults were shown grasping a mug in two different contexts: when partaking in a tea party or when clearing up after a tea party. The visual display of tea pot, jam, biscuits, plates, etc. was identical in both scenarios, as was the mug and the grasping action. The contexts were differentiated by the presence of crumbs and partially consumed cakes. The brain activity in the mirror neuron system was different for the two contexts, despite the grasping action being identical. Iacoboni et al. argued that the mirror neuron system does not simply provide a substrate for action recognition, but also for intention coding.

Iacoboni et al.'s ideas about action recognition and intention coding require that the mirror neuron system is activated only by biological actions. For example, studies of the development of intention-reading in infants have shown that infants will imitate a human hand trying (although failing) to pull apart a dumbbell apparatus, but will not read the "intentions" of a mechanical hand that fails to perform the same actions on the dumb-bell (Meltzoff, 1995; see Chapter 2). Tai et al. (2004) have demonstrated that mirror neurons do indeed seem to respond specifically to biological actions. In a study with adults, they measured mirror neuron activity to either a human hand performing manual grasping actions, or to a robot arm performing analogous actions. Mirror neuron activity was observed for the manual grasping actions performed by the human hand, but not for the actions performed by the grasping robot hand. Tai et al. (2004) argued that the mirror neuron system is biologically tuned. Although neuroimaging studies with infants and young children remain to be done, current behavioral evidence for an incremental understanding of goal-directed actions in infancy would map neatly onto such a system. Presumably, with increased experience of observing actions and carrying them out, activity in this neural system would become increasingly specific to different actions and their usual intentions, and would eventually provide a substrate for the understanding of intended actions that were not seen to be completed, as in the pioneering behavioral studies by Meltzoff and others (e.g. Meltzoff, 1995).

Rizzolatti and Craighero (2004) also made some interesting observations about the mirror neuron system with respect to imitation and language. A series of experiments with adults showed that the mirror neuron system was also active when participants imitated the motor actions of another adult, or imitated their facial expressions. In particular, cortical activation was extremely similar when the participants observed the motor behavior of another and when they actually imitated this motor behavior themselves. Rizzolatti and Craighero argued that the request to imitate leads to sensory copies of the target actions becoming active. It was speculated that the mirror neuron system thereby allows actions carried out by others to be understood by the observer, and that this might provide a neural substrate for the interpretation of gesture. Such a "sensory copy" system would also enable the translation of an observed action (such as a facial expression) into its internally felt emotional significance. As gestural communication is a precursor to spoken language, Rizzolatti and Arbib (1998) suggested that the mirror neuron system might also be the neurophysiological mechanism from which language evolved. They pointed out that the "semantics" of the mirror neuron system are inherent in the gestures used to communicate, and that through evolution the meaning of hand gestures could have been transferred to abstract sound patterns (i.e. words).

Currently, this account is completely speculative. However, as we have seen in this chapter, developmental psychologists have suggested for quite different reasons that certain classes of actions on objects (pretending), early language, and imitation are developmentally linked. This linkage could be tied to the development of the mirror neuron system. A study of imitation carried out with adolescents offers some intriguing data. The brain activity generated when imitating the facial expressions of others was measured in typically developing adolescents, and in adolescents with autism (Dapretto et al., 2006). For the children with autism, the mirror neuron system was not active. Childhood autism is thought to involve severe deficits in theory of mind. Children with autism have enormous difficulty in identifying another person's emotions and thoughts, and thus in understanding their behavior. They behave as though they are "mind blind" (Baron-Cohen, 1995). The finding that the mirror neuron system is atypical in autism could thus suggest that it plays an important role in the normative development of social cognition. Alternatively, it could mean that the normative development of social cognition is important for the typical development of the mirror neuron system. Longitudinal studies are required to find out.

Nevertheless, a number of authors have argued that the mirror system and the system for mentalizing must be distinct (Sommerville & Decety, 2006). For example, Saxe (2005) has argued that the mirror system cannot account for mental state understanding, because neuroimaging studies of mental state attribution document cortical areas outside the mirror system that are activated reliably by mental state reasoning tasks. These areas include the amygdala, the temporal poles, and medial prefrontal cortex. For example, Saxe and Kanwisher (2003) compared neural responding (via fMRI) in the false-belief task and the false-photograph task, and found that for the false-belief task responding increased in medial prefrontal cortex, the temporoparietal junction, and superior temporal sulcus. In the study by Saxe and Kanwisher (2003), additional control conditions depended on "mechanical inference" scenarios, in which subjects had to reason about the operation of invisible mechanical forces like evaporation, and scenarios containing people described from a physical perspective (e.g. hair style). As all scenarios included people, invisible mechanisms, and false representations, it was argued that the neural substrates of attributing beliefs had been isolated experimentally. In fact, however, beliefs and desires were confounded in the vignettes that formed the basis of the study (see Saxe et al., 2004). Saxe et al. (2004) went on to argue that as inhibitory control was dependent on different neural regions, false-belief attribution was distinct from inhibitory control. Clearly, many more studies will be needed before the neural substrate for mental state reasoning is understood.

SUMMARY

Social cognition and metarepresentation are linked in intimate ways. Whereas cognitive development in the foundational domains of naïve physics and naïve biology depends on veridical primary representations (e.g. of objects), cognitive development in the foundational domain of naïve psychology depends on representations of representations, or metarepresentations. To develop metarepresentational understanding, the child must "quarantine" the primary representation and take the representation itself as an object of cognition. As we have seen in this chapter, metarepresentational development depends in important ways on shared social activities such as pretending and language. Pretend play and family discussion of feelings and emotions help the young child to take desires and beliefs as entities that can be reasoned about and used to predict behavior. However, despite the critical role for communicative activities involving sharing objects with others ("shared intentionality") in social cognitive development, metarepresentational development depends also on mechanisms within individual minds. The ability to imitate is one such important individual mechanism. Intention-reading and the analysis of goal-directed actions are others.

Metarepresentations are not observable, and the development of an understanding of the mental states of others undergoes extensive development. It may be that early insights about mental states are based on an understanding of desire, which is then supplanted by belief-desire psychology. This is because desires are more closely tied to observable motivational states and to observable emotional expressions, whereas beliefs are not. However, it is also possible that the same mechanisms underpin the development of the psychological understanding of both desires and beliefs, for example intention-reading, imitation, and interpreting goal-directed actions. It may simply be more difficult to observe successful understanding by children of beliefs than of desires. Neuroimaging data are consistent with this idea. The representation of action in the brain is linked to imitation and also to intention-reading, for example in the mirror neuron system. Action recognition appears to involve an understanding of the actor's intentions. Nevertheless, mental state understanding requires more than the mirror neuron system. Belief attribution involves other neural areas as well.

A classic task in terms of measuring belief understanding has been the false-belief task. This is because making a correct prediction about the behavior of another on the basis of their *false* belief requires the child to make a prediction about behavior that goes against current reality. The development of children's understanding of false belief has been investigated very intensively, and is still the subject of controversy. More recently, it has been demonstrated that children also have difficulties with true beliefs when these no longer reflect current reality. The key insight may thus concern whether mental representations are veridical or nonveridical. What develops may be the ability to reflect on and index one's own representations, tagging their internal source so that both current reality and past reality can be kept in mind together. This would imply an important developmental role for metacognition, which is considered in Chapter 9.

Language and discourse also play important developmental roles in children's growing understanding of metarepresentation. Language enables the exchange of information about beliefs and desires, and thereby contributes to social understanding. Deaf children who lack a native language show delays in mental state understanding. Pretend play with siblings or peers is an especially rich source of discussion about mental states, and children from larger families show earlier development of a theory of mind. This suggests an additional role for pretend play in the development of understanding mental states. Language acquisition also depends on veridicality (the label should be the *correct* word), and the use of language labels by other users is the source of this veridicality (correct labels depend on social consensus). Theoretical analyses such as these suggest that language may play multiple roles in the development of metarepresentational insights.

CHAPTER 8

CONTENTS

The development of memory

8

Memory is a remarkable facility. The ability consciously to retrieve autobiographical happenings from the past— "to travel back in time in [our] own minds" (Tulving, 2002, p. 2)—may be unique to the human species. The retrieval of events and experiences from one's past is usually called "episodic memory". Episodic memory is usually contrasted with semantic memory, our generic, factual knowledge about the world, such as knowledge of concepts and language (discussed in Chapters 4 and 5). Both episodic memory and semantic memory are forms of explicit or **declarative memory**, memories that can be brought consciously and deliberately to mind. Explicit and declarative memories are typically contrasted with implicit and *procedural* memories. These are unconscious memories, indexed by changes in performance without the involvement of conscious memory content. Examples include skill learning, habit formation, associative learning, and habituation. All species appear to show implicit and procedural memory.

Cognitive psychology assumes that memory is a modular system. Semantic memory, recognition memory, working memory, implicit memory, episodic memory, and procedural memory are all considered to be distinctive in various ways. Experimentally, these different types of memory are thus usually considered independently of each other. More recently, this "modular" approach to memory has been supported by cognitive neuroscience. Different types of memory appear to rely on different brain structures. For example, episodic memory is particularly related to the hippocampus and the medial temporal lobe, whereas skill learning is particularly related to the motor cortex. Although rather few neuroimaging studies of memory have been carried out with children, information about the neural anatomy of the developed memory system has important implications for models of memory development.

Another important factor for memory research is that children (and adults) do not record events that occur in their lives into their memories verbatim. Even though it may feel as though you can remember "exactly what happened" when you went to visit your friend, your friend is bound to have a somewhat different recollection of events to you. As originally demonstrated by Bartlett (1932), children and adults *construct* memories, and the process of construction depends on prior knowledge and personal interpretation. It also depends on how much sense the memorizer can make of the temporal structure of their experiences. Very young children, for example, may not structure their experience in memorable ways, particularly if they do not understand particular experiences (e.g. being born, someone dying, being sexually abused), or if they do not have a clear temporal framework. Very young children are also still acquiring language, and language itself is important for memory. For example, language helps in rehearsing one's own experiences or in recounting them to someone else, and these verbal narratives help to establish memories more firmly. The development of memory clearly cannot be isolated from the development of other cognitive processes. Remembering is embedded in larger social and cognitive activities. Thus the knowledge structures that young children bring to their experiences may be a critical factor in explaining memory development.

It is known that infants can encode relevant information, store it, and later retrieve it, as evidenced by their ability to recall how they should play with a certain toy.

Despite this embedding of memory in other aspects of cognitive development, many studies of memory have used tasks that were purposely disembedded from larger social/cognitive activities, in order to provide a "pure" measure of the memory system of interest. An unintended result has been that the applicability of many research findings is limited. "Students of human memory ... [ignored] almost everything that people ordinarily remember. Their research did not deal with places or stories or friends or life experiences, but with lists of syllables and words ... [leading] to a preference for meaningless materials and unnatural learning tasks ..." (Neisser, 1987). Wherever possible in this chapter, I focus on studies of memory development that use less artificial memory situations and have greater "ecological validity". Finally, it is increasingly recognized that an important factor for memory development is a child's "metaknowledge" of memory processes and contents. Memory can be improved if a child is aware of explicit aspects of memorizing, such as the need for mnemonic strategies, and if a child can self-monitor his or her efficiency in memorizing and keep track of the sources of different kinds of knowledge. These metacognitive aspects of memory will be discussed in Chapter 9, where the role of "metaknowing" will be considered with respect to both memory and learning.

EARLY MEMORY DEVELOPMENT

Some aspects of early memory development have been discussed already, for example habituation, recognition memory, and memory for causal event sequences (see Chapters 1 and 2). Even very young infants show good evidence of memory in such paradigms. Although habituation and recognition are implicit forms of memory, studies of deferred imitation or of elicited imitation are generally accepted as measures of the development of declarative memory (Bauer, 2006). In deferred imitation tasks, infants are clearly bringing a past event to mind. For example, when Meltzoff (1985) showed that 14-month-olds could retain information about how to pull apart a dumb-bell toy over a 24-hour-period, he was demonstrating that the infants could encode the relevant information, store it, and retrieve it (see Chapter 1). Bauer has used both deferred and elicited imitation to track the early development of declarative memory. She has documented important changes in the reliability with which **recall** can be observed, and in the temporal extent of memory, in very young children.

Early memory for temporally ordered events

In her studies, Bauer usually requires young children to reproduce an ordered sequence of actions. Her argument is that reproduction of the ordering is a critical measure of explicit recall. The temporal ordering information must be encoded during the presentation of the event sequence, and subsequently recalled from a *representation* of the event, as the event itself has gone. For example, Bauer and Shore (1987) modeled "having a bath" to young children aged from 17–23 months by demonstrating giving a teddy bear a bath. The sequence of events was that the teddy bear's T-shirt was removed, he was put in a toy tub, and he was washed and then dried by the experimenter (in pretend mode!). The teddy bear was then handed to the child, who was asked "Can you give the dirty bear a bath?". The children proved quite capable of reproducing the modeled event sequence when tested for immediate recall.

They also remembered the correct sequence of events 6 weeks later, when they returned to the laboratory and were simply handed the teddy without prior modeling (delayed recall). These data suggest that very young children's representations of events are temporally ordered. Their event memory is not composed of a series of disorganized snapshots of individual components of the event. Instead, like adults, their representations display temporal ordering and are arranged around a goal.

Event sequences like "having a bath" are very familiar to young children, however, and this familiarity may aid temporally ordered recall. An important question is thus whether the experimenters would have found similar effects if the temporally ordered events had been novel instead of familiar. To find out, Bauer and Shore invented a novel causal event sequence called "building a rattle". During this event the experimenter modeled putting a plastic ball into a stacking cup, covering it with a slightly smaller stacking cup, and shaking the "rattle" near to her ear. The children again showed both immediate and delayed recall for the elements of the sequence, and for their temporal order. Bauer and her colleagues argued that even very young children were sensitive to the causal relations underlying event sequences from their very first experience of them, and that this early causal sensitivity meant that very young children's representations displayed goal-oriented temporal ordering, just like adults' representations.

Causal relations as an organizing principle in early episodic memories

To test the idea that causal relations play a special role in organizing the temporal order of events for young children, Bauer and Mandler (1989a) carried out a study that used two novel causal event sequences and two familiar sequences. Their subjects were younger children aged either 16 or 20 months. The novel causal event sequences were "build-a-rattle" and "make the frog jump". "Make the frog jump" involved building a see-saw by putting a wooden board onto a wedge-shaped block, putting a toy frog at one end of the board, and making him "jump" by hitting the other end of the board. The familiar event sequences were "give teddy a bath", and "clean the table". For the "clean the table" event, a wastebasket, paper towel, and empty spray bottle were used. The experimenter mimed spraying the table, wiping it with the towel, and then throwing the towel away. In order to separate temporal from causal information, Bauer and Mandler also included "novel arbitrary" event sequences. An example of a novel event whose temporal ordering was arbitrary was the "train ride" event sequence. For this event, two toy train cars were linked together. A toy driver was then put into one of the cars, and a piece of track was produced for the train to sit on. Although the events were modeled in this order, there was no causal necessity in this ordering, and so these components could be reproduced in any order without affecting the final event.

Bauer and Mandler found that recall for the temporal order of events was indeed significantly lower for the novel arbitrary events than for the novel causal events, even though recall levels for the former were still significant. Furthermore, they found that when an irrelevant component was inserted into each kind of novel event sequence (such as attaching a sticker either to one of the cups making up the rattle or to the toy train driver), then this irrelevant component was far more likely to be displaced in the causal event sequences. Attaching the sticker to the cup was frequently displaced to another position in the "building a rattle" sequence, or was even left out entirely. In contrast, attaching the sticker to the train driver was treated no differently to any of the other components in the "train ride" sequence. This finding suggests that causally related pairs of elements enjoy a privileged organizational status. Bauer and Mandler concluded that causal relations were an important organizing principle both for constructing event memories and for aiding recall. The importance of causal relations in structuring episodic memory fits nicely with the research discussed in Chapter 4, in which we saw the importance of causal information for developing and organizing semantic memory about natural kinds and artifacts (e.g. Pauen, 1996a).

Age differences in early episodic memory

Bauer and colleagues have shown convincingly that even very young children show long-term ordered recall for novel events. More recently, they have used temporal ordering tasks to explore age-related aspects of encoding and forgetting. Bauer, Wenner, Dropik, and Wewerka (2000) studied the development of explicit memory in 360 children aged from 1 to 3 years. The children were studied from the ages of either 13, 16, or 20 months, for a period of 1 year. Memory for six event sequences was tested over time. The event sequences were similar to those used in prior work, and included building a rattle and making a gong. When recall was tested, the props were provided as reminder cues, and if the props alone were insufficient to generate recall, then verbal prompts were used (e.g. "You can use this stuff to make a gong. Show me how you make a gong"). Bauer et al. found that whereas almost 80% of 13-month-olds could retain temporally ordered memories for around 1 month, over 80% of 20-month-olds retained such memories for at least 6 months. In fact, almost 70% of 20-month-olds retained these memories for at least 1 year. Developmental differences in retention are shown in Table 8.1. In related work, Carver and Bauer (1999, 2001) showed that even younger infants also retained temporally ordered memories. They reported that about 50% of 9-month-olds could retain

TABLE 8.1 Percentage of 13-, 16-, and 20-month-olds showing evidence of temporally ordered recall memory

Delay interval	Age at experience of to-be-remembered event sequences		
	20 months	16 months	13 months
1 month	100*	94*	78*
3 months	100*	94*	67
6 months	83*	72*	39
9 months	78*	50	44
12 months	67*	61	36

Data are from Bauer, Wenner, Dropik, & Wewerka (2000). An asterisk indicates that the number of children exhibiting the pattern of ordered recall (i.e., higher level of performance on previously experienced than on new event sequences) was reliably greater than chance. Because determination of chance levels is affected both by the number of observations and by the number of tied observations, identical values will not necessarily yield identical outcomes (e.g., 13-month-old 3-month delay and 20-month-old 12-month delay).

temporally ordered event sequences for a month, but not for 3 months. Infants aged 10 months could retain temporally ordered event sequences for 3 months. Hence there are developmental changes in both the reliability of explicit recall and in its temporal extent.

The encoding and retrieval of specifically autobiographical memories, however, has not been studied systematically in very young children. One reason is that it is difficult to devise robust methodologies. A second is that adults report surprisingly few autobiographical memories of the period of their lives before the age of around 3 years. This later absence of early episodic memories is often referred to as **infantile amnesia**.

Infantile amnesia is surprising given that the first 3 years of life are an active period for conceptual development, which is a form of declarative memory (semantic memory), and also for language development, which involves conscious recall of verbal knowledge. The early years also see the rapid growth of causal and psychological reasoning, which depend on a stable and efficient memory for events and their outcomes (see Chapters 3 and 6). Further, as discussed above, when measured in terms of the retention of temporally ordered events, it is clear that episodic memories are developing in infants. In fact, Bauer herself does not believe that infantile amnesia is a distinct phenomenon that deserves a separate theoretical explanation (e.g. Bauer, 2006). She argues for the developmental continuity of personal memory, suggesting that as the encoding and consolidation of memories becomes more robust with development, the quality of the traces that are stored improves. These traces thereby include more features that make memories distinctively relevant to one's self. Bauer also points out that adult patients with amnesia are very poor at the deferred imitation tasks that are easily solved by infants (McDonough, Mandler, McKee, & Squire, 1995). This supports the idea that deferred imitation taps the same memory structures that support episodic memory. Such demonstrations make it plausible that infants may be laying down autobiographical memories, even if we have not yet devised ways to measure them.

The general absence of autobiographical memories before the age of about 3 years has been repeatedly documented and observed (see Howe & Courage, 1993; Courage & Howe, 2004). Even when we feel convinced that we can recall events from our own infancy, these events often turn out to have happened to someone else. For example, the memory researcher David Bjorklund reports a vivid memory of having croup (bronchitis) as an infant:

> *My crib was covered by a sheet, but I remember looking past the bars into the living room. I can hear the whir of the vaporizer, feel the constriction in my chest, and smell the Vicks Vaporub. To this day the smell of Vicks makes my chest tighten . . .*

However, when he reminded his mother about this memory, it turned out that he had never had croup. She told him "You were such a healthy baby . . . That was your brother, Dick. You were about 3 years old then . . ." (Bjorklund & Bjorklund, 1992).

The interesting question is why we can access so few memories of the earliest period of our lives. One of the first explanations for infantile amnesia came from Freud (1938), who argued that early amnesia was caused by the repression of the emotionally traumatic events of early childhood. For Freud, the problem was not

KEY TERM

Infantile amnesia
The inability to recall autobiographic memories before the age of around 3 years.

Freud (1938) argued that infantile amnesia was caused by the repression of the emotionally traumatic events of early childhood. © Corbis.

encoding or storage, as early memories were assumed to be intact. Rather, repression was used to keep these memories from invading consciousness. Although the idea of repression can account for the active rejection of emotionally troublesome material from consciousness, it does not explain why memories for pleasant events are also later inaccessible. Another possibility is that early memories are coded in terms of physical action or pure sensation. Early memories are thus irretrievable, as they are stored in a different format to later memories, which depend on linguistically based encoding and storage. The finding that females tend to have earlier memories than males appears to be consistent with this explanation, as language development is usually more advanced in girls than in boys. According to this idea, early memories survive intact but the context in which these memories were laid down is so discrepant from the one in which we seek to retrieve them (during later childhood or adulthood) that it is impossible to make contact with the relevant memory traces (e.g. Hayne, 1990). This idea was tested in an experiment reported by Simcock and Hayne (2002).

Simcock and Hayne were interested in whether children could have verbal access to memories that were acquired when the children were preverbal. To find out, they visited children aged 27, 33, and 39 months at home, and gave them a very memorable experience. This was to play with a Magic Shrinking Machine. Children could put toys into the machine, turn some handles, and the toys would magically shrink to a much smaller size. Language skills were assessed during the visit, and of the 23 words specifically associated with the target events (e.g. the labels for the toys), the 27-month-olds knew on average 16, the 33-month-olds knew on average 19, and the 27-month-olds knew on average 20. The children were then revisited after either 6 months or a year, and their memory for the Magic Shrinking Machine was explored. Memory was tested both by eliciting verbal recall and nonverbally, for example by showing the children the machine and pictures of various toys, and asking them to choose the toys that had gone into the machine.

Simcock and Hayne (2002) reported that the children in general showed good memory of the Magic Shrinking Machine when tested with the nonverbal measures, but poor memory when tested for verbal recall, at both delays. Further, even though more relevant words had typically been acquired during the delay interval (for example, the children who had been 27 months at the time of the encoding experience now had around 21 of the 23 relevant words in their productive vocabularies rather than 16), the children never showed verbal recall for these aspects of the procedure, even though they showed nonverbal recall. Simcock and Hayne concluded that the idea that it is impossible to make contact with early memories is wrong. The children that they tested still had nonverbal access to these memories. However, the inability to translate early, preverbal experiences into language seemed to prevent these experiences from becoming part of autobiographical memory. Simcock and Hayne argued that language development therefore played a pivotal role in childhood amnesia. This idea is discussed further below.

Alternatively, it has been proposed that infantile amnesia disappears when the child gains a cognitive sense of self, argued to occur at around 2 years (for example, using data from mirror self-recognition tasks; Howe & Courage, 1993; Courage & Howe, 2004; see Chapter 3). The cognitive self is thought to provide a new organizer of information, thus facilitating the personalization of memory for events as specific events that happened "to me". However, as discussed in Chapters 3 and 7, the cognitive self may emerge earlier than 2 years. Further, even some animals seem to have cognitive selves (see Chapter 3). Another proposal has been that the memory systems that support the formation of autobiographical memories are late developing because the brain structures that underlie these systems are not functional at birth (e.g. Schachter & Moscovitch, 1984). One speculation was that the structures essential for the formation of conscious memories only begin to function properly at around 2–3 years of age. However, such arguments depended largely on drawing parallels between infant humans and infant monkeys. More recent data suggest that the maturation of the neural structures that are crucial for autobiographical memory, namely the medial temporal structures and the frontal lobes, do not map in any neat way onto infantile amnesia. In particular, whereas the medial temporal structures seem to support the formation of explicit memories by the end of the first year, the frontal lobes do not mature until the early twenties. Hence the maturation of neural structures *per se* seems unlikely to provide a satisfactory account of infantile amnesia. Recent cognitive neuroscience studies of memory are discussed at the end of this chapter.

Finally, the development of knowledge structures may be important in explaining infantile amnesia. In a similar spirit to Bauer (2006), Fivush and Hammond (1990) argued that infantile amnesia may be due to a combination of the absence of distinctive memory cues and the fact that young children have yet to learn a framework for recounting and storing events. Because young children are in the process of trying to understand the world around them, they focus on what is similar about events, namely routines. The *routine* aspects of novel events do not make good retrieval cues for future recall. Similarly, because young children do not possess their own frameworks for constructing memories, early memories are fragmented, also making them more difficult to recall.

This more sociolinguistic account explains childhood amnesia as a natural by-product of the development of the constructive process of memory itself (Nelson & Fivush, 2004). Fivush and Hammond's argument is appealing because it places infantile amnesia firmly within the context of memory development in general. According to this argument, the lack of early memories is not the result of basic structural changes in the memory system with development. Instead, it is a result of the absence of abstract knowledge structures for describing the temporal and causal sequences of events. I discuss the development of these abstract knowledge structures below. By late childhood, the routine events that young children prefer to recall have merged into *scripts* (or generic knowledge structures) about specific events like "what happens when we go to a restaurant". Childhood amnesia is therefore due to a combination of script formation and the forgetting of novel events (see also Nelson, 1993; Nelson & Fivush, 2004).

Understanding symbolic representation as an aid to memory

Abstract knowledge structures such as scripts for describing the temporal and causal sequences of events depend in part on language development, but language is not our only symbolic system. Words stand for or represent concepts and events in the everyday world, and of course we use them as symbols to encode our experiences. However, we also use other symbols to encode and communicate our experiences, such as pictorial ones. These symbols also represent or stand for objects or events, and

Children use a number of symbolic systems in addition to language, such as making gestures (pointing to things), and engaging in symbolic play.

include drawings, photographs, and sculptures. All of these symbols bring to mind something other than themselves. Children, too, use a number of symbolic systems in addition to language, for example in communication. Young children make gestures, they point to things, and they engage in symbolic (pretend) play. They also use culturally determined symbols. These include symbols such as maps and models. The use of many of these forms of symbolic coding enables children to represent information in memory in a form that will be accessible later on.

Symbolic understanding itself develops, and this development is another factor in explaining why older children have better memories than younger children. One of the most intriguing sets of experiments investigating the development of symbolic understanding comes from work on young children's understanding of models (e.g. DeLoache, 1987, 1989, 1991). The basic paradigm used in DeLoache's model studies is always the same. A 2½-or 3-year-old child is shown a scale model of a room, containing various pieces of furniture such as a couch, a dresser, a chair, and some pillows (Figure 8.1). The child is then introduced to two central characters, the stuffed toy animals Little Snoopy and Big Snoopy, who both like hiding. The scale model is introduced as Little Snoopy's room, and an adjacent room, which contains the same furniture as the model in the same spatial lay-out, is introduced as Big Snoopy's room. The child is told "Look, their rooms are just alike. They both have all the same things in their rooms!" Each correspondence is demonstrated "Look—this is Big Snoopy's big couch, and this is Little Snoopy's little couch. They're just the same".

Following this "orientation phase", the child watches as the experimenter hides one of the Snoopy toys in the appropriate room. For example, Little Snoopy might be hidden under the little couch in the model room. The child is then asked to find Big Snoopy in the real room. The child is told "Remember, Big Snoopy is hiding in the same place as Little Snoopy". Three-year-old children go straight to the big couch and find Big Snoopy; 2½-year-old children do not. They search around the big room at random, even though a memory post-test shows that they can remember perfectly well where Little Snoopy is hiding. DeLoache argues that the problem for the younger children is that they do not understand the *correspondence* between the model room and the real room. They do not seem to appreciate that they have a basis for knowing where to search for Big Snoopy.

The most compelling reason for believing that the younger children's problem lies in their lack of awareness of the correspondence between the model and the room comes from DeLoache's "magical shrinking room" studies. In these studies, 2½-year-old children were persuaded that the experimenters had built a "shrinking machine" that could shrink a doll and a room (DeLoache, Miller, & Rosengren, 1997). They were then shown where Big Snoopy was hiding in the big room, and asked to find Little Snoopy in the model room. As the children believed that the model was the shrunken big room, there was no representational relationship between the model and the room to confuse them, and indeed the children were very successful at searching for the doll in this task. DeLoache has also shown that younger children can find Big Snoopy when they are shown Little Snoopy's hiding place in a picture, which implies that they do understand the representational relation between the picture and the room (DeLoache, 1991).

Furthermore, experience with the picture task transfers to the model task. Experience with a symbolic medium that is understood (or partially understood), as pictures are, seems to facilitate the use of an unfamiliar symbolic medium (the model). Marzolf and DeLoache (1994) showed that experience with a model–room relation could help 2½-year-old children to appreciate a map–room relation. Overall, DeLoache argues that early experience with symbolic relations helps the child to use symbols in memory and in learning, and that social support is critical to the development of symbolic understanding and symbol use (DeLoache, 2004). The crucial role of culturally invented symbol systems in cognitive development was particularly highlighted by Vygotsky (1978), and is discussed further in Chapter 11.

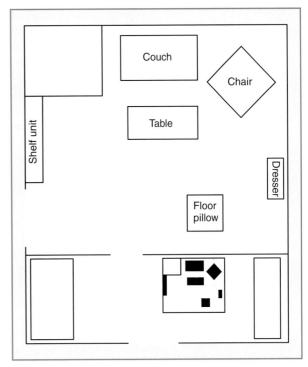

FIGURE 8.1
Diagram of the experimental room used in DeLoache's (1989) scale model studies, with the scale model shown below (the darkened areas in the model correspond to the labeled items of furniture in the room). From DeLoache (1989). Copyright © 1989 Elsevier. Reproduced with permission.

THE DEVELOPMENT OF RECOGNITION MEMORY

Recognition memory is the ability to recognize that something is familiar and has been experienced before. It is usually considered to be a form of implicit memory. We have already seen that infants have good visual recognition memories, and that individual differences in visual recognition memory in infancy are a reliable predictor of later individual differences in intelligence (see Chapter 1). Most of the other studies of memory in infancy discussed in Chapters 1 and 2 also concerned recognition memory in various forms. Habituation, which is a key measure of information processing in infancy, is a recognition measure. Experimental paradigms that use conditioned responses are also based on recognition, for example motor paradigms (such as Rovee-Collier's kick-to-work-a-mobile paradigm), and auditory paradigms (such as DeCasper and Fifer's suck-to-hear-your-mother paradigm).

Recognition memory seems to be fairly ubiquitous in animals as well as in humans, and so this early-developing memory system is far from unique. For example, pigeons can "remember" 320 pictures for 700 days when tested in a recognition memory paradigm (Vaughan & Greene, 1984). Given its ubiquity, the status of recognition memory as a *cognitive* skill can be questioned. For example, Fagan has argued that recognition memory may actually be a measure of *processing* rather than a measure of cognitive ability *per se* (see Fagan, 1992). Studies of cognitive development might thus expect to find little development in recognition memory with age. This is in fact the case.

The traditional way of examining recognition memory in young children has been to show them a series of pictures, and then to measure the number of pictures that they recognize as familiar after a certain period of time. In a classic study of this type, Brown and Scott (1971) showed children aged from 3 to 5 years a series of

100 pictures drawn from four familiar categories: people, animals, outdoor scenes/objects, and household scenes/objects. Forty-four of the pictures recurred and 12 were seen only once. The pictures that recurred were seen after a lag of 0, 5, 10, 25, or 50 items. The children's task was to say "yes" if they had seen a picture before, and "no" if the picture was novel.

Brown and Scott found that the children showed accurate recognition memory on 98% of trials. There was also little difference in recognition accuracy depending on the lag between the items. In fact, the children were equally accurate for lags of 0 and 50 pictures, showing 100% recognition accuracy for each. Accuracy levels for lags of 5 and 25 pictures were around 95%, and for a lag of 10 pictures, 98%. These remarkable levels of performance fell slightly on a long-term retention test that was given after 1, 2, 7, or 28 days. In the long-term retention test, the children were shown the 12 pictures that had been seen only once, 24 of the 44 pictures that had been seen twice, and 36 new pictures. For intervals of up to 7 days, recognition memory levels were above 94% for pictures that had been seen twice. The level was somewhat lower for pictures that had been seen only once, falling from 84% after 1 day to around 70% after 7 days. After 28 days, recognition accuracy for pictures that had been seen twice was 78%, and for pictures that had been seen only once, 56%. In a subsequent study, Brown and Scott showed that the superior memory for items seen twice was due to both the extra exposure to the items and to the need to make a judgment in the recognition task given in the first phase of the study. The previous need to make a "yes" judgment in itself seemed to act as a retrieval cue for the twice-seen items.

The excellent levels of recognition memory found in young children suggest that there is little for the developmental psychologist of memory to study here. However, interest in children's memory for what is familiar has revived recently through the study of the development of implicit memory.

Implicit memory

Implicit memory is "memory without awareness". In implicit memory tasks, children and adults behave in ways that demonstrate that they have memory for information that they are not consciously aware of having. Although most of us would measure our memories in terms of what we can *recall* rather than in terms of what we can *recognize*, the possibility that previous experiences can facilitate performance on a particular memory task even though the subject has no conscious recollection of these previous experiences is a very intriguing one. Implicit memory has also been called "unintentional memory" or "perceptual learning".

Perceptual learning tasks

One of the first studies of implicit memory in children was carried out by Carroll, Byrne, and Kirsner (1985). They measured "perceptual learning" in 5-, 7-, and 10-year-old children using a picture recognition task. In the first phase of the experiment, the children were shown some pictures and either had to say whether each picture contained a cross (crosses had been drawn at random on 33% of the pictures), or to say whether the picture was of something portable. The "cross detection" task was intended to induce "shallow processing" of the pictures at a perceptual level only, and the "portability detection" task was intended to induce "deep processing" at the level of meaning.

Memory for the previously experienced pictures was then studied in an unexpected recognition task. In this task, the children were asked to name a mixture of the pictures that they had already seen along with some new ones. Implicit memory was measured by the difference in the children's reaction times to name the old vs. the new pictures. Half of the children received this *implicit* memory task, and the other half were asked to say whether the old and the new pictures were familiar or not. The latter was the measure of *explicit* memory.

Carroll et al. predicted that implicit memory for the pictures would not vary with depth of encoding, whereas explicit memory would. In other words, deep processing should lead to better explicit memory for the previously experienced pictures than shallow processing, whereas implicit memory levels should be identical for both processing manipulations. This was essentially what they found. Carroll et al. concluded that perceptual learning (implicit memory) does not develop with age.

Fragment completion tasks

Another way of measuring whether implicit memory develops or not is to use a **fragment completion task** based either on words or on pictures. For example, Naito (1990) devised a word-fragment completion task to measure implicit memory in children aged 5, 8, and 11. The children were given some of the letters in a target word, and were asked to complete each fragment into the first meaningful word that came to mind. Although Naito used words written in Japanese characters, her task was equivalent to presenting a fragment like CH – – – Y for the target word CHERRY. This is the example given in Naito's paper, and actually the fragment CH– – –Y could also be CHEERY or CHUNKY. However, each Japanese fragment was chosen to have only *one* legitimate completion.

Prior to receiving the fragment completion task, the children were given two other tasks based on 67% of the target words. For half of these words, the children were asked to make a *category* judgment in a forced choice task ("Is this a kind of—? fruit/clothes"), intended to induce "deep" processing. For the other half of the words, they were asked to judge whether the target word contained a certain letter ("shallow" processing). Naito then measured whether more word fragments were completed correctly for the 32 previously experienced target words than for the 16 novel items in each case. She found that the "old" items were completed correctly significantly more frequently than the "new" items at all ages, and that implicit memory did not vary with depth of processing (deep vs. shallow). She also found that implicit memory levels were invariant across age group (even though a group of adults were also included in the study). In a related experiment in which children were asked to recall the target words explicitly, Naito found a strong improvement in recall with age and an effect of depth of processing. Taken together, her results suggest that implicit memory does not develop, but that explicit memory does. Naito argued that her results showed that the two types of memory were developmentally dissociable.

In *picture-fragment* completion tasks, the child is shown an increasing number of fragments of a picture of a familiar object, such as a saucepan or a telephone, until the object is recognized (Figure 8.2). If the complete object has been presented in a prior task, such as a picture-naming task, then implicit learning should result in faster recognition for fragments of previously experienced objects than for fragments of completely novel objects.

Russo, Nichelli, Gibertoni, and Cornia (1995) used a picture-completion paradigm of this type to measure implicit memory in 4- and 6-year-old children. The children

KEY TERM

Fragment completion task
Where the individual is shown fragments of words or pictures and asked to name or recall the whole object.

FIGURE 8.2
Examples of the fragmented pictures used by Russo et al. (1995). Copyright © 1995 Elsevier. Reproduced with permission.

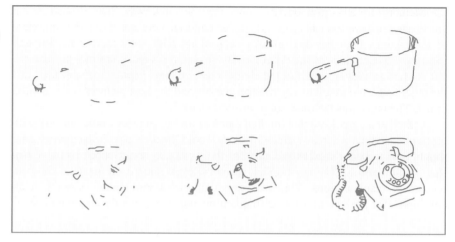

were first shown a series of 12 pictures for 3 seconds each, and were required to name each in turn. After a 10-minute break spent playing with blocks, the children were shown the fragmented versions of the familiar pictures along with fragmented versions of 12 new pictures, in random order. For each set of fragments, they were asked to say as quickly as possible what they thought the fragments were a picture of. The number of fragments that were presented was increased until the child recognized the picture. Performance in this implicit memory condition was contrasted with performance in an explicit version of the task, which was presented without time constraints. In the explicit memory task, the children were asked to use the fragments as cues to try and recall the pictures presented during the naming phase of the experiment. Russo et al. found that children of both ages recognized the familiar pictures from fewer fragments than the novel pictures, showing implicit memory. A group of young adults who were given the same picture completion task performed at similar levels to the children. Significant age differences were found in the explicit memory task, however, with the 6-year-olds showing better recall than the 4-year-olds. Russo et al. concluded that implicit memory as measured by fragment completion tasks is equivalent in children and in adults, and that the memory processes supporting implicit memory are fully developed by 4 years of age.

Perez, Peynircioglu, and Blaxton (1998) also failed to find age differences in an implicit picture-fragment completion task carried out with children aged 4 and 8 years and with university students. They added an implicit *conceptual* memory task to their study. In this task, black-and-white line drawings were presented for study, and the children were then given category labels (e.g. clothing, animals) and asked to produce the first exemplars that happened to come to mind. In an explicit version of the task, the children were given the same labels and asked to recall the pictures from those categories. Age differences were found for the explicit task, but not for the implicit task. When asked effortfully to recall the original pictures, the 4-year-olds recalled 33% of the pictures, the 8-year-olds 58% and the college students 76%. When simply asked to produce the first exemplars that came to mind, all age groups produced the names of around 45% of the previously studied pictures (a kind of priming effect).

A study carried out by Bullock Drummey and Newcombe (1995) suggested that even 3-year-olds may have fully fledged implicit memory processes. Their measure of implicit memory was the recognition of blurred pictures after long delays. Bullock

Drummey and Newcombe showed that 3-year-olds, 5-year-olds, and adults blurred versions of pictures they had seen 3 months previously in a reading book. They found that all groups showed comparable levels of implicit memory for the pictures. However, the adults had better *explicit* memory of the pictures than the children.

More recently, however, Cycowicz, Friedman, Snodgrass, and Rothstein (2000) have used the picture-fragment completion task to argue that there are some developments in implicit memory with age. Cycowicz et al. make the reasonable point that studies of explicit memory in children reveal that processes like encoding and storage show age-related improvements (see Bauer, 2006). Hence some, albeit minor, age-related improvements might be expected in implicit memory tasks. Cycowicz et al. gave children aged 5, 9, and 14 years and college students a picture-fragment completion task in which images were presented on a computer to allow easy presentation of the next level of fragmentation. All participants performed extremely well in this implicit task, correctly identifying over 90% of previously seen pictures. However, the degree of savings was lower for the youngest age group. The younger children needed more information for identifying the familiar fragmented pictures than the older children. In the explicit memory task, when the children had to recall the pictures, the usual age-related effects were found. Cycowicz et al. (2000) argued that there were developmental trends for both implicit and explicit tasks. However, they accepted that the implicit and explicit memory systems might develop at different rates.

Memory for faces

A third measure that has been used to study implicit memory in children is memory for faces. Faces have the advantage of being salient and important stimuli that are not dependent on verbal recall. For example, if the same face is presented to adult subjects on two occasions, the reaction time to recognize the face as familiar on the second occasion is dramatically reduced. This is known as a "priming" effect. Ellis, Ellis, and Hosie (1993) investigated whether young children would also show "priming" effects for faces.

In their experiment, children aged 5, 8, and 11 years were shown pictures of their classmates and of unfamiliar children, and were asked to judge whether the children were smiling or not (half were smiling) and whether the picture was of a boy or of a girl. Following this "priming" stage, the pictures of the children's classmates were presented for a second time, mixed in with previously unseen pictures of other classmates and with pictures of other unfamiliar children. On this second showing, the children were asked to judge whether the children depicted were familiar. Ellis et al. found that children of all ages were quicker to make judgments about the familiarity of the classmates that they had just seen in the priming phase of the experiment than about the familiarity of their nonprimed classmates. The amount of implicit memory as measured by the proportional differences in primed and unprimed reaction times was the same for the 5- and 8-year-olds, and was slightly less for the 11-year-olds, again suggesting that the memory processes supporting implicit memory are well developed early in childhood.

A different way to measure memory for faces is to study children's implicit memory of their classmates over time. Newcombe and Fox (1994) showed a group of 10-year-old children slides of 3- and 4-year-old children who had been their classmates in preschool. These slides were intermixed with slides of other children from the same preschool who had attended the school 5 years later. To see whether the children had implicit memories of their familiar classmates, galvanic skin response measures were recorded. The children were then shown the slides again, and were asked to say whether the depicted children were familiar and how much they liked them. The liking measure was included to see whether the children would show a preference for their previous classmates, even if they could not remember them.

Newcombe and Fox found that the children showed recognition of their former classmates according to *both* the implicit and the explicit measures. Overall recognition rates were fairly low (26% on the implicit measure and 21% on the explicit measure), but there were large individual differences in recognition rates. When the experimenters divided the children into two groups, a "high explicit recognition" group and a "low explicit recognition" group, they found that performance on the implicit recognition measure was equivalent in both groups. This is a very interesting result, as it implies that implicit memory for preschool experiences can be maintained even when explicit memories are lacking. Newcombe and Fox's data thus support Naito's (1990) suggestion that implicit and explicit memories may be developmentally dissociable.

THE DEVELOPMENT OF EPISODIC MEMORY

Unlike implicit memory, episodic memory is a memory system that involves conscious awareness. As mentioned earlier, episodic memory usually refers to memory for episodes or events in one's life, involving explicit recall of these episodes and events. In adults, episodic memory tends to be organized around "schemas", or scripts, for routine events. Each script is a "generic" or "abstract" knowledge structure that represents the temporal and causal sequences of events in very specific contexts (of course, these scripts may depend on distributed neural networks encoding actual experiences, see Chapter 4). For example, adults have a "restaurant" schema for representing the usual sequence of events when eating in a restaurant, and a "laundry" schema for representing the usual sequence of events when doing one's laundry. To study the development of episodic memory, therefore, we need to study the development of scripts and schemas. An obvious approach is to ask children about very familiar events and routines, to see whether they respond with script-like information.

Scripts or schemas are generic knowledge structures that represent the temporal and causal sequences of events in a specific context. For example, an adult will have a "laundry" schema for the usual sequence of events when doing laundry. © Royalty Free/Corbis.

The development of scripts for organizing episodic memory

Asking young children questions about familiar routines was exactly the method selected by Nelson and colleagues in their pioneering developmental work on scripts. They examined the episodic memories of 3- to 5-year-old children for events like going grocery shopping, attending birthday parties, and baking cookies. The children were simply asked to tell the experimenters "what happens" during such events. A series of ordered prompts was then used as necessary to prompt elaboration: "I know you know a lot about grocery shopping. Can you tell me what happens when you go grocery shopping? . . . Can you tell me anything else about grocery shopping? . . . What's the first thing that happens? What happens next?".

Nelson found that the youngest children gave ordered and conventionalized reports of what typically occurred during these events. For example, here is a 5-year-old telling the experimenters about going grocery shopping (Nelson, 1986; p. *ix*):

Um, we get a cart, uh, and we look for some onions and plums and cookies and tomato sauce, onions and all that kind of stuff, and when we're finished we go to the paying booth, and um, then we, um, then the lady puts all our food in a bag, then we put it in the cart, walk out to our car, put the bags in our trunk, then leave."

Research such as this shows that episodic memory is organized around general event representations from a very early age. Nelson (1993) argues that the basic ways of structuring, representing, and interpreting reality are consistent from early childhood into adulthood. This developmental argument fits nicely with the neural data on conceptual representation discussed in Chapter 4. General event representations would naturally arise from storing and interpreting repeated experiences of instances of a particular event in a distributed neural network. Over time, the core aspects of the event would be represented and activated more strongly than the details that vary with each individual experience.

As Nelson points out, scripts for routine events may thus play a very salient role in memory development. In fact, Nelson (1988) has suggested that younger children *concentrate* on remembering routines, as routine events such as going to the baby-sitter are what make the world a predictable place. The importance of this predictability means that routine events are focused on at the expense of novel and unusual events, which are forgotten. It was argued here that as distributed mental representations in memory will naturally encode what is consistent across experienced events more strongly than what is novel, the apparent developmental "focus" on the routine may be a natural consequence of how the brain encodes memories.

The relationship between scripts and novel events

However, more recent studies have shown that younger children can also remember novel and unusual events over long periods of time. In a study by Fivush and Hammond (1990), a 4-year-old recalled that, when he was 2½ "I fed my fish too much food and then it died and my mum dumped him in the toilet". Another 4-year-old told the experimenters that when he was 2½ "Mummy gave me Jonathan's milk and I threw up" (this child was lactose intolerant). Both of these events were genuine memories. These novel events had obviously made a big impression on the children concerned, as they could reproduce them accurately 18 months later! Fivush and Hammond agree with Nelson's idea that young children focus largely on routines, but suggest that children's understanding of routine events *also* helps them to understand novel events, events that differ from how the world usually works. The emotional significance of these events for the young child may also explain why they are retained so well. Emotional salience would be encoded along with the experienced event, thereby providing distinctive and additional mnemonic cues to the unusual experience.

Fivush and Hammond's suggestion that the development of scripts enables the development of memories for novel events is at first sight inconsistent with other evidence showing that young children have a tendency to *include* novel events in their scripts, however. Whereas older children can separate novel events from the routine, tagging them separately in memory as atypical, younger children display a tendency to blur the routine with the unusual. For example, Farrar and Goodman (1990) compared 4- and 7-year-old children's ability to recall novel and repeated ("script") events. In their study, the children visited the laboratory five times during a 2-week period to play "animal games". These games included making bunny and frog puppets jump fences, and having bears and squirrels hide from each other. Each game took place at a special table, and the games occurred in the same order on each visit. However, during one visit a novel event was inserted into the familiar routine (the event was two new puppets crawling under a bridge).

A week later, the children were interviewed about their experiences using both free-recall techniques and specific questions such as "What happens when you play at this table with the puppets?". The younger children frequently reported that the novel event had occurred during the script visits as well as during the single deviational visit. They appeared unable to differentiate between a typical "animal game" visit and the novel event that had occurred only once. The older children did not report that the novel event had occurred during both the script visits and the deviational visit. They were more likely to have formed separate and distinct memories for the two types of visit, tagging the novel event as separate and as a departure from the typical script.

Farrar and Goodman suggested that younger children relied on their general event memory when recalling events, and that this general memory had absorbed information from *both* the script visits and the novel visit. They concluded that the ability to establish separate memories of unusual episodes may still be developing at age 4. However, it is also possible that both groups of researchers are correct. Younger children's tendency to merge novel events with their general event memories may depend on the salience of the novel event to the child. Highly salient novel events such as those documented by Fivush and Hammond (which may be frequently "refreshed" in family contexts) may benefit from additional retrieval cues, while details of less salient events such as the deviation from the game played in Goodman's laboratory may be merged with scripts. Certainly, Fivush and her research colleagues have demonstrated good narrative recall in 3-and 4-year-olds for distinctive events that were highly salient for the child. For example, here is a child aged 46 months recalling an Easter egg hunt for a researcher:

> *I find the basket . . . I won the golden egg . . . in the tree. I found . . . candy inside different eggs. They were green, pink, yellow, orange, and umm blue. And we found candy inside. Jellybeans, suckers, and tootsies rolls and . . . and . . . different color jellybeans. . . . And yum yum yum. And we ate cupcakes with M&M sprinkles and maybe had drinks of lemonade.*

It seems likely that developments in cognitive neuroscience and connectionist modeling will help to explain the developmental relationship between remembering typical and atypical events.

Parental interaction style and the development of episodic memories

There is growing evidence that the ways in which parents interact with their children influence the development of event memories. Parents tend to ask young children fairly specific questions about shared past events, such as "Where did we go yesterday?", "Who did we see?", and "Who was there with us?" (Hudson, 1990). Repeated experience of such questions may help young children to organize events into the correct temporal and causal order, and to learn which aspects of events are the most important to recall. If this is so, then parents who ask more of these specific questions should have children with better memories. This seems to be the case. For example, in a longitudinal study of mother–child conversations about the past, Reese, Haden, and Fivush (1993) observed mother–child dyads talking about the past when the children were aged 40, 46, 58, and 70 months. The mothers were asked to talk about singular events from the past, like a special visit to a baseball game or a trip to Florida. They were asked to avoid routine events like birthday parties or Christmas, which could invoke a familiar script.

Reese et al. found that there were two distinct maternal narrative styles, which were related to the ways in which the children became able to recall their own past experiences. Some mothers consistently elaborated on the information that their child recalled and then evaluated it. Other mothers tended to switch topics and to provide less narrative structure, and seldom used elaboration and evaluation. For example, an elaborative mother who was helping her child to remember a trip to the theatre included questions like "Where were our seats?" and "What was the stage set up like?". A nonelaborative mother who was helping her child to recall a trip to Florida asked the same question repeatedly ("What kinds of animals did you see?, and what else?, and what else?"). The children of the elaborative mothers tended to remember more material at 58 and 70 months. Reese et al. suggested that **maternal elaborativeness** was a key factor in children's developing memory abilities. For example, maternal elaborativeness might be expected to lead to more organized and detailed memories, and might facilitate children's developing understanding of time. This conversational style also allows opportunities for mothers and their children to agree and disagree about the past. This negotiation could help the child to understand that the self has a unique perspective on the past.

The construction of personal histories

Researchers such as Fivush were among the first to point out that talking about past experiences with one's parents and family enables the construction of a personal history. This implies a role for social construction in the development of **autobiographical memory**. If parents focus on particular events as important or self-defining when reminiscing with young children, these events may take on salient roles in the child's autobiographical self-narrative. Alternatively, the simple opportunity to talk about the past with one's parents may enhance retention. Experiences from early childhood that are frequently rehearsed may be more likely to be recalled later in life. These hypotheses about autobiographical memory are difficult to study, as they require prospective longitudinal studies. However, at least two research groups have relevant data. Fivush and her colleagues conducted the longitudinal study discussed earlier (Reese et al., 1993). Because the repeated contacts with the families allowed an estimate of rehearsal frequency, this study was able to investigate the effects of family rehearsal on the construction of personal histories.

To explore the construction of personal histories, Fivush and Schwarzmüller (1998) interviewed some of the children who had participated in the earlier study when they were aged 8 years. Each child was asked about between four and six events that had occurred and been discussed in earlier phases of the study, when the children were aged 40, 46, 58 or 70 months. Particularly distinctive events were chosen (e.g. going to Disney World, having chicken pox). The experimenter began by saying "Today I'd like to ask you about some things you did a long time ago, and see what you remember about them". Fivush and Schwarzmüller reported that the children recalled most of the events (78%) that they were asked about, including events that had occurred before 40 months of age. However, about 80% of the information that they provided about these remembered events was new. Copies of the interview transcripts were thus mailed to the children's mothers for checking. The mothers confirmed that almost all of the extra information provided was accurate.

Highly distinctive events are thus extremely well remembered by children. Fivush and Schwarzmüller concluded that much more information had been encoded and retained by the children than they had verbally reported at the time that the events were experienced. To assess the role of family reminiscence in remembering, Fivush and Schwarzmüller scored the likely frequency of rehearsal of the different events by the families, using information gathered during prior study visits. This enabled them to produce estimates of the amount of family rehearsal of the events both at the time that the event occurred, and subsequently up to the current interview at age 8. Surprisingly, no relationship was found between the amount of rehearsal across the retention interval and the amount of information that the child recalled. Fivush and Schwarzmüller concluded that it was the experience of verbalizing the events at the time that they occurred that was critical for long-term retention. For verbal recall at least, the ability to give a narrative account of an experience at the time of experiencing it may be important for constructing a personal past. Fivush and Schwarzmüller suggested that this was because language enables children to construct extended, temporally organized representations of experienced events that are narratively coherent. Adult-guided reminiscing may help the child to learn more sophisticated forms of narrative organization. Those events which are organized in more narratively coherent ways may then become the first autobiographical memories that will be carried for a lifetime.

Bauer and colleagues, who recruited the cohort discussed earlier (Bauer et al., 2000), reached similar conclusions. For example, Van Abbema and Bauer (2005) followed up the children who had visited their laboratory five times between the ages of 1 and 3 years when these children were aged 7, 8, or 9 years. At the 3-year visit, each child had talked with their parents about six relatively unique events from the recent past. Van Abbema and Bauer were able to explore how much the children recalled about these events after a gap of 4, 5, or 6 years. Four of the six events were selected for discussion with each child. Van Abbema and Bauer found less recall of the distant events than Fivush and Schwarzmüller (1998), with the 7-year-olds recalling around 60% of the events and the older children around 35%. However, the events were generally less distinctive than those investigated by Fivush and Schwarzmüller (e.g. short-term outings; Van Abbema and Bauer found 100% recall for very distinctive events such as moving house). For the events that were recalled, the children provided as much information as they had when aged 3 years. In general, they provided more detailed narratives of the same events than when aged 3, supporting the findings of Fivush and Schwarzmüller. Van Abbema and Bauer were not able to estimate the amount of rehearsal that had occurred in the interim, but they did compare participants' memory for distant events with their memory for more recent ones (broadly, events occurring within the previous 9 months). They found that although memory for these more recent events was more detailed, there was little substantive difference between the ability to recall the recent versus distant past. They concluded that as long as the initial representation of an experienced event is strong enough, it can be retained over time.

A growing tendency to describe events from the perspective of the self was also evident. Van Abbema and Bauer noted that the function of autobiographical memory changes with age. Whereas younger children use discussion of the past to cement their understanding of their family and their role within it, older children talk about the autobiographical past to cement relationships with peers. By discussing our past with others, we "share" ourselves with our friends and deepen our social relationships. The idea that autobiographical memory serves largely social and cultural functions is a central theme in the paper by Nelson and Fivush (2004). They point out that the human ability to create a shared past allows each individual to enter a community or culture in which individuals "share a perspective on the kinds of events that make a life and shape a self" (p. 506). Nelson and Fivush point to important cultural differences in how shared reminiscing provides children with information about how to be a "self" in their culture. For example, the self-definition and self-story of the individual is seen as more important in modern Western cultures than in Asian cultures.

THE DEVELOPMENT OF EYE-WITNESS MEMORY

A special kind of episodic memory is memory for events that may not have appeared significant at the time that they were experienced. This is eye-witness memory. Studies of eye-witness memory in adults have shown that adults have remarkably poor memories for the specifics of events that they have seen. For example, adults who have witnessed a car accident in a video film can be misled into "remembering" false details such as a broken headlight simply by the experimenter asking them leading questions like "Did you see the broken headlight?" (Loftus & Zanni, 1975). If the eye-witness memory of adults is faulty, then presumably the eye-witness memory of *children* is even worse. This is an interesting research question in its own right, but it is also an important legal issue (Ceci & Friedman, 2000). As more and more children are being called as witnesses in investigations concerning physical and sexual abuse, the status of their testimony has become of paramount importance (Ceci & Bruck, 1995). In such cases, it is crucial to know whether the abuse really occurred or whether "memories" of abuse have been created as a result of repeated suggestive questioning by adults.

The accuracy of children's eye-witness testimony

Imagine that an experimenter comes to your school, takes you off to a quiet room to do a puzzle with two friends, and leaves you on your own. While you are working on the puzzle, a strange man comes into the room and messes around, dropping a pencil and fumbling with objects. He claims to be looking for the headmaster. He then steals a handbag and walks out. How much do you remember about these events? Ochsner and Zaragoza (1988, cited in Goodman & Aman, 1990) showed that 6-year-old children remembered quite a lot. The children produced more accurate statements about the other events that they had witnessed in the room and fewer incorrect statements than a group of control children who had experienced the same events except that the man had left the room without stealing the bag. The experimental group was also less suggestible, for example being less willing to select suggested misleading alternative events during a forced-choice test. This study suggests that the eyewitness testimony of young children may be no less accurate than that of adults.

The role of leading questions

Other studies, however, have found that although young children's memory for centrally important events is equivalent to that of adults, younger children are more suggestible than adults. For example, Cassel, Roebers, and Bjorklund (1996) reported a study in which 6- and 8-year-old children and adults watched a video about the theft of a bike. A week later the subjects were asked to recall the events in the video, and were asked a series of increasingly suggestive questions. Cassel et al. found that children and adults showed equivalent levels of recall for items central to the event (e.g. Whose bike was it?). However, when Cassel et al. compared the effect of repeated suggestive questioning on the 6- and 8-year-old children and the adults, they found a greater incidence of false memories in the children. Interestingly, they also found that *unbiased* leading questions such as "Did the bicycle belong to (a) the mother, (b) the boy, or (c) the girl?" were as likely to produce false memories as biased (mis)leading questions such as "The mother owned the bike, didn't she?". This is an important result, as it suggests that the mechanisms that result in false memories may be *general* ones to do with the way that the developing memory system functions, rather than *specific* ones related to false memories of negative events.

As Cassel et al.'s study relied on watching a video, we can hypothesize that leading questions may have an even *greater* effect on the recall of younger children when they actually experience an event themselves. Goodman and colleagues devised a paradigm based on a visit to a trailer (caravan) to investigate this question (Rudy & Goodman, 1991; see also Goodman, Rudy, Bottoms, & Aman, 1990). In the "trailer experiment", children aged 4 and 7 years were taken out of their classrooms to a dilapidated old trailer, chosen to be a memorable location. The children went in pairs, and once inside the trailer they played games with a strange man. One child in each pair had the important task of watching (the bystander), and the other child (the participant) played games. This enabled the experimenters to see whether the children would show similar levels of suggestibility when they were participants or bystanders at real events. The games included "Simon Says", dressing up, having your photograph taken, and tickling. During the "Simon Says" game, the children had to perform various actions including touching the experimenter's knees. These games were chosen because child sexual abuse cases frequently involve reports of being photographed, of "tickling", and of other touching.

The children were later interviewed about what had taken place in the trailer. The interview began with the interviewer asking the child to tell him or her about everything that had happened in the trailer. The interview then continued with misleading questions like "He took your clothes off, didn't he?", "How many times did he spank you?", and "He had a beard and a moustache, right?". In fact, the dressing up game did not involve removing the children's clothes, no child was spanked and the man was clean-shaven. Goodman et al. found that children of both ages recalled largely *correct* information about the games that they had played in the trailer. Neither participants nor bystanders invented information. The children were also largely accurate in their responses to specific questions about abuse, like "How many times did he spank you?", and "Did he put anything in your mouth?". The 7-year-olds answered 93% of the abuse questions correctly, and the 4-year-olds answered 83% correctly.

A related study with 3- and 5-year-olds showed that false reports of abuse did not increase when anatomically detailed dolls were provided to enable the children to *show* as well as tell what had happened (Goodman & Aman, 1990). In this study, however, the younger children *were* more susceptible to leading questions than the older children. Under the influence of misleading questions about abuse, the 3-year-olds tended to make *errors of commission* (that is, they agreed to things that had not happened) 20% of the time. Embroidery of these events was rare. In fact, the majority of commission errors occurred with the leading question "Did he kiss you?", to which the children simply nodded their heads. The 5-year-olds only made commission errors on 2 out of 120 occasions, and both of these errors were on the question "Did he kiss you?". The younger children made very few errors on the potentially more worrying misleading abuse questions such as "He took your clothes off, didn't he?" and "How many times did he spank you?".

The striking thing about Goodman's findings in these very "ecologically valid" studies is that, in the main, the children did *not* invent false reports of abuse. They were also fairly resistant to misleading questioning by the adult, and this resistance remained robust in the face of anatomically detailed dolls, a factor that might have been expected to encourage invention. More recently, Goodman and colleagues have been able to study actual child victims of abuse (Eisen, Qin, Goodman, & Davis, 2002). This was possible because the researchers worked with professionals conducting child maltreatment investigations in a large American city. As part of these investigations, 189 children aged from 3 to 17 years were taken away from their families for a 5-day period, during which extensive hospital-based examinations were carried out. The researchers were able to interview the children about aspects of these examinations, including an anogenital examination and a psychological consultation. This enabled them to assess the children's responses to misleading questions, and to explore potential relations between suggestibility, intellectual ability, and clinical ratings of psychopathology (global adaptive functioning). The children were divided into three broad age bands, 3–5 years, 6–10 years, and 11–17 years.

In all, the professional team estimated that 101 of the 189 children had been abused, 43 had been neglected, and 40 had not been abused (the status of the other 5 children could not be determined). The majority of the children were African–American (77%) and from low socioeconomic status families, thus making them rather different to the middle-class nonabused children usually studied in eye-witness memory experiments. Overall, Eisen et al. did not find that memory or suggestibility differed in maladjusted children compared to typically developing children. Abuse status was not related to the children's eye-witness memory performance. The preschoolers (3- to 5-year-olds) were more suggestible, but even they made relatively few errors in response to misleading questions about abuse (16% errors). Contrary to prediction, no relationships were found between the stress experienced by the children during the different examinations and memory performance or suggestibility. In general, more accurate memory was shown by the older children and by the more intelligent children, while less accurate memory was shown by children rated as having poor global adaptive functioning. Thus age, IQ, and overall psychopathology rather than abuse status were linked to children's eye-witness memory performance.

Other studies of young children's eye-witness testimony have also found that levels of suggestibility are higher in younger children (see Ceci & Bruck, 1993, for a review). The effects of misleading questions are almost always to increase inaccurate acquiescence (errors of commission; see Ceci & Bruck, 1995). More recently, it has been reported that if interviews are relatively unstructured, as is more common in actual forensic interviews, then misleading questions result in denials rather than in agreeing to things that have not happened (Gilstrap & Ceci, 2005). However, this novel finding requires replication. Overall, the levels of suggestibility found in different studies appear to vary with factors such as the emotional tone of the interview itself, the child's desire to please the interviewer, characteristics of both interviewer and child, and whether the child is a participant in the action or not, among others. Almost all studies find *some* age differences in suggestibility. However, it is also worth noting that leading questions are more likely to result in new disclosures than neutral questions (Gilstrap & Ceci, 2005). Hence leading questions cannot be dismissed as overall deleterious in eye-witness memory investigations with young children.

Links between the development of episodic memory and the development of eye-witness memory

In general, the developmental patterns for episodic memory and eye-witness memory are highly similar (Ceci & Bruck, 1993). Older children can generally provide more detailed and narratively coherent memories. Ceci and Bruck also suggested that the greater susceptibility of younger children to repeated questioning by adults might be related to the distinction between scripts and personal histories. As we have seen, as children develop, their autobiographical memories are increasingly described from the perspective of the self. Ceci and Bruck (1993) suggested that the overdependency of younger children on scripted knowledge could mean that suggestions made by the experimenter get included into the children's script for an event, and are thereafter reported as having actually taken place. Although this fits with Farrar and Goodman's (1990) finding that, when a novel event occurs in a standard setting, younger children tend to incorporate it into their script rather than tagging it separately, in general this suggestion has not been borne out by research (Gilstrap & Ceci, 2005). The suggestibility of younger children seems to reduce their report accuracy rather than change their memories. Because younger children sometimes agree with misleading questions, their reports contain more errors. As children get older, they seem to become less susceptible to leading questions. In general, the amount of information and the accuracy of the information that children report in a memory interview increase with age, mirroring developments in episodic memory skills (Eisen et al., 2002).

Ornstein and colleagues have made the related point that children cannot provide accurate testimony about events that they cannot remember. To examine how much children actually remember about salient, personally experienced events, Ornstein,

Gordon, and Larus (1992) investigated 3- and 6-year-old children's memories of a visit to the doctor for a physical examination. Each physical examination lasted about 45 minutes and included weighing and measuring the child, checking hearing and vision, drawing blood, checking genitalia, and listening to the heart and lungs. Ornstein et al. argued that such visits shared a number of features with instances of sexual abuse. These included physical contact with the child's body by an adult and emotional arousal due to injections and other procedures. Memory for the events in the physical examination was measured immediately after the examination was over, and after intervals of 1 and 3 weeks.

Ornstein et al. measured the children's memories by first asking them open-ended questions such as "Tell me what happened during your check-up". More detailed questions were then asked, such as "Did the doctor check any parts of your face?" and "Did he/she check your eyes?". Misleading questions were also asked, involving features of the physical examination that had not been included in an individual child's check-up. Ornstein et al. found that children in both age groups showed good recall of the physical examination immediately after it was over, recalling 82% (3-year-olds) and 92% of the features (6-year-olds), respectively. Both groups showed some forgetting of these features after 3 weeks had passed, but recall was still highly accurate, being around 71% in the 3-year-olds. Responses to misleading questions were also largely accurate. Children in both age groups were able to correctly reject misleading features most of the time, correct denials occurring on 60% of misleading questions for the 3-year-olds after a 3-week delay, and on 65% of misleading questions for the 6-year-olds. Intrusions ("remembering" features that had not in fact occurred) were also at similar levels in the two groups after the 3-week delay, being 26% for the 3-year-olds and 32% for the 6-year-olds. Ornstein et al. concluded that young children's recall of a personally experienced event was surprisingly good, supporting the findings obtained for children's memories of more positive experiences.

A different way of looking at the link between children's knowledge of routine, script-like information, and their eye-witness recall is to investigate whether children who have *more* episodic knowledge about a certain class of events are less likely to demonstrate susceptibility effects. According to this hypothesis, the possession of prior knowledge about a class of events should result in the formation of more stable memories, and these more stable memories should be less susceptible to the influence of leading questions. This hypothesis can be examined by studying the role of knowledge in children's memories, and again the work of Ornstein and colleagues provides a good example of such research.

Clubb, Nida, Merritt, and Ornstein (1993) looked at whether children's memories of what happens when you visit the doctor were linked to their knowledge and understanding of what happens during routine pediatric examinations. The children, who were 5-year-olds, were interviewed about their knowledge of physical examinations using open-ended questions like "Tell me what happens when you go to the doctor". They were then asked a series of yes–no probe questions like "Does the doctor check your heart?". Clubb et al. found that the majority of the children remembered highly salient features such as having an injection (64%), having the doctor listen to your heart (64%), and having your mouth checked (55%). Few children remembered features such as having a wrist check (5%). These percentages were then taken as an index of knowledge. A different group of 5-year-olds provided the eye-witness memory scores. This group of children had been interviewed previously about a real visit to the doctor as part of an earlier study. Clubb et al.

checked the percentages of these children who had spontaneously recalled the same features (injection, heart check, mouth check etc.) either immediately or 1, 3, or 6 weeks following their real examination. These "eye-witness memory" numbers were then correlated with the corresponding knowledge scores obtained from the first group of children.

The researchers found that the correlations between knowledge and memory were highly significant at each delay interval. From this finding, they argued that variability in knowledge in a given domain is associated with corresponding variability in recall. However, the significant correlations obtained by Clubb et al. do not tell us about the *direction* of the relationship between knowledge and memory. It could be that variability in recall determines variability in knowledge, rather than vice versa. The relationship would also be more convincing if it were demonstrated in the *same* children. Eisen et al. (2002) reported partially relevant data. In their study of maltreated children, overall the children with better event memories were also the children who provided more detail in their reports of abuse experiences. Girls also tended to provide more detailed disclosures than boys. This gender difference could reflect the role of verbal ability in constructing coherent narratives of one's personal history, as also suggested by the finding noted earlier that females tend to have earlier memories than males.

THE DEVELOPMENT OF WORKING MEMORY

Both episodic memory and eye-witness memory are aspects of long-term recall. We also have a memory system for short-term recall, which is called **working memory**. Working memory is a limited capacity "workspace" that maintains information temporarily rather than in the long term. This temporary storage allows the information to be processed for use in other cognitive tasks, such as reasoning, comprehension, and learning (e.g. Baddeley & Hitch, 1974). The information that is being maintained in working memory may either be new information, or it may be information that has been retrieved from the long-term system.

Working memory has at least three subcomponents. These are the **central executive**, the **visuospatial sketchpad**, and the **phonological loop** (Figure 8.3). The central executive is conceived of as an attentional control system, a regulatory device that co-ordinates the different working memory activities and allocates resources. The visuospatial sketchpad is thought to process and retain visual, spatial, and possibly kinesthetic information, and also to hold any verbal information that is being stored as an image. The phonological loop is a temporary phonological store which is thought to maintain and process verbal and acoustic information, the former in the form of speech sounds. It can be conceptualized as a kind of tape-loop lasting 1–2 seconds. Decay in the phonological store is fairly rapid, and so this verbal information may need to be *refreshed* or *rehearsed* by subvocal articulation. Baddeley (2000) has speculated

KEY TERMS

Working memory
A limited capacity system that maintains information on a temporary basis. It has three components: central executive, visuospatial sketchpad, and phonological loop.

Central executive
Component of working memory. It is a regulatory device that co-ordinates the different working memory activities and allocates resources.

Visuospatial sketchpad
Component of working memory that is based on visual and spatial, rather than verbal, storage.

Phonological loop
Component of working memory that uses speech sounds for coding material.

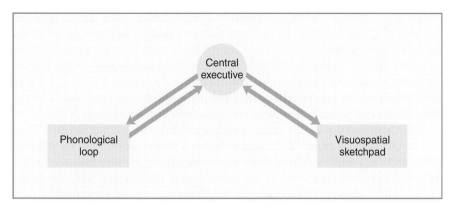

FIGURE 8.3
The model of working memory. Based on Baddeley and Hitch (1974).

that the phonological loop may have developed from processes that initially evolved for speech perception (the phonological store) and speech production (articulatory rehearsal).

Developmental psychologists have mainly been concerned with the development of the two "slave systems" of the central executive, the visuospatial sketchpad, and the phonological loop. One influential idea has been that children initially rely on visual codes in short-term memory, and then switch to phonological codes at the age of around 5 years (e.g. Conrad, 1971). The age of this switch has been seen as potentially very important, as it is similar to the age at which Piaget proposed that a fundamental shift occurred in children's logical reasoning abilities (see Chapter 11). In fact, a number of information-processing theories of cognitive development, sometimes called "neo-Piagetian" theories, are loosely based on this temporal co-occurrence. As working memory has a central role in reasoning, comprehension, and learning, it seems plausible to argue that the development of working memory must somehow be important for cognitive development in general. However, it is also possible that the development of reasoning, comprehension, and learning *in themselves* leads to improvements and developments in working memory. A detailed discussion is beyond the scope of this book, although Case (1992) and Halford (1993) are examples of authors arguing for information-processing theories of cognitive development (see also Chapter 9).

The visuospatial sketchpad

Most of the evidence for the idea that children rely on visual memory codes prior to around 5 years of age is indirect. It depends largely on showing that younger children are not susceptible to effects that are related to the use of speech sounds for coding material in working memory. As the presence of these effects is usually taken as evidence for the operation of the phonological loop (see below), the absence of these speech-based effects has been taken to imply that working memory in young children relies on the visuospatial sketchpad.

The classic study in this tradition was performed by Conrad (1971). He gave children aged 3–11 years a series of pictures to remember. The pictures had names that either sounded similar (rat, cat, mat, hat, bat, man, bag, tap), or sounded different (girl, bus, train, spoon, fish, horse, clock, hand). The children first learned to play a "matching game" with the pictures. In the matching game, one complete set of pictures was presented face-up in front of the child, and then two or three pictures from a second, duplicate, set were presented for matching. After the children had grasped the idea of matching, the experimental trials began. The experimenter set out the eight cards in the full set (using either the "sounds similar" pictures or the "sounds different" pictures), and then concealed them from view. A subset of the duplicate pictures was then presented for matching. The experimenter named each card in the duplicate set, turned the cards face-down, and then re-exposed the full set. The children had to match the face-down cards to the correct pictures.

As adults find names that sound similar more difficult to remember over short periods of time than names that sound different, Conrad expected that the children would find the "sounds similar" picture cards more difficult to match than the "sounds different" picture cards. However, this "phonological confusability" effect in adults arises because adults tend to code the picture names verbally and then to retain them in the phonological loop using rehearsal. Conrad's argument was that if a phonological confusability effect did not occur in children (i.e. if the children found the "sounds different" cards as difficult to remember as the "sounds similar" cards), then they were using a different memory code to support recall, presumably a pictorial one.

Conrad's results showed that only the younger children showed a "no difference" pattern between the two picture sets (the 3- to 5-year-olds). The memory spans of this age group for the phonologically confusable and nonconfusable pictures (measured by the number of pictures correctly recalled) were equivalent. Children aged 6 years and above showed longer memory spans for the "sounds different" picture cards than for the "sounds similar" picture cards, suggesting that they were using rehearsal strategies as a basis for recall. The possibility that the youngest subjects were also rehearsing but were idiosyncratically renaming the pictures prior to recall (e.g. "cat" as "pussy" or "Tibby", thereby effectively converting the "sounds similar" set into a "sounds different" set) was ruled out by the children's spontaneous naming behavior. The youngest children tended to speak aloud as they performed the task, and made comments like "cat goes with cat" or "cat here". This suggested that young, nonrehearsing children use some form of visual storage to remember visually presented materials.

If short-term storage in younger children is visually based, then visually similar objects should be easily confused in short-term memory, just as phonologically similar names are confused when short-term storage is phonological. This prediction is easily tested by using pictures of objects that look like each other in a memory span task, and then seeing whether visually similar objects are more difficult to remember than visually dissimilar objects. Hitch, Halliday, Schaafstal, and Schraagan (1988) devised a picture confusion memory task of this type. Their visually similar set of pictures consisted of pictures of a nail, bat, key, spade, comb, saw, fork, and pen (Figure 8.4). Their visually dissimilar set of control pictures consisted of pictures of a doll, bath, glove, spoon, belt, cake, leaf, and pig. An additional set of visually

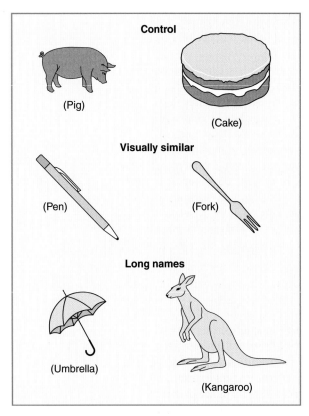

Control

(Pig)

(Cake)

Visually similar

(Pen)

(Fork)

Long names

(Umbrella)

(Kangaroo)

FIGURE 8.4

Examples of stimuli from each condition in Hitch et al.'s (1988) picture memory task. Copyright © The Psychonomic Society. Reproduced with permission.

dissimilar pictures that had long names was also used in the task. This set comprised an elephant, kangaroo, airplane, banana, piano, policeman, butterfly, and umbrella. Hitch et al. then compared 5- and 10-year-old children's memory for these pictures of familiar objects.

Hitch et al.'s memory task was similar to Conrad's, except that no matching was required. Instead, the experimenters presented each picture face-up, and then turned it over, telling the child that they would have to repeat the names of the pictures in the order in which they were shown. The 5-year-olds were given sequences of three pictures, and the 10-year-olds were given sequences of five pictures. Hitch et al. argued that, if the children were using rehearsal to remember the order of the pictures, then they should find the pictures with long names more difficult to recall than the visually similar pictures and the control pictures. However, if the children were using visual memory strategies then they should find the visually similar pictures the most difficult set to recall. Hitch et al. found that, for the 10-year-olds, the pictures with long names were the most difficult to recall. For the 5-year-olds, the visually similar pictures were the most difficult to recall, although there was a small effect of word length. Hitch et al. concluded that the tendency to use visual working memory becomes less pervasive as memory development proceeds.

All of these experiments, however, have studied the retention of *visually presented* items. Rather than showing that children rely on visual memory codes prior to around 5 years of age, it may thus be that younger children tend to rely on visual codes in working memory *when they are given visual information to remember*. This means that experimenters may be documenting a tendency in younger children to attempt to retain information in the modality in which it is presented, rather than a tendency to rely on visual memory codes. Older children may translate visually presented material into a speech code. The visual working memory effects observed by Conrad and by Hitch et al. may thus be due to children's failure to select a particular **mnemonic strategy**, rather than to an early reliance on visuospatial memory codes. We will discuss this possibility further in the next section. Such "production deficiencies" in strategy use (a production deficiency means that a child has a strategy available but does not think of using it) are common in younger children, as will be discussed when we consider strategies for reasoning.

Meanwhile, it is interesting to note that deaf children continue to rely heavily on visuospatial codes in memory, even for material that hearing children code linguistically. O'Connor and Hermelin (1973) devised a spatial span task to measure short-term recall in the deaf. In this task, three digits were presented successively on a screen, appearing in three different windows in a horizontal visual array. The left–right order did not always correspond to the temporal–sequential order of presentation. For example, the first digit to appear might be the one in the middle window. O'Connor and Hermelin found that whereas the hearing children tended to recall the digits in their *temporal order* of appearance, the deaf children recalled them in the *spatial order* of their (left–right) appearance. This suggests that the hearing children were rehearsing the digits verbally in order to remember them, while the deaf children were representing the digits as visual images.

The phonological loop

Activity in the phonological loop is usually measured by the presence of effects that are related to the use of speech sounds for coding material. For example, it is more difficult to remember words that sound similar over a short period of time (bat, cat, hat, rat, tap, mat) than words that do not. This is called the "phonological confusability" or "phonological similarity" effect. Similarly, long words like "bicycle, umbrella, banana, elephant" take longer to rehearse than short words like "egg, pig, car, boy", and so more short than long words can be retained in working memory. This is called the "word length" effect.

The number of items that can be retained in the phonological loop over a short period of time is used to provide a measure of an individual's "memory span". Memory span gives a measure of working memory capacity, and increases with age. As span length differs with different types of material, however, such as long vs. short words (and with background knowledge; see Schneider & Bjorklund, 1998), most measures of memory span are based on the retention of items like digits, which are assumed to be equally familiar to all subjects. However, number words vary in length in different languages. This can lead to different estimates of memory span in children of the same age who speak different languages. Chinese children have much longer digit spans than English children, because the Chinese number words are much shorter than the English number words (e.g. Chen & Stevenson, 1988). Welsh children have shorter digit spans than American children, as the Welsh number words are longer than the English number words. As memory span is usually one of the things measured in IQ tests, at one time it was wrongly thought that Welsh children had lower IQs than American children! Upon closer investigation, it was found that the IQ difference was an artifact of systematically lower Welsh scores on the digit span component of the test (Ellis & Hennelley, 1980).

Another important component of working memory capacity is speech rate or articulation rate, which also affects memory span. Children who articulate slowly tend to have shorter memory spans than children who can articulate more quickly, presumably because it takes them longer to rehearse individual items. Speech rate also increases with age. Because of this, it has been proposed that the development of memory span with age is entirely accounted for by developmental increases in speech rate. As older children speak more quickly than younger children, they can rehearse more information during the 1–2 seconds available in the phonological loop and can thus remember more items than the younger children, giving them longer memory spans.

As required by this proposal, speech rate and memory span are highly correlated. This connection was established in a series of studies by Hulme and colleagues, using a word repetition task (e.g. Hulme, Thomson, Muir, & Lawrence, 1984; Hulme & Tordoff, 1989). For example, in Hulme et al. (1984), children aged 4, 7, and 10 years and adults were given a pair of words, such as "apple, tiger", to repeat as quickly as they could. The number of words produced per second provided the measure of speech rate. The results showed that speech rate was linearly related to memory span: Increases in memory span were always accompanied by increases in speech rate across age. Furthermore, the relation between recall and speech rate was constant across different word lengths. When the children's memory spans for long (e.g. helicopter, kangaroo), short (e.g. egg, bus), and medium-length (e.g. rocket, monkey) words were compared, Hulme et al. found that the relationship between recall and speech rate was constant across age. This shows that, at any age, subjects can recall as much as they can say in a fixed time interval (about 1.5 seconds). Hulme et al. argued that individuals with higher speech rates could rehearse information more quickly, and could thus remember it better.

When Hitch, Halliday, Dodd, and Littler (1989) replicated Hulme et al.'s work using pictures instead of words, however, the results were rather different. With visual presentation of the words to be remembered, only the 10-year-olds showed a correlation between speech rate and memory span, as only this group appeared to spontaneously rehearse the visual inputs. With auditory presentation, all age groups showed the correlation. Thus speech rate *does* govern the number of items that can be retained in working memory, but only when the items to be remembered are presented in speech form. This is, of course, in keeping with the findings of Conrad (1971) and Hitch et al. (1988) that we discussed earlier. Younger children appear to prefer to maintain visually presented information by using a visuospatial code, whereas older children spontaneously translate visual inputs into a speech code.

Henry and Millar (1993) explain this developmental pattern by proposing that rehearsal develops out of naming behavior. They point out that younger children are frequently called upon to use naming to translate visual or tactile material into a verbal form, particularly when they enter school and rely increasingly on verbal strategies for learning and retaining information. Henry and Millar suggest that children's increasing speed and facility with naming leads to the discovery of rehearsal, and that the development of rehearsal probably explains the development of memory span after the age of about 7 years. The development of memory span prior to this point depends both on naming and on the child's familiarity with the items to be remembered. Items that are highly familiar in long-term (semantic) memory are easier to store and to retrieve. Highly familiar items also have well-specified phonological representations in the mental lexicon, and as the speech output system is used in memory span tasks for both rehearsal and recall, words with better-specified representations will require less processing, can be articulated faster, and are more easily reconstructed when memory traces deteriorate (a process termed "redintegration"; see also Roodenrys, Hulme, & Brown, 1993). According to this view, although speech rate is related to the development of memory span, speech rate is also determined by the quality of a child's phonological representations.

Henry and Millar's proposal is an interesting one, as it suggests that the *development* of working memory is intimately related to the development of long-term or semantic memory. According to their argument, the key variable that affects the capacity of working memory, speech rate, is dependent on the development of well-specified phonological representations in semantic memory, which is linked to conceptual and linguistic development. Items that have well-specified phonological representations in long-term memory are easier to redintegrate, leading to enhanced working memory. In general, these items reside in what linguists call "dense phonological neighborhoods". Phonological neighbors are words that sound similar to each other, and words with many neighbors tend to have high-probability phonotactics (see Chapter 5). There is now quite a lot of evidence that the quality of the representations of items in long-term storage affects their retention in short-term tasks. For example, Thomson, Richardson, and Goswami (2005) compared serial recall for words from dense versus sparse phonological neighborhoods in children aged 7 and 9 years. If long-term memory and working memory are linked, then children should show better retention of words residing in dense phonological neighborhoods. This should be the case even when overall item frequency is matched, as was the case for the words used in this study. Thomson et al. reported that serial recall for quadruples of words like "bone, pail, king, gum" (dense phonological neighborhoods) was indeed significantly superior to serial recall for quadruples of words like "wipe, bird, hook, leg" (sparse phonological neighborhoods). Words with better-specified phonological representations appeared to enjoy better redintegration. This supports Henry and Millar's (1993) proposal that the development of long-term memory and of short-term memory is intimately linked.

Data such as these imply that the conventional conceptual distinction between short-term and long-term memory may be only partially applicable, at least as far as the *development* of memory is concerned. Although children do use the phonological loop to maintain information over short periods of time, just like adults, its utilization appears to be gradual, depending on task features (e.g. verbal vs. pictorial input), the age of the child, and the quality of long-term representations. This pattern is reminiscent of the findings discussed earlier regarding the development of episodic memory. As the quality of a child's encoding improves, so does the quality of recall. For episodic memory, the quality of encoding refers to factors like the narrative coherence of the event representation. For working memory, the quality of encoding refers to factors like the specificity of the phonological representation. Nevertheless, in both cases, older children have more adequate representations. This suggests that Baddeley and Hitch's (1974) original proposal that working memory was a "workspace" with two slave systems that was *distinct from* long-term memory needs to be modified, at least as the memory system is developing.

THE DEVELOPMENT OF STRATEGIES FOR REMEMBERING

As adults, we often employ special strategies to help us to remember important information, especially when such information must be retained for relatively short periods of time. These strategies include rehearsing a phone number that we have just been given, or organizing information about what we need to remember to buy at the supermarket. Henry and Millar (1993) suggested that children may discover the strategy of *rehearsal* via their increasing use of naming, for example because of activities encountered in school. The emergence of strategies such as rehearsal and *organization* for remembering can also be studied in their own right. In fact, traditional answers to the question of "what is memory development the development of?" (see DeMarie & Ferron, 2003) include strategies and capacity. Memory capacity is usually measured by memory span tasks, as described above.

Younger children are surprisingly confident about their mnemonic abilities and do not seem to expect that they will need to use mnemonic strategies to improve their recall. For example, in a study conducted by Yussen and Levy (1975), half of the 4-year-olds tested predicted that they would remember all 10 items in a standard memory span task in which they were presented with 10 unrelated items to recall. In actual fact, they remembered about three! This experience did not change the children's confidence in their abilities, however. Very few of them changed their predictions about their memory capacities. Instead, they said things like "If you gave me a different list like that, I could do it!".

The emergent use of mnemonic strategies

Nevertheless, when given a specific "ecologically valid" memory task to perform, even very young children appear to have some realization that they will need to use mnemonic strategies to aid their memories. This was demonstrated in a study by Wellman, Ritter, and Flavell (1975), who told a group of 3-year-olds a story about a toy dog. Among the props used in the story were four identical plastic cups. At one point in the procedure, the experimenter put the toy dog under one of these cups, explaining that the dog would go into the dog-house while the experimenter left the room to find more things. The child was asked to remember which cup the dog was under while the experimenter was away.

During the 40 seconds that the experimenter was out of the room, most children used a variety of strategies to help them to remember which cup was the dog-house. They looked at and touched the cup hiding the dog significantly more often than the other cups, they looked at the target cup and nodded to themselves "yes", looked at the other cups and shook their heads "no", they rested their hand on the target cup, and so on. Wellman et al. also found that recall for the dog's location was more successful in the children who used these strategies than in the children who didn't. An attempt to use this procedure with 2-year-olds was thwarted by the restlessness of the children, who wouldn't keep still during the experimenter's absence.

Better success with 2-year-olds has been reported by DeLoache, Cassidy, and Brown (1985). They used a hiding game to investigate children's strategic memory for spatial locations. The children, who were aged from 18 to 24 months, watched the experimenter hide a favorite toy (e.g. Big Bird) in a natural location (e.g. under a pillow in the child's home). The children were told that Big Bird was going to hide and that they should remember where he was hiding as they would need to find him later when the bell rang. A timer was then set for 4 minutes, during which time the child took part in a number of distraction activities with other toys, organized by the experimenter. The children checked frequently on Big Bird's location during this distraction period, for example pointing at the pillow, saying "Big Bird!", and peeping underneath it. In a control condition in which Big Bird was put on top of the pillow, similar strategies were not observed. DeLoache et al. argued that this showed that the children's self-reminding behaviors were indeed strategic, as they were adopted as a function of the memory demands of the task.

Somerville, Wellman, and Cultice (1983) also succeeded in measuring strategic recall in 2-year-olds by using a highly motivating task. The task was the need to remember to buy candy at the store at a particular time specified by their mother (e.g. tomorrow morning). Memory for two events was compared, getting candy at a specified future time and removing the washing from the washing machine at a specified future time (e.g. when Daddy gets home). Children aged from 2 to 4 years all showed better memory for the highly motivating candy event, indicating an ability to plan ahead and to keep a particular event in mind. At short delays (5 minutes), even the 2-year-olds achieved a level of 80% unprompted remindings for the highly motivating event. On the low motivation task (getting the washing out of the machine), overall success with unprompted reminding was much lower, falling to 26% over long delays. Somerville et al. argued that even very young children were capable of adopting a deliberate "set" to remember at an early age.

Evidence for the strategic use of rehearsal

The spontaneous mnemonic strategies observed in these experiments were fairly task specific, however. One mnemonic strategy that is widely used by adults when they want to remember some information over a short period of time is rehearsal. Saying things to ourselves over and over again can make it easier to remember them. We saw earlier that the spontaneous use of rehearsal may not emerge until children are at school, and are having to rely increasingly on verbal strategies for learning and retaining information. This idea of a "production deficiency" in younger children's use of rehearsal is supported by the findings of a classic study of children's rehearsal, carried out by Flavell, Beach, and Chinsky (1966).

Flavell et al. asked children aged 5, 7, and 10 years to remember a set of pictures over a short delay of about 15 seconds while wearing a space helmet. The space helmet had a visor that concealed the children's eyes, but left their mouths visible. The short delay period began when the experimenter said "Visor down!", and any spontaneous rehearsal during this delay was measured by a trained lip-reader. While the visor was up, the children were shown up to seven pictures (apple, comb, moon, owl, pipe, flowers, American flag), and were required to remember between two and five of them while the visor was down. Flavell et al. found that only 10% of the 5-year-olds used a rehearsal strategy, whereas 60% of the 7-year-olds and 85% of the 10-year-olds did so. There was also some evidence from the 7-year-olds' data that the children who rehearsed more recalled more pictures. Flavell and colleagues argued that the majority of the younger children failed to rehearse because of a production deficiency. The younger children did not realize that they needed to use strategies such as rehearsal to help them to remember. As we saw earlier, younger children are also less likely to convert visually presented information into a verbal code.

Although Flavell et al.'s study did find some evidence for a relationship between the use of rehearsal and the accuracy of recall, later work has shown that the strategic rehearsal of 7-year-old children tends to be piecemeal and not particularly helpful to short-term memory. They tend to rehearse just the currently presented item, or the current item with very few other items. However, small amounts of training can lead to rapid improvement in the strategic use of rehearsal, with accompanying improvements in recall.

For example, Naus, Ornstein, and Aivano (1977) gave 8- and 11-year-old children a list of words to remember. Some of the children were told to practice the words aloud as they normally would do to themselves, and others were told to practice the words aloud by saying the word that had just been presented in a given trial along with two other words. The children who were trained how to rehearse remembered significantly more items at test than the children who were told to practice the words as they normally would to themselves. Naus et al. argued that it was the content rather than the activity of rehearsal that improved memory in list-learning tasks. The quality of rehearsal was more important than its frequency.

The fact that children can be trained to use rehearsal leaves open the question of whether younger children have the strategy of rehearsal available to them, but simply do not think of using it (a "production deficiency"). One way of finding out whether younger children's lack of rehearsal is due to a "production deficiency" is to offer them an *incentive* to use rehearsal. Kunzinger and Witryol (1984) devised an incentive-based technique that used financial rewards for studying the spontaneous use of rehearsal in 7-year-olds. They told the children that recall of some words on a list would win them 10 cents, whereas recall of others would only win them 1 cent. If children can rehearse without being trained in efficient strategy usage, then they should be more likely to rehearse "10-cent words" than "1-cent words".

Kunzinger and Witryol indeed found that the children in their study allocated more rehearsal to the "10-cent words" than to the "1-cent words". In fact, they were six times as likely to rehearse the former as the latter at the beginning of the list. In a control condition in which every word was worth 5 cents, the children rehearsed less overall. Kunzinger and Witryol argued that this was because the children in the experimental condition generalized the use of rehearsal from the "10-cent words" to the "1-cent words". The extra rehearsal allocated to the "10-cent words" also resulted in better recall. These words were recalled significantly more often than the "1-cent words" or the "5-cent words". Seven-year-olds can clearly be induced to use rehearsal, and when they do so, their memories improve.

Attractive incentives can also be used to induce memory strategies in 4-year-olds, although without apparent improvement in their memories. O'Sullivan (1993) showed 4-year-old children 15 different toys (doll, horse, ball, airplane, etc.) and told them that they would win a prize if they could remember all the toys in a recall test. Two prizes were on offer, a pencil and a box of crayons; the crayons were universally judged to be the more appealing prize. In the experiment, the toys were presented in a bag. The experimenter took them out of the bag, allowed the children to study them for 3 minutes, and then put them back into the bag. The children then spent 25 seconds drawing X's on a sheet of paper to eliminate short-term memory effects, after which the recall phase of the experiment began.

O'Sullivan found that the children who were playing to win the box of crayons showed more visual examination of the toys than the children who were playing to win the pencil, and also spent less time in "off-task" behavior. Spontaneous use of rehearsal was not observed. However, although the possibility of winning the better prize elicited significantly more efforts to remember than the possibility of winning the poorer prize, this did not translate into superior recall for the "crayons" group. Recall performance was in fact equivalent across the two incentive groups, and averaged eight items. It should be mentioned that all the children received both prizes at the end of the study!

Many other studies of the development of rehearsal in young children report broadly similar findings to the studies discussed here (see Schneider & Pressley, 1997; Schneider & Bjorklund, 1998, for reviews). Younger children seem disinclined rather than unable to rehearse. Rehearsal first appears when it is encouraged by training or by task-specific factors such as remembering a list of words, or by the use of verbal rather than visual presentation of the items to be remembered. Rehearsal is only used strategically somewhat later in development. The early lack of spontaneous rehearsal can thus be seen as a production deficiency rather than a competence deficiency. As metacognitive skills develop, children are more likely deliberately to employ strategies like rehearsal. This is discussed further in Chapter 9, in the section on metamemory.

Evidence for the strategic use of organization by semantic category

Organizational mnemonic strategies, such as sorting required grocery items into related groups and using this clustering to aid recall, show a similar developmental pattern to rehearsal. Early strategic use is largely task driven, and depends on the items to be recalled. Later strategic use is child driven, and occurs independently of the materials to be remembered.

For example, Schneider (1986) told 7- and 10-year-old children that they would be shown a set of 24 pictures, and that they should try to do anything that would help them to remember the items in the set. The sets of pictures were either defined as having "high category relatedness" (e.g. dog, cat, horse, cow, pig, mouse), or "low category relatedness" (e.g. goat, deer, hippopotamus, buffalo, monkey, lamb). In addition, the sets either had high interitem associativity according to word association norms (e.g. chair, table, bed, sofa, desk, lamp), or low interitem associativity (e.g. refrigerator, stool, bookcase, rocking chair, stove, bench).

The children were given 2 minutes to sort the pictures, and an additional 2 minutes to study them.

Schneider found that only 10% of the 7-year-olds spontaneously grouped the pictures according to their category relationships, whereas about 60% of the 10-year-olds did so. In addition, the younger children, but not the older children, were less likely to group together the items that had low interitem associativity. Whereas the 10-year-olds used categories like "furniture" to group the pictures of the stove, bench, etc., the 7-year-olds did not. Schneider argued that the use of organizational strategies in younger children depended on the degree to which the items were associated. For the 7-year-olds, high associativity *in itself* led to the use of clustering, in a largely involuntary way. By contrast, the 10-year-olds used clustering as a deliberate strategy. The older children were apparently becoming aware of the value of organizational strategies as a mnemonic. In support of his argument, Schneider found that approximately half of the 10-year-olds in his study showed systematic and strategic behavior that facilitated recall, and were aware of the value of organizational strategies.

Similar results were reported in a memory task devised by Bjorklund and Bjorklund (1985), in which 6-, 8-, and 10-year-old children were asked to recall the names of their current classmates. All of the children found this an easy task and appeared to be behaving strategically, organizing their recall in terms of grouping cues such as the seating arrangements in their classroom, the children's reading groups or boys vs. girls. However, when the experimenters asked the children how they went about remembering their classmates' names, the children were unable to outline particular strategies, suggesting that their use of clustering was involuntary. Bjorklund and Bjorklund tested this hypothesis by asking the children to use specific retrieval strategies, such as remembering all of the boys first and then all of the girls. They found that recall in this strategic condition was equivalent to recall in the free condition, when no instructions were given. Bjorklund and Bjorklund concluded that semantic associations between highly associated items can be activated with little effort, resulting in retrieval that appears to be organized and strategic when in fact it is simply a byproduct of high associativity. High associativity thus *automatically* guides the structure of recall.

However, evidence for more strategic use of semantic associativity was found in a study of younger children reported by Schneider and Sodian (1988). They asked 4-and 6-year-old children to hide 10 pictures of people (doctor, farmer, policeman) in 10 wooden houses, and then to retrieve them by matching each picture with its "twin" (a duplicate picture provided by the experimenter). The wooden houses all had roofs that could be opened and shut like boxes, and they also had magnetic stickers on the front doors to which a picture cue could be attached. The available picture cues were either functionally related to the people who were hiding (syringe, tractor, police car) or not (key, flower, lamp).

Schneider and Sodian first asked the children to perform the hiding task without the picture cues, and measured the time taken for hiding and retrieval. They then attached a picture cue to each house, and asked the children to perform the hiding and retrieval tasks a second time. Systematic use of the semantic associations between the picture cues and the targets should lead to slower hiding times on the second trial, but more accurate retrieval. This was exactly what happened. Children of both age groups spent longer hiding the people pictures on the second trial, and also remembered more locations on the second trial. Furthermore, the 6-year-olds remembered significantly more locations on the second trial than the

4-year-olds, indicating that they benefited more from the semantic associations in the cue pictures. Indeed, they were more likely to hide people at semantically appropriate locations than the younger children, hiding on average 3.63 of the possible five people appropriately, compared to 2 out of the five for the 4-year-olds.

Schneider and Sodian also reported that the older children showed more understanding of the use of retrieval cues. When asked specific questions like "Which of the games I just played with you was easier?" the 6-year-olds displayed greater conscious knowledge of the strategic use of the semantic cues than the 4-year-olds. However, even the 4-year-olds showed some knowledge of cuing as a memory aid. Furthermore, a relationship between conscious awareness of the usefulness of the cues and successful memory performance was found in both groups. Schneider and Sodian argued that the idea that preschoolers can only react automatically to highly associated cues without any awareness of their value may be misguided. Even 4-year-olds appear to have some understanding of the utility of cognitive cuing. The fact that this study used a simpler and more meaningful task from the child's point of view may also be important in eradicating the apparent production deficiency in children's spontaneous use of organization as a mnemonic strategy.

The development of multiple strategies

More recently, researchers have begun to measure whether young children use more than one strategy for remembering at a time, and whether the use of multiple strategies can benefit children's recall (e.g. Coyle & Bjorklund, 1997; DeMarie, Miller, Ferron, & Cunningham, 2004). In general, children who use more strategies do seem to recall more information. For example, DeMarie and Ferron (2003) gave children aged from 5 to 10 years three different memory tasks expected to yield different mnemonic strategies. These were a picture recall task, a selective recall task, and a picture sorting task. In the first task, children were given lists of 18 items to remember. The items were spoken by the experimenter, who placed a card depicting each item on the table as she spoke. The children were given 2 minutes to arrange the cards in any way that they liked to help them to remember the items. The cards were then concealed, and the children were asked to recall the items in any order. In the selective recall task, an apparatus with 12 doors was used. Each door had a picture on it, of either a cage or a house. Doors with cages on them concealed animals, and doors with houses on them concealed household items. The children were asked to remember where one type of item was hidden, and were given time to open the doors and check what was behind. Recall was measured by showing children pictures of the hidden items, and asking them to point to their location. In the sorting task, children were given apparatus stands which could hold cards in various positions, and were asked to place either 12 (age 5–8) or 16 (age 9–10) cards on the stand for later memory. Recall for the cards was then tested. The strategies recorded for each task included organizing and grouping cards by semantic category (task 1), selectively opening relevant doors (task 2), placing cards by semantic category (task 3), rehearsal, self-testing during learning, and semantic clustering in recall.

DeMarie and Ferron (2003) reported that even the youngest children used more than one strategy for remembering. Older children used more strategies overall than younger children. The number of strategies used across tasks was significantly but modestly correlated, for younger and for older children. Finally, strategy use was strongly correlated with successful recall. Memory capacity was also measured in this study (using span tasks), and memory capacity did not predict successful recall.

DeMarie and Ferron concluded that strategy use by young children was an important factor in memory development.

In a longitudinal study of 102 kindergarten children (6-year-olds), Schneider, Kron, Hunnerkopf, and Krajewski (2004) also investigated the role of both strategies and capacity in memory development. The children were seen on three occasions separated by 6-month intervals. Schneider et al. assessed the children's memories via an item-retention task. In this task, 20 familiar items were presented for recall (the items were from five semantic categories (namely, furniture, tools, fruit, clothes, and body parts). The children were told that they could do whatever they wanted for a 3-minute period to aid recall of these items. They were then scored for using strategies like sorting the pictures during study, clustering at recall, and rehearsal. Memory capacity was measured by a span measure.

Schneider et al. reported that both strategy use and memory capacity increased over time. Strategy use was related to better recall and children who used more strategies did particularly well. Schneider et al. were most interested in individual differences, however. They thus explored whether these general age-related increases were due to the gradual development of strategy use within individual children, or to the sudden discovery of beneficial strategies by particular children. The latter turned out to be the case. Some children ($N = 57$) were nonstrategic at the first two measurement points, and their recall was very poor. Others ($N = 9$) were consistently strategic, and showed consistently high levels of recall. Another group of 28 children discovered the organizational strategy at the second measurement point, and 21 of these showed a significant increase in recall performance. The seven children who did not were termed "utilization deficient". For these children, use of the correct strategy did not enhance recall. Surprisingly, the same was found to be true 6 months later. This subgroup of children was still showing no recall benefit from using sorting strategies. Schneider et al. reported that memory capacity was also lower in this subgroup. They concluded that memory development is characterized by a rapid transition from nonstrategic to strategic behavior for most children. Memory development does not consist of a gradual increase in strategy use. Children who were consistently strategic used strategies in more than one test of memory, and the advantages of multiple strategy use were already evident in kindergarten children.

The novice–expert distinction

The other traditional answers to the question of "what is memory development the development of?" are "knowledge" and "metamemory". Metamemory, or children's understanding about how we remember, is considered in the next chapter. Knowledge is considered here. Knowledge can also be conceptualized as expertise. It is now widely accepted that the knowledge base itself plays an important role in memory efficiency, and that experts organize their knowledge in different ways to novices. The level of prior knowledge has a critical impact on both the encoding and the storage of incoming information. Expertise also affects the efficiency of recall. One of the most interesting approaches to studying the influence of prior knowledge on cognitive development has been to contrast the performance of *novices* in a domain, who have little prior knowledge, with that of *experts*, who have a lot of prior knowledge. As such comparisons are usually confounded with age (novices are usually younger than experts), the most developmentally informative contrasts are those in which the experts are *younger than* the novices. Such contrasts are usually

KEY TERM

Novice–expert distinction
The role of the knowledge base in memory efficiency in that experts organize their knowledge in different ways than novices.

only possible in quite circumscribed domains, for example chess playing, soccer playing, and expertise in physics.

As Brown and DeLoache (1978) once called young children "universal novices", it may come as a surprise to find that young children occasionally display more expertise in circumscribed domains than older children and adults. This can occur, however, because experts and novices in a particular domain are distinguished by differences in *experience* as well as by differences in age. If you are motivated enough, it is possible to gain a lot of experience in a domain at a relatively young age. For example, some children know an amazing amount about dinosaurs, because they find this domain so interesting that they become veritable experts in dinosaur classification and behavior. Another such domain is chess. Some young chess players display a remarkable level of expertise, and regularly beat their adult opponents.

Children occasionally display more expertise in circumscribed domains than adults. Some young chess players, for example, are able to regularly beat their adult opponents.

If differences in experience distinguish novices and experts, then we can predict that differences in expertise should be correlated with differences in the structure and organization of domain memory. In a pioneering study of this question, Chi (1978) examined the factors that distinguished the memories of chess experts and chess novices. Her group of experts comprised children aged from 6 to 10 years, and her group of novices comprised graduate students who could all play chess. Chi measured the memory of both groups for "middle-game" chess positions, which involved on average 22 chess pieces. The chess players were allowed to study the chess board for 10 seconds, and were then expected to recreate the middle-game position from memory. Chi found that the children positioned 9.3 chess pieces accurately on the first trial, compared with 5.9 chess pieces for the adults. She then measured how long it took both groups to learn the *entire* middle-game position. The children took on average 5.6 trials, and the adults 8.4 trials. Expert vs. novice performance was significantly different in each case.

Although it seems plausible that the children were chess experts because they could remember more about the chess board, it is also possible that they could remember more about the chess board because they were experts. Chi argued that her data supported the latter possibility. She proposed that the child experts could see meaningful patterns in the arrays of chess pieces that were not apparent to the less-skilled adults. Schneider and colleagues tested this interpretation in a replication of Chi's study that included additional control tasks (Schneider, Gruber, Gold, & Opwis, 1993b; Figure 8.5). Schneider et al. found that recall for random as well as meaningful chess positions was better in experts than in novices. In the control task, in which the position of geometrically shaped wooden pieces had to be reconstructed on a board that did not resemble a chess board, the effect of expertise was eliminated. These findings suggest that expertise involves important *quantitative* differences in the amount of knowledge available, for example knowledge about the geometrical pattern of the chess board and the form and color of chess pieces.

The data on children's dinosaur expertise were taken to show that experts also structure their knowledge in *qualitatively* different ways from novices. Chi, Hutchinson, and Robin (1989) found that experts organized their knowledge about dinosaurs in more integrated and locally coherent ways than novices. Their knowledge was more coherent at a global level, representing superordinate information such as "meat eater" vs. "plant eater", and also at a substructural level, representing information about shared attributes such as "has sharp teeth" or "has a duckbill". Chi et al. used a picture-sorting task to establish these differences. They found that 7-year-old dinosaur experts sorted pictures of dinosaurs on the basis of several related attributes and concepts ("He had webbed feet, so that he could swim,

FIGURE 8.5
Examples of the chess
task and of the control
task (below). From
Schneider et al. (1993).
Copyright © 1993
Elsevier. Reproduced
with permission.

and his nose was shaped like a duck's bill, which gave him his name"). Seven-year-old novices sorted the same pictures on the basis of the depicted features ("He has sharp fingers, sharp toes, a big tail"). Chi and colleagues pointed out that it was easier to understand the attributes of a dinosaur (sharp teeth, webbed feet, etc.) if one knew how they were related in a causal or correlated structure. The importance of causal relations and relational mappings for conceptual development and knowledge acquisition should already be familiar from Chapters 3 and 4.

Expertise may also be more important for memory performance than general cognitive ability, at least when a particular domain like chess or soccer is the object of study. In a study of "soccer experts" carried out in Germany, Schneider and colleagues found that grade-3 soccer experts (boys and girls) recalled more information about a story concerning a soccer game than grade-7 soccer novices, and that expertise was a stronger predictor of performance than general cognitive ability, regardless of age (Schneider, Korkel, & Weinert, 1989). Similar effects have been demonstrated in adults by other researchers. For example, extensive experience of attending horse-racing meetings and calculating the odds is a better predictor of who wins money at the races than IQ (Ceci & Liker, 1986). Findings such as these suggest that the old saying "practice makes perfect" does capture something important about the development of expertise. In a longitudinal study of talented young German tennis players (the sample included Boris Becker and Steffi Graf), Schneider, Boes, and Rieder (1993a) found that the amount and level of practice was an important predictor of the rankings of the players 5 years later, as was the level of achievement motivation. Perhaps unsurprisingly, talent *per se* was only one important predictor of later tennis excellence.

Overall, studies of novices and experts show that expertise plays a crucial role in the organization and functioning of memory. An unresolved question is whether changes in expert memory are both qualitative and quantitative, or are quantitative alone. The idea that knowledge enrichment leads to *qualitative* differences in the organization of memory has some obvious parallels with proposals such as Carey's ideas about knowledge acquisition leading to conceptual change (see Chapters 4 and 6). In Chapter 4, the idea that there is true conceptual change was questioned on the grounds that cognitive neuroscience suggests that all knowledge is distributed and incremental. According to a neuroscience perspective, expertise would thus arise from incremental knowledge acquisition. This incremental acquisition of information would lead to many local changes to memories rather than to fundamental restructuring of amodal concepts. The acquisition of incremental knowledge could still lead to changes in coherence (for example, in classifying dinosaurs as plant eaters vs. meat eaters), and hence to changes in organization and structure. However, the growth of expertise may not entail *qualitative* differences in the ways that knowledge is represented. Rather, all changes in memory may be quantitative changes. Expertise may be one form of quantitative change.

The impact of cognitive neuroscience and biological constraints on theories of cognitive development is discussed more fully in Chapter 11. For now, it is comforting to learn that anyone can become an expert in certain domains if he or she is motivated enough to learn about them. Memory development depends on the depth of the knowledge base as well as on the use of explicit strategies such as rehearsal. High levels of expertise can even compensate for low levels of general intelligence in some memory tasks, such as recall tasks. The storage components of memory thus play a clear role in individual differences in some aspects of cognition.

INSIGHTS FROM COGNITIVE NEUROSCIENCE

Cognitive neuroscience studies with adults have explored the neural substrate of both implicit and explicit memory, and also of working memory. In terms of implicit memory, most work in cognitive neuroscience has focused on perceptual learning. Favored stimuli include faces, and basic-level objects such as cars and houses. Debate has centered on whether perceptual learning is domain-specific or not, and on how expertise is acquired.

For example, there appears to be a specialized area for the perceptual learning of faces in the fusiform gyrus, particularly in the right hemisphere (the "fusiform face area"; see Chapter 3). However, this same neural area may also be important in the general acquisition of expertise, since car experts show specific activation in this area for cars but not birds, whereas bird experts show specific activation for birds but not cars (Bukach, Gauthier, & Tarr, 2006). Studies using EEG have shown a specific electrophysiological component for face recognition (the N170; also discussed in Chapter 3). However, fingerprint experts show a similar N170 effect for fingerprints (Bukach et al., 2006). There are almost no studies of the mechanisms underpinning implicit learning in children. However, a fascinating fMRI study of an 11-year-old boy with autism showed robust fusiform selectivity in response to Digimon cartoon characters, in which he was obsessively interested, but not to human faces (Grelotti et al., 2005). A control autistic boy who was not interested in Digimon did not show fusiform selectivity to either the cartoon characters or to human faces. A typically developing boy interested in Pokemon showed fusiform selectivity to faces only. This pattern of results was interpreted as being due to expertise. The autistic boys presumably showed no face selectivity because their lack of mentalizing abilities (see Chapter 7) meant that they were not interested in faces. The typically developing boy, in contrast, had developed face expertise. Chess experts (adults) show specificity in the right fusiform gyrus for the spatial layout of chess boards (Righi & Tarr, 2004). Note that all these studies were of visual expertise, and not of conceptual expertise. Whereas they provide evidence that the fusiform gyrus is important in perceptual learning, they are likely to be only one component of the novice–expert shift in explicit memory discussed earlier.

Regarding explicit or declarative memory, cognitive neuroscience studies of adults suggest that areas of the frontal lobes (particularly prefrontal cortex) and medial temporal lobe structures such as the hippocampus are crucial. Adults who have damage to the medial temporal lobe system have intact short-term memory (e.g. preserved digit span) but have difficulties in acquiring new long-term memories. Memories from before the neural damage are generally retained well, suggesting that the medial temporal lobes are responsible for the consolidation of memories rather than for their long-term storage. Long-term storage is thought to depend more on the association cortices, with prefrontal structures particularly important in retrieval (Tulving, 2002) Prefrontal cortex is also likely to subserve working memory (Munakata, 2004). Munakata points out that computational modeling suggests that memory will be fractionated, as there is a computational trade-off between fast learning and slow learning. A system that specializes in learning rapidly is not suited to learning gradually, and vice versa. Hence memories that depend on rapid learning (e.g. a personal experience) will be subserved by a different system to memories that depend on incremental learning (e.g. the underlying structure of the environment, as instantiated by conceptual learning and semantic memory).

The hippocampus plays a key role in consolidating memories and in recollection, but the nature of its role is still debated (e.g. Eichenbaum, 2003). For example, one possibility is that the hippocampus plays a unique role in remembering both episodic and semantic knowledge. An interesting study of declarative memory in three children who had suffered hippocampal damage either at birth or in early life reported by Vargha-Khadem, Gadian, Watkins, Connelly, Van Paesschen, and Mishkin (1997) calls this account into question. Vargha-Khadem and colleagues studied Beth, who sustained hippocampal damage during a difficult birth; Jon, who suffered hippocampal damage during afebrile convulsions when aged 4 years; and Kate, who received toxic doses of an asthma drug at age 9, which caused seizures that left her profoundly amnesic. All three children were referred to the research team as adolescents because their parents complained that they were unable to remember the events of daily life. All three children were found to have lower than average development in terms of verbal and spatial intelligence, but to have memory quotients 16–20 points below their verbal IQs. Such a large discrepancy is indicative of amnesia in adults.

When given a variety of standardized tests, all three children performed within normal levels on tests of immediate memory but not on tests of delayed recall. All three children were also unable to remember the events of their daily lives, including conversations, visitors, and holidays, and had problems in remembering familiar environments, dates, and times (spatial and temporal deficits). **Structural imaging** of their brains revealed abnormally small hippocampi (bilaterally), with severely compromised function of the remaining tissue. Amazingly, however, this extensive damage had not interfered much with their intellectual development. All three children were in mainstream schooling, could read and spell at the level expected given their IQs, and had acquired the factual knowledge about the world that is typically called semantic memory. Thus while early hippocampal damage had had a devastating effect on the development of the children's autobiographical or episodic memory, it had not had a commensurate effect on the development of their factual knowledge, vocabulary, or comprehension skills. Vargha-Khadem et al. (1997) suggested that these children's neural damage made it unlikely that episodic memory is the only gateway to semantic memory. The children appeared to have a specific difficulty in forming context-rich episodic memories, but not in forming context-free semantic memories. Again, this points to the importance of incremental knowledge and distributed representations in the development of semantic memory.

Whereas the hippocampus is mostly developed prior to birth, the other medial temporal areas undergo important developments between 2 and 6 months, with crucial developments in the association cortices and the frontal cortex over the first 2 years of life (see Bauer, 2004, for a review). These neural changes are likely to be associated with changes in explicit memory towards the end of the first year of life, with further increases in the reliability and robustness of recall during the second year. As discussed in previous chapters, frontal cortex in particular continues to develop into adolescence and early adulthood. So, of course, does human memory.

Studies of the neural areas associated with the development of explicit memory in infants are just beginning to enter the literature. Bauer (2004) has argued that in general there is a good fit between the substantial changes in temporally ordered recall found in behavioral studies with infants and the neural data (which comes largely from animal and adult models). To study specific connections, she has carried out EEG studies with infants, using recall for the temporal order of events as her explicit memory task. For example, using the deferred imitation task with 9-month-old infants, Bauer, Wiebe, Carver, Waters, and Nelson (2003) recorded ERPs for recognition memory, delayed recognition memory, and recall 1 month later. When the infants first visited the laboratory, they watched three two-step event sequences, for example putting a toy car into an apparatus and then operating a rod to turn on a light. Each sequence was demonstrated twice, without the infant being allowed to imitate it. This experience was repeated on two more visits within the same week (the average gap between visits was 1.5 days). This was the learning phase of the experiment. Recognition memory for the learned sequences was then tested at the end of the third visit. The infants were shown pictures of the steps and end state of one familiar sequence and of one novel sequence. The electrophysiological recordings focused on activity between 260 and 870 ms following the appearance of each picture, termed a "middle latency or Nc component". The EEG was also recorded for the same pictures in a fourth visit one week later, to measure delayed recognition.

Bauer et al. (2003) reported that recordings taken on the third visit suggested that all the infants encoded the events. The Nc component showed a significantly greater negativity for the pictures of the novel sequence than for the pictures of the familiar

KEY TERM

Structural imaging
Neuroimaging to measure the structure rather than function of parts of the brain.

sequence, for all the babies. However, when tested for their recall of the event sequences a month later (using behavioral re-enactment), the babies fell into two groups. One group showed recall of at least one of the original three event sequences (46% of babies), as indicated by their accurate manipulation of the props used in the original events. The other group of babies did not (54%). Exploration of the Nc component at delayed recognition for these two groups showed that the infants who showed no behavioral evidence of recall after 1 month also showed no increased negativity to the familiar sequence after 1 week. This was suggestive of a failure of consolidation of the memories. The EEG at recall also showed group differences. The babies who recalled at least one event sequence showed a significantly shorter latency to peak amplitude for novel sequences. Bauer et al. argued that remembering was indexed by longer latency to peak amplitude, because of the reintegration processes associated with long-term recognition. Bauer (2006) has subsequently used EEG to demonstrate developmental differences in encoding. She reported that infants aged 10 months showed significantly larger ERP amplitudes compared to infants aged 9 months in the immediate recognition task used by Bauer et al. (2003). This was thought to be indicative of differential encoding. Bauer concluded that encoding and consolidation rather than retrieval are the significant sources of developmental change in early explicit memory.

Finally, the neural substrates for working memory appear to be very similar in adults and in children, with frontal and parietal areas of particular importance. For example, in a neuroimaging study of visuospatial working memory carried out with children aged from 9 to 18 years, Klingberg, Forssberg, and Westerberg (2002) reported age-related bilateral activity in the superior frontal sulcus and intraparietal cortex. Changes in working memory capacity (measured outside the scanner) were also correlated with increased activity in these two regions (both left lateralized). A strong feature of this study was that the working memory task used inside the scanner was performed as well by the younger children as by the older children. The working memory task was based on a 4 × 4 grid. Three red circles were presented sequentially in different portions of the grid, and then a final circle appeared. The participants had to decide if this final circle was in a location that had been occupied before. Age was correlated with increased brain activation during this task rather than with the amount of cortex activated. This suggests that there might be little change in the neural substrates recruited by visuospatial working memory with age. However, comparable studies of verbal working memory have not yet been carried out.

SUMMARY

This survey of some of the different types of memory that can be measured in children has shown that, whereas some memory systems develop with age, others do not. Little developmental change was found in recognition memory or in implicit memory, while large developmental changes were found to occur in episodic memory, autobiographical memory, and working memory. It was argued that these developmental changes in episodic memory may in turn explain some of the developments seen in other memory systems, such as the decrease in suggestibility found in eye-witness memory and the decline in "infantile amnesia". In general, older children provide more detailed and narratively coherent memories. It was noted that the increase in working memory capacity (memory span) seen with age may also result from the development of semantic memory, as the availability of a long-term memory representation of items seems to facilitate short-term memory performance. The *development* of short-term and long-term storage systems may thus be intimately linked, even though when measured in adults the two systems appear to be distinct (Baddeley & Hitch, 1974).

Despite the developmental changes noted in explicit memory systems, it was demonstrated that the episodic memories of even very young children represent both temporal and causal structure. This was shown using measures such as deferred imitation. Very young children can also remember distinctive events for long periods (over years), even though an important focus of early memory behavior is the development of scripts for *routine* events. Remembering is also embedded in larger social and cognitive activities, and so the ways in which parents and other carers interact with children influence the development of episodic memory. For example, mothers who use an elaborative conversational style tend to have children who have more organized and detailed memories. Talking about the past with family and friends also leads to the development of a personal history, facilitating the emergence of the autobiographical self. Language is also important because giving a narrative account of an event at the time that it was experienced seems to improve long-term retention. Although children can be susceptible to leading questions from adults, they seldom invent memories. In general, children's eye-witness testimony is accurate, and leading questions lead to inaccurate acquiescence to suggestions by the adult rather than to novel invention on the part of the child.

Cognitive neuroimaging of the development of different memory systems is in its infancy. However, there have been many recent imaging studies in adults. These studies have supported the cognitive view that the developed memory system is a fractionated system. Adult neuroimaging studies have also tended to agree concerning the localization of memory, for example with regard to the neural structures that are important for the different memory systems. From the few imaging studies available with children, it seems that there is remarkable similarity in the neural structures that support the different memory systems. For example, working memory in both children and adults depends on frontal and parietal areas. However, cognitive neuroimaging studies of children seem likely to contribute unique data to understanding human memory. For example, the study of children with very small hippocampi has suggested that semantic memory can develop normally without an intact hippocampus, whereas episodic memory cannot. In principle, neuroimaging studies with young children can also throw light on cognitive developmental debates, for example concerning implicit memory, strategy production deficiencies, the nature of expertise, and infantile amnesia.

CHAPTER 9

CONTENTS

Metacognition, reasoning, and executive function

9

Metacognition is knowledge about cognition. The idea that developing an awareness of one's own cognitive functioning might be important for cognitive development was first proposed by Flavell (1979). Flavell has defined metacognition as any cognitive activity or knowledge that takes as its cognitive object an aspect of cognitive activity. By this definition, metacognition encompasses factors such as knowing about your own information-processing skills, monitoring your own cognitive performance, regulating your own cognitive strategies to enhance your performance, knowing about the demands made by different kinds of cognitive tasks, monitoring the sources of your knowledge, and developing a theory of mind. Some aspects of metacognition are research domains in their own right. These include "metamemory" (knowledge about memory) and "**executive function**" (the monitoring and self-regulation of thought and action, the ability to plan behavior and inhibit inappropriate responses). Clearly, the link suggested by Flavell between metacognition and cognitive performance is analogous to the links discussed in Chapter 7 between metarepresentation and social cognition ("theory of mind"). In Chapter 7, we saw that to develop metarepresentations, children need to develop the ability to take a representation itself as an object of cognition. In this chapter we consider evidence that, to develop metacognition, children need to develop the ability to take cognition itself as the object of cognition.

Whereas research exploring metarepresentational development has emphasized the critical role of communicative activities involving sharing objects with others ("shared intentionality"), metacognitive development has been studied more in terms of the important mechanisms operating within individual minds (such as metamemory and executive function). The focus in metacognition research is on developing reflective awareness of one's *own* cognition rather than of the cognitions of others. As summarized neatly by Schneider and Lockl (2002), metacognition research is concerned with what the child knows about his or her own mind. Theory-of-mind research is concerned with what the child knows about somebody else's mind. Nevertheless, the two areas of research seem likely to be connected in important ways. This point has been made strongly by Kuhn (1999, 2000), who terms this general research field "meta-knowing". In an influential essay on the origins of metacognition, Wellman (1985) also emphasized the overlaps between metacognition and theory of mind, suggesting that metacognition consisted of a "large, multi-faceted theory of mind" (p. 29). In this chapter, we focus on the development of metamemory and executive function, and examine the effects of metacognitive development on reasoning and cognitive performance.

METAMEMORY

Metamemory is knowledge *about* memory. Traditionally, the development of metamemory was defined as the development of the ability to monitor and regulate one's own memory behavior (e.g. Brown, Bransford, Ferrara, & Campione, 1983). This was expected to enhance performance. As children came to understand more about how their memories worked, it was expected that they should become more sensitive to the fact that certain memory tasks will benefit from particular strategies, and they should also become more aware of their own strengths and weaknesses in remembering certain types of information (Flavell & Wellman, 1977). Similarly, as metamemory develops, children should actively begin to use mnemonic strategies to improve their encoding and retrieval of information in memory. So as metamemory improves, production deficiencies in memory tasks (see Chapter 8) should decline.

There are a number of different types of metamemory knowledge that a child can acquire. These include knowledge of oneself as a memorizer, knowledge of the present contents of one's memory, and knowledge of task demands. These can be considered aspects of declarative metamemory. Wellman (1978) argued that in addition to acquiring knowledge about these different metamemory "variables", the child needs to realize that intentional memory behavior is required ("sensitivity"). This kind of knowledge is more about procedures, requiring recognition that memory activity is necessary, and knowing the kinds of activity that may enhance performance. This has been termed procedural metamemory, "metastrategic knowing", or knowing "how" (Kuhn, 1999, 2000). Wellman and colleagues researched the metamemory variables, which they defined in terms of three different areas: knowledge about tasks (does this task require me to remember a lot of information, or a small amount?), knowledge about persons (the child's mnemonic self-concept), and knowledge about strategies (such as the benefits of rehearsal for memory performance). All variables were expected to make overlapping contributions to metamemory. Schneider and Lockl (2002) outlined further aspects of metamemory highlighted by subsequent research. These include "conditional metacognitive knowledge" (Paris & Oka, 1986); the ability to justify or explain your memory actions; and monitoring and self-regulation (Brown, Bransford, Ferrara, & Campione, 1983), encompassing the ability to select and implement memory strategies, to monitor their usefulness, and to modify them when necessary. Her analysis of metacognition led Brown to the view of the "competent information processor", a child with an efficient "executive" that regulated cognitive behaviors. Similarly, Pressley, Borkowski, and Schneider (1987) discussed the concept of the "good information processor", a child whose motivational orientation and general world knowledge enabled the automatic use of efficient learning strategies and procedures. Schneider and Lockl (2002) produced a taxonomy of metacognition summarizing developments in the field (Figure 9.1).

Metamemory variables: tasks, persons, and strategies

The different aspects of metacognition outlined in Figure 9.1 have been studied largely independently of one another. Older research focused on the development of knowledge about metamemory "variables". For example, Wellman (1978) gave 5-and 10-year-old children pictures of different memory situations to assess as either easy or difficult. An example of an easy situation was a picture of a boy who had to remember three items, whereas an example of a difficult situation was a picture of a boy who had to remember 18 items. In addition, some of the situations measured children's understanding that two different variables could *interact* to determine

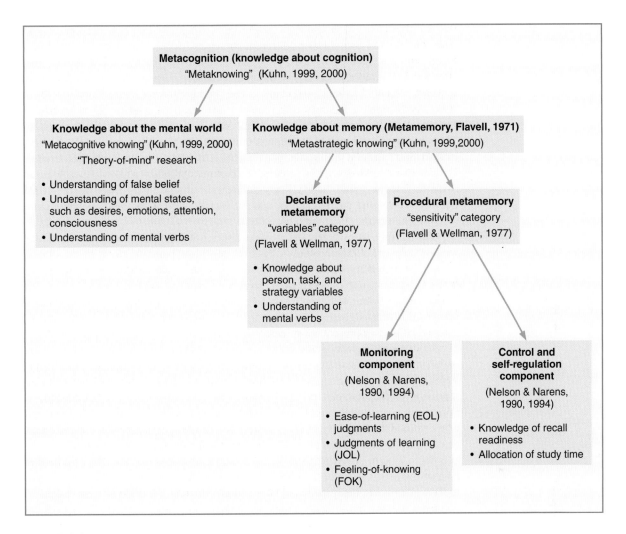

FIGURE 9.1
Schneider and Lockl's taxonomy of metacognition. From Schneider and Lockl (2002). Copyright © Cambridge University Press. Reproduced with permission.

memory difficulty. For example, a picture of a boy with 18 items to remember and a long walk during which to remember them (long recall time) was intended to be assessed as easier than a picture of a boy with 18 items to remember and a short walk during which to remember them (short recall time).

Wellman found that the 5-year-olds were as good as the 10-year-olds in judging the difficulty of memory tasks involving a single variable (such as 3 vs. 18 items). However, they were significantly worse than the 10-year-olds when the memory tasks involved interactions between variables. For example, the 5-year-olds tended to predict that both boys with 18 items to remember had equally difficult memory tasks, even though one boy had more time to remember the items than the other. The 10-year-olds rarely made such errors. Wellman concluded that the 5-year-olds could only judge memory performance on the basis of one of the relevant variables. He argued that an important aspect of the development of metamemory concerned the ability to *interrelate* the effects of different metamemory variables.

A different question about metamemory is when children first become able to assess the *relative* usefulness of different strategies for remembering. Justice (1985) asked children aged 7, 9, and 11 years to make judgments about the relative effectiveness of four alternative strategic behaviors: rehearsing, categorizing (by semantic category), looking, and naming. The children first watched a video of a child, "Lee", performing a memory task requiring the recall of a set of 12 categorizable pictures. The children were told that Lee would try to remember the pictures in different ways. For example, to demonstrate *categorization*, Lee grouped the pictures by semantic category (e.g. apple, pear, banana), and named each group aloud twice. To demonstrate *rehearsal*, Lee grouped the pictures at random and named each group twice (e.g. truck, apple, hand). For *naming*, Lee simply named each picture twice without rearranging them spatially, and for *looking*, Lee stared hard at each picture twice without rearranging them spatially.

The children were then asked to make a series of judgments about which strategy would "help Lee remember best". Each strategy was paired with all of the others, making 24 paired comparison judgments in all. The 7-year-olds made no distinction between rehearsal and categorization as the better strategy, but the 9- and 11-year-olds judged categorization to be more effective than rehearsal (which was the case in Lee's scenario). Justice suggested that some metacognitive awareness of the usefulness of categorization was present by at least 9 years of age.

More recently, Justice and colleagues have explored the contribution made by understanding how a strategy works to the efficacy of strategy use. Justice, Baker-Ward, Gupta, and Jannings (1997) showed children aged 4, 6, and 8 years video scenarios of other students trying to remember material in a variety of circumstances. For example, the video might be of a child trying to remember some pictures, and using verbal labeling of the pictures to help him or her. Alternatively, the video might be of a child trying to remember 10 things that had happened on vacation by looking at a photo album, in order to tell his/her teacher the following day. The child either labeled the events in order to aid recall ("tennis match", "museum", "shark" . . .) or looked silently at the pictures. The children viewing the videos were asked to comment on how the students shown were trying to remember, and how successful they were. Overall, four combinations of strategy and outcome were shown via these scenarios: labeling/high recall, labeling/low recall, no labeling/high recall, and no labeling/low recall. Before seeing the video scenarios, the children themselves received a picture recall task based on sets of 10 pictures. The children were told that they could do anything they liked to help them to remember, and any strategies that they used were noted by the experimenters. The children were also asked what they did to try and remember, and why these strategies might work ("How does — work to help you remember?"). The aim in each case was to examine the relations between metacognitive understanding and recall.

When their own memories were tested (recalling 10 pictures), the children participating in the study showed varying use of the labeling strategy, and varying success in remembering. In general, older children recalled more pictures than younger children, and labeling behavior (which did not differ with age) was related to recall for the older children only. Analyses of the children's understanding of their own strategic behavior showed that an important distinction was whether explanations given were mentalistic ("it helped get them in my mind") or nonmentalistic ("don't know"). Most children classified as nonmentalistic did not name labeling as a memory strategy (even if they had shown labeling behavior) and continually replied "don't know" when asked how their behavior had worked to help recall. Justice et al. (1997)

found that recall was higher for the children who gave mentalistic explanations, irrespective of age. Thus labeling was a more effective strategy for children who understood the behavior. The metamemory judgments that the children gave for the students shown memorizing in the video scenarios yielded similar findings. Children who gave mentalistic explanations of their own strategy use were more likely to demonstrate awareness of the causal relation between strategy use and performance as shown in the videos. Younger participants were in general unlikely to show awareness of this causal relation, but did show an understanding of the relationship between effort and success of recall. The data collected by Justice and colleagues suggest that older children can make more subtle judgments about the effectiveness of various memory strategies. Hence, although declarative metamemory is available in the preschool years, it also shows considerable development.

Self-monitoring and self-regulation

Another aspect of metamemory is "**self-monitoring**", which is the ability to keep track of where you are with respect to your memory goals. A related aspect is "**self-regulation**", which is the ability to plan, direct, and evaluate your own memory behavior. Both these aspects of metamemory involve executive function, and were initially studied together. More recently, the development of self-monitoring abilities has been studied in terms of ease-of-learning judgments, feeling-of-knowing, and **judgments-of-learning** (see Figure 9.1). The development of self-regulation has been studied in terms of the different aspects of executive function (e.g. planning and directing behavior). Clearly, adequate self-monitoring is necessary if self-regulation is to be successful.

An example of the integrated approach to studying children's ability to self-monitor and self-regulate their strategic memorial behavior is a study by Dufresne and Kobasigawa (1989). They examined whether 6-, 8-, 10-, and 12-year-old children could distribute their study time efficiently between easy and hard material. In their experiment, children were given two sets of booklets of paired-associate items to study. One set of booklets contained "easy" paired associates, such as *dog–cat*, *bat–ball*, and *shoe–sock*. The other set of booklets contained "hard" paired associates, such as *book–frog*, *skate–baby*, and *dress–house*. The younger children were given fewer sets of booklets, to equate task difficulty across age. The children's goal was to remember all of the pairs perfectly, and they were allowed to study the booklets until they were sure that they could remember all of the "partners". The way in which the children allocated their study time was measured by videotaping the study period, and then timing the portions of each period spent in studying either the easy or the hard booklets.

Dufresne and Kobasigawa found that the 6- and 8-year-old children did not differentiate between the easy and the hard booklets, allocating an equivalent amount of study time to each. By contrast, the 10- and 12-year-old children spent significantly longer studying the hard booklets, with the 12-year-olds spending a longer time on the hard pairs than any other group. This suggested that older children were better at self-regulating their memory behavior. Dufresne and Kobasigawa then divided the children in each age group into those who spent "more time on hard pairs" vs. those who spent "more time on easy pairs". This showed that the 8-year-olds, too, had some ability to allocate study time. More 8-year-olds spent "more time on hard pairs" than "more time on easy pairs", and this pattern was even stronger for the 10- and 12-year-olds. Only the youngest group contained more children who

Dufresne and Kobasigawa's (1989) study, which tested recall for "easy" and "difficult" paired-associate items, found that older children were better at self-regulating their memory behavior than younger children.

spent "more time on easy" problems than "more time on hard" problems, even though a separate test showed that the 6-year-olds could differentiate between the easy and the hard booklets. Dufresne and Kobasigawa argued that the younger children lacked the *metamemorial* knowledge necessary to enable them to allocate more study time to the hard pairs. Although they were able to monitor problem difficulty, they did not use this knowledge to regulate their study time accordingly. The conclusion was that while self-monitoring might be available to younger children, younger children do not necessarily use the monitored information to improve their subsequent memory performance.

Ease-of-learning judgments

One reason for this might be that younger children are less good at making predictions about their own memory performance (see Chapter 8). In the study conducted by Yussen and Levy (1975; see Chapter 8), half of the 4-year-olds tested predicted that they would remember all 10 items in a standard memory span task, but in fact recalled around three items. This aspect of self-monitoring is now termed **ease-of-learning judgments**, and is studied via paradigms in which participants are asked to predict their own ability to remember lists or texts. Participants' actual ability to remember these materials is then tested, enabling precise measurement of the accuracy of performance prediction at different ages. The classic finding is that younger children are always worse in ease-of-learning judgment paradigms (e.g. Schneider, Borkowski, Kurtz, & Kerwin, 1986). However, whether this is due to a difficulty in self-monitoring is unclear. One possibility is that younger children are more optimistic about their abilities, and that motivational factors like wishful thinking explain their unrealistic predictions. This possibility was investigated by Visé and Schneider (2000; discussed in Schneider & Lockl, 2002).

In their study, children aged 4, 6, and 9 years were asked to predict their own performance in either motor tasks (ball throwing and jumping) or memory tasks (memory-span tasks or a hide-and-seek task). The children were asked to make these predictions in two conditions. In a "wish" condition, they were asked to tell the experimenter the performance that they wished to achieve in the next trial. In an "expectation" condition, they were asked to predict the performance that they expected to achieve in the next trial. After completing the different tasks, the children were also asked to assess their performance. This post-task assessment showed that children of all ages could monitor their performance accurately, in both the motor tasks and the memory tasks. However, in general the children did not differentiate between their wishes and their expectations. Only the 9-year-olds showed a differentiation, and only for the jumping task. Visé and Schneider concluded that overestimation in younger children was due to their belief in the causal efficacy of effort. Wishful thinking occurs in part because children believe that if they try harder, then they will be able to perform as they desire. This belief in the efficacy of effort declines as children get older, leading Schneider and Lockl (2002) to conclude that ease-of-learning judgments are a better index of self-monitoring behavior in older than in younger schoolchildren.

KEY TERM

Ease-of-learning judgments
The ability to predict one's own ability to remember items, lists, or texts.

Judgments-of-learning

Judgment-of-learning tasks may provide a better indication of children's ability to monitor their own memory performance than the more traditional ease-of-learning judgments. In judgment-of-learning tasks, which usually rely on paired-associate learning of pictures, participants are asked to assess their learning: (1) immediately after studying a list of items; and (2) after a delay of a few minutes. In adults, the accuracy of judgments-of-learning is always better in the delayed condition, and judgments-of-learning on a trial by trial basis (e.g. asking participants for a judgment as they finish viewing each pair of pictures) are particularly inaccurate. Schneider, Visé, Lockl, and Nelson (2000b) studied judgments-of-learning in children aged 6, 8, and 10 years, using a paired-associate learning task. To equate levels of recall across age, the 6-year-olds were asked to recall lists of eight items (e.g. fork–mouse), the 8-year-olds were asked to recall lists of 10 items, and the 10-year-olds were asked to recall lists of 12 items. The children were told to try hard to learn the items, and were told that their job would be to recall the second picture in each pair when prompted with the first. In the immediate memory condition, children were asked for judgments-of-learning both immediately after studying each pair of pictures, and after finishing the list. After 10 minutes of unrelated activities, they were given the paired-associate recall test. In the delayed memory condition, the children were asked for judgments-of-learning for each item about 2 minutes after studying the set of pairs of pictures, and were then asked for a judgment-of-learning for the whole list. They also received the paired-associate recall test following 10 minutes of unrelated activities.

Schneider, Visé, Lockl, and Nelson (2000b) found that the accuracy of judgments-of-learning was much higher for children in the delayed condition than for children in the immediate condition, at all ages. This shows that even kindergarten children display accurate self-monitoring as indexed by judgments-of-learning, as long as judgments are delayed (mirroring effects with adults). Differences in the accuracy of judgments-of-learning for individual trials versus for the entire list were also found, again across ages. Children tended to be overconfident in their trial-by-trial judgments-of-learning and less overconfident when asked to make judgments-of-learning for the entire list. However, whereas the judgments-of-learning of the youngest children tended to overestimate actual performance, the judgments-of-learning by the 8- and 10-year-olds accurately reflected subsequent performance in the paired-associate learning task. Schneider et al. argued that developmental effects in judgments-of-learning were negligible. Both children and adults overestimate their performance in immediate judgments-of-learning, and both children and adults are fairly accurate when judgments-of-learning are delayed. Self-monitoring is hence quite proficient even in young children, although age effects in self-monitoring may emerge if task difficulty is increased. Schneider et al. suggested that developments in self-regulation rather than in self-monitoring might explain developments in metamemory in children. Certainly, this conclusion would fit the results reported by Dufresne and Kosibagawa (1989), where self-monitoring was accurate in the younger children but self-regulation was not.

Feeling-of-knowing

Although there are rather few studies of feeling-of-knowing in young children, the data converge with judgments-of-learning data in suggesting no significant developmental trends with age. There do not seem to be strong improvements in feeling-of-knowing accuracy as children get older. Rather, it seems that feeling-of-knowing can be dissociated from knowing *per se*. Feeling-of-knowing is based on the amount of information generated at retrieval, whether this information is correct or incorrect. In adults, feeling-of-knowing judgments are similar for correct information (information recalled that is accurate) and for errors of commission (information recalled that is inaccurate, leading to recall errors). Feeling-of-knowing judgments are much lower for errors of omission (information that is omitted, leading to recall errors). Similar effects appear to hold in children.

Lockl and Schneider (2002) investigated feeling-of-knowing in four groups of children aged, respectively, 7, 8, 9, and 10 years. The children were asked to give verbal definitions of words on the German version of the Peabody Picture Vocabulary Test (PPVT). The children were encouraged to continue until 30 words had been defined incorrectly (error of commission) or not defined (error of omission). Children were then trained on making absolute and relative feeling-of-knowing judgments. For absolute judgments, they were given words that had been defined either correctly or incorrectly, and were asked to rate how confident they were in selecting the correct picture for that word. For relative judgments, they were given a choice of two words, and asked to select the word for which it would be easier to choose the correct picture. Some pairs of words had both been defined correctly, some incorrectly, and for some one had been an error of commission and one an error of omission. Overall, for all ages, errors of omission were more frequent (64% of errors). The expectation was that stronger feeling-of-knowing judgments should be given to words that had previously shown errors of commission (incorrect definitions).

Lockl and Schneider then gave the children a second session in which absolute and relative feeling-of-knowing judgments were required for 10 easy words and 10 hard words. They found no age effects for either absolute or relative feeling-of-knowing judgments. Absolute feeling-of-knowing judgments were indeed stronger for errors of commission than for errors of omission, but were not as strong as feeling-of-knowing judgments for correct answers. In fact, feeling-of-knowing judgments were relatively low for all of the children in the study, and there was no increase in accuracy with age. As feeling-of-knowing judgments are also relatively low in adults, Lockl and Schneider argued that even young children possess some knowledge about their mental system when making predictions about future performance.

Studies of self-monitoring in young children using measures of feeling-of-knowing, judgments-of-learning, and judgments of ease-of-learning broadly suggest that self-monitoring by children is fairly accurate and does not develop significantly. It has hence been suggested that the important developmental process is self-regulation, or at least children's ability to link self-regulation skills to information gained from self-monitoring (Schneider & Lockl, 2002). Self-regulation will be discussed in detail in the section on executive function; studies of self-regulation in metamemory using measures such as allocation of study time (e.g. the time allocated to studying easier versus more difficult material, as in Dufresne & Kobasigawa, 1989) and knowledge of recall readiness (e.g. asking children to continue studying until they are ready for a test) suggest that younger children are not very good at using task-relevant self-regulation strategies. Effective self-regulation strategies are still developing into adolescence.

Source monitoring

Another aspect of metamemory is being able to attribute accurately the origins of one's memories, knowledge, and beliefs. The ability to make accurate decisions about sources develops markedly between the ages of 4 and 6 years. For example, Drummey and Newcombe (2002) explored source memory in children aged 4, 6, and 8 years by teaching them some new facts. An example of a new fact was "What animal cannot make any sounds?" . . . "A giraffe cannot make any sounds". Ten new facts of this kind were taught to the children, five by an experimenter and five by a puppet. A week later, the children were seen again, and the 10 facts learned previously were presented along with five novel facts of equal difficulty, and five facts expected to be already part of the child's knowledge (learned outside the experiment). For each fact, the children were asked how they knew that. If they could not answer, they were given a forced-choice recognition test asking them whether they knew this because of their parents, a teacher, the puppet, or the experimenter. Drummey and Newcombe (2002) reported that 4-year-olds correctly recalled 24% of the sources of the facts, compared to 47% and 40% for the 6- and 8-year-olds. The younger children were also much more likely to completely forget that they learned new facts as part of the experiment. The 4-year-olds falsely attributed the sources of their knowledge to their parents, the TV, or a teacher 60% of the time. By contrast, the majority of errors made by the older children were to forget whether it was the puppet or the experimenter who had told them the new fact. Drummey and Newcombe argued that the younger children were displaying "source amnesia", which is also found in patients with frontal lobe dysfunction.

Ruffman, Rustin, Garnham, and Parkin (2001) found higher levels of **source monitoring** in 8-year-old children with shorter delays. In their study, children aged 6, 8, and 10 years were shown a video about a dog named Mick. They then listened to an audiotape that repeated some of the events seen in the video, and also added some new ones. The children were then asked immediately about what had happened (e.g. "What do you think? Did the newspaper boy walk down the path to the house?"). They were also asked source questions about their knowledge ("What do you think? Did the newspaper boy walk down the path to the house in only the tape, only the video, in both, or in neither?"). Ruffman et al. reported that sources were identified correctly on 41% of occasions by the 6-year-olds, 62% of occasions by the 8-year-olds, and 70% of occasions by the 10-year-olds. They pointed out that the difficulties shown by younger children in attributing the sources of their memories had implications for eye-witness testimony (see Chapter 8). Children who cannot recall the sources of their memories may be more vulnerable to suggestibility.

In an experiment using more naturalistic events, Sluzenski, Newcombe, and Ottinger (2004) asked 4-, 6-, and 8-year-olds about the sources of their memories following either a delay of a week, or immediately. The naturalistic events were planting a seed, making a pudding, unpacking a picnic basket, and decorating a birthday invitation. Each event took around 5 minutes. The children performed two of the events with the experimenter, and imagined performing the other two events while participating in a script narrated by audiotape (e.g. "Imagine that you are going to plant a watermelon seed. Imagine that directly in front of you there is a brown pot to plant the seed in, a bag of dirt, a pair of grey gloves . . ."). When the children returned a week later, they were asked questions about the events such as "Did you actually plant a seed, or did you just imagine planting a seed?". The 4-year-olds showed accurate recall of sources for 66% of the events, compared to almost 100% accuracy for the two older groups of children. In a second experiment when source monitoring was tested immediately, over 90% of the 4-year-olds could recall whether an event had been real or imagined.

It seems likely that source monitoring develops between the ages of 4 and 8 years, and shows variation depending on the nature of the material to be remembered and its salience to the child. Younger children have more difficulty in

KEY TERM

Source monitoring
Attributing accurately the source or origins of one's memory, knowledge, and beliefs.

keeping track of the sources of their memories than older children. A number of authors have attempted to link these developments to developments in prefrontal cortex and executive function (e.g. Ruffman et al., 2001; Drummey & Newcombe, 2002). For example, it may be that the ability to identify accurately the sources of one's memories requires the ability to inhibit knowledge about inaccurate sources. At the time of writing, no firm developmental links have been demonstrated. Nonetheless, as will be seen below when we discuss metacognition and executive function, the hypothesis is a plausible one.

Metamemory and memory efficiency

Finally, an important question about metamemory is whether children with better metamemories perform better in different memory tasks. After all, if the development of the ability to monitor and regulate one's own memory behavior plays an important role in the development of memory *per se*, then children who are better at self-monitoring and at self-regulation should also remember more. Meta-analyses of the relationship between measures of metamemory and memory behavior suggest that the relation is indeed a significant one. In a meta-analysis of some of the key empirical studies of this issue (27 studies and 2231 subjects), Schneider (1985) reported an overall correlation of 0.41 between metamemory and memory performance. Schneider and Pressley (1989) reported an identical correlation in an even larger meta-analysis (of 60 publications and 7079 subjects).

Individual studies suggest the same conclusion. As we saw in Chapter 8, memory–metamemory relationships can be demonstrated even in preschool children (Schneider & Sodian, 1988). In Schneider and Sodian's hide-and-seek task involving hiding people in wooden houses (the doors of which could carry a semantic reminder cue, such as a picture of a tractor for a house containing a farmer), a significant relationship between conscious awareness of the usefulness of the semantic cues and successful memory performance was found in both 4-year-olds and 6-year-olds. Similarly, Kurtz and Weinert (1989) showed that older German children who scored highly on a general test of cognitive ability had more metacognitive knowledge (e.g. about the usefulness of clustering by semantic category for recall) than children who scored at average levels. The high-ability children also recalled more words in a list memory task in which the words could be clustered according to categories (e.g. emotions). The relationship between metamemory and memory performance also seems to be bidirectional (see Schneider & Bjorklund, 1998). Metamemory influences behavior, which in turn leads to improved metamemory. For example, a child's experience of the benefits of using a particular strategy, such as clustering words by semantic category, improves their memory performance and adds to their task-specific metamemory as well. A large-scale study of over 600 9- and 10-year-old children showed that individual differences in metamemory explained a large proportion of the variance in recall (Schneider, Schlagmuller, & Visé, 1998). Hence, as meta-knowledge about memory develops, memory performance is indeed enhanced.

METACOGNITION AND EXECUTIVE FUNCTION

Historically, research on metacognition took a number of largely unrelated forms. One aspect of study concerned the third component of working memory hypothesized by Baddeley and Hitch (1974), namely the central executive (see Chapter 8). The central executive was thought to play a central role in cognition via planning and monitoring cognitive activity. Although limited theoretically to monitoring the subprocesses of working memory (essentially the functioning and co-ordination of the phonological loop and the visuospatial sketchpad), the key role of the central executive was the top-down modulation of cognitive processes. A second aspect of the study of metacognition concerned the development of the "executive function", thought to be located in the frontal cortex. Executive function was also thought to involve the modulation of cognitive processes in a top-down manner. This aspect of metacognitive research developed out of studies with brain-injured patients with damage to frontal cortex, who exhibited poor strategic control over behavior (Milner, 1964). Similarities in the perseverative behavior of these patients and of infants performing search tasks were noted in Chapter 2. A third aspect of metacognition research concerned inhibition behaviors in young children. Young children are typically poor at inhibiting inappropriate behaviors. Interest therefore grew in the possible effects of poor **inhibitory control** on cognitive development, and the importance of individual differences in inhibitory control. These aspects of research have merged in the last decade or so into the field of executive function and metacognition. An organizing construct in this field is the assumption that younger children have inadequate strategic control over their mental processes (poor executive function), and that as they gain metaknowledge about their mental processes (metacognition, or the ability to reflect on their own cognition), strategic control improves. In general, the field is concerned with the development of conscious control over thought, emotion, and action.

One reason for the unification of these historically separate aspects of research on metacognition has been the development of cognitive neuroscience. The frontal cortex turns out to be important for working memory, for strategic control over behavior, and for the inhibition of inappropriate behaviors. An obvious question therefore was whether young children, who are not very good at strategic control nor at inhibiting inappropriate behaviors, would show the same kind of "executive deficits" exhibited by patients with damage to frontal cortex.

A typical "executive error" seen in adults with frontal cortex damage is perseverative card sorting. As discussed earlier (see Chapter 2), if a frontal patient has been sorting a pack of cards according to a particular rule (e.g. color) and the sorting rule is changed (e.g. to shape), then the patient finds it very difficult to change his or her sorting rule, and continues to sort the cards according to color. However, at the same time as making these consistent sorting errors, the patient tells the experimenter "this is wrong, and this is wrong . . ." (Diamond, 1990). It is as though the patient's behavior is under the control of his or her previous action (the patient is unable to inhibit the "prepotent" tendency to search by the old rule), rather than under the control of conscious intent. Clinical measures of card-sorting behavior, such as the neuropsychological test called the Wisconsin Card Sorting Test, typically require the patients to participate in many sorting trials, with a shift in sorting principle after each block of 10 trials. Patients with frontal lesions are found to make significantly more sorting errors and to achieve significantly fewer shifts than control subjects in the Wisconsin Card Sorting Task. Pennington (1994) has argued that "executive errors" occur when behavior is controlled by salient features of the environment, including prior actions, rather than by an appropriate rule held in mind. Executive errors are focused on cognitive inflexibility and perseveration, and will be discussed in detail below.

KEY TERM

Inhibitory control
The ability to inhibit responses to irrelevant stimuli while pursuing a cognitively represented goal.

The role of inhibition in metacognitive development was raised by Dempster (1991). Dempster argued that intelligence could not be understood without reference to inhibitory processes in the frontal cortex, and that individual differences in inhibitory processes could provide an index of the efficiency of frontal cortex in different individuals. He suggested that the critical aspect of many "frontal" tasks like card sorting was that these tasks required the suppression of *task-irrelevant* information for effective performance. For example, frontal patients need to suppress the "color rule" when asked to begin sorting the cards on the basis of the "shape rule". Impaired inhibitory functioning could thus also be an explanation for children's difficulties in the strategic control of their behavior. More recent research on inhibitory control suggests a particular role for representational conflict rather than simple response inhibition (e.g. Hughes, 1998; Carlson & Moses, 2001). Inhibitory control is also discussed in more detail below.

The role of working memory in metacognition was first raised by information-processing theories of cognitive development, although these theories did not address metacognition directly. Rather, these theories explored the general premise that children became capable of more sophisticated kinds of information-processing with development because of changes in working memory, and that this change in the processing components of working memory was the major factor in explaining developments in children's cognition. The dominant theories agreed that the amount of *processing capacity* that was available to the child changed with age, and caused developments in children's cognition. These so-called "neo-Piagetian" theories of cognitive development were effectively theories about the role of working memory in children's improved cognition with age.

For example, Pascual-Leone (1970) argued that processing space increased with age, and that as processing space ("central computing space") increased, so did the cognitive abilities of the child. A similar notion was advanced by Case (1985), whose model included a *trade-off* between "short-term storage space" (a retention component) and "operating space" (a processing component). Overall capacity ("executive processing space") was not thought to change with development, but the amount of available capacity was thought to increase as processing became more efficient (for example, via practice) and consequently took up less "space". A third neo-Piagetian model of cognitive development was proposed by Halford (1993), whose model centered on the capacity of "active" or "primary" memory. Halford defined primary memory as the memory system that held any information that was currently being processed, and he argued that the capacity of this system increased with development.

The common element central to the neo-Piagetian theories proposed by Pascual-Leone, Case, and Halford was the notion of processing capacity, which was a form of working memory or attentional capacity. These neo-Piagetian theories suggested that the size of available processing capacity placed an upper limit on cognitive performance, and that specifiable biological factors (as yet unknown) regulated the gradual shift in this upper limit with age. Cognitive development was explained by older children having more processing capacity than younger children, and qualitative improvements in cognitive performance were predicted with increasing age. These qualitative improvements were generally expected to arise from the use of more sophisticated information-processing strategies, which either increased processing capacity or were enabled by increases in processing capacity. For example, Halford (1993) argued that increases in processing capacity in working memory enabled children to use relational mappings of greater complexity. Case (1992) argued that the increased efficiency of working memory effectively created more processing capacity, thereby enabling the growth of reflection, which then made possible other cognitive advances (see Carlson, 2003). Working memory develops substantially between early childhood and adolescence, as discussed in Chapter 8.

Cognitive flexibility and executive function

In a large and systematic programme of research, Zelazo, Frye, and colleagues have investigated the development of executive function via the **Dimensional Change Card Sort task (DCCS)**. Using this task, they have shown that 3- to 4-year-old children can experience considerable difficulty in rule shifting tasks, just like frontal patients (see Zelazo, Müller, Frye, & Marcovitch, 2003, for an overview). In a now classic study, Frye, Zelazo, and Palfai (1995) introduced the "shape" and "color" sorting games. They asked children aged 3, 4, and 5 years to sort a set of cards into two trays on the basis of either shape or color. Each card depicted a single shape, a red triangle, a blue triangle, a red circle, or a blue circle. To play the "color game", the children were told that all the red ones went into one tray, and all the blue ones went into the other. The instructions were quite explicit: "We don't put any red ones in that box. No way! We put all the red ones over here, and only blue ones go over there. This is the color game . . .". After training in *both* games (color *and* shape), the children were tested for their ability to shift their sorting strategy (e.g. from color *to* shape) over three sets of five trials. On the first set of five trials, the children were given test cards to sort according to color. Having sorted this set, they were then told "OK, now we're going to play a different game, the 'shape game'. You have to pay attention". Five new test cards were then presented to sort by shape. Finally, five consecutive switching trials were administered, during which the children had to sort according to a new rule (shape or color) on each trial. Again, the instructions were quite explicit: "OK, now we're going to switch again and play a different game, the color game. You have to pay attention".

Frye et al. found that the 3- and 4-year-olds in their study experienced great difficulty in shifting their sorting strategy on the second set of five trials despite the explicit instructions from the experimenter. They typically sorted the cards correctly for the first five trials but then continued to sort by color (or shape) for the second five trials, perseveratively using the wrong rule. Performance on the final set of five trials, which required consecutive switching, was at chance level. By contrast, the older children (5-year-olds) were able to switch sorting rule in the second set of five trials, and were also able to switch sorting rule on a trial-by-trial basis during the last set of five trials. They did not show the "executive failures" characteristic of the younger children.

To make sure that the difficulties of the 3- and 4-year-olds were not due to the use of abstract and perhaps unfamiliar geometric shapes, Frye et al. carried out a similar card-sorting experiment using pictures of red and blue boats and red and blue rabbits. The children were again required to sort the cards first according to one rule, then according to a second rule, and finally to alternate between the two rules on the last set of trials. Essentially the same results as with the geometric shapes were found, although the 4-year-olds proved to be better at switching their sorting rule with the more familiar dimensions of boats and rabbits. Frye et al. also checked that the children's difficulties were not due to the use of the dimensions of shape and color *per se* by devising card-sorting tasks based on rules about number and size. Again, essentially the same results were found, with 3- and 4-year-olds showing difficulties when required to switch their sorting rule.

KEY TERM

Dimensional Change Card Sort task (DCCS) Card-sorting task that tests the ability to sort by different rules or dimensions.

On the basis of these findings, Frye et al. (1995) argued that children become able to make a judgment on one dimension while ignoring another between 3 and 5 years of age. Frye et al.'s results can also be explained by arguing that children cannot inhibit a prepotent tendency to use the pre-switch rule at will, even though the post-switch rule is known to them. To test this "executive failure" interpretation of Frye et al.'s results, we need evidence that the post-switch rules are indeed available to the younger children.

This evidence has been provided in a replication of the original card-sorting study using shape and color rules with pictures of flowers and cars (Zelazo, Frye, & Rapus, 1996). In this replication, Zelazo et al. found that 89% of the 3-year-olds who failed to use the new rule on the post-switch trials could verbally report the new rule. For example, when asked "Where do the cars go in the shape game? Where do the flowers go?" the children would point to the correct boxes, and then immediately sort according to the color rule when told "Play the shape game. Here's a flower. Where does it go?". Similar results were found even when the children received only one pre-switch trial. These findings suggested that 3-year-olds fail to use post-switch rules despite knowing these rules and despite having insufficient experience with pre-switch rules to build up a habit to sort on one dimension only. In a later study in which the children watched puppets sorting the cards, very similar results were found (Jacques, Zelazo, Kirkham, & Semcesen, 1999). The crucial point about making the puppets do the card sort is that the children no longer need to inhibit a prepotent motor response. They can simply judge whether the puppets are playing the game correctly. Jacques et al. (1999) found that the 3- to 4-year-olds that they tested consistently judged the puppets to be playing correctly when they persevered on the pre-switch rule. When the puppet sorted correctly, the children judged him to be wrong. Jacques et al. argued that the children clearly had difficulty in formulating what actions should be done when the rule was switched. These data support the view that the important factor in perseverative sorting is representational conflict rather than simple response inhibition.

Kirkham, Cruess, and Diamond (2003) argued that the reason why 3-year-olds had such difficulty with the DCCS task was that they were cognitively rather rigid. Having focused their attention on one aspect of the cards in order to sort them, they experienced great difficulty in redirecting attention to focus on what was relevant now that the rules had been changed. Kirkham et al. noted that even adults have difficulty in rule switching tasks, but their difficulty is shown by elongated reaction times rather than by sorting errors (Monsell & Driver, 2000). They then argued that children might be helped to refocus their attention if they were asked to relabel the cards before sorting them. In their experiment, 3-year-olds received the standard color- and shape-sorting tasks, but prior to sorting each card post-switch, the child was asked "What color is this one?", or "What shape is this one?". Hence the child rather than the experimenter labeled the relevant dimension post-switch. This led to 78% of the 3-year-olds tested performing correctly after the rule had been switched, compared to 42% in the standard procedure. Kirkham et al. also devised a way of making it more difficult for older children (4-year-olds) to exercise inhibitory control over their sorting. This was done by leaving the cards face-up in the sorting boxes, so that the previously correct dimension was very salient. In this "face up" condition, only 57% of 4-year-olds sorted the cards correctly post-switch, compared to 92% in the standard condition. Kirkham et al. (2003) argued that the critical feature of the DCCS was to inhibit a mind-set that was no longer relevant. Younger children have difficulty in flexibly shifting their attentional focus between conflicting representations.

By contrast, Zelazo and colleagues prefer to explain the patterns of performance observed in the DCCS as due to the ability to represent "if–then" rules (e.g. Zelazo & Frye, 1997). Older children are thought to be able to handle if–then rules of increased complexity. Complexity depends on the number of levels of embedding in a rule system. For example, if two rules apply to the same stimulus, as in the DCCS, then a new degree of embedding is required. During the first sort, the rules are simple. If the child is sorting by color, the rules are "if red, place there" and "if blue, place there". During the second sort, however, the new post-switch rules "if rabbit, place there" and "if boat, place there" must be used. Zelazo et al. (2003) argued that only older children could reflect on the incompatibility of the two sets of rules and generate a higher-order rule "If we're playing by color, then —, if we're playing by shape, then —". Age-related changes in complexity were thought to depend on changes in reflection (metacognition), which in turn were thought to depend on developments in frontal cortex. This account has been challenged, in particular by Perner (e.g. Perner & Lang, 2002). However, despite the differences in the forms of explanation that have been offered for DCCS performance, there is widespread agreement that the task provides a good measure of executive function in young children.

More recently, Zelazo and colleagues have argued for a distinction between "cool" and "hot" executive function (e.g. Zelazo & Müller, 2002). "Cool" executive function refers to "purely cognitive tasks", whereas "hot" executive function involves making decisions about events that have emotionally significant consequences. In adults, affective decision making is typically studied using gambling tasks. For example, participants are told that they can win money by choosing cards from particular decks. Typically, cards from disadvantageous decks provide higher initial gains but are associated with much larger losses over the course of the game. Cards from advantageous decks provide lower gains but also much lower losses, and are hence more rewarding overall. In a classic study, Bechara, Damasio, Damasio, & Anderson (1994) showed that adult participants typically prefer the disadvantageous decks at the outset of the game, but switch to preferring the advantageous decks as the game continues. Adult patients with lesions to orbitofrontal cortex keep selecting cards from the disadvantageous decks. These and other studies with adults suggest a link between orbitofrontal cortex and affective decision making. Kerr and Zelazo (2004) set out to study "hot" executive function in preschoolers.

To do so, they invented a gambling task suitable for children aged 3 and 4 years. It was also based on decks of cards, but the cards depicted either happy or sad faces (Figure 9.2). The children won sweets (M&Ms) for each happy face, and lost sweets for each sad face. Two decks of cards were used. Cards in the disadvantageous deck depicted two happy faces and one of zero, four, five, or six sad faces. Cards in the advantageous deck depicted one happy face and either one or no sad faces. Over the game (50 trials), it was hence more advantageous to select cards from the advantageous deck. The children were taught how to play the game, and quickly learned the correspondence between M&Ms and happy versus sad faces. They were then scored for the number of times out of 50 that they chose cards from the advantageous versus disadvantageous deck. Kerr and Zelazo found that the 3-year-olds made disadvantageous choices significantly more often than would be expected by chance. In contrast, 4-year-olds made advantageous choices significantly more often than would be expected by chance. At the individual level, however, a few 3-year-olds learned to choose cards from the advantageous deck. Kerr and Zelazo argued that "hot" executive function develops in a similar way to "cool" executive function,

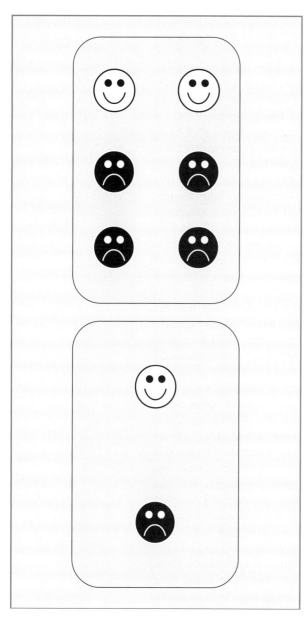

FIGURE 9.2
Examples of the cards used in Zerr and Zelazo's (2004) gambling task.

with important development between the ages of 3 and 4 years. Gambling appears to be a "conflict" measure of executive function, as the gains and losses in the two decks of cards conflict. Children must learn to respond in a way that conflicts with the salient response (here, choosing the deck offering big wins) to maximize their gain across the experiment. Again, the key developmentally appears to be managing conflicting representations.

Inhibitory control, planning, and executive function

Inhibitory control can be defined as the ability to inhibit responses to irrelevant stimuli while pursuing a cognitively represented goal (see Rothbart & Posner, 1985; Carlson & Moses, 2001). Carlson and Moses (2001) identify two types of tasks that have been used to measure inhibitory control in young children. One type of task requires children to delay gratification of a desire, for example by suppressing a prepotent response such as peeking at a gift. The second type of task requires children to respond in a way that conflicts with a more salient response. For example, in the "day/night" task, children are shown cards depicting either the sun or the moon. When they see a picture of the sun, they have to say "night". When they see a picture of the moon, they have to say "day". Performance in both of these types of task improves with age during the period from approximately 3 to 7 years.

For example, Kochanska and colleagues investigated children's ability to delay gratification of a desire in a longitudinal study of children aged on average 33 months when first seen, and 46 months when seen for the second time (Kochanska, Murray, Jacques, Koenig, & Vandegeest, 1996). These experimenters distinguished between "passive" inhibition (shyness, anxiety, fearfulness) and "active" inhibition or effortful inhibitory control. To measure the latter in young children, they designed situations in which children were tempted to violate particular standards of behavior. For example, the children were required to: (1) hold a sweet (M&M) on their tongue for up to 30 seconds before eating it; (2) wait for the experimenter to ring a bell before retrieving an M&M from under a glass cup (with the experimenter at one point lifting the bell but not ringing it); and (3) sit wearing a blindfold while the experimenter noisily wrapped a gift for the child, who was instructed not to peek. Scores on these tasks were highly correlated and were thus standardized and aggregated into one "home gift" score. Other tasks were also used, for example speaking in a whisper and moving a toy turtle slowly along a toy path. The tasks together formed an "inhibition control" battery. Kochanska et al. reported that their battery of tasks had good internal consistencies at both measurement points. The task battery correlated with maternal ratings of impulse control, and was developmentally sensitive. Kochanska et al. suggested that the tasks tapped a stable temperament variable in young children, namely inhibitory control. They also reported that girls outperformed boys at both toddler and preschool ages. Older children had better inhibitory control than younger children.

Inhibitory control in conflict tasks was studied by Diamond and Taylor (1996) using both Luria's tapping task and a day/night task. The aim of the study was to compare children's performance on two different measures of holding two pieces of information in mind while inhibiting a strong response tendency. In the tapping task, the experimenter had a wooden dowel, which she used to tap sharply on the table before handing it to the child. If the experimenter tapped once with her dowel, the child had to tap twice. If the experimenter tapped twice with her dowel, the child had to tap once. In total, 160 children, aged from 3 to 7 years, were tested. In the day/night task, on which 93 children were tested, the children were shown a black card with stars and were asked to say "day", and a white card with a sun to which they were asked to say "night". There were 16 experimental trials in each task.

Kochanska et al. (1996) reported that older children had better inhibitory control than younger children in terms of their ability to delay gratification.

Diamond and Taylor found age-related improvements in the tapping task, with group performance at around 65% correct for the 3½-year-olds and approaching ceiling for the 7-year-olds. A similar pattern was found for the day/night task, although this task was more difficult than the tapping task for most age groups. Performance in both tasks decreased in later trials, although particularly so for the day/night task (e.g. 85% of 4-year-olds tapped correctly on the first four trials compared with 67% on the last four trials, whereas 90% of 4-year-olds responded correctly on the first four day/night trials compared with 54% on the last four trials). Diamond and Taylor concluded that the ability to exercise inhibitory control over one's behavior developed between the ages of 3 and 6 years, with ceiling performance in 7-year-olds. They argued that most errors that they observed were suggestive of inhibitory failures (e.g. tapping many times instead of just once or twice) or of forgetting a rule or being unable to switch rules (e.g. always tapping once). They suggested that the growth of inhibitory control may be related to developments in frontal cortex.

A landmark study by Hughes (1998) created a battery of executive function tasks and gave them to 50 typically developing young children aged 3–4 years. Hughes set out to devise tasks that could tap the three principal factors thought to underpin executive function: inhibitory control, working memory, and attentional flexibility. To study inhibitory control, Hughes developed two tasks, a version of a hand game devised for adult frontal patients by Luria (Luria, Pribram, & Homskaya, 1964), and a detour reaching box based on the Windows task devised by Russell and colleagues (discussed in Chapter 7). In the hand game, children learned to make a pointing action and to make a fist. To play the game, both the child and the adult began with their hands behind their backs. They then showed their hands, and the children had to either make the same hand shape as the experimenter (*imitate*), or make the hand shape opposite to that exhibited by the experimenter (*conflict*). All children received both the *imitate* and *conflict* conditions, in counterbalanced orders, and were scored as successful if they achieved a run of six consecutively correct trials. In the *detour reaching* task, the children were presented with a metal box that had a large window in the front, revealing a platform containing a marble. The box had a yellow light and a green light. If the child reached directly through the window to get a marble, an infrared beam was activated and the marble fell through a trap door on the platform. However, if the yellow light was on, the child could turn a knob to break the invisible beam, and could then retrieve the marble. Children first learned this contingency, and became successful at retrieving the marble. The apparatus was then altered so that the green light was on. Now the child had to press a button which broke the beam in order to retrieve the marble. The child was encouraged to get the marble, and the number of trials needed to achieve a criterion of three successes in a row was measured (up to 15).

To measure attentional flexibility, Hughes used a color/shape set shifting task of the kind devised by Zelazo and colleagues, and also a magnets task about making patterns. In the magnets task, the child was shown a color pattern comprising 18 circles on a card, in the sequence blue–blue–red, blue–blue–red, and so on. They were then given red and blue magnets, and asked to reproduce the same pattern on a steel rule. Scoring depended on the number of correct blue–blue–red sequences made. The working memory tasks comprised a visual search task and an auditory sequencing task. In the visual search task, the child was given eight distinctive pots on a tray, and was told to place a raisin in each pot. The tray was covered with a scarf and spun around, and the child was then allowed to choose a pot and keep the raisin. The (now empty) pot was then replaced, the pots were scrambled, the tray was spun again, and the child could choose another pot. The goal was to keep selecting baited pots, to gain all the raisins, and the children were reminded on each trial to choose a pot that they hadn't yet looked in. The number of trials required to find all the raisins was scored. In the auditory sequencing task, the children were shown a book of nine pictures, each of which made a noise. After the children had checked each picture in this "noisy book", the experimenter named some of the pictures in a given order (either two items, three items, or four items). The child had to use the book to recreate the sequence of items given as a verbal list, by pressing the named pictures in turn. This generated a memory span measure for each child.

When performance on the different measures of executive function was inspected, it turned out that the 3- and 4-year-olds were at ceiling on the visual search task (finding the pots with raisins). However, effects of age (3 versus 4 years) were found for four tasks: detour reaching, Luria's hand game, auditory memory span, and the magnets task. To see whether distinct aspects of executive function could be distinguished, Hughes carried out a factor analysis controlling for verbal ability and age. This analysis suggested that the different tasks chosen did indeed load most strongly onto the expected factors of inhibitory control (detour reaching and hand game), attentional flexibility (set shifting and pattern making), and working memory (auditory span). However, when nonverbal ability was controlled as well, then the auditory working memory task loaded onto the same factor as the hand game task, while the detour reaching task had a factor of its own. Nevertheless, Hughes' data suggest that executive function can be measured in preschoolers, and that there are age-related changes in executive function in the preschool period. She concluded that executive function was a multi-faceted construct in young children.

Another important aspect of executive function is planning. Carlson and Moses (2001) gave a different battery of executive function tasks to 107 3- and 4-year-olds, and included a motor sequencing task intended to measure general executive planning ability. The executive function tasks were measures of inhibitory control, which were categorized as either delay or conflict tasks, comprising 10 tasks in all. The 10 tasks used are shown in Table 9.1. The conflict tasks comprised the day/night, grass/snow, bear/dragon, spatial conflict, and card-sort tasks. The delay tasks were the pinball task ("don't release the plunger until the experimenter says 'go' "), Kochanska's gift delay and whisper measures described earlier, the tower-building task, and a picture-matching task requiring the child to select a match from six extremely similar pictures (KRISP task). The motor sequencing measure of planning was based on a musical keyboard with four differently colored keys. The children had to play each key in turn using their index finger. After practice, they had to play consecutive sequences as fast as they could until the experimenter shouted "Stop!". Children were scored for the number of sequences that didn't skip a key or involve touching the same key twice.

Carlson and Moses reported that the children's scores on the 10 different tests of inhibitory control were moderately intercorrelated and appeared to tap a common underlying construct. The 10 measures were thus standardized and averaged to form a composite inhibitory control battery. Battery scores were found to be correlated with age, gender, and verbal ability, and also with parental scores of inhibitory control and with performance on the motor planning task. A factor analysis suggested that the different tasks in the inhibitory control battery did indeed fit the theoretical constructs of delay and conflict. Carlson and Moses (2001) concluded that inhibitory control could indeed be measured independently of age, gender, and verbal ability.

One possible drawback to the motor planning task used by Carlson and Moses (2001) is that there is no action to be planned other than playing the keyboard.

TABLE 9.1 Prepotent responses and correct responses on the inhibitory control tasks

Inhibitory control task	Prepotent response	Correct response
Day/night	Say "day" for the sun and say "night" for the moon	Say the opposite of what the picture shows
Grass/snow	Point to green for "grass," point to white for "snow"	Point to the color that is opposite to its associate
Spatial conflict	Press the button on the same side as the picture	Press the button that matches the picture, irrespective of location
Card sort	Sort by a previously successful dimension	Sort by a new dimension
Bear/dragon	Follow the commands of both animals	Do what the Bear says, but not what the Dragon says
Pinball	Release the plunger immediately	Wait for a "Go!" signal
Gift delay	Peek while E wraps gift	Wait without peeking
Tower building	Place all the blocks oneself	Give E turns placing blocks
KRISP	Point to a similar picture right away	Wait to examine all pictures before choosing exact match
Whisper	Call out the names of familiar characters	Whisper the names

E, experimenter; KRISP, Kansas Reflection-Impulsivity Scale for Preschoolers.

Hence the planning is not really cognitive in nature. To gain developmental information about the ability to plan more cognitively challenging tasks, Carlson, Moses, and Claxton (2004) carried out a second study of inhibitory control and planning, using three novel planning tasks. Forty-nine children aged 3 and 4 years were asked to complete the bear/dragon, whisper, and gift delay tasks described previously, along with a Tower of Hanoi planning task (Simon, 1975), a truck-loading task (Fagot & Gauvain, 1997), and a kitten-delivery task (Fabricius, 1988). In classic Tower of Hanoi tasks (Figure 9.3), disks have to be transferred across wooden pegs following a set of rules. Carlson et al. presented this as a "monkey jumping" game, with a Daddy monkey (large disc), a Boy monkey (medium disk), and a Baby Sister monkey (small disc). The pegs were described as trees, and the children were told that bigger monkeys could not sit on top of smaller monkeys in case they "smushed" them. Only one monkey could jump at a time, but smaller monkeys could sit on top of bigger monkeys. Various end states (e.g. all monkeys on the end peg) then had to be created by the children. In the truck-loading task, the children had to pretend to be postmen (mail carriers) delivering party invitations from a toy mail truck. Each invitation was colored differently, and had to be delivered to an appropriately colored house set along a one-way street. The child's job was to put the invitations in the truck in the correct order to ensure the shortest journey. Finally, in the kitten-delivery game, the children had to plan to minimize the distance covered in retrieving kittens from buckets placed around the room so that they could be delivered safely back to their mother. All three planning tasks were intended to require *if-if-then* reasoning as outlined by Frye, Zelazo, and colleagues (see the earlier discussion). For example, *if* invitations can only be delivered from the top of the stack, and *if* the pink house is last, *then* the pink invitation should be loaded first.

FIGURE 9.3
The Tower of Hanoi task.

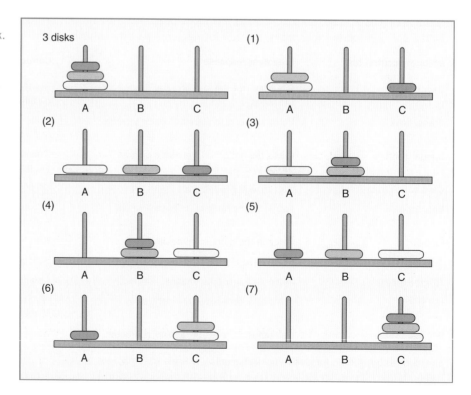

Carlson et al. (2004) reported that both 3- and 4-year olds performed at about the same level on the Tower of Hanoi and kitten-delivery tasks, but there were developmental improvements in the truck-loading task. No task showed floor effects. Performance on the truck-loading and Tower of Hanoi tasks was significantly related, but kitten delivery was not related to these tasks. When relations between the planning and the inhibitory control tasks were explored, no significant correlations survived controls for age and verbal ability. Carlson et al. (2004) concluded that planning and inhibitory control were largely independent constructs in executive function, and that both developed dramatically in the preschool years. This is consistent with the conclusions from metamemory research discussed above, that the core developmental factor is self-regulation. Efficient planning and efficient inhibitory control are required for effective self-regulation.

Executive function and theory of mind

As noted at the beginning of this chapter, it seems very likely that there will be important commonalities between developing reflective awareness of one's *own* cognition (metacognition) and developing reflective awareness of the cognitions of *others* (theory of mind). In fact, during the last decade there has been an explosion of research on this question about developmental connections. The major focus has been on the potential developmental relationship between executive function and theory of mind (e.g. Frye et al., 1995; Russell, 1996; Hughes, 1998; Perner & Lang, 2000).

Many studies have now shown that there are significant correlations between performance on executive function tests and performance on theory-of-mind tests such as the false-belief task, even when age and intelligence are controlled. In particular, measures of inhibitory control and of working memory show strong associations with false-belief tasks. Theoretically, this is believed to reflect the need to suppress irrelevant perspectives when keeping track of false beliefs (inhibitory control) and to keep multiple perspectives in mind (working memory; see Carlson et al., 2004). Perhaps surprisingly, planning does not seem to be related to performance in theory-of-mind tasks.

For example, in her landmark study, Hughes (1998) gave her 3- and 4-year-old participants six theory-of-mind tasks, two false-belief tasks, two tasks requiring an explanation of why a doll held a false belief, and two measures of deception. The false-belief tasks involved: (1) false location, which was a version of the Maxi and his chocolate task discussed in Chapter 7; and (2) false content, which was a version of the sticking plaster task discussed in Chapter 7. Hughes found that all the theory-of-mind measures were correlated with her measures of inhibitory control and working memory, whereas the attentional flexibility measure (based on set shifting) was correlated only with deception. Once age, verbal ability, and nonverbal ability were controlled, inhibitory control and attentional flexibility were significantly related to deception only, and relations with working memory became nonsignificant. Davis and Pratt (1995) used forward and backward digit span to measure working memory in 54 children aged 3–5 years, and also administered two false-belief tasks (the Smarties task and an appearance–reality task using a sponge/ rock), two false-photograph tasks, and a measure of vocabulary. They found that the backward digit span task was a unique predictor of children's ability to pass the false-belief and false-photograph tasks, even when age and vocabulary were controlled. Forward digit span did not show the same relationships. Carlson and Moses (2001) included four theory-of-mind tasks in their study of 107 preschoolers: two false-belief tasks (false location and false contents), an appearance–reality task, and a deception task. Children's performance on the inhibitory control battery (based on 10 tasks) was significantly correlated with their performance on the theory-of-mind battery, and this relationship remained significant after controls for age, verbal ability, and gender. No measure of nonverbal ability was taken for this sample. The planning measure (motor sequencing) was not related to performance on the theory-of-mind battery after controls for age and verbal ability.

Similar findings were reported by Carlson et al. (2004), who included more measures of planning in their battery of executive function tasks. In this study, the theory-of-mind tasks were false-belief tasks (false location and false contents) and appearance–reality tasks. When the relative contributions to theory of mind made by the inhibitory control measures versus the planning measures were explored, it was found that only inhibitory control was significantly related to theory of mind once age and verbal ability were controlled. Significant relations between planning and theory of mind did not survive in these more stringent analyses. Multiple regression analyses showed that whereas inhibitory control still explained significant unique variance in theory-of-mind performance when verbal ability and planning were entered into the equations first, planning did not explain significant unique variance in theory-of-mind performance when verbal ability and inhibitory control were entered into the equations first. Carlson et al. concluded that individual differences in the inhibitory control aspects of executive function rather than in the planning aspects were related to theory-of-mind performance. They suggested that conflict inhibition (i.e. inhibitory control tasks based on conflict rather than on delay) might lie at the heart of the relation between executive function and theory of mind. This interpretation suggests that the common link is the need to manage conflicting representations. Again, however, nonverbal ability was not measured in this study, so the extent to which individual differences in cognitive ability might explain the links found between executive function and theory of mind remains unclear.

Perner and colleagues have suggested a different explanation for the robust relation between executive-function tasks and theory-of-mind tasks (e.g. Perner & Lang, 1999; Lang & Perner, 2002). In a meta-analysis of studies conducted up until 1999, Perner and Lang (1999) showed that overall the effect size for the correlation between executive function and theory of mind (with age partialled out) was 1.08, a large effect size (effect sizes over 0.8 are considered to be large). They proposed that, at around 4 years of age, children come to understand that mental states are "causally efficacious". In other words, children come to understand that mental representations are causally responsible for a person's actions or behaviors. Lang and Perner (2002) compared children's understanding of why their knee jerked when tapped sharply by the experimenter (an involuntary reflex) with children's understanding of false belief in a false-location task. The children were also given the DCCS task and Luria's hand game as measures of executive function. In the knee-jerk task, the children were asked if they moved their leg on purpose. The goal was to see whether they understood that the knee jerk was not under their own intentional control.

Lang and Perner (2002) reported that all measures were strongly correlated in the 69 4-year-olds that they tested. Performance in the false-belief task was significantly related to performance in the knee-jerk task, the DCCS, and the hand game. Lang and Perner argued that understanding belief, understanding the involuntary nature of reflexes, and executive function as measured by the ability to inhibit prepotent responses all depended on a common developmental factor. The common factor was said to be the understanding of mental states as representations that are causally responsible for action. Although this is an interesting idea, it is undermined by the data now available showing that an understanding of false belief develops before the age of 4 years (see Chapter 7). There is emergent understanding that mental states determine action and behavior before executive functions are well-established, and before children understand the involuntary nature of reflexes. The 4-year-olds tested by Lang and Perner did not seem to understand the involuntary nature of reflexes, as 52% said that they *had* meant to move their leg on both knee-jerk trials. Also, some of the studies of "desire psychology" and "belief desire psychology" (discussed in Chapter 7) suggest that children are developing an understanding of how mental states are causally responsible for action well below the age of 4 years.

Cognitive developmental neuroscience and executive function

As demonstrated by the patient data discussed earlier, executive function is thought to be intimately related to the frontal cortex. As the frontal cortex is a brain region whose structure matures relatively late, and as the functional integration of other neocortical regions with frontal cortex is necessarily affected by the maturation of those regions, the classic view is that advances in cognitive development in the later childhood years are related to maturational changes in frontal cortex (Goldman-Rakic, 1987). Recently, it has been possible to explore this hypothesis directly, by giving children different executive function tasks while imaging their brain activity. A number of correlations between frontal activity and performance in executive function tasks have been reported.

For example, Bunge and colleagues gave a measure of response inhibition (a go/no-go task) and a measure of interference suppression (a flanker task, described below) to children aged from 8 to 12 years and to adults, measuring brain activity using fMRI (Bunge, Dudukovic, Thomason, Vaidya, & Gabrieli, 2002). Both tasks were based on simple visual displays involving arrows and geometrical shapes (Figure 9.4). In the flanker task, participants were asked to press a button on the left when the central arrow was pointing to the left, and a button on the right when the central arrow was pointing to the right. The central arrow was flanked by irrelevant shapes (e.g. diamonds: neutral trials). Interference was introduced by making the flanking shapes arrows that were pointing in the wrong direction (incongruent trials). Alternatively, the flankers could be arrows pointing in the correct direction (congruent trials). In no-go trials, the arrow was flanked by crosses. When crosses appeared, participants were instructed not to press any button. Behaviorally, the children were poorer than the adults in the incongruent and the no-go trials, although accuracy levels for the children were over 90%.

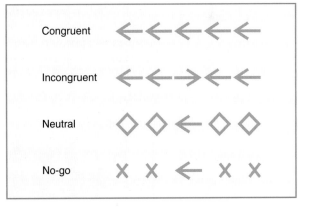

The brain imaging data showed that interference suppression in the children was associated with left prefrontal activity. In particular, left ventrolateral prefrontal cortex was more active in children when suppressing interference, whereas right ventrolateral prefrontal cortex was more active in adults. When those children best at

FIGURE 9.4
An example of the visual display used by Bunge et al. (2002). From Bunge et al. (2002). Copyright © 2002 Elsevier. Reproduced with permission.

suppressing interference were studied separately (i.e. by selecting children with equivalent behavioral performance to adults), more extensive activation of left ventrolateral prefrontal cortex was found rather than an expertise-related change to right ventrolateral prefrontal activity. For response inhibition (the go/no-go task), similar results were found. The children still failed to activate right ventrolateral prefrontal cortex, even when only those children whose behavioral performance was similar to adults were selected. However, during response inhibition, children who performed well did activate a subset of the neural regions recruited by adults, suggestive of different time courses for cognitive control in the two kinds of task.

A complementary study by Durston and colleagues used fMRI to study inhibitory control processes in children aged 8 years and adults (Durston, Thomas, Yan, Uluğ, Zimmerman, & Casey, 2002). They used a more child-friendly go/no-go paradigm based on Pokemon characters (Figure 9.5). Children were instructed to press a button in response to any character except Meowth ("catch all the Pokemon except for Meowth"). The number of "go" trials preceding a no-go trial was varied (one, three, or five go trials could precede a no-go trial). It was expected that children would find it more difficult to inhibit responding when more "go" trials were used. Behaviorally, the frequency of no-go errors did indeed increase, being 8% for one preceding "go" trial, 12.5% for three trials, and 14.5% for five trials. In this study, the children and adult participants activated the same neural regions during response inhibition. Activity was greater in children, and was focused bilaterally in ventrolateral prefrontal cortex, right dorsolateral prefrontal cortex and the right parietal lobe. In adults, the degree of activation in the ventral prefrontal regions was correlated with the number of preceding "go" trials, whereas for children it was high in all conditions. Clearly, this study differed from that of Bunge et al. (2002) in terms of the presence of adult-like right ventrolateral prefrontal activity. Task differences might provide part of the explanation, as the study by Durston and colleagues used a highly motivating task. In adults, right inferior frontal gyrus is considered critical to response inhibition in go/no-go tasks (Aron, Fletcher, Bullmore, Sahakian, & Robbins, 2003).

Two other tasks have also been used in neuroimaging studies of executive function development in children. These are the **Stroop task** and the oculomotor response suppression task. The Stroop task, in which participants are required to name the ink color that is used to present written words, is another classic measure

FIGURE 9.5
The no-go trial preceded by three go trials (other characters from the Pokemon series). The instruction to subjects was to "catch all the Pokemon except for Meowth" by pressing the thumb button on a button box. From Durston et al. (2002). Reproduced with permission from Blackwell Publishing.

go   go   go   no-go   go

4 sec

of frontal function that is performed poorly by frontal patients (e.g. Vendrell, Junque, Pujol, Jurado, Molet, & Grafman, 1995). For example, if the word *red* is presented in green ink, participants need to say "green", but word reading is more automatic than color naming. Because the competing color term "red" is activated by reading, saying "green" to the word *red* takes significantly longer than saying "green" if the letter string XXX is printed in green. Interference is not found in the other direction, that is, participants are no slower to read "red" when the ink color is green than when the ink color is black. Schroeter, Zysset, Wahl, and von Cramon (2004) used **fNIRS** (functional near-infrared spectroscopy) to compare brain activity in 10-year-old children and adults in a color-word matching Stroop task (Figure 9.6). For children, activity in left lateral prefrontal cortex was dependent on Stroop interference, but activity in right lateral prefrontal cortex was not. A similar pattern was found in adults. The left-lateralization observed in both populations was explained by the linguistic requirements of the Stroop task (i.e. the automatic activation of word-reading processes, which are left lateralized; see Chapter 10). Activation in dorsolateral prefrontal cortex was found to increase with development. Adleman et al. (2002) also investigated neural activity in the Stroop task, comparing children aged 10 and 14 years with 20-year-old adults in an fMRI paradigm. They also found a linear relationship between development and activation in left lateral prefrontal cortex, with additional activity in the left parietal cortex and left anterior cingulate.

The oculomotor response suppression task requires participants to voluntarily stop a reflexive eye movement to a prepotent visual stimulus and to move their gaze instead to a mirror location in the other visual field. For example, if participants are fixating a cross in the center of a computer screen and a large red blob appears to the right of the cross, the natural response is to move the eyes to the large red blob. In the oculomotor response suppression task, participants must instead move their eyes to the same (empty) location in the left visual field (an antisaccade). In adults and monkeys, making an antisaccade engages dorsolateral prefrontal cortex, posterior parietal cortex, and the anterior cingulate, as well as sensory and visual areas. Luna and colleagues gave the oculomotor response suppression task to children aged 10 and 15 years and compared neural activation to adults using fMRI (Luna et al., 2001). In order to isolate the neural activity related to response inhibition, prosaccade trials were also used, in which a green blob appeared. If the blob was green, the task was to move the eyes to look at the blob (i.e. the participants could make the natural saccade to the prepotent stimulus). The youngest children made many errors in the task, and it was only in adolescence that greater brain activity was observed in dorsolateral prefrontal cortex. Adolescents exhibited more activity in this region than either children or adults. Luna et al. concluded that the efficient top-down modulation of reflexive acts continues to develop into adulthood.

Overall, therefore, cognitive neuroimaging studies provide converging evidence for the importance of the maturation of the frontal cortex and the functional integration of other neocortical regions with the frontal cortex in the development of executive function. However, all studies to date are correlational. It is unclear whether structural developments in the brain enable the development of executive

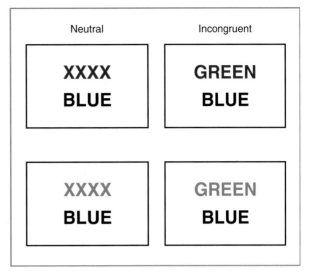

FIGURE 9.6
Examples of the trials for the color-word matching Stroop task. "Does the color of the upper word correspond with meaning of the lower word?" For the upper two examples, the correct answer would be "no"; for the lower two examples, the correct answer would be "yes". From Schroeter et al. (2004). Copyright © 2004 Elsevier. Reproduced with permission.

KEY TERM

fNIRS (functional near-infrared spectroscopy) Allows neuroimaging of brain activation by tracking blood flow via changes in hemoglobin.

function in children, or whether cognitive-behavioral developments in inhibitory control cause changes in the brain. To date, neural activity associated with planning has not been studied in children, although, as we saw in Chapter 8, developments in working memory are also associated with frontal and parietal regions. As more developmental neuroimaging studies are conducted, it should become possible to distinguish cause and effect. For example, longitudinal neuroimaging studies of children with superior executive function or of children with deficits in executive function might begin to disentangle cause and effect, as might studies of interventions targeted at improving executive function or metacognition.

METACOGNITION AND REASONING

To date, there has been rather little research on the potential effects of developments in metacognition on young children's spontaneous reasoning. This is surprising. In the few studies that have explored links between metacognition and reasoning, the efficiency of children's reasoning is usually markedly improved by encouraging children to reflect on their reasoning processes (e.g. Brown, 1978). One reason for the paucity of studies might be that inductive and deductive reasoning appear to be available early in development, and to function in highly similar ways in children and in adults. Despite early views that reasoning was age dependent and content independent (see Brown, 1990), it has become clear that children do not gradually become efficient all-purpose learning machines. Children do not acquire and apply general reasoning strategies irrespective of the domain in which they are reasoning (and neither do adults; see Goswami, 2002). Rather, inductive and deductive reasoning show remarkable continuity across the lifespan. **Inductive reasoning** and **deductive reasoning** are influenced by similar factors and are subject to similar heuristics and biases in both children and adults.

Traditionally, the development of reasoning and problem solving was thought to involve the acquisition of logical rules. Therefore, development was studied by seeing whether children could acquire isolated logical rules in completely unfamiliar situations. These studies were largely of deductive reasoning, as deductive reasoning problems can be solved without (or despite) real-world knowledge. In a deductive reasoning problem, there is only one logically valid answer. For example, if a child is given the two premises "All cats bark" and "Rex is a cat" (see Dias & Harris, 1988), there is only one logical deduction. Rex is a cat, all cats bark, therefore Rex must also bark. The logical deduction is counterfactual (it goes against children's real-world knowledge about the facts associated with cats), but counterfactual deductions are still logically valid.

By contrast, there is no logical justification of induction (Hume, 1748). Inductive inferences may not be logically valid, but they are still very useful in human reasoning. Generalizing on the basis of a known example, making an inductive inference from a particular premise, or drawing an analogy are all examples of inductive reasoning. Conceptual development involves reasoning on the basis of known examples, and as we saw in Chapter 4, this kind of induction is taken for granted in young children. Even babies can make inductive inferences and create perceptual and conceptual prototypes (see also Chapter 2). The most important constraint on inductive reasoning is similarity. A typical inductive reasoning problem might take the form "Humans have spleens. Dogs have spleens. Do rabbits have spleens?" (see Carey, 1985). In the absence of any knowledge about spleens, it is impossible to know whether rabbits have spleens. However, as two other mammals apparently have spleens, it seems likely that rabbits might have spleens too. If the problem had been phrased as "Dogs have spleens. Bees have spleens. Do humans have spleens?", then the induction becomes less intuitively compelling. Humans are reasonably similar to dogs but they are not similar to bees. Perhaps humans don't have spleens? As we will see, the development of inductive reasoning has been studied most comprehensively in terms of the ability to reason by analogy. The ability to make inductive generalizations from examples has been accepted as early developing, but has been argued to be distinct from analogy. This is because inductive generalizations can be made on the basis of similarities in appearance ("surface similarity"), whereas the core to reasoning by analogy is relational similarity. The hallmark of **analogical reasoning** has been seen as the ability to apply the *relational similarity constraint* (Goswami, 1992), that is, to constrain inductive inferences on the basis of relational similarity.

KEY TERM

Analogical reasoning
The ability to reason from a familiar or known problem to a novel one by identifying relational correspondences between the two.

Reasoning by analogy

Analogical induction plays an important role in the history of science. An early example of reasoning by analogy was Archimedes' insight into the value of using water displacement to quantify mass when comparing different substances. According to the story (see Goswami, 1992), Archimedes had been asked to calculate whether base metal had been substituted for gold in an ornate and intricately designed crown that had been commissioned by his king. Archimedes knew the weight per volume of pure gold, but the crown was so ornate that he could not measure its volume. Unable to reach a solution, he went home and had a bath. According to the legend, he then cried "Eureka, I've got it". When he stepped into his bath, he had noticed that his body displaced a certain volume of water. By making an analogy between his body and the crown, the mathematical solution to calculating the gold in the crown became available: immerse the crown in water and see whether the volume of water that was displaced was equivalent to that displaced by pure gold. This kind of "insight" is a classic example of inductive reasoning.

Analogies are used whenever we recall familiar past situations in order to deal with novel ones, whether metacognitively (via effort) or not. When reasoning by analogy "We face a situation, we recall a similar situation, we match them up, we reason, and we learn" (Winston, 1980). To solve a new problem by using an analogy, we need to find the *correspondences* between the previously encountered problem and the novel one. This enables us to "match up" the two situations. We then need to transfer knowledge from the familiar problem to the novel one. The identification of these correspondences usually requires *relational* reasoning. The solution to one problem can usually be applied to a different problem if similar sets of relations link different sets of objects in the two problems.

This point can be illustrated by thinking about some of the analogies that have led to new discoveries in science. One of the most famous was Kekule's (1865) new theory about the molecular structure of benzene, which he discovered on the

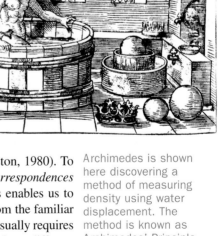

ARCHIMEDES erster erfinder scharpffsinniger vergleichung/ Wag vnd Gewicht/durch aufffluß des Wassers.

Archimedes is shown here discovering a method of measuring density using water displacement. The method is known as Archimedes' Principle. This kind of "insight" is a classic example of inductive reasoning.
© Archivo Iconografico, S.A./Corbis.

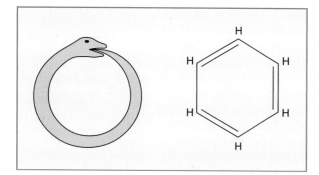

basis of an analogy to a visual image that he had of a snake biting its own tail (Figure 9.7; see Holyoak & Thagard, 1995, for other examples). The carbon atoms in benzene are arranged in a ring, which shares visual similarity with a snake biting its tail, even though the objects in the analogy bear no resemblance to each other at all. The similarity is purely relational—in this case, arrangement of an object or objects in a ring. Sometimes, however, there are similarities in the objects *as well as* in the relations in an analogy. An example is the invention of Velcro, which was developed in 1948 after Georges de Mestral noticed that burdock burrs stuck to his dog's coat because they were covered with tiny hooks (see Holyoak & Thagard, 1995). Velcro shares "surface" similarity (similarity of appearance) as well as relational similarity (capacity to stick tight via hooks) with burdock burrs.

Most research on the development of analogical reasoning has examined whether children can recognize relational similarities between previously encountered problems and novel ones (i.e. identify correspondences), and whether they can use relational reasoning to solve analogies (the question of transfer). Related questions have been how early children are able to make relational mappings, and whether children can map relational similarities in the *absence* of surface similarities (e.g. Gentner, 1989). I will focus here on the first two of these questions, as the related questions have been covered to some extent in earlier chapters. For example, research discussed in Chapter 2 showed that even babies can make rudimentary analogies, suggesting that relational mapping abilities are present from very early in life. Similarly, research discussed in Chapter 4 showed that surface similarities between problems are not necessary for young children to use analogies. The "personification" analogy that children use to help them to develop conceptual knowledge about biological kinds (making analogies from people to dogs and plants) is a good example. More detailed discussion of these points is available in Goswami (1992, 1996, 2001). Further, both of these analogical processes are improved by metacognition. Identifying correspondences and transferring relations are facilitated by encouraging children to reflect on what they are doing—a metacognitive strategy.

The use of relational reasoning in childhood

The question of whether children have the cognitive ability to make relational mappings has been investigated largely through studies using item analogies, which provide a pure measure of relational reasoning. In an item analogy, the relation between two items A and B must be mapped to a third item C in order to complete the analogy with an appropriate D term. For example, to complete the item analogy "bird is to nest as dog is to —?" (*bird : nest :: dog : —?*), children must map the relation *lives in* that links *bird* to *nest* to the item *dog* to reason that *dog-house* is the correct solution to the analogy.

Item analogies can be given to quite young children, as long as they are set in familiar domains (see Goswami, 1991, 1992). For example, a 4-year-old can be given the analogy *bird : nest :: dog : dog-house* by presenting the task in the form of a game about constructing sequences of pictures (e.g. Goswami & Brown, 1990).

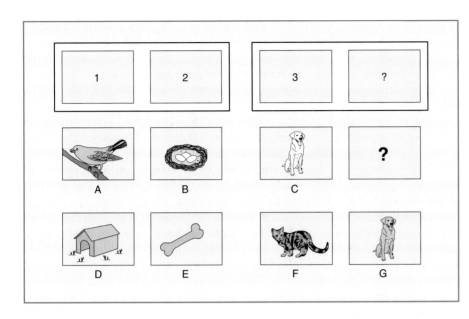

FIGURE 9.8
The game board (top row), analogy terms (middle row), and correct answer and distractors (bottom row) used for the analogy bird : nest : : dog : dog-house by Goswami and Brown (1990). Copyright © 1990 Elsevier. Reproduced with permission.

Here is 4-year-old Lucas trying to predict which picture he needs to complete the picture sequence *bird : nest :: dog: —?*, depicted in Figure 9.8.

> *Bird lays eggs in her nest [the nest in the B-term picture contained three eggs]—dog—dogs lay babies, and the babies are—umm—and the name of the babies is puppy!*

Lucas used the relation "type of offspring" to solve the analogy. The solution that the experimenters had intended, however, was "dog-house", as they had linked the A and B terms by the alternative relation "lives in". Following his verbal prediction, Lucas was shown the available completion pictures for the analogy, which did not in fact include a picture of a puppy. Instead, they depicted a *dog-house*, a *bone*, another *dog*, and a *cat*. Lucas was not interested in these pictures, as he was quite certain that his answer was correct:

> *I don't have to look [at the distractor pictures]—the name of the baby is puppy!*

In the end, when Lucas was persuaded to look at the different solution pictures designed by the experimenters, he decided that the picture of the *dog-house* was the correct response. This shows the strength and flexibility of young children's analogical reasoning skills. Of course, *puppy* was an equally correct solution to the analogy given the A and B terms in the picture sequence, and Lucas' defense of his solution suggests that he fully understood the relational mapping constraint that determined the correct solution. Nevertheless, he could use this constraint flexibly when faced with alternative solutions to work out another correct answer.

Analogical reasoning as measured by the A : B :: C : D item analogy format is thus available by at least age 4 (Goswami & Brown, 1990). If the same format is used to explore analogies based on causal relations, such as *cutting* or *melting* (e.g. *apple : cut apple :: playdoh : cut playdoh*; *chocolate : melted chocolate :: snowman : melted snowman*), then even 3-year-old children succeed in the item analogy task

(Goswami & Brown, 1989). It is difficult to use the item analogy format to demonstrate analogical competence in children younger than 3, however, because of the abstract nature of the task. With children younger than 3, it is necessary to devise ingenious *problem analogies* to show analogical reasoning at work.

In problem analogies, a young child is faced with a problem that they need to solve. Let us call this problem B. The use of an analogy from a previously experienced problem, problem A, offers a solution. The measure of analogical reasoning is whether the children can use the solution from problem A to solve problem B. We have already discussed one such problem analogy task, the "reaching-for-a-toy" task devised to study analogical problem solving in infants and toddlers (e.g. Brown, 1990; Chen, Sanchez, & Campbell, 1997). This problem analogy format has also been extended to 2-year-olds.

Singer-Freeman (2005) devised a series of analogies for 2-year-olds using real objects and models. Her analogies were based on the simple causal relations of *stretching, fixing, opening, rolling, breaking,* and *attaching.* For example, a child might watch the experimenter stretching a loose rubber band between two plexiglass poles in order to make a "bridge" that she could roll an orange across ("Look what I'm going to do, I'm going to use this stuff to roll the orange! Stretch it out, put it on . . . wow, that's how I roll the orange!"). After an opportunity to roll the orange by themselves, the children were given a transfer problem involving a loose piece of elastic, a toy bird, and a model with a tree at one end and a rock at the other. They were asked "can you use this stuff to help the bird fly?". The intended solution was to stretch the elastic from the tree to the rock, and to "fly" the bird along it. In a third analogy problem, the children were asked to "give the doll a ride" by stretching some ribbon between two towers of different heights that were fixed to a base board. Children in a control condition were simply asked to "help the bird fly" and "give the doll a ride" without first seeing the base analogy of rolling the orange.

Singer-Freeman found that whereas only 6% of the children in the control condition thought of the *stretching* solution to the transfer problem, 28% of 30-month-olds in the analogy condition did so, and this figure rose to 48% following hints to use an analogy ("You know what? To help the bird fly, we have to change this", said while pointing to the elastic). When the same hint was given to the children in the control condition, only 14% thought of the *stretching* solution. Although these performance levels may appear modest, they are comparable to the spontaneous levels of analogical transfer found in adults. Problem analogy studies conducted with adults typically find spontaneous transfer levels of around 30%, at least in unfamiliar problem scenarios (e.g. Gick & Holyoak, 1980). More recent work with young children (4-year-olds) also reports around 30% successful transfer when no metacognitive support is offered to help the children to notice the analogy (Tunteler & Resing, 2002).

Metacognition and reasoning by analogy

Of course, in problem analogy tasks children have to *notice* the analogy as well as to perform the relational mapping correctly. Noticing relational similarities or correspondences between previously encountered problems and novel ones may require children to reflect upon their knowledge, in other words, to exercise some metacognitive control. The ability to notice or recognize relational similarities between problems has been investigated via problem analogy tasks. The factors that influence whether young children notice relational similarities between problems were most extensively examined by Brown and colleagues (e.g. Brown, Kane, & Echols, 1986; Brown & Kane, 1988; Brown, Kane, & Long, 1989). For example, Brown et al. (1986) gave 4- and 5-year-old children the "Genie" problem invented by Holyoak, Junn, and Billman (1984) to try to solve, and then demonstrated the solution. The children's ability to notice the correspondences between the Genie problem and a series of analogous problems was then measured in a variety of different conditions, some of which encouraged metacognitive reflection.

In the "Genie" problem, a genie is about to move from one location to another. He needs to take some precious jewels with him, and his problem is how to move them from the old location to the new location without damaging them in any way. His solution is to roll his magic carpet into a tube, and then to roll the jewels through this tube. The children in Brown et al.'s study were shown the Genie problem via a toy scenario with toy props. They then enacted the solution with the experimenter, rolling up a piece of paper that represented the magic carpet, and rolling the jewels through the paper tube. In order to help the children to extract the *goal structure* of the problem, they were asked a series of questions to make them reflect on key aspects of the problem-solving process including "Who has a problem?", "What did the genie need to do?", and "How does he solve his problem?". The children were then shown another problem intended to be analogous to the genie's, which also involved toy props. This was the "Easter Bunny" problem. An Easter Bunny needed to deliver a lot of eggs to children in time for Easter, but had left things a bit late. A friend had offered to help him, but the friend was on the other side of a river, and so the eggs had to be transported across the river to this friend without getting wet. The idea was that the Easter Bunny could use an analogous solution to the genie by rolling his blanket (a piece of paper) into a tube and rolling the eggs across the river through this tube.

Brown et al. found that 70% of the children in the reflective questioning group noticed this analogy spontaneously. However, only 20% of children in a control group noticed the analogy by themselves. This control group had also experienced the Genie problem, but had not been questioned about the goal structure of the story. Hence they had not received the metacognitive manipulation. Brown's conclusion from this and a series of similar studies was that children found it easy to recognize relational similarities between previously encountered problems and novel ones as long as they had represented the relational structure of the previously encountered problem in memory. Questioning by the experimenter facilitated this representational process, as it encouraged the children to reflect upon and represent the important relations that enabled the character to achieve his goal. Brown then investigated the effects of metacognitive support on children's analogical reasoning by investigating the effects of experiencing a *series* of analogies, and of being *taught* to look for analogies during problem solving ("learning-to-learn"; e.g. Brown & Kane, 1988; Brown et al., 1989).

In Brown's metacognitive studies, two novel paradigms were devised, labeled the A–B–A–C paradigm and the A1–A2/B1–B2/C1–C2 paradigm. In the first paradigm, children were introduced to problem A and were asked to solve it by themselves (which they were typically unable to do). They were then given an easier problem B, which was actually similar in terms of relational correspondences to problem A. Following successful solution of problem B, problem A was readministered, along with gentle hints about its similarity to problem B. A novel problem C was then given, to measure spontaneous analogical transfer. In the A–B–A–C paradigm, the solution to be transferred was always the same. In the A1–A2/B1–B2/C1–C2 paradigm, the children were transferring three *different* solutions, one each for problem pairs A, B, and C. The solution to problem A1 was analogous to the solution to problem A2, the solution to problem B1 was analogous to the solution to problem B2, and the solution to problem C1 was analogous to the solution to problem C2. In this paradigm, Brown argued that the children were forming a "learning set" to look for analogies. In each case, the metacognitive component was implicit rather than explicit—the children had to figure out the similarities by responding to the hints from the experimenter.

For example, in Brown et al.'s (1989) investigation of the A–B–A–C paradigm, Holyoak et al.'s (1984) Genie paradigm formed the core of the procedure. Children aged 7 were given the Genie problem to solve by themselves with toy props including a real toy carpet, and when they failed, they were given the Easter Bunny problem described above. The experimenter helped them to solve the Easter Bunny problem before representing the Genie problem. The children were told that problem B would help them, as the two problems were "just the same". Finally, a novel problem C was administered (this was about a farmer who had to transfer ripe cherries across a fallen tree without damaging them). Brown and colleagues were most interested in performance with problem C. Success with problem C would indicate that the children had extracted "meta-knowledge" about trying to use analogies. Children's performance was compared to that of control children who had simply received the same problems in the A–B–A–C order without any of the help or hints given to the experimental group.

The results showed that 98% of the children in the metacognitive group solved problem C by rolling up paper, whereas only 38% of children in the control group generated the rolling solution. The children were "learning-to-learn", learning to use analogy even though they were never instructed explicitly in how the problems were alike. Similar "learning-to-learn" effects were demonstrated in the A1–A2/B1–B2/C1–C2 paradigm with even younger children. Here children aged 3, 4, and 5 years learned to transfer different solutions (stacking objects, pulling objects, swinging over obstacles) between problem pairs. At the same time, as they progressed through the problem sequence, they extracted an abstract notion of the usefulness of problem solving by analogy. When performance on the final problem, C2, was assessed, 85% of 3-year-olds, 95% of 4-year-olds, and 100% of 5-year-olds were successful in problem solving by analogy (Brown et al., 1989).

Brown's work shows that even very young children can extract meta-knowledge that facilitates inductive reasoning following hints, as long as they have rich conceptual representations of the domain being studied, and as long as they are interested in the subject matter. The early age at which analogies appear suggests that they provide a powerful logical tool for explaining and learning about the world. Analogies also contribute to both the acquisition of knowledge and the reorganization of knowledge. As children's knowledge about the world becomes richer, the structure of their knowledge becomes deeper, and more complex relationships are represented, enabling deeper or more complex analogies. This means that, as children learn more about the world, the type of analogies that they make will change. For example, as we saw in the chapter on conceptual development (Chapter 4), conceptual development depends both on the enrichment of knowledge and on making analogical mappings between domains (Carey & Spelke, 1994). To date, there are rather few research studies about the role of analogies in knowledge acquisition and knowledge reorganization. Nevertheless, analogical reasoning and relational mappings are widely acknowledged to play an important role in cognitive development (e.g. Carey, 1985).

Deductive logic and deductive reasoning

Another early-developing mode of logical reasoning is deductive reasoning. Problems that can be solved by deductive reasoning have only one right answer. The problem solver deduces this answer on the basis of the logical combination of the premises presented in the problem. For example, we use deductive logic to solve *syllogisms*, which are problems like the following:

All cats bark.
Rex is a cat.
Does Rex bark?

Given these premises, the only possible answer is that yes, Rex does bark. Although the premises in this example are obviously contrary to fact, as in the real world cats cannot bark, the plausibility or potential truth of the premises does not matter as far as the logical deduction is concerned. When children are given syllogisms to solve, the test of deductive reasoning is not whether the premises are counter-factual or not, but whether the child can draw the correct deductive inference. The critical test is whether the children can recognize that the premises, whatever they may be, *logically imply* the conclusions.

Syllogistic reasoning

Experimental research has shown that even quite young children can make deductive inferences about counterfactual premises. The problem about whether Rex barks or not was posed to 5- and 6-year-olds in an experiment by Dias and Harris (1988; see Table 9.2). In addition to "contrary facts" problems, such as whether Rex barks, Dias and Harris also gave children a selection of "known facts" problems ("All cats miaow. Rex is a cat. Does Rex miaow?"), and "unknown facts" problems ("All hyenas laugh. Rex is a hyena. Does Rex laugh?"). One group of children in the experiment was given the reasoning problems in a "play" mode. In this condition, toy cats, dogs, and hyenas were presented and were made to miaow, bark, and laugh by the experimenter. A second group was simply told the premises in the problems without any toys or demonstrations, and asked to judge the conclusion.

Dias and Harris found that the children in the "play" group performed at or close to ceiling on all the different problem types. They were able to reason deductively whether the problems were contrary to fact, used known facts, or used unknown facts. In contrast, the children in the verbal group only showed high levels of responding in the "known facts" problems ("All cats miaow. Rex is a cat. Does Rex miaow?"). These problems could have been solved by using real-world knowledge rather than by using deductive logic.

In a follow-up experiment using only the "contrary facts" problems, Dias and Harris tried

TABLE 9.2	Examples of the counterfactual syllogisms used by Dias and Harris (1988)	
"Yes" answers		**"No" answers**
(What noise do cats make?)		(Where do fishes live?)
All cats bark.		All fishes live in trees.
Rex is a cat.		Tot is a fish.
Does Rex bark?		Does Tot live in water?
(What are books made of?)		(What colour is milk?)
All books are made of grass		All milk is black.
Andrew is looking at a book		Jane is drinking some milk.
Is it made of grass?		Is her drink white?
(What colour is snow?)		(What colour is blood?)
All snow is black.		All blood is blue.
Tom touches some snow.		Sue has blood on her hand.
Is it black?		Is it red?
(How do birds move?)		(What is the temperature of ice?)
All birds swim.		All ice is hot.
Pepi is a bird.		Ann has some ice.
Does Pepi swim?		Is it cold?

presenting the premises verbally to *both* groups of children. Their aim was to rule out the possibility that the presence of the toy animals was acting as a memory prompt for the children in the "play" group. This time, the children in the "play" group were told that they should pretend that the experimenter was on another planet, and that everything on that planet was different. For example, the experimenter would say "All cats bark. On that planet I saw that all cats bark", using a "make-believe" intonation, and would then verbally present the syllogism. In these "make-believe" conditions, the levels of reasoning shown by the "play" group remained close to ceiling. In a later study (Dias & Harris, 1990), children as young as 4 were found to be capable of syllogistic reasoning. This effect was robust whether the premises were presented as referring to another planet, were presented using a make-believe intonation, or were presented using visual imagery. Dias and Harris concluded that young children were capable of deductive reasoning, even about counterfactual premises, as long as logical problems were presented in the context of play.

Leevers and Harris (2000) went on to show that the play context was not critical to children's capacity for deductive logic, however. Leevers and Harris gave 4-year-old children counterfactual syllogisms similar to those used by Dias and Harris, but the children in their study were simply told to *think* about the problems (e.g. "I want you to *think about* it. I want you to close your eyes and make a picture in your head so the *x* that you are *thinking about*, in the picture in your head . . ."). Examples of the problems used by Leevers and Harris included "All snow is black. Len is a snowman made of snow. Is Len white?", and "All ladybirds have stripes on their backs. Daisy is a ladybird. Is Daisy spotty?". The 4-year-olds showed good syllogistic reasoning, and this transferred to new counterfactual problems given 2–3 weeks later without the mental imagery instructions. Leevers and Harris argued that their manipulations may have improved counterfactual reasoning because they encouraged the children to process the premises mentally instead of dismissing them as absurd. This idea was supported by the types of justifications given by the successful children. These were largely theoretical in nature. For example, one 4-year-old girl commented "All ladybirds have stripes on their back. But they don't" before reasoning that Daisy's ladybird was not spotty. Syllogistic reasoning thus appears to be present by at least 4 years of age.

Conditional reasoning and the selection task

Another widely used measure of deductive reasoning is the **selection task**, developed by Wason (1966). In the selection task, the subject is told about a certain (conditional) state of affairs "if *p* then *q*". For example, the subject might be told "If a letter is sealed, then it has a 5d stamp on it". The task for the subject is to decide on the minimum number of pieces of evidence that are needed to validate the rule. The pieces of evidence available are usually *p* (e.g. a sealed letter, shown face-down), *q* (e.g. a letter with a 5d stamp, shown face-up), *not-p* (e.g. an unsealed letter, shown face-down), and *not-q* (e.g. a letter with a 4d stamp, shown face-up; Figure 9.9). Most adult subjects can solve the selection task when the problem is presented in a familiar context such as sorting letters in the post office (Johnson-Laird, Legrenzi, & Sonino-Legrenzi, 1972). The correct answer is that the minimum pieces of evidence required are *p* and *not-q*. This answer is given by the majority of adult subjects in tasks using familiar contexts, but in more formal versions of the same task performance can be as low as 10% correct. A typical formal version of the selection

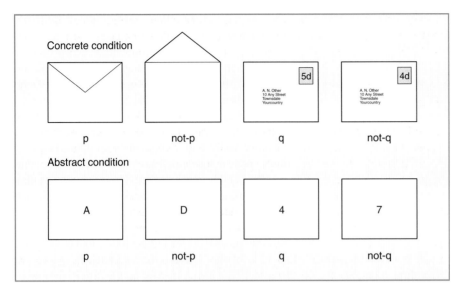

task is "if there is a vowel on one side of a card, there is an even number on the other side" (see Wason & Johnson-Laird, 1972).

Cheng and Holyoak (1985) have argued that this huge discrepancy in adults' ability to use deductive logic in the selection task depends on whether the selection task taps into familiar knowledge structures called *pragmatic reasoning schemas*. Pragmatic reasoning schemas describe permission scenarios in real life. For example, adults frequently encounter permission rules such as "If you want this letter to arrive tomorrow, it must go first class", "If you are 18, you can drink alcohol in a pub", and "If you are 17, you can legally drive a car". Children probably encounter even more permission rules than adults. These may include "If it is 9 o'clock, you must be in bed", "If you are wearing your school blazer, you must wear your school cap", and "If the whistle has gone, you are not allowed to stay in the playground". Following Cheng and Holyoak's logic, we can predict that children should also show successful deductive reasoning in the selection task if it taps into a familiar type of permission schema.

This idea was tested by Light, Blaye, Gilly, and Girotto (1989), who devised permission rules that would be interpretable to 6- and 7-year-old children. They used two rules: "In this town, the police have made a rule which says that all the trucks must be outside of the center" and "In this game, all the mushrooms must be outside of the center of the board". The first rule, which was designed to have underlying pragmatic force, was demonstrated by showing the children a game board with a brown center and a white surround (Figure 9.10). Pictures of trucks and cars were shown inside and outside the center area. The second rule, which was designed to be arbitrary, was demonstrated using the same board but with pictures of flowers and mushrooms inside and outside the center area instead of trucks and cars. Two trucks (or mushrooms) and one car (or flower) were always shown in the brown center of the board, and one truck (or mushroom) and three cars (or flowers) were always shown in the white surround.

The children's first job was to rearrange the pictures on the game board so that they obeyed the rule (e.g. moving the two offending trucks out of the town center).

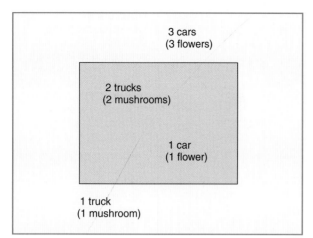

3 cars
(3 flowers)

2 trucks
(2 mushrooms)

1 car
(1 flower)

1 truck
(1 mushroom)

FIGURE 9.10
Schematic depiction of
the game board used to
test children's
understanding of
permission rules by Light
et al. (1989). Copyright
© 1989 Elsevier.
Reproduced with
permission.

The experimenter then tested the children's understanding of the rule by carrying out a potential violation. The violation was moving a picture of a car or a flower outside the center and asking if that disobeyed the rule (this was permissible). Next, the children themselves were asked to move a picture so that it *did* disobey the rule. Finally, a version of the selection task was given. The children were shown the game board with two pictures on it, both upside-down, one in the brown area and one in the white area. The children were asked: (1) which picture they would need to turn over to check whether the rule had been disobeyed; (2) whether the picture that they had turned over disobeyed the rule; and (3) whether the other picture disobeyed the rule. Light et al. found that 45% of the 6-year-olds and 77% of the 7-year-olds succeeded in answering these three components of the selection task correctly in the truck condition. However, only 5% of the 6-year-olds and 23% of the 7-year-olds succeeded in the mushroom condition.

These results suggest that 6- and 7-year-old children, like adults, can use deductive logic in the selection task as long as an appropriate permission schema has been activated. Furthermore, Light et al. showed that activation of a permission schema in a *pragmatic* context could transfer to an *abstract* context. Some of the children who were successful in the truck task were then given an abstract version of the selection task involving squares and triangles ("all the triangles must be in the center"). Fifty-nine per cent of the successful 7-year-olds and 30% of the successful 6-year-olds showed transfer from the truck task to the triangles. Light et al. argued that this showed that the children understood the logic behind their correct choices in the truck version of the selection task. The children were using their grasp of the pragmatics of permission and inhibition to help them to solve the task, and this understanding was then transferred to the triangles.

More recently, Harris and Nunez (1996) have shown that even 3- and 4-year-olds are sensitive to the pragmatics of permission and inhibition in the selection task. Harris and Nunez used a variety of story formats to present different permission rules, and then asked the children to select the correct picture from a set of four that depicted a breach of the rule. For example, in one study using familiar permission rules, the children were told: "This is a story about Sally. One day Sally wants to play outside. Her Mum says that if she plays outside, she must put her coat on". The children were then shown four pictures, a picture of Sally outside with her coat on, a picture of Sally outside without her coat on, a picture of Sally inside with her coat on, and a picture of Sally inside without her coat on (Figure 9.11). The children were asked to select the picture in which the protagonist was breaking the permission rule ("Show me the picture of where Sally is being naughty and not doing what her mum told her"). This required them to select the picture that depicted the combination of *p* and *not-q*.

The majority of children in both age groups chose the picture of Sally outside without her coat on. Similar results were found when the children were asked about novel rules ("Carol's Mum says if she does some painting she should put her helmet on"). Obviously, Harris and Nunez's paradigm is less demanding than the traditional selection task paradigm, as they required their subjects to select the picture that depicted the combination of *p* and *not-q* rather than to make an independent identification of *p* and *not-q*. Nevertheless, their conclusion that 3- and 4-year-old children are quite capable of identifying breaches of a permission rule seems a convincing one. Furthermore, they argued that children's grasp of permission rules was not restricted to *familiar* rules, as the link between condition and action could be quite arbitrary. Even so, the actions and conditions used by Harris and Nunez in their unfamiliar condition (painting, wearing a cycling helmet) were in themselves familiar to the children. The links were not quite as arbitrary as in the formal versions of the selection task used with adults ("if there is a vowel on one side of a card, there is an even number on the other side").

Metacognition and conditional reasoning

Markovits (e.g. Markovits, 2000; Markovits & Barrouillet, 2002) has argued for a role for metacognition in successful conditional reasoning by children. He has suggested important developmental links between conditional reasoning, working memory capacity, and inhibition. In general, Markovits accepts that younger children can solve conditional reasoning tasks. For example, Markovits and Barrouillet (2002) proposed that children did have an understanding of "if–then" propositions, that this understanding was inherently relational, and that rich linguistic and pragmatic experiences supported this understanding. They argued that conditional reasoning depended on relational mappings and was based on relational structures (in a similar fashion to reasoning by analogy).

For example, they proposed that when children were given a simple "if–then" statement (e.g. "If it rains, then the street will be wet"), they constructed a mental representation of the major premise based on prior knowledge (e.g. their prior experience of rain causing streets and fields to get wet). This mental representation represented relational structure, in terms of elements (streets, fields) and relations between elements (wetting by rain) in the environment. However, the mental representation was thought to be held in working memory, which has limited capacity. This capacity was also therefore affected by the cognitive demands made by retrieving the familiar relational structure and the cognitive demands made by inhibiting irrelevant aspects of this structure. Because retrieval processes were assumed to be less efficient for younger children than for older children, because younger children were assumed in general to have less relevant knowledge than older children, and because younger children were less good at inhibiting inappropriate information (as in the case of counterfactuals, for example), conditional reasoning overall was accordingly said to be less efficient in younger children than older ones. As can be seen, this developmental argument about conditional reasoning shares features with the development of both executive function (e.g. inhibiting inappropriate information) and metacognition (e.g. adopting efficient retrieval processes). A direct link was also assumed, as the ability metacognitively to reflect

FIGURE 9.11

The set of choice pictures used to test children's understanding of the permission rule "If Sally wants to play outside, she must put her coat on". From Harris and Nunez (1996). Reproduced with permission from Blackwell Publishing.

on one's own reasoning processes was assumed to aid reasoning efficiency. However, Markovits and Barrouillet (2002) also argued that developmental changes are to be expected in the number of relational schemas that can be processed by young children (following Halford, 1993). Given the difficulty of making a distinction between the number of relations and relational knowledge discussed earlier, this final assumption seems unnecessary.

SUMMARY

Metacognition, or developing an awareness of one's own cognitive functioning, is important for many aspects of cognitive development. The study of metacognition focuses on reflective awareness of one's *own* cognition, contrasting with the development of reflective awareness of the cognitions of others, which is theory of mind. Children with good metacognitive skills are "good information processors". They can use metacognitive strategies to improve their memories, for example by adopting efficient strategies for remembering. They can monitor their own performance, keeping track of where they are with respect to their memory goals, and they can evaluate their memory behavior. They can also self-regulate their own memory behavior, for example by planning and directing their own activities. Self-monitoring behaviors appear to develop relatively early. For example, there is little change with age in ease-of-learning judgments, judgments-of-learning, and feeling-of-knowing. Self-regulation appears to undergo more protracted development. The development of self-regulation is intimately related to the development of executive function.

Executive function refers to the control aspects of gaining awareness of one's mental processes. Strategic control over one's mental processes is thought to improve as metacognition develops. Executive function involves cognitive flexibility, for example in shifting attentional focus between conflicting representations. It also involves the ability to exercise conscious control over one's thoughts, actions, and emotions. Inhibitory control can be measured both by delay tasks (e.g. delaying gratification of a desire) and by conflict tasks (e.g. responding in a way that conflicts with a more salient response, as in the "day/night" task). A central factor in the development of inhibitory control appears to be the cognitive ability to manage conflicting representations. Planning is another important aspect of executive function, as is the development of working memory. Performance in executive function tasks is strongly correlated with performance in theory-of-mind tasks, and it is the inhibitory control aspects of executive function that appear to underpin this robust relationship. Although developments in executive function are widely linked to developments in frontal cortex, current neuroimaging studies cannot tell us whether structural developments in the brain enable the development of executive function, or vice versa. Logically, the changes documented in frontal cortex could reflect cognitive-behavioral developments rather than cause them. Ways in which neuroimaging might be used to disentangle cause and effect in cognitive development are discussed further in Chapter 11.

In contrast to executive function, inductive and deductive reasoning show remarkable similarities in children and adults. The same factors seem to govern successful reasoning in both age groups, and similar levels of spontaneous performance are found in both children and adults when unfamiliar versions of the different experimental paradigms are administered. In Chapter 8, we saw that similar effects have been observed in studies of memory, with remarkable continuity from childhood to adulthood in certain kinds of memory, such as implicit memory and recognition memory. We also saw that the effects on particular memory systems of using unfamiliar stimuli and paradigms were highly similar in children and in adults. This is probably a general cognitive phenomenon. Attempts to design "pure" measures of reasoning or memory, in which the reasoning or memory process is measured *independently* of the context in which it is required, are generally counter-productive to high levels of performance in both children and adults. When familiar, "child-centered" materials are used, then even very young children show efficient reasoning. They can reason by analogy, they can solve problems requiring deductive logic, and they can display successful conditional reasoning. However, metacognitive awareness and reflection improves performance for all these kinds of reasoning. Knowledge about your own reasoning skills, and actively monitoring your own performance, enable you to behave strategically to improve efficiency. "Meta-knowing" is important for cognitive performance of all kinds (Kuhn, 2000).

CHAPTER 10

CONTENTS

Reading and mathematical development

10

Various symbolic systems have been invented during the course of human development and are now instrumental in shaping cognitive development. Vygotsky (see Chapter 11) called these symbolic systems "**sign systems**", and pointed out that they have transformed culture and society. To participate fully in their cultural and social environments, therefore, children need to acquire these sign systems. The most ubiquitous symbolic systems are orthographic systems (e.g. the alphabet) and the number system (e.g. Arabic numerals). Other symbolic systems include art, musical notation, and maps. As Vygotsky pointed out, these symbolic systems enabled human cognition to develop beyond the constraints of biology. As well as responding to direct stimulation from the environment, humans can organize their cognitive behavior by creating and using symbols that can be responded to psychologically, such as print and Arabic digits. The acquisition of both print and Arabic number requires social transmission (e.g. by teachers), but also requires some cognitive prerequisites on the part of the child. After all, the original cultural invention of these symbol systems by our forebears was possible because of certain aspects of human cognition. This will be the focus of this chapter: the cognitive developmental origins of literacy and numeracy. Detailed treatment of their further development is beyond the scope of this book.

Cognitive neuroscience has contributed a number of studies of reading development and developmental dyslexia in children, and a few studies relevant to numerical development and dyscalculia. Whereas it is accepted that the acquisition of literacy is parasitic on language development, the argument has been made that the human brain has dedicated neural circuits for recognizing numerosity. This has led to a debate about whether number knowledge is "innate", and to claims that there are "two distinct core systems of numerical representations . . . [which] therefore do not emerge through individual learning or cultural transmission" (Feigenson, Dehaene, & Spelke, 2004). In contrast, reading is widely accepted to require individual learning and cultural transmission. Reading is not thought to be innate, and similarly language is no longer considered to be the product of an innate "language acquisition device" (LAD; see Chapter 5). As both reading and number are symbolic systems, it seems likely that number as a symbolic system builds upon the mental representations for objects and quantities identified by researchers like Feigenson et al. (2004). It is not clear that these mental representations are in themselves a number system. The perspective adopted here is that certain physiological/cognitive structures, on which number knowledge builds, are shared with other species. Although at present there are no data suggesting that other species share the cognitive structures upon which reading builds, it is possible that there are some physiological/cognitive evolutionary antecedents. For example, animals may be able to recognize some prosodic parameters of spoken

Apes produce calls with pure tonal notes which are reminiscent of the multisyllabic babbling sounds produced by 8-month-old babies.

language (e.g. domestic animals appear to show some sensitivity to the emotional content of language, which is prosodically determined). If evolutionary antecedents are found for the physiological/cognitive structures that support literacy, they seem likely to involve the prosodic aspects of auditory processing (which yield phonological information; see Chapter 5). For example, apes produce calls with pure tonal notes, repetition, rhythm, and phrasing that are reminiscent of the multisyllabic babbling sounds produced by babies at around 8 months (ape "singing"; see Masataka, 2007). Rats can distinguish Dutch from Japanese on the basis of prosodic (rhythmic) cues (Toro et al., 2003).

READING DEVELOPMENT

Different cultures have invented different symbol systems for representing spoken language. For example, China and Japan use character-based scripts, whereas most European languages use the alphabet. These different types of printed symbol share one core feature, which is that they are a visual code for spoken language. Reading is essentially the cognitive process of understanding speech written down. Meaning is communicated via print. Skilled readers access meaning directly from this visual code, but phonology does not become irrelevant. In fact, phonological activation appears mandatory during reading, even by highly skilled readers (see Ziegler & Goswami, 2005). However, languages differ in the units of sound that are represented by print. This has been termed a difference in psycholinguistic "grain size". Japanese characters (called *Kana*) represent individual syllables. Chinese characters (called *Kanji*) represent morphemes. The alphabet represents phonemes, although it does so with more transparency in some languages than in others. For example, Italian, Greek, and Spanish are all highly consistent in their spelling–sound correspondences: one letter makes only one sound. English, Danish, and French are markedly less consistent: one letter can make multiple sounds. Consider the letter "a" in English, which makes different sounds in the highly familiar words *man*, *make*, *car*, and *walk*. These two factors of phonological complexity and orthographic transparency lead to cross-cultural differences in reading acquisition by children.

Phonological awareness and learning to read

As we saw in Chapter 5, an important part of language acquisition is phonological development. Children need to learn the sounds and combinations of sounds that are permissible in a particular language, so that their brains can develop phonological representations of the sound structure of individual words. As might be expected, there are individual differences in the quality of the phonological representations developed by children. These individual differences turn out to be very important for reading development. The cognitive skills required for reading are usually described by the umbrella term "**phonological awareness**". Phonological awareness refers to a child's ability to detect and manipulate the component sounds that comprise words, at different grain sizes.

In Chapter 5, phonological development was discussed largely in terms of syllables and phonemes. We saw that the prosodic cues that are exaggerated in infant-directed speech, namely changes in pitch, duration, and stress, carried important information about word boundaries and about how sounds were ordered into words. We also saw that the physical changes where languages placed the boundaries determining phonemes were not random. Rather, general auditory perceptual abilities seemed to influence where these "basic cuts" were made. In addition to awareness of syllables and phonemes, an important level of phonological awareness for literacy acquisition is awareness of "onset-rime" units. *Onsets* and *rimes* represent a grain size intermediate between syllables and phonemes. While the primary phonological processing unit across the world's languages is the syllable, each syllable comprising a word can be decomposed into onsets, rimes, and phonemes in a hierarchical fashion. This is shown in Figure 10.1. The onset-rime division of the syllable depends on dividing at the vowel. In English, words like *sing*, *sting*, and *spring* all share the same rime, the sound made by the letter string "ing". The onset of *sing* is /s/, the onset of *sting* is /st/, and the onset of *spring* is /spr/. These onsets comprise one, two, and three phonemes respectively. However, in many languages in the world, syllable structure is simple. Syllables are CV (consonant–vowel) units. Hence for many languages, onsets, rimes, and phonemes are equivalent. Each onset and each rime in the syllable is also a single phoneme.

The development of phonological awareness appears to follow a very similar developmental sequence across languages. Children first gain awareness of syllables, then of onset-rime units, and finally of phonemes. Although infants can distinguish different phonemes (see Chapter 5), the ability to reflect on one's knowledge of the sound structure of words develops gradually, particularly at the phonemic level. Hence phonological awareness is also called **metalinguistic awareness**, highlighting the fact that the child needs to become consciously aware of knowledge that is already present in the mental lexicon. Whereas metalinguistic awareness of syllables and onset-rimes appears to develop before learning to read, direct tuition is usually required for phonemic awareness to develop. The intimate relationship between becoming a reader and becoming phonemically aware means that phonemic awareness develops at a faster rate for children who are learning to read transparent

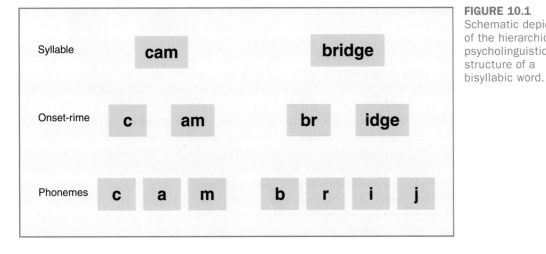

FIGURE 10.1
Schematic depiction of the hierarchical psycholinguistic structure of a bisyllabic word.

orthographies (e.g. Italian and Greek children) than for children who are learning to read opaque orthographies (e.g. English and French children).

Becoming aware of syllables

In a pioneering study, Liberman, Shankweiler, Fischer, and Carter (1974) devised a tapping task to measure syllable awareness in prereading children. They gave American children aged from 4 to 6 years a small stick, and asked them to tap once for words that had one syllable (*dog*), twice for words that had two syllables (*dinner*), and three times for words that had three syllables (*president*). A criterion of six correct responses in a row was required for children to be accorded **syllabic awareness**. This criterion was reached by 46% of the 4-year-olds, 48% of the 5-year-olds, and 90% of the 6-year-olds. The 4- and 5-year-olds were prereaders, and the 6-year-olds had been learning to read for about a year.

Another measure used to assess syllabic awareness in young children is the counting task. Devised by the Russian psychologist Elkonin (1963), in the counting task children are given plastic counters and are asked to use them to represent the number of syllables in words of increasing length. Treiman and Baron (1981) gave a syllable-counting task to 5-year-old prereaders. For example, if the experimenter said "butter", the child had to set out two counters. Treiman and Baron (1981) also reported good syllable awareness in these prereaders. Treiman and Zukowski (1991) devised a same–different task to assess syllable-level skills. In this task, the children were introduced to a puppet who felt happy when he heard two words that had some of the same sounds in them. The children had to listen to pairs of words like "hammer–hammock" and "compete–repeat", repeat them, and then decide whether the puppet would like them. The first pair of words shares the first syllable, and the second pair of words shares the second syllable, so the puppet should like both of these pairs. In contrast, pairs of words like "delight–unique" and "plastic–heavy" do not share sounds, so the puppet should dislike these pairs. Treiman and Zukowski reported that 100% of 5-year-olds, 90% of 6-year-olds, and 100% of 7-year-olds succeeded in this task.

These different tasks suggest that syllable awareness has developed in young children before they learn to read. Similar data has been found in deletion tasks (deleting a syllable from a word, e.g. "party–part"; see Bruce, 1964); in tasks requiring children to say "just a little bit" of a word (e.g. "Peter–Pete"; see Fox & Routh, 1975); and blending tasks (blending together two syllables to form a word, e.g. "sis" + "ter" makes *sister*; Anthony, Lonigan, Burgess, Driscoll, Phillips, & Cantor 2002). These tasks have been given to children as young as 3 years of age, who perform above chance at the syllable level. Clearly, there are some task-dependent factors, as the success level seems to vary with the different tasks. For example, same–different judgment tasks appear to be easier than tapping tasks. However, without giving a range of tasks to the *same children*, it is difficult to be sure about the relative cognitive demands made by tasks like tapping, counting, blending, and same–different judgment. The key finding is that at the syllable level, children as young as 3 years perform at above-chance levels in *all* of these tasks.

Similar results are found in other languages. For example, Cossu, Shankweiler, Liberman, Katz, and Tola (1988) gave the *tapping* task to Italian prereaders aged 4 and 5 years, and to schoolchildren being taught to read, aged 7–8 years. The children were asked to tap once for each syllable in words like "*gatto*", "*melone*", and "*termometro*". Syllable awareness was shown by 67% of the 4-year-olds, 80% of the 5-year-olds, and 100% of the school-age sample. Durgunoglu and Oney (1999) gave the tapping task to Turkish kindergartners. Performance was 94% correct. Hoien, Lundberg, Stanovich, and Bjaalid (1995) gave the *syllable-counting* task to 128 Norwegian preschoolers aged on average 6 years 11 months. For the syllable task, the children had to make pencil marks for each syllable in a word (e.g. "telephone" = three marks). The children performed at 83% correct. Counting tasks were also given to German preschoolers by Wimmer, Landerl, Linortner, and Hummer (1991) and to French kindergartners by Demont and Gombert (1996). The German preschoolers performed at 81% correct in the syllable-counting task, and the French children performed at 69% correct. Durgunoglu, Nagy, and Hancin-Bhatt (1993) used a blending task to assess phonological awareness at the syllable level in Spanish-speaking children living in the USA. The children were asked to blend pairs of syllables into words (e.g. "do-ce"). Performance was 85% correct. Hence, just like English-speaking children, Italian, Norwegian, French, Turkish, Spanish, and German children seem to have good syllable awareness before receiving literacy teaching.

"Hey, diddle, diddle! The cat and the fiddle, the cow jumped over the moon". The nursery rhyme may be helpful in establishing onset-rime awareness in preschool children.

Becoming aware of onsets and rimes

As the nursery rhyme is an intimate part of an English-speaking childhood, it might be expected that **onset-rime awareness** is also well-developed in young children prior to schooling. Popular nursery rhymes have strong rhythms that emphasize syllabification ("HUMP-ty DUMP-ty sat on a wall"), and many nursery rhymes contrast rhyming words in ways that distinguish the onset from the rime (e.g. "Twinkle Twinkle Little Star" rhymes "star" with "are"; "Incy Wincy Spider" rhymes "spout" with "out"). The most widely used measure of onset-rime awareness in preschool children is the oddity task devised by Bradley and Bryant (1978). In this task, children are asked to select the "odd word out" of a group of three words on the basis of either the initial sound, the medial sound, or the final sound (e.g. bus, bun, *rug*; *pin*, bun, gun; top, *doll*, hop). The initial sound task can be solved on the basis of the different onset, and the medial and final sound tasks can be solved on the basis of the different rime. Bradley and Bryant (1983) gave the oddity task to around 400 preschool English children aged 4 and 5 years. The children scored above chance levels in both the onset and rime versions of the task, with average performance being 56% correct with onsets and 71% correct with rimes.

Another task used to measure onset-rime awareness is the same–different judgment task. For example, Treiman and Zukowski (1991) asked their children whether the puppet would like word pairs like "plank–plea" (shared onset), and "spit–wit" (shared rime). Fifty-six per cent of the 5-year-olds, 74% of the 6-year-olds, and 100% of the 7-year-olds made accurate judgments. Blending and segmentation have also been used to study onset-rime awareness, with similar results. For example, Anthony et al. (2003) asked children to help a puppet to blend units like "h" and "at" into *hat*. Children can also be asked to complete nursery rhymes, enabling younger children to be tested. Bryant, Bradley, Maclean, and Crossland (1989) asked 3-year-olds to complete familiar nursery rhymes such as "Jack and Jill went up the —? [hill]". Five nursery rhymes were used for testing, and only one of the 64 3-year-olds in the study knew none of these nursery rhymes. On average, the children knew about half of the nursery rhymes (they could score 1 for partially completing the rhymes and 2 for fully completing them, making a total possible score of 10; the mean score for the group was 4.5). Onset-rime awareness is clearly present in English-speaking children prior to schooling.

KEY TERM

Onset-rime awareness
Dividing the syllable at the vowel, as in s–ing, str–ing.

Again, rhyme awareness is also found prior to literacy tuition in other languages. Chukovsky (1963) collected a large corpus of Russian children's language games and poems, and noted that the children were fascinated by rhymes. For example, Tania, aged 2½ years, made up the following poem:

> *Ilk, silk, tilk*
> *I eat Kasha with milk.*
> *Ilks, silks, tilks,*
> *I eat Kashsa with milks.*

The oddity task has been given to prereaders in a variety of languages. For example, Wimmer, Landerl, and Schneider (1994) developed a version for German kindergartners, testing 138 children. They used four words to increase task difficulty for these older children (German children do not go to school until age 6). The onset task was made up of words like "Korn, Kopf, *Rock*, Korb", and the two rime tasks were made up of words like "Bund, Hund, *Wand*, Mund" (middle sound different), and "Haus, *Baum*, Maus, Laus" (end sound different). The children were tested about 4 months before beginning schooling, which meant that they were prereaders aged on average 6 years. Wimmer et al. reported that performance was above chance, and that the onset task was more difficult than the rime task for these children (44% correct vs. 73% correct, respectively). Ho and Bryant (1997) gave Chinese 3-year-olds a rhyme oddity task, and found that performance was 68% correct. Hoien et al. (1995) gave their Norwegian preschoolers a match-to-sample rhyme task, in which children had to select the one picture out of three that rhymed with a target picture. Performance was 91% correct. Porpodas (1999) devised a Greek version of the oddity task. He reported that first-grade children in Greece scored 90% correct. As with syllables, therefore, children across languages seem to develop good onset-rime awareness prior to receiving literacy teaching.

Becoming aware of phonemes

The same is not true for the development of phoneme awareness. Although some children in some studies in some languages (e.g. Turkish, Czech; see Goswami & Ziegler, 2006) have been reported to develop some phoneme awareness prior to schooling, in general studies find that phoneme awareness develops as a result of direct teaching, usually the direct teaching of literacy. This is not particularly surprising, as the phoneme is not a natural speech unit. This was discussed briefly in Chapter 5, where we saw that the concept of a phoneme is an abstraction from the physical stimulus. For example, the "a" phoneme in "bat" and "back" is not exactly the same physical sound, and neither is the "p" phoneme in "pit" and "spoon". In natural speech, acoustic features such as voicing determine phonetic differences (such as the difference between /p/ and /b/). Via prototype formation, the brain groups some similar but nonidentical sounds (called allophones) as the phoneme /b/, and many other similar but nonidentical sounds as the phoneme /p/. This grouping depends on acoustic features. The mechanism for learning about the abstract unit of the phoneme seems to be learning about letters. Letters are used to symbolize phonemes, even though the physical sounds corresponding (for example) to the "P" in *pit* and *spoon* are rather different. Hence the development of **phonemic awareness** depends in part on the consistency with which letters symbolize phonemes. Accordingly, there is cross-language divergence in the rate of development of phonemic awareness.

This has been shown using a variety of cognitive tasks. One task that has been used in many languages is phoneme counting. For example, Wimmer et al. (1991) gave a phoneme-counting task to their German preschoolers, Demont and Gombert (1996) gave a phoneme-counting task to their French kindergartners, Hoien et al. (1995) gave a phoneme-counting task to their Norwegian preschoolers, and Durgunoglu and Oney (1999) gave a phoneme-tapping task to their Turkish kindergartners. The German children performed at 51% correct, the French children at 2% correct, the Norwegian children at 56% correct, and the Turkish children at 67% correct. The Italian children studied by Cossu et al. (1988) were also given a phoneme-tapping task. Criterion was reached by 13% of the 4-year-olds and 27% of the 5-year-olds. By contrast, 97% of the school-aged sample (who were being taught to read) reached criterion. One reason for this variability in results is that not all of the studies of kindergartners checked that the children were prereaders, but another is that the written languages varied in transparency. In English, counting tasks at the phoneme level are generally performed rather poorly. For example, Liberman et al. (1974) reported levels of 0% correct at the phoneme level for their 4-year-olds, and 17% correct for their 5-year-olds. By age 6, when the children had been learning to read for about a year, phoneme tapping was at 70% correct. Studies of first-grade children by Tunmer and Nesdale (1985) and of second-grade children by Perfetti, Beck, Bell, and Hughes (1987) report success levels of 71% and 65%, respectively. By the end of first grade, children learning to read transparent languages typically score at much higher levels than this (e.g. Turkish: 94%; Greek: 100%; German: 92%; see Durgunoglu & Oney, 1999; Harris & Giannouli, 1999; Wimmer et al., 1991). By contrast, Demont and Gombert (1996) found that by the end of grade 1, French children scored 61% in phoneme-counting tasks, very similar to the achievement levels shown by English children.

Again, similar effects of **orthographic transparency** are found with other tasks. For example, using the same–different judgment task, Treiman and Zukowski (1996) reported that 25% of American 5-year olds could recognize shared beginning phonemes ("steak–sponge") and final phonemes ("smoke–tack"), compared with 39% of 6-year-olds. By 7 years, performance was at 100% correct. Goswami and East (2000) tested phoneme awareness in English 5-year-olds using an oddity task (final phoneme shared, as in *cliff, drum, swam*), a blending task, and a segmentation task. They found difference performance levels depending on which task was used. The 5-year-olds scored 0% correct in the phoneme-segmentation task, 54% correct in the phoneme-blending task, and 37% correct in the oddity task. In Greek first-grade children, Porpodas (1999) found a performance level of 98% correct for phoneme deletion. Using a final phoneme-deletion task (in which children had to delete the final phoneme in spoken consonant–vowel–consonant (CVC) nonwords), Durgunoglu and Oney (1999) reported that Turkish first-grade children scored 98% correct. Ideally, rather than relying on cross-sectional comparisons, the same children should be followed longitudinally in order to track developmental relationships. Nevertheless, the general picture is clear. Phoneme awareness develops at different rates in children who are learning to speak and read different languages.

Theoretically, it has been proposed that there are at least two language-dependent reasons for this (Ziegler & Goswami, 2005, 2006). One is the phonological structure of the syllable. As noted above, for many of the world's languages, the most frequent syllable type is CV. For these languages, onset-rime segmentation of the syllable is equivalent to phonemic segmentation. An Italian child who segments early-acquired words like "*Mamma*" and "*casa*" (house) at the onset-rime level will thereby arrive

KEY TERM

Orthographic transparency
Consistency of symbol to sound (grapheme–phoneme) matching.

at the phonemes comprising these words (e.g. /m/ /a/ /m/ /a/). Only 5% of English monosyllables follow the CV pattern (see De Cara & Goswami, 2002; examples are "go" and "see"). The most frequent syllable type in English is CVC ("cat", "dog", "soap"). Other phonological factors might also contribute to the relative ease or difficulty of becoming aware of phonemes. For example, languages differ in the sonority profile of their syllables. Vowels are the most sonorant sounds, followed in decreasing order by glides (e.g. /w/), liquids (e.g. /l/), nasals (e.g. /n/), and obstruents (e.g. /p/). Whereas the majority of syllables in English end with obstruents (almost 40%), the majority of syllables in French either end in liquids or have no coda at all (almost 50%).

The second important factor in explaining cross-language differences in phonemic awareness is orthographic transparency. Some languages have a 1 : 1 mapping between letters and sounds. For these languages, letters correspond consistently to one phoneme. Examples include Greek, German, Spanish, and Italian. Other languages have a 1 : many mapping between letters and sounds. A good example is English. Some letters or letter clusters can be pronounced in more than one way, for example O in "go" and "to", EA in "speak" and "steak", and G in "magic" and "bag" (see Berndt, Reggia, & Mitchum, 1987; Ziegler, Stone, & Jacobs, 1997). It is much easier to become aware of phonemes if one letter consistently maps onto one and the same phoneme. It is relatively difficult to learn about phonemes if a letter can be pronounced in multiple ways (see Ziegler & Goswami, 2005, 2006, for more detailed arguments). This theoretical analysis predicts that children learning to read in languages like Italian and Spanish should find it easiest to become aware of phonemes. They are learning languages with predominantly CV syllables, so that onset-rime segmentation and phonemic segmentation are equivalent, and their written language consistently represents one phoneme by one letter. Children learning to read in languages like German should have a more difficult time, because spoken syllables are complex in structure (in fact, German has the same syllable structure as English). Nevertheless, German has a 1 : 1 mapping from letter to sound, facilitating the process of becoming aware of phonemes. It is children who are learning to read in languages like English and French who should have the most difficult time. These children are learning languages with a complex syllable structure and an inconsistent orthography. In fact, cross-language comparisons indeed suggest that it takes children longer to learn about phonemes in languages like English and French than in languages like Italian and Spanish. This is shown in Table 10.1.

TABLE 10.1 Data (% correct) collated from studies comparing phoneme counting in different languages in kindergarten or early grade 1

Language	% phonemes counted correctly
Greek[1]	98
Turkish[2]	94
Italian[3]	97
Norwegian[4]	83
German[5]	81
French[6]	73
English[7]	70
English[8]	71
English[9]	65

1, Harris & Giannouli, 1999; 2, Durgunoglu & Oney, 1999; 3, Cossu et al., 1988; 4, Hoien et al., 1995; 5, Wimmer et al., 1991; 6, Demont & Gombert, 1996; 7, Liberman et al., 1974; 8, Tunmer & Nesdale, 1985; 9, Perfetti et al., 1987 and grade 2 children.

Longitudinal connections between phonological awareness and reading

Despite cross-language variability in the rate at which children acquire phoneme awareness, preschool differences in phonological sensitivity appear to predict reading and spelling development across languages. The strongest research designs measure phonological awareness prior to school entry, and then explore whether individual differences in phonological awareness predict children's performance in standardized tests of reading and spelling 2 or 3 years later. Other cognitive variables that might cause a longitudinal relationship, such as individual differences in intelligence or in memory, are also measured and are then controlled in the longitudinal analyses. This enables the researchers to measure whether there is a *specific* connection between phonological awareness and progress in literacy.

In one of the first longitudinal studies to demonstrate a specific connection, Bradley and Bryant (1983) followed up the 400 preschool children to whom they had administered the oddity task at ages 4 and 5 years. At follow-up, the children were aged on average 8 and 9 years. The children were given standardized tests of reading, spelling, and reading comprehension, and their performance was adjusted for age and IQ. Bradley and Bryant found high correlations between performance on the oddity task at ages 4 and 5 and reading and spelling performance 3 years later. When the effects of IQ and memory were removed in multiple regression equations, the oddity task accounted for up to 10% of unique variance in reading. In a study with 3-year-olds reported by Bryant, Maclean, Bradley, and Crossland (1989), a significant relationship between nursery rhyme knowledge at age 3 and success in reading and spelling at ages 5 and 6 was found, again controlling for factors such as social background and IQ. Similar results with English-speaking samples have been reported by a number of other research groups. For example, Baker, Fernandez-Fein, Scher, and Williams (1998) measured nursery rhyme knowledge in 39 kindergarten children and reported that it was the strongest predictor of word attack and word identification skills measured in grade 2. Rhyme knowledge at time 1 accounted for 36% and 48% of unique variance in reading at time 2, respectively. The second strongest predictor of reading at time 2 was letter knowledge, which accounted for an additional 11% and 18% of the variance, respectively.

Similar longitudinal connections between phonological awareness and reading have been found in other languages. In a landmark study, Lundberg, Olofsson, and Wall (1980) gave 143 Swedish children a range of phonological awareness tests in kindergarten. The tests used included syllable blending, syllable segmentation, rhyme production, phoneme blending, phoneme segmentation, and phoneme reversal. When Lundberg et al. examined the predictive relationships between these tests and reading attainment in second grade, both the rhyme test and the phoneme tests were found to be significant predictors of reading almost 2 years later. In a German replication of Bradley and Bryant's study, Wimmer et al. (1994) followed up the 183 German kindergartners who had received the oddity task at age 6 (in kindergarten) one year later (at grade 1), and again when they were almost 10 years old. Wimmer et al. reported that performance in the oddity task was only minimally related to reading and spelling progress in German children when they were 7–8 years old (the same age as the English children in Bradley and Bryant's study). However, at the 3-year follow-up, when the children were aged on average 9 years 9 months, rime awareness (although not onset awareness) was significantly related to both reading and spelling development. In the study with Norwegian preschoolers by Hoien et al. (1995) mentioned earlier, the children were given measures of syllable, onset-rime, and phoneme awareness. When reading was tested in first grade, it was found that syllable, rhyme, and phoneme awareness all made independent contributions to variance in reading. In the study with Chinese preschoolers mentioned earlier, Ho and Bryant (1997) gave the rime oddity task to 100 Chinese children at age 3 years, and measured their progress in reading and spelling 2 years later. Phonological awareness was found to be a significant predictor of reading even after other factors such as age, IQ, and mother's educational level had been controlled. Individual differences in phonological sensitivity hence predict individual differences in reading attainment across languages, even for children who are learning to read nonalphabetic scripts. Because the children are so young, the measures of phonological sensitivity used in these longitudinal studies are usually syllable, onset, and rime measures. Although different tasks measure phonological awareness at different "grain sizes", the general assumption is that syllable, onset-rime, and phoneme measures are all tapping the same cognitive construct, namely "phonological awareness" (Anthony et al., 2003).

Training children's phonological skills: the impact on reading

As always in developmental psychology, however, the existence of a robust longitudinal association between factor A (e.g. phonological awareness) and outcome B (e.g. literacy) does not in itself show a causal relationship. To test whether a developmental relationship is a causal one, an intervention study is required. In the area of reading and spelling, there are now many such intervention studies, because improving children's literacy is an important goal for governments in many cultures. However, not every training study has followed a stringent research design. When carrying out studies aimed at isolating causal variables in developmental psychology, it is crucial to have the correct control groups (Goswami, 2003a). In the case of phonology and reading, it is important that some groups of children receive an intervention designed to improve their performance that does not manipulate phonological sensitivity. When exploring causality, it is not sufficient to compare a group of children who receive a phonological intervention with a group of children who do not. Although the children in such "unseen" control groups are receiving training in reading from their classroom teachers, they are not receiving the individualized attention of an eager researcher who is piloting a special new training programme. Effects due simply to participating in an intervention are called "Hawthorne" effects. They arise not from cognitive changes due to targeted training but from the generalized motivational and self-esteem effects of participating in something extra and unusual. This aspect of receiving an intervention, as well as the cognitive aspects of the intervention itself, must be controlled if a training study is to provide unambiguous information about cognitive variables.

One training study that did follow a stringent research design was that of Bradley and Bryant (1983; mentioned earlier). As part of their study, Bradley and Bryant selected the 65 children in their cohort of 400 who had performed most poorly in the oddity task when they were aged 4 and 5 years. These 65 children were divided into four matched groups, three of which were provided with 2 years of specialized training. One group, the phonological awareness group, was given training in grouping words on the basis of sound. This was done using a picture-sorting task and various word games. For example, the children were taught to put the pictures of a *hat*, a *rat*, a *mat*, and a *bat* together when grouping by rhyme (Figure 10.2). During the course of the 2 years, the children were taught to group words by a variety of grain sizes, namely onset, rime, vowel phonemes, and coda phonemes. A control group spent the same amount of time with the same researchers and the same games, but learned to group words by semantic category. For example, in the picture card

FIGURE 10.2
Bradley and Bryant (1983) used word games to teach children to group words on the basis of sound.

game they might group the cards into "farmyard animals". A second experimental group also did the phonology picture and word games, but in addition spent the second year of the study matching plastic letters to shared phonology. For example, they learned to use plastic letters to represent the rime "at" in words like *hat*, *rat*, and *mat*. The fourth group of children was an unseen control group. Following the intervention, the children who had received training in phonological awareness alone were 4 months ahead in reading and spelling than the children in the semantic control group (a nonsignificant difference). The children in the group who had had both phonological awareness and plastic letters training were a significant 8 months further on in reading than the children in the semantic control group, and 12 months further on in spelling, even after adjusting post-test scores for age and IQ. Compared with the children who had spent the intervening period in the unseen control group, the phonology + plastic letters group were an astonishing 24 months further on in spelling, and 12 months in reading. Clearly, combining phonological awareness training with instruction in orthography–phonology relations yields the largest benefits.

Again, training studies in other languages have reported similar beneficial effects (e.g. Danish: Lundberg, Frost, & Petersen, 1988; and German: Schneider, Kuespert, Roth, Visé, and Marx, 1997; Schneider, Roth, & Ennemoser, 2000). For example, Schneider et al. (2000) developed a 6-month metalinguistic training program covering syllables, rhymes, and phonemes for young German children. They then indentified 138 German children as being "at risk" for dyslexia while in kindergarten on the basis of rhyme production, rhyme matching, and syllable segmentation skills that were significantly poorer than those of German control kindergartners. Schneider et al. developed an innovative research design in which *all* of the children designated "at risk" received training. One group received metalinguistic training alone, a second group received letter–sound training alone, and a third group received combined phonological + letter–sound training. Progress in reading and spelling for these three experimental groups was then compared with that of children from the same kindergartens who had never been at risk for reading difficulties. As might be expected from the results reported by Bradley and

Bryant (1983), the German children receiving the phonological + letter–sound training program had the best outcome. A year into first grade, this group showed comparable attainment in literacy with those children who had never been at risk and who had received no training. The other two training groups were still significantly impaired in literacy attainment in comparison with those children who had never been at risk. The importance of phonology was demonstrated by the finding that the "at risk" group who had received letter–sound training alone, without metalinguistic training, either performed at comparable levels in later reading and spelling progress to the "metalinguistic training alone" group, or performed at lower levels than this group. Clearly, training either phonological awareness alone or letter–sound recoding alone is insufficient for effective progress in literacy. Training one set of skills without the other will not prevent literacy difficulties. The cognitive profiles of children with developmental dyslexia in different languages will be discussed later in this chapter.

Learning to decode in different languages

So far, we have seen that the two factors of phonological complexity and orthographic transparency lead to cross-cultural differences in the emergence of phoneme awareness in children learning to read different languages, but that phonological awareness at all grain sizes (syllable, onset-rime, phoneme) is a significant predictor of reading acquisition across the world's languages. As might be expected, the factors of phonological complexity and orthographic transparency also lead to cross-cultural differences in the rate at which children learn to decode printed symbols into sound. Children who are learning to read spoken languages with simple (CV) syllables and consistent letter–sound correspondences acquire decoding skills most rapidly (for example, Italian and Spanish children). Cross-language differences in phonological complexity and orthographic transparency also have effects on the brain. Both the grain size of lexical representations and the reading strategies that children develop for decoding show systematic differences across orthographies (Ziegler & Goswami, 2005).

A detailed analysis of these differences is beyond the scope of this book (see Ziegler & Goswami, 2005, 2006, for detail), and in general there are more developmental similarities than differences across languages. We will focus on the similarities here. The similarities arise from the learning problem facing a child who is attempting to learn the orthographic system that their culture uses as a visual code for spoken language. Beginning readers across languages are faced with three problems: availability, consistency, and the granularity of symbol-to-sound mappings. The *availability* problem reflects the fact that not all phonological units are accessible prior to reading. As we have seen, phonemes in particular may be inaccessible to prereaders, and the speed with which phonemic awareness develops varies with orthographic consistency. The grain sizes that are most accessible prior to reading (syllables and onset-rimes) hence may not correspond to the visual symbols used to represent phonology. We can predict that a Japanese child, who is learning visual symbols that represent syllables (an early-developing grain size), will be at an advantage compared with an English child, who is learning letters that represent phonemes (a later-developing grain size, at least for languages where onset-rime units are not equivalent to phonemes).

The **consistency problem** refers to the fact that the alphabet represents phonemes with more transparency in some languages than in others. As discussed earlier, Italian,

KEY TERM

Consistency problem
The fact that the alphabet represents phonemes with more transparency in some languages than in others.

Greek, and Spanish are all highly consistent in their spelling–sound correspondences. For these languages, one letter makes only one sound for reading. English, Danish, and French are markedly less consistent in their spelling–sound correspondences, as in reading one letter can make multiple sounds. Sound–spelling consistency can vary across languages as well. Whereas most alphabetic languages are inconsistent for sound–spelling correspondence, with one sound corresponding to more than one letter (a 1 : many relationship), some languages are consistent for spelling as well as for reading (e.g. Italian, Serbo-Croatian). In terms of initial acquisition, "feedforward inconsistency" (from spelling to sound) appears to be most influential in slowing development (see Ziegler & Goswami, 2005). English has an unusually high degree of "feedforward inconsistency", and this appears to cause problems for beginning readers in English, who have to decode words like "though", "cough", "through", and "bough".

Finally, the **granularity problem** refers to the fact that there are many more orthographic units to learn when access to the phonological system is based on bigger grain sizes as opposed to smaller grain sizes. That is, there are more words than there are syllables, there are more syllables than there are rimes, there are more rimes than there are graphemes, and there are more graphemes than there are letters (graphemes are alphabetic units that make a single sound, for example the phoneme /f/ can be represented by the grapheme "ph"). It seems likely that reading proficiency in a particular language will depend on the resolution of all three of these problems, a resolution which will of necessity vary by orthography (see Ziegler & Goswami, 2005, 2006, for detail). For example, children learning to read English must develop multiple strategies in parallel in order to become successful readers. They need to develop whole-word recognition strategies in order to read words like "cough" and "yacht", they need to develop rhyme analogy strategies in order to read irregular words like "light", "night", and "fight", and they need to develop grapheme–phoneme recoding strategies in order to read regular words like "cat", "pen", and "big".

For many of the world's languages, children need to develop grapheme–phoneme recoding strategies only in order to become highly skilled readers. Languages like German, Italian, Turkish, and Finnish can be read very successfully in letter-by-letter fashion. Indeed, experiments across orthographies suggest that children learning to read these languages do rely on grapheme–phoneme recoding, and that this strategy develops to an efficient level within the first months of learning to read (e.g. Cossu, Gugliotta, & Marshall, 1995; Wimmer, 1996; Durgunoglu & Oney, 1999). Various cognitive "hallmarks" suggest a reliance on grapheme–phoneme recoding. One is a length effect: children who are applying grapheme–phoneme correspondences should take longer to read words with more letters/phonemes. Children learning to read consistent orthographies like Greek show reliable length effects compared to children learning to read English (e.g. Goswami, Porpodas, & Wheelwright, 1997). Another is skilled nonword reading: children applying grapheme–phoneme correspondences should be as efficient at reading letter strings that do not correspond to real words (e.g. *grall*, *tegwump*) as they are at reading letter strings that do correspond to real words (*ball*, *wigwam*). Young readers of consistent orthographies like German are usually much better at reading nonwords like "grall" than reading-level-matched English children (Frith, Wimmer, & Landerl, 1998). Of course, there is more than one way of reading a nonword. A nonword like "grall" can either be read by applying grapheme–phoneme correspondences, or can be read by analogy to a familiar real word like *ball*. German children show no difference in reading accuracy for nonwords that can be read by analogy compared with nonwords that cannot be read by analogy. English children do show a difference. For example, when given nonwords that could be read by analogy to real English words (e.g. *dake* [cake], *murn* [burn]), English children were more accurate than when given phonologically matched nonwords that could not (e.g. *daik*, *mirn*; see Goswami, Ziegler, Dalton, & Schneider, 2003). German children showed no difference; they also read the nonwords very efficiently when the two types of nonword (large grain size, small grain size) were mixed together into one list. English children, in contrast, showed a strategy switching cost with the mixed list (they were apparently alternating between using rime analogies and using grapheme–phoneme recoding).

When the efficiency of grapheme–phoneme recoding strategies is compared in children who are learning to read different languages during the first year of reading instruction, there is a clear advantage for children who are learning to read consistent alphabetic orthographies. In the largest cross-language study carried out to date, scientists in 14 of the countries comprising the European Union in 2000 measured simple word and nonword reading in first-grade children attending schools using "phonics"-based (grapheme–phoneme-based) instructional programs (Seymour, Aro, & Erskine, 2003). The word and nonword items were matched for difficulty across the languages, and length of tuition in reading was also equated, although the ages of the children differed. The age differences were unavoidable, as (for example) children in England and Scotland begin school at age 5, whereas Scandinavian children begin school at age 7. The data are shown in Table 10.2. As can be seen, the efficiency of grapheme–phoneme recoding approached ceiling level during the first year of teaching for most of the European languages. Children learning to read languages like Finnish, German, Spanish, and Greek were decoding both words and nonwords with accuracy levels above 90%, In contrast, children learning to read French (79% correct), Danish (71% correct), and Portuguese (73% correct) were not as advanced, reflecting the reduced orthographic consistency of these languages. The children learning to read in English showed the slowest rates of acquisition, reading 34% of the simple words correctly and 29% of the simple nonwords. When followed up a year later, these children were achieving levels of 76% for real words and 63% for nonwords, still short of the early efficiency shown by the Finnish and Germans. This is not surprising, of course. The English children were learning a symbol system with inconsistent correspondences at the phoneme level, and they also had to match these symbols to phonemes that were embedded in complex syllables. These two factors of phonological complexity and orthographic transparency make the learning problem more challenging for a young reader of English.

TABLE 10.2 Data (% correct) adapted from the cost A8 study of grapheme–phoneme recoding skills for monosyllables in 14 European languages (Seymour, Aro, & Erskine, 2003)

Language	Familiar real words	Nonwords
Greek	98	97
Finnish	98	98
German	98	98
Austrian German	97	97
Italian	95	92
Spanish	95	93
Swedish	95	91
Dutch	95	90
Icelandic	94	91
Norwegian	92	93
French	79	88
Portuguese	73	76
Danish	71	63
Scottish English	34	41

Developmental dyslexia

The two critical factors of phonological complexity and orthographic transparency also lead to cross-cultural differences in the manifestation of **developmental dyslexia**. Developmental dyslexia has been found in all languages in the world so far studied (see Smythe, Everatt, & Salter, 2004, for review). The core problem in developmental dyslexia is a phonological one. Children with developmental dyslexia seem to have brains that are less efficient in one or more of the processes required for phonological development. Although there is debate over whether the difficulties lie at the phoneme level (e.g. Tallal, 2004), for example in perceiving the rapid acoustic cues that distinguish phonemes, or at the syllable level (e.g. Goswami et al., 2002) in terms of perceiving auditory cues to rhythm and stress, there is agreement that children with developmental dyslexia have not developed well-specified phonological representations of the sound structure of the individual words in their mental lexicons (Snowling, 2000). Despite typically having wide vocabularies and high IQ, children with developmental dyslexia in different languages experience difficulties in three kinds of phonological task. These are phonological awareness tasks (e.g. the tapping task, the oddity task), tasks requiring phonological short-term memory (such as digit span; see Chapter 8), and "rapid automatized naming tasks", which require children to name familiar items like colors, pictures, or digits as fast as they can. Children diagnosed with developmental dyslexia find it difficult to perform these phonological tasks in languages as diverse as Chinese (Ho, Law, & Ng, 2000), Japanese (Kobayashi, Kato, Haynes, Macaruso, & Hook, 2003), German (Wimmer, 1993), and English (Bradley & Bryant, 1978). Of course, as the specificity of phonological representations changes with reading experience, it is also important to compare children with dyslexia with younger children who are reading at the same level as they are (a "reading level" or "RL match" design). Matching for reading level goes some way to equating the experience of the brain with print. If the phonological skills of the dyslexic children are inferior even to those of these younger children, then it can be assumed that any cognitive deficits found are fundamental, rather than a simple consequence of poorer reading experience.

The phonological deficit has now been established in developmental dyslexia using RL match designs in many languages (see Goswami, 2003b, for an overview). For example, Bradley and Bryant (1978) gave 10-year-old English children with developmental dyslexia the oddity task described earlier, and compared their performance with that of 7-year-old typically developing readers. The children with dyslexia were significantly worse than the younger controls in each version of the oddity task. For onsets, they scored 54% correct compared with 89% for the younger children, for the middle sound different (rime) task they scored 75% correct compared with 94% correct for the younger RL controls, and for the final sound different (rime) task they scored 81% correct compared with 97% correct for the 7-year-olds. In a study of German children with developmental dyslexia, Landerl, Wimmer, and Frith (1997) gave an onset-rime Spoonerism task to 11-year-old German dyslexics, 11-year-old German CA (chronological age) controls, and 8-year-old German RL controls. The Spoonerism task required the children to substitute onsets between two words (e.g. "boat"–"fish" to "foat"–"bish"). When performance was scored in terms of correct Spoonerisms (i.e. "foat"–"bish"), the German dyslexic group made significantly more errors than both their RL and CA controls (German dyslexic group = 37% correct, RL controls = 57% correct, CA controls = 68% correct).

KEY TERM

Developmental dyslexia
Children who may have wide vocabularies and high IQs but who have difficulty in reading and spelling.

Despite this common cognitive deficit across languages, the manifestation of developmental dyslexia varies markedly with the language that the child is learning to read. As might be expected given the patterns of normative development seen across cultures, children with dyslexia who are learning to read transparent orthographies develop better decoding skills than children with dyslexia who are learning to read opaque languages. Similarly, children with dyslexia who learn spoken languages with a simple (CV) syllable structure become more competent than children with dyslexia who learn spoken languages with a complex syllable structure. This developmental pattern means that reading levels can be very accurate in older children with developmental dyslexia who are learning to read consistent orthographies. An accuracy deficit in reading is often only visible earlier in the developmental process. However, reading remains extremely slow and effortful even in these consistent orthographies. This speed impairment means that the children are functionally dyslexic, even if decoding is relatively accurate. For example, recoding a sentence to sound can take so long that the beginning of the sentence is lost from short-term memory, meaning that reading comprehension is severely affected. In addition, spelling skills remain poor in children with developmental dyslexia who are learning consistent orthographies. In fact, developmental dyslexia is more usually diagnosed on the basis of poor spelling in these languages. The persistent difficulties with spelling likely reflect the 1 : many correspondence between sound and spelling in most alphabetic orthographies (discussed earlier).

Illustrative studies can be described for the consistent orthographies German (by Wimmer, 1993, 1996) and Greek (by Porpodas, 1999). Porpodas (1999) selected a sample of 16 Greek first-graders with literacy difficulties out of an initial cohort of 564 children. The dyslexic children were at least 2 standard deviations below the other children in spelling accuracy, and at least 1 standard deviation below the other children in decoding time. Porpodas then compared these children to a sample of 16 CA-matched control Greek children from the same cohort. All children were given a set of 24 two- and three-syllable nonwords to try and read. The nonwords were created by changing the initial and middle letters of real words. Porpodas reported that the Greek dyslexic children read 93% of these nonwords correctly, compared to 97% for the CA controls. Although this was a significant difference, even the struggling Greek readers were clearly very accurate. They took twice as long as the typically developing children to recode the nonwords to sound, however. When given a Greek version of the oddity task, the poor readers scored 51% correct, and the controls scored 89% correct.

Wimmer (1996) reported on the reading skills of a group of German children in grade 1 who later became dyslexic. The children were given simple nonwords like "*Mana*" (Mama) and "*Aufo*" (Auto = car) to read. Wimmer found that 7 out of 12 children who later became dyslexic read less than 60% of these nonwords accurately, compared to an average performance of 96% correct for beginning readers who did not subsequently become dyslexic. In a phoneme reversal task given at the same time (e.g. reverse "ob" to "bo"), the to-be-dyslexic children scored on average 22% correct, compared to an average of 69% correct for the control children. In fact, 42% of the dyslexic children could not attempt the phonological task at all. Wimmer (1993) reported on the reading and phonological skills of the dyslexic group when they were 10-year-olds. In a timed nonword reading task based on "Italian"-type nonwords with open syllables ("*ketu*", "*heleki*", "*tarulo*"), the children with dyslexia scored as well as RL controls, reading on average 92% of items correctly. They also performed as well as younger RL controls in a phoneme awareness task requiring them to substitute one vowel phoneme for another (e.g. "*Mama ist krank*" to "*Mimi ist krink*"). Both groups succeeded on 86% of trials. Clearly, after 3 years of reading instruction, the German dyslexics had developed accurate phonological recoding skills. They had also used print–sound relationships to improve the quality of their phonological representations, as they were now performing at comparable levels in phonological awareness tasks to RL controls. However, they were still significantly poorer than CA controls, who scored 95% correct in the vowel substitution task.

The overwhelming amount of cross-language evidence for phonological deficits in developmental dyslexia, particularly during early development, means that the accepted cognitive explanation for developmental dyslexia is that affected children have a specific problem with phonology. The phenotype of developmental dyslexia is also defined by phonology in genetic studies, usually via poor performance in phonological awareness tasks and poor nonword reading. Some of the genes involved in dyslexia have already been mapped. Most studies exploring heritability have been family and twin studies, particularly in English (e.g. Gayan et al., 1999; Gayan & Olson, 2001). Of course, the idea of "genes for dyslexia" does not make sense, as reading is a culturally determined activity. Whereas a child's genes *can* determine their eye color, they cannot determine the child's reading level. Rather, children at genetic risk for dyslexia are those with a genetic risk of phonological difficulties. The extent to which these phonological difficulties translate into a reading difficulty depends on environmental factors. For example, children whose carers actively develop their phonological awareness via language games, nursery rhymes, and so on may be able to compensate to some extent for genetic predisposition. Levels of association reported so far in behavioral and molecular genetics are not strong enough to translate into reliable predictors of risk for a single child (Fisher & Francks, 2006).

A carer may help to compensate to some extent for a child's genetic predisposition to dyslexia through the use of phonological improvement tools, such as language games and nursery rhymes.

Cognitive neuroimaging studies of reading and developmental dyslexia

So far, most neuroimaging studies of reading development and developmental dyslexia have been carried out with English-speaking children. Given that English is an unusually difficult language to learn to read, this is a pity. The neural networks that are developed by a brain learning to read the English orthography might be somewhat different to the neural networks that are developed by a brain learning to read a more transparent orthography. On the other hand, given the central role of phonological awareness in learning to read all orthographies, some of the findings from imaging studies in English seem likely to translate into other languages. Across spoken languages, the neural networks that develop for language are left-lateralized to the frontal and temporal areas of the brain. The neural networks that develop for reading also seem to be left-lateralized, comprising a network of frontal, temporoparietal, and occipitotemporal regions.

FIGURE 10.3
In the "false-font" task used by Turkeltaub et al. (2003) subjects were instructed to press a button held in their right hand if the stimulus contained an ascender or "tall letter" or a button held in their left hand if it did not. In the examples given here, "sauce" would be given a "no" response, as would the first false-font string shown. The word "alarm" would be given a "yes", as would the second false-font string. From Turkeltaub et al. (2003). Copyright © 2003 Macmillan Magazines Limited. Reproduced with permission.

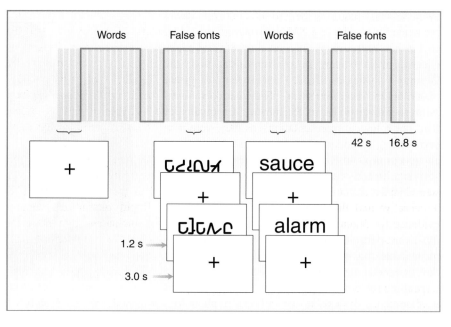

In a neuroimaging study of normative development using fMRI, Turkeltaub, Gareau, Flowers, Zeffiro, and Eden (2003) measured neural activation in children and young adults aged from 7 years to 22 years while they were performing a "false-font" task. The false-font task is based on meaningless symbols that have similar visual features to letters (Figure 10.3), and is designed to mimic the demands of reading an alphabetic script. The children were asked to detect certain features such as ascenders (b, d, and k are examples of letters with ascenders). This task was chosen because the 7-year-olds could perform it as well as the adults. This is an important consideration in developmental studies. If a key task is performed more poorly by one group compared to another, then differences in neural activity could simply reflect these differences in expertise rather than any differences linked to development itself. Turkeltaub et al. argued that comparison of the neural activity found when detecting features like ascenders in real words with the neural activity found during the false-font task yielded a measure of "implicit reading". The implicit reading-related activity in the college students was found to depend on the left hemisphere sites identified in studies of adults, including left posterior temporal and left inferior frontal cortex and also right inferior parietal cortex. To explore developmental effects, Turkeltaub et al. then restricted the analyses to children under the age of 9 years. Now the main area engaged was left posterior superior temporal cortex (traditionally considered the focus of phonological activity, and thus thought to be engaged during grapheme–phoneme translation). As reading developed, activity in left temporal and frontal areas increased, while activity in right posterior areas declined. This pattern suggested that reading-related activity in the brain becomes more left-lateralized with development.

Turkeltaub et al. (2003) also explored the neural activation associated with the three core measures of phonological processing used in studies of developmental dyslexia, namely phonological awareness, phonological short-term memory, and rapid automatized naming. Although activity in all three tasks was highly interrelated, Turkeltaub et al. were able to explore potential functional differences by calculating partial correlations between activated brain regions and each of the three measures while controlling for the effects of the other two measures. They reported that the three different measures did seem to correlate with distinct patterns of brain activity. Phonological awareness appeared to depend on a network of areas in left posterior superior temporal cortex, and inferior frontal gyrus. The degree of activity in this region depended on the level of children's phonological skills. Left posterior superior temporal cortex was also the region identified by the analyses of children below 9 years of age, suggesting again that phonological recoding to sound is the route into reading. Activity in the inferior frontal gyrus increased with reading ability. Phonological short-term memory (measured by digit span) appeared to depend on left intraparietal sulcus. This is a dominant site for working memory in adults (see Chapter 8). Digit span activation was also found in the middle frontal gyri (bilaterally) and the right superior temporal sulcus. Rapid automatized naming appeared to depend on a different, bilateral network, including right posterior superior temporal gyrus, right middle temporal gyrus, and left ventral inferior frontal gyrus. Interpretation of this right-lateralized pattern requires further studies.

Neuroimaging studies of children with developmental dyslexia have also been carried out. In one study, Shaywitz et al. (2002) studied 70 children with dyslexia aged on average 13 years, and compared them to 74 11-year-old typically developing controls (although the controls were not matched for reading level). Using fMRI, the children were scanned while performing a variety of reading-related tasks. These were letter identification (e.g. are t and V the same letter?); single-letter rhyme (e.g. do V and C rhyme?); nonword rhyming (e.g. do *leat* and *jete* rhyme?); and reading for meaning (e.g. are *corn* and *rice* in the same semantic category?). To isolate the chief brain regions involved in each task, the neural activity in each condition was contrasted with neural activity in a baseline condition, which was based on line-orientation judgments (e.g. do [\\V] and [\\V] match?). The main finding was that the children with developmental dyslexia showed underactivation in the core brain areas for reading, namely the left frontal, temporal, parietal, and occipital sites. In addition to this underactivity, the children with developmental dyslexia activated right-hemisphere sites, largely in temporoparietal cortex. Individual differences in performance on a standardized test of nonword reading were found to be significantly correlated with the degree of activation in left posterior inferior temporal regions. Therefore the data showed a nice brain–behavior correlation. One drawback of the study, however, was that there were group differences in behavioral performance in some of the component tasks. In the nonword rhyming measure, for example, the controls (79%) were significantly better than the children with dyslexia (59%). This means that some of the differences in activation could reflect differing levels of expertise rather than differences core to having developmental dyslexia. Inclusion of a reading-level-matched control group, comprising younger children who were matched to the dyslexics for performance in the reading-related tasks, would have aided interpretation of the data.

One attractive feature of neuroimaging is that it can reveal changes in neural organization following intervention. For example, if an intervention is targeted at improving phonological skills, then neuroimaging can show whether neural activity in the regions supporting phonology changes or normalizes subsequent to the intervention. If any behavioral changes found are due to Hawthorne effects, then the neural networks supporting phonology should not be the primary locus of change. A number of fMRI studies of targeted phonological remediation have now been carried out (e.g. Simos et al., 2002; Temple et al., 2003; Shaywitz et al., 2004; see Goswami, in press, for an overview). These studies all show that neural activity in the left-lateralized sites for reading normalizes (i.e. increases) following intervention. For example, Shaywitz and colleagues carried out a training study based on three groups of children aged from 6 to 9 years (Shaywitz et al., 2004). One group comprised children with a diagnosed reading disability who were receiving a daily targeted intervention based on phonology. A second group comprised children with a diagnosed reading disability who were receiving the typical community-based interventions on offer in their schools. The children in the third group were nonimpaired controls. The children receiving the targeted remediation improved their reading accuracy and reading fluency and also their reading comprehension. Comparing brain activation following remediation to fMRI scans taken before the intervention began, Shaywitz et al. (2004) reported that these children showed increased activation in the left posterior temporal and inferior frontal regions associated with efficient reading in typically developing children. The reading-disabled children who were receiving community-based interventions did not show comparable gains, neither behaviorally nor neurally (in fact, these were really an unseen control group, as they did not receive any extra attention during the study). Although the data are consistent with Shaywitz et al.'s claim that training programs for developmental dyslexia must be based on phonology, a seen control group (for example, receiving semantic training) is required in order to strengthen this conclusion. If the seen control group does not show improvements in reading, and if increased activation in the left-lateralized sites for reading is not found for this group, then there would be a stronger neural case for arguing the merits of phonological remediation.

The current neuroimaging literature on reading development and developmental dyslexia highlights again the importance of research designs in studies of causal factors in development. Neuroimaging studies to date have been correlational in nature, or have omitted important control groups, making it difficult to distinguish cause from effect. As a final example, we will consider a neuroimaging study of children with developmental dyslexia in a language other than English. This is a study of eight Chinese children with developmental dyslexia, carried out by Siok, Perfetti, Jin, and Tan (2004). The children were compared with CA-matched controls and were asked to carry out reading-related tasks while in the fMRI scanner. One was a homophone judgment task, in which the children had to decide whether two different Chinese characters made the same sound (an English homophone is *beach–beech*). This task tapped orthography–phonology connections. The other was a character decision task, in which the children saw one Chinese character and had to decide whether it was a real word or not. This task tapped orthography–semantic relations. Interestingly, during the homophone judgment task, the Chinese dyslexics did not demonstrate the reduced activation in left temporoparietal regions that would typically be found in developmental dyslexia in English. Instead, they showed reduced activity in the left middle frontal gyrus, an area involved in visuospatial analysis. Siok et al. thus argued that whereas the biological marker for reading disability in English was reduced left temporoparietal activation, for Chinese it was reduced activation of left middle frontal gyrus. Although this argument is consistent with their data, again a control group matched for reading level is required in order to be sure. Reduced activation in left middle frontal gyrus might be expected for the level of reading achieved by the children with dyslexia. These children were significantly worse in the homophone judgment task than their controls, and were also significantly slower to make their judgments. If younger children who achieve the same performance in the homophone judgment task do not show the same imaging profile, then the finding is more likely to be related to the causes of developmental dyslexia in Chinese.

MATHEMATICAL DEVELOPMENT

Unlike cognitive neuroimaging studies of reading development, which have largely confirmed what was already known about children's development from cognitive behavioral work, cognitive neuroimaging studies of number have offered a novel explanation for a confusing and contradictory developmental literature. This is because pioneering work concerning the mental representation of mathematical knowledge by Dehaene and his research group has generated the "triple code" model of the representation of number in the brain. Cognitive neuroimaging work, largely with adults, has suggested that there are three numerical coding systems in distinct areas of the brain. One is a visually based code for Arabic numerals (visual number forms) in the fusiform gyrus. The second is a linguistic system for storing "number facts". Multiplication tables and overlearned arithmetic knowledge such as "2 + 2 = 4" appeared to be stored in left-lateralized language areas (left angular gyrus), just like other overlearned verbal sequences such as the days of the week and the months of the year. Most provocatively, Dehaene and colleagues have also produced evidence for a "general number sense" in the parietal lobes (an area important for spatial cognition). From this evidence (discussed below), Dehaene has argued for an approximate, **analog magnitude representation** in the human brain, in the horizontal intraparietal sulcus. He has also shown that animals, too, have such magnitude representations. As the idea of an approximate magnitude representation is important for organizing the literature on infant performance in behavioral tests of numerical cognition, I will discuss the cognitive and neuroimaging data supporting this claim first.

The analog magnitude representation

An analog representational format suggests that, when the brain makes comparisons between continuous quantities, some kind of internal continuum is used. This internal continuum is an analog of the external stimulus. For example, when judging size, weight, or number, the brain might be relying on a representation of quantitative information where part of the relevant cortical area codes smaller quantities and a closely related area codes larger quantities. In the case of number, an analog representation would imply that numbers are not stored mentally as discrete entities reflecting exact quantities, but as approximations of quantity. Hence as quantities get larger, the representations for these numbers would get less precise. The representation for 10 would be more precise than the representation for 100 or 1000.

Cognitive data

Both cognitive and neuroimaging data support the idea that different properties of the physical world are represented in the human brain in analog form. This was first noticed by psychophysicists, who were interested in people's ability to make different physical comparisons between, for example, lines of different lengths and squares of different luminance. They discovered that for a wide range of stimuli, the threshold of stimulus discrimination increased with stimulus intensity. This relationship was formalized as **Weber's law**. Weber's law captures the fact that our ability to make physical discriminations is ratio-sensitive. Our performance depends on the proportion by which stimuli differ on the relevant dimension. Dehaene's insight was to argue that the same ratio-sensitive analog representation was used for quantity (number).

An analog representation codes quantity in an imprecise, approximate way. This means that number discrimination should be ratio-sensitive. If adults have to solve numerical tasks without using language, they indeed behave in ways that are ratio-sensitive. For example, if they have to decide whether they see 12 dots in a briefly presented display, they are less precise with 10 or 11 dots than with 4 or 20 dots (van Oeffelen & Vos, 1982). If adults have to decide under speeded conditions whether an Arabic numeral is larger or smaller than 5, they are slower and less accurate with numbers close to 5 (like 4 and 6) than with numbers distant from 5 (like 1 or 9). This is called the *symbolic distance effect*, and is a marker of analog coding (Moyer & Landauer, 1967). The ratio-dependence of number discrimination is found in other species, too. For example, when rats are trained to press a lever a certain number of times, they make more and more errors as the target number increases (Mechner, 1958; Meck & Church, 1983). Rats are less precise at discriminating larger numbers than smaller ones, even when the numerical distance is the same. For example, when comparing 2 and 4, the numerical distance is 2 and the ratio is 1 : 2. When comparing 16 and 18, the numerical distance is still 2, but the ratio is 8 : 9—rather close to 1. Similarly, if monkeys are given a choice of two piles of chocolate pieces (Washburn & Rumbaugh, 1991), their performance will be worse when the ratio of chocolate in the two piles becomes close to 1 (see Dehaene et al., 1998, for a useful review). Dehaene pointed out that infants, too, appear to be ratio-sensitive in their discrimination of quantities.

As discussed briefly in Chapter 2, infant studies of number discrimination depend on variations of the habituation technique. Typically, infants are habituated to a display representing one number, and then a new number is presented. If dishabituation occurs, it is assumed that the infants can distinguish the two quantities. As discussed, Cooper (1984) used habituation to show that 10-month-old infants could distinguish relations such as "greater than" and "less than". Wynn (1992a) used habituation to explore whether babies could add and subtract small numbers. She found that babies dishabituated when the "wrong" answer to addition or subtraction problems involving 1 and 2 was presented. From these data, she argued that infants could compute the numerical results of simple arithmetical operations. More recent investigators have focused on possible confounds between changes in number and changes in basic perceptual variables like total surface area in the infancy research. They have demonstrated that when number versus perceptual variables is varied systematically in visual paradigms, infants do not appear to respond on the basis of number (see Clearfield & Mix, 1997; Feigenson, Carey, & Spelke, 2002). However, when experiments on infant number do control for perceptual variables in the displays, it turns out that infants aged 6 months can, for example, discriminate 8 from 16, but not 8 from 12 (see Xu & Spelke, 2000). Similarly, they can discriminate 16 from 32 when perceptual variables are controlled, but not 1 from 2 (Xu, Spelke, & Goddard, 2005), and they can discriminate 4 from 8, but not 2 from 4 (Xu, 2003).

If infants are using an analog magnitude representation to make judgments about quantity, this would provide a neat explanation for their ratio-sensitive behavior with

KEY TERM

Weber's law
Statement that our ability to make physical discriminations is ratio-sensitive, e.g. that the threshold to discriminate between amount of stimuli increases with stimulus intensity.

numbers larger than around 3 or 4. The ratio for the comparison of 8 to 16 is 1 : 2, whereas for the comparison of 8 with 12 it is 2 : 3, therefore closer to 1. Accordingly, infants do worse with 8 to 12 than with 8 to 16. The ratio for 16 : 32 and for 4 : 8 is also 1 : 2, therefore infants perform well. The apparent ratio dependence of infant sensitivity to numbers larger than around 3 can thus be explained by a reliance on the analog magnitude representation. As the analog representation codes magnitude in an imprecise, approximate way, it yields two important properties concerning infants' representations of quantity. One is that the representation of numerically close quantities is similar (e.g. 4 and 5, 9 and 10). Another is that the precision of coding gets worse and worse for larger and larger quantities. Infants, therefore, are responding to quantity rather than to number.

What about numbers smaller than 3 or 4? When perceptual variables are controlled, infants appear unable to distinguish 1 from 2 (Xu et al., 2005). It has been argued that small numbers depend on a different representational process, called "**subitizing**". Subitizing yields precise representations of distinct individuals (e.g. Feigenson et al., 2004), and refers to the fast enumeration of the numerosity of very small sets, namely 1, 2, and 3. Subitizing is thought to be influenced more by perceptual processes, and this assumption explains infant sensitivity to perceptual variables like total surface area when judging smaller numbers. Studies with adults also show a difference in behavioral performance with the numbers 1, 2, and 3 compared to larger numbers. For example, in tasks requiring the identification of the number of dots in a briefly presented display, reaction times were the same for the numbers 1, 2, and 3. Above 3, reaction time increased steadily with display size (e.g. Kaufman, Lord, Reese, & Volkmann, 1949). The discrimination of small numbers may thus depend on fast, automatic processes that do not involve the analog magnitude representation. Early in development, these discriminations may not reflect number *per se* either. This idea is discussed later, in the section on language and number.

Analog magnitude representation in older children

A number of studies suggest that older children also use an analog magnitude representation to make judgments about quantity. For example, Huntley-Fenner and Cannon (2000) asked children aged 3, 4, and 5 years to compare two rows of black squares, and to decide whether one row had more squares. The rows of black squares contained between 1 and 15 squares, and varied systematically in their ratio and their interval distance. Ratios were 1 : 1, 1 : 2, or 2 : 3, and for the latter ratios the interval distance varied from 1 to 5. Hence the ratio 1 : 2 was tested by comparisons between 1 and 2, 2 and 4, 3 and 6, 4 and 8, and 5 and 10. The ratio 2 : 3 was tested by comparisons between 2 and 3, 4 and 6, 6 and 9, 8 and 12, and 10 and 15. Examples of the stimuli are shown in Figure 10.4. The children's counting skills were also measured. Huntley-Fenner and Cannon reported that most children made their choices without counting the arrays, and that those children who did count did so on only a minority of trials (average = 8 of the 19 trials). Counting did not improve accuracy: the "counters" were correct on 70% of trials and the noncounters on 67% of trials. Consistent with the analog magnitude representation account, the children were significantly more successful in choosing the numerically larger row for the displays with a ratio of 1 : 2 (81% correct) than for the displays with a ratio of 2 : 3 (53% correct), at all ages.

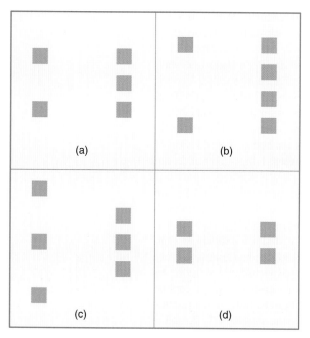

FIGURE 10.4

Examples of the stimuli used by Huntley-Fenner and Cannon (2000). From Huntley-Fenner and Cannon (2000). Reproduced with permission from Blackwell Publishing.

Although the data reported by Huntley-Fenner and Cannon (2000) are consistent with reliance on an analog magnitude representation, they did not control for perceptual variables in their displays (apart from row length). Barth, La Mont, Lipton, Dehaene, Kanwisher, and Spelke (2005a) asked 5-year-olds to compare the numerosity of two arrays of dots, a red array and a blue array. The children were asked to decide whether there were more blue dots or more red dots. To control for perceptual variables, dots could either be the same size in the two displays or of different sizes. The overall area occupied by the arrays could either be the same or different. These displays controlled for surface area, but not for summed contour length. The magnitude comparison task was presented via an animated display (Figure 10.5). The ratios used for red versus blue dots were 5 : 3 and 3 : 5. Barth et al. reported that the 5-year-olds in their study performed at above chance level in all the displays. As performance did not vary with the perceptual variables being controlled, they argued that this showed a reliance on an analog magnitude representation for number. In a further experiment controlling for contour length, similar results were found. Barth et al. argued that their data showed a reliance on primitive approximate number representations.

In related work, Barth, La Mont, Lipton, and Spelke (2005b) used similar animated displays to test magnitude comparisons by 5-year-olds for displays of 10–58 dots, presented very briefly to preclude counting. This time three ratios were used, 0.57, 0.67, and 0.80. On half of the trials, dot size, total contour length, summed dot area, and density were negatively correlated with number. On the other half of the trials, they were positively correlated. If children were relying on perceptual variables to make their magnitude judgments, then they should be wrong systematically in the former (negatively correlated) set of trials. Barth et al. reported that the 5-year-olds performed well above chance level (67% correct), and showed a significant effect of ratio. As ratio approached one, performance declined. As ratio-dependence is the signature of the analog magnitude representation, Barth et al. argued that children's judgments depended on this abstract and nonlinguistic system. A similar ratio-dependence was found in a cross-modal version of the task, in which one set of dots was presented auditorially ("Now you'll hear the red dots. Are there more blue dots, or more red dots?"). Again, performance was significantly above chance, in fact children were as accurate in the cross-modal task as in the visual comparison task.

Using a number estimation task, Huntley-Fenner (2001) found further evidence consistent with reliance on the analog magnitude representation, this time in children aged from 5 to 7 years. The children were shown an array of either 5, 7, 9, or 11 black squares on a computer screen, for an extremely brief presentation (250 ms). The display was then masked, and the children were asked to point out the numerosity of the array using a number line from 1 to 20. Overall the children received 40 trials for each numerosity (160 trials in all). Huntley-Fenner reported that there was no improvement over trial number in the task, suggesting that perceptual learning of the

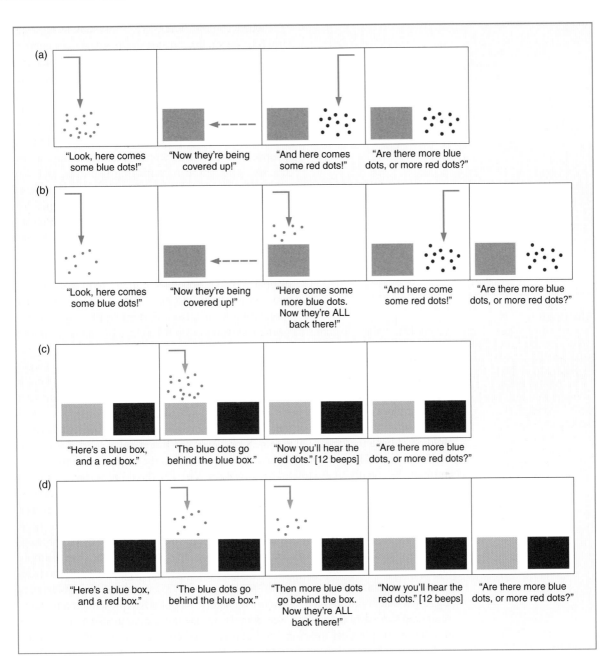

FIGURE 10.5

The magnitude comparison task used by Barth et al. (2005). (a) Comparison of visual arrays. (b) Addition and comparison of visual arrays. (c) Comparison of visual arrays and auditory sequences. (d) Addition and comparison of visual arrays and auditory sequences. From Barth et al. (2005). Copyright © 2005 National Academy of Sciences, U.S.A. Reproduced with permission.

task was not occurring. There was, however, a systematic change in the distribution of responses proportional to target quantity, which is another signature of the analog magnitude representation. The standard deviations of the children's estimates increased proportionally to the means of their estimates (Figure 10.6). Huntley-Fenner concluded

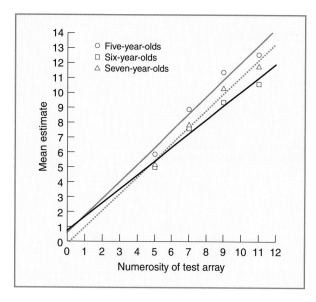

FIGURE 10.6
Five-, 6-, and 7-year-olds' mean estimates graphed as a function of the display numerosity. Participants' estimates increased proportionally to the presented numerosity. From Huntley-Fenner (2001). Copyright © 2001 Elsevier. Reproduced with permission.

that when children were asked to estimate number, they relied upon their analog magnitude representation.

Similar conclusions were reached by Jordan and Brannon (2006) using a numerical similarity task. Six-year-old children were first trained to match exact numbers using a touch-sensitive computer screen. For example, a computer display would show a target number of dots, say two dots. The display would then disappear, and two new displays would be shown side by side, one also containing two dots, and one containing, say, eight dots. The child's job was to touch the display with two dots. Perceptual variables were controlled. Once the child had learned the task, the arrays were changed so that an exact match was no longer presented. Instead, the child had to choose the most similar match. For example, if the target display was four dots, the child might have to choose between two dots and eight dots. Children were not explicitly told to select the most similar number, but were told to "play the game, the same way you played before . . . Just make your best guess. I'm sure you'll do a good job, you've been doing so well".

In fact, although the target displays varied in number, the choices were always between 2 versus 8 and 3 versus 12. This enabled the researchers to calculate whether the children judged smaller targets as nearer to the small value in each case, and larger targets as nearer to the large value. If similarity judgments are made according to an analog representation of the dimension being tested, then the probability that children choose the larger value (e.g. 8 or 12) as the target value increases should itself increase. This follows Weber's law. In addition, the target value for which children are equally likely to choose 2 or 8 (or 3 or 12) should be at the geometric mean (the square root of the product of those two numbers). This is the point of subjective similarity on an analog magnitude representation. If the representation of number is linear, then the point of subjective similarity should be the arithmetic mean (e.g. 5 or 7.5). Jordan and Brannon (2006) reported that the probability of choosing 8 or 12 indeed increased with the numerosity of the target, and that the point of subjective similarity was indeed the geometric mean. This pattern confirmed the predictions made by Weber's law. Jordan and Brannon argued that their data suggested that children were relying on an analog magnitude representation to make numerical similarity judgments. Remarkably, Jordan and Brannon also demonstrated that the psychophysical functions for the 6-year-old children were identical to those of rhesus monkeys trained in the same task. This is consistent with Dehaene's (1997) suggestion of an evolutionarily grounded approximate magnitude representation found in animals and in man.

Neuroimaging data

The general neural claim for the analog magnitude representation is that there is a supra-modal representation for number in intraparietal cortex, which corresponds to an evolutionarily driven "number sense" (e.g. Dehaene, et al., 1998). This intraparietal area is thought to be particularly concerned with knowledge of numerical quantities and their relations. Dehaene, Spelke, Pinel, Stanescu, and

Tsivkin (1999) compared brain activation using fMRI for two arithmetic tasks in adults, one involving exact addition (e.g. $4 + 5 = 9$) and one involving approximate addition (e.g. $4 + 5 = 8$). They reported that during exact calculation participants showed greatest relative activation in a left-lateralized area in the inferior frontal lobe, traditionally regarded as a language area. During approximate calculation, participants showed greatest relative activation in a bilateral parietal area involved in visuospatial processing. Dehaene et al. also used EEG to track the precise time course of brain activation. They found that the ERPs to exact versus approximate trial blocks were already different by 400 ms, before the possible answers to the additions were displayed. Dehaene et al. argued that their data supported the idea that exact calculation relies on knowledge of "number facts" or verbal associations stored in the language areas of the brain. Approximate calculation relies on visuospatial parietal networks, which support a language-independent representation of quantity.

In a related fMRI experiment (Pinel, Dehaene, Rivière, & Le Bihan, 2001), adults were given a number comparison task involving two-digit numbers from 30 to 99, and were asked to decide whether a given number was smaller than or larger than 65. The numbers used were classified as either close to 65 (60–64, 66–69), intermediate from 65 (50–59, 70–79), or distant from 65 (30–49, 80–99). In a second condition, the numbers were spoken rather than presented visually. Both conditions yielded a behavioral distance effect, with faster reaction times for more distant numbers. Numerical distance also had an effect on the degree of brain activation in the parietal cortex, for both conditions. There was greater activity for smaller distances. Pinel et al. argued that the finding that brain activation decreased quasi-monotonically with increasing numerical distance suggested a semantic representation for number in the left and right inferior parietal areas, based on analog magnitude. More recently, Dehaene, Piazza, Pinel, and Cohen (2003) carried out a meta-analysis of different neuroimaging studies with adults that involved number processing. By comparing activations across studies and tasks, they argued that the core of the analog magnitude representation was the bilateral horizontal segment of the intraparietal sulcus. This area was active whenever adults had to access the meanings of the quantities that numbers represented, or the proximity relations of numbers.

Cantlon, Brannon, Carter, and Pelphrey (2006) used fMRI to explore the neural correlates of the analog magnitude representation in 4-year-old children. They devised a task suitable for both children and adults, and compared neural activity in both groups. The task involved viewing a series of visual displays of 16 circles (Figure 10.7). The circles were colored blue, and could vary in size, density, visual surface area, and spatial arrangement. There were two types of deviant trial. Occasionally, participants would see a display of 32 circles instead of 16 circles. This was a number deviant trial. At other times, they would see a display of 16 squares or 16 triangles instead of circles. This was a shape deviant trial. Deviants and standards were carefully constructed so that perceptual variables such as cumulative surface area and density overlapped (in fact, the standard for some participants was 32 instead of 16, and number deviants could be in the ratio of 1 : 2 or 2 : 1, so number deviants could be 16 or 64). Cantlon et al. reported that number deviants led to increased activation in the right intraparietal sulcus for children across conditions, and to increased bilateral activation in the same area for adults. Shape deviants led to increased activation in visual areas such as the fusiform gyrus for both groups. Cantlon et al. concluded that the intraparietal sulcus is recruited for nonsymbolic numerical processing early in development, before formal schooling has begun.

FIGURE 10.7
A schematic depiction of the visual displays used by Cantlon et al. (2006). From Cantlon, Brannon, Carter, and Pelphrey (2006).

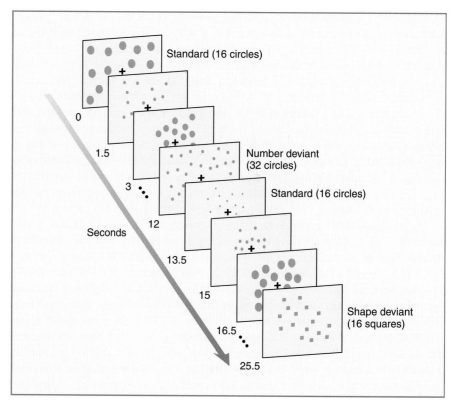

Temple and Posner (1998) used EEG to explore the neural basis of the distance effect in 5-year-old children and compared brain activation to that of adults given the same task in a previous study. As will be recalled, the distance effect is one of the hallmarks of the analog magnitude representation. Temple and Posner asked the children to make judgments concerning whether numbers presented on a computer screen were larger than or smaller than 5. The numbers (1, 4, 6, and 9) were either represented by Arabic digits or by groups of dots. The children had to press a response key as rapidly as possible to make their judgment. The distance effect is shown when reaction times (RTs) to smaller distances (e.g. deciding that 6 is larger than 5) are longer than RTs to larger distances (e.g. deciding that 9 is larger than 5). The task is shown in Figure 10.8. Temple and Posner reported that the components of the EEG waveform affected by distance were remarkably similar in the children and the adults. Neural distance effects also occurred at very similar time points in both groups (approximately 200 ms after stimulus onset), even though the children showed much longer response times than the adults. Most children did not actually press the response key until over 1.5 seconds after stimulus onset, compared to around half a second for adults. The distance effect was also centered on the same parietal electrodes. Temple and Posner argued that the same parietal cerebral circuit underpinned abstract magnitude comparisons by children and by adults. Although more cognitive neuroimaging studies with children are required, current evidence is consistent with the proposal that there is an analog magnitude representation in the intraparietal sulcus that represents approximate number meaning for both children and adults.

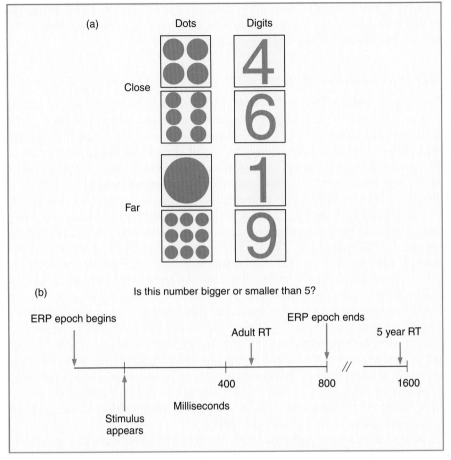

FIGURE 10.8
Temple and Posner asked children to make judgments concerning whether numbers or dots presented on a computer screen were larger than or smaller than 5. From Temple and Posner (1998). Copyright © 1998 National Academy of Sciences, U.S.A. Reproduced with permission.

Counting

Given the existence of an approximate analog magnitude representation for quantity, and a possible second representational system for small numbers, which is precise and distinct, what is the role of individual learning and culture in mathematical development? Clearly, the role is enormous. Even if both representational systems are accepted to be part of our physiology, with clear evolutionary antecedents, there is a large difference between selecting 3 crackers rather than 2, or distinguishing 8 dots from 16 dots, and having a symbolic number system. Developmentally, acquisition of a symbolic number system probably begins with counting. Young children learn to count when they are relatively young, but it is not clear that they understand what they are doing when they are counting (e.g. Piaget, 1952). Counting appears to be learned first as a linguistic routine. Gradually, children learn the principles underlying counting (Gelman & Gallistel, 1978). For example, they come to understand the principle of **cardinality**, which is the understanding that all sets with the same number are qualitatively equivalent. They also come to understand the principle of **ordinality**, which is the understanding that numbers come in an ordered scale of magnitude. The count sequence represents this ordered scale of magnitude, and a number label, such as "five", represents the fact that five horses is the equivalent amount to five biscuits. The language of the count sequence captures number

KEY TERMS

Cardinality
Understanding that all sets with the same number are qualitatively equivalent.

Ordinality
Understanding that numbers come in an ordered scale of magnitude, i.e. that 5 is greater than 4.

meaning in terms of both a distinctive individual quantity and an ordinal entity with a fixed place among other numerical entities. Hence the count sequence enables the precise interpretation of any number—in nonanalog fashion.

The development of counting

Counting by young children has been studied extensively. By the age of around 3 years, most children can recite the number words "one" through to "five" while pointing to one object at a time (e.g. Gelman & Gallistel, 1978; Fuson, 1988). From their studies of counting, Gelman and Gallistel argued that children as young as 2 years used number words in systematic ways. These ways suggested some appreciation of the principles underlying counting, namely cardinality, ordinality, and one-to-one correspondence. One-to-one correspondence is important for counting, as in order to count accurately it is necessary to count each member of a set once and only once. Each label must be used for one unique object. Gelman and Gallistel (1978) did not claim a full understanding of cardinality, or of ordinality, from children's early counting behavior, however. The count principle relevant to cardinality was suggested to be the recognition that the last number counted represents the value of the set (this is termed the "cardinal word principle" by Wynn, 1990). The count principle relevant to ordinality was the need to count in a stable order, using the same oral sequence each time. These principles do not fully capture the understanding of symbolic number. As pointed out by Bryant and Nunes (2002), cardinality is also about the relations between sets of numbers, and ordinality is also about an ordered scale of magnitude, and these aspects of numerical understanding are not captured by behaviors such as counting in a stable order. Nevertheless, children's early counting is suggestive of some insight into what number words mean. For example, even very young children do not give one object when asked for 2, 3, or 4 (Wynn, 1990).

One of the first systematic studies of counting was reported by Saxe (1977). He gave children aged 3, 4, and 7 years (who could all count up to nine on a pretest) a range of counting tasks in order to trace underlying development. For example, the children were shown an array of beads (up to nine) and were asked to "put out just the same number"; they were shown some drawn circles and asked to "draw just the same number" themselves; they were asked to give a puppet on the table "just the same number [of model animals] to eat" as another puppet underneath the table; and they were shown two linear arrays (e.g. 9 toy horses, 11 toy pigs) and asked "Are there just the same number of pigs and horses, or does one have more?" Children who did not count spontaneously in these tasks were prompted to do so (e.g. the experimenter asked "Would counting help?"). Saxe reported that the accuracy of counting rose sharply between ages 3 and 4 years. He also observed a developmental shift from "prequantitative" counting (where counting was not used in order to produce the same number), and "quantitative" counting, where it was. For example, a prequantitative child might count 14 toy ducks and then count 6 toy fish, and say that there are the same number "because I counted". A quantitative child would count the toy ducks and fish accurately using one-to-one correspondence.

Saxe then carried out a longitudinal study, following a group of 3-year-old children for 18 months, using the same counting tasks. As in the cross-sectional study, a change from prequantitative to quantitative counting was found with age. Saxe suggested that progression from prequantitative to quantitative counting was related to the accuracy of counting, because both were regulated by the "same cognitive development". Saxe's suggestion was that this cognitive development was the acquisition of one-to-one

By the age of around 3 years, most children can recite the number words "one" through to "five" while pointing to one object at a time.

correspondence. Once the "logic" underlying counting was understood, children began to construct quantitative counting strategies, and counting accuracy improved. However, Saxe speculated that a different developmental process might apply to the counting of small numbers. Indeed, work on children's counting behavior with small numbers has not made much reference to one-to-one correspondence.

The best-known research on counting with small numbers is that of Wynn (1990, 1992a). Wynn (1990) created the "give a number" task based on toy dinosaurs for children aged 2.5 years, 3 years, and 3.5 years. The dinosaurs were presented in a pile on the table, and the children were asked to give a puppet a certain number of dinosaurs. For example, they were asked "Could you give Big Bird two dinosaurs to play with, just give him two and put them here . . . can you get two dinosaurs for Big Bird?". Children were asked to give the puppet one, two, three, five, or six toys. They were then asked to check that they had given the correct number (to prompt counting behavior), and they were also prompted to fix things if counting revealed the incorrect number ("But Big Bird wanted two. How can we make it so there's two?"). The children tested appeared to respond in one of two ways. They either systematically counted the toys or they grabbed a handful for Big Bird. In fact, only four of the oldest children qualified as "counters". The "grabbers" tended to respond accurately if Big Bird wanted one dinosaur, showed a trend towards systematicity for two dinosaurs, but otherwise did not even approximate the number asked for. Wynn concluded that the grabbers did not understand Gelman and Gallistel's (1978) cardinal word principle (that is, they did not understand that counting determines numerosity). A follow-up study supported this conclusion. A new group of 2- to 3-year-olds were administered the "give-a-number" task along with a counting task and a "give some" task (e.g. "Give Big Bird some toy pigs"). Wynn found that each child succeeded up to a certain numerosity, and then failed for all higher ones. The shift from grabbing to counting appeared to occur at around 3½ years. Wynn suggested that a major conceptual change in children's understanding of counting occurred at this time. After acquiring the number words "one", "two", and "three" in sequence, children then acquired the meaning of *all* the number words in their counting range.

To explore these possibilities developmentally, Wynn (1992) carried out a 7-month longitudinal study of 2- to 3-year-olds, using the give-a-number task and two related tasks: a "how-many" task and a "point-to-x" task. In the how-many task, children were asked to count sets of two to six items and were then asked "So how many are there?". In the point-to-x task, children were shown pictures of two sets, and were asked for a specific number x (e.g. "Can you show me the three flowers?"). Children were tested for all combinations of numbers for which they appeared to have cardinal knowledge. For example, a child who could reliably give 2 in the give-a-number task would be tested with 2 versus 3, 3 versus 4, 1 versus 3, and 1 versus 4. This procedure checked for knowledge of the cardinal meanings of 2 and 3, and the partial meanings of 3 and 4. Performance in the give-a-number task was used to compute the highest number that children could succeed consistently in giving, which then determined developmental group (I, II, III, IV). Children in group I could distinguish 1 from 2; those in group II could distinguish 1, 2, and 3; those in group III could distinguish 1, 2, 3, and 4; and those in group IV could distinguish 1, 2, 3, 4, and 5. Even group I children could count accurately to numbers higher than these (e.g. in group I most children counted accurately to 5).

Wynn's longitudinal data supported her claim that children learn the cardinal meanings of the smaller number words sequentially, and then simultaneously learn the cardinal meanings of the remaining number words in their counting range. Once the children knew the cardinal meaning of 4, they also seemed simultaneously to understand 5 and 6. Children who knew the cardinal meanings of all the number words used counting in both the give-a-number and the point-to-*x* tasks, whereas those who knew the cardinal meanings of only the smaller number words did not. However, even very young children understand that number words refer to specific numerosities. The youngest children tested (2½ years) could identify "two" and "three" in the point-to-*x* task when each number was paired with one, even though they could not consistently give Big Bird two items.

One current debate in the counting literature is whether younger children simply regard all larger number words as referring to "a lot". Rather than conceiving of number words for larger numbers as corresponding to specific numerosities, perhaps they do not even conceive of large, exact numerosities at all. It is argued that extensive experience of using the count labels might result in conceptual change. Because younger children can individuate objects up to around 3 or 4, perhaps they understand the number words "one", "two", "three", and "four" to mean sets of these sizes, but understand number words larger than 4 to mean "a lot". On this view, learning to count would allow children to "bootstrap" their way to a concept of large exact numbers, a concept that was not present prior to acquiring this language (e.g. Carey, 2004). For example, based on Wynn's (1990, 1992a) data and other data, Le Corre, Van de Walle, Brannon, and Carey (2006) have argued that the developmental "shift" to becoming a "cardinal principle" knower requires a qualitative shift in children's representation of number. Prior to this shift, children learn the meanings of "one", "two", and "three" by mapping these number words onto the outputs of a subitizing process that determines small cardinal values without counting. Number words beyond "four" are only mapped onto analog magnitudes after children have constructed the count principles. Le Corre et al. (2006) argue that the acquisition of counting as a representation of number requires the construction of a new representational format. This representational format does not underpin accurate counting for 1, 2, and 3. They suggest that each child must recreate the construction of the natural number system for themselves. This process of recreation is thought to depend on exposure to the verbal count sequence.

This claim for conceptual change in number understanding has proved a controversial one (e.g. Rips, Asmuth, & Bloomfield, 2006). We can illustrate this debate via a boy aged 2½ years (tested by Sarnecka and S. Gelman, 2004), who was given a rather small amount of chocolate candies. This boy protested "I like some *plenty*! I like some *too much*! I like some *lot*! I like some *eight*!". Did this child equate "eight" with a lot, or did he expect that "eight" was a large and exact numerosity that was more candies than he had been given? To find out, Sarnecka and Gelman tested a whole group of children aged from 2 years 7 months to 3 years 6 months. The children were first given a pretest, in which they were asked to give puppets one, two, three, five, or six erasers in order to sort them into the groups of understanding defined by Wynn (1992a). The aim was to find children who did not yet know the meaning of "six". Seventeen children were identified in groups I, II, and III, and were then given the "six-versus-a-lot" task. The idea was to see whether the children would treat "six" and "a lot" as synonymous.

The "six-versus-a-lot" task proceeded as follows. The children were introduced to a game about putting pennies into bowls. They were then told:

"I'm going to put six pennies in here [one bowl], and six pennies in here [another bowl]. All right! So this bowl has six pennies and this bowl has six pennies. Here are some more pennies [pours all remaining pennies into one of

the two bowls]. Okay, now I'm going to ask you a question about six pennies. Which bowl has six pennies?"

Alternatively, they were told:

"I'm going to put a lot of pennies in here [places six pennies in a bowl], and a lot of pennies in here [places six pennies in another bowl]. All right! So this bowl has a lot of pennies and this bowl has a lot of pennies. Here are some more pennies [pours all remaining pennies into one of the two bowls]. Okay, now I'm going to ask you a question about a lot of pennies. Which bowl has a lot of pennies?"

Experiments such as the "six-versus-a-lot" coins task demonstrate that acquisition of the count sequence enables children to conceive of the precise interpretation of a given number.

Garnecka and Gelman predicted that if children conceived of "six" as a precise and large numerosity, then they should not choose the bowl with the most pennies in the "six" condition, but they should be happy to choose it in the "a lot" condition. However, if they conceived of "six" as "a lot", then they should also choose the fullest bowl of pennies in the "six" condition. The data showed that even children at level I did not conceive of "six" and "a lot" as synonymous. The children almost never chose the fuller bowl in the "six" condition, but they chose it around half the time in the "a lot" condition. Garnecka and Gelman argued that children did not treat the quantifier "a lot" as specific, but did treat the number word "six" as specific. Even unmapped number words (i.e. the child does not yet have the exact mapping between "six" and sets of 6 items) are treated as referring to exact numerosities. In contrast to the claim made by Le Corre et al. (2006), children in Wynn's groups I, II, and III do appear to have a notion of exact numerosity for large numbers.

Experiments such as these support the idea that the acquisition of the count sequence helps children to conceive of the precise interpretation of any number. Counting captures number meaning for the child, in terms of both a distinctive individual quantity and an ordinal entity with a fixed place in a sequence. Even before the child has fully mapped this sequence, experience with the language of counting provides social and cultural support for cognitive development. Cultural transmission of the count sequence enables children to organize their cognitive structures for number (i.e. to organize subitizing and the analog magnitude representation into a coherent system). This may not require conceptual change so much as conceptual reorganization and redescription. However, this debate requires more than behavioral evidence. Further cognitive neuroscience studies are required to identify the nature of the development of the underlying mental representations for number.

Note, however, that the claim that learning to count might facilitate the development of a symbolic number system in children does not preclude the possibility that, with development, language and number become independent. Indeed, we know from adult patient data that number skills can be preserved even when the comprehension and production of language has been severely compromised (e.g. by semantic dementia; see Remond-Besuchet, Noel, Seron, Thioux, Brun, & Aspe 1999). Patients can have exceptional calculation abilities even when they have lost considerable linguistic skills.

The role of language in counting

Similarly, the idea that learning the count sequence is an important developmental step in acquiring a symbolic system of number does not mean that children lack any concept of larger numbers prior to learning counting language (see Carey, 2004; Gelman & Butterworth, 2005, for debate). For example, Gelman and Butterworth have argued strongly that it is not necessary to have a system of number names in order to have a concept of larger numbers. They define the concept of numerosity as the cognitive equivalent of cardinality, and argue that having the concept of "one" is sufficient for numerosity. By adding "one" as many times as we wish, we can develop concepts of distinct numerosities and their infinity (although see Rips et al., in press, for logical objections). On the other hand, Gelman and Butterworth (2005) agree that possessing a system of number names is helpful in learning to enumerate sets and in calculation. Further, it seems likely that the fact that counting also provides a concrete representation for the ordinal aspects of number might be important developmentally.

One way to test this idea is to see whether cross-cultural differences in the set of number names have any cognitive consequences. Some languages use language labels that provide more concrete support for the ordinal aspects of number than other languages. For example, the Asian spoken numeral system specifies precisely what is represented by each number in terms of place value. Rather than using opaque labels for numbers above ten (eleven, twelve, thirteen . . .), these numbers are labeled ten-one, ten-two, ten-three, ten-four, and so on. Twenty is labeled two-tens, 43 is labeled four-tens-three, eighty is labeled eight-tens, and so on. There is also clear phonetic distinction of number labels. Whereas English uses the phonetically similar labels "fourteen" and "forty" for quite distant numbers in terms of their place value, in Chinese, Japanese, and Korean the labels are the distinctive "ten-four" and "four-tens". According to a linguistic analysis, the Asian spoken numeral system could assist the development of cognitive representations for number meanings and their ordinal aspects.

Miura, Kim, Chang, and Okamoto (1988) asked children from China, Japan, Korea, and America to construct numbers from sets of wooden blocks (ten blocks and unit blocks, hence 12 would require one ten block and two units). All participants were in first grade, and were aged on average 6 or 7 years. The children were asked to read numbers presented on cards, and were then asked to represent the numbers using the blocks. They were also asked whether they could show each number in a different way using the blocks. The numbers tested were 11, 13, 28, 30, and 42. Miura et al. (1988) found that 91% of the American first-graders used unit blocks to represent these numbers on the first trial. Sixty-six per cent of these children then could not make a correct representation on the second trial (i.e. they could not use the ten blocks correctly). In contrast, 81% of the Chinese children, 83% of the Korean children, and 72% of the Japanese children used the ten blocks when representing the numbers on the first trial. Over 90% of these children could also make an alternative correct construction on the second trial, either by using the unit blocks or by using ten blocks and more than nine unit blocks (e.g. 28 as one ten block and 18 units). Miura et al. concluded that the cognitive representation of numbers differed for the Asian and American children. By first grade, place value was an integral component of numerical representations for the Asian children, but not for the American children. These differences in cognitive representation were ascribed to language. However, there is evidence that the cognitive differences found may be more apparent than real. When children are shown how to use the ten units in practice trials before the experiment, then English-speaking children's performance becomes statistically equivalent to that of Japanese children (63% for the English children, 87% for the Japanese; see Saxton & Towse, 1998).

Linguistic effects on the cognitive representation of symbolic number could arise earlier in development, during the acquisition of counting language. Hodent,

Bryant, and Houdé (2005) have argued that the number words that toddlers learn could have specific effects on number understanding, contrasting French and English. Hodent et al. pointed out that in French, the number word for "one", "*un*", is also used to distinguish singular and plural ("*un*" = "a", "*des*" = "some"). They hypothesized that the fact that the same label is used to represent singularity in the count sequence (*un, deux, trois* . . .) and when contrasting "one" with "a lot" could lead to interference for young children who are attempting to judge the accuracy of simple computations, such as $1 + 1 = 3$. Indeed, Houdé (1997) found that French-speaking 2-year-olds accepted simple sums such as $1 + 1 = 3$ "because there are lots". Hodent et al. hence contrasted the performance of French toddlers with that of English toddlers in simple computational problems analogous to those used with infants by Wynn (1992a; see Chapter 2). Mickey Mouse dolls or Barbar the Elephant dolls were used to present simple arithmetic problems. Hodent et al. predicted that French toddlers, but not English toddlers, should experience difficulties with sums like $1 + 2 = 4$, when the starting point of the operation was singular. However, neither nation was expected to experience difficulties when the starting point of the operation was plural, as in $2 + 1 = 4$. This was exactly what Hodent et al. found. The French 2-year-olds were significantly worse than the English 2-year-olds for the sum $1 + 2 = 4$ only. By 3 years of age, this cross-cultural difference had disappeared. Hodent et al. argued that language played a role in the cognitive representation of small numbers during a precise window of symbolic number development.

The converse idea, that it is not necessary to have a system of number names in order to have an idea of larger numbers, has also been supported by linguistic studies. One example is studies of indigenous tribes in the Amazon, who lack counting words. In particular, the Piraha only have the number words "one", "two", and "many" (Gordon, 2004). The Piraha do not even use the words "one" and "two" consistently. The Munduruku have number words from one to five (Pica, Lemer, & Izard 2004). The words "one", "two", and "three" are used consistently, but not the words "four" or "five". Above 5, the Munduruku show little consistency in how they use words like "some", "many", or "small quantity". Despite this lack of counting language, both tribes did very well in nonverbal number tasks involving set sizes up to 80. For example, in one task participants were asked to point to the display of dots in a pair of displays that was more numerous. Interestingly, the performance of both tribes suggested the use of Weber's law. As the ratio of the to-be-compared quantities approached 1, discrimination performance decreased. Further, accuracy in number discrimination decreased as target numbers increased. Both tribes hence appeared to be using the analog magnitude representation as a basis for their responses.

One developmental function of acquiring the count sequence might thus be to *detach* numerosity from the approximate analog representation. Number names enable any number to be interpreted precisely in nonanalog fashion. The experimental studies of children learning to count reviewed above support this idea. They suggest that children start to treat number words as referring to specific, unique numerosities even before they know exactly which numerosity each word refers to (e.g. Sarnecka & Gelman, 2004). According to this analysis, counting is very important for the development of a symbolic number system.

The development of other skills with numbers, such as addition, subtraction, multiplication, and division, cannot be described in this book due to space constraints. Certainly, the understanding of numbers as exact quantities will be important for developing accurate calculation skills. There are also other cognitive prerequisites for understanding mathematical procedures, however, and a thorough review is offered by Nunes and Bryant (1996). For example, the understanding of Piagetian reversibility and inversion (see Chapter 11) is likely to be related to the understanding of additive composition—that numbers are composed of other numbers, and hence that $4 + 5 = 9$, and $9 - 5 = 4$. The understanding of sharing is likely to be related to the understanding of division. Even preschoolers are good at sharing toys or sweets between a group of children, but this does not mean that they understand that the more potential recipients, the smaller the bounty per child. The understanding of ratio (one-to-many correspondence) appears to be important for multiplicative and proportional reasoning. Other Piagetian logical operations such as class inclusion are also important for mathematical reasoning. These logical operations are discussed in Chapter 11.

SUMMARY

Acquisition of the two dominant symbol systems in our culture, the alphabet and Arabic number, depends on different cognitive prerequisites. For the alphabet and other orthographies, the key is phonological development. Phonological development is a natural part of language acquisition, but there are individual differences in the quality of the phonological representations developed by children. These individual differences predict individual differences in the acquisition of literacy. Children with better phonological awareness acquire reading more easily. Children who experience unusual difficulties in developing well-specified phonological representations, perhaps because of problems in auditory processing, are at risk for developmental dyslexia.

Across languages, there is an apparently universal developmental sequence for acquiring phonological awareness of syllables, onsets, and rimes (larger grain sizes). Children learning very different spoken languages (e.g. English versus Chinese) develop syllable and onset-rime awareness prior to schooling. For phonological awareness of phonemes, there is cross-language divergence. Phoneme awareness typically develops in response to learning to read, and it develops more rapidly in children who are learning to read transparent alphabetic orthographies. These children also learn to decode faster than children who are learning to read less consistent orthographies. Hence for reading, the nature of the symbol system itself affects cognitive development. For typically developing children, however, these cognitive differences are transient in nature. Most children learn to read, whether they are learning a consistent alphabetic orthography, an inconsistent alphabetic orthography, or a nonalphabetic orthography. The neural systems underpinning skilled reading show more similarity than divergence across orthographies (Paulesu et al., 2001).

Acquisition of the number system depends on an analog magnitude representation that codes quantity via an internal continuum, and on automatic perceptual processes (referred to as "subitizing") that code the numerosity of very small sets (1, 2, and 3). The neural basis of the analog magnitude representation has been identified, and appears to function in similar ways in 4- and 5-year-old children and adults. The acquisition of the number system also depends on language. The acquisition of the count sequence, which is first learned as a verbal routine, appears to be very important for developing an understanding of symbolic number. The language of the count sequence seems to help children to organize their physiological/cognitive structures for number. The small numbers yielded by subitizing, and the larger approximate quantities yielded by the analog magnitude representation, can be coded precisely in nonanalog fashion by using the count sequence. The count sequence thus provides a linguistic structure for two of the central principles of a symbolic number system—the cardinal principle that numbers mean a distinctive individual quantity, and the ordinal principle that each number has a fixed place among other numerical entities that is dependent on increasing magnitude.

This account of the development of a symbolic number system provides a classic example of Vygotsky's idea that symbol systems transform human cognitive development. Cultural transmission of the count sequence to young children plays an important role in organizing the physiological/cognitive structures upon which the number system is built. Similarly, cultural transmission of the alphabet (and other orthographies) transforms the representation of spoken language. The physiological/cognitive structures for spoken language, and particularly for phonology, underpin the acquisition of literacy, but these structures are also transformed by literacy. As Frith (1998, p. 1051) observed, learning the alphabet is like catching a virus. "This virus infects all speech processing, as now whole word sounds are automatically broken up into sound constituents. Language is never the same again". For both reading and number, symbol systems enable cognition to develop beyond the constraints of biology. According to the data reviewed here, neither numerical nor orthographic representations are innate. Cognitive development is required. Both reading and number depend on pre-existing neural representations for coding visual and auditory information. However, both depend also on the child learning culturally determined symbolic systems, which shape cognitive development in particular ways.

CHAPTER 11

CONTENTS

Theories of cognitive development

Theories of cognitive development are explanatory systems that account for the data regarding "what develops". The most comprehensive theory of cognitive development has been Piaget's theory of logical development. Piaget was by training a biologist, and in his theory the primary causal mechanism for building knowledge was the adaptation to and refinement of existing cognitive "schemes" by the environment. Knowledge was constructed by the child as a consequence of his or her active experiences with the external world. An alternative explanatory account of cognitive development was proposed by Vygotsky, a Russian psychologist trained in philology. His theory had a more cultural focus, recognizing the key role of social interaction in cognitive development, and the important role of adults in mediating cultural knowledge for children and in supporting them in acquiring it. More recently, as cognitive neuroscience has become more prominent in exploring cognition, connectionist modeling has provided an explanatory framework for thinking about cognitive development. We have seen some examples in this book. Connectionism has generated models of how complex cognition (e.g. conceptual development; see Chapter 4) can arise from the learning activity of simple on-off nodes in a connected network. These computer networks are intended to be analogous to networks of neurons, which can either fire action potentials or not fire them. Hence connectionism can, in principle, explain cognitive development in terms of simple networks that learn complex structure from "input". None of these explanatory frameworks is completely satisfactory. Given the increasing importance of insights from cognitive neuroscience, the future of cognitive developmental theorizing seems likely to follow a hybrid route. Contemporary theories of cognitive development must acknowledge the importance of knowledge construction (Piaget) and of the social world (Vygotsky). At the same time, contemporary theories must be consistent with biological constraints on how the brain actually learns. A new theoretical framework for explaining how the brain learns is neuroconstructivism. This framework covers biological aspects of cognitive development, such as changes in the physical structure of the brain with learning, and consequent changes in the functional organization of the brain, using concepts such as "enbrainment". These different explanatory frameworks will be discussed in turn, and then analyzed in terms of the experiments that have been discussed in earlier chapters.

PIAGET'S THEORY

Piaget's fundamental interest was in the origins of knowledge, and he applied the principles of biology to the study of the development of knowledge in children.

One of his central assumptions was that knowledge structures (or schemes) adapt themselves to their environments. Piaget suggested that the cognitive system would naturally seek equilibrium, and that cognitive development was caused by two processes. These were "**accommodation**" and "**assimilation**". Accommodation was the process of adapting cognitive schemes for viewing the world (general concepts) to fit reality. Assimilation was the complementary process of interpreting experience (individual instances of general concepts) in terms of current cognitive schemes. As every cognitive equilibrium can be only partial, every existing equilibrium must evolve towards a higher form of equilibrium—towards a more adequate form of knowing. This process of knowledge evolution was thought to drive cognitive development. When one cognitive scheme became inadequate for making sense of the world, it was replaced by another.

Stages in cognitive development

Piaget is usually characterized as proposing a stage model of cognitive development, as his observations led him to propose that a major overhaul of current cognitive schemes occurred four times between infancy and adulthood. Hence he proposed four major cognitive stages in logical development, corresponding to four successive forms of knowing. During each of these stages, children were hypothesized to think and reason in a different way. Each stage was thought to require fundamental cognitive restructuring on the part of the child. However, Piaget recognized that the acquisition of each new way of thinking would not necessarily be synchronous across all the different domains of thought (see Chapman, 1988). Instead, he argued that the chronology of the stages might be extremely variable, and that such variability might also occur within a given stage.

Piaget's stages, and their approximate ages of occurrence, were:

1. The **sensory-motor period**: 0–2 years.
2. The period of pre-operations: 2–7 years.
3. The period of concrete operations: 7–11 years.
4. The period of formal operations: 11–12 years on.

Sensory-motor cognition was based on the infant's physical interactions with the world. The onset of representational thought came as pre-operational thinking developed, involving the internalization of action on the mental plane. When the results of such internalizations (called compositions) became mentally reversible, concrete operational cognition developed, marking the beginning of truly mental operations. Finally, during formal operational cognition, certain concrete operations became linked together, marking the onset of scientific thought. The ages of attainment that Piaget gave for the different cognitive stages were only approximations. For example, he suggested that the concrete operations of class inclusion and seriation (see below) might pursue slightly different developmental courses, the former being related to linguistic development and the latter to perceptual development. Nevertheless, the key idea was of an internal programming of cognitive change, based on states of "disequilibrium" between the child's mental states and the external world.

KEY TERMS

Accommodation
Adapting and changing cognitive schemes (general concepts) in a way that allows the world view to better fit reality.

Assimilation
Interpreting new experiences in terms of familiar (i.e. current) schemes.

Sensory-motor period
0–2 years: six stages of development, cognitive development as the infant's physical interactions with the world.

The sensory-motor stage

One of Piaget's major claims, a claim that has received support from data from cognitive neuroscience, was that thought develops from action. In his view, a "logic of action" existed prior to, and in addition to, the logic of thought. In Piaget's terms, a practical logic of relations and classes in terms of sensory-motor action was the precursor of the representational logic of relations and classes that emerged at the concrete operational stage. Piaget pointed out that babies are born with many means of interacting with their environment. Their sensory systems are functioning at birth, as we saw in Chapter 1. Babies also have a range of motor responses that are ready for use, such as sucking and grasping. Piaget argued that the presence of these reflexes meant that babies were born with the potential to know everything about their worlds, even though at birth they knew almost nothing. These basic abilities allowed infants to gain knowledge of the world and to build up hypotheses about it. Piaget's baby was conceptualized as busily interpreting and reinterpreting perceptual information in the light of his or her hypotheses, hypotheses that were drawn from sensory-motor experiences in the everyday world.

Piaget identified six substages of development within the sensory-motor stage. The first was the modification of reflexes. For example, the baby could learn to modify its sucking reflex in order to fit the contours of its mother's nipple (accommodation). At the same time, the baby assimilated the sucking response to an increasing range of objects, and gradually became able to distinguish between objects that would satisfy hunger and objects that would not. The second stage was called primary circular reactions. A circular reaction is a repetitive behavior. Babies seem to enjoy engaging in repetitive behaviors, and another important insight of Piaget's was that this repetition might have cognitive value. The first repetitive behaviors were concerned with the self, and thus Piaget labeled them "primary". Primary circular reactions involved the recreation of sensory experiences. A good example is thumb sucking.

The third sensory-motor stage was called secondary circular reactions. Secondary repetitive behaviors involve the outside world. For example, a baby might seek to recreate interesting events in its environment, such as dropping an object. The circular reaction would be to repeatedly drop the object without getting bored—a behavior that also requires repetitive behavior on the part of the baby's caretaker, who has to repeatedly pick the object up! The fourth stage was called the co-ordination of circular reactions. At this point, the baby became able to co-ordinate a series of behaviors in order to attain a goal. Piaget called this goal-oriented behavior "means–ends" behavior. An example is pulling on a blanket so that a desired toy at the edge of the blanket moves to a location within the baby's reach.

Thumb sucking is an example of Piaget's primary circular reactions, which involve the repetition of behaviors in order to relive a particular sensory experience.

The fifth sensory-motor stage was called tertiary circular reactions. By this stage, babies' ability to recreate events in the outside world had become more sophisticated. Stage 5 infants could conduct different trial-and-error explorations in order to determine the results of certain actions. For example, a baby may repeatedly drop an object in a variety of ways in order to examine the different trajectories that the object will take. The focus of interest for the infant is the variation of these trajectories, rather than the repetition of the action of dropping (as in secondary circular reactions). Such actions can be viewed as hypothesis-testing behavior, and Piaget argued that tertiary circular reactions led to the discovery of the spatial and causal relations between the objects involved.

The final stage of sensory-motor cognition was called the interiorization of schemes. At this point, the baby became able to anticipate the consequences of certain actions, and thus to work out the sequence of actions required to attain a desired goal prior to performing the actions themselves. This anticipation occurred via mental combination of the actions and their consequences, without the need for trial-and-error exploration. The interiorization of schemes hence marked the *cognitive* representation of actions and their consequences. These representations were detached from immediate action and were liberated from direct perception— they were fully symbolic. According to Piaget, stage 6 of sensory-motor cognition marked the beginning of conceptual thought.

Probably the most famous example of how Piaget thought that sensory-motor information led to the development of conceptual thought was his analysis of object permanence. Piaget measured the emerging conception of the permanence of objects by studying the development of babies' *searching behavior*. As we saw in Chapter 2, infants begin to search for partially hidden objects at the age of around 4–5 months. However, an object must be partially visible for the infant to try and retrieve it. By around 9 months, the infant becomes able to search for fully hidden objects. Now the A-not-B error appears. Search behavior is apparently determined by previously successful actions. By around 12 months, the A-not-B error disappears. As long as the infants see the object being moved to a new hiding location, they can retrieve it over multiple hidings. Piaget acknowledged that this behavior indicated an understanding of the object itself and of its relation to other objects, but noted that search difficulties remained when displacement was "invisible" (i.e. not witnessed by the infant). A full conception of objects was only allowed once invisible displacements were solved, at around 18 months. Now the infant could find objects wherever they were hidden. For Piaget, this marked the attainment of a cognitive representation of the object, detached from motor action and from sensory perception. More direct measures of mental representations, for example by using neuroimaging, suggest that relying on search behavior to index cognitive representations was misguided (see Chapter 2).

Evaluation

Clearly, Piaget was wrong about how early cognitive representations develop. However, if we allow much younger babies the ability to develop cognitive representations, even for objects that are out of view, then Piaget's description of sensory-motor cognition is actually remarkably consistent with the current data on infant development discussed in Chapters 1 and 2. The idea that sensory-motor responses are a primary source of information for infants must be correct, and the idea that sensory-motor behaviors play an important role in knowledge acquisition fits with statistical learning (which is primarily sensory), learning by imitation (primarily motor), learning by analogy, and explanation-based learning. Piaget argued that sensory-motor responses were foundational because of the "logic of action". Sensory-motor behaviors *became* thought. In 1998, I argued that this was unlikely. However, the neuroimaging data now available suggest that this idea is very plausible. Similar ideas are now proposed by the adult literature on "embodied cognition". The recognition of the distributed nature of mental representations also supports the view that sensory-motor representations are part of thought. For example, in Chapter 4 we saw that sensory-motor experiences associated with different concepts like "cup" are retained as part of the concept of a cup. Cognition appears to be embedded and not amodal. Piaget's view that the development of the object concept took 18 months to achieve was incorrect. However, his focus on the importance of action and his recognition that the repetition and recreation of sensory-motor experience were an important means of learning were fundamental insights into infant cognition.

Piaget's ideas about the interiorization of action are also interesting in the light of more recent infant data. Piaget argued that sensory-motor behaviors became representational via interiorization, and that this interiorization occurred via "motor analogies". For example, he had noticed that his own children imitated certain spatial relations that they had observed in the physical world with their own bodies. They imitated the opening and closing of a match-box by opening and closing their hands and mouths. Piaget suggested that this behavior showed that the infants were trying to understand the mechanism of the match-box through a motor analogy, reproducing a kinesthetic image of opening and closing. This is reminiscent of the "like me" analogy discussed in Chapter 3. Although that analogy was discussed in relation to the development of social cognition, Piaget is using a similar explanatory framework involving motor imitation for understanding the physical world. An outstanding empirical question is whether action provides a separate and autonomous source of knowledge from representational or reflective understanding. Given the massive interconnectivity in the brain, it seems unlikely that we develop separate and autonomous sources of knowledge about anything in the world. However, this is an empirical question, and is hotly debated in adult cognition (e.g. Caramazza & Mahon, 2003). As noted in earlier chapters, sources of knowledge that are intimately linked during development may achieve a degree of independence in the developed system (e.g. language and number; see Chapter 10). Hence empirical longitudinal data are required to answer this question.

In Piaget's theory, analogies were also thought to play a role in the generalization of sensory-motor schemes to new objects. In fact, Piaget argued that analogical transfer was rapid once a new physical concept had been understood. Commenting on the acquisition of the "pull" schema (the ability to use string-like objects as a "means for bringing"), Piaget wrote:

> *Let us note that once the new schema is acquired, it is applied from the outset to analogous situations. The behavior pattern of the string is without any difficulty applied to the watch chain. Thus, at each acquisition we fall back on the application of familiar means to new situations. (Piaget, 1952, p. 297, cited by Brown, 1990)*

As discussed in Chapter 2, recent experiments on analogy have supported Piaget's view. Simple relational mappings are available to infants as young as 3 months (see Greco, Hayne, & Rovee-Collier, 1990), and are readily transferred to new objects (e.g. to novel mobiles).

The pre-operational and concrete operational stages

In order to document cognitive changes beyond stage 6 of sensory-motor cognition, Piaget investigated children's understanding of the properties of concrete objects and the relations between those objects. The set of logical concepts that described classes of objects and their relations were called the "concrete operations". Children were thought to develop a full understanding of the properties and relations of concrete objects rather gradually, between the ages of around 2 and 7 years. The key concrete operations were children's understanding of transitive relations between objects of different lengths or heights ("transitivity"), children's understanding of classes of objects and their part-whole relations ("class inclusion"), and children's understanding of addition, subtraction, and equivalence ("conservation"). Along with related logical concepts such as **seriation**, these operations of transitivity, class inclusion, and conservation have been the main focus of later research.

Piaget's explanation for these logical developments was that during **pre-operational** cognition, the schemes or concepts of sensory-motor thought were redeveloped in the mental realm. For example, the interiorization of operations such as addition and subtraction on concrete objects led to the representation of the formal properties of whole numbers, such as that $2 + 2 = 4$ simultaneously implies that $4 - 2 = 2$. The recognition of the "reversibility" of this operation was thought to be a critical feature of concrete operational cognition. The functional units of thought were not isolated concepts and judgments, but an integrated system of reversible and interdependent structures:

> The child can grasp a certain operation only if he is capable, at the same time, of correlating operations by modifying them in different, well-determined ways—for instance, by inverting them . . . the operations always represent reversible structures which depend on a total system . . . (Piaget, 1952, p. 252)

The main characteristics of pre-operational thought were that it was **egocentric**, in that the child perceived and interpreted the world in terms of the self, that it displayed **centration**, in that the child tended to fix on one aspect of a situation or object and ignore other aspects, and that it displayed a lack of **reversibility**, in that the child was unable mentally to reverse a series of events or steps of reasoning. The pre-operational child was thus seen as prelogical, having a subjective and self-centered grasp of the world. As with sensory-motor cognition, these insights clearly capture aspects of young children's behavior in certain situations. The acquisition of the concrete operations was thought to be marked by the gradual waning of egocentricity. Children became able to "decenter" or to consider multiple aspects of a situation simultaneously, and they became able to grasp "reversibility" or the ability to understand that any operation on an object simultaneously implied its inverse. Piaget argued that

KEY TERMS

Seriation
Understanding that objects can form an ordered series in term of their physical or psychological attributes.

Pre-operational
2–7 years: symbolic development (e.g. language) and developing understanding of the properties of concrete objects and the relations between these objects.

Egocentric thought
Perception and interpretation of the world in terms of the self (e.g. inability to "put oneself in another's shoes").

Centration
Tendency to focus on one aspect of a situation or object and ignore other aspects.

Reversibility of thought
Inability mentally to reverse a series of events or steps of reasoning.

the organization of the concrete operations could be described in terms of mathematical groupings, for example $A + A' = B$ (class inclusion), $A > B$, $B > C$, therefore $A > C$ (transitivity), and $A = B$, A transforms to A', therefore $A' = B$ (conservation). Piaget's idea was that cognitive structures developed to mirror mathematical logic. The psychological reality of the logical structures representing truly logical thought and their reversibility could be represented formally. Most subsequent research on pre-operational and concrete operational thought has neglected Piaget's focus on mathematical groupings, however. Instead, it has focused on whether logical concepts like conservation, transitivity, and class inclusion are present at an earlier age than Piaget supposed. Rather than assuming that children who fail a Piagetian logical task are incompetent, recent research explores the possibility that children's knowledge becomes obscured by misleading aspects of the tasks. Younger children, with their poorer executive skills, may be unable to inhibit responses triggered by these misleading aspects (see Houdé, 2000, for an interesting analysis).

Transitivity

One key logical concept identified by Piaget was **transitivity** (the transitive inference). Transitive relations hold between any entities that can be organized into an ordinal series, and are fundamental to basic mathematical concepts such as measuring. Piaget and Inhelder (1956) proposed that a typical transitive inference problem of the form "If Tom is bigger than Mark, and Mark is bigger than John, who is bigger, Tom or John?" could not be solved until concrete operational reasoning had been acquired. Children's ability to make these kinds of transitive inferences before the age of 6–7 years has been hotly debated. Much of the debate focused on an experiment carried out by Bryant and Trabasso (1971), which showed that even 4-year-olds could make transitive inferences as long as they were trained to remember the premises comprising the inferential problem. This suggested that the logical ability to make a transitive inference was present in quite young children, and that sensory-motor concepts did not have to be redeveloped in the mental realm.

Bryant and Trabasso used a five-term series ($A > B > C > D > E$) in order to provide a true test of inferential ability for 4-, 5-, and 6-year-old children. In a five-term series, two components will be both "larger" and "smaller". These components are B and D ($B > C$, $A > B$; $D > E$, $C > D$). In a three-term series, in contrast, A is always large and C is always small ($A > B > C$). If children are trained to remember the premises $A > B$ and $B > C$ in a three-term series, then in theory they could work out the relationship between A and C without using a transitive inference, by remembering that A is large and that C is small. However, when children are trained to remember the premises in a five-term series, a memory strategy will not work for an inference about the relationship between B and D. B and D have been both large and small.

Bryant and Trabasso's (1971) paradigm was based on colored wooden rods. Children were shown five rods (red, white, yellow, blue, and green), each of which was a different length (3, 4, 5, 6, and 7 inches long). The rods were always presented in pairs. For example, the child might learn that blue was larger than red, and that red was larger than green. The rods were presented via a container box that had holes of different depths bored into it, so that only one inch of each rod was seen in any training trial. During this training phase of the experiment, the child was asked which rod was taller (or shorter). After making a choice, the two rods were removed from

KEY TERM

Transitivity
Understanding that the relationship between two items that cannot be compared directly may be inferred by reference to a third or more intermediaries, e.g. John is taller than Paul, Paul is taller than Peter, who is taller, John or Peter?

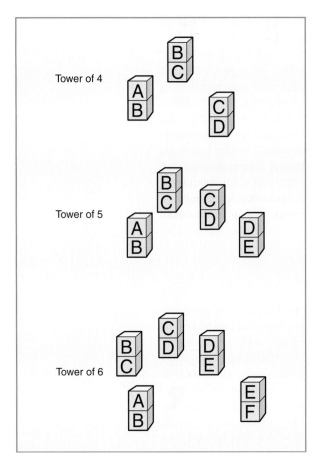

FIGURE 11.1
Examples of the premise towers used by Pears and Bryant (1990). The letters A, B, C, D, E, and F denote different colors. Copyright © The British Psychological Society. Reproduced with permission.

the container and shown to the child, providing direct visual feedback about their relative length. During the testing phase of the experiment, the children were asked to make a comparison without feedback regarding the true length of the rods. As well as the four direct comparisons on which they had been trained (A > B, B > C, C > D, D > E), the children were asked about the six possible inferential comparisons in a random order (A ? C, A ? D, A ? E, B ? D, B ? E, C ? E). For the critical B ? D comparison, 78% of the 4-year-olds, 88% of the 5-year-olds, and 92% of the 6-year-olds were successful. Bryant and Trabasso concluded that children at all three age levels were able to make genuine transitive inferences very well.

This conclusion did not go undisputed (see Breslow, 1981, for a useful review). One problem with the rods task was that the container used during the comparisons provided children with a visual reminder of which were the "long" rods and which were the "short" rods. For example, for the critical B ? D comparison, rod B was necessarily near the "long" end of the box and rod D was near the "short" end of the box. This spatial cue might have enabled the children to solve the comparison correctly by associating the respective rods with the large or the small end points of the box. Pears and Bryant (1990) thus eliminated the memory load in the transitive task completely, by using visible premises. Children were shown pairs of colored bricks presented in little "towers" one on top of the other. The child's task was to build a complete tower of bricks from single bricks of the appropriate colors, using the premise pairs as a guide.

Before being allowed to build the target towers, the children were asked a series of inferential questions such as "Which will be the higher in the tower that you are going to build, the yellow brick or the blue one?". Three kinds of tower had to be constructed during the experiment: four-brick towers (involving three premises), five-brick towers (involving four premises), and six-brick towers (involving five premises). To take a five-brick tower as an example, if the little towers showed red on top and blue beneath (RtB), blue on top and green beneath (BtG), green on top and yellow beneath (GtY), and yellow on top and white beneath (YtW), then the target tower was (Rt Bt Gt Yt W). The different kinds of problems used are shown in Figure 11.1. Pears and Bryant found that the children were significantly above chance in their performance on two-thirds of the critical inferential questions. From this finding, they argued that 4-year-olds do possess the ability to make transitive inferences, at least about the continuum of space.

Conservation and invariance

Another logical concept investigated by Piaget was **conservation**, which is the ability to conserve quantity across changes in appearance. This logical operation underpins the understanding of invariance, an important logical insight that in turn underpins the number system and gives stability to the physical world. Children who understand the principle of invariance understand that simply changing the appearance of a quantity does not affect the amount that is present, as the change in appearance is reversible. Changes in one dimension can be compensated for by changes in another. Piaget designed the conservation task as a measure of children's understanding of the principle of invariance.

In the conservation task, children's understanding of invariance was assessed by asking them to compare two initially identical quantities, one of which was then transformed. For example, a child could be shown two rows of five beads arranged in 1 : 1 correspondence, or two glasses of liquid filled to exactly the same level (Figure 11.2). An adult experimenter would then alter the appearance of one of these quantities while the child was watching. For example, the adult could pour the liquid

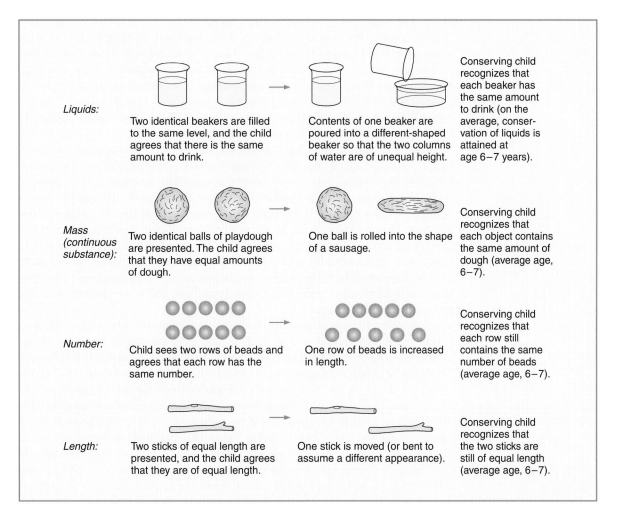

FIGURE 11.2

Examples of different versions of the conservation task. From Schaffer (1985). Adapted from *Developmental Psychology: Childhood and Adolescence*. By D. R. Schaffer. Copyright © 1996, 1993, 1989, 1985 Brooks/ Cole Publishing Company, Pacific Grove, CA 93950, a division of International Thompson Publishing, Inc.

from one of the glasses into a shorter, shallower beaker, or could spread out the beads in one of the rows so that the row looked longer. Piaget's experimental question was whether children understood that quantity remained invariant despite these changes in perceptual appearance. The answer to this question appeared to be "no". Most children below the age of around 7 who were given the conservation task told the experimenter that there was now less water in the shallower beaker, or that there were more beads in the spread-out row.

The simplest way to test children's understanding of invariance, however, would have been to show them a single quantity, such as a glass of liquid or a row of pennies, and then to transform the appearance of this single quantity. As pointed out by Elkind and Schoenfeld (1972), the traditional conservation task involved a hidden transitive inference. In the traditional task, the child is shown two identical quantities, Q1 and Q2, and one is then transformed (e.g. Q1 to Q1A). The child is usually asked "Is there more, less, or the same as before?". To answer correctly, the child must reason that: (1) quantity 1 = quantity 2 (Q1 = Q2); (2) quantity 1 has changed to quantity 1A, but the two are still equivalent (Q1 = Q1A); and therefore (3) that quantity 1A = quantity 2 (Q1A = Q2; see Table 11.1). The child is being asked to conserve equivalence rather than to conserve invariance. Elkind and Schoenfeld hence compared the "conservation of identity" (one entity is transformed) with the conservation of equivalence by 4- and 6-year-old children. The children had little difficulty in judging the invariance of a single quantity, but the 4-year-olds were poor at judging quantitative equivalence. Some understanding of the conservation of quantity is thus present by age 4.

Most investigators who have used the traditional conservation task, however, have replicated Piaget's findings. Children even make conservation errors when they are reasoning about natural transformations in equivalence paradigms. For example, if children are shown two rows of toy boats floating in a pool, and then one row is allowed to drift apart so that it appears longer than the other row, the children claim that there are more boats in the longer row (Miller, 1982). Children can even fail in identity paradigms. For example, Miller (1982) showed that if children are told to watch their classmates playing a game of "Simon Says", and Simon Says "spread out" or "bunch together", the children making the conservation judgments claim that there are more children when the group is spread out, and fewer children when the group is bunched together.

One aspect of conservation that has come under the spotlight is the pragmatics of the traditional Piagetian conservation task. The intentional structure of the experimenter's nonlinguistic behavior is at variance with the answer that is desired. The child is asked a question about two quantities ("are there more, less, or the same?"), an adult carries out an apparently salient transformation, and then asks them the same question again. If someone asks you the same question twice, it usually means that you should change your answer. The experimental set-up may lead children to answer the question that they think the tester plans to ask, rather than attending to the precise question that is in fact asked. Donaldson (1978), Rose and Blank (1974), and Siegal (1991) have all argued that different aspects of the pragmatics of the conservation task may mislead children into giving nonconserving responses.

TABLE 11.1	The hidden transitive inference in the traditional conservation task		
Step (A):	Q1	=	Q2
Step (B):	Q1	=	Q1A
(therefore, via transitive inference)			
Step (C):	Q1A	=	Q2

Based on Elkind and Schoenfeld, 1972.

Perhaps the most compelling study for the influence of pragmatics was the ingenious "naughty teddy" paradigm devised by McGarrigle and Donaldson (1975). In their studies, 4- and 5-year-old children were told that they would play a special game with the experimenter. The children were shown a cardboard box containing a teddy bear, and were told that the teddy was very naughty and was liable to escape from his box from time to time and try to "mess up the toys" and "spoil the game". The conservation materials were then brought out (e.g. two rows of counters in one-to-one correspondence). The child was asked "Are there more here or more here or are they both the same number?". All of a sudden, the naughty teddy appeared and altered the length of one of the rows by shoving the counters together. The teddy received the appropriate scolding and the children were then asked again: "Are there more here or more here or are they both the same number?". Under these conditions of an accidental transformation of the arrays, the majority of 4- and 5-year-old children in the experiment gave conserving responses.

However, given the findings of Miller (1982) concerning natural transformations, it must be asked whether children who experience accidental versions of the conservation task are receiving a proper test of conservation. Piaget's idea was that younger children make mistakes because they tend to focus on one perceptual dimension of the transformed quantity and ignore the compensating dimension. In exciting and accidental paradigms, the children may not actually look at the transformed arrays (see Bryant, 1982). One way to explore whether there is genuine logical development in the conservation task is to study the same children over time. Siegler (1995) has used a "microgenetic" method to study the mastery of number conservation in 5-year-olds using a task based on rows of buttons.

Siegler tried to induce cognitive change by giving the children different types of feedback in a conservation training paradigm. Three types of training were studied during four successive training sessions. One group of 5-year-olds was simply told whether their answers to different problems were correct or incorrect (the "feedback" training group). Children in a second group were asked to explain their reasoning, and were then given feedback concerning the correctness of their answers to the problems (a kind of explanation-based learning). Members of a third group received feedback about their answers, and were then asked by the experimenter "How do you think I knew that?". This last type of training required the children to explain the experimenter's reasoning. This condition was expected to encourage the children to search for the causes of the observed events. This third condition indeed had the largest effect on conservation performance. Learning in this condition was found to involve two distinct realizations: that relative length did not predict which row had the greatest number of objects, and that the type of quantitatively relevant transformation did (i.e. whether buttons were added to or subtracted from the rows, or whether the appearance of the rows was altered by lengthening or shortening).

Interestingly, understanding of the importance of the type of transformation did not lead to the immediate rejection of the less advanced forms of reasoning, even when the same problem was presented several times during the experiment. Instead, children's understanding of conservation occurred gradually rather than suddenly. Siegler also found large individual differences in children's ability to benefit from having to explain the experimenter's reasoning. The children who benefited most tended to be those who had displayed greater variability of reasoning in the pretest. Siegler concluded that children use several types of reasoning before as well as during transitional periods of cognitive development. He suggested that an "overlapping waves" model of logical development may be more appropriate, with certain ways of thinking being prevalent at different times. Siegler's data may also be understood in terms of the child's growing efficiency in inhibiting misleading aspects of the transformations. As will be recalled, we saw in Chapter 6 that adults who have learned Newtonian physics still activate misleading representations based on impetus theories of motion. Those adults who are better at inhibiting these misleading representations are more accurate in reasoning tasks (Petitto & Dunbar, in press). Cognitive neuroscience studies of children experiencing Siegler's paradigms would be very interesting. This might offer a way of testing Houdé's (2000) hypothesis about the role of inhibitory processes in logical development.

Class inclusion

The third major logical operation among Piaget's concrete operations was **class inclusion**. The logical concept of class inclusion involves understanding that a set of items can be simultaneously part of a combined set and part of an embedded set. For example, imagine a bunch of six flowers, four of which are red and two of which are white. The combined set is the six flowers, and the embedded sets are the white flowers and the red flowers. To see whether young children understand the logical concept of class inclusion, Piaget devised the class inclusion task. The child was shown a combined set, such as the flowers, and was then asked "Are there more red flowers or more flowers here?". Children younger than approximately 6 years of age usually responded that there were more red flowers. Piaget argued that children could only deal with the parts or with the whole separately. They could not think about the flowers in two ways simultaneously as they lacked reversibility—just as they could not simultaneously think about total length and gap size when trying to judge the quantity in a row of pennies.

Markman and Seibert (1976) argued instead that the children could be failing to make part–whole comparisons because Piaget's class inclusion question sounded a bit strange. In natural speech, we do not usually contrast a whole and a part by asking "Are there more red flowers or more flowers here?". For a part–part comparison we would ask "Are there more red flowers or more white flowers?", and for a part–whole comparison we might say "Are there more red flowers, or are there more flowers in the bunch?". The use of the term "bunch" is a natural linguistic device for referring to a collection of objects. Collections have some degree of internal organization and form natural units which are marked in the spoken language. Collection terms alert language users to wholes rather than parts. Piaget's class inclusion question relies on the repeated use of the class (part) term "flower", which might make the listener assume that a part–part comparison was required.

To test this idea, Markman and Seibert contrasted 5- to 6-year-old children's class inclusion performance in two different versions of the class inclusion task. In one version, the standard class inclusion question was asked using Piaget's class-term format. In the second version, the class inclusion question was asked using the collection terms found in natural language. The children in the collection version of the experiment were asked about four different types of collection, a bunch of grapes, a class of children, a pile of blocks, and a family of frogs. For example, the children were shown some grapes and told:

Here is a bunch of grapes, there are green grapes and there are purple grapes, and this is the bunch. Who would have more to eat, someone who ate the green grapes or someone who ate the bunch?

The children in the standard version of the experiment were asked about the same stimuli (grapes, children etc.), but were told:

> *Here are some grapes, there are green grapes and there are purple grapes. Who would have more to eat, someone who ate the green grapes or someone who ate the grapes?*

Markman and Seibert found that the children performed at a significantly higher level when the collection term was used to pose the class inclusion question (70% correct) than when the class term was used (45% correct). They argued that this showed that the psychological coherence of collections was greater than that of classes, as collections are more readily conceptualized as wholes. The data suggest that even 4-year-olds have the logical concept of class inclusion. They appear illogical because the unnatural language of the standard class inclusion task induces them to make part–part comparisons.

Markman and Seibert's results were replicated by Fuson, Lyons, Pergament, Hall, and Kwon (1988) with 5- and 6-year-olds, and also by Hodges and French (1988) with younger children (3- and 4-year-olds). Fuson et al. also found that experience with the collection terms transferred to classic Piagetian class inclusion problems employing class terms. However, Dean, Chabaud, and Bridges (1981) argued that collection terms could facilitate performance in the class inclusion task simply because collection terms imply large numbers. They pointed out that if children interpret collection nouns as synonymous with "a lot", then their performance on the class inclusion question would improve simply because of the connotation of a large number of objects. Dean et al. gave 5- and 6-year-old children part–whole problems in which the collection term was used to describe the part rather than the whole. For example, Dean et al. told the children:

> *Here are some ants, some red ants and some brown ants. Suppose the red ants were an army, but the brown ants were not an army. Do you think there are more in the army of red ants, or more ants?*

Forty-five per cent of children responded that there were more red ants, even though they could see that there were fewer red ants than brown ants in the display. Dean et al. argued that these errors showed the influence of the "large number" connotation of collection terms.

A different way of understanding these data is to accept that language can bias our cognitive responses. Armies are usually enormous, and perhaps the children assumed that the red ants visible on the table were only representatives of the whole army. Even adult logic can be misled by clever wording, which is a staple of the advertising industry. The real question with respect to Piaget's theory is whether the logical structures of class inclusion, transitivity, and conservation are available to young children. Regarding class inclusion reasoning, the structural organization of the family is a highly familiar example of an inclusive set (see Halford, 1993). Most young children know that a family is made up of parents and children. The combined set of the family thus has two natural embedded sets, adults and children. These embedded sets also have their own natural language labels ("parents", "children"). Goswami and Pauen (2005) investigated whether family structure could provide a useful analogy for more traditional class inclusion problems involving piles of blocks and bunches of balloons.

The children in Goswami and Pauen's study (4- to 5-year-olds) had all failed the traditional Piagetian class inclusion task, which was given as a pretest ("Are there more red flowers or more flowers?"). They were then shown a toy family, for example a family of toy mice (two large mice as parents, three small mice as children) or a family of yo-yos (two large yo-yos as parents, three small yo-yos as children). Their job was to create analogous families (two parents and three children) from an assorted pile of toy animals (such as fluffy toy bears, ladybirds, ducks, and crocodiles) or from a pile of other toys (such as toy cars, spinning tops, balls, and helicopters). After the children had correctly created four families that were analogous to the mice/yo-yo families (having two parents and three children), they were given four class-inclusion problems involving toy frogs, sheep, building blocks, and balloons. The class inclusion problems were posed using collection terms ("group", "herd", "pile", "bunch"). A control group of children received the same class-inclusion problems using collection terms, but did not receive an analogy training session in which they learned to create families. The results showed that the children in the "create-a-family" condition solved more of the class inclusion problems. They appeared to be using analogies to family structure.

Evaluation

This survey of some of the key experiments that have challenged Piaget's view that pre-operational children lack logical concepts like class inclusion and transitivity has been necessarily brief. However, it has echoed many of the conclusions reached in Chapter 9. "Pure" measures of reasoning, in which logical abilities are measured independently of the context in which they are required, are difficult to devise. When familiar, "child-centered" materials are used, and when attention is paid to linguistic and nonlinguistic aspects of the experimental set-up, then the logic of the concrete operations appears to be understood by 4-year-olds. Furthermore, as also seen in Chapter 9, these experiments document the facilitatory effects of accessing familiar relational or organizational structures on children's performance in reasoning tasks. For example, in deductive reasoning, Harris and Nunes (1996) and Light et al. (1989) found that the activation of an appropriate permission schema helped children to reason successfully in the selection task. In this chapter, we have seen that a family structure scenario or a tower-building scenario can reveal logical competence with class inclusion or with transitivity. In terms of logical development, the concrete operations appear to be similar to deductive and inductive reasoning. Children reason in similar ways to adults, but are more easily misled by interfering variables such as contextual variables, because they are worse at inhibiting irrelevant information.

Developmentally, therefore, sensory-motor cognition does not seem to be redeveloped in the mental realm, as Piaget argued. Instead, the crucial factors in explaining development appear to be the augmentation of sensory-motor knowledge by increasing experience, some of which is active and some of which is transmitted by language (discussed below). Logical development is more likely to depend on the ability to reflect metacognitively on one's knowledge, and efficiently to inhibit competing knowledge that is interfering with the application of logic. With developments in metacognition and executive function, children can apply concepts like transitivity and invariance in a strategic way to new situations. Houdé (2000) offers an interesting example of this framework for explaining cognitive development that is based on inhibition. Thoughtful treatments of Piaget's theory that disagree with the arguments given in this chapter can be found in Chapman (1988), Smith (1992), and Smith (2002).

Formal operational thought

According to Piaget's theory, cognitive change beyond the concrete operational period depended on the emerging ability to take the results of concrete operations and to generate hypotheses about their logical relationships. This "formal operational" reasoning became available at the age of approximately 11 or 12 years. Piaget described this level of reasoning as "operating on operations", or "second-order" reasoning:

> *This notion of second-order operations also expresses the general characteristic of formal thought—it goes beyond the framework of transformations bearing directly on empirical reality (concrete operations) and subordinates it to a system of hypothetico-deductive operations, i.e. operations which are possible.*
> *(Inhelder & Piaget, 1958, p. 254)*

Piaget characterized formal operational reasoning in terms of the ability to apply a formal system such as propositional logic to the elementary operations concerning classes of objects and their relations. Again, the underlying idea was that cognitive structures developed to mirror mathematical logic.

Piaget described the basis of this propositional logic in terms of the combinatorial system describing all 16 possible binary relations between the entities p, q, *not-p*, and *not-q* (such as the conditional rule "if p then q"; discussed in Chapter 9). He also described the subsystem of transformations that could operate on these relations (such as finding the inverse relation or the reciprocal relation). This latter analysis has been called the INRC grouping (I for identity of the relation, N for negation or inverse, R for reciprocity, and C for correlation). The presence of these binary combinatorial relations, and of the INRC operations, was thought to be the hallmark of **formal operational thought**. As with concrete operational thought, however, most subsequent research has neglected Piaget's focus on mathematical groupings, and has focused instead on younger children's performance in the tasks that Piaget used to demonstrate the presence of the formal operations.

Formal operational tasks

Formal operational thought was scientific thought, as Piaget believed that the attainment of the formal operations allowed the child to represent alternative hypotheses and their deductive implications. Indeed, many of Piaget's tests for the presence of formal operational structures involved scientific tasks, such as discovering the rule that determines whether material bodies will float or sink in water, discovering the rule between weight and distance that will enable a balance beam to balance, and discovering the rule that governs the oscillation of a pendulum. All of these rules were part of the combinatorial or INRC groupings. For example, the rule governing the behavior of the balance beam is an inverse proportional relation between weight and distance (that simultaneously increasing the weight and distance on one arm of the balance is equivalent to decreasing the weight and increasing the distance on the other arm). Discovery of such proportionality was thought to be a key feature of formal operational reasoning.

Piaget's experimental method was to allow children to manipulate the independent variables (e.g. the length of the string and the weight of the bob in the pendulum task), and then see whether they could arrive at the correct rule. Most children did not manage to discover the appropriate rules before the age of around 11 years. For example, in the pendulum task, children needed to use strings of different lengths and bobs of different weights in order to discover that the period of a pendulum is a function of its length. As children usually began the task by believing that the weight of the bob must be an important factor in determining the oscillation of the pendulum, they needed to hold the length of the string constant while experimenting with a variety of weights in order to conclude that weight alone does not affect the pendulum's period. Children younger than 11 to 12 years usually failed to see the necessity for holding other variables such as string length constant, and thus failed to reason according to Piaget's combinatorial system (use of the system can be expressed as follows: If p is "increases in the period of oscillation", and q is "decreases in the length of the string", then p implies q and vice versa). Piaget argued that children who manipulated the two variables correctly showed an awareness of this combination, and also of all the other possible combinations in the group, since the other combinations were discarded as being irrelevant to the problem at hand. More recent experiments suggest that the key determinants of scientific reasoning in these paradigms may be somewhat different, however. For example, the work of Howe on scientific reasoning has suggested that hypothesis testing only changes conceptual knowledge when children debate outcomes with their peers or teachers (e.g. Howe, Tolmie, Duchak-Tanner, & Rattray, 2000). Nine-year-olds who debated their conceptual knowledge before beginning a scientific task (about shadows) and reached a consensus, and who then tested that consensual hypothesis experimentally as a group, did show conceptual changes in understanding.

The emphasis on the discovery of proportionality as a key factor in formal operational reasoning also led Piaget to include reasoning by analogy among his formal operational tasks. His logic was simple. As a full appreciation of the possible relations between objects was a concrete operational skill, the construction of relations between those relations must be a formal operational skill. Analogical reasoning was higher-order reasoning in the sense that the simple relations in an analogy ("lower-order relations") had to be linked by a relation at a higher level in order to make the analogy valid. Analogies also involved proportional reasoning, as an analogy like "Rome is to Italy as Paris is to France" (Rome : Italy :: Paris : France) was logically equivalent to a proportional expression like $3 : 4 = 15 : 20$.

Evaluation

Evidence discussed in earlier chapters has shown that formal operational reasoning is available prior to adolescence in a variety of paradigms. For example, in Chapter 9 we discussed a series of experiments showing that the ability to reason by analogy is present in children as young as 2–3 years of age (e.g. Goswami & Brown, 1989, 1990; Singer-Freeman, 2005). In Chapter 6, we analyzed a number of experiments on scientific reasoning. In the balance scale task, we saw that 9-year-olds could use the multiplicative integration rule to link weight and distance (Wilkening & Anderson, 1991). When the ability to combine information about different dimensions was tested using the barking dog and fleeing animals task (requiring the integration of time and velocity to judge distance), even 5-year-olds showed an ability to use multiplicative rules (Wilkening, 1982). Wilkening (1982) noted that this finding completely contradicted Piaget's notion that time had to be derived from information about speed and distance, and that the operations for deriving time required formal operational reasoning. Chapter 6 also reviewed work on hypothesis testing by children and their understanding of the deductive implications of evidence (e.g. as conclusive or inconclusive; Sodian et al., 1991; Ruffman et al., 1993). It was shown that although younger children can fail to test hypotheses in a systematic way, can omit to control for confounding variables, and tend to seek confirmatory rather than disconfirmatory evidence, adults will behave in the same ways in certain circumstances. Meanwhile, the work of Howe and colleagues showed that 9-year-olds can evaluate scientific hypotheses by testing relevant variables when they are working in collaborative peer groups supported by teachers.

Again, the core factors in successful formal operational reasoning appear to be familiarity and context or circumstance, including educational context. Successful scientific reasoning can be promoted by teachers who guide students in testing hypotheses that have been reached through group discussion and consensus (Howe & Tolmie, 2003). Recall that Blaisdell et al. (2006) found that rats tested in food prediction scenarios made the causal inferences predicted by causal Bayes nets on the basis of purely observational learning (Chapter 6). They also correctly differentiated between common-cause models, causal chains, and direct causal links. Data such as these suggest that any model of logical development based on qualitatively different kinds of reasoning becoming available at different ages will be wrong. Instead, the core factors to explore with respect to developmental changes in reasoning might be familiarity and context (including contextual support, e.g. from teachers), metacognition, and language.

Nevertheless, Piaget's core idea that cognitive structures mirror mathematical systems was very insightful. Similar arguments have been applied here to the learning brain. For example, mathematical algorithms for extracting causal structure from covariation data (such as causal Bayes nets) have been important for showing that, in principle, simple learning systems can extract causally accurate information from perceptual data (see Chapter 6). Similarly, systems that can learn the patterns or regularities in environmental input captured by conditional probabilities can, in principle, acquire complex cognitive structures like language and concepts (see Chapters 4 and 5). Although the INRC grouping chosen by Piaget may not have been the appropriate mathematical model for cognition, future empirical work may supplant machine learning algorithms like causal Bayes nets and explanation-based learning. Again, the critical data will be empirical data about what children (and animals) learn, and how they learn it.

VYGOTSKY'S THEORY

The notion that developmental changes in reasoning might be better explained by factors such as familiarity, context, metacognition, and language fits well with the theoretical emphasis of Vygotsky's theory of cognitive development. Vygotsky recognized the importance of language and of cultural context in cognitive development. Although he did not live long enough to generate the wealth of experimental data contributed by Piaget, his ideas about cognitive development were of comparable importance. Whereas Piaget focused on how the individual child constructed knowledge for him- or herself, Vygotsky argued that knowledge originated in socially meaningful activity and was shaped by language. Social context and culture were crucial in explaining cognitive development, and language played an essential role in the organization of "higher psychological functions" (Vygotsky, 1978, p. 23). Language was seen as the primary symbolic system that

Lev Semeonovich Vygotsky, 1896–1934, recognized the key role of language and social interaction in cognitive development.

children could respond to psychologically. Language hence mediated cognition. Vygotsky argued that cognition developed prior to language, as demonstrated by the cognitive activities of babies. However, "the most significant moment in the course of intellectual development . . . occurs when speech and practical activity, two previously completely independent lines of development, converge" (p. 24). This convergence was marked by egocentric or private speech, which Vygotsky interpreted as fundamental in organizing the child's cognitive activities. Egocentric speech was seen as part of goal-directed behavior. Eventually, children were thought to internalize egocentric speech as the "inner speech" that organized mental life.

Vygtosky conceptualized early thought as prelinguistic, and early language as preintellectual, with purely social functions:

In the first year of the child's life (that is, during the preintellectual stage of development in speech), we find rich development in the social function of speech. The relatively complex and rich social contact of the child leads to a very early development of a "means of contact" . . . babbling, behavioral displays and gestures emerge as a means of social contact. (Vygotsky, 1934, p. 88)

Via the stage of egocentric speech, language gradually became internalized and became the means of organizing thought. Vygotsky pointed out that when children were put into problem-solving situations, they:

. . . not only act in attempting to achieve a goal, they also speak. As a rule, this speech arises spontaneously and continues almost without interruption throughout the experiment. It increases and is more persistent every time the situation becomes more complicated and the goal more difficult to attain. Attempts to block it . . . are either futile, or lead the child to "freeze up" (Vygotsky, 1978, p. 25)

Vygotsky argued that language was as important as action in attaining goals, and that language and action were part of "one and the same complex psychological function" (p. 25). Language enabled children to disconnect themselves from the immediate, concrete situation and to generate possibilities and plans for solving problems. Language was also thought to play a role in controlling the child's own behavior—by speaking of their intentions, children guided their actions. Finally, language enabled children to ask adults to help them, thus acting as a problem-solving tool. In fact, Vygotsky suggested that children did not at first distinguish the roles played by the child and the helper in problem solving, experiencing a "syncretic whole". When this "social speech" became internalized, children effectively appealed to themselves for help. Language and thought were also inevitably interdependent. One example given by Vygotsky was visual perception (Vygotsky, 1978). Initially, children use language to label their visual perceptions, thus enhancing individual objects in the visual field ("ball", "car"). Soon, however, language can be used to create a "time field" in addition to the visual–spatial field of current perception. The child can now view changes in the immediate situation from the viewpoint of past activities, and can act in the present from the viewpoint of the future. Language enabled the child's field of attention to embrace "a whole series of potential perceptual fields that form successive, dynamic structures over time" (Vygotsky, 1978, p. 36). Vygotsky speculated that animals cannot do this, and noted that the ability to combine past and present perceptual fields via language also enabled reconstructive memory:

> *Created with the help of speech, the time field for action extends both forward and backward ... [creating] the conditions for the development of a single system that ... encompasses two new functions: intentions and symbolic representations of purposeful action. (p. 36–37).*

Sociocultural tools for mediating knowledge

As well as language, Vygotsky identified a number of "**sign systems**" or cultural semiotic systems that enabled the symbolic representation of knowledge. These included drawing pictures, writing, reading, using number systems, maps, and diagrams. These symbolic systems were seen as psychological tools for organizing cognitive behavior. Cognitive development, therefore, did not just happen in the brain of the individual child. Rather, it depended on interactions between the child and the cultural tools available for mediating knowledge. These interactions with cultural tools first depended on interpersonal communication with adults and other teachers, and were then internalized by the child, the tools (symbols) thereby becoming internal mediators of cognitive processes. Sign systems had a crucial role in an individual's intellectual development, as they extended the operation of psychological processes beyond the individual. For example, memory could be extended by recording memories in writing, or by drawing a picture of a salient event, thereby fundamentally changing the memory itself via symbolic activity. Wertsch has called this "mediated cognition" (e.g. Wertsch, 1985; Rowe & Wertsch, 2002). Because these symbol systems are the product of sociocultural evolution (they are not reinvented by each individual), Vygotsky saw sign systems as social in nature. Children gained access to these psychological tools because of the social/cultural context in which they developed, and because of face-to-face communication and interaction with others. Hence the communicative and intellectual functions of sign systems were inherently related.

The interrelatedness of social and cognitive processes in the child was repeatedly emphasized in Vygotsky's writings:

> *Sign-using activity in children is neither simply invented nor passed down by adults ... within a general process of development, two qualitatively different lines of development, differing in origin, can be distinguished: the elementary processes, which are of biological origin ... and the higher psychological functions, of sociocultural origin .. the history of child behavior is born from the interweaving of these two lines. (Vygotsky, 1978, p. 46)*

By elementary processes, Vygotsky meant basic perceptual processes such as vision, touch and hearing, and basic aspects of behavior such as goal-directed action and social communication. Two fundamental forms of cultural behavior were thought to emerge in infancy, psychological tool use and language. Both were mediated by adults. Psychological tools meant tools invented by human society, such as signs, symbols, and concepts. The combination of psychological tool use and language in

KEY TERM

Sign systems
Cultural semiotic systems; psychological tools that enable the symbolic representation and organization of knowledge, which include drawing pictures, writing, reading, using number systems, maps, and diagrams.

psychological activity changed psychological functioning in a profound way, enabling higher levels of cognitive activity in the child. These higher levels of cognition were thought to be specific to human beings. Only humans had mediated cognition, as animals do not create artificial signs to communicate with each other:

> We know that social interaction such as that found in the animal world . . . is not mediated by speech or any other system of signs .. [this] is social interaction of only the most primitive or limited type . . . (Vygotsky, 1934, p. 11)

The zone of proximal development

In addition to his emphasis on the social and cultural nature of cognitive development, Vygotsky illustrated the importance of learning from others to cognitive development. He rejected the Piagetian idea that development unfolds according to its own timetable, without any influence from school learning. For Vygtosky, development could not be independent of learning, particularly during the school years. Clearly, learning began prior to schooling, and:

> ". . . any learning a child encounters in school always has a previous history. For example, children begin to study arithmetic in school, but long beforehand they have had some experience with quantity . . . children have their own preschool arithmetic, which only myopic psychologists could ignore. (Vygotsky, 1978, p. 84)

But school learning introduced something fundamentally new into the child's development. This something new was captured by Vyogtsky's concept of the "**zone of proximal development**". This concept captured the insight that "what children can do with the assistance of others might be in some sense even more indicative of their mental development than what they can do alone" (Vygotsky, 1978, p. 85).

While acknowledging that it was important to measure a child's actual level of development, for example via tests of mental function, Vygotsky argued that it was also important to investigate how much further a child could go under the guidance of a teacher. He gave the example of two children who entered school aged 10 years, and who could deal with standardized tasks up to the degree of difficulty typical of the 8-year level. These two children would have a mental age of 8 years. However, suppose the experimenter then showed them different ways of dealing with some of the problems. Suppose that with assistance one child could deal with problems up to a 12-year-old's level, the other with problems up to a 9-year-old's level. Vygotsky argued that mentally these children were clearly not the same. They differed in terms of their zone of proximal development. He defined this as:

> The distance between the actual developmental level, as determined by independent problem solving, and the level of potential development as determined through problem solving under adult guidance or in collaboration with more capable peers. (Vygotsky, 1978, p. 86)

The zone of proximal development enabled a prospective rather than retrospective characterization of cognitive development.

The concept of a zone of proximal development has had a profound impact in education. Vygotsky's insight that school learning can affect a child's cognitive development is important for how we set about teaching children in schools. For example, the zone of proximal development contradicts the notion that learning should be matched with the child's developmental level. Learning can change the child's developmental level, and hence it is better for teachers to discover the child's zone of proximal development and teach to that in order for instruction to bring optimal benefits. Vygotsky's view that school learning mediated cognitive development in the middle childhood years can be illustrated by his

According to Vygotsky, since learning can change a child's developmental level, it would be optimally beneficial for a child to be taught in line with his or her zone of proximal development, rather than at his or her current developmental level. © Royalty-Free/Corbis.

contrast between *scientific* and *spontaneous* concepts. Spontaneous concepts are defined as those generated by children on the basis of their observations and experiences. Sometimes these concepts are wrong (an example is the medieval impetus theory of motion, discussed in Chapter 6). Scientific concepts were thought to be acquired consciously and effortfully in school, and were thought to transform students' knowledge. For example, scientific concepts were thought to restructure spontaneous concepts and raise them to a higher level (an example might be restructuring the erroneous impetus theory of motion into a Newtonian theory).

Although Vygotsky himself did not produce evidence for these ideas, neo-Vygotskians did attempt to explore them empirically. As discussed in Chapter 9, syllogistic reasoning was originally considered a form of higher-level reasoning. Vygotsky's student Luria carried out an extensive study of syllogistic reasoning in peasants living in remote villages of Uzbekistan and Kirghizia (Luria, 1976). He found evidence apparently suggesting that these unschooled peasants were incapable of syllogistic reasoning, being hampered by an "empirical bias". For example, Uzbekistan is a hot, plains region, which does not have snow. When unschooled villagers from Uzbekistan were given syllogisms such as "In the Far North, where there is snow, all bears are white. Novaya Zemla is in the Far North. What color are the bears there?", they did very poorly (Luria, 1976). They would give responses along the lines of "I cannot tell, you would have to ask people who had been there and seen the bears". Even when syllogisms were based on familiar information, such as the factors that affect the growth of cotton, invoking an unfamiliar setting led to logical failures. With premises such as "Cotton grows well where it is hot and dry. England is cold and damp. Can cotton grow there or not?", these villagers refused to commit themselves, although some would make pertinent observations (e.g. "If it's cold there, it won't grow. If the soil is loose and good, it will"). Neo-Vygotskians argued that such data showed the dominant role of schooling in the development of higher-order logical thought (see Karpov, 2005, p. 175).

As we saw in Chapter 9, however, even 4-year-olds can use syllogistic reasoning when premises are familiar, and with appropriate manipulations (e.g. a make-believe world) they can make logical deductions about counterfactuals as well. Anthropologists have also challenged this simplistic view of the effects of schooling (e.g. Cole & Scribner, 1974). Despite lacking firm empirical evidence, however, Vygotsky's idea that school learning can systematically target the zone of proximal development and transform knowledge is a very important one. Russian neo-Vygotskians (e.g. Karpov, 2005) have also stressed that joint activity with adults is critical to the effective use of the zone of proximal development in teaching. Verbal mediation is not enough to optimize learning. The adult must mediate the child's acquisition, mastery, and internalization of new content via shared activity.

Neo-Vygotskians argue that mediation should begin with the adult explaining and modeling the procedure or material to be learned. The adult should then involve the child in joint performance of this procedure or material, thereby creating the zone of proximal development of a new mental process. The child's mastery and internalization of the material should then be guided until the adult can begin to withdraw, eventually passing responsibility for further development to the child. Karpov (2005) argues that while some instructional programs that have been developed to exploit Vygotsky's ideas about mediated cognition and the zone of proximal development fulfil neo-Vygotskian criteria, others do not. An example of a successful instructional program is "reciprocal teaching", designed to improve reading comprehension by Palincsar and Brown (1984). Reciprocal teaching begins with the teacher modeling the optimal strategies for reading comprehension to a small group of children. These strategies include summarizing what has been read and predicting what will happen next. First the teacher leads the group in analyzing the text in accordance with these strategies, and gradually leadership passes to the children.

Vygotsky argued that a full understanding of the zone of proximal development also entailed a re-evaluation of the role of imitation in learning. He suggested that, using imitation, children are capable of doing much more in collective activity or under the guidance of adults:

> Learning awakens a variety of internal developmental processes that are able to operate only when the child is interacting with people in his environment and in cooperation with his peers. Once these processes are internalized, they become part of the child's independent developmental achievement . . . learning is not development, however properly organized learning results in mental development and sets in motion a variety of developmental processes that would be impossible apart from learning. Thus, learning is a necessary and universal aspect of the process of developing culturally organized, specifically human, psychological functions. (Vygotsky, 1978, p. 90)

Sadly, Vygotsky died before he could carry out a systematic analysis of what the internal developmental processes activated by education were and which aspects of the educational process led to the internalization that caused further cognitive development. However, he recognized the importance of investigating the relations between the cognitive levels achieved with adult or peer guidance and the internalization of these levels, both for understanding cognitive development and for assessing the value of school learning:

> If successful [this research] should reveal to the teacher how developmental processes stimulated by the course of school learning are carried through inside the head of each individual child. The relevance of this internal, subterranean developmental network of school subjects is a task of primary importance for psychological and educational analysis. (Vygotsky, 1978, p. 91)

Surprisingly, such research still remains to be done. Neo-Vygotskians have focused instead on an approach called "theoretical learning", which offers an interesting alternative to the constructivist learning pedagogies based on Piaget's theory. In theoretical learning, children are not required to rediscover scientific knowledge for themselves. Instead, they are taught precise definitions of scientific concepts. They then master and internalize the procedures related to these concepts by using the conceptual knowledge that they have been taught to solve subject-domain problems. This is said to lead to cognitive benefits, as children eventually adopt a general strategy of searching for a general principle or theory when faced with new problems in new domains, hence demonstrating "formal-logical thought" (see Karpov, 2005, pp. 182–202). One reason why researchers have not tackled the question of "how developmental processes stimulated by the course of school learning are carried through inside the head of each individual child" may be the complexity of the research question. As Vygotsky noted, cognitive development was unlikely "to follow school learning the way a shadow follows the object that casts it . . . extensive and highly concrete research based on the concept of the zone of proximal development is necessary to resolve the issue" (Vygotsky, 1978, p. 91).

Play

Vygotsky also recognized the importance of play for child development, although this aspect of his theorizing has received less attention. Vygotsky argued that the world of the imagination fulfilled a crucial psychological function in development, enabling children to realize desires that could not otherwise be fulfilled (e.g. being the mother):

> *We often describe a child's development as the development of his intellectual functions, every child stands before us as a theoretician who, characterized by a higher or lower level of intellectual development, moves from one stage to another. But if we ignore a child's needs . . . we will never be able to understand his advance from one developmental stage to the next . . . it is impossible to ignore the fact that the child satisfies certain needs in play. (Vygotsky, 1978, p. 92–93)*

Vygotsky thought that the imagination represented a specifically human form of cognitive activity, was absent in animals, and arose during the preschool years: "Like all functions of consciousness, it originally arises from action" (Vygotsky, 1978, p. 93). Vygotsky argued that the defining characteristic of play was the creation of an imaginary situation. Play was not simply symbolic, because of the role of motivation. Play also involved rules of behavior.

Vygotsky illustrated his ideas with an example of two sisters who decided to "play" at being sisters:

> *The vital difference . . . is that the child in playing tries to be what she thinks a sister should be. In life the child behaves without thinking that she is her sister's sister. In the game of sisters . . . both are concerned with displaying their sisterhood . . . both acquire rules of behavior . . . they dress alike, talk alike . . . as a result of playing, the child comes to understand that sisters possess a different relationship to each other than to other people. What passes unnoticed by the child in real life becomes a rule of behavior in play. (Vygotsky, 1978, p. 94–95)*

For Vygotsky, play enabled the child to act in a purely cognitive realm, rather than relying on motivational incentives supplied by external things. For infants and toddlers, *things* decide action: doors demand to be opened, staircases to be climbed, switches to be operated. Vygotsky suggested that early in development, perception and motives were interdependent: "Every perception is a stimulus to activity" (Vygotsky, 1978, p. 96). In play, *things* lost their determining force and the child acted independently of what was seen. In play, thought was separated from objects and action arose from ideas rather than from things. A piece of wood became a doll and a stick became a horse. Symbolic play was crucial developmentally, as the meaning of things to the child was no longer dominated by their status as real objects in the perceptual world. In play, their meanings could be detached from perceptual reality (as in the mental decoupling discussed by Leslie, 1987; see Chapter 3). Vygotsky argued that play provided a critical bridge between the perceptual/ situational constraints of early childhood, and adult thought, which was totally free of situational constraints.

According to Vygotsky's analysis of play, a central developmental function was that the "rules of the game" required children to act against their immediate impulses. This enabled the development of self-regulation:

> *At every step the child is faced with a conflict between the rules of the game and what he would do if he could suddenly act spontaneously . . . he achieves the maximum display of willpower when he renounces an immediate attraction in the game (such as candy, which by the rules of the game he is forbidden to eat because it represents something inedible). Ordinarily, a child experiences subordination to rules in the renunciation of something he wants, but here subordination to a rule and renunciation of action on immediate impulse are the means to maximum pleasure. Thus, the essential attribute of play is a rule that has become a desire. (Vygotsky, 1978, p. 99)*

Hence play facilitated the development of self-regulation, as the child's desire in playing was to control his or her immediate impulses. Vygotsky pointed out that play also enabled children to decouple action from meaning. In infancy and toddler-hood, actions were dominant over meaning, as children could do more than they could understand:

> *Internal and external action are inseparable: imagination, interpretation and will are the internal processes carried by external action . . . [in play] action retreats to second place . . . just as operating with the meaning of things leads to abstract thought . . . the ability to make conscious choices occurs when the child operates with the meaning of actions. (Vygotsky, 1978, p. 101)*

Meaning is detached from action by means of a different action. A child who wishes to ride a horse stamps the ground and imagines herself riding a horse, rather than performing the actions required to ride a real horse.

Vygotsky thus regarded play as a major factor in cognitive development. He also argued that play itself created a zone of proximal development:

> *In play a child always behaves beyond his average age, above his daily behavior; in play it is as though he were a head taller than himself . . . play contains all developmental tendencies in a condensed form and is itself*

a major source of development . . . action in the imaginative sphere, in an imaginary situation, the creation of voluntary intentions, and the formation of real-life plans and volitional motives—all appear in play and make it the highest form of preschool development . . . From the point of view of development, creating an imaginary situation can be regarded as a means of developing abstract thought. The corresponding development of rules leads to actions on the basis of which the division between work and play becomes possible, a division encountered at school age as a fundamental fact. (Vygotsky, 1978, pp. 102–103)

Russian neo-Vygotskians have developed this idea further, arguing that teachers have an important role in creating a zone of proximal development for play. For example, Karpov (2005, p. 142) notes that some groups of children (for example, children of low socioeconomic status) engage in little sociodramatic play, and that some teachers regard sociodramatic play as a waste of time. Adult mediation is required to initiate or extend sociodramatic play, for example in explaining real-world situations like attending a hospital clinic and explaining the causes of adult actions in those situations. The goal is for play to become "a micro-world of active experiencing of social roles and relationships" (see Karpov, 2005, p. 140). Russian neo-Vygotskians have also argued that the motive to engage in imaginary play (i.e. to fulfill desires that cannot be fulfilled otherwise) leads in turn to the motive to study at school:

> Vygotsky regarded play as a major factor in cognitive development and argued that play itself created a zone of proximal development where children behaved beyond their age.

> *One of the major outcomes of sociodramatic play is that, by the end of the period of early childhood, children become dissatisfied with such a pseudo-penetration into the world of adults . . . the only "real" and "serious" role that is available for the child in an industrialized society . . . is the role of a student in school. (Karpov, 2005, p. 153)*

Karpov notes, however, that empirical evidence to support this idea is currently lacking.

In other areas, the Russian neo-Vygotskians have produced quite a lot of empirical evidence to support Vygotsky's major ideas, and have also augmented them. Karpov's (2005) elegant survey of a literature primarily available in Russian is extremely useful for illustrating this extension of Vygotsky's ideas. For example, regarding Vygotsky's theory about the role of play in the development of self-regulation, the Russian neo-Vygotskians noted that the child's internal desire was not the only critical factor. The child's playmates exerted an important regulatory function as well. Karpov (2005, p. 157) cites Elkonin's observation of 6-year-old boys playing at being fire-fighters. One boy is the chief fire-fighter, another is the driver of the fire engine, others are fire-fighters. Play begins, the chief shouts "Fire", everyone takes a seat in the engine, and the driver pretends to drive. When they reach the fire, the fire-fighters jump out to extinguish the fire. The driver jumps out too, as this is the most fun part of the game, but the others remind him that he is the driver and that he has to stay with the fire engine. So the boy returns to sit in the engine.

This mutual regulation coupled with the child's own growing abilities to suppress immediate desires is said to lead to the development of self-regulation. This occurs first in the zone of proximal development provided by play, and eventually in nonplay situations. Karpov (2005, p. 158) cites further relevant data from Manuilenko (1948). In this study, children aged from 3 to 7 years were required to stand motionless for as long as they could. For example, they had to stand motionless alone in a room, alone in a room in the play context of being "a sentry", or they had to be a sentry in a room full of their playmates. The children were able to stand still longest in the third situation. The playmates were monitoring the sentry, and this helped him to stand still for longer. Again, the zone of proximal development provided by play enabled superior performance to the actual developmental level of self-regulation (Karpov, 2005). Karpov notes that, to date, Russian neo-Vygotskians have not provided causal evidence for Vygotsky's idea that imaginary play leads to the development of self-regulation in nonplay situations. However, he points out that Western psychologists have provided some relevant data, for example in demonstrating links between pretend play, theory of mind, and executive function (see Chapters 7 and 9).

Evaluation

Vygotsky's theory of cognitive development has probably had a bigger impact on education than on developmental psychology. This is unsurprising, as Vygotsky accorded education a key role in cognitive development, whereas Piaget did not. Yet, ironically, Russian neo-Vygotskians argue persuasively that many of these educational impacts have involved misunderstandings of Vygotsky's ideas, such as the idea of the zone of proximal development and the idea that all meaning is socially constructed (Karpov, 2005). Vygotsky's notion of the zone of proximal development was a sophisticated one, which recurred in other spheres of activity such as play, and which required sensitive mediation by adults. Similarly, although Vygotsky argued that cognitive development originated in socially meaningful activity, he also argued that teachers should teach children directly the knowledge that has been acquired over the course of human sociocultural evolution. He did not argue that children should be always scaffolded and supported to discover this knowledge for themselves.

A critical aspect of Vygotsky's theory for cognitive development is the idea that language and other symbol systems play a causal role in organizing cognition. For Vygotsky, language is as important as action. In Western psychology, there has been less emphasis on the causal role of language as a symbol system, as the focus has been more on how children discover knowledge for themselves, primarily via action. Vygotsky's emphasis on the importance of interpersonal communication for learning in young children has more parallels with Western cognitive developmental work. For example, in areas such as theory of mind and social cognition (see Chapter 7), the importance of communication within families and with peers is becoming a central aspect of empirical investigation (e.g. Dunn et al., 1991a). Vygotsky's emphasis on the world of the imagination and the value of sociodramatic play is also reflected in more recent Western psychology (e.g. Lillard, 2002). However, to my knowledge, there are no systematic Western research programs exploring Vygotsky's ideas about the rule-based aspects of children's imaginative play and the possible effects on the development of self-regulation and metacognition. Instead, Western research programs for improving metacognition tend to be procedurally based and not play-focused (see Schneider & Lockl, 2002). However, Vygotsky's ideas about how play will lead to an appetite for school are less compelling.

COGNITIVE NEUROSCIENCE: TOWARDS A NEW THEORETICAL FRAMEWORK

Throughout this book, we have seen that new insights from cognitive neuroscience are requiring us to adapt traditional approaches to understanding cognitive development. Traditional constructs such as "constraints on learning", "modules", and the contrast between "domain-general" and "domain-specific" analyses are changing in light of new understandings, particularly concerning the distributed nature of neural (mental) representations. Some of these adaptations offer alternative theoretical frameworks for explaining cognitive development. I will discuss two such frameworks here, "**neuroconstructivism**" and "connectionism". Finally, I will consider what the experiments discussed in this book suggest concerning a new theoretical framework for cognitive development. Whereas aspects of both neuroconstructivism and connectionism are crucial for generating a new theoretical framework for cognitive development, neither is currently able to incorporate the critical roles of social–cognitive factors such as intention-reading and communication. Similarly, neither approach currently incorporates the role played by cognitive factors internal to the child, such as imaginative play and inner speech. Language, by its very nature, provides an amodal symbolic system for cognitive development, a means for organizing the child's inner mental life, and (as Vygotsky put it) a "time field for action" extending both backwards and forwards. It seems likely that inputs like language and imaginative play, generated by the child and then responded to psychologically by the child, will by their very nature be extremely difficult for the connectionist modeler to specify.

Neuroconstructivism

Neuroconstructivism explains the mechanisms of cognitive change by considering the biological constraints on the neural activation patterns that comprise mental representations. These biological constraints affect brain development, and hence will affect the development of the neural substrates underpinning mental representations. According to neuroconstructivism, environmental experiences are key to development, as they will change the brain's "hardware", leading to changes in the nature of representations, which in turn lead to new experiences and further changes to the neural systems (Westermann, Mareschal, Johnson, Sirois, Spratling, & Thomas, 2007, p. 75; see also Mareschal et al., 2007). By acknowledging the key role of the environment (broadly defined), neuroconstructivism avoids neural reductionism. "Algorithm and hardware change each other in development . . . they cannot be studied in isolation" (p. 75).

Neuroconstructivism is based on the notion of biological "constraints", but describes these as constraints on *development* rather than as constraints on learning (Table 11.2). One such constraint is the biological action of genes. Genes cannot turn themselves "on" or "off", but require signals to tell them to do so. These signals can originate within the cell, outside the cell, or outside the organism. Therefore, as discussed in the Foreword, genetic activity is modified by neural, behavioral, and external environmental events. To describe cognitive development adequately, all of these interactions must be understood. For example, low levels of the neurotransmitter serotonin are associated with depressed cognition. Maternal and

TABLE 11.2   Biological constraints on neuroconstructivism, following Westermann et al., 2007

Constraint	Example
Genes	Genes do not encode structure deterministically, e.g. gene expression is influenced by the environment
Encellment	Development of neurons is constrained by the cellular environment
Enbrainment	The brain is not really modular, as the functional properties of individual regions are constrained by their connectivity
Embodiment	The brain is in a body, which is embedded in a physical and social environment
Ensocialment	The social and physical environment constrains the emergence of neural representations
Interactions between constraints	The interactive working of these constraints shapes the neural structures that form the basis of mental representations

infant serotonin levels are correlated in monkeys, and also correlate with insecure attachment. Hence logically, low serotonin could be associated with aberrant maternal care or with shared genes (or both). Neuroconstructivism points out that a full understanding of these interactions is required to explain the development of disorders of cognition such as depression (Gottleib, 2007).

A second important constraint identified by neuroconstructivism is "**encellment**", the fact that the development of neurons is constrained by their cellular environments. Neural activation patterns themselves constitute "experiences" for the neural networks involved, and this experience of connection patterns (plus underlying morphology) is hypothesized to affect the ways in which progressively more complex representations are formed. A similar biological constraint is "**enbrainment**", which refers to the fact that the functional properties of brain regions are constrained by their interactions with other regions, for example via feedback processes and top-down interactions. These interregional interactions will affect the development of the neural structures involved and therefore of neural representations. "Embodiment" is an analogous constraint. Embodiment refers to the fact that the brain is in a body, and that the body will act as a "filter" for information from the environment. The ways in which the senses function will hence constrain the development of mental representations. The body also allows the infant to manipulate the environment. "The embodiment view emphasizes that pro-activity in exploring the environment is a core aspect of cognitive development . . . the child . . . selects the experiences from which to learn" (Westermann et al., 2007, p. 78).

The final constraint on development discussed by Westermann et al. (2007) is called "ensocialment". Social aspects of the environment will have profound effects on social and behavioral development, for example by affecting gene expression. Westermann et al. (2007) argue that putting these constraints together (and acknowledging that they will interact with each other) constitutes a theoretical framework for cognitive development. "Put together, in the development of cognitive processing, these constraints form an interactive network shaping the neural structures that form the basis of mental representations." (p. 79). Although the

KEY TERMS

Encellment
The development of neurons is constrained by their cellular environments.

Enbrainment
The functional properties of brain regions are constrained by their codevelopment with other regions.

proactivity of the child is stressed theoretically, the emergence of the neural representations supporting cognitive behavior is said to be strongly constrained by the ontological history of the individual: "The events occurring at a given time constrain the range of possible adaptations available to the system in the future" (Westermann et al., 2007, p. 80). The authors note that this notion of *progressive specialization* is shared with constructivist theories of cognitive development, such as Piaget's theory.

Neuroconstructivism has many appealing features but it does not yet provide a comprehensive theory of cognitive development. A focus on the biological constraints that affect the development of the neural structures and neural networks that underlie cognitive processing is very important. These biological constraints affect cognitive theories. A good example is theories of conceptual development, as discussed in Chapter 4. There we saw that neuroimaging studies showed the distributed nature of conceptual representations. The activation of particular concepts by adults produced neural activation in the sensory modalities associated with those concepts and in association areas recording the conjunction of particular sets of sensory information (e.g. Barsalou et al., 2003). It was suggested that, developmentally, this would mean that there is no amodal or abstract "concept" for entities such as "robins" or "cups" that are held in a separate conceptual system. Rather, the "cup" network would be activated to different degrees depending on the context in which the "cup" concept was activated. It was also suggested that such a modality-specific system would lend itself naturally to development. As infants and children gained more conceptual knowledge about the world, modality-specific knowledge would change, and at the same time the conjunctions in association areas would change. Children's concepts could thus naturally differ from those of adults, depending on the sensory and social/emotional information being attended to. This kind of explanatory framework for conceptual development would arise naturally from neuroconstructivism.

Another appealing feature is that neuroconstructivism allows developmental disorders to be explained via altered constraints on brain development that thereby alter the developmental trajectory (Karmiloff-Smith, 2007). This was discussed in Chapter 10, when we considered causal explanations for developmental dyslexia. As discussed, the core problem in developmental dyslexia is a (cognitive) phonological deficit. One explanation of this cognitive deficit may be that children with developmental dyslexia have brains that are less efficient in one or more of the processes required for phonological development. These were suggested to be basic auditory processes (see Goswami, 2003a). Altered sensory functioning could explain why children with developmental dyslexia do not develop well-specified phonological representations of the sound structure of the individual words in their mental lexicons. Another important theoretical implication of neuroconstructivism is that adult cognition can only be fully understood by considering cognitive development. Adult cognition is an outcome of development, and so developmental constraints must be taken seriously in formulating adult cognitive theories. This is a central message of this book. The importance of developmental constraints has also been argued in specific areas of adult cognition, such as skilled reading (see Ziegler & Goswami, 2005, for a discussion of developmental shortcomings of the "dual route" model of reading).

However, as currently conceptualized, neuroconstructivism relies heavily on analogies from sensory neuroscience. Constraints such as encellment and enbrainment have been largely derived from the behavior of cells and neural networks in the visual cortex. For example, if axons have committed themselves to particular connections, they cannot become uncommitted. As *cognitive* neuroscience gathers pace, different constraints may become apparent. For example, for the cognitive system it is not clear that "The events occurring at a given time constrain the range of possible adaptations available to the system in the future" (Westermann et al., 2007, p. 80). This is only likely to be partially true, as cognitive knowledge is so distributed. In fact, it may not even be true of the sensory systems traditionally used as examples in sensory neuroscience, such as visual development in kittens. The development of visual cortical connections in kittens was thought to be irreversibly constrained by rearing environment (e.g. Blakemore & Cooper, 1970), but was later shown to be more malleable than originally supposed (e.g. Rauschecker & Singer, 1981). Certainly, the cognitive system appears much more malleable than the sensory systems in terms of the range of future available adaptations.

The fundamental point is that there is always a role for learning in human cognition. For example, recent cultural innovations have required the cognitive system to become adaptive in novel ways (e.g. in using new technologies). Pensioners can learn to use computers and mobile telephones. Obviously, biological constraints will affect how new interactive networks are formed during this new learning, and how the neural structures that form the basis of new mental representations are shaped. But a more efficient level of theoretical description may be a cognitive one. For example, individual differences in whether pensioners become efficient computer users are likely to reflect factors such as encapsulated knowledge, motivation to learn, and self-belief. Describing these cognitive variables may be as useful (or more useful) for theories of cognitive development as trying to understand every aspect of encellment or enbrainment.

Certainly, there is ample data to show that novel inputs late in life can alter neural structures. An example is the development of the hippocampus in London taxi drivers (see Goswami, 2004, for more examples). London taxi drivers must pass an examination to demonstrate detailed knowledge of the street map of London, called "The Knowledge". London taxi drivers show enlarged hippocampal formations compared to adults who do not drive taxis, and hippocampal volume is correlated with the amount of time spent as a taxi driver (Maguire et al., 2000). Although neuroconstructivism emphasizes the proactive child, a comprehensive theory of cognitive development requires an analysis of whether "the range of possible adaptations available to the system in the future" is ever restricted for the cognitive system. The effects of different types of learning on the brain (e.g. learning by imitation versus learning by analogy), the important roles of motivation and metacognition, and the role of representations internal to the child that themselves affect cognitive development (such as language) will be greater than those captured by constraints such as "ensocialment". This caveat is discussed further below, with respect to connectionist models.

Connectionism

Whereas neuroconstructivism aims to capture development, connectionism is concerned with learning. Connectionists build computational models of cognition. The computational architecture in these models is built from networks of simple processing units. Each unit has an output that is a simple numerical function of its inputs. This is intended as a loose representation of a neural network. Cognitive entities such as concepts or aspects of language are represented by patterns of

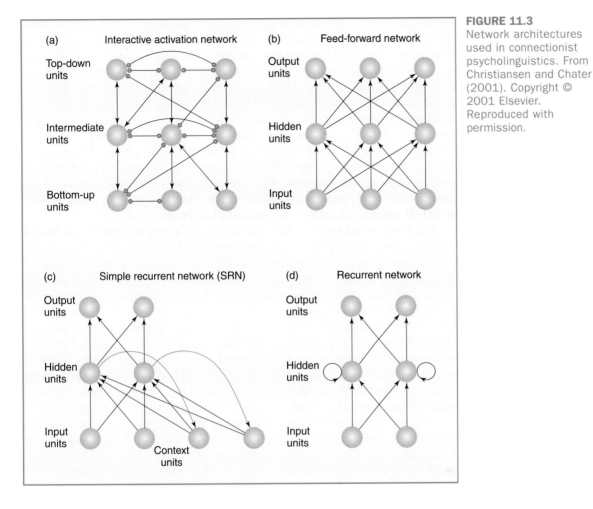

FIGURE 11.3
Network architectures used in connectionist psycholinguistics. From Christiansen and Chater (2001). Copyright © 2001 Elsevier. Reproduced with permission.

activation across several units, just as representations are distributed in the brain. Early connectionist models were bottom-up, in that information could only flow forwards in the models (Figure 11.3). The input units received experimenter-determined information intended to be representative of the input of a given cognitive type, such as language. This information was fed forwards to a layer of "hidden" units, a layer of units lying between the input and output units that "learned" features of the input and fed the output units. A major contribution of early connectionist models was the *in-principle demonstration* that a simple network could learn the structure of the input (e.g. linguistic structure). This apparently showed that structure could be learned in the absence of innate knowledge (e.g. about language).

Connectionist models have continued to grow in computational sophistication. The invention of new algorithms has allowed hidden units to affect input units as well as output units, leading to the development of simple recurrent networks and of interactive activation networks (see Figure 11.3). In adult cognition, such networks have been used to demonstrate further important *in-principle effects*. One was that bottom-up processing could generate effects that had been assumed from behavioral data to require top-down processing. For example, phoneme restoration (i.e. recreating a "missing" phoneme that has been obliterated by someone coughing when hearing speech) was shown to be possible in the absence of knowledge about real words if a network was trained on statistical regularities at the phoneme level (Pitt & McQueen, 1998). Hence, in principle, phoneme restoration need not be a top-down, lexical effect— although of course, this in-principle demonstration does not mean that phoneme restoration is *not* a top-down effect. Similarly, it was shown that words could be segmented from the speech stream on the basis purely of bottom-up, statistical information (Christiansen, Allen, & Seidenberg, 1998). Connectionist models of adult speech processing, sentence processing, language production, and reading aloud have converged to show that aspects of language and language processing can be successfully captured without assuming discrete symbolic representations (Christiansen & Chater, 2001). Prior to connectionism, most cognitive theories assumed symbolic representations, which were discrete or amodal in form and all-or-nothing in terms of functionality (they were either engaged during a cognitive task, or not). This is the metaphor of the "algebraic" mind (see Elman, 2005).

Since the advent of connectionism, the possibility of distributed and graded representations must be taken seriously. Distributed representations have already been discussed, but graded representations are also important. A representation can be graded in terms of (for example) the number of relevant neurons firing, their firing rates, the coherence of the firing patterns, and how "clean" they are for signaling the appropriate information (see Munakata, 2001). Graded representations offer an alternative explanation of behavioral dissociations, for example in infant looking and search behavior (see Munakata, 2001, for more examples). As we saw in Chapter 2, babies appear to attend to certain variables such as height at different ages in occlusion events (4 months) versus containment events (7 months) versus covering events (12 months). Rather than postulating separable cognitive systems for, say, occlusion events versus containment events, it could be that a weaker representation of a hidden object suffices for occlusion events than for containment events. Similarly, in principle, graded representations can explain apparent double dissociations, when one group succeeds on task A but not task B, whereas another group succeeds on task B but not task A. Double dissociations are seen in adult cognitive neuropsychology as evidence for functional separation. Connectionism shows that rather than indexing separable systems these double dissociations could, in principle, arise from graded representations (see Munakata, 2001).

Connectionist models can also demonstrate computational trade-offs that may be relevant for explaining the development of different types of cognitive system, such as semantic memory versus episodic memory. For example, a single system can either learn rapidly, with nonoverlapping representations, or slowly, using overlapping representations. A system that learns rapidly could be crucial for the development of episodic memory (Munakata & McClelland, 2003). As discussed in Chapter 8, episodic memory is memory for episodes or events in one's life, and involves explicit recall of these episodes and events, for example meeting a particular person at a particular place. Episodic memories must be encoded quickly and kept distinct from other episodic memories, such as meeting another person at the same place. In contrast, semantic memory is our generic, factual knowledge about the world, such as our knowledge of concepts and language. These kinds of memories are better learned slowly, with overlapping representations that collapse across particular instances. Munakata and McClelland (2003) argued that different aspects of the memory system might rely on different types of learning, and hence show the observed specializations (for example, the hippocampus might specialize in fast learning while posterior cortex specializes in slow learning). This is an important in-principle idea. However, as discussed in Chapter 8, Vargha-Khadem and colleagues (1997) showed that children with hippocampal damage have preserved semantic memory, but grossly impaired episodic memory. These dissociations are explicable in terms of the kind of learning required for each type of memory system, but not if the hippocampus is hypothesized to specialize in fast learning.

There are fewer connectionist models of aspects of *cognitive development*, but again existing models have demonstrated important in-principle effects for learning by naïve systems. For example, "critical period" effects, when learning appears to be particularly effective during a particular developmental time window, can arise in neural networks that rely on error-driven learning (via the back-propagation algorithm; see Figure 11.3) even though the underlying learning mechanism remains constant in these models. A "novice" back-propagation system is very responsive to learning from its errors, whereas an "expert" system is less responsive, hence more entrenched in its learning. This could explain why it is easier to learn a first language early in life than a second language later in life (see Johnson & Munakata, 2005). During learning of the first language, learning becomes entrenched, and so the system is less sensitive to errors when learning the second language. On the other hand, if both languages are acquired at the same time, before learning has become entrenched, both languages are learned easily.

The error-correction learning algorithm underlying entrenchment is only one possible form of learning that can be adopted by connectionist models. If a model depends on "Hebbian" learning (units that "fire together, wire together", so that the response that the system makes to received inputs is strengthened over time), it becomes difficult to reorganize the system when a new learning environment is experienced. This form of entrenchment is suggested to underlie the critical period effects found for learning native phonemes (see Chapter 5). For example, Munakata and McClelland (2003) suggested that this kind of entrenchment could explain why Japanese native speakers find it difficult to learn the English /l/–/r/ distinction. These two phonemes are the same (single phoneme) in Japanese, and Hebbian learning would produce a single representation for this phoneme, which would continue to be strengthened by input comprising *both* English /l/'s and /r/'s. Hence the system would never learn to distinguish English /l/ and /r/. However, it is possible behaviorally to train Japanese adults to recognize the English /l/–/r/ distinction using auditory–visual training methods (Hardison, 2003). This suggests that entrenchment is not a necessary characteristic of linguistic critical period phenomena in humans.

Another important in-principle effect is that so-called "U-shaped curves" in development, such as the apparent decline and then recovery in the accuracy of young children's use of the past tense rule (see Chapter 5), can arise from item-based learning (Rumelhart & McClelland, 1986). There is no need to invoke symbolic rules of grammar. The statistical structure of the input is sufficient for nonmonotonic changes in performance when the frequency of different forms is taken into account. Such demonstrations led to important debates about the nature of the input in language learning, and about whether there was sufficient information in the input alone (e.g. the language tokens experienced by the child) to explain the complexity of the system that was learned (e.g. natural language). Elman (2005) discusses this general issue in terms of the "poverty of the stimulus" argument. Prior to connectionism, a popular view was that extra innate "preknowledge" was required to fully explain language learning, as the actual input experienced by the child was too impoverished to explain the complexity of language development. An example of such innate preknowledge was the language acquisition device postulated by Chomsky (1957; see Chapter 5). Elman showed that connectionist models can learn compositional and hierarchical structure from learning conditional probabilities in the input, and from using more powerful learning algorithms such as Bayes nets (see Chapter 6 for a discussion of Bayes nets in casual learning). Connectionist models of language acquisition hence demonstrate that, in principle, the available input is rich enough to enable a simple network that learns according to different statistical algorithms to behave like a child's brain acquiring language.

Elman (2005) has identified two challenges for connectionist models of cognitive development. One is to capture social cognition, and the other is to capture the fact that infants and children are not passive learners, but are instead active learners with motivations and desires. Elman makes the key point that children may not attend to "the input" in the same way that the connectionist model does—"the input" is not necessarily equivalent to what is taken in. This point draws attention to a larger point concerning the value of connectionist models for cognitive development, which is that they can only model learning in terms of decisions about the input that have been taken a priori by the modeler. These decisions are necessarily limited by current behavioral data and theories about the structure of the input. For example, we saw in Chapter 4 that Quinn and Johnson (1997, 2000) produced a successful connectionist model of conceptual development that learned the contrastive concepts of animals and furniture. From information about (for example) the different leg lengths associated with tables, chairs, dogs, and cats, the model first devoted large numbers of hidden units to coding the "global level" of animals versus furniture. Subsequently, it devoted more and more hidden units to distinctions in attributes such as leg length that yielded the "basic level" of categorization.

As noted in Chapter 4, however, the infant brain might be attending to aspects of the stimuli that have not been considered by the experimenters. Therefore, these aspects will not have been built into the connectionist simulation. The example given for conceptual development was that infants might devote attention to features that afford actions, such as "being graspable". Hence connectionist models of conceptual development must also include features of the input such as action affordance. Further, we know from cognitive neuroscience studies that actions on objects are coded by a special neural system, the mirror neuron system. We also know that mirror neurons are tuned to respond to biological actions (Tai et al., 2004). As argued in Chapter 4, all of these different aspects of the input must be taken into account when developing an adequate connectionist model of how young children develop conceptual knowledge from their real-world experience. This is why the in-principle demonstrations from connectionism are currently more important for theories of cognitive development than the successes of particular models in supporting particular theories (e.g. in suggesting a "global to basic" shift in infant categorization; see Chapter 4).

Another example of this general point concerns language acquisition. As discussed in Chapter 5, Kuhl et al. (2003) showed that babies did not learn language from the television. Even though these babies received the same amount and quality of (Mandarin Chinese) "input" from videos as babies who were interacting with real people, being exposed to "the input" was not sufficient for learning. Although it is important to know, in principle, that aspects of cognitive development can be captured by models that apply statistical algorithms to complex input, in practice connectionism may never be able to offer a complete theoretical account of cognitive development. Too much depends on the design decisions made by the modeler when constructing a given connectionist network. For example, the initial state of "knowledge" of the network, the nature of its input and output representations, the patterns of connectivity that it can form, and the learning algorithms that it will use will all determine the conclusions that can be drawn regarding cognitive development. The optimistic view would be that once all of these modeling decisions are understood in detail, we will have a comprehensive theory of the constraints on learning that might need to operate if children are to make the best use of the knowledge available in their learning environments. The alternative view is that whereas connectionist models have a crucial role to play in helping us to understand how complex cognition can arise without assuming symbolic thought, they are inherently limited by their reliance on statistical algorithms and capturing "the input".

As Vygotsky made clear, part of the input for human cognitive development is internal. There are internal mediators of cognitive processes that are very important for cognitive development, such as inner speech, the imagination, and pretending. It is doubtful that computational models will ever be able to capture aspects of the "input" such as these. However, new generations of computational models are evolving all the time. For example, "embodied" models of cognition simulate not only the internal cognitive architecture of the "mind", but also the organism's body and the physical world that it inhabits (Schlesinger, 2001). Such models have sensors and motor effectors, for example "muscles" that affect fixation points. These models are currently rather simple (e.g. a simple "eye" that learns to track moving objects in the visual field). Nevertheless, the fact that these "agent-based" models possess bodies that also provide input for learning is important given the key role of action in the development of cognition.

Towards a new theoretical framework

How can we draw together the important insights gained from neuroconstructivism and connectionism and the equally important insights contributed by the traditional cognitive developmental theories of Piaget and Vygotsky? The answer that I will sketch out here attempts to combine our new knowledge about the power of simple learning mechanisms to represent conceptual structure with our "old" knowledge about the importance of language and imaginative pretend play, knowledge construction, direct teaching, and being part of a community to cognitive development. Essentially, the new theoretical frameworks of neuroconstructivism and connectionism help us to understand how the brain creates cognitive representations from perceptual input. The old theoretical frameworks help us to understand how the activities of the child and the parent/sibling/peer/teacher enrich and develop these emergent conceptual representations into a rich and sophisticated cognitive system.

Mechanisms of learning

Sensory *statistical learning* is a crucial part of cognitive development. In Chapter 1, we saw that visual statistical learning is extremely efficient even early in infancy, particularly for dynamic stimuli. In particular, the infant visual system tracks conditional probabilities in the visual world, and by tracking and coding these conditional probabilities, represents relational and causal structure. For example, 2-month-old infants can track visual transitional probabilities between abstract geometric shapes, and 3-month-old infants can learn prototypes for abstract geometric shapes. They can also recognize vehicles and animals on the basis of motion cues alone (Arterberry & Bornstein, 2001). Three-month-old infants represent spatial relations such as "above" and "below", and 3½-month-old girls expect occluded objects to continue to exist. Simple learning algorithms represent both the relational and causal aspects of visual events, so that perceptual structure yields conceptual information. For example, the perceptual structure of "event categories" such as containment, occlusion, and support yields conceptual knowledge concerning the kinds of objects that (for example) should be able to contain other objects. Cross-modal connections are present from birth, although there is an important role for learning. Hence sensory information from different modalities can specify the same object or event. In monkeys, mirror neurons respond *both* to the sound of paper ripping and to the visual depiction of someone tearing up a newspaper. Babies, too, are likely to have the same kind of neural system.

In Chapter 2, we saw that a perceptual–structural analysis of the dynamic spatial and temporal behavior of objects yields not only conceptual entities such as event categories and vehicles versus animals, but also powerful conceptual frameworks about causal mechanisms. For example, the perceptual system assumes causality and animacy in the absence of conflicting information. Perception of dynamic interrelations in the everyday world of objects and events gives rise to causal information about structure. Hence, by default, perception supplies information about both the physical world of inanimate objects and the mental world of animate agents. For example, cross-modal information about the world of objects and events yields a lot of data about the laws governing physical interactions between objects (for example, a sound can specify whether one is watching a collision event or not). The babies' own actions also lead to rapid learning. In Chapter 2, we saw infants both learning by imitation and learning by analogy, as instantiated by learned "means–ends" behaviors like pulling apart a dumbbell, and using objects like cloths and strings to move a desirable toy within reach.

In Chapter 2, we also considered the potential importance of insights from machine learning algorithms to cognitive development. Machines are capable of **"explanation-based learning"**, which depends on constructing causal explanations for phenomena on the basis of single training examples (De Jong, 2006). Experiments in machine learning have shown that a machine can generalize from a single example by explaining to itself why the training example is an instantiation of a concept that is being learned. Background knowledge (prior domain knowledge) is used to constrain the inferences made. As noted in Chapter 2, Baillargeon has pointed out that infants are faced with similar problems in learning, and may also be capable of constructing causal explanations from experiencing single phenomena. This was demonstrated by "teaching experiments". For example, Wang and Baillargeon (2005) showed that if 9-month-old babies were exposed to critical events demonstrating the importance of the variable *height* for covering events, then they became sensitive to this variable three months earlier than other babies. Experimental manipulation of the frequency with which key variables were experienced affected the age at which infants learned about them. Explanation-based learning provides a mechanism for the development of causal explanatory frameworks, and also creates a natural role for the importance of individual experience in learning. As discussed in Chapter 6, causal explanation plays a critical role in cognitive development.

Machines also learn causal structure via algorithms called *causal Bayes nets*. Real-world information about temporal order and statistical covariation apparently enables babies and children to build knowledge about causal structure and causal strength using (it is assumed) similar algorithms. Babies and children learn causal information both by "seeing" and by "doing" (see Chapters 2 and 6). They can make causal inferences on the basis of perceptual input alone, but active experience is important for ruling out invalid inferences. For example, intervening in a causal system enables children to distinguish covariation that is causal from covariation that is incidental. Causal learning and causal reasoning can be both "bottom-up" and "top-down". Although the basis of causal inference is statistical (e.g. as exemplified by the power of Bayes nets), background knowledge and context will affect the causal inferences that are drawn from particular patterns of temporal and covariation data. Infants and children construct explanatory causal frameworks from perceptual information and from information gained via action. These frameworks are central to cognitive development, and their explanatory power is captured by the constructivist account of Piaget.

In Chapter 5, we saw that similar powerful statistical learning mechanisms were at work in the auditory domain. Here infants' ability to track conditional probabilities enabled them to extract the structural properties of auditory input. This yielded information about the phonotactic patterns of language (the sounds that make up the language, and the orders in which they can be combined), and information about word boundaries. As discussed, the physical changes where languages place phonetic boundaries are not random. General auditory perceptual abilities explain why infants are sensitive to the acoustic boundaries that separate phonetic categories in all human languages from birth. The infants then rapidly *learn* the locations of the phonetic boundaries that are important for *their* language, using statistical learning mechanisms (Kuhl, 2004, 2007). The infants track conditional probabilities to create prototypes for different phonemes. They are also sensitive to other auditory parameters such as rhythm and stress, which help them with word segmentation, with tracking the emotional content of speech, and with the marking of new information (via motherese or infant-directed speech). The production of language structures by the infant herself is also very important for learning. Infant babble imitates the intonational prosody of the adult language, and enables infants to try out syllables and other phoneme combinations. Hearing yourself produce babble is important for learning, and deaf babies show restricted babble and this soon falls away, whereas deaf babies born to signing parents babble with their hands. This "hand babble" is produced repetitively and reflects the general prosodic contours of natural sign languages. Both deaf and hearing babies are thus discovering and producing the most rudimentary structures of the natural language to which they are exposed. Again, perceptual learning mechanisms coupled with action extract structure that has cognitive content.

Learning by imitation is another important aspect of gaining cognitive expertise. Imitation enables infants to re-experience sensory events such as speech and the trajectories of falling objects and to learn more about them by doing so. In Chapter 3, we saw that learning by imitation is also crucially important for social cognition. Imitation is present from birth. Neonatal imitation shows that infants can recognize cross-modal equivalences between acts that they see others perform and their own felt bodily movements. Meltzoff (2002, 2007) has argued that this recognition of self–other equivalences functions as a "like me" analogy. By connecting the visible bodily actions of others with their own internal states, infants can feel what it is like to do the act that was seen. The recognition of self–other equivalence in action then enables infants to realize that others have perceptions and emotions that are also "like me". This provides a foundation for understanding the actions, goals, and psychological states of others. Bodily analogies may also help in understanding physical systems. For example, we saw earlier in this chapter that Piaget observed his own babies imitating the opening and closing of boxes by opening and closing their hands.

Infants also learn social contingencies from very early indeed. Adults can make their social behavior contingent upon infant attempts to communicate, and so contingency learning may also help infants to become aware of themselves as a separate (bodily) self with their own intentional and affective states. Infants are also very interested in goal-directed actions by other agents and in where agents look. This makes them attend in particular to input relevant to understanding intentionality. Indeed, by 9 months infants can distinguish whether another agent is unable or unwilling to give them a desired toy, and by 14 months infants will imitate intended acts by another agent, even if these acts are never witnessed. By 8–10 months, typically developing infants show proto-declarative pointing, demonstrating communicative intentions of their own. The infants wants to share attention with another, which is truly intersubjective, as there is shared *psychological* ground (both infant and sharer know that they are sharing attention; see Tomasello & Carpenter, 2007). The infant is already part of communicative activities involved in sharing objects before the age of 12 months, and the concomitant sharing of psychological states can be termed "shared intentionality" (Chapter 7; see also Tomasello & Carpenter, 2007). Shared intentionality is crucial for social cognitive development, and is also linked to language development (see Chapter 3).

Learning by analogy is the fourth kind of learning that has been shown to play an important role in cognitive development. Inductive reasoning operates from early in development, as shown in Chapter 4 when we considered categorization. Generalizing on the basis of a known example is the basis of categorization, and examples can be objects, events, actions, or even mental states. When generalization depends on perceptual similarity, this is not usually treated as analogy. However, when generalization depends on structural (relational) similarity, then it is treated as analogy. As we saw in Chapter 4, perceptual similarity and structural similarity are usually highly correlated. Perceptual similarity usually means that objects also share deeper nonobservable characteristics (such as the features "has a heart" and "has blood inside" shared by biological kinds). In fact, when perceptual similarity and structural similarity are pitted against one another, even young children go with structural similarity (Gelman & Coley, 1990). This tendency is enhanced by language. When category membership labels are provided, even 2-year-olds go with structural similarity over perceptual appearance. Consistency of labeling by adults further supports categorization (Waxman & Braun, 2005).

We also saw in Chapter 4 that the patterns of induction made during categorization may be constrained by the perceptual system itself. For example, the nature of observed motion may determine whether inductions are made to similar animate or inanimate entities, perhaps because one type of motion is perceived by special neurons that are biologically tuned (mirror neurons). Cognitive neuroscience studies have also shown that sensory information is always retained when concepts are recognized. As discussed in Chapter 4, the distributed nature of conceptual representation lends itself naturally to development. We also saw that the existence of distributed representations might mean that a central tenet of some theories of conceptual development, the assumption of conceptual change, is incorrect. One example is scientific reasoning. The level of knowledge that can be abstracted from perceptual causal information about different entities has in important cases been transcended by modern physics and biology. However, when this knowledge is taught, it does not appear to restructure conceptual understanding, "carving the world at different joints" (Carey & Spelke, 1994). Instead, both the naïve knowledge and the taught knowledge may be maintained together. Inhibitory mechanisms may then determine which kind of knowledge dominates once a particular problem is encountered (Petitto & Dunbar, in press). A similar case can be made for number (see Chapter 10). Rather than indicating conceptual change, children's use of count labels may be another example of children using language to organize their mental life in the way proposed by Vygotsky. Language may enable conceptual reorganization and redescription rather than the construction of a new representational format. For example, imaging data suggest that the "old" representational formats (e.g. the parietal representation for approximate magnitude) are still activated during simple number tasks (e.g. Ansari, Garcia, Lucas, Harmon, & Dhital, 2005), even if the primary activation is in other areas (e.g. frontal areas).

Language, gesture, pretend play, and the imagination

In Chapter 5, we examined language acquisition in depth. Our survey provided evidence consistent with Vygotsky's thesis that language is the primary symbolic system that children respond to psychologically. The first communicative skill that emerged developmentally was word comprehension. Children understand the referents intended by words by 8–10 months. The second communicative skill to emerge was the use of gesture. Gesture has communicative intent, as it is a way of producing meanings for others to understand. Gesture plays a key role in enhancing the effectiveness of communication in early language development, and is gradually replaced by word production. Children begin producing more words between 11 and 13 months of age. It has been argued that gesture provides a "cognitive bridge" between comprehension and production. Goldin-Meadow and Wagner (2005) have argued that gesture plays an additional cognitive role in development. Gestures can communicate important information about what the child understands in a given cognitive domain, which can be sensed by their teachers, who will alter their input accordingly. Goldin-Meadow and Wagner (2005) offer a number of demonstrations in different cognitive domains that children's use of gestures reflects what they are thinking, even when they are unable to verbalize these thoughts explicitly. They show that gesture–speech "mismatches" are often found when children are on the verge of making progress on a particular cognitive task. For example, children who are on the verge of understanding the Piagetian conservation of liquid may give a verbal nonconserving response based on the different height of the liquids, while at the same time gesturing to the experimenter that one container is wide and shallow, and the other is tall and narrow (see Figure 11.2). Children who produce gesture–speech mismatches are more likely to make progress when given relevant instruction than children who do not.

Vygotsky argued that one of the symbolic functions of language was that it enabled children to disconnect themselves from the immediate, concrete situation and to generate possibilities and plans. He also noted that language can be used to create a "time field" in addition to the visual–spatial field of current perception, enabling the child to view changes in the immediate situation from the viewpoint of past activities, and to act in the present from the viewpoint of the future. We saw a number of examples of this disconnection and time field at work in Chapter 8, when we considered episodic memory development. Very early autobiographical memories are fragmented, as children do not yet have sufficient language to rehearse their own experiences to themselves and form an autobiographical self-narrative. Language development enables children to construct extended, temporally organized representations of experienced events that are narratively coherent. We also saw that remembering is embedded in larger social and cognitive activities. As children experience repeated events with other people, they develop schemas or scripts that encode the typical temporal and causal structure of routine events. Again, language helps children to structure and encode their experiences. Reminiscing within families also aids the development of autobiographical memories. Whereas younger children use discussion of the past to cement their understanding of their family and their role within it, older children talk about the autobiographical past to cement relationships with peers (Van Abbema & Bauer, 2005).

However, in Chapter 7, we saw that action might help young children to disconnect themselves from the immediate concrete situation before language does. This action is pretend play, and the disconnection is the beginning of metarepresentation (Leslie, 1987). For example, when pretending that a banana is a telephone, the child must decouple the *primary* representation of the banana given by the sensory systems (yellow, edible object) from the pretend representation of telephone receiver. A crucial aspect of cognition is that our primary representations are veridical. However, when we pretend, the primary representation is "quarantined" from the pretend representation, and the pretend representation is a metarepresentation—a representation of a primary representation. Through pretend, the child is manipulating her cognitive relations to information, and taking a representation as the object of cognition. Leslie (1987) argued that the emergence of pretence marks the beginning of the capacity to understand cognition itself—to understand thoughts as entities. Language has a similar function of providing a medium for reflecting on and knowing about our own thoughts. Language and pretending are intimately connected, for example, social partners use language to help young children to understand pretend situations. Adult scaffolding of pretend play is another example of shared intentionality.

Both language and imaginative pretend play share two core developmental functions: they enable children to reflect upon and regulate their own cognitive behavior, and they enable a deeper understanding of the mind. The reflection/regulation functions of language and pretend play relate to metacognition. As the child develops metacognitive abilities, cognition itself can become the object of cognition. We saw in Chapter 9 that developing an awareness of one's own cognitive functioning is the key to cognitive development once the foundational domains are established. As metacognition develops, children become able to monitor their own cognitive performance and regulate their own cognitive strategies, they become aware of the demands made by different kinds of cognitive tasks, and they become able to monitor the sources of their knowledge. Most measures of reflection and self-regulation (e.g. executive measures) are significantly correlated with verbal ability. Hence language has an important enabling function with respect to metacognition. The self-regulation of thought and action (executive function) has been a particular focus of study. The assumption has been that as children gain metaknowledge about their cognitive processes (metacognition), their strategic control over their mental processes (executive function) will improve. The data discussed in Chapter 9 suggest that this is indeed the case. This picks up Vygotsky's idea that language enables children to engage in problem solving and planning. During this developmental process, the abilities to deal with *conflicting* representations and to develop inhibitory control over thoughts and actions are particularly important. As is also discussed in Chapter 9, gaining insight into one's own cognitive processes benefits the development of both inductive and deductive reasoning.

The function of imaginative play in enabling children to reflect upon and regulate their own cognitive behavior has not been an object of study in the West, but has been studied by the neo-Vygotskian psychologists in Russia (see Karpov, 2005). Vygotsky argued that the imagination represented a specifically human form of cognitive activity. He argued that a central developmental function of pretend play was that the "rules of the game" required children to act against their immediate impulses, thereby helping them to gain inhibitory control over their thoughts and actions. For example, 3- to 7-year-old children can stand motionless for much longer when playing at being "a sentry", particularly when their friends are there to monitor whether they stay in role. Western psychology has focused more on the other aspect of imaginative play referred to above: its important role in enabling a deeper understanding of mind ("theory of mind"). As we saw in Chapter 7, many studies by Dunn and others have shown that pretend play with siblings and peers is closely linked to developing a deeper understanding of the minds of others. Sociodramatic role play helps children to gain insights into the beliefs, desires, and intentions of other agents. Sociodramatic play also requires negotiation with friends regarding the plot and each other's roles. This results in extensive mental state discourse, whereby language can exert important effects on the development of theory of mind.

Hence the second core developmental function of language and pretend play referred to above: their roles in enabling a deeper understanding of mind. The linguistic discussion about feelings, thoughts, and desires that is part of imaginative play is important for helping children to understand the contents of other minds. Conversations and communication about the mind play a pivotal role in acquiring an understanding of other minds, whether this communication is part of shared imaginative play or part of family discourse. Children engaged in pretend play have to enquire, argue, and reflect about why people behave in the ways that they do. Children in families also engage in considerable discourse about feelings and emotions. As shown for example by Dunn et al. (1991a), there are important links between family dialog about feelings and children's later understanding of the emotions and beliefs of others. As Schneider and Lockl (2002) pointed out, metacognition research is concerned with what the child knows about his or her own mind, while theory-of-mind research is concerned with what the child knows about somebody else's mind. Both types of cognitive development, however, depend on both language and the imagination. As Vygotsky argued, both pretend play and language allow meaning to be detached from perceptual reality, enabling the development of abstract thought. Via language and action, children can take their own cognitive processes as the objects of cognition.

Vygotsky also argued that in play, a child behaves "beyond his average age, above his daily behavior; in play it is as though he were a head taller than himself" (Vygotsky, 1978, pp. 102–103). This is the zone of proximal development, the notion that what children can achieve with the assistance of others is the true measure of their cognitive development. The Russian neo-Vygotskians have stressed that joint activity is critical to the effective use of the zone of proximal development in teaching (Karpov, 2005). The child's acquisition, mastery, and internalization of new content must be mediated via shared activity. Vygotsky argued that collaborative activity was important for cognitive development, because it enabled cultural "sign systems" to be transmitted that in themselves led to cognitive development, and because children were capable of doing much more in collective activity (for example, by imitation) or under the guidance of others than they could do alone: "Learning awakens a variety of internal developmental processes that are able to operate only when the child is interacting with people in his environment and in cooperation with his peers" (Vygotsky, 1978, p. 90). This idea has recently received new impetus from investigations of the "pedagogical stance" by Gergely, Csibra, and their colleagues. For example, Csibra and Gergely (2006) proposed that humans are adapted to spontaneously transfer relevant cultural knowledge to conspecifics and to fast-learn the contents of such teaching via a species-specific social learning system that is "pedagogy". In their terms, "pedagogy" is a neglected aspect of the triadic interactions with objects that infants and their caretakers engage in. One function of these triadic interactions is *epistemic*, namely to provide infants with reliable, new, and relevant information about the objects concerned. Knowledge transfer during these triadic interactions is thought to be triggered by communicative cues such as eye contact and the use of motherese. Although not part of Csibra and Gergely's argument, it is easy to imagine that this species-specific social learning system also enables cultural knowledge transfer to older children via collaborative learning in the zone of proximal development. As Gergely, Egyed, and Kiraly (2007) point out, such a system requires a default assumption about other agents, which is that they are trustworthy and benevolent sources of universally shared cultural knowledge. As children get older, they become more selective about who is regarded as trustworthy (Harris, 2007).

The promise of cognitive neuroscience

As noted above, it seems unlikely that connectionist models will ever be able to capture the richness of the internal mediators of cognitive processes, such as inner speech and imaginative pretend play, and the collaborative aspects of learning, such as shared intentionality and the zone of proximal development. However, at some level, this must be possible. The biological constraints identified by neuroconstructivism and the learning constraints identified by connectionism must be at work in creating the brains of children who are able to respond psychologically to language, pedagogy, and the imagination. How will cognitive neuroscience enable us to gain a deeper understanding of how cognitive development happens? One interesting possibility has been sketched by Clark (2006). Although Clark's argument is about language, it is relevant to all aspects of the cognition-enhancing symbol systems that have emerged from human sociocultural activity (recall that Vygotsky included concepts as a culturally determined symbolic system).

Clark argues that the entire cognitive system should be conceptualized as a "loose-knit, distributed representational economy" (p. 373). Some elements in the economy might conflict with other elements in the economy, but this is inevitable as there is no homunculus or "single central reasoning engine" that determines cognition. Rather, there are many interacting parts of the overall reasoning machinery that can be maintained at the same time. The activity of all these parts is cognition. Hence children may indicate more cognitive insight via gesture than they can indicate via explanation, or they may be able to regulate their own thoughts and actions when playing in ways that they cannot yet manage in the absence of pretend. There is no all-knowing, inner "central executive" that governs what is "known" and that orchestrates development. Rather, there is a "vast parallel coalition of more-or-less influential forces whose largely self-organizing unfolding makes each of us the thinking beings that we are" (Clark, 2006, p. 373).

Cognitive neuroscience appears to be revealing just such a vast parallel coalition of mental representations, knowledge, and forces. It is also beginning to reveal what some of these "self-organizing unfolding" processes might be. For example, in neuroconstructivism we see that cognitive development depends in part on the interactions between the neural structures in this vast parallel coalition, in part on the "embodiment" of the brain (with the sensory systems acting as filters for the "input"), and in part on the cellular environments themselves. Therefore, we can explore whether the cognitive representations developed by a child who is growing up in a stressful environment are affected by the atypical cellular environments created by the constant activation of the stress hormones. We can explore whether the cognitive representations developed by a child who has a mildly impaired auditory system are affected by the quality of the information about the external world provided by that auditory system. The interactions and interconnections between neural structures will develop differently in each case. Eventually, it is possible that cognitive neuroscience will develop to the point where we can measure how the brain responds psychologically to complex "inputs" such as language, pedagogy, and the imagination. In practice, however, we already understand quite a lot about these psychological responses from cognitive behavioral work. This has been illustrated by our discussion in this chapter of influential theories of cognitive development.

How will cognitive neuroscience take theories of cognitive development forward?

Cognitive neuroscience methods, with their potential for revealing directly the nature of mental representations and how they change in response to certain factors, are exciting tools for cognitive developmental psychology. However, their inherent limitations must be recognized. As stressed repeatedly in this book, current cognitive neuroimaging studies focus on *where* in the brain something is happening, and show *correlations* between neural activity and behavior. They do not yet tell us much about developmental causality. For example, they do not show that a particular developmental ability depends on the development of a particular neural structure, despite much speculation along these lines in some fields (for example, the idea that the development of frontal cortex plays a causal role in the development of inhibitory control, see Chapter 9). In fact, it is not clear that neuroimaging studies could ever reveal causation of this type. Neural structures change in response to input, and this input can be cognitive–behavioral input, as stressed by neuroconstructivism. Logically, the changes documented in a neural structure, such as frontal cortex, could reflect cognitive–behavioral developments rather than cause them. The most exciting ways in which cognitive neuroimaging can contribute to understanding cognitive development would seem to be: (1) in revealing more about developmental trajectories; (2) in revealing more about the "vast coalition" of mental representations and how they interact; and (3) in adding to our understanding of how sensory input gives rise to cognitive knowledge. In particular, longitudinal studies are required.

For example, regarding (1), we could explore the neurodevelopmental trajectory of acquiring knowledge about animates. This seems likely to begin with sensory analyses of motion and with cross-modal information about agents. It seems likely that multiple representations of aspects of the visual appearance, typical sounds, smells, and textures of different animates are acquired with experience, and maintained in a distributed network of knowledge that is represented both in primary sensory areas and in conjunction areas that record the co-activation of particular sets of neurons (and hence enable cognitive activity such as prototype formation). These multiple representations are by necessity also linked to emotions (e.g. which animates are frightening), beliefs (e.g. which animates are trustworthy), and intentions (e.g. which animates can I try and learn from?). Cognitive neuroimaging could show us which aspects of the neural system for acquiring knowledge about animates develop first, which neural structures become connected to this core system, how information flows through the system in response to different inputs, and which neural interactions are key in determining output. These kinds of knowledge will affect our cognitive theories. For example, we might learn that a structure like the amygdala, which is thought to be crucial for understanding emotions like fear, is a core part of the system for representing knowledge about animates. The amygdala is also thought by some researchers to play a particular role in autism (e.g. Baron-Cohen et al., 1999). This knowledge about neural connections would then constrain our cognitive developmental theories, for example about how knowledge about animate agents links to the development of theory of mind (which is impaired in individuals with autism).

It also seems likely that deviations in any part of the trajectory of normative development could have serious repercussions for cognitive development. For example, a baby whose sensory system did not yield normative information about biological motion could be at risk for autism, because this low-level sensory anomaly in acquiring knowledge about animates could eventually lead to impaired theory of mind (e.g. Plaisted, Saksida, Alcantara, & Weisblatt, 2003). Any or none of these possibilities could be true. One important aspect of cognitive neuroscience methods is that they can yield unique information about the development of mental representations to help us to find out. One of the great potentials of cognitive neuroscience methods for cognitive development lies in the early identification of neural markers for risk (see Goswami, 2004, 2006). However, in order to identify these neural markers, we need extensive longitudinal information about typical neurodevelopment. This information will be very complex, but in principle it is possible to acquire it.

Regarding (2), the "vast coalition" of mental representations and how they interact, conceptual development is one area where this kind of information would be very informative for theory. Children experience many instances of different kinds of concepts, and this experience is not simply perceptual and action-based, but context-dependent. For example, in developing a concept like "hammer", experiences of games with toy hammers will be recorded along with experiences of watching adults using real hammers or of holding a real hammer oneself. It seems that multiple aspects of each experience are registered by the brain, and are activated together when new instances of the same concept are encountered. Hence core features of hammer experiences (e.g. the action of hammering) will be activated more strongly than variable aspects (e.g. whether the hammer is a yellow plastic toy or a real hammer made of steel and wood). This type of process could be the neural basis for Lakoff's (1986) observation that what we *understand* as properties of concepts depends on our interactive functioning with our environment. Medin (1989) argued that people have implicit assumptions about the structure of the world and about the underlying nature of categories, and that these beliefs are represented in the categories that they develop as "essences". If this assumed process of multiple distributed representation could be measured neurodevelopmentally, it might help us to understand how (for example) these essences emerge.

This type of investigation would also yield insights into how semantics emerge from conceptual experience. The distributed representations beginning to be revealed by cognitive neuroscience seem to give rise to apparently amodal semantic knowledge. This can be knowledge about objects like hammers or cups, but it can also be abstract semantic knowledge like knowledge about truth or justice. Longitudinal study of the neurodevelopmental trajectory of conceptual development could give us important insights into why the developed semantic system appears to be amodal, symbolic, and enduring in form. High-level concepts must be formed from low-level percepts (Markman & Dietrich, 2000), but must also incorporate context in order to explain the effects of background knowledge and context in human reasoning.

This brings us to (3), the potential for cognitive neuroscience to add to our understanding of how sensory input gives rise to cognitive knowledge. This type of investigation seems particularly important, as it is not well-understood. Traditionally, "the input" was thought to be too impoverished to enable sensory input to give rise to cognitive knowledge, as discussed earlier (e.g. Elman, 2005). The problem was therefore avoided by postulating preknowledge like the language acquisition device, by assuming naïve theories in babies, or by postulating core knowledge or innate biases, such as the essentialist bias. Cognitive activity that appears to be guided by preknowledge, naïve theories, innate biases, or core knowledge may in fact arise simply because the neural architecture of our sensory systems processes perceptual information in certain ways. Understanding whether this is the case is particularly important for a comprehensive new theory of cognitive development. This is the perspective offered by neuroconstructivism and connectionism. Coupled with neural imaging of what actually happens in the brain as a child develops language or concepts, this perspective should provide particularly rich information about development. Understanding how sensory input gives rise to cognitive knowledge has the potential to impact our understanding of typical cognitive development, atypical cognitive development, and the patterns of breakdown in the adult system that are studied by neuropsychologists.

The truly ambitious goal for a new theory of cognitive development informed by cognitive neuroscience is to cross and integrate the disciplinary boundaries of biology, culture, cognition, emotion, perception, and action (see Diamond, 2007). Social, emotional, and cultural influences on cognition must become equal partners with biological, sensory, and neurological influences. As Diamond argues, development is a life-long process, and we must pay more than lip-service to the complexity of human experience. Ultimately, it is this very complexity that enables the remarkable cognitive developmental changes that are observed as babies develop into children, and children develop into adults. All of this complexity shapes the brain. Because cognitive neuroscience methods enable us to measure this shaping directly, they have the potential to play an innovative role in developing new explanatory frameworks to enable us to truly understand cognitive development.

References

Adleman, N. E., Menon, V., Blasey, C. M., White, C. D., Warsofsky, I. S., Glover, G. H., & Reiss, A. L. (2002). A developmental fMRI study of the Stroop color–word task. *NeuroImage*, *16*, 61–75.

Akhtar, N., & Tomasello, M. (1997). Young children's productivity with word order and verb morphology. *Developmental Psychology*, *33*, 952–965.

Amsel, E., Goodman, G., Savoie, D., & Clark, M. (1996). The development of reasoning about causal and noncausal influences on levers. *Child Development*, *67*, 1624–1646.

Amsterdam, B. (1972). Mirror self-image reactions before age two. *Developmental Psychobiology*, *5*, 297–305.

Anderson, J. R. (1990). *Cognitive Psychology and Its Implications*, 3rd Edition. Hillsdale, NJ: Lawrence Lawrence Erlbaum Associates, Inc.

Anderson, N. H. (1991). *Contributions to Information Integration Theory: Vol. III. Developmental.* Hillsdale, NJ: Lawrence Erlbaum Associates, Inc.

Ansari, D., Garcia, N., Lucas, E., Harmon, K., & Dhital, B. (2005). Neural correlates of symbolic number processing in children and adults. *NeuroReport*, *16*, 1769–1773.

Anthony, J. L., Lonigan, C. J., Burgess, S. R., Driscoll, K., Phillips, B. M., & Cantor, B. G. (2002). Structure of preschool phonological sensitivity: overlapping sensitivity to rhyme, words, syllables, and phonemes. *Journal of Experimental Child Psychology*, *82*, 65–92.

Anthony, J. L., Lonigan, C. J., Driscoll, K., Phillips, B. M., & Burgess, S. R. (2003). Phonological sensitivity: A quasi-parallel progression of word structure units and cognitive operations. *Reading Research Quarterly*, *38(4)*, 470–487.

Aron, A. R., Fletcher, P. C., Bullmore, E. T., Sahakian, B. J., & Robbins, T. W. (2003). Stop-signal inhibition disrupted by damage to right inferior frontal gyrus in humans. *Nature Neuroscience*, *6(2)*, 115–116.

Arterberry, M. E., & Bornstein, M. H. (2001). Three-month-old infants' categorization of animals and vehicles based on static and dynamic attributes. *Journal of Experimental Child Psychology*, *80*, 333–346.

Aslin, R. N. (2007). What's in a look? *Developmental Science*, *10*, 48–53.

Astington, J. W. (2001). The future of theory-of-mind research: understanding motivational states, the role of language, and real-world consequences. *Child Development*, *72(3)*, 685–687.

Atkinson, J., & Braddick, O. (1989). Development of basic visual functions. In A. M. Slater & G. Bremner (Eds.), *Infant Development* (pp. 7–41). Hove, UK: Lawrence Erlbaum Associates.

Atran, S. (1994). Core foundations vs. scientific theories. In L. A. Hirschfeld & S. A. Gelman (Eds.), *Mapping the Mind* (pp. 316–340). New York: Cambridge University Press.

Baddeley, A. D. (2000). The episodic buffer: A new component of working memory? *Trends in Cognitive Sciences*, *4*, 417–423.

Baddeley, A. D., & Hitch, G. (1974). Working memory. In G. H. Bower (Ed.), *The Psychology of Learning and Motivation* (Vol. 8, pp. 47–90). London: Academic Press.

Bahrick, L. E., & Watson, J. S. (1985). Detection of intermodal proprioceptive–visual contingency as a basis of self perception in infancy. *Developmental Psychology*, *21*, 963–973.

Baillargeon, R. (1986). Representing the existence and location of hidden objects: Object permanence in 6- and 8-month-old infants. *Cognition*, *23*, 21–41.

Baillargeon, R. (1987a). Object permanence in 3.5- and 4.5-month-old infants. *Developmental Psychology*, *23*, 655–664.

Baillargeon, R. (1987b). Young infants' reasoning about the physical and spatial properties of a hidden object. *Cognitive Development*, *2*, 179–200.

Baillargeon, R. (2001). Infants' physical knowledge: Of acquired expectations and core principles. In E. Dupoux (Ed.), *Language, Brain and Cognitive Development: Essays in Honour of Jacques Mehler* (pp. 341–361). Cambridge, MA: MIT Press.

Baillargeon, R. (2002). The acquisition of physical knowledge in infancy: A summary in eight lessons. In U. Goswami (Ed.), *Handbook of Childhood Cognitive Development* (pp. 47–83). Oxford: Blackwell.

Baillargeon, R. (2004). Infants' physical world. *Current Directions in Psychological Science*, *13*, 89–94.

Baillargeon, R., & DeVos, J. (1991). Object permanence in young infants: Further evidence. *Child Development*, *62*, 1227–1246.

Baillargeon, R., & DeVos, J. (1994). Qualitative and quantitative reasoning about unveiling events in 12.5- and 13.5-month-old infants. Unpublished manuscript, University of Illinois.

Baillargeon, R., & Gelman, R. (1980). *Young children's understanding of simple causal sequences: Predictions and explanations.* Paper presented to the meeting of the American Psychological Society, Montreal, 1980.

Baillargeon, R., & Graber, M. (1987). Where is the rabbit? 5.5-month-old infants' representation of the height of a hidden object. *Cognitive Development*, *2*, 375–392.

Baillargeon, R., & Graber, M. (1988). Evidence of location memory in 8-month-old infants in a non–search AB task. *Developmental Psychology*, *24*, 502–511.

Baillargeon, R., & Wang, S.-H. (2002). Event categorization in infancy. *Trends in Cognitive Sciences*, *6*, 85–93.

Baillargeon, R., DeVos, J., & Graber, M. (1989). Location memory in 8-month-old infants in a non-search AB task: Further evidence. *Cognitive Development, 4,* 345–367.

Baillargeon, R., Graber, M., De Vos, J., & Black, J. (1990). Why do young infants fail to search for hidden objects? *Cognition, 36,* 255–284.

Baillargeon, R., Li, J., Ng, W., & Yuan, S. (in press). An account of infants' physical reasoning. In A. Woodward & A. Needham (Eds.), *Learning and the Infant Mind.* New York: Oxford University Press.

Baillargeon, R., Needham, A., & De Vos, J. (1992). The development of young infants' intuitions about support. *Early Development & Parenting, 1,* 69–78.

Baillargeon, R., Spelke, E. S., & Wasserman, S. (1985). Object permanence in 5-month-old infants. *Cognition, 20,* 191–208.

Baker, L., Fernandez-Fein, S., Scher, D., & Williams, H. (1998). Home experiences related to the development of word recognition. In J. L. Metsala, & L. C. Ehri (Eds.), *Word Recognition in Beginning Literacy.* Mahwah, NJ: Lawrence Erlbaum Associates, Inc.

Baldwin, D. A., & Markman, E. M. (1989). Establishing word–object relations: A first step. *Child Development, 60,* 381–398.

Baron-Cohen, S. (1989a). Perceptual role-taking and protodeclarative pointing in autism. *British Journal of Developmental Psychology, 7,* 113–127.

Baron-Cohen, S. (1989b). The autistic child's theory of mind: A case for specific developmental delay. *Journal of Child Psychology and Psychiatry, 30,* 285–297.

Baron-Cohen, S. (1995). *Mindblindness: An Essay on Autism and Theory of Mind.* Boston: MIT Press.

Baron-Cohen, S. Ring, H. A., A. Ring, Wheelwright, S. Bullmore, E. T., Brammer, M. J., Simmons, A., & Williams, S. C. R. (1999). Social intelligence in the normal and autistic brain: an fMRI study. *European Journal of Neuroscience, 11(6),* 1891–1898.

Barsalou, L. W., Simmons, W. K., Barbey, A. K., & Wilson, C. D. (2003). Grounding conceptual knowledge in modality-specific systems. *Trends in Cognitive Sciences, 7,* 84–91.

Barth, H., LaMont, K., Lipton, J., Dehaene, S., Kanwisher, N., & Spelke, E. S. (2005a). Nonsymbolic arithmetic in adults and young children. *Cognition, 98,* 199–222.

Barth, H., LaMont, K., Lipton, J., & Spelke, E. S. (2005b). Abstract number and arithmetic in preschool children. *Proceedings of the National Academy of Sciences, 102(39),* 14116–14122.

Bartlett, F. C. (1932). *Remembering.* Cambridge: Cambridge University Press.

Bates, E., Camaioni, L., & Volterra, V. (1975). The acquisition of performatives prior to speech. *Merrill Palmer Quarterly, 21,* 205–226.

Bates, E., Devescovi, A., & Wulfeck, B. (2001). Psycholinguistics: A cross-language perspective. *Annual Review of Psychology, 52,* 369–398.

Bauer, P. J. (2004). Getting explicit memory off the ground: Steps toward construction of a neuro-developmental account of changes in the first two years of life. *Developmental Review, 24,* 347–373.

Bauer, P. J. (2006). Constructing a past in infancy: A neuro-developmental account. *Trends in Cognitive Sciences, 10,* 175–181.

Bauer, P. J., & Mandler, J. M. (1989a). One thing follows another: Effects of temporal structure on 1- to 2-year-olds' recall of events. *Developmental Psychology, 25,* 197–206.

Bauer, P. J., & Mandler, J. M. (1989b). Taxonomies and triads: Conceptual organisation in one- to two-year-olds. *Cognitive Psychology, 21,* 156–184.

Bauer, P. J., & Shore, C. M. (1987). Making a memorable event: Effects of familiarity and organisation on young children's recall of action sequences. *Cognitive Development, 2,* 327–338.

Bauer, P. J., Dow, G. A., & Hertsgaard, L. A. (1995). Effects of prototypicality on categorisation in 1- to 2-year-olds: Getting down to basic. *Cognitive Development, 10,* 43–68.

Bauer, P. J., Wenner, J. A., Dropnik, P. L., & Wewerka, S. S. (2000). Parameters of remembering and forgetting in the transition from infancy to early childhood. *Monographs of the Society for Research in Child Development, 65(4),* Serial no. 263.

Bauer, P. J., Wiebe, S. A., Carver, L. J., Waters, J. M., & Nelson, C. A. (2003). Developments in long-term explicit memory late in the first year of life: Behavioral and electrophysiological indices. *Psychological Science, 14,* 629–635.

Bechara, A., Damasio, A. R., Damasio, H., & Anderson, S. W. (1994). Insensitivity to future consequences following damage to human prefrontal cortex. *Cognition, 50,* 7–15

Becker, J. (1994). 'Sneak shoes', 'sworders' and 'nose beards': A case study of lexical innovation. *First Language, 14(2),* 195–211.

Behne, T., Carpenter, M., Call, J., & Tomasello, M. (2005a). Unwilling versus unable: Infants' understanding of intentional action. *Developmental Psychology, 41,* 328–337.

Behne, T., Carpenter, M., & Tomasello, M. (2005b). One-year-olds comprehend the communicative intentions behind gestures in a hiding game. *Developmental Science, 8,* 492–499.

Benedict, H. (1979). Early lexical development: Comprehension and production. *Journal of Child Language, 6,* 183–200.

Berko, J. (1958). The child's learning of English morphology. *Word, 14,* 150–177.

Berndt, R. S., Reggia, J. A., & Mitchum, C. C. (1987). Empirically derived probabilities for grapheme-to-phoneme correspondences in English. *Behavior Research Methods, Instruments, & Computers, 19,* 1–9.

Bertenthal, B. I., Proffitt, D. R., Spetner, N. B., & Thomas, M. A. (1985). The development of infant sensitivity to biomechanical motions. *Child Development, 56,* 531–543.

Bigelow, A. E., MacLean, K., & Proctor, J. (2004). The role of joint attention in the development of infants' play with objects. *Developmental Science, 7(5)*, 518–526.

Bjorklund, D. F., & Bjorklund, B. R. (1985). Organisation vs. item effects of an elaborated knowledge base on children's memory. *Developmental Psychology, 21*, 1120–1131.

Bjorklund, D. F., & Bjorklund, B. R. (1992). *Looking at Children: An Introduction to Child Development.* Pacific Grove, CA: Brooks/Cole.

Blaisdell, A. P., Sawa, K., Leising, K. J., & Waldmann, M. R. (2006). Causal reasoning in rats. *Science, 311*, 1020–1022.

Blakemore, C., & Cooper, G. (1970). Development of the brain depends on the visual environment. *Nature, 228*, 477–478.

Bloom, L. (1973). *One Word at a Time.* Paris: Mouton.

Bogartz, R. S., Shinskey, J. L., & Speaker, C. J. (1997). Interpreting infant looking: The event set × event set design. *Developmental Psychology, 33*, 408–422.

Bonatti, L., Peña, M., Nespor, M., & Mehler, J. (2005). Linguistic constraints on statistical computations: The role of consonants and vowels in continuous speech processing. *Psychological Science, 16*, 451–459.

Bornstein, M. H., & Sigman, M. D. (1986). Continuity in mental development from infancy. *Child Development, 57*, 251–274.

Bortfeld, H., Morgan, J., Golinkoff, R., & Rathbun, K. (2005). Mommy and me: Familiar names help launch babies into speech stream segmentation. *Psychological Science, 16*, 298–304.

Bowerman, M. (1982). Reorganizational processes in lexical and syntactic development. In E. Wanner & L. R. Gleitman (Eds.), *Language Acquisition: The State of the Art.* New York: Cambridge University Press.

Bowlby, J. (1969). *Attachment, Vol. 1 of Attachment and Loss.* London: Hogarth Press/New York: Basic Books.

Bowlby, J. (1971). *Attachment and Loss.* London: Routlege or Harmondsworth: Penguin Books.

Bowlby, J. (1973). *Separation: Anxiety & Anger. Vol. 2 of Attachment and Loss.* London: Hogarth Press.

Bradley, L., & Bryant, P. E. (1978). Difficulties in auditory organization as a possible cause of reading backwardness. *Nature, 271*, 746–747.

Bradley, L., & Bryant, P. E. (1983). Categorising sounds and learning to read: A causal connection. *Nature, 310*, 419–421.

Braine, M. (1963). The ontogeny of English phrase structure: The first phase. *Language, 39*, 1–13.

Braine, M. (1971). The acquisition of language in infant and child. In C. Reed (Ed), *The Learning of Language.* New York: Appleton-Century-Croft.

Bremner, J. G. (1988). *Infancy.* Oxford: Blackwell.

Breslow, L. (1981). Re–evaluation of the literature on the development of transitive inferences. *Psychological Bulletin, 89*, 325–351.

Bretherton, E., & Beeghly, M. (1982). Talking about internal states: The acquisition of an explicit theory of mind. *Developmental Psychology, 18*, 906–921.

Brooks, R., & Meltzoff, A. N. (2002). The importance of eyes: How infants interpret adult looking behavior. *Developmental Psychology, 38*, 958–966.

Brooks, R., & Meltzoff, A. N. (2005). The development of gaze following and its relation to language. *Developmental Science, 8*, 535–543.

Brown, A. L. (1978). Knowing when, where and how to remember: A problem of metacognition. In R. Glaser (Ed.), *Advances in Instructional Psychology, Vol. 1.* Hillsdale, NJ: Lawrence Erlbaum Associates, Inc.

Brown, A. L. (1990). Domain-specific principles affect learning and transfer in children. *Cognitive Science, 14*, 107–133.

Brown, A. L., & DeLoache, J. S. (1978). Skills, plans and self-regulation. In R. S. Siegler (Ed.), *Children's Thinking: What Develops?* Hillsdale, NJ: Lawrence Erlbaum Associates, Inc.

Brown, A. L., & Kane, M. J. (1988). Preschool children can learn to transfer: Learning to learn and learning by example. *Cognitive Psychology, 20*, 493–523.

Brown, A. L., & Scott, M. S. (1971). Recognition memory for pictures in preschool children. *Journal of Experimental Child Psychology, 11*, 401–412.

Brown, A. L., Bransford, J. D., Ferrara, R. A., & Campione, J. C. (1983). Learning, remembering and understanding. In J. H. Flavell & E. M. Markman (Eds.), *Handbook of Child Psychology, Vol. 3.* New York: Wiley.

Brown, A. L., Kane, M. J., & Echols, C. H. (1986). Young children's mental models determine analogical transfer across problems with a common goal structure. *Cognitive Development, 1*, 103–121.

Brown, A. L., Kane, M. J., & Long, C. (1989). Analogical transfer in young children: Analogies as tools for communication and exposition. *Applied Cognitive Psychology, 3*, 275–293.

Brown, J. R., Donelan-McCall, N., & Dunn, J. (1996). Why talk about mental states? The significance of children's conversations with friends, siblings and mothers. *Child Development, 67*, 836–849.

Brown, R., & Hanlon, C. (1970). Derivational complexity and order of acquisition in child speech. In R. Hayes (Ed.), *Cognition and the Development of Language.* New York: Wiley.

Bruce, D. J. (1964). The analysis of word sounds. *British Journal of Educational Psychology, 34*, 158–170.

Bryant, P. E. (1982). *Piaget: Issues and Experiments.* Leicester: The British Psychological Society.

Bryant, P., & Nunes, T. (2002). Children's understanding of mathematics. In U. Goswami (Ed.), *Blackwell Handbook of Childhood Cognitive Development* (pp. 412–439). Oxford: Blackwell.

Bryant, P. E., & Trabasso, T. (1971). Transitive inferences and memory in young children. *Nature, 232*, 456–458.

Bryant, P. E., Bradley, L., MacLean, M., & Crossland, J. (1989). Nursery rhymes, phonological skills and reading. *Journal of Child Language, 16*, 407–428.

Bryant, P. E., MacLean, M., Bradley, L. L., & Crossland, J. (1990). Rhyme and alliteration, phoneme detection, and learning to read. *Developmental Psychology, 26,* 429–438.

Bukach, C. M., Gauthier, I., & Tarr, M. J. (2006). Beyond faces and modularity: The power of an expertise framework. *Trends in Cognitive Sciences, 10,* 159–166. (Erratum in *10,* pp. 243).

Bullock Drummey, A., & Newcombe, N. (1995). Remembering vs. knowing the past: Children's implicit and explicit memory for pictures. *Journal of Experimental Child Psychology, 59,* 549–565.

Bullock, M., & Gelman, R. (1979). Preschool children's assumptions about cause and effect:Temporal ordering. *Child Development, 50,* 89–96.

Bullock, M., Gelman, R., & Baillargeon, R. (1982). The development of causal reasoning. In W. J. Friedman (Ed.), *The Developmental Psychology of Time* (pp. 209–254). New York: Academic Press.

Bunge, S. A., Dudukovic, N. M., Thomason, M. E., Vaidya, C. J., & Gabrieli, J. D. E. (2002). Immature frontal lobe contributions to cognitive control in children: evidence from fMRI. *Neuron, 33,* 301–311.

Bush, G., Luu, P., & Posner, M. I. (2000). Cognitive and emotional influences in the anterior cingulate cortex. *Trends in Cognitive Sciences, 4,* 215–222.

Bushnell, I. W. R., McCutcheon, E., Sinclair, J., & Tweedie, M. E. (1984). Infants' delayed recognition memory for colour and form. *British Journal of Developmental Psychology, 2,* 11–17.

Butterworth, G. (1977). Object disappearance and error in Piaget's stage 4 task. *Journal of Experimental Child Psychology, 23,* 391–401.

Butterworth, G. (1998). What is special about pointing in babies? In F. Simion & G. Butterworth (Eds.), *The Development of Sensory, Motor and Cognitive Capacities in Early Infancy: From Perception to Cognition* (pp. 171–190). Hove, UK: Psychology Press.

Callaghan, T., Rochat, P., Lillard, A., Claux, M.L., Odden, H., Itakura, S., Tapanya, S., & Singh, S. (2005). Synchrony in the onset of mental-state reasoning: Evidence from five cultures. *Psychological Science, 16,* 378–384.

Callanan, M., & Oakes, L. M. (1992). Preschoolers' questions and parents explanations: Causal thinking in everyday activity. *Cognitive Development, 7,* 213–233.

Cameron-Faulkner, T., Lieven, E., & Tomasello, M. (2003). A construction based analysis of child directed speech. *Cognitive Science, 27,* 843–873.

Cantlon, J. F., Brannon, E. M., Carter, E. J., & Pelphrey, K. A. (2006). Functional imaging of numerical processing in adults and 4-year-old children. *PLOS Biology, 4(5),* 0844–0854.

Caramazza, A., & Mahon, B. Z. (2003). The organization of conceptual knowledge: the evidence from category-specific semantic deficits. *Trends in Cognitive Sciences, 7(8),* 354–361.

Carey, S. (1978). The child as word learner. In M. Halle, J. Bresnan, & G. A. Miller (Eds.), *Linguistic Theory and Psychological Reality.* Cambridge, MA: MIT Press.

Carey, S. (1985). *Conceptual Change in Childhood.* Cambridge, MA: MIT Press.

Carey, S. (2004). On the origin of concepts. In J. Miller (Ed.), *Daedalus. 133* (pp. 59–68). Cambridge, MA: MIT Press.

Carey, S., & Gelman, R. (1991). *The Epigenesis of Mind: Essays on Biology and Cognition.* Hillsdale, NJ: Lawrence Erlbaum Associates, Inc.

Carey, S., & Spelke, E. (1994). Domain-specific knowledge and conceptual change. In L. A. Hirschfeld & S. A. Gelman (Eds.), *Mapping the Mind,* pp. 169–200. New York: Cambridge University Press.

Carlson, S. M. (2003). Executive function in context: Development, measurement, theory, and experience. *Monographs of the Society for Research in Child Development, 68(3),* Serial no. 274, 138–151.

Carlson, S. M., & Moses, L. J. (2001). Individual differences in inhibitory control and children's theory of mind. *Child Development, 72,* 1032–1053.

Carlson, S. M., Moses, L. J., & Claxton, L. J. (2004). Individual differences in executive functioning and theory of mind: An investigation of inhibitory control and planning ability. *Journal of Experimental Child Psychology, 87,* 299–319.

Carpendale, J. I. M., & Lewis. C. (2004). Constructing an understanding of mind: The development of children's social understanding within social interaction. *Behavioural and Brain Sciences, 27,* 79–151.

Carpenter, M., Akhtar, N., & Tomasello, M. (1998a). Fourteen- through 18-month-old infants differentially imitate intentional and accidental actions. *Infant Behavior & Development, 21,* 315–330.

Carpenter, M., Call, J., & Tomasello, M. (2005). Twelve- and 18-month-olds copy actions in terms of goals. *Developmental Science, 8,* F13–F20.

Carpenter, M., Nagell, K., & Tomasello, M. (1998b). Social cognition, joint attention, and communicative competence from 9 to 15 months of age. *Monographs of the Society for Research in Child Development, 63(4),* Serial no. 255.

Carroll, M., Byrne, B., & Kirsner, K. (1985). Autobiographical memory and perceptual learning: A developmental study using picture recognition, naming latency and perceptual identification. *Memory & Cognition, 13,* 273–279.

Carver, L. J., & Bauer, P. J. (1999). When the event is more than the sum of its parts: Nine-month-olds' long-term ordered recall. *Memory, 7,* 147–174.

Carver, L. J., & Bauer, P. J. (2001). The dawning of a past: The emergence of long–term explicit memory in infancy. *Journal of Experimental Psychology: General, 130,* 726–745.

Case, R. (1985). *Intellectual Development: Birth to Adulthood.* New York: Academic Press.

Case, R. (1992). Neo-Piagetian theories of child development. In R. J. Sternberg & C. J. Berg (Eds.), *Intellectual Development* (pp. 161–196). Cambridge: Cambridge University Press.

Casey, B. J., Galvan, A., & Hare, T. A. (2005). Changes in cerebral functional organization during cognitive development. *Current Opinion in Neurobiology, 15,* 239–244.

Cassell, W. S., Roebers, C. E. M., & Bjorklund, D. F. (1996). Developmental patterns of eyewitness responses to repeated and increasingly suggestive questions. *Journal of Experimental Child Psychology*, *61*, 116–133.

Cassidy, J., & Shaver, P. R. (Eds.) (2002). *Handbook of Attachment Theory, Research and Clinical Application*. London: Guilford Press.

Ceci, S. J., & Bruck, M. (1993). The suggestibility of the child witness: A historical review and synthesis. *Psychological Bulletin*, *113*, 403–439.

Ceci, S. J., & Bruck, M. (1995). *Jeopardy in the Courtroom*. Washington, DC: American Psychological Association.

Ceci, S. J., & Friedman, R. D. (2000). The suggestibility of children: Scientific research and legal implications. *Cornell Law Review*, *86*, 34–108.

Ceci, S. J., & Liker, J. (1986). A day at the races: A study of IQ, expertise and cognitive complexity. *Journal of Experimental Psychology: General*, *115*, 255–266.

Cernoch, J. M., & Porter, R. H. (1985). Recognition of maternal axillary odors by infants. *Child Development*, *56*, 1593–1598.

Chapman, M. (1988). *Constructive Evolution: Origins and Development of Piaget's Thought*. Cambridge: Cambridge University Press.

Chen, C., & Stevenson, H. W. (1988). Cross-linguistic differences in digit span of preschool children. *Journal of Experimental Child Psychology*, *46*, 150–158.

Chen, Z., Campbell, T., and Polley, R. (1995). *From Beyond to Within Their Grasp: The Rudiments of Analogical Problem Solving in 10- and 13-month-old Infants*. Poster presented at the Biennial Meeting of the Society for Research in Child Development, Indianapolis, IN, March 1995.

Chen, Z., Sanchez, R. P., & Campbell, T. (1997). From beyond to within their grasp: The rudiments of analogical problem solving in 10- and 13-month-olds. *Developmental Psychology*, *33*, 790–801.

Cheng, P. W., & Holyoak, K. J. (1985). Pragmatic reasoning schemas. *Cognitive Psychology*, *17*, 391–416.

Cheour, M., Ceponiene, R., Lehtokoski, A., Luuk, A., Allik, J., Alho, K., & Näätänen, R. (1998). Development of language-specific phoneme representations in the infant brain. *Nature Neuroscience*, *1*, 351–353.

Chi, M. T. H. (1978). Knowledge structure and memory development. In R. S. Siegler (Ed.), *Children's Thinking: What Develops?* (pp. 73–96). Hillsdale, NJ: Lawrence Erlbaum Associates, Inc.

Chi, M. T. H., Hutchinson, J. E., & Robin, A. F. (1989). How inferences about novel domain-related concepts can be constrained by structured knowledge. *Merrill-Palmer Quarterly*, *35(1)*, 27–62.

Chomsky, N. (1957). *Syntactic Structures*. The Hague/Paris: Mouton.

Chouinard, M., & Clark, E. (2003). Adult reformulations of child errors as negative evidence. *Journal of Child Language*, *30*, 637–669.

Christiansen, M. H., & Chater, N. (2001). Connectionist psycholinguistics: Capturing the empirical data. *Trends in Cognitive Sciences*, *5(2)*, 82–88.

Christiansen, M. H., Allen, J., & Seidenberg, M. (1998). Learning to segment speech using multiple cues: a connectionist model. *Language and Cognitive Processes*, *12 (2/3)*, 221–268.

Chukovsky, K. (1963). *From Two to Five*. Berkeley, CA: University of California Press.

Clark, A. (2006). Language, embodiment, and the cognitive niche. *Trends in Cognitive Sciences*, *10(8)*, 370–374.

Clark, E. V. (1973). Non-linguistic strategies and the acquisition of word meanings. *Cognition*, *2*, 161–182.

Clark, E. V. (2003). *First Language Acquisition*. Cambridge: Cambridge University Press.

Clark, E. V. (2004). How language acquisition builds on cognitive development. *Trends in Cognitive Sciences*, *8*, 472–478.

Clearfield, M. W., & Mix, K. S. (1999). Number versus contour length in infants' discrimination of small visual sets. *Psychological Science*, *10*, 408–411.

Clubb, P. A., Nida, R. E., Merritt, K., & Ornstein, P. A. (1993). Visiting the doctor: Children's knowledge and memory. *Cognitive Development*, *8*, 361–372.

Cohen, L.B (1988). An information processing approach to infant development. In L. Weiskrantz (Ed.), *Thought Without Language* (pp. 211–228). Oxford: Oxford University Press.

Cohen, L. B., & Caputo, N. F. (1978). *Instructing infants to respond to perceptual categories*. Paper presented at the Midwestern Psychological Association Convention, Chicago, IL.

Cole, M., & Scribner, S. (1974). *Culture and Thought*. New York: John Wiley & Sons.

Conrad, R. (1971). The chronology of the development of covert speech in children. *Developmental Psychology*, *5*, 398–405.

Cooper, R. G. (1984). Early number development: Discovering number space with addition and subtraction. In C. Sophian (Ed.), *The Origins of Cognitive Skills* (pp. 157–192). Hillsdale, NJ: Lawrence Erlbaum Associates, Inc.

Cornell, E. H. (1979). Infants' recognition memory, forgetting and savings. *Journal of Experimental Child Psychology*, *28*, 359–374.

Cornell, E. H., & Bergstrom, L. I. (1983). Serial position effects in infant's recognition memory. *Memory & Cognition*, *11*, 494–499.

Cossu, G., Gugliotta, M., & Marshall, J. (1995). Acquisition of reading and written spelling in a transparent orthography: Two non parallel processes? *Reading & Writing*, *7(1)*, 9–22.

Cossu, G., Shankweiler, D., Liberman, I. Y., Katz, L., and Tola, G. (1988). Awareness of phonological segments and reading ability in Italian children. *Applied Psycholinguistics*, *9*, 1–16.

Courage, M. L., & Howe, M. L. (2004). Advances in early memory development research: Insights about the dark side of the moon. *Developmental Review*, *24*, 6–32.

Coyle, T. R., & Bjorklund, D. F. (1997). Age differences in, and consequences of, multiple- and variable-strategy use on a multitrial sort-recall task. *Developmental Psychology*, *33*, 372–380.

Csibra, G., & Gergely G. (2006). Social learning and social cognition: the case for pedagogy. In Y. Munakata & M. H. Johnson (Eds). *Processes of Change in Brain and Cognitive Development. Attention and Performance XXI* (pp. 249–274). Oxford: Oxford University Press.

Csibra, G., Bíró, S., Koós, O., & Gergely, G. (2003). One-year-old infants use teleological representations of actions productively. *Cognitive Science*, *27*, 111–133.

Curtin, S., Mintz, T. H., & Christiansen, M. H. (2005). Stress changes the representational landscape: Evidence from word segmentation. *Cognition*, *96*, 233–262.

Cutler, A., & Norris, D. (1988). The role of strong syllables in segmentation for lexical access. *Journal of Experimental Psychology: Human Perception and Performance*, *14*, 113–121.

Cutting, J. E., Proffitt, D. R., & Kozlowski, L. T. (1978). A biomechanical invariant for gait perception. *Journal of Experimental Psychology*: *Human Perception & Performance*, *4*, 357–372.

Cycowicz, Y. M., Friedman, D., Snodgrass, J. G., & Rothstein, M. (2000). A developmental trajectory in implicit memory is revealed by picture fragment completion. *Memory*, *8*, 19–35.

Dale, P. S. (1980). Is early pragmatic development measurable? *Journal of Child Language*, *7*, 1–12.

Dapretto, M., Davies, M. S., Pfeifer, J. H., Scott, A. A., Sigman, M., Bookheimer, S. Y., & Iacoboni, M. (2006). Understanding emotions in others: Mirror neuron dysfunction in children with autism spectrum disorders. *Nature Neuroscience*, *9*, 28–30.

Das Gupta, P., & Bryant, P. E. (1989). Young children's causal inferences. *Child Development*, *60*, 1138–1146.

Davis, H. L., & Pratt, C. (1995). The development of children's theory of mind: The working memory explanation. *Australian Journal of Psychology*, *47(1)*, 25–31.

de Boysson-Bardies, B., Sagart, L., & Durand, C. (1984). Discernible differences in the babbling of infants according to target language. *Journal of Child Language*, *11*, 1–15.

De Cara, B., & Goswami, U. (2002). Statistical Analysis of similarity relations among spoken words: Evidence for the special status of rimes in English. *Behavioural Research Methods and Instrumentation*, *34(3)*, 416–423.

Dean, A. L., Chabaud, S., & Bridges, E. (1981). Classes, collections and distinctive features: Alternative strategies for solving inclusion problems. *Cognitive Psychology*, *13*, 84–112.

DeCasper, A. J., & Fifer, W. P. (1980). Of human bonding: Newborns prefer their mother's voices. *Science*, *208*, 1174–1176.

DeCasper, A. J., & Spence, M. J. (1986). Prenatal maternal speech influences newborns' perception of speech sounds. *Infant Behaviour & Development*, *9*, 133–150.

Dehaene, S. (1997). *The Number Sense: How the Mind Creates Mathematics*. New York: Oxford University Press.

Dehaene, S., Dehaene–Lambertz, G., & Cohen, L. (1998). Abstract representations of numbers in the animal and human brain. *Trends in Neuroscience*, *21(8)*, 355–361.

Dehaene, S., Piazza, M., Pinel, P., & Cohen, L. (2003). Three parietal circuits for number processing. *Cognitive Neuropsychology*, *20*, 487–506.

Dehaene, S., Spelke, E., Pinel, P., Stanescu, R., & Tsivkin, S. (1999). Sources of mathematical thinking: behavioral and brain-imaging evidence. *Science*, *284*, 970–974.

Dehaene-Lambertz, G., & Gliga, T. (2004). Common neural basis for phoneme processing in infants and adults. *Journal of Cognitive Neuroscience*, *16*, 1375–1387.

Dehaene-Lambertz, G., Dehaene, S., & Hertz-Pannier, L. (2002). Functional neuroimaging of speech perception in infants. *Science*, 298, 2013–2015.

Dehaene-Lambertz, Hertz-Pannier, L., Dubois, J., Mériaux, S., Roche, A., Sigman, M., & Dehaene, S. (2006). Functional organization of perisylvian activation during presentation of sentences in preverbal infants. *PNAS*, *103(38)*, 14240–14245.

DeJong, G. (2006). Toward robust real-world inference: A new perspective on explanation-based learning. In J. Firnkranz, T. Scheffer, & M. Siliopoulou (Eds.), *ECML06, the Seventeenth European Conference on Machine Learning* (pp. 102–113). Berlin: Springer Verlag.

DeLoache, J. S. (1987). Rapid change in the symbolic functioning of very young children. *Science*, *238*, 1556–1557.

DeLoache, J. S. (1989). Young children's understanding of the correspondence between a scale model and a larger space. *Cognitive Development*, *4*, 121–139.

DeLoache, J. S. (1991). Symbolic functioning in very young children: Understanding of pictures and models. *Child Development*, *62*, 736–752.

DeLoache, J. S. (2004). Becoming symbol-minded. *Trends in Cognitive Sciences*, *8*, 66–70.

DeLoache, J. S., Cassidy, D. J., & Brown, A. L. (1985). Precursors of mnemonic strategies in very young children's memory. *Child Development*, *56*, 125–137.

DeLoache, J. S., Miller, K. F., & Rosengren, K. S. (1997). The credible shrinking room: Very young children's performance with symbolic and non-symbolic relations. *Psychological Science*, *8*, 308–313.

DeMarie, D., & Ferron, J. (2003). Capacity, strategies, and metamemory: Tests of a three-factor model of memory development. *Journal of Experimental Child Psychology*, *84*, 167–193.

DeMarie, D., Miller, P. H., Ferron, J., & Cunningham, W. (2004). Path analysis tests of theoretical models of children's memory performance. *Journal of Cognition and Development*, *5*, 461–492.

Demont, E., & Gombert, J. E. (1996). Phonological awareness as a predictor of recoding skills and syntactic awareness as a predictor of comprehension skills. *British Journal of Educational Psychology*, *66*, 315–332.

Dempster, F. N. (1991). Inhibitory processes: A neglected dimension of intelligence. *Intelligence*, *15*, 157–173.

Dennett, D. 1978. *Brainstorms: Philosophical Essays on Mind and Psychology*. Cambridge: Bradford Books/MIT Press.

DeVries, J. I. P., Visser, G. H. A., & Prechtl, H. F. R. (1984). Fetal mortality in the first half of pregnancy. In H. F. R. Prechtl (Ed.), *Continuity of Neural Functions from Prenatal to Postnatal Life* (pp. 46–64). Oxford: Blackwell.

Diamond, A. (1985). The development of the ability to use recall to guide action, as indicated by infants' performance on A-not-B. *Child Development*, *56*, 868–883.

Diamond, A. (1988). Differences between adult and infant cognition: Is the crucial variable presence or absence of language? In L. Weiskrantz (Ed.), *Thought without Language* (pp. 337–370). Oxford: Clarendon Press.

Diamond, A. (1990). Developmental time course in human infants and infant monkeys, and the neural bases of inhibitory control in reaching. *Annals of the New York Academy of Science*, *608*, 637–676.

Diamond, A. (2007). Interrelated and interdependent. *Developmental Science*, *10(1)*, 152–158.

Diamond, A., & Taylor, C. (1996). Development of an aspect of executive control: Development of the abilities to remember what I said and to "do as I say, not as I do". *Developmental Psychology*, *29(4)*, 315–334.

Dias, M. G., & Harris, P. L. (1988). The effect of make-believe play on deductive reasoning. *British Journal of Developmental Psychology*, *6*, 207–221.

Dias, M., & Harris, P. L. (1990). The influence of the imagination on reasoning by young children. *British Journal of Developmental Psychology*, *8*, 305–318.

DiLalla, L. F., Thompson, L. A., Plomin, R., Phillips, K., Fagan, J. F., III , Haith, M. M., Cyphers, L. H., & Fulker, D. W. (1990). Infant predictors of preschool and adult IQ: A study of infant twins and their parents. *Developmental Psychology*, *26*, 759–769.

Dodd, B. (1979). Lipreading in infancy: Attention to speech in and out of synchrony. *Cognitive Psychology*, *11*, 478–484.

Dollaghan, C. A. (1994). Children's phonological neighbourhoods: Half empty or half full? *Journal of Child Language*, *21*, 257–271.

Donaldson, M. (1978). *Children's Minds*. Glasgow: William Collins.

Drummey, A. B., & Newcombe, N. S. (2002). Developmental changes in source memory. *Developmental Science*, *5*, 502–513.

Dufresne, A., & Kobasigawa, A. (1989). Children's spontaneous allocation of study time: Differential and sufficient aspects. *Journal of Experimental Child Psychology*, *47*, 274–296.

Dunbar, K., & Fugelsang, J. (2005). Scientific thinking and reasoning. In K. J. Holyoak & R. G. Morrison (Eds.), *Cambridge Handbook of Thinking and Reasoning* (pp. 705–725). Cambridge: Cambridge University Press.

Duncan, J., & Owen, A. M. (2000). Common regions of the human frontal lobe recruited by diverse cognitive demands. *Trends in Neurosciences*, *23*, 475–483.

Dunn, J., & Cutting, A. L. (1999). Understanding others, and individual differences in friendship interactions in young children. *Social Development*, *8*, 201–219.

Dunn, J., Brown, J., & Beardsall, L. (1991a). Family talk about feeling states and children's later understanding of others' emotions. *Developmental Psychology*, *27*, 448–455.

Dunn, J., Brown, J., Slomkowski, C., Tesla, C., & Youngblade, L., (1991b). Young children's understanding of other people's feelings and beliefs: Individual differences and their antecedents. *Child Development*, *62*, 1352–1366.

Durgunoglu, A. Y., & Oney, B. (1999). A cross-linguistic comparison of phonological awareness and word recognition. *Reading & Writing*, *11*, 281–299.

Durgunoglu, A. Y., Nagy, W. E., & Hancin-Bhatt, B. J. (1993). Cross-language transfer of phonological awareness. *Journal of Educational Psychology*, *85*, 453–465.

Durston, S., Thomas, K. M., Yan, Y., Uluğ, A. M., Zimmerman, R. D., & Casey, B. J. (2002). A neural basis for the development of inhibitory control. *Developmental Science*, *5(4)*, F9–F16.

Eichenbaum, H. (2003). How does the hippocampus contribute to memory? *Trends in Cognitive Sciences*, *7*, 427–429.

Eimas, P. D., & Quinn, P. C. (1994). Studies on the formation of perceptually based basic-level categories in young infants. *Child Development*, *65*, 903–917.

Eimas, P. D., Siqueland, E. R., Jusczyk, P., & Vigorito, J. (1971). Speech perception in infants. *Science*, *171*, 303–306.

Eisen, M., Qin, J. J., Goodman, G. S., & Davis, S. (2002). Memory and suggestibility in maltreated children. *Journal of Experimental Child Psychology*, *83*, 167–212.

Elkind, D., & Schoenfeld, E. (1972). Identity and equivalence conservation at two age levels. *Developmental Psychology*, *6*, 529–533.

Elkonin, D. B. (1963). The psychology of mastering the elements of reading. In B. Simon & J. Simon (Eds.) *Educational Psychology in the USSR*. Stanford, CA: Stanford University Press.

Ellis, H. D., Ellis, D. M., & Hosie, J. A. (1993). Priming effects in children's face recognition. *British Journal of Psychology*, *84*, 101–110.

Ellis, N. C., & Hennelly, R. A. (1980). A bilingual word-length effect: Implications for intelligence testing and the relative ease of mental calculation in Welsh and English. *British Journal of Psychology*, *71*, 43–51.

Elman, J. L. (2005). Connectionist models of cognitive development: where next? *Trends in Cognitive Sciences*, *9(3)*, 111–117.

Fabricius, W. V. (1988). The development of forward search planning in preschoolers. *Child Development, 59*, 1473–1488.

Fagan, J. F. III (1984). The relationship of novelty preferences during infancy to later intelligence and later recognition smemory. *Intelligence, 8*, 339–346.

Fagan, J. F. III (1992). Intelligence: A theoretical viewpoint. *Current Directions in Psychological Science, 1*, 82–86.

Fagot, B. I., & Gauvain, M. (1997). Mother–child problem solving: Continuity through the early childhood years. *Developmental Psychology, 33*, 480–488.

Fantz, R. L. (1961). The origin of form perception. *Scientific American, 204*, 66–72.

Fantz, R. L. (1966). Pattern discrimination and selective attention as determinants of perceptual development from birth. In A. H. Kidd & J. J. Rivoire (Eds.), *Perceptual Development in Children* (pp. 143–173). New York: International Universities Press.

Farrar, M. J., & Goodman, G. S. (1990). Developmental differences in the relation between script and episodic memory: Do they exist? In R. Fivush & J. Hudson (Eds.), *Knowing and Remembering in Young Children*. New York: Cambridge University Press.

Farroni, T., Csibra, G., Simion, F., & Johnson, M. H. (2002). Eye contact detection in humans from birth. *Proceedings of the National Academy of Sciences, 99*, 9602–9605.

Fearon, P., & Morgan, C. (2006). Environmental factors in schizophrenia: the role of migrant studies. *Schizophrenia Bulletin, 32(3)*, 405–408.

Feigenson, L., Carey, S., & Spelke, E. S. (2002). Infants' discrimination of number vs. continuous extent. *Cognitive Psychology, 44*, 33–66.

Feigenson, L., Dehaene, S., & Spelke, E. S. (2004). Core systems of number. *Trends in Cognitive Sciences, 8(7)*, 307–314.

Fenker, D. B., Waldmann, M. R., & Holyoak, K. J. (2005). Accessing causal relations in semantic memory. *Memory & Cognition, 33*, 1036–1046.

Fenson, L., & Ramsay, D. S. (1981). Effects of modeling action sequences on the play of twelve-, fifteen-, and nineteen-month-old children. *Child Development, 52*, 1028–1036.

Fenson, L., Dale, P. S., Reznick, J. S., Bates, E., Thal, D., & Pethick, S. (1994). Variability in early communicative development. *Monographs of the Society for Research in Child Development, 59(5)*, Serial no. 242.

Fernald, A. (1993). Approval and disapproval: Infant responsiveness to vocal affect in familiar and unfamiliar languages. *Child Development, 64*, 657–674.

Fernald, A., & Mazzie, C. (1991). Prosody and focus in speech to infants and adults. *Developmental Psychology, 27*, 209–221.

Fiser, J., & Aslin, R. N. (2002). Statistical learning of new visual feature combinations by infants. *Proceedings of the National Academy of Sciences, 99*, 15822–15826.

Fisher, S. E., & Francks, C. (2006). Genes, cognition and dyslexia: Learning to read the genome. *Trends in Cognitive Sciences, 10*, 250–257.

Fivush, R., & Hammond, N. R. (1990). Autobiographical memory across the preschool years: Toward reconceptualising childhood amnesia. In R. Fivush & J. Hudson (Eds.), *Knowing and Remembering in Young Children*. New York: Cambridge University Press.

Fivush, R., & Schwarzmüller, A. (1998). Children remember childhood: Implications for childhood amnesia. *Applied Cognitive Psychology, 12*, 455–473.

Flavell, J. H. (1971). First discussant's comments: What is memory development the development of? *Human Development, 14*, 272–278.

Flavell, J. H. (1979). Metacognition and cognitive monitoring: A new area of cognitive-developmental inquiry. *American Psychologist, 34*, 906–911.

Flavell, J. H., & Wellman, H. M. (1977). Metamemory. In R. Kail, & J. Hagen (Eds.), *Perspectives on the Development of Memory and Cognition*. Hillsdale, NJ: Lawrence Erlbaum Associates, Inc.

Flavell, J. H., Beach, D. R., & Chinsky, J. H. (1966). Spontaneous verbal rehearsal in a memory task as a function of age. *Child Development, 37*, 283–299.

Flavell, J. H., Flavell, E. R., & Green, F. I. (1983). Development of appearance–reality distinction. *Cognitive Psychology, 15*, 95–120.

Fodor, J. (2000). *The Mind Doesn't Work That Way: The Scope and Limits of Computational Psychology*. Cambridge, MA: MIT Press.

Fox, B., & Routh, D. K. (1975). Analyzing spoken language into words, syllables, and phonomes: A developmental study. *Journal of Psycholinguistic Research, 4(4)*, 331–342.

Fox, N. A., Henderson, H. A., Marshall, P. J., Nichols, K. E., & Ghera, M. M. (2005). Behavioral inhibition: Linking biology and behaviour within a developmental framework. *Annual Review of Psychology, 56*, 235–262.

Fremgen, A., & Fay, D. (1980). Overextensions in production and comprehension: A methodological clarification. *Journal of Child Language, 7*, 205–211.

Freud, S. (1938). The psychopathology of everyday life. In A. A. Brill (Ed.), *The Writings of Sigmund Freud* (pp. 317–385). New York: Modern Library.

Friedrich, M., & Friederici, A. D. (2004). N400-like semantic incongruity effect in 19-month-olds: processing known words in picture contexts. *Journal of Cognitive Neuroscience, 16(8)*, 1465–1477.

Friedrich, M., & Friederici, A. D. (2005). Phonotactic knowledge and lexical-semantic processing in one-year-olds: Brain responses to words and nonsense words in picture contexts. *Journal of Cognitive Neuroscience, 17(11)*, 1785–1802.

Friedrich, M., & Friederici, A. D. (2006). Early N400 development and later language acquisition. *Psychophysiology, 43*, 1–12.

Frith, C. D., & Frith, U. (2006). The neural basis of mentalising. *Neuron, 50*, 531–534.

Frith, U. (1998). Editorial: Literally changing the brain. *Brain, 121*, 1051–1052.

Frith, U., & Frith, C. D. (2003). Development and neurophysiology of mentalizing. *Philosophical Transactions of the Royal Society: Biological Sciences, 358*, 459–473.

Frith, U., Wimmer, H., & Landerl., K. (1998). Differences in phonological recoding in German- and English-speaking children. Scientific *Studies of Reading, 2*, 31–54.

Frye, D., Zelazo, P. D., & Palfai, T. (1995). Theory of mind and rule-based reasoning. *Cognitive Development, 10*, 483–527.

Fugelsang, J. A., & Dunbar, K. N. (2005). Brain-based mechanisms underlying complex causal thinking. *Neuropsychologia, 43*, 1204–1213.

Fugelsang, J. A., Stein, C. B., Green, A. E., & Dunbar, K. N. (2004). Theory and data interactions of the scientific mind: Evidence from the molecular and the cognitive laboratory. *Canadian Journal of Experimental Psychology, 58*, 86–95.

Fuson, K. C. (1988). *Children's Counting and Concepts of Number*. New York: Springer-Verlag.

Fuson, K. C., Lyons, B., Pergament, G., Hall, J. W., & Kwon, Y. (1988). Effects of collection terms on class inclusion and on number task. *Cognitive Psychology, 20*, 96–120.

Gallagher, H. L., & Frith, C. D. (2003). Functional imaging of 'theory of mind'. *Trends in Cognitive Sciences, 7*, 77–83.

Gayan, J., & Olson, R. K. (2001). Genetic and environmental influences on orthographic and phonological skills in children with reading disabilities. *Developmental Neuropsychology, 20*, 483–507.

Gayan, J., Smith, S. D., Cherny, S. S., Cardon, L. R., Fulker, D. W., Kimberling, W. J., Olson, R. K., Pennington, B., & DeFries, J. C. (1999). Large quantitative trait locus for specific language and reading deficits in chromosome 6p. *American Journal of Human Genetics, 64*, 157–164.

Gelman, R. (1990). First principles organise attention to and learning about relevant data: Number and the animate–inanimate distinction as examples. *Cognitive Science, 14*, 79–106.

Gelman, R., & Butterworth, B. (2005). Number and language: How are they related? *Trends in Cognitive Sciences, 9(1)*, 6–10.

Gelman, R., & Gallistel, C. R. (1978). *The Child's Understanding of Number*. Cambridge, MA: Harvard University Press.

Gelman, R., Bullock, M., & Meck, E. (1980). Preschooler's understanding of simple object transformations. *Child Development, 51*, 691–699.

Gelman, S. (1988). The development of induction within natural kind and artifact categories. *Cognitive Psychology, 20*, 65–90.

Gelman, S. A. (2004). Psychological essentialism in children. *Trends in Cognitive Sciences, 8*, 404–409.

Gelman, S. A., & Coley, J. D. (1990). The importance of knowing a dodo is a bird: Categories and inferences in 2-year-old children. *Developmental Psychology, 26*, 796–804.

Gelman, S. A., & Gottfried, G. M. (1993). *Causal explanations of animate and inanimate motion*. Unpublished manuscript.

Gelman, S. A., & Kremer, K. E. (1991). Understanding natural cause: Children's explanations of how objects and their properties originate. *Child Development, 62*, 396–414.

Gelman, S. A., & Markman, E. M. (1986). Categories and induction in young children. *Cognition, 23*, 183–209.

Gelman, S. A., & Markman, E. M. (1987). Young children's inductions from natural kinds: The role of categories and appearances. *Child Development, 58*, 1532–1541.

Gelman, S. A., & Opfer, J. (2002). Development of the animate–inanimate distinction. In U. Goswami (Ed.), *Blackwell Handbook of Childhood Cognitive Development* (pp. 151–166). Malden, MA: Blackwell.

Gelman, S. A., & Wellman, H. M. (1991). Insides and essences: Early understandings of the non-obvious. *Cognition, 38*, 213–244.

Gelman, S. A., Coley, J. D., & Gottfried, G. M. (1994). Essentialist beliefs in children: The acquisition of concepts and theories. In L. A. Hirschfeld & A. S. Gelman (Eds.), *Mapping the Mind: Domain Specificity in Cognition and Culture* (pp. 341–365). Cambridge, MA: Cambridge University Press.

Gentner, D. (1989). The mechanisms of analogical learning. In S. Vosniadou & A. Ortony (Eds.), *Similarity and Analogical Reasoning* (pp. 199–241). Cambridge: Cambridge University Press.

Gergely, G. (2001). The obscure object of desire: 'Nearly, but clearly not, like me': Contingency preference in normal children versus children with autism. *Bulletin of the Menninger Clinic, 65*, 411–426.

Gergely, G., & Csibra, G. (2003). Teleological reasoning in infancy: The naïve theory of rational action. *Trends in Cognitive Sciences, 7*, 287–292.

Gergely, G., Bekkering, H., & Király, I. (2002). Rational imitation in preverbal infants. *Nature, 415*, 755.

Gergely, G., Egyed, K., & Király, I. (2007). On pedagogy. *Developmental Science, 10(1)*, 139–146.

Gergely, G., Nádasdy, Z., Csibra, G., & Bíró, S. (1995). Taking the intentional stance at 12 months of age. *Cognition, 56*, 165–193.

Gibson, E. J., & Walk, R. D. (1960). The "visual cliff". *Scientific American, 202*, 64–71.

Gick, M. L., & Holyoak, K. J. (1980). Analogical problem solving. *Cognitive Psychology, 12*, 306–355.

Gillan, D. J., Premack, D., & Woodruff, G. (1981). Reasoning in the chimpanzee I: Analogical reasoning. *Journal of Experimental Psychology: Animal Behaviour Processes, 7*, 1–17.

Gilmore, R. O., & Johnson, M. H. (1995). Working memory in infancy: Six-month-olds' performance on two versions of the oculomotor delayed response task. *Journal of Experimental Child Psychology, 59*, 397–418.

Gilstrap, L. L., & Ceci, S. J. (2005). Reconceptualizing children's suggestibility: Bidirectional and temporal properties. *Child Development*, *76*, 40–53.

Gleason, J. B. (1980). The acquisition of social speech and politeness formulae. In H. Giles, W. P. Robinson & S. M. P. (Eds.), *Language: Social Psychological Perspectives*. Oxford: Pergamon.

Goldfield, B.A., & Reznick, J. S. (1990). Early lexical acquisition: Rate, content and the vocabulary spurt. *Journal of Child Language*, *17*, 171–183.

Goldin-Meadow, S., & Wagner, S. M. (2005). How our hands help us learn. *Trends in Cognitive Sciences*, *9(5)*, 234–241.

Goldman-Rakic, P. S. (1987). Development of cortical circuitry and cognitive function. *Child Development*, *58*, 601–622.

Goodman, G. S., & Aman, C. (1990). Children's use of anatomically detailed dolls to recount an event. *Child Development*, *61*, 1859–1871.

Goodman, G. S., Rudy, L., Bottoms, B. L., & Aman, C. (1990). Children's concerns and memory: Issues of ecological validity in the study of children's eyewitness testimony. In R. Fivush & J. Hudson (Eds.), *Knowing and Remembering in Young Children* (pp. 331–346). New York: Cambridge University Press.

Gopnik, A., Glymour, C., Sobel, D. M., Schulz, L. E., Kushnir, T., & Danks, D. (2004). A theory of causal learning in children: Causal maps and Bayes nets. *Psychological Review*, *111*, 3–32.

Gopnik, A., Sobel, D., Schultz, L., & Glymour, C. (2001). Causal learning mechanisms in very young children: Two-, three-, and four-year-olds infer causal relations from patterns of variation and covariation. *Developmental Psychology*, *37(5)*, 620–629.

Gordon, P. (2004) Numerical cognition without words: Evidence from Amazonia. *Science*, *306*, 496–499.

Goswami, U. (1991). Analogical Reasoning: What develops? A review of research and theory. *Child Development*, *62*, 1–22.

Goswami, U. (1992). Analogical reasoning in children. Part of the series *Developmental Essays in Psychology*. London: Lawrence Erlbaum Associates.

Goswami, U. (1996). Analogical reasoning and cognitive development. *Advances in Child Development and Behaviour*, *26*, 91–138.

Goswami, U. (1998). *Cognition in Children*. Hove, UK: Psychology Press.

Goswami, U. (2001). Analogical reasoning in children. In Gentner, D., Holyoak, K. J., and Kokinov, B. N. (Eds.), *The Analogical Mind: Perspectives from Cognitive Science* (pp. 437–470). Cambridge, MA: MIT Press.

Goswami, U. (2002). Inductive and deductive reasoning. In U. Goswami (Ed.), *Blackwell's Handbook of Childhood Cognitive Development* (pp. 282–302). Oxford: Blackwell.

Goswami, U. (2003a). Why theories about developmental dyslexia require developmental designs. *Trends in Cognitive Sciences*, *7*, 12.

Goswami, U. (2003b). Phonology, learning to read and dyslexia: A cross-linguistic analysis. In V. Csepe (Ed.), *Dyslexia: Different Brain, Different Behaviour* (pp. 1–40). The Netherlands: Kluwer Academic

Goswami, U. (2004). Neuroscience and education. *British Journal of Educational Psychology*, *74*, 1–14.

Goswami, U. (2006). Neuroscience and education: from research to practice? *Nature Reviews Neuroscience*, *7*, 406–413.

Goswami, U. (in press). Basic processes in reading: Insights from neuroscience. In D. Olson (Ed.), *Cambridge Handbook of Literacy*. Cambridge, Cambridge University Press.

Goswami, U., & Brown, A. (1989). Melting chocolate and melting snowmen: Analogical reasoning and causal relations. *Cognition*, *35*, 69–95.

Goswami, U., & Brown, A. L. (1990). Higher-order structure and relational reasoning: Contrasting analogical and thematic relations. *Cognition*, *36*, 207–226.

Goswami, U., & East, M. (2000). Rhyme and analogy in beginning reading: Conceptual and methodolgical issues. *Applied Psycholinguistics*, *21*, 63–93.

Goswami, U., & Pauen, S. (2006). The effects of a 'family' analogy on class inclusion reasoning by young children. *Swiss Journal of Psychology*, *64*, 115–124.

Goswami, U., & Ziegler, J. C. (2006). Fluency, phonology and morphology: A response to the commentaries on becoming Literate in different languages. *Developmental Science*, *9(5)*, 451–453

Goswami, U., Porpodas, C., & Wheelwright, S. (1977). Children's orthographic representations in English and Greek. *European Journal of Psychology of Education*, *12*, 273–292.

Goswami, U., Thomson, J., Richardson, U., Stainthorp, R., Hughes, D, Rosen, S., & Scott, S. K. (2002). Amplitude envelope onsets and developmental dyslexia: A new hypothesis. *Proceedings of the National Academy of Sciences*, *99(16)*, 10911–10916.

Goswami, U., Ziegler, J., Dalton, L., & Schneider, W. (2003). Nonword reading across orthographies: How flexible is the choice of reading units? *Applied Psycholinguistics*, *24*, 235–247.

Gottleib, G. (2007). Probabilistic epigenesis. *Developmental Science*, *10(1)*, 1–11.

Greco, C., Hayne, H., & Rovee-Collier, C. (1990). The roles of function, reminding and variability in categorization by 3-month-old infants. *Journal of Experimental Psychology: Learning, Memory & Cognition*, *16*, 617–633.

Grelotti, D. J., Klin, A. J., Gauthier, I., Skudlarski, P., Cohen, D. J., Gore, J. C., Volkmar, F. R., & Schultz, R. T. (2005). fMRI activation of the fusiform gyrus and amygdale to cartoon characters but not to faces in boy with autism. *Neuropsychologia*, *43*, 373–385.

Haake, R. J., & Somerville, S. C. (1985). The development of logical search skills in infancy. *Developmental Psychology*, *21*, 176–186.

Hagmayer, Y., Sloman, S. A., Lagnado, D. A., & Waldmann, M. R. (2007). Causal reasoning through intervention. In A. Gopnik & L. Schulz (Eds.), *Causal Learning: Psychology, Philosophy, and Computation* (pp. 88–100). Oxford: Oxford University Press.

Haith, M. M. (1998). Who put the cog in infant cognition? Is rich interpretation too costly? *Infant Behavior & Development, 21*, 167–179.

Haith, M. M., Hazan, C., & Goodman, G. S. (1988). Expectation and anticipation of dynamic visual events by 3.5-month-old babies. *Child Development, 59*, 467–479.

Halford, G. S. (1993). *Children's Understanding: The Development of Mental Models*. Hillsdale, NJ: Lawrence Erlbaum Associates, Inc.

Hardison, D. (2003). Acquisition of second-language speech: effects of visual cues, context and talker variability. *Applied Psycholinguistics, 24*, 495–522.

Harris, M., & Giannouli, V. (1999). Learning to read and spell in Greek: The importance of letter knowledge and morphological awareness. In M. Harris & G. Hatano (Eds.), *Learning to Read and Write: A Cross-Linguistic Perspective* (pp. 51–70). Cambridge: Cambridge University Press.

Harris, P. L. (2007). Trust. *Developmental Science, 10(1)*, 135–138.

Harris, P. L., & Nunez, M. (1996). Understanding of permission rules by preschool children. *Child Development, 67*, 1572–1591.

Harris, P. L., Brown, E., Marriott, C., Whittall, S., & Harmer, S. (1991). Monsters, ghosts, and witches: Testing the limits of the fantasy–reality distinction in young children. *British Journal of Developmental Psychology, 9*, 105–123.

Hart, B. H., & Risley, T. R. (1995). *Meaningful Differences in the Everyday Experience of Young American Children*. Baltimore, MD: Paul H. Brookes.

Hauk, O., Johnsrude, I. S., & Pulvermuller, F. (2004). Somatotopic representation of action words in human motor and premotor cortex. *Neuron, 41*, 301–307.

Hayes, L. A., & Watson, J. S. (1981). Neonatal imitation: Fact or artifact? *Developmental Psychology, 17*, 655–660.

Hayne, H. (1990). The effects of multiple reminders on long-term retention in human infants. *Developmental Psychobiology, 23*, 453–477.

Heibeck, T. H., & Markman, E. M. (1987). Word learning in children: An examination of fast mapping. *Child Development, 58*, 1021–1034.

Heider, F., & Simmel, M. (1944). An experimental study of apparent behavior. *American Journal of Psychology, 57*, 243–59.

Henderson, L. M., Yoder, P. J., Yale, M. E., & McDuffie, A. (2002). Getting to the point: Electrophysiological correlates of protodeclarative pointing. *International Journal of Developmental Neuroscience, 20*, 449–458.

Henry, L. A., & Millar, S. (1993). Why does memory span improve with age? A review of the evidence for two current hypotheses. *European Journal of Cognitive Psychology, 5*, 241–287.

Hepper, P. G. (1988). Foetal 'soap' addiction. *The Lancet, 11 June*, 1347–1348.

Hepper, P. G. (1992). Fetal psychology: An embryonic science. In J. G. Nijhuis (Ed.), *Fetal Behaviour: Developmental and Perinatal Aspects* (pp. 129–156). Oxford: Oxford University Press.

Hepper, P. G., Wells, D. L., & Lynch, C. (2005). Prenatal thumb sucking is related to postnatal handedness. *Neuropsychologia, 43*, 313–315.

Hespos, S. J., & Baillargeon, R. (2001a). Reasoning about containment events in very young infants. *Cognition, 78*, 207–245.

Hespos, S. J., & Baillargeon, R. (2001b). Infants' knowledge about occlusion and containment events: A surprising discrepancy, *Psychological Science, 12*, 140–147.

Hespos, S. J., & Baillargeon, R. (2006). Décalage in infants' knowledge about occlusion and containment events: Converging evidence from action tasks. *Cognition, 99*, B31–B41.

Hitch, G. J., Halliday, S., Dodd, A., & Littler, J. E. (1989). Development of rehearsal in short-term memory: Differences between pictorial and spoken stimuli. *British Journal of Developmental Psychology, 7*, 347–362.

Hitch, G. J., Halliday, S., Schaafstal, A. M., & Schraagen, J. M. (1988). Visual working memory in young children. *Memory & Cognition, 16(2)*, 120–132.

Ho, C. S.-H., & Bryant, P. (1997). Phonological skills are important in learning to read Chinese. *Developmental Psychology, 33*, 946–951.

Ho, C. S.-H., Law, T. P.-S., & Ng, P. M. (2000). The phonological deficit hypothesis in Chinese developmental dyslexia. *Reading & Writing, 13*, 57–59.

Hodent, C., Bryant, P., & Houdé, O. (2005). Language-specific effects on number computation in toddlers. *Developmental Science, 8*, 420–423.

Hodges, R. M., & French, L. A. (1988). The effect of class and collection labels on cardinality, class-inclusion and number conservation tasks. *Child Development, 59*, 1387–1396.

Hoien, T., Lundberg, L., Stanovich, K. E., & Bjaalid, I. K. (1995). Components of phonological awareness. *Reading & Writing, 7*, 171–188.

Holyoak, K. J., & Thagard, P. (1995). *Mental Leaps: Analogy in Creative Thought*. Cambridge, MA: MIT Press.

Holyoak, K. J., Junn, E. N., & Billman, D. O. (1984). Development of analogical problem-solving skill. *Child Development, 55*, 2042–2055.

Hood, B. M. (1995). Gravity rules for 2- to 4-year-olds? *Cognitive Development, 10*, 577–598.

Hood, B. M., Wilson, A., & Dyson, S. (2006). The effect of divided attention on inhibiting the gravity error. *Developmental Science, 9*, 303–308.

Hood, L., & Bloom, L. (1979). What, when, and how about why: A longitudinal study of the early expressions of causality. *Monographs of the Society for Research in Child Development, 44(6)*, Serial no. 181.

Hornik, R., Risenhoover, N., & Gunnar, M. (1987). The effects of maternal positive, neutral, and negative affective communications on infant responses to new toys. *Child Development, 58,* 937–944.

Houdé, O. (1997). The problem of deductive competence and the inhibitory control of cognition. *Current Psychology of Cognition, 16,* 108–113.

Houdé, O. (2000). Inhibition and cognitive development: object, number, categorization, and reasoning. *Cognitive Development, 15,* 63–73.

Howe, C. J., & Tolmie, A. (2003). Group work in primary school science: discussion, consensus and guidance from experts. *International Journal of Educational Research, 39,* 51–72.

Howe, C. J., Tolmie, A., Duchak–Tanner, V., & Rattray, C. (2000). Hypothesis testing in science: Group consensus and the acquisition of conceptual and procedural knowledge. *Learning and Instruction, 10,* 361–391.

Howe, M. L., & Courage, M. L. (1993). On resolving the enigma of infantile autism. *Psychological Bulletin, 113,* 305–326.

Hudson, J. A. (1990). The emergence of autobiographical memory in mother–child conversation. In R. Fivush & J. Hudson (Eds.), *Knowing and Remembering in Young Children.* New York: Cambridge University Press.

Hughes, C. (1998). Executive function in preschoolers: Links with theory of mind and verbal ability. *British Journal of Developmental Psychology, 16,* 233–253.

Hughes, C., & Dunn, J. (1998). Understanding mind and emotion: Longitudinal associations with mental-state talk between young friends. *Developmental Psychology, 34,* 1026–1037.

Hughes, C., & Dunn, J. (2000). Hedonism or empathy: Hard-to-manage children's moral awareness, and links with cognitive and maternal characteristics. *British Journal of Developmental Psychology, 18,* 227–245.

Hughes, C., Dunn, J., & White, A. (1998). Trick or treat?: Uneven understanding of mind and emotion and executive dysfunction in hard-to-manage preschoolers *Journal of Child Psychology & Psychiatry, 39,* 981–994.

Hughes, C., White, A., Sharpen, J., & Dunn, J. (2000). Antisocial, angry and unsympathetic: 'Hard to manage' preschoolers' peer problems, and possible cognitive influences. *Journal of Child Psychology & Psychiatry, 41,* 169–179.

Hulme, C., & Tordoff, V. (1989). Working memory development: The effects of speech rate, word length, and acoustic similarity on serial recall. *Journal of Experimental Child Psychology, 47,* 72–87.

Hulme, C., Thomson, N., Muir, C., & Lawrence, A. (1984). Speech rate and the development of short-term memory span. *Journal of Experimental Child Psychology, 38,* 241–253.

Hume, D. (1748/1999). *Enquiry Concerning Human Understanding.* Sections IV–VII (paras. 20–61), pp. 25–79. Oxford: Oxford University Press.

Huntley-Fenner, G. (2001). Children's understanding of number is similar to adults' and rats': Numerical estimation by 5- and 7-year-olds. *Cognition, 78,* B27–B40.

Huntley-Fenner, G., & Cannon, E. (2000). Preschoolers' magnitude comparisons are mediated by a preverbal analog mechanism. *Psychological Science, 11(2),* 147–152.

Iacoboni, M., Molnar–Szakacs, I., Gallese, V., Buccino, G., Mazziotta, J. C., & Rizzolatti, G. (2005). Grasping the intentions of others with one's own mirror neuron system. *PLOS Biology, 3,* 529–535.

Inagaki, K., & Hatano, G. (1987). Young children's spontaneous personification as analogy. *Child Development, 58,* 1013–1020.

Inagaki, K., & Hatano, G. (1993). Young children's understanding of the mind–body distinction. *Child Development, 64,* 1534–1549.

Inagaki, K., & Hatano, G. (2004). Vitalistic causality in young children's naïve biology. *Trends in Cognitive Sciences, 8,* 356–362.

Inagaki, K., & Sugiyama, K. (1988). Attributing human characteristics: Developmental changes in over- and under-attribution. *Cognitive Development, 3,* 55–70.

Jackson, P. L., Meltzoff, A. N., & Decety, J. (2006). Neural circuits involved in imitation and perspective-taking. *Neuroimage, 31,* 429–439.

Jacques, S., Zelazo, P. D., Kirkham, N. Z., & Semcesen, T. K. (1999). Rule selection and rule execution in preschoolers: An error-detection approach. *Developmental Psychology, 35,* 770–780.

Jenkins, J. M., & Astington, J. W. (1996). Cognitive factors and family structure associated with theory of mind development in young children. *Developmental Psychology, 32,* 70–78.

Johansson, G. (1973). Visual perception of biological motion and a model for its analysis. *Perception & Psychophysics, 14,* 201–211.

Johnson, M. H. (1997). *Developmental Cognitive Neuroscience: An Introduction.* Oxford: Blackwell.

Johnson, M. H. (2005). *Developmental Cognitive Neuroscience,* 2nd Edition, Oxford: Blackwell.

Johnson, M. H., & Munakata, Y. (2005). Processes of change in brain and cognitive development. *Trends in Cognitive Sciences, 9,* 152–158.

Johnson-Laird, P. N., & Wason, P. C. (1977). A theoretical analysis of insight into a reasoning task. In P. N. Johnson-Laird & P. C. Wason (Eds), *Thinking: Readings in Cognitive Science.* Cambridge: CUP.

Johnson-Laird, P. N., Legrenzi, P., & Sonino-Legrenzi, M. (1972). Reasoning and a sense of reality. *British Journal of Psychology, 63,* 395–400.

Jones, S. S., & Smith, L. B. (1993). The place of perception in children's concepts. *Cognitive Development, 8,* 113–139.

Jordan, K. E., & Brannon, E. M. (2006). A common representational system governed by Weber's law: Nonverbal numerical similarity judgments in 6-year-olds and rhesus macaques. *Journal of Experimental Child Psychology, 95,* 215–229.

Joseph, R. (2000). Fetal brain behaviour and cognitive development. *Developmental Review, 20,* 81–98.

Jusczyk, P. W., & Aslin, R. N. (1995). Infants' detection of the sound patterns of words in fluent speech. *Cognitive Psychology*, 29, 1–23.

Jusczyk, P. W., Houston, D. M., & Newsome, M. (1999). The beginnings of word segmentation in English-learning infants. *Cognitive Psychology*, 39, 159–207.

Justice, E. M. (1985). Categorisation as a preferred memory strategy: Developmental changes during elementary school. *Developmental Psychology*, 6, 1105–1110.

Justice, E. M., Baker-Ward, L., Gupta, S., & Jannings, L. R. (1997). Means to the goal of remembering: Developmental changes in awareness of strategy use–performance relations. *Journal of Experimental Child Psychology*, 65, 293–314.

Kail, R. (1991). Processing time declines exponentially during childhood and adolescence. *Developmental Psychology*, 27, 259–266.

Kaiser, M. K., McCloskey, M., & Profitt, D. R. (1986). Development of intuitive theories of motion: Curvilinear motion in the absence of external forces. *Developmental Psychology*, 22, 67–71.

Kaiser, M. K., Profitt, D. R., & McCloskey, M. (1985). The development of beliefs about falling objects. *Perception & Psychophysics*, 38, 533–539.

Kaminski, J., Call, J., & Fischer, J. (2004). Word learning in a domestic dog: Evidence for fast mapping. *Science*, 304, 1682–1683.

Karmiloff-Smith, A. (2007). Atypical epigenesis. *Developmental Science*, 10(1), 84–88.

Karpov, Y. V. (2005). *The Neo-Vygotskian Approach to Child Development*. New York: Cambridge University Press.

Kaufman, E. L., Lord, M., Reese, T. W., & Volkmann, J. (1949). The discrimination of visual number. *American Journal of Psychology*, 62, 498–525.

Kaufman, J., Csibra, G., & Johnson M. H. (2003a). Representing occluded objects in the human infant brain. *Proceedings of the Royal Society of London B (Suppl.)*, 270, S140–S143.

Kaufman, J., Mareschal, D., & Johnson, M. H. (2003b). Graspability and object processing in infants. *Infant Behavior and Development*, 26, 516–528.

Keane, M. K. (1988). *Analogical Problem Solving*. Chichester, UK: Ellis Horwood.

Keil, F. C. (1987). Conceptual development and category structure. In Neisser, U. (Ed.). *Concepts and Conceptual Development: Ecological and Intellectual Factors in Categorisation* (pp. 175–200). Cambridge: Cambridge University Press.

Keil, F. C. (1989). *Concepts, Kinds and Cognitive Development*. Cambridge, MA: MIT Press.

Keil, F. C. (1991). The emergence of theoretical beliefs as constraints on concepts. In S. Carey & R. Gelman (Eds.), *The Epigenesis of Mind: Essays on Biology & Cognition* (pp. 237–256). Hillsdale, NJ: Lawrence Erlbaum Associates, Inc.

Keil, F. C. (1994). The birth and nurturance of concepts of domains: The origins of concepts of living things. In L. A. Hirschfeld & S. A. Gelman (Eds.), *Mapping the Mind* (pp. 234–254). New York: Cambridge.

Keil, F. C. (2006). Explanation and understanding. *Annual Review of Psychology*, 57, 227–54.

Keil, F. C., & Batterman, N. (1984). A characteristic-to-defining shift in the development of word meaning. *Journal of Verbal Learning & Verbal Behaviour*, 23, 221–236.

Kekule, F. A. (1865). *Bulletin of the Society of Chemistry France (Paris)*, 3, 98.

Kerr, A., & Zelazo, P. D. (2004). Development of "hot" executive function: the children's gambling task. *Brain and Cognition*, 55, 148–157.

Kirkham, N. Z., Cruess, L., & Diamond, D. (2003). Helping children apply their knowledge to their behaviour on a dimension-switching task. *Developmental Science*, 6, 449–467.

Kirkham, N. Z., Slemmer, J. A., & Johnson, S. P. (2002). Visual statistical learning in infancy: Evidence for a domain general learning mechanism. *Cognition*, 83, B35–B42.

Kisilevsky, B. S., & Low, J. A. (1998). Human fetal behaviour: 100 years of study. *Developmental Review*, 18, 1–29.

Klahr, D., Fay, A. L., & Dunbar, K. (1993) Heuristics for scientific experimentation: A developmental study. *Cognitive Psychology*, 24, 111–146.

Klingberg, T., Forssberg, H., & Westerberg, H. (2002). Increased brain activity in frontal and parietal cortex underlies the development of visuospatial working memory capacity during childhood. *Journal of Cognitive Neuroscience*, 14(1), 1–10.

Kobayashi, M., Kato, J., Haynes, C. W., Macaruso, P., & Hook, P. (2003). Cognitive linguistic factors in Japanese children's reading. *Japanese Journal of Learning Disabilities*, 12, 240–247.

Kochanska, G., Murray, K., Jacques, T. Y., Koenig, A. L., & Vandegeest, K. (1996). Inhibitory control in young children and its role in emerging internalization. *Child Development*, 67, 490–507.

Koenig, M. A., & Echols, C. H. (2003). Infants' understanding of false labeling events: the referential roles of words and the speakers who use them. *Cognition*, 87, 179–208.

Kopera-Frye, K., Dehaene, S., & Streissguth, A. P. (1996). Impairments of number processing induced by prenatal alcohol exposure. *Neuropsychologia*, 34, 1187–1196.

Koslowski, B. (1996). *Theory and Evidence: The Development of Scientific Reasoning*. Cambridge, MA: MIT Press.

Koslowski, B., & Masnick, A. (2002). Causal reasoning. In U. Goswami (Ed.), *Handbook of Child Cognitive Development* (pp. 257–281). Oxford: Blackwell.

Kotovsky, L., & Baillargeon, R. (1998). The development of calibration-based reasoning about collision events in young infants. *Cognition*, 67, 311–351.

Kozhevnikov, M., & Hegarty, M. (2001). Impetus beliefs as default heuristic: Dissociation between explicit and implicit knowledge about motion. *Psychonomic Bulletin and Review*, 8, 439–453.

Krist, H., Fieberg, E. L., & Wilkening, F. (1993). Intuitive physics in action and judgement: The development of knowledge about projectile motion. *Journal of Experimental Psychology: Learning, Memory & Cognition, 19*, 952–966.

Kuhl, P. K. (1986). Reflections on infants' perception and representation of speech. In J. Perkell & D. Klatt (Eds.), *Invariance and Variability in Speech Processes*. Norwood, NJ: Ablex.

Kuhl, P. K. (1991). Human adults and human infants show a "perceptual magnet effect" for the prototypes of speech categories, monkeys do not. *Perception & Psychophysics, 50*, 93–107.

Kuhl, P. K. (2004). Early language acquisition: Cracking the speech code. *Nature Reviews Neuroscience, 5*, 831–843.

Kuhl, P. K. (2007). Is speech learning 'gated' by the social brain? *Developmental Science, 10(1)*, 110–120.

Kuhl, P. K., Tsao. F.-M., & Liu, H.-M. (2003). Foreign-language experience in infancy: Effects of short-term exposure and social interaction on phonetic learning. *Proceedings of the National Academy of Sciences, 100*, 9096–9101.

Kuhl, P. K., Williams, K. A., Lacerda, F., Stevens, K. N., & Lindblom, B. (1992). Linguistic experience alters phonetic perception in infants by 6 months of age. *Science, 255*, 606–608.

Kuhlmeier, V. A., Wynn, K., & Bloom, P. (2003). Attribution of dispositional states by 12-month-olds. *Psychological Science, 14*, 402–408.

Kuhn, D. (1989). Children and adults as intuitive scientists. *Psychological Review, 96*, 674–689.

Kuhn, D. (1999). Metacognitive development. In L. Balter & C. S. Tamis-LeMonda (Eds), *Child Psychology: A Handbook of Contemporary Issues* (pp. 259–286). New York: Psychology Press.

Kuhn, D. (2000). Theory of mind, metacognition, and reasoning: A life-span perspective. In P. Mitchell & K. J. Riggs (Eds), *Children's Reasoning and the Mind* (pp. 301–326). Hove, UK: Psychology Press/Taylor & Francis.

Kuhn, D. (2005). *Education for Thinking*. Harvard, MA: Harvard University Press.

Kuhn, D., Amsel, E., & O'Loughlin, M. (1988). *The Development of Scientific Thinking Skills*. San Diego, CA: Academic Press.

Kuhn, D., Garcia-Mila, M., Zohar, A., & Andersen, C. (1995). Strategies of Knowledge Acquisition. *Monographs of the Society for Research in Child Development, 60*, Serial no. 4.

Kunzinger, E. L., & Witryol, S. L. (1984). The effects of differential incentives on second-grade rehearsal and free recall. *Journal of Genetic Psychology, 144*, 19–30.

Kurtz, B. E., & Weinert, F. E. (1989). Metamemory, memory performance and causal attributions in gifted and average children. *Journal of Experimental Child Psychology, 48*, 45–61.

Lagnado, D. A., Waldmann, M. R., Hagmayer, Y., & Sloman, S. A. (2007). Beyond covariation: Cues to causal structure. In A. Gopnik & L. Schulz (Eds.), *Causal Learning: Psychology, Philosophy, and Computation* (pp. 154–172). Oxford: Oxford University Press.

Lakoff, G. (1986). *Women, Fire and Dangerous Things: What Categories Tell Us about the Nature of Thought*. Chicago: University of Chicago Press.

Lamsfuss, S. (1995). *Regularity of movement and the animate–inanimate distinction*. Poster presented at the Biennial Meeting of the Society for Research in Child Development, Indianapolis, IN, March 1995.

Landerl, K., Wimmer, H., & Frith, U. (1997). The impact of orthographic consistency on dyslexia: A German–English comparison. *Cognition, 63*, 315–334.

Lang, B., & Perner, J. (2002). Understanding of intention and false belief and the development of self-control. *British Journal of Developmental Psychology, 20*, 67–76.

Le Corre, M., Van de Walle, G., Brannon, E. M., & Carey, S. (2006). Re-visiting the competence/performance debaate in the acquisition of the counting principles. *Cognitive Psychology, 52*, 130–169.

Leevers, H. J., & Harris, P. L. (2000). Counterfactual syllogistic reasoning in normal four-year-olds, children with learning disabilities, and children with autism. *Journal of Experimental Child Psychology, 76*, 64–87.

Leslie, A. M. (1987). Pretense and representation: The origins of "theory of mind". *Psychological Review, 94*, 412–426.

Leslie, A. M. (1994). ToMM, ToBY and Agency: Core architecture and domain specificity. In L. A. Hirschfeld & S. A. Gelman (Eds.), *Mapping the Mind* (pp. 119–148). New York: Cambridge University Press.

Leslie, A. M. (2005). Developmental parallels in understanding minds and bodies. *Trends in Cognitive Sciences, 9*, 459–462.

Leslie, A. M., & Keeble, S. (1987). Do six-month-old infants perceive causality? *Cognition, 25*, 265–288.

Liberman, I. Y., Shankweiler, D., Fischer, F. W., & Carter, B. (1974). Explicit syllable and phoneme segmentation in the young child. *Journal of Experimental Child Psychology, 18*. 201–212.

Light, P. H, Blaye, A., Gilly, M., & Girotto, V. (1989). Pragmatic schemas and logical reasoning in 6- to 8-year-old children. *Cognitive Development, 4*, 49–64.

Lillard, A. S. (2002). Pretend play and cognitive development. In U. Goswami (Ed.), *Handbook of Cognitive Development* (pp. 188–205). London: Blackwell.

Lipska, B. K., & Weinberger, D. R. (2002). A neurodevelopmental model of schizophrenia: Neonatal disconnection of the hippocampus. *Neurotoxicity Research, 4*, 469–475.

Liszkowski, U., Carpenter, M., Henning, A., Striano, T., & Tomasello, M. (2004). Twelve-month-old infants point to share attention. *Developmental Science, 7*, 297–307.

Lockl, K., & Schneider, W. (2002). Developmental trends in children's feeling-of-knowing judgements. *International Journal of Behavioral Development, 26(4)*, 327–333.

Loftus, E. F., & Zanni, G. (1975). Eyewitness testimony: The influence of the wording of a question. *Bulletin of the Psychonomic Society, 5*, 86–88.

Lohmann, H., & Tomasello, M. (2003). The role of language in the development of false belief understanding: A training study. *Child Development, 74*, 1130–1144.

Löw, A., Bentin, S., Rockstroh, B., Silberman, Y., Gomolla, A., Cohen, R., & Elbert T. (2003). Semantic categorization in the human brain: spatiotemporal dynamics revealed by magnetoencephalography. *Psychological Science, 14*, 367–372.

Luna, B., Thulborn, K. R., Munoz, D. P., Merriam, E. P., Garver, K. E., Minshew, N. J., Keshavan, M. S., Genovese, C. R., Eddy, W. F., & Sweeney, J. A. (2001). Maturation of widely distributed brain function subserves cognitive development. *NeuroImage, 13*, 786–793.

Lundberg, I., Frost, J., & Petersen, O. (1988). Effects of an extensive programme for stimulating phonological awareness in pre-school children. *Reading Research Quarterly, 23*, 163–284.

Lundberg, I., Olofsson, A., & Wall, S. (1980). Reading and spelling skills in the first school years predicted from phonemic awareness skills in kindergarten. *Scandanavian Journal of Psychology, 21*, 159–173.

Luo, Y., & Baillargeon, R. (2005). When the ordinary seems unexpected: Evidence for incremental physical knowledge in young infants. *Cognition, 95*, 297–328.

Luria, A. R. (1976). *Cognitive Development: Its Cultural and Social Foundations*. Cambridge, MA: Harvard University Press.

Luria, A. R., Pribram, K. H., & Homskaya, E. D. (1964). An experimental analysis of the behavioral disturbances produced by a left frontal arachnoidal endothelioma (meningioma). *Neuropsychologia, 2*, 257–280.

Maguire, E. A., Gadian, D. G., Johnsrude, I. S., Good, C. D., Ashburner, J., Frackowiak, R. S. J., & Frith, C. D. (2000). Navigation-related structural change in the hippocampi of taxi drivers. *PNAS, 97*, 4398–4403.

Mandel, D. R., Jusczyk, P. W., & Pisoni, D. B. (1995). Infants' recognition of the sound patterns of their own names. *Psychological Science, 6(5)*, 314–317.

Mandler, J. M. (1990). Recall of events by preverbal children. In A. Diamond (Ed.), *The Development and Neural Bases of Higher Cognitive Functions* (pp. 485–516). New York: New York Academy of Sciences.

Mandler, J. M. (1992). How to build a baby II: Conceptual primitives. *Psychological Review, 99*, 587–604.

Mandler, J. M. (2004a). *The Foundations of Mind: Origins of Conceptual Thought*. Oxford: Oxford University Press.

Mandler, J. M. (2004b). Thought before language. *Trends in Cognitive Sciences, 8(11)*, 508–513.

Mandler, J. M., & Bauer, P. J. (1988). The cradle of categorisation: Is the basic level basic? *Cognitive Development, 3*, 247–264.

Mandler, J. M., & McDonough, L. (1993). Concept formation in infancy. *Cognitive Development, 8*, 291–318.

Mandler, J. M., & McDonough, L. (1995). Long-term recall of event sequences in infancy. Special Issue: Early memory. *Journal of Experimental Child Psychology, 59*, 457–474.

Mandler, J. M., Bauer, P. J., & McDonough, L. (1991). Separating the sheep from the goats: Differentiating global categories. *Cognitive Psychology, 23*, 263–298.

Manuilenko, Z. V. (1948). Razvitie proizvolnogo povedeniya u detei goshkolnogo vozrasta [The development of voluntary behaviour in preschoolers]. *Izvestiya APN RSFSR, 14*, 43–51.

Marcus, G. F., Pinker, S., Ullman, M., Hollander, M., Rosen, T., & Xu, F. (1992). Overregularization in language acquisition. *Monographs of the Society for Research in Child Development, 57*, Serial no. 228.

Mareschal, D., & Johnson, M. H. (2003). The "what" and "where" of object representations in infancy. *Cognition, 88*, 259–276.

Mareschal, D., Johnson, M. H., Sirois, S., Spratling, M., Thomas, M., & Westermann, G. (2007). *Neuroconstructivism: Vol. 1: How the Brain Constructs Cognition*. Oxford: Oxford University Press.

Mareschal, D., Plunkett, K., & Harris, P. L. (1999) A computational and neuropsychological account of object-oriented behaviours in infancy. *Developmental Science, 2*, 306–317.

Markman, A. B., & Dietrich, E. (2000). Extending the classical view of representation. *Trends in Cognitive Sciences, 4(12)*, 470–475.

Markman, E. M., & Seibert, J. (1976). Classes and collections: internal organization and resulting holistic properties. *Cognitive Psychology, 8*, 561–577.

Markovits, H. (2000). A mental model analysis of young children's conditional reasoning with meaningful premises. *Thinking and Reasoning, 6(4)*, 335–348.

Markovits, H., & Barrouillet, P. (2002). The development of conditional reasoning: A mental model account. *Developmental Review, 22(1)*, 5–36.

Markson, L., & Bloom, P. (1997). Evidence against a dedicated system for word learning in children. *Nature, 385*, 813–815.

Marzolf, D. P., & DeLoache, J. S. (1994). Transfer in young children's understanding of spatial representations. *Child Development, 65*, 1–15.

Masataka, N. (2007). Music, evolution and language. *Developmental Science, 10(1)*, 35–39.

Massey, C. M., & Gelman, R. (1988). Preschooler's ability to decide whether a photographed object can move itself. *Developmental Psychology, 24*, 307–317.

McCloskey, M. (1983). Intuitive physics. *Scientific American, 248*, 122–130.

McCune-Nicolich, L. (1981). Toward symbolic functioning: Structure of early pretend games and potential parallels with language. *Child Development, 52*, 785–797.

McDonough, L., Mandler, J. M., McKee, R. D., & Squire, L. R. (1995). The deferred imitation task as a nonverbal measure of declarative memory. *Proceedings of the National Academy of Sciences, 92*, 7580–7584.

McGarrigle, J., & Donaldson, M. (1975). Conservation accidents. *Cognition, 3*, 341–350.

McKenzie, B. E., & Bigelow, E. (1986). Detour behaviour in young human infants. *British Journal of Developmental Psychology, 4*, 139–148.

McKenzie, B. E., & Over, R. (1983). Young infants fail to imitate facial and manual gestures. *Infant Behaviour & Development, 6*, 85–95.

McKenzie, B. E., Day, R. H., & Ihsen, E. (1984). Localisation of events in space: Young infants are not always egocentric. *British Journal of Developmental Psychology, 2*, 1–10.

Mechner, F. (1958). Probability relations within response sequences under ratio reinforcement. *Journal of the Experimental Analysis of Behavior, 1*, 109–121.

Meck, W. H., & Church, R. M. (1983). Selective adjustment of the speed of internal clock and memory processes. *Journal of Experimental Psychology: Animal Behaviour Processes, 9*, 171–201.

Medin, D. L. (1989). Concepts and conceptual structure. *American Psychologist, 44*, 1469–1481,

Medin, D. L., & Schaffer, M. M. (1978). Context theory of classification learning. *Psychological Review, 85*, 207–238.

Mehler, J., Lambertz, G., Jusczyk, P. W., & Amiel-Tison, C. (1986). Discrimination de la langue maternelle par le nouveau-né. *Comptesrendus de l'Académie des Sciences de Paris, 303*, Série III, 637–640.

Meins, E. (1997). *Security of Attachment and the Social Development of Cognition*. Hove, UK: Psychology Press.

Meins, E., & Fernyhough, C. (1999). Linguistic acquisitional style and mentalising development: The role of maternal mind-mindedness. *Cognitive Development, 14*, 363–380.

Meins, E., Fernyhough, C., Wainwright, R., Das Gupta, M., Fradley, E., & Tuckey, M. (2002). Maternal mind-mindedness and attachment security as predictors of theory of mind understanding. *Child Development, 73*, 1715–1726.

Meltzoff, A. N. (1985). Immediate and deferred imitation in 14- and 24-month-old infants. *Child Development, 56*, 62–72.

Meltzoff, A. N. (1988a). Infant imitation after a 1-week delay: Long-term memory for novel acts and multiple stimuli. *Developmental Psychology, 24*, 470–476.

Meltzoff, A. N. (1988b). Infant imitation and memory: Nine-month-olds in immediate and deferred tests. *Child Development, 59*, 217–225.

Meltzoff, A. N. (1988c). Imitation of televised models by infants. *Child Development, 59*, 1221–1229.

Meltzoff, A. N. (1990). Foundations for developing a concept of self: The role of imitation in relating self to other and the value of social mirroring, social modeling, and self practice in infancy. In D. Cicchetti & M. Beeghly (Eds.), *The Self in Transition: Infancy to Childhood* (pp. 139–164). Chicago: University of Chicago Press.

Meltzoff, A. N. (1995a). Understanding the intentions of others: Re-enactment of intended acts by 18-month-old children. *Developmental Psychology, 31*, 838–850.

Meltzoff, A. N. (1995b). What infant memory tells us about infantile amnesia: Long-term recall and deferred imitation. *Journal of Experimental Child Psychology, 59*, 497–515.

Meltzoff, A. N. (2002). Imitation as a mechanism for social cognition: Origins of empathy, theory of mind and the representation of action. In U. Goswami (Ed.), *Blackwell Handbook of Childhood Cognitive Development* (pp. 6–25). Oxford: Blackwell.

Meltzoff, A. N. (2007). 'Like me': A foundation for social cognition. *Developmental Science, 10(1)*, 126–134.

Meltzoff, A. N., & Borton, R. W. (1979). Intermodal matching by human neonates. *Nature, 282*, 403–404.

Meltzoff, A. N., & Decety, J. (2003). What imitation tells us about social cognition: A rapprochement between developmental psychology and cognitive neuroscience. *Philosophical Transactions of the Royal Society: Biological Sciences, 358*, 491–500.

Meltzoff, A. N., & Moore, M. K. (1977). Imitation of facial and manual gestures by human neonates. *Science, 198*, 75–78.

Meltzoff, A. N., & Moore, M. K. (1983). Newborn infants imitate adult facial gestures. *Child Development, 54*, 702–709.

Mendelson, R., & Shultz, T. R. (1975). Covariation and temporal contiguity as principles of causal inference in young children. *Journal of Experimental Child Psychology, 22*, 408–412.

Mervis, C. B. (1987). Child-basic object categories and early lexical development. In U. Neisser (Ed.). *Concepts and Conceptual Development: Ecological and Intellectual Factors in Categorisation* (pp. 201–233). Cambridge: Cambridge University Press.

Mervis, C. B., & Pani, J. R. (1980). Acquisition of basic object categories. *Cognitive Psychology, 12*, 496–522.

Michotte, A. (1963). *The Perception of Causality*. Andover, UK: Methuen.

Miller, S. A. (1982). On the generalisability of conservation: A comparison of different kinds of transformation. *British Journal of Psychology, 73*, 221–230.

Mills, D., Prat, C., Stager, C., Zangl, R., Neville, H., & Werker, J. (2004). Language experience and the organization of brain activity to phonetically similar words: ERP evidence from 14- and 20-month-olds. *Journal of Cognitive Neuroscience, 16*, 1452–1464.

Milner, A. D., & Goodale, M. A. (1995). *The Visual Brain in Action*. Oxford: Oxford University Press.

Milner, B. (1963). Effects of brain lesions on card sorting. *Archives of Neurology, 9*, 90–100.

Milner, B. (1964). Some effects of frontal lobectomy in man. In J. M. Warren & K. Akert (Eds.), *The Frontal Granular Cortex & Behavior* (pp. 313–334). New York: McGraw-Hill.

Mitroff, S. R., Scholl, B. J., & Wynn, K. (2004). Divide and conquer: How object files adapt when a persisting object splits into two. *Psychological Science, 15,* 420–425.

Miura, I. T., Kim, C. C., Chang, C.-M., & Okamoto, Y. (1988). Effects of language characteristics on children's cognitive representation of number: cross–national comparisons. *Child Development, 59,* 1445–1450.

Mix, K. S., Levine, S. C., & Huttenlocher, J. (1997). Numerical abstraction in infants: Another look. *Developmental Psychology, 33,* 423–428.

Moll, H., & Tomasello, M. (2004). 12- and 18-month-old infants follow gaze to spaces behind barriers. *Developmental Science, 7,* F1–F9.

Monsell, S., & Driver, J. (2000). Banishing the control homunculus. In S. Monsell & J. Driver (Eds.), *Control of Cognitive Processes: Attention and Performance XVIII* (pp. 3–32). Cambridge MA: MIT Press

Moore, C., & Corkum, V. (1994). Social understanding at the end of the first year of life. *Developmental Review, 14,* 349–372.

Moore, D., Benenson, J., Reznick, S. J., Peterson, M., & Kagan, J. (1987). Effect of auditory numerical information infants' looking behaviour: Contradictory evidence. *Developmental Psychology, 23,* 665–670.

Moro, Ch., & Rodríguez, C. (1998). Towards a pragmatical conception of the object: The construction of the uses of the objects by the baby in the pre-linguistic period. In M. Lyra & J. Valsiner (Eds.), *Child Development within a Culturally Structured Environment, Vol. IV.* (pp. 53–72). Norwood, CT: Ablex.

Moyer, R. S., & Landauer, T. K. (1967). Time required for judgments of numerical inequality. *Nature, 215,* 1519–1520.

Mumme, D., Fernald, A., & Herrera, C. (1996). Infants' responses to facial and vocal emotional signals in a social referencing paradigm. *Child Development, 67,* 3219–3237.

Munakata, Y. (2001). Graded representations in behavioral dissociations. *Trends in Cognitive Sciences, 5(7),* 309–315.

Munakata, Y. (2004). Computational cognitive neuroscience of early memory development. *Developmental Review, 24,* 133–153.

Munakata, Y., & McClelland, J. L. (2003). Connectionist models of development. *Developmental Science, 6,* 413–429.

Munakata, Y., Casey, B. J., & Diamond, A. (2004). Developmental cognitive neuroscience: Progress and potential. *Trends in Cognitive Sciences, 8(3),* 122–128.

Mundy, P., Card, J., & Fox, N. (2000). EEG correlates of the development of infant joint attention skills. *Developmental Psychobiology, 36,* 325–338.

Mundy, P., Hogan, A., & Doehring, P. (1996). *A Preliminary Manual for the Abridged Early Social Communication Scales.* Coral Gables, FL: University of Miami. Online. Available: www.psy.miami.edu/faculty/pmundy

Murphy, G. L. (1982). Cue validity and levels of categorisation. *Psychological Bulletin, 91,* 174–177.

Myers, N. A., Clifton, R. K., & Clarkson, M. G. (1987). When they were very young: Almost-threes remember two years ago. *Infant Behaviour & Development, 10,* 128–132.

Naatanen, R., & Picton, T. W. (1987). The N1 wave of the human electric and magnetic response to sound: A review and an analysis of the component structure. *Psychophysiology, 24,* 375–425.

Naito, M. (1990). Repetition priming in children and adults: Age-related differences between implicit and explicit memory. *Journal of Experimental Child Psychology, 50,* 462–484.

Naus, M. J., Ornstein, P. A., & Aviano, S. (1977). Developmental changes in memory: The effects of processing time and rehearsal instructions. *Journal of Experimental Child Psychology, 23,* 237–251.

Neisser, U. (1987). *Concepts and Conceptual Development: Ecological and Intellectual Factors in Categorisation.* Cambridge: Cambridge University Press.

Nelson, K. (1986). *Event Knowledge: Structure and Function in Development.* Hillsdale, NJ: Lawrence Erlbaum Associates, Inc.

Nelson, K. (1988). The ontogeny of memory for real events. In U. Neisser & E. Winograd (Eds.), *Remembering Reconsidered: Ecological and Traditional Approaches to the Study of Memory* (pp. 244–276). New York: Cambridge University Press.

Nelson, K. (1993). The psychological and social origins of autobiographical memory. *Psychological Science, 4,* 7–14.

Nelson, K., & Fivush, R. (2004). The emergence of autobiographical memory: A social cultural developmental theory. *Psychological Review, 111,* 486–511.

Nelson, T. O., & Narens, L. (1990). Metamemory: A theoretical framework and new findings. In G. H. Bower (Ed.), *The Psychology of Learning and Motivation* (Vol. 26, pp. 125–141). New York: Academic Press.

Nelson, T. O., & Narens, L. (1994). Why investigate metacognition? In J. Metcalfe & A. P. Shimamura (Eds.), *Metacognition: Knowing about Knowing* (pp. 1–25). Cambridge, MA: MIT Press.

Newcombe, N., & Fox, N. (1994). Infantile amnesia: Through a glass darkly. *Child Development, 65,* 31–40.

Nicolich, L. M. (1977). Beyond sensori-motor intelligence: Assessment of symbolic maturity through analysis of pretend play. *Merrill-Palmer Quarterly, 23,* 89–101.

Noles, N. S., Scholl, B. J., & Mitroff, S. R. (2005). The persistence of object file representations. *Perception & Psychophysics, 67,* 324–334.

Nunes, T., & Bryant, P. (1996). *Children Learning Mathematics.* Oxford: Blackwell.

O'Connor, N., & Hermelin, B. (1973). Spatial or temporal organisation of short–term memory. *Quarterly Journal of Experimental Psychology, 25,* 335–343.

O'Sullivan, J. T. (1993). Preschoolers' beliefs about effort, incentives and recall. *Journal of Experimental Child Psychology, 55,* 396–414.

Ochsner, J. E., & Zaragoza, M. S. (1988). *The accuracy and suggestibility of children's memory for neutral and criminal eyewitness events*. Paper presented at the American Psychology and Law Meetings, Miami, FL.

Oller, D. K. (1980). The emergence of the sounds of speech in infancy. In G. Yeni-Komshian, J. Kavanaugh, & C. Ferguson (Eds.), *Child Phonology* (pp. 93–112). New York: Academic Press.

Oller, D. K., & Eilers, R. (1988). The role of audition in infant babbling. *Child Development, 59*, 441–449.

Onishi, K. H., & Baillargeon, R. (2005). Do 15-month-old infants understand false beliefs? *Science, 308*, 255–258.

Ornstein, P. A., Gordon, B. N., & Larus, D. M. (1992). Children's memory for a personally-experienced event: Implications for testimony. *Applied Developmental Psychology, 6*, 49–60.

Palincsar, A. S., & Brown, A. L. (1984). Reciprocal teaching of comprehension—fostering and monitoring activities. *Cognition and Instruction, 1*, 117–175.

Paris, S. G., & Oka, E. R. (1986). Children's reading strategies, metacognition, and motivation. *Developmental Review, 6*, 25–56.

Pascual-Leone, J. (1970). A mathematical model for the transition rule in Piaget's developmental stages. *Acta Psychologica, 32*, 301–345.

Pauen, S. (1996a). *Wie klassifizieren Kinder Lebewesen und Artefakte? Zur Rolle der Erscheinung und Funktion von Objektteilen*. University of Tuebingen, Germany.

Pauen, S. (1996b). Children's reasoning about the interaction of forces. *Child Development, 67*, 2728–2742.

Pauen, S. (2002). Evidence for knowledge-based category discrimination in infancy. *Child Development, 73*, 1016–1033.

Pauen, S., & Wilkening, F. (1997). Children's analogical reasoning about natural phenomena. *Journal of Experimental Child Psychology, 67*, 90–113.

Paulesu, E., J.-F. Démonet, J.-F., Fazio, F., McCrory, E., Chanoine, V., Brunswick, N., Cappa, S. F., Cossu, G., Habib, M., Frith, C. D., & Frith, U. (2001). Dyslexia: Cultural diversity and biological unity. *Science, 291(5511)*, 2165–2167.

Pears, R., & Bryant, P. (1990). Transitive inferences by young children about spatial position. *British Journal of Psychology, 81*, 497–510.

Peccei, J. S. (2005). *Child Language: A Resource Book for Students*. London: Routledge.

Pennington, B. F. (1994). The working memory function of the prefrontal cortices: Implications for developmental and individual differences in cognition. In M. M. Haith, J. Benson, R. Roberts, & B. F. Pennington (Eds.), *The Development of Future Oriented Processes* (pp. 243–289). Chicago: University of Chicago Press.

Perez, L. A., Peynircioglu, Z. F., & Blaxton, T. A. (1998). Developmental differences in implicit and explicit memory performance. *Journal of Experimental Child Psychology, 70*, 167–185.

Perfetti, C. A., Beck, I., Bell, L., & Hughes, C. (1987). Phonemic knowledge and learning to read are reciprocal: A longitudinal study of first grade children. *Merrill-Palmer Quarterly, 33*, 283–319.

Perner, J., & Lang, B. (1999). Development of theory of mind and executive control. *Trends in Cognitive Sciences, 3(9)*, 337–344.

Perner, J., & Lang, B. (2000). Theory of mind and executive function: Is there a developmental relationship? In S. Baron-Cohen, H. Tager-Flusberg & D. Cohen (Eds.), *Understanding Other Minds: Perspectives from Autism and Developmental Cognitive Neuroscience*, 2nd Edition (pp. 150–181). Oxford: Oxford University Press.

Perner, J., & Lang, B. (2002). What causes 3-year-olds' difficulty on the dimensional change card sorting task? *Infant & Child Development, 11*, 93–105.

Perner, J., & Ruffman, T. (2005). Infants' insight into the mind: How deep? *Science, 308*, 214–216.

Perner, J., Ruffman, T., & Leekam, S. R (1994). Theory of mind is contagious; you catch it from your sibs. *Child Development, 65*, 1224–1234.

Perris, E. E., Myers, N. A., & Clifton, R. K. (1990). Long-term memory for a single infancy experience. *Child Development, 61*, 1796–1807.

Peterson, C., & Siegal, M. (1998). Changing focus on the representational mind: Concepts of false photographs, false drawings and false beliefs in deaf, autistic and normal children. *British Journal of Developmental Psychology, 16*, 301–320.

Petitto, L. A., & Dunbar, K. N. (in press). New findings from educational neuroscience on bilingual brains, scientific brains, and the educated mind. In K. Fischer & T. Katzir (Eds.), *Building Usable Knowledge in Mind, Brain and Education*. Cambridge: Cambridge University Press.

Petitto, L. A., & Marentette, P. F. (1991). Babbling in the manual mode: Evidence for the ontogeny of language. *Science, 251*, 1483–1496.

Petitto, L. A., Holowka, S., Sergio, L. E., Levy, B., & Ostry, D. J. (2004). Baby hands that move to the rhythm of language: Hearing babies acquiring sign language babble silently on the hands. *Cognition, 93*, 43–73.

Piaget, J. (1952). *The Child's Conception of Number*. London: Routledge Kegan Paul.

Piaget, J. (1954). *The Construction of Reality in the Child*. New York: Basic Books.

Piaget, J. (1960). The general problems of the psychobiological development of the child. In J. M. Tanner & B. Inhelder (Eds.), *Discussions on Child Development* (Vol. 4) (pp. 3–27). London: Tavistock.

Piaget, J., & Inhelder, B. A. (1956). *The Child's Conception of Space*. London: Routledge Kegan Paul.

Pica, P., Lemer, C., & Izard, V. (2004). Exact and approximate arithmetic in an Amazonian indigene group. *Science, 306(5695)*, 499–503.

Pinel, P., Dehaene, S., Rivière, D., & LeBihan, D. (2001). Modulation of parietal activation by semantic distance in a number comparison task. *Neuroimage, 14,* 1013–1026.

Pitt, M. A., & McQueen, J. M. (1998). Is compensation for coarticulation mediated by the lexicon? *Journal of Memory and Language, 39,* 347–370.

Plaisted, K., Saksida, L., Alcantara, J., & Weisblatt, E. (2003). Towards an understanding of the mechanisms of weak central coherence effects: experiments in visual configural learning and auditory perception. *Philosophical Transcripts of the Royal Society, London. Series B. Biological Science, 358,* 375–386.

Plotnik, J. M., de Waal, F. B. M., & Reiss, D. (2006). Self–recognition in an Asian elephant. *PNAS, 103,* 45, 17053–17057.

Porpodas, C. D (1999). Patterns of phonological and memory processing in beginning readers and spellers of Greek. *Journal of Learning Disabilities, 32,* 406–416.

Premack, D., & Woodruf, G. (1978). Does the chimpanzee have a theory of mind? *Behavioral and Brain Sciences, 4,* 515–526.

Pressley, M., Borkowski, J. G., & Schneider, W. (1987). Good strategy users coordinate metacognition and knowledge. In R. Vasta & G. Whitehurst (Eds.), *Annals of Child Development* (Vol. 5, pp. 89–129). Greenwich, CT: JAI Press.

Quinn, P. C. (1994). The categorisation of above and below spatial relations by young infants. *Child Development, 65,* 58–69.

Quinn, P. C. (2002). Category representation in infants. *Current Directions in Psychological Science, 11,* 66–70.

Quinn, P. C., & Eimas, P. D. (1986). On categorisation in early infancy. *Merrill-Palmer Quarterly, 32,* 331–363.

Quinn, P. C., & Johnson, M. H. (1997). The emergence of category representations in infants: A connectionist analysis. *Journal of Experimental Child Psychology, 66,* 236–263.

Quinn, P. C., & Johnson, M. H. (2000). Global before basic category representations in connectionist networks and 2-month-old infants. *Infancy, 1,* 31–46.

Rakoczy, H., Tomasello, M., & Striano, T. (2005). On tools and toys: How children learn to act on and pretend with 'virgin objects'. *Developmental Science, 8(1),* 57–73.

Rauschecker, J. P., & Singer, W. (1981). The effects of early visual experience on the cat's visual cortex and their possible explanation by Hebb synapses. *Journal of Physiology, 310,* 215–239.

Reese, E., Haden, C. A., & Fivush, R. (1993). Mother–child conversations about the past: Relationships of style and memory over time. *Cognitive Development, 8,* 403–430.

Remond-Besuchet, C., Noel, M.-P., Seron, X., Thioux, M., Brun, M., & Aspe, X. (1999). Selective preservation of exceptional arithmetical knowledge in a demented patient. *Mathematical Cognition, 5(1),* 41–63.

Repacholi, B. M., & Gopnik, A. (1997). Early reasoning about desires: Evidence from 14- and 18-month-olds. *Developmental Psychology, 33,* 12–21.

Rieser, J. J., Doxey, P. A., McCarrell, N. J., & Brooks, P. H. (1982). Wayfinding and toddlers' use of information from an aerial view of a maze. *Developmental Psychology, 18,* 714–720.

Riggs, K. J., & Simpson, A. (2005). Young children have difficulty ascribing true beliefs. *Developmental Science, 8(3),* F27–F30.

Righi, G., & Tarr, M. J. (2004). Are chess experts any different from face, dird, or Greeble experts? *Journal of Vision, 4,* 504a.

Rips, L. J., Asmuth, J., & Bloomfield, A. (2006). Giving the boot to the bootstrap: how not to learn the natural numbers. *Cognition, 101,* B51–B60.

Rizzolatti, G., & Arbib, M. (1998). Language within our grasp. *Trends in Neurosciences, 21,* 188–194.

Rizzolatti, G., & Craighero, L. (2004). The mirror neuron system. *Annual Review of Neuroscience, 27,* 169–192.

Rizzolatti, G., Fogassi, L., & Gallese, V. (2001). Neurophysiological mechanisms underlying the understanding and imitation of action. *Nature Reviews Neuroscience, 2,* 661–670.

Rochat, P., Morgan, R., & Carpenter, M. (1997). Young infants' sensitivity to movement information specifying social causality. *Cognitive Development, 12,* 537–561.

Rodríguez, C. (2007). Object use, communication and signs. The triadic basis of early cognitive development. In J. Valsiner & A. Rosa (Eds.), *The Cambridge Handbook of Socio-cultural Psychology* (pp. 257–276). New York: Cambridge University Press.

Rolls, E. T. (1999*). The Brain and Emotion.* Oxford: Oxford University Press.

Roodenrys, S., Hulme, C., & Brown, G. (1993). The development of short-term memory span: Separable effects of speech rate and long-term memory. *Journal of Experimental Child Psychology, 56,* 431–442.

Rosch, E. (1978). Principles of categorisation. In E. Rosch & B. B. Lloyd (Eds.), *Cognition and Categorisation.* Hillsdale, NJ: Lawrence Erlbaum Associates, Inc.

Rosch, E., & Mervis, C. B. (1975). Family resemblances: Studies in the internal structure of categories. *Cognitive Psychology, 7,* 573–605.

Rosch, E., Mervis, C. B., Gray, W. D., Johnson, M. D., & Boyes-Braem, P. (1976). Basic objects in natural categories. *Cognitive Psychology, 8,* 382–439.

Rose, S. A., & Blank, N. (1974). The potency of context in children's cognition: An illustration through conservation. *Child Development, 45,* 499–502.

Rose, S. A., & Feldman, J. F. (1995). Prediction of I. Q. and specific cognitive abilities at 11 years from infancy measures. *Developmental Psychology, 31,* 685–696.

Rose, S. A., Feldman, J. F., & Jankowski, J. J. (2001). Visual short-term memory in the first year of life: Capacity and recency effects. *Developmental Psychology, 39,* 539–549.

Rose, S. A., Feldman, J. F., & Jankowski, J. J. (2004). Infant visual recognition memory. *Developmental Review, 24,* 74–100.

Rosengren, K. S., Gelman, S. A., Kalish, C. W., & McCormick, M. (1991). As time goes by: Children's early understanding of growth in animals. *Child Development, 62,* 1302–1320.

Rothbart, M. K., & Posner, M. I. (1985). Temperament and the development of self-regulation. In L. C. Hartlage & C. F. Telzrow (Eds.), *The Neuropsychology of Individual Differences: A Developmental Perspective* (pp. 93–123). New York: Plenum Press.

Rovee-Collier, C. K. (1993). The capacity for long-term memory in infancy. *Current Directions in Psychological Science, 2,* 130–135.

Rovee-Collier, C. K., & Hayne, H. (1987). Reactivation of infant memory: Implications for cognitive development. *Advances in Child Development and Behaviour, 20,* 185–238.

Rovee-Collier, C. K., Schechter, A., Shyi, G. C. W., & Shields, P. (1992). Perceptual identification of contextual attributes and infant memory retrieval. *Developmental Psychology, 28,* 307–318.

Rovee-Collier, C. K., Sullivan, M. W., Enright, M., Lucas, D., & Fagen, J. W. (1980). Reactivation of infant memory. *Science, 208,* 1159–1161.

Rowe, S., & Wertsch, J. (2002). Vygotsky's model of cognitive development. In U. Goswami (Ed.), *Blackwell Handbook of Childhood Cognitive Development.* Oxford: Blackwell.

Rowland, C. F., & Pine, J. M. (2000). Subject– auxiliary inversion errors and wh- question acquisition: What children do know? *Journal of Child Language, 27,* 157–181.

Rudy, L., & Goodman, G. S. (1991). Effects of participation on children's reports: Implications for children's testimony. *Developmental Psychology, 27,* 527–538.

Ruffman, T., Perner, J., Olson, D., & Doherty, M. (1993). Reflecting on scientific thinking: Children's understanding of the hypothesis–evidence relation. *Child Development, 64,* 1617–1636.

Ruffman, T., Rustin, C., Garnham, W., & Parkin, A. J. (2001). Source monitoring and false memories in children: Relation to certainty and executive functioning. *Journal of Experimental Child Psychology, 80,* 95–111.

Rumelhart, D. E., & Abrahamson, A. A. (1973). A model for analogical reasoning. *Cognitive Psychology, 5,* 1–28.

Rumelhart, D. E., & McClelland, J. (1986). On learning the past tenses of English verbs. In D. E. Rumelhart, J. L. McClelland, & The PDP Research Group (Eds.), *Parallel Distributed Processing* (Vol. 2, pp. 216–271). Cambridge, MA: MIT Press.

Russell, J. (1996). *Agency: Its Role in Mental Development.* Hove, UK: Psychology Press.

Russell, J. (2005). Justifying all the fuss about false belief. *Trends in Cognitive Sciences, 9,* 307–308.

Russell, J., Mauthner, N., Sharpe, S., & Tidswell, T. (1991). The "windows task" as a measure of strategic deception in preschoolers and autistic subjects. *British Journal of Developmental Psychology, 9,* 331–349.

Russo, R., Nichelli, P., Gibertoni, M., & Cornia, C. (1995). Developmental trends in implicit and explicit memory: A picture completion study. *Journal of Experimental Child Psychology, 59,* 566–578.

Saffran, J. R., Aslin, R. A., & Newport, E. L. (1996). Statistical learning by 8-month-old infants. *Science, 274,* 1926–1928.

Sarnecka, B. W., & Gelman, S. A. (2004). Six does not just mean a lot: Preschoolers see number words as specific. *Cognition, 92,* 329–352.

Saxe, G. B. (1977). A developmental analysis of notational counting. *Child Development, 48,* 1512–1520.

Saxe, R. (2005). Against simulation: The argument from error. *Trends in Cognitive Science, 9(4),* 174–179.

Saxe, R., & Kanwisher, N. (2003). People thinking about thinking people: fMRI investigations of theory of mind. *NeuroImage, 19,* 1835–1842.

Saxe, R., Carey, S., & Kanwisher, N. (2004). Understanding other minds: Linking developmental psychology and functional neuroimaging. *Annual Review of Psychology, 55,* 87–124.

Saxton, M., & Towse, J. N. (1998). Linguistic relativity: The case of place-value in multi-digit numbers. *Journal of Experimental Child Psychology, 69(1),* 66–79.

Scaife, M., & Bruner, J. (1975). The capacity for joint visual attention in the infant. *Nature, 253,* 265–266.

Schachter, D. L., & Moscovitch, M. (1984). Infants, amnesics and dissociable memory systems. In M. Moscovitch (Ed.), *Infant Memory: Its Relation to Normal and Pathological Memory in Humans and Other Animals* (pp. 173–216). New York: Plenum Press.

Schaffer, D. R. (1996). *Developmental Psychology: Childhood and Adolescence.* Pacific Grove, CA: Brooks/Cole Publishing.

Scheier, C., Lewkowicz, D. J., & Shimojo, S. (2003). Sound induces perceptual reorganization of an ambiguous motion display in human infants. *Developmental Sciences, 6,* 233–244.

Schlesinger, M. (2001). Building a better baby: embodied models of infant cognition. *Trends in Cognitive Sciences, 5(4),* 139.

Schleussner, E., Schneider, U., Arnscheidt C., Kähler, C., Haueisen, J., & Seewald, H. J. (2004). Prenatal evidence of left–right asymmetries in auditory evoked responses using fetal magnetoencephalography. *Early Human Development, 78,* 133–136.

Schlottmann, A., Allen, D., Linderoth, C., & Hesketh, S. (2002). Perceptual causality in children. *Child Development, 73,* 1656–1677.

Schneider, W. (1985). Developmental trends in the metamemory–memory behaviour relationship: An integrative review. In D. L. Forrest-Pressley, G. E. MacKinnon, & T. G. Waller (Eds.), *Cognition, Metacognition and Human Performance* (Vol. 1, pp. 57–109). Orlando, FL: Academic Press.

Schneider, W. (1986). The role of conceptual knowledge and metamemory in the development of organisational processes in memory. *Journal of Experimental Child Psychology, 42,* 218–236.

Schneider, W., & Bjorklund, D. F. (1998). Memory. In W. Damon (Ed.), *Handbook of Child Psychology*, 5th Edition (pp. 467–521). New York: John Wiley & Sons.

Schneider, W. & Lockl, K. (2002). The development of metacognitive knowledge in children and adolescents. In T. Perfect & B. Schwartz (Eds.), *Applied Metacognition*, (pp. 224–247). Cambridge: Cambridge University Press.

Schneider, W., & Pressley, M. (1989). *Memory Development Between 2 and 20*. New York: Springer.

Schneider, W., & Pressley, M. (1997). *Memory Development Between 2 and 20*, 2nd Edition. Hillsdale, NJ: Lawrence Erlbaum Associates, Inc.

Schneider, W., & Sodian, B. (1988). Metamemory–memory behaviour relationships in young children: Evidence from a memory-for-location task. *Journal of Experimental Child Psychology*, *45*, 209–233.

Schneider, W., Boes, K., & Rieder, H. (1993a). Performance prediction in adolescent top tennis players. In J. Beckmann, H. Strang, & E. Hahn (Eds.), *Aufmerksamkeit und Energetisierung*. Goettingen: Hogrefe.

Schneider, W., Borkowski, J. G., Kurtz, B. E., & Kerwin, K. (1986). Metamemory and motivation: A comparison of strategy use and performance in German and American children. *Journal of Cross-Cultural Psychology*, *17*, 315–336.

Schneider, W., Gruber, H., Gold, A., & Opwis, K. (1993b). Chess expertise and memory for chess positions in children and adults. *Journal of Experimental Child Psychology*, *56*, 328–349.

Schneider, W., Korkel, J., & Weinert, F. E. (1989). Domain-specific knowledge and memory performance: A comparison of high- and low-aptitude children. *Journal of Educational Psychology*, *81*, 306–312.

Schneider, W., Kron. V., Hunnerkopf. M., & Krajewski, K. (2004). The development of young children's memory strategies: First findings from the Wurzburg Longitudinal Memory Study. *Journal of Experimental Child Psychology*, *88*, 193–209.

Schneider, W., Kuespert, P., Roth, E., Vise, M., & Marx, H. (1997). Short- and long-term effects of training phonological awareness in kindergarten: Evidence from two German studies. *Journal of Experimental Child Psychology*, *66*, 311–340.

Schneider, W., Roth, E., & Ennemoser, M. (2000a). Training phonological skills and letter knowledge in children at-risk for dyslexia: A comparison of three kindergarten intervention programs. *Journal of Educational Psychology*, *92*, 284–295.

Schneider, W., Schlagmuller, M., & Visé, M. (1998). The impact of metamemory and domain-specific knowledge on memory performance. *European Journal of Psychology of Education*, *13*, 91–103.

Schneider, W., Visé, M., Lockl, K., & Nelson, T. O. (2000b). Developmental trends in children's memory monitoring: Evidence from a judgment-of-learning task. *Cognitive Development*, *15*, 115–134.

Scholl, B. J., & Tremoulet, P. D. (2000). Perceptual causality and animacy. *Trends in Cognitive Sciences*, *4*, 299–309.

Schroeter, M. L., Zysset, S., Wahl, M., & von Cramon, D. Y. (2004). Prefrontal activation due to Stroop interference increases during development—an event-related fNIRS study. *NeuroImage*, *23*, 1317–1325.

Schulz, L., & Gopnik, A. (2004). Causal learning across domains. *Developmental Psychology*, *40*, 162–176.

Scott, S. K., & Johnsrude, I. S. (2003). The neuroanatomical and functional organization of speech perception. *Trends in Neurosciences*, *26*, 100–107.

Sedlak, A. J., & Kurtz, S. T. (1981). A review of children's use of causal inference principles. *Child Development*, *52*, 759–784.

Sekuler, R., Sekuler, A. B., & Lau, R. (1997) Sound alters visual motion perception. *Nature*, *385*, 308.

Seymour, P. H. K., Aro, M., & Erskine, J. M. (2003). Foundation literacy acquisition in European orthographies. *British Journal of Psychology*, *94*, 143–174.

Shaywitz, B. A., Shaywitz, S. E., Pugh, K. R., Mencl, W. E., Fullbright, R. K., Skudlarski, P., Constable, R. T., Marchione, K. E., Fletcher, J. M., Lyon, G. R., & Gore, J. C. (2002). Disruption of posterior brain systems for reading in children with developmental dyslexia. *Biological Psychiatry*, *52(2)*, 101–110.

Shaywitz, B. A., Shaywitz, S. E., Blachman, B. A., Pugh, K. R., Fullbright, R. K., Skudlarski, P., Mencl, W. E., Constable, R. T., Holahan, J. M., Marchione, K. E., Fletcher, J. M., Lyon, G. R., & Gore, J. C. (2004). Development of left occipitotemporal systems for skilled reading in children after a phonologically-based intervention. *Biological Psychiatry*, *55(9)*, 926–933.

Shimizu, Y. A., & Johnson, S. C. (2004). Infants' attribution of a goal to a morphologically unfamiliar agent. *Developmental Science*, *7*, 425–430.

Shultz, T. R. (1982). Rules of causal attribution. *Monographs of the Society for Research in Child Development*, *47(1)*, Serial no. 194.

Shultz, T. R., & Kestenbaum, N. R. (1985). Causal reasoning in children. *Annals of Child Development*, *2*, 195–249.

Shultz, T. R., & Mendelson, R. (1975). The use of covariation as a principle of causal analysis. *Child Development*, *46*, 394–399.

Shultz, T. R., & Ravinsky, F. B. (1977). Similarity as a principle of causal inference. *Child Development*, *48*, 1552–1558.

Shultz, T. R., Fisher, G. W., Pratt, C. C., & Rulf, S. (1986). Selection of causal rules. *Child Development*, *57*, 143–152.

Shultz, T. R., Pardo, S., & Altmann, E. (1982). Young children's use of transitive inference in causal chains. *British Journal of Psychology*, *73*, 235–241.

Siegal, M. (1991). *Knowing Children: Experiments in Conversation and Cognition*. Hillsdale, NJ: Lawrence Erlbaum Associates, Inc.

Siegal, M., & Beattie, K. (1991). Where to look first for children's knowledge of false beliefs. *Cognition*, *38*, 1–12.

Siegler, R. S. (1978). *Children's Thinking: What Develops?* Hillsdale, NJ: Lawrence Erlbaum Associates, Inc.

Siegler, R. S. (1995). How does change occur: A microgenetic study of number conservation. *Cognitive Psychology, 28*, 225–273.

Siegler, R. S., & Liebert, R. M. (1974). Effects of contiguity, regularity and age on children's causal inferences. *Developmental Psychology, 10*, 574–579.

Sigman, M., Cohen, S. E., Beckwith, L., & Parmelee, A. H. (1986). Infant attention in relation to intellectual abilities in childhood. *Developmental Psychology, 22*, 788–792.

Sigman, M., Cohen, S. E., Beckwith, L., Asarnow, R., & Parmelee, A. H. (1991). Continuity in cognitive abilities from infancy to 12 years of age. *Cognitive Development, 6*, 47–57.

Simcock, G., & Hayne, H. (2002). Breaking the barrier: Children do not translate their preverbal memories into language. *Psychological Science, 13*, 225–231.

Simon, H. A. (1975). The functional equivalence of problem solving skills. *Cognitive Psychology, 7*, 268–288.

Simon, T. J., Hespos, S. J., & Rochat, P. (1995). Do infants understand simple arithmetic? A replication of Wynn (1992). *Cognitive Development, 10*, 253–269.

Simons, D. J., & Keil, F. C. (1995). An abstract to concrete shift in the development of biological thought: the *insides* story. *Cognition, 56*, 129–163.

Simos, P. G., Fletcher, J. M., Bergman, E., Breier, J. I., Foorman, B. R., Castillo, E. M., Davis, R. N., Fitzgerald, M., and Papanicolaou, A. C. (2002). Dyslexia-specific brain activation profile becomes normal following successful remedial training. *Neurology, 58*, 1203–1213.

Singer-Freeman, K. E. (2005). Analogical reasoning in 2-year-olds: The development of access and relational inference. *Cognitive Development, 20(2)*, 214–234.

Siok, W. T., Perfetti, C. A., Jin, Z., and Tan, L. H. (2004). Biological abnormality of impaired reading is constrained by culture. *Nature, 431*, 71–76.

Sirois, S., & Mareschal, D. (2002). Models of habituation in infancy. *Trends in Cognitive Sciences, 6*, 293–298.

Slater, A. M. (1989). Visual memory and perception in early infancy. In A. M. Slater & G. Bremner (Eds.), *Infant Development* (pp. 43–71). Hove, UK: Lawrence Erlbaum Associates.

Slater, A. M., Morison, V., & Rose, D. (1983). Perception of shape by the new-born baby. *British Journal of Developmental Psychology, 1*, 135–142.

Slaughter, V. (1998). Children's understanding of pictorial mental representations. *Child Development, 69*, 321–332.

Sluzenski, J., Newcombe, N. S., & Ottinger, W. (2004). Changes in reality monitoring and episodic memory in early childhood. *Developmental Science, 7*, 225–245.

Smiley, S., & Brown, A. L. (1979). Conceptual preferences for thematic or taxonomic relations: A nonmonotonic age trend from preschool to old age. *Journal of Experimental Child Psychology, 28*, 249–257.

Smith, L. (1992). *Jean Piaget: Critical Assessments* [4 volumes]. London: Routledge.

Smith, L. (2002). Piaget's model. In U. Goswami (Ed.), *Blackwell Handbook of Childhood Cognitive Development* (pp. 515–537). Oxford: Blackwell.

Smythe, I., Everatt, J., & Salter, R. (Eds.) (2004). *The International Book of Dyslexia*. Chichester: John Wiley & Sons.

Snowling, M. J. (2000). *Dyslexia*. Oxford: Blackwell.

Sodian, B., Zaitchek, D., & Carey, S. (1991). Young children's differentiation of hypothetical beliefs from evidence. *Child Development, 62*, 753–766.

Somerville, S. C., & Capuani-Shumaker, A. (1984). Logical searches of young children in hiding and finding tasks. *British Journal of Developmental Psychology, 2*, 315–328.

Somerville, S. C., Wellman, H. M., & Cultice, J. C. (1983). Young children's deliberate reminding. *Journal of Genetic Psychology, 143*, 87–96.

Sommerville, J. A., & Decety, J. (2006). Weaving the fabric of social interaction: Articulating developmental psychology and cognitive neuroscience in the domain of motor cognition. *Psychonomic Bulletin & Review, 13*, 179–200.

Sommerville, J. A., Woodward, A. L., & Needham, A. (2005). Action experience alters 3-month-old infants' perception of others' actions. *Cognition, 96*, B1–B11.

Sophian, C., & Somerville, S. C. (1988). Early developments in logical reasoning: Considering alternative possibilities. *Cognitive Development, 3*, 183–222.

Sorce, J. F., Emde, R. N., Campos, J., & Klinnert, M. D. (1985). Maternal emotional signaling: Its effect on the visual cliff behavior of 1-year-olds. *Developmental Psychology, 21*, 195–200.

Spelke, E. S. (1976). Infants' intermodal perception of events. *Cognitive Psychology, 8*, 553–560.

Spelke, E. S. (1991). Physical knowledge in infancy: Reflections on Piaget's theory. In S. Carey & R. Gelman (Eds.), *The Epigenesis of Mind: Essays on Biology and Cognition* (pp. 133–169). Hillsdale, NJ: Lawrence Erlbaum Associates, Inc.

Spelke, E. S. (1994). Initial knowledge: Six suggestions. *Cognition, 50*, 431–445.

Spelke, E. S., Phillips, A. T., & Woodward, A. L. (1995). Infants' knowledge of object motion and human action. In D. Sperber, A. J. Premack, & D. Premack (Eds.), *Causal Cognition: A Multidisciplinary Debate* (pp. 44–78). Oxford: Clarendon Press.

Spinozzi, G., Lubrano, G., & Truppa, V. (2004). Categorization of above and below spatial relations by tufted capuchin monkeys (*Cebus apella*). *Journal of Comparative Psychology, 118*, 403–412.

Starkey, P., & Cooper, R. G. (1980). Perception of number by human infants. *Science, 210*, 1033–1035.

Starkey, P., Spelke, E. S., & Gelman, R. (1983). Detection of intermodal numerical correspondences by human infants. *Science, 222*, 179–181.

Stechler, G., & Latz, E. (1966). Some observations on attention and arousal in the human infant. *Journal of the American Academy of Child Psychology, 5*, 517–525.

Striano, T., Henning, A., & Stahl, D. (2005). Sensitivity to social contingencies between 1 and 3 months of age. *Developmental Science, 8*, 509–519.

Surian, L., Caldi, S., & Sperber, D. (2007). Attribution of beliefs by 13-month-old infants. *Psychological Science, 18*, 580–586.

Sutton, J., Smith, P. K., & Swettenham, J. (1999). Social cognition and bullying: Social inadequacy or skilled manipulation? *British Journal of Developmental Psychology, 17*, 435–450.

Swingley, D. (2005). 11-month-olds' knowledge of how familiar words sound. *Developmental Science, 8*, 432–443.

Symons, D. K. (2004). Mental state discourse, theory of mind, and the internalization of self–other understanding. *Developmental Review, 24*, 159–188.

Tai, Y. F., Scherfler, C., Brooks, D. J., Sawamoto, N., & Castiello, U. (2004). The human premotor cortex is 'mirror' only for biological actions. *Current Biology, 14*, 117–120.

Tallal, P. (2004). Improving language and literacy is a matter of time. *Nature Reviews Neuroscience, 5*, 721.

Temple, E., & Posner, M. I. (1998). Brain mechanisms of quantity are similar in 5-year-olds and adults. *Proceedings of the National Academy of Sciences of the U. S. A., 95*, 7836–7841.

Temple, E., Deutsch, G. K., Poldrack, R. A., Miller, S. L., Tallal, P., Merzenich, M. M., & Gabrieli, D. E. (2003). Neural deficits in children with dyslexia ameliorated by behavioral remediation: Evidence from functional MRI. *Proceedings of the National Academy of Sciences, 100*, 2860–2865.

Thomson, J., Richardson, U., & Goswami, U. (2005). Phonological similarity neighborhoods and children's short-term memory: Typical development and dyslexia. *Memory and Cognition, 33*, 1210–1219.

Toda, S., & Fogel, A. (1993). Infant response to still-face situation at 3- and 6-months. *Developmental Psychology, 29*, 532–538.

Tomasello, M. (1988). The role of joint-attentional processes in early language acquisition. *Language Sciences, 10*, 69–88.

Tomasello, M. (1990). Cultural transmission in the tool use and communicatory signalling of chimpanzees? In S. Parker & K. Gibson (Eds.), *Language and Intelligence in Monkeys and Apes: Comparative Developmental Perspectives* (pp. 274–311). Cambridge: Cambridge University Press.

Tomasello, M. (1995). Joint attention as social cognition. In C. Moore & P. J. Dunham (Eds), *Joint Attention: Its Origins and Role in Development* (pp. 103–130). Hillsdale, NJ: Lawrence Erlbaum Associates, Inc.

Tomasello, M. (2000). Do young children have adult syntactic competence? *Cognition, 74*, 209–253.

Tomasello, M. (2006). Acquiring linguistic constructions. In D. Kuhn & R. Siegler (Eds.), *Handbook of Child Psychology* (pp. 255–298). New York: John Wiley & Sons.

Tomasello, M., & Carpenter, M. (2007). Shared intentionality. *Developmental Science, 10(1)*, 121–125.

Tomasello, M., Akhtar, N., Dodson, K., & Rekau, L. (1997). Differential productivity in young children's use of nouns and verbs. *Journal of Child Language, 24*, 373–387.

Tomasello, M., Striano, T., & Rochat, P. (1999). Do young children use objects as symbols? *British Journal of Developmental Psychology, 17*, 563–584.

Toro, J. M., Trobalon, J. B., & Sebastian-Galles, N. (2003). The use of prosodic cues in language tasks by rats. *Animal Cognition, 6*, 131–136.

Treiman, R., & Baron, J. (1981). Segmental analysis: Developmental and relation to reading ability. In G. C. MacKinnon & T. G. Waller (Eds.), *Reading Research: Advances in Theory and Practice*, Volume III. New York: Academic Press.

Treiman, R., & Zukowski, A. (1991). Levels of phonological awareness. In S. Brady & D. Shankweiler, (Eds.). *Phonological Processes in Literacy* (pp. 67–83). Hillsdale, NJ: Lawrence Erlbaum Associates, Inc.

Treiman, R., & Zukowski, A. (1996). Children's sensitivity to syllables, onsets, rimes and phonemes. *Journal of Experimental Child Psychology, 61*, 193–215.

Tremoulet, P., & Feldman, J. (2000). Perception of animacy from the motion of a single object. *Perception, 29*, 943–951.

Tulving, E. (2002). Episodic memory: From mind to brain. *Annual Review of Psychology, 53*, 1–25.

Tunmer, W. E., & Nesdale, A. R. (1985). Phonemic segmentation skill and beginning reading. *Journal of Educational Psychology, 77*, 417–527.

Tunteler, E., & Resing W. C. M (2002). Spontaneous analogical transfer in 4-year-olds: a microgenetic study. *Journal of Experimental Child Psychology, 83*, 149–166.

Turkeltaub, P. E., Gareau, L., Flowers, D. L., Zeffiro, T. A., & Eden, G. F. (2003). Development of neural mechanisms for reading. *Nature Neuroscience, 6(7)*, 767–773.

Tzourio-Mazoyer, N., De Schonen, S., Crivello, F., Reutter, B., Aujard, Y., & Mazoyer, B. (2002). Neural correlates of woman face processing by 2-month-old infants. *NeuroImage, 15*, 454–461.

Ungerer, J. A., Zelazo, P. R., Kearsley, R. B., & O'Leary, K. (1981). Developmental changes in the representation of objects in symbolic play from 18 to 31 months of age. *Child Development, 52*, 186–195.

Ungerleider, L. G., & Mishkin, M. (1982). Two cortical visual systems. In D. J. Ingle, Goodale, M. A., & R. J. W. Mansfield (Eds.), *Analysis of Visual Behaviour*. Cambridge, MA: MIT Press.

Vaish, A., & Striano, T. (2004). Is visual reference necessary? Vocal versus facial cues in social referencing. *Developmental Science, 7*, 261–269.

van Abbema, D. L. V., & Bauer, P. J. (2005). Autobiographical memory in middle childhood: Recollections of the recent and distant past. *Memory, 13*, 829–845.

van Oeffelen, M. P., & Vos, P. G. (1982). Configuration effects on the enumeration of dots: counting by groups. *Memory and Cognition, 10(4)*, 396–404.

Vargha-Khadem, F., Gadian, D. C., Watkins, K. E., Connelly, A., Van Paesschen, W., & Mishkin, M., (1997). Differential effects of early hippocampal pathology on episodic and semantic memory. *Science, 277,* 376–380.

Vaughan, W. J., & Greene, S. L. (1984). Pigeon visual memory capacity. *Journal of Experimental Psychology: Animal Behavior Processes, 10,* 256–271.

Vendrell, P., Junque, C., Pujol, J., Jurado, M. A., Molet, J., & Grafman, J. (1995). The role of prefrontal regions in the Stroop task. *Neuropsychologia, 33(3),* 341–352.

Viennot, L. (1979). Spontaneous reasoning in elementary dynamics. *European Journal of Science Education, 1,* 205–221.

Vihman, M. M., Nakai, S., DePaolis, R. A., & Halle, P. (2004). The role of accentual pattern in early lexical representation. *Journal of Memory and Language, 50,* 336–353.

Vintner, A. (1986). The role of movement in eliciting early imitations. *Child Development, 57,* 66–71.

Visalberghi, E., & Fragaszy, D. (1990). Do monkeys ape? In S. Parker & K. Gibson (Eds.), *Language and Intelligence in Monkeys and Apes: Comparative Developmental Perspectives* (pp. 247–273). Cambridge: Cambridge University Press.

Visé, M., & Schneider, W. (2000). Determinanten der Leistungsvorhersage bei Kindergarten- und Grundschulkindern: Zur Bedeutung metakognitiver und motivationaler Einflussfaktoren. *Zeitschrift für Entwicklungspsychologie und Pädagogische Psychologie, 32,* 51–58.

Volterra, V., & Erting, C. (1990). *From Gesture to Language in Hearing and Deaf Children.* Berlin: Springer-Verlag.

Vygotsky, L. (1978). *Mind in Society.* Cambridge, MA: Harvard University Press.

Waldmann, M. R., & Hagmayer, Y. (2005). Seeing versus doing: Two modes of accessing causal knowledge and processing effort. *Journal of Experimental Psychology: Learning, Memory, and Cognition, 31,* 216–227.

Waldmann, M. R., Hagmayer, Y., & Blaisdell, A. P. (2006). Beyond the information given: Causal models in learning and reasoning. *Current Directions in Psychological Science, 15,* 307–311.

Wang, S., & Baillargeon, R. (2005). Inducing infants to detect a physical violation in a single trial. *Psychological Science, 16,* 542–549.

Wang, S., & Baillargeon, R. (in press). Can infants be "taught" to attend to a new physical variable in an event category? The case of height in covering events. *Cognitive Psychology.*

Wang, S., Baillargeon, R., & Paterson, S. (2005). Detecting continuity violations in infancy: A new account and new evidence from covering and tube events. *Cognition, 95,* 129–173.

Washburn, D. A., & Rumbaugh, D. M. (1991). Ordinal judgements of numerical symbols by macaques (*Macaca mulatta*). *Psychological Science, 2(3),* 190–193.

Wason, P. C. (1966). Reasoning. In B. Foss (Ed.), *New Horizons in Psychology.* Harmondsworth, UK: Penguin Books.

Wason, P. C., & Johnson-Laird, P. N. (1972). *Psychology of Reasoning: Structure and Content.* Cambridge, MA: Harvard University Press.

Watson, J. S. (1994). Detection of self: The perfect algorithm. In S. T. Parker, R. W. Mitchell, & M. L. Boccia (Eds.), *Self-awareness in Animals and Humans: Developmental Perspectives* (pp. 131–148). New York: Cambridge University Press.

Waxman, S. R. (1990). Linguistic biases and the establishment of conceptual hierarchies: Evidence from preschool children. *Cognitive Development, 5,* 123–150.

Waxman, S. R., & Braun, I. (2005). Consistent (but not variable) names as invitations to form object categories: New evidence from 12-month-old infants. *Cognition, 95,* B59–B68.

Waxman, S. R., & Lidz, J. (2006). Early word learning. In D. Kuhn & R. Siegler (Eds.), *Handbook of Child Psychology, 6th Edition* (Vol. 2, pp. 299–335). New York: John Wiley & Sons.

Waxman, S. R., & Markov, D. B. (1995). Words as invitations to form categories: Evidence from 12- to 13-month-old infants. *Cognitive Psychology, 29,* 257–302.

Weber, C., Hahne, A., Friedrich, M., & Friederici, A. D. (2004). Discrimination of word stress in early infant perception: electrophysiological evidence. *Cognitive Brain Research, 18,* 149–161.

Wellman, H. M. (1978). Knowledge of the interaction of memory variables: A developmental study of metamemory. *Developmental Psychology, 14,* 24–29.

Wellman, H. M. (1985). The origins of metacognition. In D. L. Forrest-Pressley, G. E. MacKinnon, & T. G. Waller (Eds.), *Metacognition, Cognition and Human Performance* (pp. 1–31). Orlando, FL: Academic Press.

Wellman, H. M. (2002). Understanding the psychological world: Developing a theory of mind. In U. Goswami (Ed.), *Childhood Cognitive Development* (pp. 167–187). Oxford: Blackwell.

Wellman, H. M., & Gelman, S. A. (1992). Cognitive development: Foundational theories of core domains. *Annual Review of Psychology, 43,* 337–375.

Wellman, H. M., & Gelman, S. A. (1998). Knowledge acquisition in foundational domains. In W. Damon, D. Kuhn, & R. Siegler (Eds.), *Handbook of Child Psychology, 5th Edition, Volume 2, Cognition, Perception and Language* (pp. 523–573). New York: John Wiley & Sons.

Wellman, H. M., & Woolley, J. D. (1990). From simple desires to ordinary beliefs: The early development of everyday psychology. *Cognition, 35,* 245–275.

Wellman, H. M., Ritter, K., & Flavell, J. (1975). Deliberate memory development in the delayed reactions of very young children. *Developmental Psychology, 11,* 780–787.

Wellman, H. M., Somerville, S. C., & Haake, R. J. (1979). Development of search procedures in real-life spatial environments. *Developmental Psychology, 15,* 530–542.

Werker, J. F., & Tees, R. C. (1984). Cross-language speech perception: Evidence for perceptual reorganization during the first year of life. *Infant Behavior and Development, 7,* 49–63.

Wertsch, J. V. (1985). *Vygotsky and the Social Formation of Mind.* Cambridge, MA: Harvard University Press.

Westermann, G., Mareschal, D., Johnson, M. H., Sirois, S., Spratling, M. W., & Thomas, M. S. C. (2007). Neuroconstructivism. *Developmental Science, 10(1),* 75–83.

Whiten, A., & Ham, R. (1992). On the nature and evolution of imitation in the animal kingdom: Reappraisal of a century of research. In P. B. Slater, J. S. Rosenblatt, C. Beer, & M. Milinski (Eds.), *Advances in the Study of Behaviour* (pp. 239–283). San Diego, CA: Academic Press.

Wilkening, F. (1981). Integrating velocity, time and distance information: A developmental study. *Cognitive Psychology, 13,* 231–247.

Wilkening, F. (1982). Children's knowledge about time, distance and velocity interrelations. In W. J. Friedman (Ed.), *The Developmental Psychology of Time* (pp. 87–112). New York: Academic Press.

Wilkening, F., & Anderson, N. H. (1991). Representation and diagnosis of knowledge structures in developmental psychology. In N. H. Anderson (Ed.), *Contributions to Information Integration Theory: Volume III. Developmental* (pp. 43–80). Hillsdale, NJ: Lawrence Erlbaum Associates, Inc.

Wilkening, F., & Huber, S. (2002). Children's intuitive physics. In U. Goswami (Ed.), *Blackwell Handbook of Childhood Cognitive Development* (pp. 349–370). Oxford: Blackwell.

Wimmer, H. (1993). Characteristics of developmental dyslexia in a regular writing system. *Applied Psycholinguistics, 14,* 1–33.

Wimmer, H. (1996). The nonword reading deficit in developmental dyslexia: evidence from children learning to read German. *Journal of Experimental Child Psychology, 61,* 80–90.

Wimmer, H., & Perner, J. (1983). Beliefs about beliefs: Representation and constraining function of wrong beliefs in young children's understanding of deception. *Cognition, 13,* 103–128.

Wimmer, H., Landerl, K., & Schneider, W. (1994). The role of rhyme awareness in learning to read a regular orthography. *British Journal of Developmental Psychology, 12,* 469–484.

Wimmer, H., Landerl, K., Linortner, R., & Hummer, P. (1991). The relationship of phonemic awareness to reading acquisition: More consequence than precondition but still important. *Cognition, 40,* 219–249.

Winston, P. H. (1980). Learning and reasoning by analogy. *Communications of the ACM, 23(12),* 689–703.

Winterer, G., & Weinberger, D. R. (2004). Genes, dopamine and cortical signal-to-noise ratio in schizophrenia. *Trends in Neurosciences, 11,* 683–690.

Woodward, A. L. (1998). Infants selectively encode the goal object of an actor's reach. *Cognition, 69,* 1–34.

Woodward, A. L. (2003). Infants' developing understanding of the link between looker and object. *Developmental Science, 6,* 297–311.

Woodward, A. L., & Guajardo, J. J. (2002). Infants' understanding of the point gesture as an object-directed action. *Cognitive Development, 17,* 1061–1084.

Woolfe, T., Want, S., & Siegal, M. (2002). Signposts to development: Theory of mind in deaf children. *Child Development, 73,* 768–778.

Wynn, K. (1990). Children's understanding of counting. *Cognition, 36,* 155–193.

Wynn, K. (1992a). Addition and subtraction by human infants. *Nature, 358,* 749–750.

Wynn, K. (1992b). Children's acquisition of the number words and the counting system. *Cognitive Psychology, 24,* 220–251.

Xu, F. (2002). The role of language in acquiring object kind concepts in infancy. *Cognition, 85,* 223–250.

Xu, F. (2003). Numerosity discrimination in infants: Evidence for two systems of representations. *Cognition, 89,* B15–B25.

Xu, F., & Carey, S. (1996). Infants' metaphysics: The case of numerical identity. *Cognitive Psychology, 30,* 111–153.

Xu, F., & Spelke, E. S. (2000). Large number discrimination in 6-month-old infants. *Cognition, 74,* B1–B11.

Xu, F., Spelke, E. S., & Goddard, S. (2005). Number sense in human infants. *Developmental Science, 8,* 88–101.

Youngblade, L. M., & Dunn, J. (1995). Individual differences in young children's pretend play with mother and sibling: Links to relationships and understanding of other people's feelings and beliefs. *Child Development, 66,* 1472–1492.

Younger, B. A. (1985). The segregation of items into categories by 10-month-old infants. *Child Development, 56,* 1574–83.

Younger, B. A. (1990). Infants' detection of correlations among feature categories. *Child Development, 61,* 614–620.

Younger, B. A., & Cohen, L. B. (1983). Infant perception of correlations among attributes. *Child Development, 54,* 858–867.

Younger, B. A., & Cohen, L. B. (1985). How infants form categories. In G. Bower (Ed.), *The Psychology of Learning and Motivation: Advances in Research and Theory* (pp. 211–247). New York: Academic Press.

Yussen, S. R., & Levy, V. M. (1975). Developmental changes in predicting one's own span of short-term memory. *Journal of Experimental Child Psychology, 19,* 502–508.

Zaitchik, D. (1990). When representations conflict with reality: The preschooler's problem with false beliefs and "false" photographs. *Cognition, 35,* 41–68.

Zelazo, P. D., & Frye, D. (1997). Cognitive complexity and control: A theory of the development of deliberate reasoning and intentional action. In M. Stamenov (Ed.), *Language Structure, Discourse, and the Access to Consciousness* (pp. 113–153). Amsterdam: John Benjamins.

Zelazo, P. D., & Müller, U. (2002). Executive functions in typical and atypical development. In U. Goswami (Ed.), *Handbook of Childhood Cognitive Development* (pp. 445–469). Oxford: Blackwell.

Zelazo, P. D., Frye, D., & Rapus, T. (1996). An age-related dissociation between knowing rules and using them. *Cognitive Development, 11,* 37–63.

Zelazo, P. D., Müller, U., Frye, D., & Marcovitch, S. (2003). The development of executive function in early childhood. *Monographs of the Society for Research in Child Development, 68(3),* Serial no. 274.

Zeskind, P. S., Sale, J., Maio, M. L., Huntington, L., & Weiseman J. R. (1985). Adult perceptions of pain and hunger cries: A synchrony of arousal. *Child Development, 56,* 549–554.

Ziegler, J. C., & Goswami, U. (2005). Reading acquisition, developmental dyslexia and skilled reading across languages: A psycholinguistic grain size theory. *Psychological Bulletin, 131(1),* 3–29.

Ziegler, J. C., & Goswami, U. (2006). Becoming literate in different languages: similar problems, different solutions. *Developmental Science, 9,* 429–453.

Ziegler, J. C., Stone, G. O., & Jacobs, A. M. (1997). What's the pronunciation for -OUGH and the spelling for /u/? A database for computing feedforward and feedback inconsistency in English. *Behavior Research Methods, Instruments, & Computers, 29,* 600–618.

Zinober, B., & Martlew, M. (1985). The development of communicative gestures. In M. Barret (Ed.), *Children's Single Word Speech* (pp. 183–215). Chichester, UK: John Wiley & Sons.

Author index

Subject index